CLUSTERS OF GALAXIES

Cover illustration :
An X-ray image of the Coma cluster of galaxies obtained by the ROSAT satellite
(by courtesy of S.D.M. White et al.)

XXIXth Rencontre de Moriond
XIVth Moriond Astrophysics Meetings
Méribel, Savoie, France - March 12-19, 1994

CLUSTERS OF GALAXIES
Series : Moriond Astrophysics Meetings

ISBN 2-86332-167-6
Copyright 1994 by Editions Frontières

EDITIONS FRONTIERES
B. P. 33
91192 Gif-sur-Yvette Cedex - France

Printed in Singapore

Proceedings of the XXIXth RENCONTRE DE MORIOND
XIVth Moriond Astrophysics Meetings
Méribel, Savoie, France   March 12-19, 1994

CLUSTERS OF GALAXIES

edited by
F. Durret
A. Mazure
J. Trân Thanh Vân

EDITIONS
FRONTIERES

The Astrophysics Session of the XXIXth Rencontre de Moriond

CLUSTERS OF GALAXIES

International Advisory Committee

M. Arnaud   *(Saclay)*
J. Audouze   *(Paris)*
H. Bohringer   *(Garching)*
F. Combes-Bottaro   *(Paris)*
A. Dressler   *(Pasadena)*
F. Durret   *(Paris)*
R. Ellis   *(Cambridge, U.K.)*
A. Evrard   *(Ann Arbor)*
A. Fabian   *(Cambridge, U. K.)*
D. Gerbal   *(Paris)*
G. Giuricin   *(Trieste)*
N. Kaiser   *(Toronto)*
P. Katgert   *(Leiden)*
A. Mazure   *(Montpellier)*
Y. Mellier   *(Toulouse)*
J.-L. Puget   *(Orsay)*
E. Salvador-Sole   *(Barcelona)*
C. Sarazin   *(Charlottesville)*
J. Trân Thanh Vân   *(Orsay)*
J. Tyson   *(Murray Hill)*
S. White   *(Cambridge, U.K.)*

Program Committee

F. Durret   *(Paris)*
A. Mazure   *(Montpellier)*
S. White   *(Cambridge, U.K.)*

94' RENCONTRES DE MORIOND

The XXIXth Rencontres de Moriond were held in 1994 in Villars-sur-Ollon, Switzerland, and in Méribel les Allues, Savoie, France.

The first meeting took place at Moriond in the French Alps in 1966. There, experimental as well as theoretical physicists not only shared their scientific preoccupations but also the household chores. The participants in the first meeting were mainly French physicists interested in electromagnetic interactions. In subsequent years, a session on high energy strong interactions was also added.

The main purpose of these meetings is to discuss recent developments in contemporary physics and also to promote effective collaboration between experimentalists and theorists in the field of elementary particle physics. By bringing together a relatively small number of participants, the meeting helps to develop better human relations as well as a more thorough and detailed discussion of the contributions.

This concern of research and experimentation of new channels of communication and dialogue which from the start animated the Moriond meetings, inspired us to organize a simultaneous meeting of biologists on Cell Differenciation (1970) and to create the Moriond Astrophysics Meeting (1981). In the same spirit, we have started this year a new series on Condensed Matter Physics. Common meetings between biologists, astrophysicists, condensed matter physicists and high energy physicists are organized to study the implications of the advances in one field into the others. I hope that these conferences and lively discussions may give birth to new analytical methods or new mathematical languages.

At the XXIXth Rencontres de Moriond in 1994, four physics sessions, one astrophysics session and one biology session were held :

* January 22-29   "Particle Astrophysics, Atomic Physics and Gravitation"

                              "Coulomb and Interference Effects in small electronic structures"

* March 12-19   "Electroweak Interactions and Unified Theories"

                              "Clusters of Galaxies"

* March 19-26   "QCD and High Energy Hadronic Interactions"

                              " Rencontre de Biologie - Méribel "

I thank the organizers of the XXIXth Rencontres de Moriond :

- E. Adelberger, R. Ansari, A. Blanchard, F. Boehm, G. Chardin, C. Cohen-Tannoudji, T. Damour, O. Fackler, J. Faller, E. Fischbach, G. Fontaine, G. Gerbier, E. Giacobino, Y. Giraud-Héraud, G. Greene , I. Grenier, B. Guiderdoni, E. Hinds, J. Kaplan, B. Kayser, R. Pain, S. Petcov and J. Wilkerson for the session on Particle Astrophysics, Atomic Physics and Gravitation,

- H. Bouchiat, D. C. Glattli, D. Mailly and M. Sanquer for the Condensed Matter Physics session,

- P. Binetruy, A. Blondel, R. Cahn, G. Coignet, L. Fayard, P. Fayet, J.-M. Frère, L. Krauss, L. Moscoso, C. Savoy and C. Verzegnassi for the Leptonic session,

- F. Durret, A. Mazure and S. White for the Astrophysics session,

- P. Aurenche, E. Berger, A. Capella, D. Denegri, L. Montanet, B. Pietrzyck, D. Schiff, and C. Voltolini for the Hadronic session,

- A. Adoutte, M. Fellous, P. Goldstein, M. A. Gransbastien, J. C. Kader, M. Solignac, P. Sonigo, K. Trân Thanh Vân and A. Ullman for the Biology meeting,

and the conference secretaries : G. Ambonati, L. Besson, V. Chopin, S. Desbarbieux, C. Douillet, D. Josephson, A. Lecoeur, A. S. Lécuiller, F. Lefevre, D. Levêque, L. Norry, F. and N. Osswald, A. M. Perrin, J. Raguideau, R. Scattergood, V. Sobek and F. Warin.

I am also grateful to Mrs S. Müller, Ms B. Gautron, Mr C. Dallery, Ms M. Favet, Mr. P. Bernard Granger, and Mr R. Theveniot who contributed through their hospitality and cooperation to the well-being of the participants enabling them to work in a relaxed atmosphere.

These Rencontres were sponsored by the Centre National de la Recherche Scientifique (INSU, SPM and FP), the Institut National de Physique Nucléaire et de Physique des Particules (IN2P3) and the Commissariat à l'Energie Atomique (DAPNIA). The workshop on Particle Astrophysics, Atomic Physics and Gravitation was also sponsored by the National Science Foundation and the Moriond Astrophysics meeting by the Centre National d'Études Spatiales, the Institut d'Astrophysique de Paris and the Ministère de l'Enseignement Supérieur et de la Recherche (programme ACCESS). I would like to express my thanks to their encouraging support.

I sincerely wish that a fruitful exchange and an efficient collaboration between the physicists, the astrophysicists and the biologists will arise from these Rencontres as from the previous ones.

J. Trân Thanh Vân

Avant-propos

Les XIVèmes Rencontres de Moriond en Astrophysique se sont tenues à Méribel du 12 au 19 mars 1994 sur le sujet "Les Amas de Galaxies".

Ce sujet a été choisi en raison de l'importance des amas de galaxies en astrophysique extragalactique et en cosmologie, pour des raisons à la fois théoriques et observationnelles.

Premièrement, les amas sont les plus grandes structures en quasi-équilibre dans l'Univers, et présentent des structures complexes, mettant en jeu diverses composantes (les galaxies, le gaz émetteur X, la matière noire). Ce sont, en particulier, les objets les mieux adaptés à la recherche de matière sombre et à l'étude de sa distribution spatiale, par l'analyse d'images en rayons X, d'observations optiques des mouvements des galaxies dans les amas, et de la distortion d'objets d'arrière-plan par effet de lentille gravitationnelle.

Deuxièmement, du fait que les échelles de temps de l'effondrement et de la relaxation des amas sont à peine plus courtes que l'âge de l'Univers, l'hypothèse d'équilibre hydro-statique est elle-même sujette à caution, et il est probable qu'un certain nombre de tels systèmes sont encore en formation. Par conséquent, les amas de galaxies peuvent contraindre les mécanismes de formation des grandes structures de l'Univers et de distribution de la matière dans ces structures.

Troisièmement, l'interaction entre le gaz intergalactique dans les amas et le fond diffus micro-onde (effet Sunyaev-Zeldovich) peut produire des fluctuations significatives et observables dans ce fond diffus; l'amplitude de telles fluctuations peut alors contraindre l'évolution des amas. De plus, l'observation de cet effet sur des amas individuels peut donner des indications précieuses sur la structure du gaz, et peut permettre de déterminer certains paramètres cosmologiques.

Enfin, d'un point de vue observationnel, une énorme quantité de données a été accumulée ces dernières années, aux longueurs d'onde optiques (arcs gravitationnels, vitesses radiales, images du Télescope Spatial Hubble), X (satellites GINGA, BBXRT, ROSAT, ASCA) et radio (galaxies individuelles, halos radio, effet Sunyaev-Zel'dovich). De plus, des amas à des décalages spectraux de l'ordre de 1 sont maintenant en cours d'étude avec le Télescope Spatial Hubble et avec de grands télescopes au sol. Ces données, couplées à des modélisations théoriques, donnent de nouveaux renseignements sur la structure, l'origine et l'évolution des amas et des grandes structures de l'Univers.

Les Editeurs

Foreword

The XIVth "Rencontres de Moriond" were held in Méribel on march 12-19, 1994 on the topic "Clusters of Galaxies".

This subject was chosen because clusters of galaxies are critically important in extragalactic astronomy and cosmology for both theoretical and observational reasons.

First of all, clusters are the largest quasi-equilibrium structures in the Universe, and show a complex structure involving a variety of interacting components (galaxies, X-ray emitting gas, dark matter). They are, in particular, the best objects in which to search for dark matter and to analyze its spatial distribution (by using X-ray maps, optical observations of the motions of cluster galaxies, and studies of the distortion of background objects by gravitational lensing).

Second, because the collapse and relaxation timescales of clusters are only slightly smaller than the age of the Universe, the hypothesis of hydrostatic equilibrium is itself open to question, and indeed many systems are probably still forming. As a result, clusters can constrain the formation mechanisms of larger scale structures and the matter distribution within them. Third, the interaction between the intergalactic gas in clusters and the cosmic microwave background (the Sunyaev-Zel'dovich effect) can produce significant and observable fluctuation in the cosmic microwave background; the observed amplitude of such fluctuations can therefore constrain cluster evolution. Furthermore, observation of this effect in individual clusters gives important clues to the structure of the gas and may provide an independent route to the determination of cosmological parameters.

Finally, on the observational side, a large amount of new data has been acquired during the past few years at optical (gravitational arcs, radial velocities, Hubble Space Telescope images), X-ray (from the GINGA, BBXRT, ROSAT, ASCA satellites) and radio (individual galaxies, radio halos, the Sunyaev-Zel'dovich effect) wavelengths. In addition clusters at redshifts of order unity are now being studied with the Hubble Space Telescope and with large ground-based telescopes. Coupled with theoretical modelling, these data are giving new insights into the structure, origin, and evolution of clusters and of large-scale structure.

The Editors

XXIXTH RENCONTRES DE MORIOND

XIVTH MORIOND ASTROPHYSICS MEETING "CLUSTERS OF GALAXIES "

Méribel , March 12-19, 1994

CONFERENCE PROGRAMME

SATURDAY MARCH 12

Afternoon : Registration
18:30   J. Tran Thanh Van : Welcome and Practical Information
18:40   News on Dark Matter in Galaxies and Clusters
        Françoise Combes
19:15   Status of the searches for gravitational microlensing events
        by dark objects in the galactic halo (MACHO and EROS collaborations)
        Michel Spiro
19:50   Welcome by the Director of the Tourism Office of Méribel
20:15   Welcome cocktail
20:45   Dinner

SUNDAY MARCH 13

8:30   Introduction to the meeting, programme preview
       Florence Durret and Alain Mazure
9:00   Cluster dynamics and cluster masses (I)
       David Merritt
10:00   Coffee break
10:30   Dynamics of cluster formation (I)
        Simon White

16:30   Observed structure within clusters (I)
        Michael West
17:30   Fractal cold gas as galactic dark matter, consequences for cluster structure (C)
        Daniel Pfenniger
17:50   Luminosity functions of poor clusters (C)
        Hank Donnelly
18:10   Coffee break
18:30   The internal dynamics of ESO Key-programme and other clusters of galaxies (C)
        Roland den Hartog
18:50   Optical sizes of 100 galaxy clusters (C)
        Giuliano Giuricin
19:10   Structure in the Virgo cluster (C)
        Brent Tully
19:30   New survey in the central parts of the Coma cluster (C)
        Andrea Biviano
19:50   The relation between M^* and M1 in the luminosity function of cluster galaxies (C)
        Dario Trevese
20:10   A search for intracluster light in Abell 665 (C)
        Eric Gaidos

WEDNESDAY MARCH 16

8:30   Enrichment of the intracluster medium (I)
       Monique Arnaud
9:30   Iron production and circulation in clusters (C)
       Alvio Renzini
9:50   ROSAT studies of compact galaxy groups (C)
       Trevor Ponman
10:10 Coffee break
10:30 The Sunyaev-Zel'dovich effect in clusters (I)
       Michael Jones

AFTERNOON AND EVENING : joint meeting with the physicists

17:00 Galaxy clusters and cosmology (I)
       Carlos Frenk
18:00 Theory of quark and lepton masses (I)
       Pierre Ramond
18:35 Coffee break
19:10 General Relativity and experiment (I)
       Thibault Damour
19:55   Dark matter (I)
       Alvaro de Rujula

THURSDAY MARCH 17

8:30   Simulations of cluster evolution (I)
       August Evrard
9:30   Models of the IGM with ejection from galaxies (C)
       Christopher Metzler
9:50   Simulations of the evolution of the ICM (C)
       Julio Navarro
10:10 Coffee break
10:30 Simulations of clusters using adaptive PPPM + SPH (C)
       Peter Thomas
10:50 The mass function in the adhesion model (C)
       Bérengère Dubrulle
11:10 The fundamental plane of galaxy clusters (C)
       Alberto Cappi

17:00 Theory of cluster evolution (I)
       Nick Kaiser
18:00 X-ray emission and S-Z effect induced by the hot gas in clusters : implications for cosmology (C)
       Sergio Colafrancesco
18:20 Coffee break
18:40 cD galaxies in double clusters (C)
       Frank Baier
19:00 The cosmology/group of galaxies connection (C)
       Gary Mamon
19:20 Mass function of relaxed objects in the peak model formalism (C)
       Eduard Salvador-Solé
19:40 Mass mapping in X-ray luminous clusters (C)
       Ian Smail
20:00 The autocorrelation of rich clusters in the MDM scenario (C)
       George Rhee

FRIDAY MARCH 18

8:30   Theory of large-scale structure (I)
       George Efstathiou
9:30   Nearby superclusters: flows and anisotropies (C)
       Roberto Scaramella
9:50   Coffee break
10:10 Clusters and superclustering (I)
       Will Sutherland
11:10 Cluster formation and QSOs as its tracers (C)
       Vladimir Lukash

16:30 Observations of lensing by clusters (I)
       Geneviève Soucail
17:30 Coffee break
17:50 Theory of lensing by clusters (I)
       Jordi Miralda-Escude
18:50 Simulations of lensing by clusters (C)
       Joachim Wambsganss
19:10 POSTER SESSION

SATURDAY MARCH 19

8:30   Conference summary and directed discussion
       Dick Bond

10:30 End of meeting

CONTENTS

Poster papers

Invited and contributed Papers

NEWS ON DARK MATTER IN GALAXIES AND CLUSTERS

Françoise Combes
DEMIRM, Observatoire de Paris
61 Av. de l'Observatoire, F-75 014 Paris, France

Daniel Pfenniger
Observatoire de Genève, CH-1290 Sauverny, Switzerland

Abstract. Major progresses have been made this last year towards a better knowledge of the invisible mass. Michel Spiro will talk in details about the micro-lensing experiments and their promising results; the ROSAT satellite has provided extended X-ray maps of the hot gas, which traces dark matter in galaxy clusters: they reveal lower amounts of dark matter in clusters than was previously derived; the dark to visible mass in clusters is not larger than its value in spiral galaxies. It was shown, by X-ray data and gravitational lenses analysis that the dark matter density is highly peaked towards the cluster centers. A new dark matter candidate has also been proposed, in the form of cold and fractal molecular gas that could be present around most late-type spiral galaxies and account for the observed flat rotation curves.

I – ROTATION CURVES OF SPIRAL AND IRREGULAR GALAXIES

The best evidence until now of the existence of dark matter is provided by the HI gas rotation curves of spiral galaxies. Already, the optical rotation curves obtained with ionised gas (Hα) were found to be surprisingly flat (e.g. Rubin et al. 1980), but they do not extend enough outside the optical disk to unambiguously require the presence of dark matter. On the contrary, the radio rotation curves obtained up to 3–4 optical radii with HI at 21cm, are maintained flat so far out that the presence of a dark component is unavoidable (e.g. Bosma 1981, van Albada et al. 1985).

A – HUBBLE SEQUENCE

More recently, it has been realised that the fraction of dark matter depends on the morphological type: it is increasing along the Hubble sequence, from Sa to Sd (also called "early" and "late" galaxies respectively), and maximises for dwarf irregulars. The Hubble sequence was until now characterised by five main parameters monotonously varying from Sa to Sd: 1) the decreasing bulge-to-disk luminosity ratio, indicating that the mass concentration decreases along the sequence; 2) the increasing gas fraction; 3) the decreasing total mass; 4) the decreasing fraction of heavy elements, processed in stars; and 5) the increasing pitch angle, i.e., the spiral arms being more wound for early-type galaxies.

From enhanced sensitivity HI observations in gas-poor early-type galaxies, falling rotation curves have been discovered (Casertano & van Gorkom 1991, Salucci & Frenk 1989). This means that early-type galaxies *have proportionally less dark matter.*

On the other side of the sequence, dwarf irregulars are observed with rising rotation curves (e.g. Carignan & Freeman 1988). Dwarfs spirals *have proportionally more dark matter.* Since the Hubble sequence is also a mass (or luminosity) sequence, it emerges that the dark-to-luminous mass decreases with total visible mass (Persic & Salucci 1993).

These new results should be re-enforced with larger statistics. It is of prime importance, for instance, to find several galaxies with no evidence at all of dark matter. This will provide strong constraints on non-baryonic dark matter models, and even rule out modified Newtonian gravity hypotheses.

The Hubble sequence is not only a classification of galaxies according to their morphology; the galaxy disks may evolve in a short time-scale (less than 10^9 yrs) along the sequence, through numerous dynamical instabilities, such as the formation and dissolution of spiral waves and bars (Pfenniger et al. 1994). The non-axisymmetric waves produce gravity torques that drive the mass towards the center: a galaxy then evolves from late to early types (Sd to Sa), increasing its luminous mass, and its mass concentration; at the same time, star-formation consumes the gas and increases the heavy element content. The evolution cannot be the other way around, since mass concentration, star formation, and nucleosynthesis are irreversible processes. The fact that during the evolution, the luminous mass increases, while the dark mass fraction decreases suggests that the dark matter has been transformed into stars, particularly because disk galaxies like the Galaxy are too fragile structures to afford a substantial mass accretion in or at the periphery of the optical disk (Tóth & Ostriker 1992). This is only possible if the dark matter around galaxies is composed mainly of hydrogen and helium gas, not yet condensed in compact objects.

B – MAXIMUM DISK

How well do we know the radial distribution and exact amount of dark matter in spiral galaxies? How much mass is associated with visible stars?

The M/L mass-to-light ratio for the stellar population depends on age, metallicity, and the overall colours. Tinsley (1981) has computed the variations of M/L with (B-V) colour, from 1 to 10 for red to blue galaxies. She deduced already at that time that since the total (dynamical) mass to luminosity ratio was not varying as much, the fraction of dark matter was higher in blue galaxies, i.e. in the late-types of the Hubble sequence. The possibility to vary M/L for stars, according to their age and colour, makes the maximum disk hypothesis tenable for most galaxies: i.e., it is possible to explain the rotation curve in the inner parts of the galaxy by maximising the contribution of the visible matter in fitting M/L. No dark matter is then required within the optical disk. Recently, Buchhorn et al. (1994) have succeeded to fit the observed $H\alpha$ rotation curves of 97% galaxies in a sample of about 500: they compute the gravitational potential of the galaxy from the red image (less perturbed by extinction), assuming a constant M/L as a function of radius. The derived rotation curve fits surprisingly well the kinematical $H\alpha$ data; it remains quite flat, except for small-scale wiggles, tracing the streaming motions associated with spiral arms. Of course, the choice of a lower M/L for the stars is still possible, within the uncertainties; however the precise fits of these wiggles is a strong argument in favor of the maximum disk, since any spherically distributed dark matter will not follow so tightly the spiral arm streaming motions.

When the rotation curve is flat, the radial distribution of dark matter corresponds to an isothermal component, the density varying as r^{-2} in the extended parts of the disk, and the projected surface density as r^{-1}. In some cases, however, not only isothermal distributions, but also r^{-3} or r^{-4} asymptotic laws for the density are possible (Lake & Feinswog 1989).

The main argument against the maximum disk hypothesis rises within non-baryonic dark matter scenarios. It is indeed difficult to imagine a hollow dark matter component, with a central hole filled in by the baryonic matter, if the dark and luminous matter components are physically different and independent (one is spherical, the other one flattened). However, this argument is no longer valid if both types of matter are two forms belonging to the same physical component, and simply one form converts into the other one within some radius.

C – CONSPIRACY

The flatness of most rotation curves has been considered a puzzle, since it implies a conspiracy between two supposedly independent dynamical components: the visible disk and the spherical dark halo. We have seen already that this flatness is no longer universal, rotation curves having tendencies to rise for late-types and fall for early-type galaxies. But yet, most intermediate types have a flat curve.

When the curve is flat already within the optical disk, the visible matter alone can account for it (e.g. Freeman 1993). The problem is to explain the continuity of the curve in the outer parts, dominated by dark matter. Several scenarios have been proposed, arguing that dark matter is dragged by baryonic infall (Blumenthal et al. 1986). But in dark matter dominated dwarfs the predicted core radius of the total mass is too short with respect to the observations (Moore 1994).

The conspiracy is of course no longer a problem if the dark and luminous matter are two aspects of the same dynamical component, one phase being progressively transformed in the other, during galaxy evolution.

II – CLUES FROM THE GAS

A – RADIAL DISTRIBUTION OF GAS AND DARK MATTER

The atomic gas serves as a tracer of dark matter, since only HI is visible in the outer parts of spiral disks. There is moreover some evidence that the gas and dark matter are intimately related. From the flat rotation curves, the surface density of dark matter σ_{DM} varies asymptotically as $1/r$, and the HI surface density σ_{HI} is also observed to vary in $1/r$. Bosma (1981) was the first to notice a constant ratio of σ_{DM}/σ_{HI} as a function of radius in spiral galaxies. The constant ratio has been confirmed by many authors (Sancisi & van Albada 1987, Puche et al. 1990), and varies between 10 and 20 according to morphological type (Broeils 1992).

B – 3D DISTRIBUTION: POLAR RINGS AND THICKNESS OF HI PLANES

Albeit many observational efforts, it has not been possible until now to determine with certainty the 3D-shape of the dark matter distribution.

Polar rings, i.e., material orbiting almost perpendicular to the main plane of the galaxy were a good hope to test the 3D distribution of mass, and in particular the shape of dark matter. Much work has been devoted to this problem but with controversial results (Whitmore et al 1987; Sackett & Sparke 1990). The modelling is in fact confronted with many difficulties, the main one being intrinsic to the formation mechanism: gas settling in the polar ring and then forming stars. Due to gas clouds collisions, a polar ring cannot form in a galaxy that has already a gaseous component at the same radii in the equatorial plane. Therefore, the equatorial velocities are not determined at the same radius as the polar ones, and the flattening of the halo cannot be directly determined (Reshetnikov & Combes 1994).

Warps and their problematic longevity have long been an argument in favor of spherical dark halos, since the time-scale of differential precession is then considerably enlarged. However, the warp lines of nodes are not observed to be wound as they should even at radii where the disk dominates the mass, and other explanations involving gas accretion and short life-time are now considered more plausible (Binney 1992).

As well as the HI kinematics in the galaxy plane being used to test the radial distribution of mass, the HI velocity dispersion and height can be used to test the mass distribution perpendicular to the plane. In the isothermal sheet model of a thin plane, the height $h(r)$ of the gaseous plane is $h(r) = \sigma_v^2(r)/\pi G\mu(r)$, where $\sigma_v(r)$ is the z-velocity dispersion, and $\mu(r)$ the total surface density, within the gaseous plane. Since the HI gas z-velocity dispersion has been observed constant in the outer parts of face-on galaxies (Shostak & van der Kruit 1984; Dickey et al. 1990), the HI characteristic height as a function of radius gives the amount of dark matter $\mu(r)$ included within the HI plane. In the Milky Way, the height $h(r)$ is increasing linearly with radius (Merrifield 1992), and its precise value is that expected if all the dark matter was flattened at least as much as the flaring HI plane. In M31, Brinks & Burton (1984) also discovered a flaring linear with radius.

C – GAS RESERVOIRS AROUND MOST SPIRAL GALAXIES

It has long been known that intermediate-type spiral galaxies have formed stars at about a constant rate along the Hubble time (Kennicutt 1983). Infall of gas has been invoked to solve the problem of gas consumption by star formation (Larson et al. 1980), and even the maintenance of spiral structure needs the replenishment of the dissipative component (Toomre 1990). Recently Braine & Combes (1993) have found that interacting galaxies appear to possess more visible gas than isolated ones, as if galaxy interactions would suddenly reveals more gas. This could be due to the driving of the gas towards the center by tidal torques, if there exists an outer gas reservoir.

III – A NEW CANDIDATE FOR DARK MATTER: COLD H_2

All these arguments about galaxy evolution and gas properties led us to propose a new model for dark matter around spiral galaxies (Pfenniger, Combes, & Martinet 1994; Pfenniger & Combes 1994). The idea of diffuse gas has been eliminated since the beginning by the Gunn-Peterson test (Gunn & Peterson 1965): if the Universe was filled by an homogeneous diffuse gas, we should detect it in the spectrum of remote quasars, as an absorption trough starting at the redshift of the quasar. This test could be done for atomic gas (21cm line), or ionised gas (Lyα) etc...

But the gas could be in a clumpy and fragmented structure as it is observed in nearby molecular clouds. It has been proposed by several authors that the interstellar medium is distributed in a fractal structure, over at least 4 orders of magnitude in scale (e.g., Scalo 1985; Falgarone et al. 1992). We extrapolate this fractal down by 2 orders of magnitude in scale, since structures as small as $10 - 20$ AU are detected in the interstellar gas (HI VLBI interferometry: Diamond et al. 1989, proper motions when passing in front of quasars: Fiedler et al. 1987, or pulsars: Cognard et al. 1993). The physical structure of this fractal will be detailed in another contribution in this conference. By physical arguments, we deduce that the building blocks of the fractal, the "clumpuscules", have masses of the order of Jupiters (10^{-3} $M_\odot$), volumic densities of 10^{10} H cm^{-3}, and surface densities of 10^{25} H cm^{-2}. The gas is in molecular form, and in thermal equilibrium with the 3 K cosmic background.

IS THAT GAS OBSERVABLE AROUND GALAXIES?

Most of the mass is in the form of H_2 molecules, which unfortunately do not radiate at low excitation, since by symmetry they have no dipole moment (no emission of rotational lines). In molecular clouds, H_2 is traced by the CO emission. This is highly dependent on metallicity, and CO emission is expected to disappear far away from the optical disk, where the gas is deficient in heavy elements. High-energy γ rays are also a good tracer of all nucleons, since they are produced in the interaction between cosmic rays and matter. However, the main sources of cosmic rays are supernovae and other stars, and therefore this tracer is again restricted to the optical disk.

Since the gas is cold, any emission would not be easily detected against the background, and may be the best hope is to detect it in absorption. Already many absorption lines corresponding to the HI atomic gas are detected in the spectrum of quasars: along some line of sights, up to 100 Lyα absorbing systems have been detected, and represent the well-known Lyα forest. These absorption lines correspond to moderate column densities, between 10^{15} to 10^{20} H cm^{-2}; if they are associated to galaxies they imply an equivalent cross-section, corresponding to a radius of about $R = 200 - 400$ kpc, at $z = 2.5$ (Sargent 1988). UV observations with the Hubble Space Telescope have recently revealed that the absorbing systems are still numerous at low redshift (Morris et al. 1991; Bruhweiler et al. 1993). These absorbing systems could be the envelopes of dense and massive molecular clumps.

At the present temperature of the background radiation (2.7 K), it is highly probable that some of the H_2 has become solid. At the average density of the clumpuscules, the phase transition occurs at 3 K. If H_2 ice is present in the shape of snow flakes, they can be efficiently coupled to the background radiation, and radiate themselves like a black-body. This will also occur in the presence of a small amount of dust. The emission of these particles could then be detected by faint fluctuations of the microwave background.

Let us mention also that these clumpuscules are not compact enough to produce micro-lensing for stars in the Large Magellanic Clouds. However, on the line of sight of a remote quasar (at least at 100 Mpc distance), intervening clumpuscules or larger clumps of the fractal structure could produce, by micro-lensing, the observed non-intrinsic variability of these quasi-punctual sources (cf. Hawkins 1993).

IV – GALAXY CLUSTERS

The X-ray emission of the hot gas in galaxy clusters has been explored with enhanced sensitivity by the satellite ROSAT, for 4 years now. More clusters have been detected, and in the brightest clusters, the hot gas has been studied at a much larger distance from the cluster center. Within the hypothesis of hydrodynamical equilibrium, the hot gas is a tracer of the cluster potential, and the total mass has been determined at larger cluster radii. A comparative analysis of groups and clusters have shown that the total mass-to-light ratio decreases with the size of the object (David et al. 1994). For the largest clusters, which contain also the greatest fraction of hot gas, the M/L ratio begins to decreases, the dark matter becomes luminous. This M/L ratio never rises much above that for spiral galaxies. Previous estimates of larger M/L relied on virial estimates, and on the hypothesis of isotropic motions in the outer parts of clusters, which is not verified since these outer parts are not relaxed.

The radial distribution of dark matter has been determined more accurately from a deeper analysis of X-ray data. The results are consistent with a very small (unresolved) core radius of dark matter: much smaller than that of the hot gas (Gerbal et al. 1992; Briel et al. 1992; Durret et al. 1994). This is confirmed independently by the gravitational lens method for total mass determination, when arcs and mini-arcs are present (Hammer 1991, Wu & Hammer 1993). This more concentrated distribution suggests that the dark matter is baryonic in order to dissipate energy and cool to a lower temperature than the hot gas (Briel et al. 1992).

A – COOLING FLOWS

The hot gas in the center of clusters reaches the density threshold for thermal instability, and its cooling time falls below the Hubble time: it then cools down very quickly (Rees & Ostriker 1977). The rate of cooling has been measured, of the order of $\dot{M} = 10^2 \, M_\odot/\text{yr}$ (e.g. Fabian 1987). But the cooled gas has never been detected, a puzzle that several scenarios have tried to get round, including star formation with biased initial mass functions. Recently, X-ray absorption has revealed the existence of a large mass of gas in the center of clusters (White et al. 1991; Allen et al. 1993).

Since this gas is not seen in HI (emission, absorption, O'Dea et al. 1994), it could be hidden in the form of molecular clouds (White et al. 1991; Ferland et al. 1994; Fabian, this meeting). Several tentatives of CO detection have been made in vain (Grabelsky & Ulmer 1990; Mc Namara & Jaffe 1994; Antonucci & Barvainis 1994; Braine & Dupraz 1994). The low temperature of the molecular gas, and its low filling factor, if it is distributed in small dense clumps, can easily explain these non-detections.

In the hypothesis of cold gas as dark matter, the hot gas comes from the heating of some of the cold gas of the outer parts of galaxies during cluster formation. Since the mass of this cold gas in late-type galaxies is one or two orders of magnitudes than the visible mass, it is easy to explain the domination of the hot gas mass in clusters, between 2 and 8 times the galaxy visible masses (Edge & Stewart 1991). During cooling flows the gas resumes its cold phase, and falls down the cluster potential well, accounting for the small core radii.

B – BARYON FRACTION OF THE TOTAL MASS OF A CLUSTER

The new X-ray data allow to make a more accurate mass account within galaxy clusters. From stellar luminosity, hot X-ray gas, the visible baryonic matter is already a fraction $0.15 \, h_{50}^{-3/2}$ of the total mass (White et al. 1993).

But standard big-bang nucleosynthesis constrain Ω_b below $0.09\,h_{50}^{-2}$ (Smith et al. 1993). This is hardly compatible with $\Omega = 1$, unless most of the non-baryonic dark matter has been maintained outside of clusters, by some formation mechanism. White et al. (1993) show that this cannot be accounted for by dissipative effects during cluster formation, and conclude:
- either that Ω is much lower than 1,
- or the theory of standard big-bang nucleosynthesis is wrong.

Let us mention that a model of universe, where dark matter is only baryonic, is not ruled out by observations. In X-ray clusters, the visible mass, including the hot gas, is only 10 times lower than the total dynamical mass. The total Ω inferred is of the order of 0.05, still compatible with the standard big-bang nucleosynthesis.

V – CONCLUSIONS

The enhanced sensitivity of ROSAT X-ray data have not revealed the presence of more dark matter on large scales. In fact, the dark matter becomes visible in rich clusters as hot emitting gas. This implies that the fraction of baryonic matter in clusters becomes larger and larger, incompatible with the joint hypothesis of standard big-bang nucleosynthesis (BBN) and $\Omega = 1$. On the other hand, at the galaxy scale, the amount of baryons is still insufficient to meet the lower bound of BBN, so that there must exist some baryonic dark matter. This could exist in the shape of brown dwarfs, as might have been seen by micro-lensing experiments (e.g. Spiro, this meeting). Or this baryonic dark matter could be in the form of cold molecular gas in the outer parts of galaxies. This gas will then be available for star formation, all along the galaxy life-time, explaining galaxy evolution along the Hubble sequence. The fractal structure of this medium is simply the generalisation of what is observed in nearby molecular clouds at slightly higher temperatures: $5-15$ K. The cold gas is in statistical equilibrium with the cosmic background radiation at 2.7 K. This new candidate has the advantage of providing a natural origin of the hot gas in clusters, and explaining the observed high baryonic fraction in strong X-ray clusters.

REFERENCES

Allen S.W., Fabian A.C., Johnstone R.M., et al.: 1993, MNRAS 262, 901
Antonucci R., Barvainis R.: 1994, AJ 107, 448
Binney J.J.: 1992, ARAA 30, 51
Bosma A.: 1981, AJ 86, 1971
Blumenthal G.R., Faber S.M., Flores R., Primack J.R: 1986, ApJ 301, 27
Braine J., Dupraz C.: 1994, A&A 283, 407
Briel U.G., Henry J.P., Böhringer H.: 1992, A&A 259, L31
Broeils A.: 1992, "Dark and visible matter in spiral galaxies", PhD Thesis, Rijksuniversiteit Groningen
Bruhweiler F.C., Boggess A., Norman D.J., Grady C.A., Urry M.C., Kondo Y.: 1993, ApJ 409, 199
Buchhorn M. et al.: 1994, preprint (work presented in Freeman 1993)
Brinks E., Burton W.B.: 1984, A&A 141, 195
Carignan C., Freeman K.C.: 1988, ApJ 332, L33
Casertano S., van Gorkom J.H.: 1991, AJ 101, 1231
Cognard I., Bourgois G., Lestrade J-F. et al.: 1993, Nature, 366, 320
David L.P., Forman W., Jones C.: 1994, Nature, in press
Diamond P.J., et al.: 1989, ApJ 347, 302
Dickey J.M., Hanson M.M., Helou G.: 1990, ApJ 352, 522
Durret F., Gerbal D., Lachièze-Rey M., Lima-Neto G., Sadat R: 1994, A&A, in press

Edge A.C., Stewart G.C.: 1991, MNRAS 252, 428
Fabian A.C.: 1987, in "Large Scale Structures in the Universe", Saas-Fee Advanced Course 17, L. Martinet, M. Mayor (eds.), Geneva Observatory, Geneva, p. 1
Falgarone E., Puget J.-L., Pérault M.: 1992, A&A 257, 715
Ferland G.J., Fabian A.C., Johnstone R.M.: 1994, MNRAS 266, 399
Fiedler R.L., Dennison B., Johnston K.J., Hewish A.: 1987, Nature 326, 675
Freeman K.C.: 1993, in "Physics of Nearby Galaxies, Nature or Nurture?" T.X. Thuan, C. Balkowski, J.T.T. Van (eds.), Editions Frontières, Gif-sur-Yvette, p. 201
Gerbal D., Durret F., Lima-Neto G., Lachièze-Rey M.: 1992, A&A 253, 77
Grabelsky D.A., Ulmer M.P.: 1990, ApJ 355, 401
Gunn J.E., Peterson B.A.: 1965, ApJ 142, 1633
Hammer F.: 1991, ApJ 383, 66
Hawkins M.R.S.: 1993, Nature 366, 242
Kennicutt R.: 1983, ApJ 272, 54
Lake G., Feinswog L.: 1989, AJ 98, 166
Larson B., Tinsley B.M., Caldwell C.N.: 1980, ApJ 237, 692
McNamara B.R., Jaffe W.: 1994, A&A 281, 673
Merrifield M.R.: 1992, AJ 103, 1552
Moore B.: 1994, "The nature of dark matter", preprint submitted to Nature
Morris S.L., Weymann R.J., Savage B.D., Gilliland R.L.: 1991, ApJ 377, L21
O'Dea C.P., Baum S.A., Maloney P.M. et al.: 1994, ApJ, in press
Persic M., Salucci P.: 1993, MNRAS 261, L21
Pfenniger D., Combes F., Martinet L.: 1994, A&A 285, 79
Pfenniger D., Combes F.: 1994, A&A 285, 94
Puche D., Carignan C., Bosma A.: 1990, AJ 100, 1468
Rees M.J., Ostriker J.: 1977, MNRAS 179, 541
Reshetnikov V., Combes F.: 1994, A&A, in press
Rubin V.C., Ford W.K., Thonnard N.: 1980, ApJ 238, 471
Sackett P.D., Sparke L.S.: 1990, ApJ 361, 408
Salucci P., Frenk C.S.: 1989, MNRAS 237, 247
Sancisi R., van Albada T.S.: 1987, in "Dark Matter in the Universe" IAU Symp. 117, J. Kormendy, G.R. Knapp (eds.), Reidel, Dordrecht, p. 67
Sargent W.L.W.: 1988, in "QSO absorption lines", J. Blades, D. Turnshek, C. Norman (eds.), Cambridge University Press, p. 1
Scalo J.M.: 1985, in "Protostars and Planets II", D.C. Black, M.S. Matthews (eds.), University of Arizona Press, Tucson, p. 201
Shostak G.S., van der Kruit P.C.: 1984, A&A 132, 20
Smith M.S., Kawano L.H., Malaney R.A.: 1993, ApJS 85, 219
Tinsley B.M.: 1981, MNRAS 194, 63
Toomre A.: 1990, in "Dynamics and Interactions of Galaxies", R. Wielen (ed.), Springer-Verlag, p. 292
Tóth G., Ostriker J.P., 1992, ApJ 389, 5
van Albada T.S., Bahcall J.N., Begeman K., Sancisi R.: 1985, ApJ 295, 305
White D.A., Fabian A.C., Johnstone R.M. et al.: 1991, MNRAS 252, 72
White S.D.M., Navarro J.F., Evrard A.E., Frenk C.S.:1993, Nature 366, 429
Whitmore B.C., McElroy D.B., Schweizer F.: 1987, ApJ 314, 439
Wu X.P., Hammer F.: 1993, MNRAS 262, 187

CLUSTER DYNAMICS AND CLUSTER MASSES

DAVID MERRITT and KARL GEBHARDT
Department of Physics and Astronomy, Rutgers University
Piscataway, NJ 08855

ABSTRACT

In spite of the promise of new techniques for constraining the mass distribution in galaxy clusters, much remains to be learned from galaxy orbital velocities. This article reviews the theory of potential estimation in hot dynamical systems like galaxy clusters. An analysis is presented of the Coma cluster, based on a sample of ~1500 galaxies with probable membership, of which ~450 have measured velocities. The Coma data are shown to be consistent with a model in which the dark matter density falls roughly as r^{-3} inside of ~1.5 Mpc ($H_0 = 50$), with, perhaps, a transition to a slower falloff at larger radii. We find no significant evidence for a core in either the galaxy number densities or the mass distribution.

1. Introduction

Since Zwicky's[1] realization that the gravitational mass of the Coma cluster greatly exceeds the mass in stars, there has been no compelling reason to assume that the spatial distribution of the dark matter bears any relation to the density profile defined by the galaxies. But until recently, techniques for determining the gravitational potential $\Phi(r)$ have failed to yield strong, model-independent constraints on the dark matter distribution. Happily, this situation is about to change. New data from X-ray observatories (as described by K. Yamashita, H. Böhringer and R. Mushotzky at this meeting) are providing the first detailed information about the dependence of the gas temperature on position in galaxy clusters, information which will eventually translate into strong constraints on the potential. And new techniques – such as mass-mapping using gravitational lenses – are beginning to provide estimates of the matter distribution that are free of the assumptions of dynamical equilibrium and spherical symmetry (G. Soucail, J. Miralda-Escude and I. Smail, this meeting).

At the same time, the more classical approach based on measurements of discrete galaxy velocities bears re-examining due to the large data sets that are now becoming available. Here we review the theory of kinematical mass estimation in "hot" dynamical systems like galaxy clusters. We argue that much of the past work in this field has suffered from a confusion between "model fitting" and "statistical estimation." While it is easy to construct a model that is consistent, in some weak sense, with the kinematical data, such models are often highly nonunique. Most authors have based their mass estimation algorithms on the velocity dispersion profile defined by the galaxies, thus guaranteeing that their solution for $\Phi(r)$ will be degenerate. Furthermore, the estimation of quantities like $\rho(r)$, the mass density profile, is strongly "ill-conditioned" in the sense understood by statisticians,[2] meaning that the use of *ad hoc* parametrized models is guaranteed to severely bias the answer *regardless* of the quality of the data. While many of the published algorithms are very sophisticated, and a few are reasonably nonparametric, we show that most of these accomplish nothing more than an evaluation of the virial theorem, and hence tell us little that is unique or compelling about the distribution of dark matter.

Even in a precisely spherical and relaxed cluster, reasonably model-independent estimates of $\Phi(r)$ and $\rho(r)$ require large data sets as well as numerical algorithms that can use the complete information contained within a discrete set of positions and velocities. Below we analyze the Coma cluster and conclude that a fairly wide range of models is consistent with the currently existing kinematical data. In models where the galaxy velocities are close to isotropic near the cluster center, the inferred dark-matter density falls roughly as r^{-3} in the inner parts of the cluster, with no strong evidence for a core. At larger radii, $r \gtrsim 1.5$ Mpc ($H_0 = 50$ km s^{-1} Mpc^{-1}), we find marginal evidence for a slower falloff of ρ with r, implying a total mass for the Coma cluster that could be several times larger than the standard value based on a naive application of the virial theorem. Larger kinematical samples may eventually allow us to choose between these models.

Recent work (as reviewed by M. West at this meeing) has demonstrated the prevalence of substructure and departures from dynamical equilibrium in many galaxy clusters. Here we ignore such complications, even though they might seriously bias estimates of the mass distribution as inferred from kinematical data. Our aim is to demonstrate the difficulty of the potential estimation problem even in the idealized spherical case, as a starting point for more sophisticated studies.

2. Potential Estimation in Hot Systems

Dynamical masses of stellar or galactic systems are usually estimated from the line-of-sight velocities of some set of luminous tracers orbiting in the overall potential. Rough estimates of the mass are often based on the virial theorem, which for a spherical system is

$$\langle v^2 \rangle = \langle r \cdot \nabla \Phi \rangle, \tag{1}$$

with $\langle v^2 \rangle$ the mean square velocity of some sample orbiting in the potential $\Phi(r)$. In a spherical system, $\langle v^2 \rangle$ is equal to three times the mean square line-of-sight velocity, independent of any assumptions about the velocity anisotropy. In nonspherical systems (which certainly include galaxy clusters), the virial theorem contains a geometrical factor that depends on intrinsic shape and orientation, both of which are typically unknown. More serious, however, is the unknown radial dependence of Φ. Without some information about the relative distribution of dark and luminous components, the virial theorem places only order-of-magnitude constraints on the total mass, even in the spherical case, and says virtually nothing about the central density or scale length of the matter that determines the potential.[10,21] Most of the cluster "virial masses" quoted in the literature were derived from a form of the virial theorem which assumes that the mass is attached to, or has the same overall spatial distribution as, the galaxies. If mass does not follow light, these estimates are worth very little.

One might hope to do better by constructing the velocity dispersion profile of the galaxies, since this function contains information about the variation with radius of the kinematical quantities. But the extra information helps surprisingly little. Idealizing a galaxy cluster as a nonrotating spherical system, the Jeans equation states

$$\frac{d\Phi}{dr} = -\frac{1}{\nu}\frac{d(\nu\sigma_r^2)}{dr} - \frac{2}{r}\left(\sigma_r^2 - \sigma_t^2\right). \tag{2}$$

Eq. (2) contains the two velocity dispersions $\sigma_r(r)$ and $\sigma_t(r)$, measured along and tangential to the radius vector. The observed velocity dispersion at every projected radius is a complicated average along the line of sight of these two intrinsic components, and contains too little information to determine both functions independently. As a result, many different $\Phi(r)$'s can be made equally consistent with an observed velocity dispersion profile by varying the assumed dependence of anisotropy on radius. This problem is widely recognized, but it is rarely emphasized just how great the indeterminacy is if no *a priori* constraints are placed on the galaxy orbits or on the distribution of the mass. Given *perfect* measurements of the surface density and velocity dispersion profiles of a set of galaxies in a spherical cluster, the central mass density is uncertain by *several orders of magnitude*, even if one imposes the reasonable constraint that $\rho(r)$ be a declining function of radius.[3] The total mass is uncertain by a smaller, but still large, factor – roughly an order of magnitude in the case of measured profiles like those in the Coma cluster. The shapes of the galaxy orbits in the more extreme models are not very likely to occur in nature, but the dependence of quantities like the mass density on the assumed kinematics is so strong that even mild departures from isotropy can imply huge changes in the mass density.

However the amount of information in a large sample of line-of-sight velocities is much greater than that contained within the velocity dispersion profile alone. For example, if one knew the maximum line-of-sight velocity at every projected radius R, one would have a secure limit on depth of the potential at every intrinsic radius $r = R$, namely $\Phi(r = R) \leq -v_{max}^2(R)/2$, independent of any assumptions about orbital shapes. In galaxy clusters, this approach is not very useful, since it requires measurement of the poorly-defined wings of the velocity distribution and even then only imposes a lower limit on the depth of the potential.

We can do even better by making use of the complete distribution of line-of-sight velocities. In a spherical cluster, define the "projected distribution function" $N(R, V)$ such that $N(R, V)dV$ is the surface density at R of galaxies with radial velocities in the range V to $V + dV$. At a given $R = R_0$, the function $N(R_0, V)$ is the so-called "line profile," the distribution of line-of-sight velocities at that projected radius. The integral of N over V is the surface density profile of the kinematic sample; the first moment of N over V is proportional to the line-of-sight rotational velocity profile (typically negligible for galaxy clusters); the second moment gives the line-of-sight velocity dispersion profile; etc. Although — remarkably, given the importance of the question — no one has yet proven mathematically that $N(R, V)$ contains enough information to uniquely determine the gravitational potential even in a spherical system, there is good reason to believe that it constrains the potential very tightly, and perhaps uniquely.[3-6] For instance, the line profiles $N(R_0, V)$ have distinctly different shapes in systems dominated by eccentric or circular orbits (Fig. 1). This fact suggests that we can determine the velocity anisotropy directly from the shapes of the line profiles, and then use the Jeans equation (1), with the known anisotropy, to infer the mass distribution.

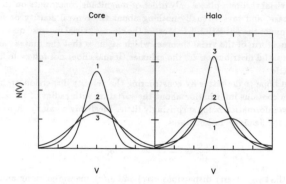

Fig. 1. Line-of-sight velocity distributions in a spherical cluster containing galaxies on three kinds of orbits. (1) Nearly circular orbits; (2) isotropic velocities; (3) strongly eccentric orbits. The left and right panels represent the appearance of the line profiles near the apparent center and in the halo, respectively.

Since the velocity dispersion profile itself tells us little about $\Phi(r)$, it follows that almost all of the kinematically-derivable information about the potential is contained within these finer details of the line-of-sight velocity distribution – crudely speaking, in the deviations of the line profiles from Gaussians (although the line profiles in even a precisely isotropic cluster need not be exactly Gaussian). This is a discouraging result, since modest departures from spherical symmetry or equilibrium in a galaxy cluster might substantially affect the shapes of these curves. In addition, rather large data sets – containing, perhaps, several hundred or even thousand velocities – are needed to construct reliable estimates of $N(R, V)$, even in a spherical cluster.

A nagging question is how to interpret past work on mass distributions in galaxy clusters as inferred from galaxy velocities. Almost all of these studies were based on the velocity dispersion profile alone – the additional (and essential) information contained within $N(R, V)$ was not used (perhaps in part because of the small size of most cluster data sets). We might expect these studies to have reached no very definite conclusions about the form of $\Phi(r)$, at least in cases where the velocity anisotropy was left as a free function to be determined by the data. On the contrary, however, many of these papers contain definite statements about the preferred form of the potential and of the galaxy kinematics – statements which appear to be justified, since the authors typically show that a particular model represents the data best. For instance, dynamical studies of the Coma cluster[7-11] often conclude that the best-fit model is one in which mass approximately follows light, and the galaxy velocities are roughly isotropic. How should we interpret these statements? Is there some objective sense in which these "best-fit" models are more likely than other models?

All of the Coma cluster studies cited above were "parametric": a set of convenient mathematical functions were postulated for representing the dynamical quantities of interest – e.g. the components of the galaxy velocity dispersion tensor,[9,10] or the phase-space density of the galaxies,[7,8,11] etc. – and the parameters of the assumed functions were then varied to maximize the goodness-of-fit of the spatially projected models to the number density and velocity dispersion profiles.

One danger of parametric techniques is that there almost always exists a single choice of parameters for which the model fits the data best, even if the underlying problem is mathematically degenerate – that is, even if the data, assumed complete and error-free, are insufficient to constrain the solution uniquely. This is because a single member of the parametric family will usually lie closest, in function space, to the region containing the set of possible, exact solutions. This single function will be selected by the optimization routine as the one that best matches the data, even though a more flexible representation of the unknown function would have yielded a range of equally-good solutions. In such cases, the "best-fit" model has no physical significance whatsoever; it is purely an artifact of the particular choice of parametric representation, since a different representation would have yielded a different "best-fit" model.

A simple experiment demonstrates the relevance of these arguments to the potential estimation problem. Suppose that we specify the observed number density and velocity dispersion profiles, $\Sigma(R)$ and $\sigma_p(R)$, of a spherical cluster. Suppose we represent the unknown distribution function describing the galaxies as a sum of basis functions, e.g.

$$f(E, L^2) = \sum_{i,j=1}^{n} c_{ij}(-E)^i L^{2j}, \tag{3}$$

where n is the number of terms retained in the expansion. By allowing f to depend on the orbital angular momentum L we permit the velocity distribution to be anisotropic. For any assumed potential $\Phi(r)$, we can then vary the c_{ij} to optimize the fit of the projected f to the measured profiles. Repeating this experiment with a family of trial potentials, we can find the pair of functions $\{\Phi, f\}$ that best reproduces $\Sigma(R)$ and $\sigma_p(R)$.

Fig. 2 shows the result for a $\Phi(r)$ defined by two parameters, core radius R_c and total mass M. The plotted contours represent the mean square deviation of the best-fit model from the "observed" profiles, in the assumed potential. When n, the number of basis functions representing f, is small, these contours single out a particular set of values R_c, M as most likely. (The lowest-order term in Eq. 3 gives the exact f from which the "observed" profiles were generated; thus, the peak in Fig. 2a lies very close to the true potential.) As n is increased, the χ^2 contours become peculiarly elongated; when $n = 15$, there is no longer a single best-fit potential, but instead a curved region in (R_c, M) space along which the goodness of fit is nearly constant. Thus, when the representation of the unknown f is strongly parametrized, the algorithm gives what appears to be a unique solution for the potential; while a more flexible representation for f reveals that a large number of forms for the potential are equally likely. Clearly, the "best-fit" potential in the first frame is simply an artifact; a different choice of basis set in the expansion (3) would have singled out a different point on the (R_c, M)-plane as optimum.

Most of the published studies of the mass distribution in galaxy clusters were based on parametrized representations with $n = 2$ or 3. As Fig. 2a shows, it is not surprising that these studies were able to find "optimum" values for the parameters defining the potential. Dejonghe[11] adopted the same series representation as in Eq. (3) for f, and used $n = 9$ terms in the expansion. His plots of goodness-of-fit for the Coma cluster (his figures 1 and 2) look very much like Fig. 2b here: Dejonghe also found a narrow ridge in potential parameter space along which χ^2 was nearly constant, with no well-defined maximum. Ironically, Dejonghe's treatment of the Coma data, which was algorithmically much superior to the others cited above, placed the *weakest* limits on the form of the potential, since his algorithm was the most flexible and hence best able to represent the wide range of f's corresponding to different potentials.

The open curve in Fig. 2c is the relation between M and R_c defined by the virial theorem, Eq. (1). Since the quantity $\langle v^2 \rangle$ is determined uniquely by the adopted profiles $\Sigma(R)$ and $\sigma_p(R)$, the virial theorem implies a relation between the two parameters R_c and M that define the adopted potential. It is apparent that the ridge of nearly-constant χ^2 in Fig. 2c is simply following this virial theorem curve. In other words, almost any potential that is consistent with the virial theorem can reproduce the kinematical data equally well. Thus, one way to interpret the results of past studies of the mass distribution in galaxy clusters is to say that these authors – with the help of sometimes formidable numerical machinery – did nothing more than to evaluate the virial theorem.

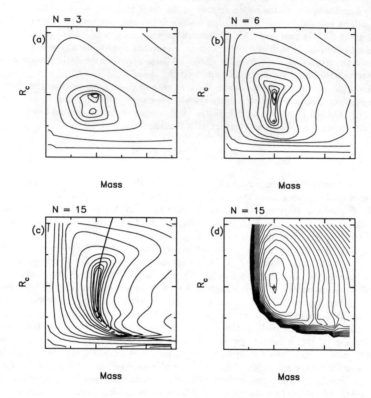

Fig. 2. Four attempts to find the "best-fit" potential from radial velocity data. In panels (a)-(c), the goodness of fit is defined as the mean square deviation of the theoretical $\Sigma(R)$ and $\sigma_p(R)$ from the data; N is the number of basis functions used to approximate f. Panel (d) shows contours of constant likelihood, as defined in the text; the + marks the correct solution. The solid line in (c) is the curve defined by the virial theorem.

[The fact that the "best-fit" models for the Coma cluster are often characterized by a nearly constant mass-to-light ratio and by a nearly isotropic velocity distribution has a simple explanation. It so happens that the Coma data *are* well described by such a model, as first shown by Rood *et al.*[7] Many authors – perhaps subconciously – adopt parametrized families for functions like $f(E, L^2)$ or $\sigma_r(r)$ that contain as a special case an isotropic distribution function with a number density profile close to that of the Coma galaxies. Their optimization routine then returns this model, or one similar to it, as the best fit.]

It is possible to modify the algorithm just described to make use of the complete information contained within a discrete set of positions and velocities. One simply replaces the functional describing the goodness of fit – taken above to be the mean-square deviation of the model profiles from the observed profiles $\Sigma(R)$ and $\sigma_p(R)$ – by the *likelihood* that the particular set of R's and V's would have been observed if the model were correct. That is, one varies f and Φ to optimize

$$\mathcal{L} = \prod_{data} N(R_i, V_i) \tag{4}$$

where $N(R_i, V_i)$ is the value of the projected distribution function corresponding to the model $\{f, \Phi\}$ at the data point R_i, V_i. This modification is moderately difficult from a technical point of view, since it requires the computation of the line profiles for every considered f and Φ.[12] But Fig. 2d shows that the extra effort is justified: the "most likely" potential, here computed from a sample of 300 positions and velocities, is now well-defined and very close to the correct one. (The regions of zero probability in Fig. 2d correspond to potentials for which at least one of the measured velocities V_i exceeds the escape velocity at $r = R_i$.) By evaluating goodness of fit via the likelihood rather than χ^2, the algorithm is forced to take account of the full distribution of line-of-sight velocities, and not just the dispersions, when judging the adequacy of a model.

Although encouraging, this experiment is still parametric in its representation of $\Phi(r)$. There might easily exist some very different $\Phi(r)$, not contained within the family of functions considered, that is equally consistent with the data. In fact numerical experiments show that – while data sets of a few hundred velocities can place usefully tight constraints on a potential characterized by only two free parameters, as in the example presented above – such data can not be used to make very model-independent statements about $\Phi(r)$.[12] The reason is that many more than a few hundred velocities are needed to accurately determine the line-of-sight velocity distributions $N(R, V)$. Furthermore, features in the line profiles that one might be tempted to attribute to anisotropy may be due in a real cluster to departures from equilibrium or spherical symmetry. Perhaps the most we can hope to accomplish in galaxy clusters is to falsify some interesting, simple model – e.g. a spherical model in which mass follows light, or in which the velocity distribution is everywhere isotropic, etc. – by comparing the detailed distribution of velocities in the model with that in the observed cluster.

3. The Coma Cluster

A. Biviano (this meeting) describes an ongoing project to measure a large number of galaxy velocities in the Coma cluster. One motivation for this study is to look for evidence in the kinematics for substructure or departures from equilibrium. Here we present an analysis of the existing velocity data under the assumption that Coma is spherical and relaxed. We discuss the consistency of this assumption at the end.

One simple way to compute $\Phi(r)$ from the kinematical data, without assuming *ad hoc* forms for the unknown functions, is to suppose that the distribution of galaxy velocities is everywhere isotropic. The intrinsic velocity dispersion is then given by the deprojection of the observed velocity dispersion profile:

$$\nu(r)\sigma^2(r) = -\frac{1}{\pi} \int_r^\infty \frac{d(\Sigma\sigma_p^2)}{dR} \frac{dR}{\sqrt{R^2 - r^2}}, \tag{5}$$

with $\nu(r)$ the spatial density of the galaxies, obtained by deprojecting the surface density:

$$\nu(r) = -\frac{1}{\pi} \int_r^\infty \frac{d\Sigma}{dR} \frac{dR}{\sqrt{R^2 - r^2}}. \tag{6}$$

The mass within r then follows from Eq. (2):

$$GM(r) = -r\sigma^2 \left(\frac{d\ln\nu}{d\ln r} + \frac{d\ln\sigma^2}{d\ln r} \right), \tag{7}$$

and the mass density is

$$\rho(r) = \frac{1}{4\pi r^2} \frac{dM}{dr}. \tag{8}$$

Here we are treating the galaxies as if they were ions in an X-ray emitting gas; the quantity $\sigma^2(r)$ plays the role of $kT(r)/m$ in the gas.

Eqs. (5) - (8) define an "inverse problem" with a unique solution $\rho(r)$, given smooth estimates of $\Sigma(R)$ and $\sigma_p(R)$. Astronomers tend to solve such problems by postulating a model, then projecting it into observable space and comparing with the data. But statisticians are fond of noting that the use of parametrized models for the solution of inverse problems is extremely dangerous, even if (unlike the case discussed in the previous section) the inverse problem has a *mathematically* unique solution. The reason is that the quantities of interest are usually related to the data via differentiations. For instance, $\rho(r)$ depends on a second derivative of $\nu(r)$ (Eqs. 7 and 8), and ν is itself a deprojection, i.e. derivative, of Σ (Eq. 6). Any small error in the choice of parametrized model to represent $\Sigma(R)$ or $\sigma_p(R)$ will be amplified enormously in the computation of $\rho(r)$. At one level, this means simply that accurate estimation of quantities like the mass density requires high-quality data. But regardless of the quality of the data, one has a much better chance of finding the correct solution if the modeling is carried out nonparametrically. This is because a nonparametric function estimate will tend to follow the curvature implied by the data, rather than imposing a shape that is likely to be subtly wrong, even if it fits the data well in a χ^2 sense.

A uniformly consistent way of solving ill-conditioned inverse problems like this one[13] is to construct smooth estimates of the input functions (here Σ and σ_p) directly from the data, using a nonparametric algorithm, then to operate mathematically on these smooth functions to produce estimates of the functions of interest (i.e. Φ, ρ). Confidence bands on the estimates can be constructed via the bootstrap.[14] The instability due to the inversion is dealt with by simply using a larger smoothing length on the data when constructing the estimates of Φ or ρ, than would be appropriate for the estimates of the data functions Σ or σ_p themselves.[15] By contrast, parametric techniques deal with the instability by brute force, and are almost certain to bias the answer regardless of the quality or quantity of the data.

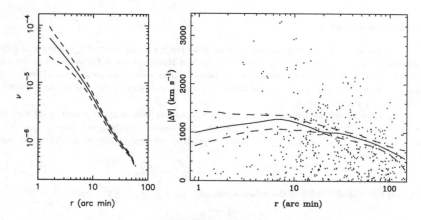

Fig. 3. Nonparametric estimates of the number density profile $\hat{\nu}(r)$ and line-of-sight velocity dispersion profile $\hat{\sigma}_p(R)$ defined by the Coma galaxies. The points in the right-hand panel are the 433 measured velocities from the compilation of T. Bird & M. King. Dashed lines are 90% confidence bands on the estimates.

Accordingly, Fig. 3 shows nonparametric estimates of $\nu(r)$ and $\sigma_p(R)$ for the Coma galaxies. The estimate $\hat{\nu}(r)$ was computed from a sample of 1480 galaxies identified as likely members by Mellier *et al.*,[16] using a "maximum penalized likelihood" algorithm[17] with Abell's[18] choice of cluster center. Interestingly, $\hat{\nu}(r)$ does not look very similar to any of the functional forms that are usually fit to it, such as the lowered isothermal sphere. Instead there is a roughly power-law cusp inside of 10', with $\hat{\nu} \propto r^{-1}$. The estimate $\hat{\sigma}_p(R)$ was computed from a set of 433 galaxies with measured velocities, as compiled by T. Bird and M. King. The "LOWESS" regression algorithm of W. S. Cleveland[19] was used. Both estimates are highly uncertain at radii $R \lesssim 3'$ due to the small number of bright galaxies near the center.

Fig. 4a gives the estimated mass density as a function of radius in the isotropic model, obtained by applying eqs. (7) and (8) to $\hat{\nu}$ and $\hat{\sigma}_p$. $\hat{\rho}(r)$ falls roughly as r^{-3} over most of the cluster in this model, although there is a hint of a core inside of a few hundred kpc; however the 90% confidence bands are consistent with a pure power law even at small radii.

Although consistent – by construction – with the data as presented in Fig. 3, this isotropic model might still be inconsistent with the full set of velocities in Coma. Fig. 5 shows estimates of the line profiles $N(R, V)$ at three radii in the Coma cluster, as computed with an adaptive kernel algorithm[20] using galaxies from the Bird-King sample grouped in three radial annuli. Shown for comparison are the line profiles predicted by the isotropic model just discussed; the latter were computed from

$$N(R, V) = \pi \int_{R^2}^{r_{max}^2(V)} \frac{dr^2}{\sqrt{r^2 - R^2}} \int_0^{-2\Phi(r)-V^2} f\left[v'^2/2 + V^2/2 + \Phi(r)\right] dv'^2, \qquad (9)$$

with the isotropic distribution function $f(E)$ computed from $\hat{\nu}$ and $\hat{\Phi}$ via Eddington's equation. (For clarity, we have omitted confidence bands on the model $N(R, V)$'s.) While the overall agreement is reasonable, there are some apparently signficant differences. The velocity distribution near the center of Coma is more peaked near $V = 0$ than in the model, perhaps indicative of an anisotropic subpopulation at the cluster center. At intermediate radii, the Coma velocity distribution is somewhat bimodal; at large radii, the distribution is once again nearly symmetric, but the mean has shifted by about 150 km s^{-1} from the mean velocity near the center. Furthermore, the model profile is somewhat less peaked than the true profile at large radii.

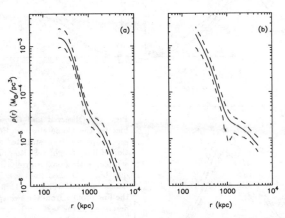

Fig. 4. Nonparametric estimates of the mass density profile $\hat{\rho}(r)$ in the Coma cluster. (a) Isotropic model; (b) anisotropic model ($r_a = 60' \approx 2.4$ Mpc). Dashed lines are 90% confidence bands on the estimates; $H_0 = 50$ km s^{-1} Mpc^{-1}.

We can test the sensitivity of the predicted $N(R, V)$ to the assumption of isotropy by varying the assumed kinematics – taking care to leave fixed the detailed dependence of Σ and σ_p on radius. In other words, we vary *both* $\Phi(r)$, as well as the anisotropy $\beta(r) = 1 - \sigma_t^2/\sigma_r^2$, in such a way as to leave Σ and σ_p unchanged. One natural (though admittedly parametric) choice for describing the internal kinematics is $\sigma_r^2/\sigma_t^2 = 1 + r^2/r_a^2$, where the anisotropy radius r_a defines where the galaxy velocities begin to become strongly radial. For any choice of r_a, one can then derive $\Phi(r)$ using a set of equations similar to those given above for the isotropic case.[21] There then exists a simple (though not unique) anisotropic distribution function $f(E + L^2/2r_a^2)$ that yields the observed $\hat{\nu}(r)$ in this potential.[22] $N(R, V)$ can be computed from this f via a Monte-Carlo algorithm.

The results are shown in Figs. 4 and 5, for $r_a = 60' \approx 2.4$ Mpc. The predicted mass density profile is still well described as $\rho \propto r^{-3}$ near the cluster center, but becomes much flatter at large radii to compensate for the assumed anisotropy. (Values of r_a less than about $40'$ yield a non-monotonic, and eventually negative, mass density profile; thus the model shown here with $r_a=60'$ is close to the maximally anisotropic allowed by this form of β.) The predicted line-of-sight velocity distributions (Fig. 5) differ from those in the isotropic model only at large radii, where the preponderance of radial orbits predicts a more peaked profile, as in fact seen in the Coma data. However the predicted difference between the two models, even at large radii, is not much greater than the uncertainty in the estimates of the Coma line profiles themselves, suggesting that the current sample of ~450 velocities is barely large enough to distinguish between these two very different models. This result is not surprising: since both the area and the width of the curves in each frame of Fig. 5 are fixed by construction, the only way these curves can differ is in their detailed shapes, and large numbers of discrete velocities are required to detect such deviations with certainty.[23]

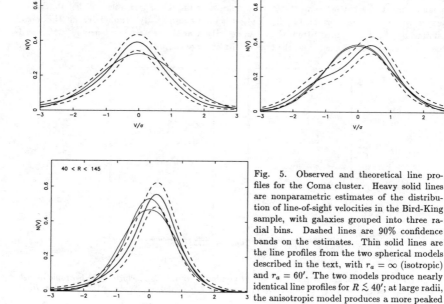

Fig. 5. Observed and theoretical line profiles for the Coma cluster. Heavy solid lines are nonparametric estimates of the distribution of line-of-sight velocities in the Bird-King sample, with galaxies grouped into three radial bins. Dashed lines are 90% confidence bands on the estimates. Thin solid lines are the line profiles from the two spherical models described in the text, with $r_a = \infty$ (isotropic) and $r_a = 60'$. The two models produce nearly identical line profiles for $R \lesssim 40'$; at large radii, the anisotropic model produces a more peaked profile.

Because $\hat{\rho}(r)$ rises more steeply into the center of Coma than the galaxy number density, the local mass-to-light ratio increases sharply at small radii in both of the models presented here, by a factor of ~ 3-5 between 1 Mpc and 300 kpc.

We note that the Coma line profiles are reasonably symmetric, with no strong indications of substructure. Larger velocity samples, such as that of Biviano *et al.*, should tell us whether the slight asymmetries seen in Fig. 5 are indicative of substructure or are simply finite-sample fluctuations. (The circular orbital time exceeds H_0^{-1} at $r \approx 100' \approx 4$ Mpc in our isotropic model, so we would not expect Coma to be completely relaxed at the largest radii for which we have data. But even at smaller radii, the X-ray emission[24] and galaxy positions[25] show evidence for subgroupings and ongoing formation.) The presence of dynamically-significant substructure is potentially the most serious problem facing cluster mass determinations based on galaxy velocities.

4. Conclusions

Even in a perfectly spherical and stationary cluster, estimation of the radial dependence of the dark matter density from line-of-sight velocity data is a hard problem. One always has the freedom to "adjust" the assumed dependence of velocity anisotropy on radius to compensate for changes in the assumed mass distribution, in such a way that the galaxy velocity dispersion profile remains precisely unchanged. But most past studies have begun by reducing all of the kinematical data to a velocity dispersion profile; the "optimum" models found in these studies can accordingly be shown to be numerical artifacts, resulting from the use of *ad hoc* parametrized functions to describe the galaxy velocity distribution function or its moments. Almost all of the information about the radial dependence of the potential is contained within the fine details of the line-of-sight velocity distribution $N(R, V)$. Furthermore, very different dynamical models – constructed so as to reproduce exactly the number density and velocity dispersion profiles defined by the galaxies – can yield very similar $N(R, V)$'s. Distinguishing between these different models, even in the idealized spherical case, requires large samples of discrete velocities, $N \gtrsim 1000$. If the cluster is nonspherical or out of equilibrium, even larger velocity samples (and more sophisticated algorithms) would be needed to constrain $\Phi(r)$ in a model-independent way. We have shown that the existing velocity data for the Coma cluster are reasonably consistent with an equilibrium model in which the mass density falls off as $\sim r^{-3}$ for $r \lesssim 1.5$ Mpc, with, perhaps, a more gradual falloff at larger radii; the total mass of the cluster is poorly defined by these data but could be several times the value derived by assuming that mass follows light.

Acknowledgements

We are indebted to T. Bird and M. King for giving us their compilation of Coma velocities in machine-readable form.

References

1. F. Zwicky, *Helv. Phys. Acta.* **6** (1933) 110.
2. F. O'Sullivan, *Stat. Sci.* **1** (1986) 502.
3. H. Dejonghe and D. Merritt, *Astrophys. J.* 531 **391** (1992).
4. S. M. Kent, *Mon. Not. R. Astron. Soc.* **247** (1991) 702.
5. D. Merritt, *Astrophys. J.* **413** (1993) 79.
6. O. Gerhard, *Mon. Not. R. Astron. Soc.* **265** (1993) 213.
7. H. J. Rood, T. L. Page, E. C. Kintner and I. R. King, *Astrophys. J.* **175** (1972) 627.
8. S. M. Kent and J. E. Gunn, *Astron. J.* **87** (1982) 945.
9. M. E. Bailey, *Mon. Not. R. Astron. Soc.* **201** (1982) 271.
10. L. S. The & S. D. M. White, *Astron. J.* **92** (1986) 1248.

11. H. Dejonghe, *Astrophys. J.* **343** (1989) 113.
12. D. Merritt and P. Saha, *Astrophys. J.* **409** (1993) 75.
13. G. Wahba, *Spline Models for Observational Data* (SIAM: Philadelphia) (1990) p. 19.
14. B. Efron, *The Jackknife, the Bootstrap and Other Resampling Plans* (SIAM: Phila- delphia) (1982).
15. D. W. Scott, *Multivariate Density Estimation* (Wiley: New York) (1992) p. 131.
16. Y. Mellier *et al.*, *Astron. Astrophys.* **199** (1988) 67.
17. D. Merritt and B. Tremblay, *Astron. J.* **108** (1994).
18. G. O. Abell, *Ann. Rev. Astron. Astrophys.* **3** (1965) 1.
19. W. S. Cleveland, *J. Am. Stat. Assoc.* **74** (1979) 829.
20. B. W. Silverman, *Density Estimation for Statistics and Data Analysis* (Chapman and Hall: London) (1986) p. 100.
21. D. Merritt, *Astrophys. J.* **313** (1987) 121.
22. D. Merritt, *Astron. J.* **90** (1985) 1027.
23. M. Merrifield and S. M. Kent, *Astron. J.* **99** (1990) 1548.
24. S. D. M. White, U. G. Briel and J. P. Henry, *Mon. Not. R. Astron. Soc.* **261** (1993) L8.
25. Y. Mellier, G. Mathez, A. Mazure, B. Chauvineau and D. Proust, *Astron. Astrophys.* **199** (1988) 67.

SUBSTRUCTURE: CLUES TO CLUSTER FORMATION

Michael J. West

Sterrewacht Leiden, The Netherlands

Abstract

Observational evidence of substructure in clusters of galaxies is briefly reviewed, and its implications discussed. Current estimates suggest that many, perhaps most, clusters harbor substructure in their galaxy and/or gas distribution. Quantitative analysis of the frequency and properties of subclustering can provide important cosmological constraints, as well as insights to cluster and galaxy formation.

1 INTRODUCTION

Back in the halcyon days of Zwicky and Abell, clusters of galaxies were generally assumed to be dynamically-relaxed systems that were well described by equilibrium models. Today, however, a growing abundance of optical, x-ray and redshift data has revealed that many clusters are much more complex systems than originally thought. Substructure – localized concentrations of galaxies and/or gas within an otherwise smooth cluster mass distribution – appears to be a common feature of many, perhaps most, clusters[1].

2 OBSERVATIONS

2.1 Substructure: The Local Group

With hindsight, it probably should not have come as any great surprise that many clusters have substructure. The nearest cluster to us, our own Local Group, has long been known to have two distinct mass concentrations. Figure 1 shows the Local Group as it would appear to an observer at the Celestial Pole; the galaxy distribution is strongly clustered around the two dominant galaxies, M31 and the Milky Way.

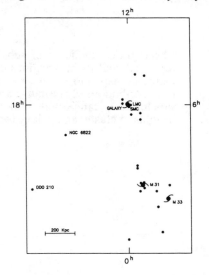

Figure 1. The distribution of Local Group galaxies as seen from the Celestial Pole (from van den Bergh 1989[2]). Note the strong clumping of galaxies around the two dominant members, M31 and the Milky Way.

2.2 Substructure: The Virgo Cluster

The nearest rich cluster to us, the Virgo cluster, also exhibits substructure. More than 30 years ago, de Vaucouleurs[3] suggested that the Virgo cluster is composed of several distinct but overlapping subclumps which have different galaxy populations and kinematics. More recently, Binggeli, Tammann & Sandage[4] mapped the galaxy

distribution in the Virgo cluster in great detail, concluding that Virgo shows a pronounced "double structure" with prominent subclusters around the bright galaxies
M87 and M49, as well as a number of other smaller clumps (see Figure 2).

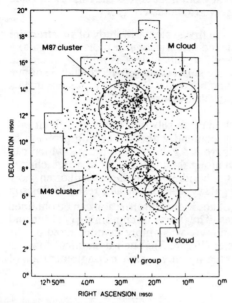

Figure 2. Projected distribution of
Virgo cluster galaxies (from Binggeli
et al. 1987). Prominent subclusters
are circled.

2.3 Substructure: Abell Clusters

With the systematic cataloguing of clusters by Abell[5] and Zwicky[6] it became
possible to explore substructure in a statistical way using large samples of clusters.

The first study to address the question of substructure in Abell clusters was by
Abell, Neyman & Scott[7]. These authors developed a statistical test for substructure
and then applied it to the projected galaxy distribution in seven clusters. Their
conclusion was that 5 out of 7 clusters had evidence of substructure, a result which
is quite similar to more modern studies.

Many optical studies of substructure in Abell clusters have since been published.
Obviously it is not possible to review all of them in the limited space available here,
so instead the following is a list of those papers which I feel have had the greatest
impact on the field. The reader should bear in mind that this is a personal view, and
a different author might give a different list, however the papers presented below
should be a fair representation of the work that has been done to date.

• *Baier 1977-84.* In a series of papers, Baier[8 – 11] and collaborators presented isodensity contour plots of the projected galaxy distribution in a large number of Abell clusters. These papers were the first to suggest that substructure might be very common in clusters, although they did not address the important issue of the statistical significance of the observed subclustering.

• *Geller and Beers 1982*[12]. This was the first systematic study of substructure in galaxy clusters. These authors produced density contour plots of the galaxy distribution in 65 clusters and then identified subclusters as regions where the local density contrast smoothed over some small scale was more than 3σ above the background fluctuations. They concluded that $\sim 40\%$ of clusters in this sample exhibited statistically significant substructure.

• *Bothun et al. 1983*[13]. Detecting bona fide substructure is a difficult task with galaxy positions alone; one must contend with the nagging problem of contamination by foreground and background galaxies and groups which can masquerade as substructure when seen along the line of sight to a rich cluster. Moreover, clusters with only a few tens or hundreds of members will often show apparent clumpiness in their projected galaxy distribution as a result of Poisson fluctuations[14]. However, a great deal of additional information can be obtained from radial velocities of cluster galaxies. The power of combining position and velocity information to look for substructure was amply demonstrated by the Bothun et al. study of the Cancer cluster (Figure 3). Their dynamical analysis revealed that the Cancer "cluster" is in reality only a chance conglomeration of five unrelated groups.

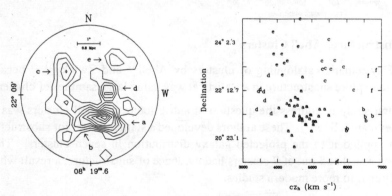

Figure 3. The Cancer cluster (from Bothun et al. 1983). The left panel shows isodensity contours of the projected galaxy distribution. The right panel shows a plot of galaxy declination versus radial velocity. The Cancer cluster is seen to be composed of five distinct subgroups (denoted a – e).

• *Dressler & Shectman 1988*[15]. This seminal study employed an extensive dataset of positions and radial velocities for over 1000 galaxies in 15 Abell clusters together with a sensitive test for substructure. By searching for localized correlations between positions and velocities that would be a telltale signature of dynamical subgroupings, these authors found that at least 30% – 40% of the clusters in their sample had statistically significant substructure.

- *Fitchett & Webster 1987*[16]; *Mellier et al. 1988*[17]. These and other papers (see refs. 11, 18, 19) claimed evidence of substructure in the core of the Coma cluster, a result which has since been confirmed by Einstein and ROSAT x-ray imaging (see refs. 20 - 22). These studies had an important impact on the field by challenging the long-held belief that Coma – the quintessential rich cluster – had already reached a tranquil, post-virialized state. If the Coma cluster could have substructure, then clearly many other clusters might also!

It should be mentioned that Zwicky[23] too alluded to substructure in clusters. However, this was due in part to Zwicky's considerably looser definition of what constitutes a galaxy cluster; many of the low density "clusters" identified by Zwicky were actually extended supercluster regions, with the "subclusters" corresponding to individual groups and clusters.

2.4 Substructure: X-ray Observations

X-ray studies of substructure offer a number of advantages over optical studies. Because the x-ray emission is proportional to the square of the local matter density, the distribution of hot intracluster gas can provide a more sensitive probe of variations in the cluster mass distribution. And unlike optical studies, which are inherently limited by counting statistics from at most a few hundred cluster galaxies, x-ray observations can readily increase the ratio of signal to noise by integrating longer to collect more photons. Furthermore, x-ray studies of substructure are less susceptible to line-of-sight contamination.

Early imaging observations with the Einstein satellite revealed that a number of Abell clusters are in fact "double clusters" composed of two roughly equal-mass components[24]. More recently, Jones and Forman[25] and Stern et al.[22] examined the x-ray morphologies of 208 clusters observed with Einstein (see Figure 4), concluding that at least 22% of these clusters, and possibly as many as 40%, show unambiguous evidence of substructure. This is likely to be a *lower* limit on the true fraction of clusters with substructure, since improved x-ray resolution and more photons would undoubtedly increase the number of detected substructures.

ROSAT observations have also provided dramatic evidence of substructure in a number of clusters. Briel et al.[26] showed that Abell 2256 contains a secondary clump that is in the process of merging with the main cluster. Similarly, White et al.[20] identified a number of subclusters within the Coma cluster, including a large subcluster centered on NGC 4839 that appears to be falling into the Coma at present. These and other ROSAT discoveries have emphasized that substructure may lurk anywhere – even in the cores of very rich clusters like Coma and Abell 2256.

Abell 514   Abell 1750

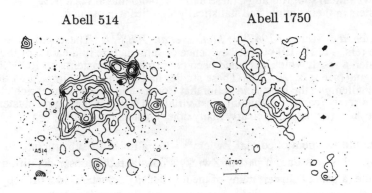

Figure 4. X-ray isointensity contours for two clusters with obvious substructure (from Jones & Forman 1992).

2.5   Substructure: Gravitational Lenses

Additional evidence for substructure comes from studies of gravitational lenses, which provide a direct means of probing the dark matter distribution in clusters. In a number of clusters the observed positions, orientations and curvatures of the giant luminous arcs and smaller arclets strongly suggest the presence of multiple mass concentrations[27 – 30]

2.6   The Bottom Line

The overwhelming majority of observational studies to date indicate that substructure is common in *at least* 30% of rich clusters. Recent work suggests that as many as 50% to 75% of clusters may contain substructure[31 – 34]. Indeed, given the trend over the past decade, it would not be too surprising if eventually *all* clusters are found to have some substructure when examined with sufficient resolution.

3   WHAT CAN WE LEARN FROM SUBSTRUCTURE?

The prevalence of substructure among clusters today strongly suggests that we are currently in the epoch of cluster formation. If clusters are dynamically young, then they may still retain traces of the conditions at the time of their formation. Hence substructure can provide valuable information about the early universe, galaxy and cluster formation, and a host of other topics. Some examples are given below.

3.1 Cosmological Parameters: $\Omega_0, P(k)$

It is well known that the formation of structure by gravitational instability depends sensitively on the cosmological density parameter Ω and on the primordial spectrum of density fluctuations $P(k)$. In a low density universe, density fluctuations cease growing at early epochs ($z \sim \Omega_0^{-1}$), whereas in a high-Ω universe structure formation continues unabated to the present. Richstone, Loeb & Turner[35] had the clever idea of using substructure to determine the current rate of cluster formation, and thereby place constraints on the value of Ω_0. As Figure 5 shows, cluster evolution is expected to be a strong function of Ω_0. Richstone et al. concluded that the observational evidence for 30% or more of clusters with substructure requires that $\Omega_0 \gtrsim 0.5$.

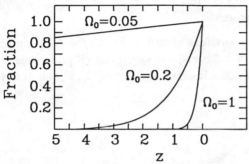

Figure 5. The fraction of present-day clusters formed by redshift z in universes with different values of Ω_0 (after Richstone et al. 1992).

There are, however, some complications. Most importantly, estimates of Ω_0 depend on the timescale for subcluster disruption, which is unknown (e.g., if individual subclusters survived for a Hubble time then the fraction of clusters with substructure today would tell us nothing about the formation rate of clusters). Richstone et al. made the reasonable assumption that subclusters would be destroyed within a dynamical time, however this should be checked with numerical experiments. Furthermore, one cannot easily separate Ω_0 from $P(k)$, since the abundance and mass function of subclusters, as well as the timescale for their disruption, will depend on the spectrum of density fluctuations[14]. Nevertheless, the basic idea behind the Richstone et al. approach is sound, and their results provide rather compelling evidence in favor of a high-density universe.

Studies of clusters at earlier epochs can also place interesting limits on the rate of cluster evolution. The CNOC[36] collaboration has begun an ambitious project to study a number of the richest clusters at redshifts $z \simeq 0.2 - 0.5$, one of the goals being to examine the dynamical state of these clusters.

It is interesting to note that substructure may also provide a means of reconciling the seemingly paradoxical evidence for low and high values of Ω_0. The abundance of clusters with substructure today indicates a high-density universe, yet dynamical mass estimates from clusters consistently yield low values of $\Omega_0 \simeq 0.1$. A possible resolution to this quandary comes from N-body simulations[37 − 39] which have shown that segregation of galaxies from dark matter can develop rapidly within subclusters, and that this segregation is preserved after subclusters merge to form clusters. A consequence of this "dynamical bias" is that the virial theorem may underestimate the true masses of clusters today by as much as an order of magnitude; hence the observed values of $\Omega_0 \simeq 0.1$ from cluster dynamics could be consistent with a true value of $\Omega_0 \simeq 1$.

3.2 Clusters in Relation to Large-Scale Structures

As "fossil" remains from earlier stages of cluster formation, substructure can provide important clues about the formation process.

Consider the Coma cluster and its environs shown in Figure 6. As discussed earlier, this cluster has a number of subclusters; the supergiant elliptical galaxies NGC 4889 and NGC 4874 reside in two subclusters in the core of Coma, and ROSAT

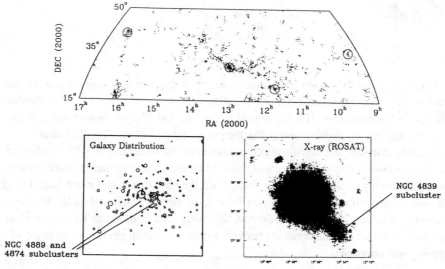

Figure 6. Top panel: the galaxy distribution in the region of the Coma cluster and its environs. Circles denote Abell clusters. Bottom panels: the distribution of subclusters in the Coma cluster (optical data are from Mellier et al. 1988; ROSAT image is from White et al. 1993).

observations have revealed a third large subcluster associated with NGC 4839. Interestingly, the distribution of these subclusters appears to follow roughly the same orientation as the local filamentary supercluster in which Coma is embedded; this suggests that the distribution of subclusters may be correlated with the surrounding large-scale matter distribution.

West, Jones & Forman[40] have used Einstein observations[22] to examine the distribution of subclusters in a large number of clusters. Because most clusters are too distant for the surrounding filamentary structure to be seen in existing galaxy surveys, Abell clusters were used as tracers of the surrounding large-scale structure. For clusters with two or more x-ray peaks, the position angle between the component subclusters was compared with the position angle from the cluster to each neighboring Abell cluster within a distance of 10 h^{-1} Mpc. Figure 7 illustrates the method more clearly, together with the results. If subclusters are randomly distributed with respect to the surrounding distribution of Abell clusters, then θ should be uniformly distributed between 0° and 90°. What one sees instead is that the observed distribution is strongly skewed towards small values of θ, which indicates that subclusters tend to share the same orientation as the surrounding supercluster. We also find that when multiple subclusters are present in a cluster they frequently have a collinear arrangement.

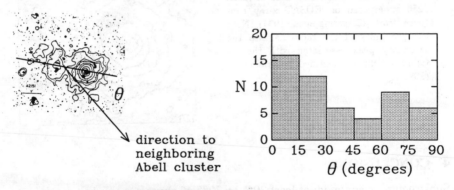

Figure 7. Left panel: schematic representation of the method used to examine subcluster orientations. Right panel: the distribution of observed values of θ (from West, Jones & Forman 1994).

These results suggest a picture in which cluster formation proceeds by mergers of subclusters along large-scale filamentary features in the galaxy distribution. Such a formation process has important implications for the shapes, orientations and kinematics of clusters.

3.3 cD Galaxies, Cooling Flows, and Radio Sources

Substructure also has important implications for our understanding of galaxy formation. For example, the well-known difficulty of forming massive cD galaxies via mergers and accretion in present-day clusters is ameliorated if they instead formed within subclusters at earlier epochs[41, 42]. The question of cD peculiar velocities also appears to be closely related to substructure[34, 43 − 45].

Growing observational evidence suggests that there may also be an important connection between substructure and radio emission in clusters. Radio halos − enigmatic regions of diffuse radio emission in clusters that do not appear to be associated with any galaxy − may find a possible explanation as a result of recent subcluster mergers[46, 47] As Figure 8 shows, for example, the diffuse radio halo in Abell 2256 is located quite close to the infalling subcluster. Additionally, there is interesting evidence that cluster radio galaxies may serve as beacons for identifying recent subcluster mergers[48].

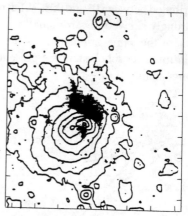

Figure 8. The diffuse radio halo in Abell 2256 superposed on ROSAT x-ray contours (from Röttgering et al. 1994). Note the proximity of the radio halo to the secondary peak associated with the infalling subcluster identified by Briel et al. (1991).

4 CONCLUSIONS

Substructure is common; at least 30% to 70% of clusters studied to date appear to have multiple mass concentrations. The once orthodox view of clusters of galaxies as simple, dynamically-relaxed systems is clearly no longer tenable.

Substructure can provide a wealth of information about such diverse topics as cluster and galaxy formation, cosmology, and the intracluster medium. Happily, we can be assured of rapid progress in the next few years.

Acknowledgements. I thank my collaborators Christine Jones, Bill Forman and everyone in the CNOC group. I also thank the Netherlands Foundation for Research in Astronomy (ASTRON) and the Leids Kerkhoven-Bosscha Fonds for financial support.

REFERENCES

1) For earlier reviews on this subject see M.J. Fitchett 1988 in The Minnesota Lectures on Clusters of Galaxies and Large-Scale Structure, ed. J.M. Dickey (ASP Conf.Ser.,5), 143 and also M.J. Geller 1984, Comments Astrophys., 10, 47
2) van den Bergh, S., 1989, Astron. Astrophys. Rev., 1, 111
3) de Vaucouleurs, G., 1961, ApJS, 6, 213
4) Binggeli, B., Tammann, G.A. & Sandage, A., 1987, AJ, 94, 251
5) Abell, G.O., 1958, ApJS, 3, 211
6) Zwicky, F., et al., 1961-1968, Catalog of Galaxies and Clusters of Galaxies, Vols. 1-6, Pasadena, California Institute of Technology
7) Abell, G.O., Neyman, J. & Scott, E.L., 1964, AJ, 69, 529
8) Baier, F.W., 1977, Astr. Nach., 298, 151
9) Baier, F.W. & Ziener, R., 1977, Astr. Nach., 298, 87
10) Baier, F.W., 1983, Astr. Nach., 304, 211
11) Baier, F.W., 1984, Astr. Nach., 305, 175
12) Geller, M.J. & Beers, T.C., 1982, PASP, 94, 421
13) Bothun, G.D., Geller, M.J., Beers, T.C. & Huchra, J.P., 1983, ApJ, 268, 47
14) West, M.J., Oemler, A. & Dekel, A., 1988, ApJ, 327, 1
15) Dressler, A. & Shectman, S.A., 1988, AJ, 95, 985]
16) Fitchett, M.J. & Webster, R.L., 1987, ApJ, 317, 653
17) Mellier, Y., et al., 1988, A&A, 199, 67
18) Rood, H.J., 1974, ApJ, 188, 451
19) Valtonen, M.J. & Byrd, G.G., 1979, ApJ, 230, 655
20) White, S.D.M., Briel, U.G. & Henry, J.P., 1993, MNRAS, 261, L8
21) Davis, D.S. & Mushotzky, R.F., 1993, AJ, 105, 409
22) Stern, C., Jones, C., Hughes, J. & Forman, W., 1994, to be submitted to ApJ
23) Zwicky, F., 1957, Morphological Astronomy (Berlin:Spinger-Verlag)
24) Forman, W., et al., 1981, ApJ, 243, L133
25) Jones, C. & Forman, W., 1992, in Clusters and Superclusters of Galaxies, ed. A.C. Fabian (Dordrecht: Kluwer), p. 49
26) Briel, U.G., et al., 1991, A&A, 246, L10
27) Grossman, S.A. & Narayan, R., 1989, ApJ, 334, 637
28) Pelló, R., et al., 1991, ApJ, 366, 405
29) Miralda-Escudé, J., 1993, ApJ, 403, 497
30) Kneib, J., et al., 1993, A&A, 273, 367
31) Mohr, J.J., 1993, ApJ, 413, 492
32) Salvador-Solé, E., Sanromà, M., & González-Casado, G., 1993, ApJ, 402, 398
33) Escalera, E., et al., 1994, ApJ, 423, 539
34) Bird, C., 1994, AJ, in press
35) Richstone, D., Loeb, A. & Turner, E.L., 1992, ApJ, 393, 477
36) Carlberg, R.G., et al., 1994, JRASC, 88, 39
37) West, M.J. & Richstone, D.O., 1988, ApJ, 335, 532
38) Carlberg, R.G., & Couchman, H.M.P., 1989, ApJ, 340, 47
39) Serna, A., Alimi, J.-M. & Scholl, H., 1994, ApJ, in press
40) West, M.J., Jones, C. & Forman, W., 1994, in preparation
41) Merritt, D., 1985, ApJ, 289, 18
42) Tremaine, S., 1990, in Dynamics and Interactions of Galaxies, ed. R. Wielen (Berlin: Springer-Verlag), p. 394
43) Malumuth, E.M., et al., 1992, AJ, 104, 495
44) Bird, C., 1994, ApJ, 422, 480
45) Oegerle, W.R. & Hill, J.M., 1994, AJ, in press
46) Fabian, A.C. & Daines, S.J., 1991, MNRAS, 252, 17p
47) Röttgering, H.J.A., et al., 1994, ApJ, in press
48) Burns, J.O., et al., 1994, ApJ, 423, 94

FRACTAL COLD GAS AS DARK MATTER
IN GALAXIES AND CLUSTERS

Daniel Pfenniger
Observatoire de Genève, CH-1290 Sauverny, Switzerland

Françoise Combes
DEMIRM, Observatoire de Paris
61 Av. de l'Observatoire, F-75 014 Paris, France

Abstract. The conjecture that dark matter in galaxies is mostly cold fractal gas exposed in another paper at this conference is developed in the more general context of the thermodynamics of the ideal isothermal gas subject to gravitational instability. This simple gas model already contains the contrary ingredients able to prevent an asymptotic equilibrium: any growing gravothermal singularity evaporates in a finite time, and any tendency to uniform gas is gravitationally unstable. The paradox is simply resolved by allowing fractal states, which are then scale-free and steady *in average*, but non-differentiable and time-dependent.

If we apply to clusters the lessons learned with galaxies, we are led to the conclusion that gas in clusters at a temperature much below the virial temperature should also adopt a fractal structure and become inhomogeneous. The same instrumental biases acting at galactic scale and preventing the detection of the smallest and coldest sub-resolution clumps in the fractal are then even more relevant for cluster gas measurements.

The large baryonic mass observed in the cluster hot gas and the morphology-density relation suggest also gaseous dark matter in spirals. If this dark gas component remains undetected in spirals, the same instrumental biases should hold in clusters, where cooling hot gas disappears from detection near the centre.

1. EVOLUTION OF GALAXIES AND GALACTIC DARK MATTER

Nowadays many hints point toward a secular evolution of galaxies much faster than classically envisioned in the 60's[1]. In particular at the scale of galaxy clusters or galaxy groups the morphology-density relation (e.g. [2]) and the Butcher-Oemler effect indicate possible major modifications of galaxies in much less than the Hubble time. At the scale of galaxies the better understanding of mergers[3], galaxy dynamics[4], and the observations of metal rich and blue bulges[5] also indicate that galaxies are still changing today, with probable sub-Gyr phases of evolution. If the Hubble sequence is an evolutionary sequence, then the only reasonable evolutionary sense is from Sm-Sd to Sa, because all the irreversible processes such as bulge formation, star formation and heavy elements enrichment are increasing this way[6].

Now the M/L ratio along the Hubble sequence decreases from more than 100 in dwarf irregulars to nearly normal for visible matter (≈ 10) in Sa's. Admitting regular processes dark matter cannot be removed selectively during galaxy evolution because the total mass of galaxies increases from Sd to Sa (e.g. [7]). Also it is dynamically ruled out to accrete more than a few percents of matter within an already formed stellar disk without heating or destroying it[8],[9]. But it remains possible to accrete large amounts of angular momentum rich and dissipative matter at the disk periphery, as in high resolution cosmological simulations with gas (e.g. [10]). So the simplest hypothesis is to assume that during the secular evolution of isolated disk galaxies dark matter transforms into stars. The only way to achieve this is to have most dark matter in some gaseous form beyond the optical disks.

The small amount of dark matter in Sa galaxies and stellar disks puts a constraint on the amount of non-gaseous dark matter, such as brown dwarfs, black-holes, or other dark matter candidates in the original mix making late-type spirals. Since the amount of dark matter in early-type spirals is at most of the order of the visible matter, it means that in late-type spirals the fraction of non-gaseous dark matter is less than about 10%.

The obvious problem with gaseous dark matter is then to explain why the mass of gas as usually determined from HI and CO observations is, although proportional to dark matter, insufficient by a large factor (≈ 20). By critically reviewing the knowledges we have about interstellar gas, we can state the following[11]: interstellar gas is typically very inhomogeneous and multi-phase, covering decades of density and temperature ranges; in gravitating systems such as galaxies only gas at a temperature higher than the virial temperature ($\approx 10^4$ K in galaxies, $\approx 10^7$ K in clusters) tends to be smooth. Colder gas tends to be highly lumpy, without necessarily forming immediately stars or Jupiters (since it is still there!). This is indicative that gravitation rules the clumpiness of the gas by the Jeans' instability condition. Also observations of the local ISM show that most of the commonly measured gas mass is in a cold form and fills only a few percents of the volume, an unusual fluid indeed.

With today's observational constraints it appears that a large range of a priori possible clumps at subparsec scales can hardly be detected. These clumps might be even colder, down to 2.7 K, than those we can presently measure ($\gtrsim 5$ K). Neglecting the highly clumpy state of cold gas at sub-resolution scale is evaluated to account for the systematic discrepancy between dark matter and HI in the outer gaseous galactic disks[11].

2. THERMODYNAMICS OF THE JEANS UNSTABLE IDEAL GAS

Several major problems of astrophysics would appear clearer if the following idealised problem would be first understood: *What is the asymptotic state of an ideal gas (made of small perfectly elastic particles) contained in a box and maintained at a temperature sufficiently low to reach the gravitational (Jeans) instability?* Before introducing more complex physical ingredients, it is important to understand this simple model, because otherwise one might miss important aspects of cosmic gas physics.

In a spherical container of radius r the equilibrium state of a hot enough gas is the isothermal sphere (see e.g. [12], p. 500). However, below a critical temperature ($kT < 0.4\,GMm/r$), no equilibrium state does exist. (M is the total gas mass, and m the particle mass.) Some parts may temporarily collapse and heat indefinitely (the gravothermal catastrophe), but this departure from thermodynamical equilibrium diverges toward a state equivalent to a finite mass isolated system, which evaporates completely in a finite time; this occurs by increasing the central density and temperature, but also by decreasing the total collapsing mass (see e.g. [12], p. 523). This contrary behaviours between the beginning and end of a singularity show that in a such Jeans unstable isothermal gas any tendency to collapse is soon prevented by evaporation, but also any tendency to uniformity is prevented by Jeans' instability. The asymptotic state can only be dynamical.

On the other hand, we expect also that the average behaviour should become scale-free, since no scale between the largest and smallest sizes (given by the box and the particle) is involved in the process. Of course in space no wall confines gas, yet the problem remains because an isothermal sphere requires then an infinite mass. Having a finite mass the whole gas blob evaporates in about 100 crossing times (see e.g. [12], p. 525). So the paradox persists, in no way a cold ideal gas in isothermal conditions can find an asymptotic state of rest.

A solution to this paradox is suggested by observations and simulations. Molecular clouds are observed to be fractal over at least 4 decades, from 100 down to 0.1 pc[13],[14], and shearing sheet experiments of self-gravitating and Jeans unstable layers develop long-range and time-dependent correlations[15] which appear typical of fractals. The asymptotic state is indeed scale-free but dynamical: a fractal state in which clumps exist at every scale, but collide, merge, or disrupt so that the statistical ensemble is *in average* steady and scale-free. The thermodynamics of fractal systems is today in the infancy (e.g. [16]).

A fractal state for interstellar gas is very different from the classical picture of fiducial round clouds of determined scale. Not only it has never been possible to show that such clouds are stable over a long time, but also the particular retained size of these clouds has been chosen for purely convenience reasons. In the literature several attempts have been made to "deconstruct" the fiducial interstellar cloud model, yet despite its obvious crudeness, the model is still alive by lack of alternative picture.

3. REAL COLD COSMIC GAS

In practice no gas is ideal at every scale, and there always exists an upper and lower scale at which the geometrical fractal model breaks. A largest scale in a galaxy is determined by differential rotation ($\sim (d\ln\Omega/dr)^{-1}$), but the smallest scale must be determined by the microphysics. Without invoking complications such as magnetic fields, a simple possibility has been given[11] involving first order opacity properties of ideal gas in a black-body radiation field[17]: the scale at which there is a transition from the isothermal to the adiabatic regime. In cold conditions near 3 K, for a mix of H_2 and He this transition occurs at solar system sizes, with a corresponding mass of the order of Jupiter. This mass is proportional to $T^{1/4}\mu^{-9/4}$, so is slowly variable with T, but more strongly dependent on the molecular weight μ. Interestingly, above the H_2 and H ionization temperatures μ decreases from about 2.3 to 0.63, and the critical mass increases by a factor ~ 30, from about 0.003 $M_\odot$ at $T \approx 2000$ K to about 0.1 $M_\odot$ at $T \approx 8000$ K[11], crossing rapidly the brown dwarf regime, which suggests a link with the stellar IMF cutoff below 0.1 $M_\odot$.

Recently, Ferland et al.[18] have computed in detail the cooling of uniform gas in cluster conditions taking into account many coupling channels of matter with radiation. They find that indeed cooling may proceed efficiently from millions of K down to 3 K.

In star formation problems it is usually assumed that an adiabatic proto-star cloud collapses in isolation. Yet we have estimated that on the contrary, if the cold gas has a fractal dimension $D \approx 1.5 - 2.0$, as derived from the empirical Larson relations $M \sim r^D$ in Galactic molecular clouds, the collision time is similar or shorter than the crossing time at every scale, so the isolation hypothesis does not hold[11]. The clump collisions are then slightly supersonic, which is appropriate to disrupt clumps trying to collapse further in the adiabatic regime. At higher temperature, above the H-ionization, the fractal dimension D becomes smaller than 1, and then the collision time increases allowing deeper adiabatic collapses (assuming initially the empirical properties of the fractal gas in the Galaxy).

4. CLUSTER EVOLUTION AND DARK MATTER

The above considerations have some applications to clusters. Taking the observational facts at face: the morphology-density relation shows that nearly all spiral galaxies are transformed into early-type galaxies or completely destroyed when crossing clusters. The high hot gas mass fraction found in clusters implies that dark matter in spirals is also at least for such a fraction in the form of gas, presumably cold. If cold gas in spiral galaxies is able to escape detection, the same can be expected to happen in clusters. The most natural scale ($\approx 10 - 50\,\mathrm{AU}$) of cold gas at low temperature is hardly accessible with present instruments. Since cluster dark matter profiles follow hot gas profiles except near the center, it is therefore likely that a substantial fraction of the cluster dark matter is also in the form of cold fractal gas. The higher fraction of dark matter in the dense conditions at cluster centers would result naturally from the higher cooling rate of the hot gas becoming cold 3 K gas.

REFERENCES
[1] Eggen O.J., Lynden-Bell D., Sandage A.R., 1962, ApJ 136, 768
[2] Whitmore B.C., 1993, in: Physics of Nearby Galaxies, Nature or Nurture?, T.X. Thuan, C. Balkowski, J.T.T. Van (eds.), Editions Frontières, Gif-sur-Yvette, p. 351
[3] Barnes J., Hernquist L., Schweizer F.: 1991, Sci. Am. 265, 40
[4] Pfenniger D., 1992, in: Physics of Nearby Galaxies, Nature or Nurture?, T.X. Thuan, C. Balkowski, J.T.T. Van (eds.), Editions Frontières, Gif-sur-Yvette, p. 519
[5] Rich M., 1992, in: Physics of Nearby Galaxies, Nature or Nurture?, T.X. Thuan, C. Balkowski, J.T.T. Van (eds.), Editions Frontières, Gif-sur-Yvette, p. 153
[6] Pfenniger D., Combes F., Martinet L.: 1994, A&A 285, 79
[7] Broeils A.: 1992, "Dark and visible matter in spiral galaxies", PhD Thesis, Rijksuniversiteit Groningen
[8] Tóth G., Ostriker J.P., 1992, ApJ 389, 5
[9] Pfenniger D., 1993, in: Galactic Bulges, IAU Symp. 153, H. Dejonghe, H. Habing (eds.), Kluwer, Dordrecht, p. 387
[10] Evrard A.E., 1992, in: Physics of Nearby Galaxies, Nature or Nurture?, T.X. Thuan, C. Balkowski, J.T.T. Van (eds.), Editions Frontières, Gif-sur-Yvette, p. 375
[11] Pfenniger D., Combes F.: 1994, A&A 285, 94
[12] Binney J., Tremaine S., 1987, Galactic Dynamics, Princeton Univ. Press, Princeton
[13] Scalo J., 1990, in: Physical Processes in Fragmentation and Star Formation, R. Capuzzo-Dolcetta et al. (eds.), Kluwer, Dordrecht, p. 151
[14] Falgarone E., 1992, in: Astrochemistry of Cosmic Phenomena, P.D. Singh (ed.), Kluwer, Dordrecht, p. 159
[15] Toomre A., Kalnajs A.J.: 1991, in: Dynamics of Disc Galaxies, B. Sundelius (ed.), Göteborg Univ., Göteborg, p. 341
[16] Beck C., Schögl F., 1993, "Thermodynamic of chaotic systems, an introduction", Cambridge Univ. Press, Cambridge
[17] Rees M.J.: 1976, MNRAS 176, 483
[18] Ferland G.J., Fabian A.C., Johnstone R.M.: 1994, MNRAS 266, 399

LUMINOSITY FUNCTIONS OF POOR CLUSTERS

R. Hank Donnelly
Dept. of Astronomy/Whitin Observatory
Wellesley College, Wellesley, MA 02181 USA

ABSTRACT

Since the identification of the Abell Galaxy Cluster Sample in the 1950's observational cosmologists have been interested in the characteristics of these systems. However, until recently little more than their most basic properties, such as morphology and distance (from a small sample of member velocities), has been known. Some fundamental questions still remain unanswered. Do clusters form from field galaxies? Have they evolved significantly since their formation? Is their morphological type an indicator of their age? With the advent of wide-field imaging CCD's and multi-plexing spectroscopic instruments considerably more information has been accumulated for the richer clusters (those with memberships > 50). However, the poorer clusters, which potentially represent a transitional phase from field to the richer clusters, have received relatively little attention.

This paper presents the results of a deep photometric survey of three poor clusters of galaxies out to 0.5 Abell radii. Data were taken in both V and I bands from the Johnson-Kron-Cousins system and are complete to a limiting magnitude of $V = 19.5^m$. The three clusters are located at essentially the same redshift ($z = 0.07$) and span the full range of Rood-Sastry morphological types. While the surface distributions support the morphological typing, comparison of the three luminosity functions shows no indication of an evolutionary sequence. A composite luminosity function is presented for comparison with samples at other redshifts and richness classes.

1 Introduction

Galaxy Clusters, because they are so massive, represent excellent probes for studying the formation of structure in the Universe. In a hierarchical model, objects this large should still be relatively young, and young clusters would argue in favor of a high value of Ω. Thus we wish to know how old this class of objects is. Ideally, we would study the dispersion of the velocities of the member galaxies via their redshifts, however, it is still rather rare to have even moderately complete velocity information for a given cluster. We need some sort of secondary indicator of age. Struble and Rood[1] suggested that the surface distribution, or morphological type, should correlate with age. Many authors have also suggested that the faint end slope of the luminosity function – α (using a Schechter formalism) – would be a good indicator. This assumes that as the cluster evolves, the fainter galaxies will be more and more dominated by the brighter (and more massive) galaxies due to galactic cannibalism and merger events.

Our understanding of the luminosity function has evolved from one where it appeared that the luminosity function was universal – no difference between the field and the rich clusters – to a clear distinction between them. It now appears that the luminosity function is dependent upon the morphological mix of galaxies in the environment in question. Each Hubble type has its own luminosity function, and the overall luminosity function in some location is a composite of many sub-functions.

Of interest now is the universality of the luminosity function *within* galaxy clusters. The variation in size has previously been unexplored as free parameter. Earlier work[2], which suggested that all clusters were the same, was limited by the depth of the survey, and thus the number of points to be fit by a potential luminosity function. Often the depth of the data extended to just beyond the inflection point at M_*.

This sample contains three clusters: Abell 1800, Abell 568 and Abell 2630. These clusters were selected because while they span the range of Rood-Sastry (RS) morphological types (A1800- cD, A568- C7, A2630- Ic) they are all Abell Richness Class 0 (number of galaxies brighter than m_3+2 less than 50) and they all lie at essentially the same redshift ($z \sim 0.07$). For these clusters we have V and I band data complete to a depth of $V = 19.5^m$ and a radius from the cluster center of $0.73h^{-1}$ Mpc (half an Abell radius). In absolute magnitude the depth is to approximately -18.6^m and is roughly 1.5 magnitudes deeper than previous work[2]. At this depth the number of galaxies found was: A1800- 127, A568- 170, A2630- 94. The details of the data reduction and extraction as well as the catalog of sources and their light curves will appear soon[3].

2 Background Subtraction

The precise removal of interlopers that have been projected onto a cluster is essentially impossible without redshifts and often (this sample included) these are unavailable. However, a *qualitative* removal can be performed via the use of a Background Luminosity Function (BLF). The validity of this procedure is dependent upon the uniformity at large scales of the background. The precise BLF that is used can vary widely from author to author even using the same approach[4,5]. Further, because the BLF will have a different log-log slope than the cluster– otherwise there is little point in subtracting it– the strength of the effect of the BLF will depend upon the total number of galaxies in the cluster. Unless the BLF in a given magnitude interval is nearly the same as the total number of galaxies in that same interval, i.e. we are *strongly* dominated (90%) by the background, the subtraction of a BLF will have little to no effect.

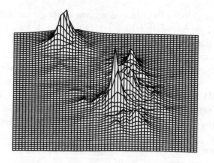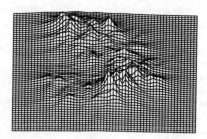

Figure 1: Density maps of the bright(left) and faint samples for Abell 1800. The orientation is such that top to bottom is North to South and left to right is East to West, with the height being representative of the local density of galaxies.

For this sample, we observed four "empty" fields near A1800, the cluster with the largest number of nearby ($< 10°$) clusters. We found good agreement with the I band data from Lilly et al.[6]. Unfortunately, the Lilly data did not extend brighter than $I = 18.0^m$ and there was no V band data. To eliminate this incompleteness we adapted the BLF from the ACO catalog[5]. This BLF could not be extended reliably beyond $V = 18.5^m$, however by shifting it 0.8^m a reasonable composite BLF was generated in combination with Lilly's data. This shift is consistent with the color expected from a typical field spiral which should dominate the BLF.

Using this BLF we expected to find 69 (of 127) in A1800, 51 (of 170) in A568 and 49 (of 94) in A2630 background galaxies. This sample was strongly dominated by the numbers in the fainter magnitude bins. In the interval from $V = 18.5^m$ to 19.5^m there are 48, 35 and 34 background galaxies. This suggested separating the sample into two components: a bright cluster dominated sample and a faint background dominated sample. Locating our divider at $V = 18.5^m$, the cluster galaxies comprise 68% (A1800), 84% (A568) and 73%(A2630) of the bright sample and 23% (A1800), 52%(A568) and 11%(A2630) of the faint sample. We expect the surface distribution, surface density and mean color of the galaxies in the cluster to be very different from that of the field, thus a comparison of these two samples should help us determine the quality of our BLF.

The first result from the examination of the surface distributions is that the RS morphological type appears to be a robust parameter. Originally, the RS type was determined from only the ten brightest galaxies, however even at the depth of this study ($\sim 2.5^m$ deeper) the clusters still exhibit the characteristics of each morphological class.

Secondly, the faint samples trace the same distribution as the bright samples. The surface density for the bright and faint components in A1800 is shown in Figure 1 as a representative example. This is rather surprising given that we expected the field to have a uniform density on the surface of the sky and that any random fluctuations would be randomly located. Even more intriguing is the result that the worst correlation occurred in A568– the cluster with the it strongest cluster contribution in the faint component. This "washing out" at faint magnitudes (and by extension smaller masses) would be consistent with relaxed distribution.

The radial surface density also showed a strong correlation between the two components in all three clusters. The cluster centers were determined using the techniques developed by Ulmer, Wirth and Kowalski[7] and were in excellent agreement.

As a final comparison, we examined the mean colors of contained within each magnitude bin. For the bright, cluster dominated component we found: $\overline{V}$=15:$\overline{VI}$=1.22, $\overline{V}$=16:$\overline{VI}$=1.18, $\overline{V}$=17:$\overline{VI}$=1.17, $\overline{V}$=18:$\overline{VI}$=1.16. These colors compare favorably with those determined by Lauberts[8] for elliptical galaxies. For the faint sample with a $\overline{V}$=19 the color is $\overline{VI}$=1.10 considerably redder than what we would have expected for a sample presumably dominated by spiral galaxies.

All of these comparisons suggest that the BLF we have constructed, even though it is in good agreement with previous results is too aggressive. This could potentially *artificially* flatten the luminosity function decreasing the faint end slope and thus implying an older more evolved system.

3   Luminosity Functions

Both the raw and background subtracted luminosity functions for all three clusters are presented in Figure 2. A simple visual inspection strongly suggests that the luminmosity functions of all three clusters agree. This is contrary to what we would expect if the variation in morphology represented an evolutionary sequence. In an evolutionary sequence we would expect the faint end slope to flatten with increasing age due to dynamical interactions between the galaxies. We have fit linear least squares solutions to the luminosity functions after 16th magnitude and then solved for a Schechter faint end slope, α, via the formula: $\alpha = -2.5 * slope - 1$. These values are given in Table 1. The agreement between clusters is quite good. The I band data begins to become incomplete fainter than $I = 18.5^m$ due to lack of or poor detection in the V band. As a consequence a mean color was used in the photometric solution as an estimate for objects fainter than this limit to extend the depth of the luminosity function. The variation in the I band fits is due this extension as is demonstrated by fitting the I band luminosity functions excluding the last magnitude bin.

The largest variance in slope occurs for the background subtracted fit of A568. An allusion was made above to the fact that A568's distribution was the most "relaxed" looking suggesting that it was more evolved, however this one variation in slope is in the opposite sense, i.e. it is steeper rather than flatter.

It seems that these objects represent a class that is uniform in *evolutionary* development. Combining all three clusters together we find faint end slopes of $\alpha_V = -1.85 \pm 0.15$ and $\alpha_I = -1.58 \pm 0.17$. We note that this is *steeper* than Lugger's (and previous work's) fits for richer clusters, possibly suggesting that these poor clusters are the progenitors of larger objects.

4   Summary

From this work the results are: 1) the RS morphological class appears to a be robust parameter, but not an evolutionary index, 2) the BLF's commonly used may be too agressive, especially for the poorer clusters, and 3) the faint end slopes are suggestive that the poor clusters may represent a transitional stage from the field environment to a rich cluster. Velocity information on these objects will help to further clarify these results and we look forward to reporting on them when they are available.

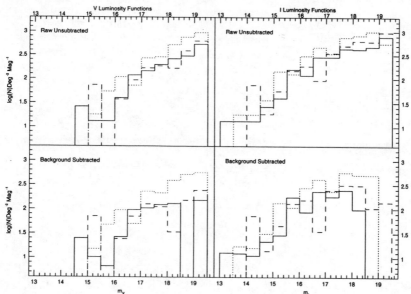

Figure 2: Luminosity functions for the three clusters. A1800 is represented by a solid line, A568 by the dotted line and A2630 by the dashed line. The upper two panels are raw luminosity functions while the lower ones have had a background luminosity function removed from them.

Fit	A1800	A568	A2630
V_{raw}	-1.80 ± 0.10	-1.88 ± 0.1	-1.88 ± 0.1
I_{raw}	-1.55 ± 0.1	-1.33 ± 0.2	-1.70 ± 0.2
I_{raw}^{*}	-1.53 ± 0.2	-1.53 ± 0.1	-1.75 ± 0.3
V_{sub}	-1.50 ± 0.2	-1.90 ± 0.2	-1.55 ± 0.3
I_{sub}	-1.08 ± 0.4	-1.28 ± 0.2	-1.15 ± 0.3

Table 1: Faint End Slopes. The "*raw*" fits are using all observed galaxies as opposed to the "*sub*" fits which use the background subtracted luminosity functions. The "***" I band fit excludes the faintest magnitude bin because it is likely to be affected by incompleteness.

REFERENCES

1) Struble, M.F. and Rood, H.J. 1982, *ApJ Supp*, **87**, 7.
2) Lugger, P.M. 1986, *ApJ*, **303**, 535.
3) Donnelly, R.H. 1994, (*in preparation*)
4) Dressler, A. 1980, *ApJ Supp*, **42**, 565.
5) Abell, G.O., Corwin, H.G. and Olowin, R.P. 1989, *ApJ Supp*, **70**, 1.
6) Lilly, S.J., Cowie, L.L., and Gardner, J.P. 1991, *ApJ*, **369**, 79.
7) Ulmer, M.P., Wirth, G.D. and Kowalski, M.P. 1992, *ApJ*, **397**, 430.
8) Lauberts, A. 1984, *A+A Supp*, **58**, 249.

INTERNAL DYNAMICS OF ESO KEY-PROGRAMME CLUSTERS

R. den Hartog*, A. Biviano, A. Mazure, P. Katgert*, P. Dubath, E. Escalera, P. Focardi,
D. Gerbal, G. Giuricin, B.J.T. Jones, O. Le Fèvre, M. Moles, J. Perea, G. Rhee
*) *Sterrewacht Leiden, 2300 RA, Leiden, the Netherlands*

Abstract

We discuss the construction of a volume-limited sample from a set of 89 clusters, observed by the ESO Key-programme for Rich Clusters of Galaxies, and a supplement of 37 clusters from the literature. We define the 3-dimensional Abell richness class R_{3D} and compute the spatial density of clusters with $R_{3D} \geq 1$. With the sample of 43 $R_{3D} \geq 1$ clusters we construct the cumulative distribution of σ_V. It shows good agreement with the distribution of X-ray temperatures, and we conclude that the so-called β-problem is absent. From comparison with the results of numerical models for the standard CDM scenario we conclude that a bias parameter $b = 2.5$ is required. Finally, we discuss the presence of luminosity segregation in our clusters. It turns out that only the brightest cluster members have systematically lower velocities.

1 The construction of a volume-limited sample

One of the goals of the ESO Key-programme for Rich Clusters of Galaxies was to collect redshifts and magnitudes for a complete, volume-limited sample of the 140 $R \geq 1$ ACO clusters [1] in a cone around the SGP defined by $b \leq -30°$ and $\delta \leq 0°$, out to $z = 0.1$, or $m_{10} = 16.9$. During 35 nights on the ESO 3.6m we have obtained 4003 redshifts in 89 clusters. Depending on the richness, between 1 and 3 Optopus aperture plates were observed for each cluster, yielding between 10 and 120 redshifts. R-band magnitudes were obtained from a combination of CCD and photographic photometry. The observations and methods will be discussed in greater detail in a forthcoming paper [12]. We have supplemented our sample with another 1042 redshifts in 37 clusters from the literature.

To construct from this collection a volume-limited sample of clusters the following steps are taken:

First, cluster members must be separated in redshift space from fore- and background galaxies. We have defined the redshift limits on either side of the cluster using the first gap between adjacent galaxies that was larger than 900 km/s. The value of 900 km/s is an optimal value given the aperture and average depth of the individual surveys. For $N \geq 10$ groups both N or σ_V change very little when the gapsize is varied by a few 100 km/s, or when more elaborate schemes, e.g. gaps weighted with N or σ_V, are used.

Second, we deal with the projection effects along the line of sight by introducing a 3-dimensional equivalent of Abell's richness class, R_{3D}. We find that on average 75% of the measured redshifts is in the main system, while 25% is in fore- and background. Thus of the 50 galaxies that are required within $[m_3, m_3 + 2]$ and 1.5 h^{-1} Mpc around the centre to have a $R = 1$ cluster, on average 38 are within the cluster itself. So we define that $R_{3D} \geq 1$ if the Abell counts times the fraction of measured redshifts that are in the main system, $C_{3D} = C_{Abell} \times f_{main} \geq 38$.

Third, we define an optimal depth for the sample. To compute a useful value of σ_V at least 10 velocities are required [9]. If we divide the volume out to $z = 0.1$ into 10 concentric shells, we find that we have sampled the $N \geq 10$ clusters out to $z = 0.08$ with a roughly constant spatial density;

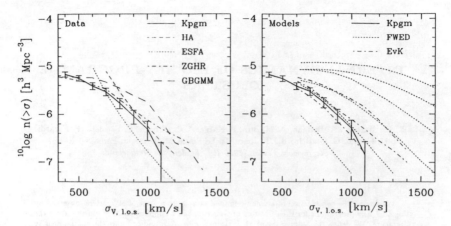

Figure 1: *a.* The cumulative distribution of velocity-dispersions, corrected for incompleteness and interlopers. Also shown are four distributions from the literature, two from optical surveys [9, 18], and two from X-ray surveys [6, 10], converted to velocity dispersions assuming $\beta = kT_X/\mu m_H \sigma_V^2 = 1$. *b.* Comparison with the cumulative σ_V distributions from standard CDM N-body simulations for different values of the bias factor b. The dotted lines are the functions by FWED [8] (corrected for the softening effect). The values of b are 1.0, 1.3, 1.6, 2.0, 2.5 and 3.0 (top to bottom). The dashed-dotted lines are the (preliminary) functions by van Kampen [15] for values of b of 2.0, 2.4 and 2.8 (top to bottom).

beyond this redshift the density drops by a factor half. Therefore we take $z = 0.08$ as the sample limit, bringing the sampled volume to $1.0 \times 10^7 h^{-3} \text{Mpc}^3$. Of the 56 $N \geq 10$ clusters closer than $z = 0.08$ 43 have $R_{3D} \geq 1$.

Fourth, we have to correct for the incompleteness of this sample of 43 clusters. Three corrections are important: (1) for spatial incompleteness, (2) for the clusters with $N < 10$ and (3) for the fraction of $R = 0$ clusters that nevertheless have $R_{3D} \geq 1$. Because we have at least one redshift for 133 clusters that are in the original cone, the spatial completeness is well under control. Using the correlation between m_{10} and z (in the cone) and the distribution of f_{main} we estimate that we are missing 25 from the $N < 10$ clusters and 6 more from the clusters with $38 \leq C_{\text{Abell}} \leq 49$ but for which $C_{3D} \geq 38$. Because we can compute for each cluster that could thus have been in our sample the probability that it would have been observed with a certain C_{3D}, we can estimate the completeness as a function of C_{3D}.

Taking these corrections into account we estimate the true amount of clusters with $R_{3D} \geq 1$ in our sample to be 74. Hence the comoving spatial density is $7.1 \times 10^{-6} h^3 \text{Mpc}^{-3}$, which is close to the values found by other groups [2, 13, 14, 18].

2 The distribution of velocity dispersions

In order to compute the cumulative distribution of velocity dispersions, $n(> \sigma_V)$, we first correct the σ_V in clusters with $N \geq 50$ for interloper galaxies, that were not removed by the gapper routine. We apply a new, iterative method that uses the combined information of velocities and positions to identify galaxies that are unlikely to belong to the cluster [5]. Removal of these interlopers may reduce σ_V with as much as 30%.

Figure 1a shows $n(> \sigma_V)$ computed from the 43 clusters with $C_{3D} \geq 1$. We find less high-σ_V clusters than other groups [9, 18], mainly because our interloper correction has reduced most of the very high values. For the higher σ_V the agreement with the distribution functions for X-ray temperatures $n(> T_X)$ [6, 10] is remarkably good. *We conclude that the systematical difference between σ_V^2 and T_X, also known as the β-problem, is absent.*

We compare in Figure 1b our $n(> \sigma_V)$ to the results of the cosmological N-body simulations by FWED [8] and van Kampen [15] for the standard $\Omega = 1$ CDM scenario with various values of the bias parameter b.

The volume of the FWED simulations is huge, 0.7 times our sample volume, containing 52 $R = 1$ clusters. Consequently, the mass resolution is low, and the scale length for force softening is large: $0.28 (1 + z)^{-1} h^{-1}$ Mpc. Van Kampen [16] found that the velocity dispersion of the dark matter in clusters which were modelled with softening scales as large as FWED's is typically 80% of the value for clusters in identical simulations, but run with a much smaller softening length of 10 h^{-1} kpc.

Van Kampen's models that we used for Fig. 1b [15] differ from those of FWED in that each cluster is simulated individually with an ≈ 200 times higher mass resolution, using the constrained random-field technique, and galaxies are formed during the cluster evolution. Comparing van Kampen's $n(> \sigma_V)$ with the functions of FWED (corrected for the softening effect), we find a remarkable similarity. Note in particular the coincidence of the two models for $b = 2.0$.

The observed $n(> \sigma_V)$ implies for both models a value of $b \simeq 2.5 - 2.6$. This value is also found for the standard CDM model from matching the two-point correlation function with the observed one [4], and is consistent with the results of FWED. However, it is uncomfortably large in the light of the COBE observations of the CMBR which indicate that $b \simeq 1.0$ [7, 17].

3 Luminosity Segregation

A low value of b could still be compatible with our observations if the measured values of σ_V are systematically lower than the σ_V of the dark matter (or the galaxies) in the above models. This situation can occur if dynamical friction is important in the evolution of the clusters, but somehow missed in the models. Because the frictional force $F_{\mathrm{fric}} \propto M_{\mathrm{gal}}^2$, we expect heavy galaxies to move slower than light galaxies. Of course, we can only test the hypothesis of luminosity segregation, i.e. that bright galaxies move slower than faint galaxies. We find in Figure 2 that there is indeed an effect for the clusters observed in the Key-programme. However, a system that undergoes dynamical friction evolves towards equipartition of kinetic energy. Fig. 2 shows that the effect we see is not consistent with energy equipartition, neither for a constant M/L of the galaxies, nor for a varying M/L, as this would imply $M/L \propto L^{2.5}$, which seems very unlikely in the light of the fundamental plane relations. Moreover, only the 1% brightest galaxies contribute to the first and second bin, so the effect can not have any impact on the measured values of σ_V. This seems to confirm the results of theoretical studies that also found little evidence for velocity bias [3, 11]. It is clear that luminosity segregation can not prevent the conclusion that *only standard CDM models with a high bias parameter $b \simeq 2.5$ are consistent with the observed $n(> \sigma_V)$ function.*

Probably a better interpretation of the effect is that the brightest galaxies have formed by mergers, in which orbital energy is converted into internal energy of the remnants. Interestingly, if we omit the brightest galaxy in each cluster, the effect almost disappears, as illustrated by the open symbols in Fig. 2. *Hence, only the BCMs in our sample have systematically lower velocities.*

Acknowledgements. We thank Eelco van Kampen for many helpful discussions and use of his unpublished models.

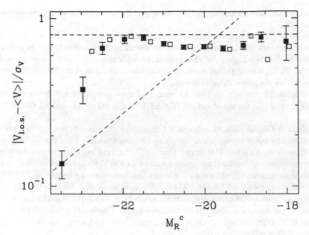

Figure 2: The velocity with respect to the cluster as a function of absolute R-band magnitude. Solid markers were computed from $N \geq 10$ Kpgm clusters with the brightest member included, open markers from the same clusters without the BCM. The horizontal dashed line indicates the expectation value of the velocity in a Maxwellian distribution, while the tilted line corresponds to equipartition of kinetical energy with constant a M/L-ratio for the galaxies.

References

[1] Abell, G.O., Corwin, H.G., Olowin, R.P., 1989, ApJS, 70, 1

[2] Bahcall, N.A., Soneira, R.M., 1983, ApJ, 270, 20

[3] Cen, R., Ostriker, J.P., ApJL, 399, L113

[4] Davis, M., Efstathiou, G., Frenk, C.S., White, S.D.M, 1985, ApJ, 292, 371

[5] den Hartog, R.H., Katgert, P., 1994, in preparation

[6] Edge, A.C., Stewart, G.C., Fabian, A., Arnaud, K.A., 1990, MNRAS, 245, 559

[7] Efstathiou, G., Bond, J.R., White, S.D.M., 1992, MNRAS, 258, 1p

[8] Frenk, C.S., White, S.D.M., Efstathiou, G., Davis, M., 1990, ApJ, 351, 10 (FWED)

[9] Girardi, M., Biviano, A., Giuricin, G., Mardirossian, F., Mezzetti, M., 1993, ApJ, 404, 38

[10] Henry, J.P., Arnaud, K.A., 1991, ApJ, 372, 410

[11] Katz, N., Hernquist, L., Weinberg, D.W., ApJL, 399, L109

[12] Mazure, A., Katgert, P., Biviano, A., den Hartog, R.H., Dubath, P., et al., 1994, in preparation

[13] Peacock, J.A., West. M.J., 1992, MNRAS, 259, 494

[14] Scaramella, R., Zamorani, G., Vettolani, G., Chincarini, G., 1991, AJ, 101, 342

[15] van Kampen, E., 1994a, in preparation

[16] van Kampen, E., 1994b, MNRAS, in press

[17] Wright, E.L., Meyer, S.S., Bennett, C.L., Boggess, N.W., Cheng, E.S., 1992, ApJL, 396, L13

[18] Zabludoff, A.I., Geller, M.J., Huchra, J.P., Ramella, M., 1993, AJ, 106, 1301

OPTICAL RADII
OF 90 GALAXY CLUSTERS

M. Girardi[1,2], A. Biviano[3], G. Giuricin[1,2], F. Mardirossian[1,2], and M. Mezzetti[1,2]

(1) SISSA, via Beirut 4, 34013 - Trieste, Italy
(2) Dipartimento di Astronomia, Università degli Studi di Trieste, Trieste, Italy
(3) Institut d'Astrophysique de Paris, 98bis bd Arago, 75014 Paris, France

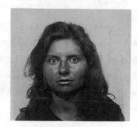

Abstracts

We analyze the density profiles and virial radii for a sample of 90 nearby clusters, using galaxies with available redshifts and positions. Each cluster has at least 20 redshifts measured within an Abell radius, and all the results come from galaxy sets of at least 20 members.

Most of the density profiles of our clusters are well fitted by hydrostatic-isothermal-like profiles. The slopes we find for many cluster density profiles are consistent with the hypothesis that the galaxies are in equilibrium with the binding cluster potential.

The virial radii correlate with the core radii at a very high significance level. The observed relationship between the two size estimates is in agreement with the theoretical one computed by using the median values of the density profile parameters fitted on our clusters.

Introduction

The distribution functions of observational cluster quantities, such as radii, velocity dispersions, masses, luminosities and X-ray temperatures, can provide strong constraints both on cosmological scenarios and on the internal dynamics of these systems. In this paper, we obtain estimates of cluster sizes for a large data-sample of 90 clusters, and we examine the relationships between these sizes and other cluster properties. In particular, we deal with the estimates of the core radius and virial radius[1], for increasing apertures of 0.5, 0.75, 1 $h^{-1} Mpc$ (we adopt H_0=100 km s^{-1}). We use the hydrostatic-isothermal models in order to fit the galaxy distribution of clusters, by assuming the following surface density profile

$$\sigma(r) = \frac{\sigma_0}{[1 + (r/R_c)^2]^\alpha} \tag{1}$$

where σ_0 is the *central projected galaxy density* and R_c is the *core radius*. This model corresponds for $r >> R_c$ to a *volume* $-$ *density* $\rho(r) \propto r^{-2\alpha-1}$. The well-known King profile corresponds to the model of Eq.(1) with $\alpha = 1$. As emphasized by Sarazin[2], it may be noted that very different values of R_c for the same cluster have been obtained by different authors. In the present paper we compute the $2D$-projected virial radius (i.e. not de-projected by the classical value of $\pi/2$),

$$R_v = \frac{N^2}{\sum_{1 \ i\neq j}^{N} R_{ij}^{-1}}, \tag{2}$$

where N is the number of cluster members and R_{ij} is the projected distance between the $i-$ and the $j-$member.

We based our analysis on a sample of 90 nearby ($z < 0.15$) clusters, each one with at least 20 measured redshifts of cluster members within 1.5 $h^{-1} Mpc$. The procedure adopted to reject non-cluster members is similar to that described in Girardi et al.[3]. The cluster center is defined as a biweight mean of the velocities, right ascensions and declinations. We pay particular attention to problems of magnitude incompleteness and to the possible presence of subclustering in our sample, which is tested according to Dressler & Schectman 's procedure[4].

Analysis and Results

In order to obtain the values of R_c, we fitted the observed galaxy distributions to hydrostatic-isothermal models on the hypothesis of spherical symmetry. For this purpose, we adopted the Maximum Likelihood method which takes directly into account the positions of individual galaxies, and does not require any binning of the data[2]. In the first step we allowed R_c and α to vary from 0 to 1 and from 0.5 to 1.5, respectively; we rejected values of R_c and α outside the above-mentioned intervals. Bad fits are rejected by a Kolmogorov-Smirnov test. In a second stage of the investigation, we decided to fix the value of α at the median value obtained in the two-parameter-fitting procedure (α=0.8). By reducing the free parameters to one, R_c, we were able to better constrain the size-estimates. The median values of $R_{c,0.5,\alpha=0.8}$ and $R_{c,0.75,\alpha=0.8}$ are equal to 0.11 $h^{-1}\,Mpc$ and 0.12 $h^{-1}\,Mpc$; their distributions do not differ, according to the KS- and Sign-test. This suggests that our estimates of the core-radii are quite stable within half an Abell radius. The median values of $R_{v,0.5}$ and $R_{c,0.75}$ are equal to 0.49 $h^{-1}\,Mpc$ and 0.67 $h^{-1}\,Mpc$. The analysis of the errors of R_v and R_c suggests that the dispersion of the values of R_v and R_c is partially intrinsic, and not mainly induced by the errors involved.

Both the core and the virial radius describe the galaxy distribution inside the cluster, so the existence of a relation between these two quantities is quite natural. This functional dependence can be easily derived when one knows the density profile. On the hypothesis that the models we use fit cluster density distributions, we obtain the following relation

$$R_v = R_c \cdot F(A/R_c), \tag{3}$$

where A is the aperture considered and $F(A/R_c)$ is fairly well represented by the relation

$$F(A/R_c) = 1.193 \,(A/R_c) \,\frac{1 + 0.032 \,(A/R_c)}{1 + 0.107 \,(A/R_c)}. \tag{4}$$

In our data sample the values obtained for the core and virial radii are very well correlated. The observational relations between core and virial radii are in good agreement with the respective theoretical relations, described via eq.(3) and obtained with our ($\alpha = 0.8$) profiles. We also investigated the existence of a correlation between R_v (and R_c) and other optical cluster quantities, such as the Abell richness, the morphological types by Bautz-Morgan and by Rood-Sastry and the robust velocity dispersions[3]: we found no strong evidence of correlation. The distribution function of X-ray core radii - for 18 clusters in common[4] - does not differ from that of our optical core radii.

Our cluster set is not volume-complete. Therefore, in order to estimate the cosmic distributions for our cluster core and virial radii, we normalized our observational distributions to a complete cluster sample[3], using the richness distrbution of ACO cluster catalog[5], which is nominally complete for clusters with $z \leq 0.2$ and richness class $R \geq 1$.

In conclusion, most of our cluster profiles ($\sim 90\%$) are fitted by hydrostatic-isothermal-like profiles with $\alpha = 0.8$; in this model both the galaxies and the gas are in equilibrium with the binding cluster potential. In fact, the slope of our best-fit profiles is similar to that of X-ray cluster profiles[4]. Therefore we agree with the analysis of Bahcall and Lubin[6], who suggested a value of $\alpha = 0.7 \pm 0.1$ in order to resolve the β-discrepancy.

References

1) Bahcall, N.A. 1977, Ann.Rev. A&A, Vol.15, 505

2) Sarazin, C.L. 1986, Rev.Mod.Phys., 58, 1.

3) Girardi, M., Biviano, A., Giuricin, G., Mardirossian, F., & Mezzetti, M. 1993, ApJ, 404, 38

4) Jones, C., & Forman, W. 1984, ApJ, 276, 38

5) Abell, G.O., Corwin, H.G.Jr., & Olowin, R.P. 1989, ApJS, 70, 1, ACO

6) Bahcall, N.A., & Lubin, L.M. 1993, preprint

THE MASS OF THE VIRGO CLUSTER INFERRED FROM INFALL

R. Brent Tully
Institute for Astronomy, University of Hawaii
Honolulu, HI 96822, USA

and

Edward J. Shaya
Physics Department, University of Maryland
College Park, MD 20742, USA

Abstract

Least Action models of the observed positions and velocities of galaxies in the Local Supercluster lead to preferred solutions with $\beta = \Omega_\circ^{0.6}/b = 0.35$, or $M/L \sim 200 M_\odot/L_\odot$ if $b = 1$. However, these solutions do not provide enough mass to the Virgo Cluster to create the extended 'triple-value' region about it that is observed (with turn-around at a radius of $\sim 0.5 D_v$). It is necessary to augment the mass assigned to the Virgo Cluster by a factor of 2 to 2.5 with respect to the large-scale value of M/L to properly position three groups of galaxies deep within the infall region. $(M/L)_{virgo} \sim 400 - 500 M_\odot/L_\odot$ is needed if $b = 1$. The Least Action solutions indicate that the orbits of galaxies near to the cluster have acquired considerable angular momentum.

Introduction

Modeling the influx of galaxies onto the potential well of a galaxy cluster results in a measurement of the mass of the cluster[2]. It is a particularly interesting measurement because it is not confined to the central regions of the cluster like most other procedures but rather provides an estimate of the mass distribution out to the scales of the infalling material, which can be many megaparsecs away. This report will be about modeling involving the Least Action methodology[3,4,5,9]. Before getting into these new models, we recall what we had already learned with a simpler description[8].

The study of a decade ago was based on the standard equations of General Relativity for a spherically symmetric bound shell. Hence, the description was fully non-linear but it required the unreasonable assumption about mass symmetry. The main constraints are offered by galaxies raining down on the Virgo Cluster from a restricted quadrant referred to as the Virgo Southern Extension. This region is *not* superimposed on the cluster, but contiguous with it on the plane of the sky extending to several times the cluster radius. Galaxies are clearly displaced from uniform Hubble expansion in a way consistent with a generic triple-value inflow pattern[6]. Enough of the galaxies have distance estimates that the geometry of the volume is crudely understood. Constraints are imposed on the spherical model by the *envelope* of radial velocities as a function of line of sight. The mass of the cluster was determined to amount to $7 \times 10^{14}(D_v/15)M_\odot$ where D_v is the distance to the Virgo Cluster, fiducially taken at 15 Mpc.

A strong conclusion of the study of a decade ago was that there is a major influx of spiral-rich systems into the Virgo Cluster, with of order 60 cataloged galaxies expected to reach the cluster in the next 3 Gyr. The mass-to-light ratio for the cluster is $520(15/D_v)M_\odot/L_\odot$. The most puzzling conclusion from that earlier study was that this amount of mass in the cluster is already enough to explain the modest retardation from Hubble expansion we feel at the Local Group even though only 20% of the light within a sphere centered on Virgo and extending to our radius is actually within the cluster. The inference was that the mass associated with galaxies outside the cluster but within our radius of it must have much lower M/L values than that of the cluster itself; we determined an *upper limit* of $70(15/D_v)M_\odot/L_\odot$.

The most obvious failing of that earlier study is with the assumption of spherical symmetry. The analysis that will now be described is non-linear and non-parametric. Mass is assumed to follow the distribution of the light, although there is freedom to modify the detailed recipe. It will be interesting to see how the new results compare with the old ones.

Least Action

Our procedures are described in the references given in the first paragraph so only some important points will be recalled here. The Least Action analysis involves a substitution of initial boundary conditions for missing final boundary conditions. We know three of the six elements of phase space for galaxies today (α, δ positions on the sky and radial velocities), and a fourth (distances) can be crudely measured in a fraction of cases. The three uncertain elements of phase-space location today can be replaced by the reasonable assumption that initial velocities were negligible (ie, initial random motions were adiabatically damped with the expansion of the universe and today's peculiar velocities have developed as a result of gravitational perturbations). If one makes the further assumption that the orbits of the constituents of the sample have never intersected (alternative assumptions are possible) then paths for the constituents can be determined by searching for an extremum of the action: the integral of the Lagrangian of the ensemble through time.

The quality of the description of the current light/mass distribution is a critical component of the analysis. We use a union of the *Nearby Galaxies Catalog*[7] and the *IRAS 1.2 Jy sample*[1] restricted to $V < 3000$ km/s. The individual galaxies are combined into groups with a local-density/crossing-time criterion that assures the statistical validity of the assumption that constituent paths have not intersected (ie, the constituents are groups or individual galaxies with relative crossing times greater than the age of the universe). Each constituent has a known blue luminosity that will be directly related to a mass assignment.

We start with a given assumption about the M/L assignment and a choice of cosmological model (Ω_o, Λ). An iterative procedure is followed to get fits to the observables (α, δ, V) because our calculations actually require (α, δ, distance) as input. Hence, we assume a distance for each mass carrier, look for a least action solution which gives us model velocities for the carriers, compare the radial component with observed velocities, then iterate by selecting new distances that give velocities in better agreement with observations. After about 10 iterations we are selecting distances that result in velocities that agree with observations. For the fraction of carriers with direct distance measurements, these measurements can be compared with the model distances that have just been found. These measured to model differences contribute to a χ^2 estimator that provides a measure of the quality of the fit. Then other M/L and cosmological model choices can be considered in an attempt to search for a minimum χ^2 value.

The Virgo Cluster Region

There is a well defined infall region within the structure known as the Virgo Southern Extension. For the present discussion, our particular concern is with three groups of galaxies called 11+2, 11-3, and 11-4 in the *Nearby Galaxies Catalog*[7] (see Table II). The group velocities are respectively 0.74, 1.89, and 1.55 times the Virgo Cluster velocity while their measured distances are respectively 0.83, 0.87, and 0.65. If one compares with a spherical infall model (Ref. 8, Fig. 4) then the triple-value expectation distance ratios are respectively (0.39, **1.00**, 1.37 for group 11+2), (**0.86**, **0.86**, 1.96 for group 11-3), and (**0.68**, 0.92, 1.73 for 11-4), where the underlined numbers are the distances with respect to Virgo closest to Hubble expansion and the bold numbers those closest to measurements.

It is seen that measured distances in these cases are in best agreement with either of the two triple-value choices within the Virgo turn-around radius rather than the third choice found outside turn-around and nearest to the Hubble expansion expectation. It can be appreciated that a different Least Action solution may be available for each triple-value choice. The challenge is to specify models which get the triple-value distances 'right' within the constraints of the measurements.

For simplicity, the present discussion will be restricted to the *unbiased* case where the mass is fully described by the M/L assignment and, hence, $\Omega_o = (M/L)/(M/L)_{crit}$. (The critical value for closure of the universe in our units is $(M/L)_{crit} \sim 1300 M_\odot/L_\odot$.) There is a family of acceptable solutions that include cases with bias, $b \neq 1$; best M/L choices scale as $\Omega_o^{0.6}$.

Here is the important point, indeed, the motivation for this paper. *With our simplest assumption of M/L = constant in the Least Action analysis, we cannot simultaneously get a good fit to the overall supercluster sample and to the triple-value region.* Our best fits for the entire sample are given with $M/L \sim 200 M_\odot/L_\odot$ (whence $\Omega_o \sim 0.15$; $\beta = \Omega_o^{0.6}/b \sim 0.35$). However, in these cases the triple-value region around Virgo is very small and the groups that were discussed above are not captured by it. There needs to be more mass within their radius of the cluster. In order to get these groups acceptably near their measured distances, we need to assign $(M/L)_{virgo} \sim 400 - 500 M_\odot/L_\odot$.

One might imagine that the discrepancy between preferred field and cluster M/L values might disappear at high bias since larger M/L choices are preferred overall. However, the requirements for more mass associated with the cluster increase almost (not quite) as fast, and for all reasonably values of Ω_o it is still the case that $(M/L)_{virgo} \sim 2 - 2.5(M/L)_{supercluster}$.

The new results can be compared with the spherically-symmetric models. Comparable values are being found for the cluster mass ($400 - 500 M_\odot/L_\odot$ versus $520 M_\odot/L_\odot$) These results are in good agreement within the present uncertainties, as might have been expected since the spherical approximation would be best in close proximity to the cluster. However, now we are finding M/L values in the supercluster outside the cluster $\sim 200 M_\odot/L_\odot$, three times the upper limit from the spherical analysis.

The Least Action solutions that we are finding produce orbits with *considerable angular momentum* for the groups infalling onto Virgo. This condition in itself illustrates a violation of the old spherical symmetry assumptions. Indeed, the old 'triple-value' picture becomes more complicated and ambiguous with non-radial infall.

Acknowledgements: Jim Peebles is involved in the collaboration to develop a Least Action model for the Local Supercluster and Mike Pierce is participating in the measurement of galaxy distances. This research is supported by the US National Science Foundation.

References

1) Fisher, K.B. 1992, Ph.D. Dissertation, U. California Berkeley.

2) Hoffman, G.L., Olson, D.W., and Salpeter, E.E. 1980, *Astrophys. J.*, **242**, 861.

3) Peebles, P.J.E. 1989, *Astrophys. J. (Letters)*, **344**, L53.

4) Peebles, P.J.E. 1990, *Astrophys. J.*, **362**, 1.

5) Shaya, E.J., Peebles, P.J.E., and Tully, R.B. 1993, *Cosmic Velocity Fields: 9th IAP Astrophys. Meeting*, 11-17 July, Paris, France.

6) Tonry, J.M., and Davis, M. 1981, *Astrophys. J.*, **246**, 680.

7) Tully, R.B. 1988, *Nearby Galaxies Catalog*, (Cambridge: Cambridge University Press).

8) Tully, R.B., and Shaya, E.J. 1984, *Astrophys. J.*, **281**, 31.

9) Tully, R.B., Shaya, E.J., and Peebles, P.J.E., 1993, *Evolution of the Universe and Its Observational Quest: Yamada Conf. XXXVII, 8-12 June, Tokyo, Japan.*

A NEW SURVEY IN THE CENTRAL PARTS OF THE COMA CLUSTER

A. Biviano[1], F. Durret[1,2], D. Gerbal[1,2]
O. Le Fèvre[2], C. Lobo[1,3], A. Mazure[4], E. Slezak[5]

[1] Institut d'Astrophysique, CNRS, 98bis Bd Arago, F-75014 Paris, France
[2] DAEC, URA 173, Observatoire de Paris-Meudon, F-92195 Meudon Cedex
[3] Centro de Astrofísica da Universidade do Porto, Rua do Campo Alegre 823, 4100 Porto, Portugal
[4] GRAAL, Université Montpellier II, C.P.072, F-34097 Montpellier Cedex
[5] Observatoire de la Côte d'Azur, B.P. 229, F-06304 Nice Cedex 4

ABSTRACT

We have observed the central regions of the Coma cluster both spectroscopically and photometrically, and doubled the number of galaxies with redshifts members of Coma in a field of 40×20 arcmin^2. For these galaxies, we derive the luminosity function and find it to be well fitted by a gaussian up to a magnitude $b_J = 17.3$. A preliminary analysis of our new catalogue indicates that substructures are present in the cluster and suggests that bound populations may be present around the brightest galaxies.

Until recently, the Coma cluster was considered as a prototype of rich and relaxed clusters (see e.g. Kent & Gunn 1982, The & White 1986, Merritt 1987). However, recent studies, both at optical and X-ray wavelengths have shown that substructures appeared to be present, even in the cluster core (Baier 1984, Fitchett & Webster 1987, Mellier et al. 1988, White et al. 1993). This motivated our new investigation of the dynamical properties of the central regions of Coma.

OBSERVATIONS

Using the MOS-SIS spectrograph at the Canada-France-Hawaii Telescope, we observed a field of about 48×24 arcmin^2 centered on the two brightest central galaxies of Coma, and a field of 10×10 arcmin^2 centered on NGC 4839. We obtained 275 reliable redshifts, out of which 77 were already available in the litterature. Our final catalogue, including the litterature data, has about 500 objects with velocities and b$_J$ magnitudes within the area covered by the Godwin et al. (1983) catalogue (hereafter GMP); the GMP catalogue is photometrically complete up to magnitudes b$_J = 20$.

We also obtained V band photometric data, which are presently being reduced; our photometric catalogue will be complete to a magnitude $V_{26.5} \sim 22$.

LUMINOSITY FUNCTION

In our catalogue, we have selected the galaxies most likely belonging to Coma. For this purpose, we applied several selection criteria in the redshift space; all gave comparable results, and we chose the velocity range given by a 3σ clipping (Yahil & Vidal 1977) : 3800-9900 km s^{-1} , leading to a catalogue of 391 galaxies.

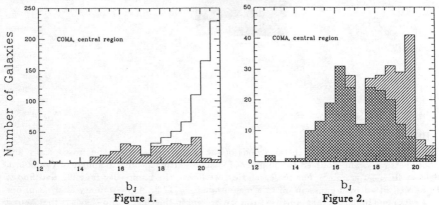

Figure 1.   Figure 2.

Fig. 1 shows the histogram of magnitudes for galaxies in the GMP catalogue limited to the central region of 48×24 arcmin^2; the hatched histogram superimposed corresponds to galaxies for which we have redshifts. This figure shows that our sample is complete in redshift up to magnitude b$_J \simeq 17$, and almost complete (95%) up to b$_J \simeq 18$.

In Fig. 2 is displayed the same magnitude histogram as in Fig. 1 (single hatched), as well as the magnitude histogram for galaxies with velocities in the 3800-9900 km s^{-1} range defined above. From this figure, it can be seen that the contamination by foreground and background galaxies becomes prohibitive at magnitudes above $b_J \sim 19$.

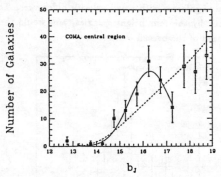

Figure 3.

We have calculated the luminosity function for galaxies belonging to Coma up to magnitude $b_J = 19$, applying the correction for incompleteness based on the ratio of the histograms of Fig. 1. This differential luminosity function is shown in Fig. 3. The error bars were calculated assuming Poisson statistics for the number of galaxies in each magnitude bin. A fit with a Schechter (1976) function with a fixed value of $\alpha = -1.25$ is shown (dashed line). This fit is rejected at a 97% confidence level. We find that a gaussian of mean value $\mu = 16.3 \pm 0.1$ and dispersion $\sigma = 0.9 \pm 0.1$ is a good fit to the black points (which roughly correspond to the magnitude interval in which our sample is complete). Similar results are found from new frames in the V band, showing that they are not due to the incompleteness of the GMP catalogue. The idea that the luminosity function for the brightest galaxies in a cluster could be fitted by a gaussian was discussed by Sandage et al. (1985) for the Virgo cluster. Thompson & Gregory (1993) made a similar fit for Coma galaxies and found parameter values for the gaussian inconsistent with ours.

SUBSTRUCTURE IN COMA

We have run a simple Dressler & Schechtman (1988) test for the presence of substructure in the central region of Coma (see above) and find that subclustering is present with a 98.6% probability.

As a first stage to this investigation, we considered that the brightest cluster members could be located in different subgroups, as suggested both by the isopleth map at optical wavelengths (Mellier et al. 1988) and by the ROSAT X-ray map (White et al. 1993). We selected galaxies in circles of radii 210 arcsec around the four bright galaxies NGC 4874, 4889, 4911 and 4839; the value of 210 arcsec was chosen because it corresponds approximately to half the distance between the two central brightest members.

In each circle, we computed for each galaxy the difference between its velocity V and that of the central galaxy V_C. The histogram of $V-V_C$ is shown in Fig. 4 for all circles (excluding the four central galaxies), with poissonian error bars plotted. We tried to fit this distribution

60

with a single gaussian with a fixed mean of zero and a fixed dispersion equal to that computed for the whole sample (1014 km s^{-1}). We are unable to reject statistically such a fit although there is a hint of an excess of galaxies with small velocity differences. These galaxies would belong to groups dominated by the four bright galaxies, and would therefore constitute a population differing from that of the overall cluster.

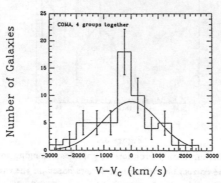

Figure 4.

V−V$_c$ (km/s)

CONCLUSIONS

With our new catalogue of 500 galaxies likely members of Coma, we have shown that the luminosity function is well described by a gaussian up to a magnitude b_J=17.3. A more detailed investigation will be described in Biviano et al. (in preparation). We will derive a much more complete luminosity function from our photometric data presently under reduction. The present analysis of the cluster structure does not lead to definite conclusions, and will be completed using more refined techniques, such as wavelet analysis (see e.g. Escalera & Mazure 1992).

REFERENCES

Baier F.W., 1984, Astron. Nachr. 305, 175
Dressler A., Schechtman S.A., 1988, AJ 95, 985
Escalera E., Mazure A., 1992, ApJ 388, 23
Fitchett M.J., Webster R.A., 1987, ApJ 317, 653
Godwin J.G., Metcalfe N., Peach J.V., 1983, MNRAS 202, 113
Kent S.M., Gunn J.E., 1982, AJ 87, 945
Mellier Y., Mathez G., Mazure A., Chauvineau B., Proust D., 1988, A&A 199, 67
Merritt D., 1987, ApJ 313, 121
Sandage A., Binggeli B., Tammann G., 1985, AJ 90, 1759
Schechter P., 1976, ApJ 203, 297
The L.S., White S.D.M., 1986, AJ 92, 1248
Thompson L.A., Gregory S.A., 1993, AJ 106, 2197
White S.D.M., Briel U.G., Henry J.P., 1993, MNRAS 261, L8
Yahil A., Vidal N.V., 1977, ApJ 214, 347

M_1 - M^* CORRELATION IN GALAXY CLUSTERS

Dario Trèvese, Giuseppe Cirimele and Benedetto Appodia
Istituto Astronomico, Università di Roma "La Sapienza",
via G. M. Lancisi 29, I-00161 Roma, Italy

Abstract

Photographic F band photometry of a sample of 36 Abell clusters has been used to study the relation between the magnitude M_1 of the brightest cluster member and the Schechter function parameter M^*. Clusters appear segregated in the M_1-M^* plane according to their Rood & Sastry class. We prove on a statistical basis that on average, going from early to late RS classes, M_1 becomes brighter while M^* becomes fainter. The result agrees with the predictions of galactic cannibalism models, never confirmed by previous analyses.

1. Introduction

A Schechter-like luminosity function (LF) is consistent with the observed galaxy cluster LFs and with a theory of direct hierarchical clustering (Press & Schechter[1], Bond et al.[2]). Galaxy merging has been invoked to modify the Schechter-like shape and reconcile the local LF with faint galaxy count and redshift distribution (see Cavaliere & Menci[3] and refs. therein) According to a galactic cannibalism model (Ostriker and Tremaine[4]), Hausman and Ostriker[5]), brightest cluster members grow at the expense of the other massive galaxies, which are most affected by dynamical friction and this should cause a negative correlation between the magnitude M_1 of the brightest cluster member and the characteristic magnitude M^* of a fitting Schechter[6] LF.

Dressler[7] derived an indication that M_1 and M^* are negatively correlated from a study of 12 rich clusters. However, subsequent studies of 9 Abell clusters (Lugger[8] (L86)) and 12 clusters (Oegerle and Hoessel[9] (OH89)) found no evidence for any relation between M_1 and M^*. These results were interpreted as indications against the Dressler[7] claim and the prediction of cannibalism model.

A uniform study of a large sample of nearby galaxy clusters has been undertaken (Flin et al.[10], Trèvese et al.[11] (T92), Trèvese, Cirimele and Flin[12]) to derive their statistical properties. In this paper we report preliminary results of a new analysis of the M_1-M^* relation based on a subsample of 36 Abell clusters, more than three times larger than each of the previous samples, from which we obtain a statistically significant evidence of a new type of negative M_1-M^* correlation, related to the fact that M_1 becomes brighter and M^* fainter going from early to late Rood & Sastry [13] cluster types.

2. M_1 - M^* correlation

The data were obtained from F-band photographic plates taken with the 48-inch Palomar Schmidt Telescope (Hickson[14]). Plate scanning and data reduction is described in T92. Rel-

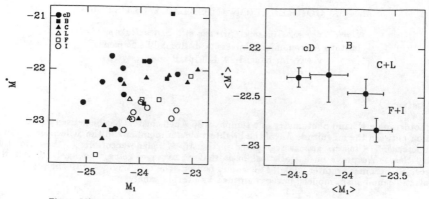

Fig. 1. M^* vs M_1 for the clusters sample
Different symbols refer to RS classes

Fig. 2. M^* vs M_1 averaged over
subsamples corresponding to RS classes.

Table 1. The clusters sample

Abell	z	RS	BM	Abell	z	RS	BM	Abell	z	RS	BM
A76	0.0416	L	II-III	A655	0.1240	cD	I-II	A1775	0.0717	B	I
A147	0.0438	I	III	A656	0.136*	cD	I-II	A2028	0.0772	I	II-III
A151	0.0526	cD	II	A671	0.0494	C	III	A2040	0.0456	C	III
A157	0.103*	B	II	A779	0.0226	cD	I-II	A2052	0.0348	cD	I-II
A260	0.0348	F	II	A1132	0.1363	B	III	A2056	0.0763	C	II-III
A278	0.0896	I	III	A1377	0.0514	B	III	A2065	0.0721	C	III
A407	0.0470	I	II	A1413	0.1427	cD	I	A2073	0.113*	I	III
A505	0.0543	cD	I	A1570	0.156*	I	II-III	A2096	0.108*	C	III
A569	0.0196	B	II	A1589	0.0718	C	II-III	A2124	0.0654	cD	I
A637	0.136*	C		A1661	0.1671	F	III	A2593	0.0433	F	II
A646	0.1303	I	III	A1689	0.1810	C	II-III	A2657	0.0414	F	III
A649	0.124*	cD	II	A1700	0.119*	L	III	A2670	0.0745	cD	I-II

The asterisk indicates that z has been estimated from the Abell z-m_{10} relation.

ative photometry has been computed for 55 clusters (Trèvese, Cirimele and Flin[12]) and the absolute calibration has been obtained using published photometric data for the 36 clusters listed in table 1 where the redshifts and RS types are also reported. Color transformation and K-correction from Schneider et. al.[15], have been taken in to account. We estimate an uncertainty in the zero point of the magnitude scale of a few tenth of a magnitude.

The LFs were determined inside circular regions with a fixed radius of $R_3 = 1.7/z$ arc min, corresponding to 3 Mpc for $H_o = 50\ Km\ s^{-1}\ Mpc^{-1}$, $q_o = 1$. The galaxy samples were corrected statistically for the background density and a uniform magnitude limit $m_3 + 3$ was adopted for all clusters. The LFs where then fitted with a Schechter[6] function $\Phi(L)dL = \Phi^* \left(\frac{L}{L^*}\right)^\alpha exp\left(-\frac{L}{L^*}\right) d\left(\frac{L}{L^*}\right)$, using a maximum likelihood algorithm. Each LF has been fitted with $\alpha = -1.25$ (Schechter[6]) and M^* as free parameter excluding the first ranked galaxy (see OH89). Figure 1 shows the distribution of the 36 clusters of our sample in the M_1-M^*

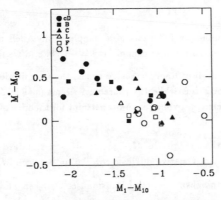

Fig. 3. $M_1 - M_{10}$ versus $M^* - M_{10}$
Different symbols refer to RS classes

plane. We obtain a positive correlation coefficient $r = 0.48$ and an associated probability $P(> r) = 3 \cdot 10^{-3}$, apparently in contrast with the negative, though non significant, correlation found by Dressler[7]. This could be interpreted as an evidence against the selective depletion of the bright end of the luminosity function, predicted by the galactic cannibalism model of Hausman and Ostriker[5]. However, as can be seen in Figure 1, the clusters are segregated in the M_1-M^* plane according to their RS class. Dividing the sample into four groups, corresponding to the RS classes F+I, C+L, B and cD respectively, to collect enough objects in each group. The average values $< M_1 >$ and $< M^* >$ of each group are negatively correlated as seen in Figure 2. The effect is due to the fact that $< M_1 >$ becomes brighter, while $< M^* >$ becomes fainter, going from early to late RS types, consistently with the prediction of the cannibalism model.

The observed positive M_1-M^* correlation can be due, at least in part, to uncertainties in the photometric calibration of the plates, since any shift of the magnitude scale affects by the same amount all the galaxy magnitudes. However part of this positive correlation could be intrinsic in nature, e.g. cluster may originate with luminosity functions differing, to a first approximation, by a global shift in absolute magnitude. Assuming as a standard candle the magnitude M_{10} of the tenth brightest member we can plot, see Figure 3, $(M^* - M_{10})$ versus $(M_1 - M_{10})$, which are independent of the calibration uncertainties and appear negatively correlated. Also a partial correlation analysis indicates the same effect. The global correlation coefficients between M_1, M^* and M_{10} are all positive : $r_{1,*}=0.54$, $r_{1,10}=0.82$ and $r_{*,10}=0.87$. The partial correlation: $r_{1,*;10} = (r_{1,*} - r_{*,10} \cdot r_{1,10})/((1 - r_{*,10}^2) \cdot (1 - r_{1,10}^2))^{\frac{1}{2}}$ which represents the 'intrinsic' correlation between M_1 and M^* is $r_{1,*;10} = -0.61$ with an associated probability $P(> |r|) = 8 \cdot 10^{-5}$.

The effect is statistically significant, thus providing a new constraint for any model of cluster formation and evolution.

3. Conclusions

We have determined the luminosity functions of a sample of 36 Abell clusters and fitted them with Schechter-like profiles, assuming a canonical $\alpha = -1.25$, and we find that:

- On average, going from early to late Rood & Sastry types, the magnitude M_1 of the bright cluster member becomes brighter, while the characteristic magnitude M^* is fainter. The effect is statistically significant, providing a new constraint for theories of cluster formation and evolution.

- Including in the study also the magnitude M_{10}, assumed as a standard candle, a partial correlation analysis confirms a negative intrinsic correlation between M_1 and M^*.

- These results support the cannibalism model of Hausman & Ostriker, at variance with previous analyses.

Part of the positive $M_1 - M^*$ correlation is caused by uncertainties in the absolute photometry while part could be intrinsic in nature.

References

1) Press,W.H., Schetcher,P., 1974 *Astrophys. J.* **187**, 425

2) Bond,J.R., Cole,S., Efstathiou,G., Kaiser,N., 1991 *Astrophys. J.* **379**, 440

3) Cavaliere,A. and Menci,N., 1993 *Astrophys. J.* **407**, L9

4) Ostriker,J.P., Tremaine,S.D., 1975 *Astrophys. J.* **202**, L113

5) Hausman,M.A ,Ostriker,J.P., 1978 *Astrophys. J.* **224**, 320

6) Schetcher,P., 1976 *Astrophys. J.* **203**, 297

7) Dressler,A., 1978 *Astrophys. J.* **223**, 765

8) Lugger, P.M., 1986 *Astrophys. J.* **303**, 535 (L86)

9) Oegerle,N.R., Hoessel,J.G., 1989 *Astron. J.* **98**,, 1523 (OH89)

10) Flin,P., Hickson,P., Pittella,G., 1988 in *Large scale structure in the universe. Observational and Analytical Methods* eds. Seiter W.C., Duerbeck H.W., Tacke W. (Springer Verlag) p. 179

11) Trevese,D., Flin,P., Migliori,L., Hickson,P., Pittella G., 1992 *Astron. Astrophys. Suppl. Ser.* **94**, 327 (T92)

12) Trevese,D., Cirimele,G., Flin,P., 1992 *Astron. J.* **104**, 3

13) Rood,H.J., Sastry,G., 1971 *Publ. Astr. Soc. Pacific* **83**, 313

14) Hikcson,P., 1977 *Astrophys. J.* **217**, 16

15) Schneider,D.P., Gunn,J.E., Hoessel,J.G., 1983 *Astrophys. J.* **264**, 337

A MEASUREMENT OF DIFFUSE LIGHT IN ABELL 665

Eric J. Gaidos

Department of Physics and Center for Space Research 37-618A,

Massachusetts Institute of Technology, 77 Massachusetts Avenue,

Cambridge, MA 02139

The distribution of diffuse light associated with the cD galaxy and cluster potential of A665 ($z = 0.18$) has been characterized using deep 10'x10' R-band images obtained at the Michigan-Dartmouth-MIT Observatory 1.3 m McGraw-Hill Telescope. My preliminary analysis measured the surface brightness profile to a distance of 1.6 h_{50}^{-1} from the cD center and a photon noise level of 30 magnitudes/square arc second using the statistical techniques of Uson et al (1991). I find that the cD galaxy maintains a steep profile to 600 h_{50}^{-1} kpc and that there is a possible extended halo at $\mu \approx 28$ reaching to the edge of my images. The latter structure must be confirmed after a more careful treatment of bright stars in the field of view. If the halo is real, it has a total luminosity of approximately $25L_*$.

Introduction

The possible existence of diffuse emission from clusters of galaxies has motivated observational searches since Zwicky found that a large fraction of the mass might lie undetected in the Coma cluster (Zwicky, 1933). Measurements of intracluster light are a direct means of establishing upper limits on the mass to light ratio of the so-called dark matter that is now inferred from its pervasive gravitational influence in the universe. Sciama (1982) and Melott (1984) have proposed that certain astrophysical observations could be explained if some of this dark matter were composed of neutrinos with a mass of a few eV which undergo electromagnetic decay with a lifetime of order 10^{23} seconds. Such particles might produce an excess background light in the direction of galaxy clusters.

However, there are several other reasons for detecting and characterizing intracluster light. Galaxy clusters often contain a cD galaxy with an extended halo. The morphology of the halo, specifically, the degree to which the halo is smooth or contains fine structure, could be used to distinguish between theories of cD galaxy formation. A very smooth halo would suggest that the cD galaxy formed in the primordial collapse and virialization of the inner cluster, while a clumpier halo would indicate a cD forming from tidal debris or even entire cannibalized galaxies. Galaxy collisions are seen to produce tidal arms and debris; measuring the total luminosity of faint debris would place an upper limit on the total number of collisions suffered by the cluster members over the age of the cluster (Miller, 1983; Meritt, 1984). Surface brightness measurements of intracluster light would also constrain the amount of cluster cooling flow gas that can be deposited in low-mass stars (O'Connell & McNamara, 1988; Fabian et al, 1991). If the material creating the diffuse light is virialized, its surface brightness distribution can be used to provide useful constraints on the cluster potential shape for comparison with X-ray isophotes (see Buote & Tsai, these proceedings) or to assist with models of gravitational lensing by clusters (Soucail, private communication). The outer halos of giant ellipticals galaxies and cD galaxies may be dominated by globular clusters, as in the case of M87. There have been recent attempts to characterize distant globular cluster populations using the surface brightness fluctuations technique developed by Tonry (Wing & Harris, in press). Potentially, diffuse light observations could be used to pave the way for application of the technique to cD galaxies in low-redshift clusters.

The search for diffuse light in clusters of galaxies not associated with the individual galaxy members has a long, if unspectacular, history. Both the instrumentation and analysis techniques have evolved significantly. Oemler (1973) studied the surface brightness profile of the cD galaxy in Abell 2670 using both Schmidt and prime-focus Palomar plates. He found that the cD galaxy extended to a size of 1 Mpc. Thuan & Kormendy (1977) were among many who attempted to masure the the the diffuse background light light in the Coma cluster. They also used photographic plates. Melnick et al(1977) employed photelectric measurements to place an upper limit of 25% for the ratio of diffuse light to total cluster light. Partridge and collaborator used the then-nascent CCD imager technology (Partridge, 1990) to search for intracluster light in several clusters. These early attempts suffered from the limitations of the poor calibration of photographic plates, the difficult background-correction of 'single-pixel' photoelectric photometry, and the small field of view of the available CCD detectors. More recently, Uson *et al* (1991) obtained R-band CCD images in a cross-shaped mosaic of Abell 2029 (z = 0.08). They found that the cD galaxy possessed a smooth halo that followed a deVeaucouleurs Law to 700 h_{50}^{-1} kpc and had a total luminosity of 220 L_*.

Observations & Analysis

The cluster of galaxies Abell 665 was identified as the richest in the Abell catalog and has had been the object of many observations, including at X-ray energies by the EINSTEIN, ROSAT, and ASCA satellites and at at centimeter wavelengths in measurements of the Sunyaev-Zeldovich effect. My optical observations were made at the 1.3 m McGraw-Hill telescope of the Michigan-Dartmouth-MIT Observatory on Kitt Peak in December, 1993 and February, 1994. The detector was a Tektronix 2048^2 thick CCD with 10.9 x 10.9 arc-minute field of view and a KPNO R filter was used. A series of 5- and 10-minute images of the central A665 field totalling 5.5 hours was obtained. Sky flats were constructed for each night from images obtained from an unrelated but contemporaneous survey of faint radio sources. The images were bias-subtracted, flattened and mapped into a single 10x10 arc-minute mosaic using NOAO IRAF image processing routines.

I report here the preliminary analysis of this co-added image and a few tentative results. The procedure is based primarily on the techniques used by Uson *et al* (1991). The pixels were binned into elliptical annuli of 5000 pixels each. The ellipticity (e = 0.3) and position angle were chosen to match that of the inner isophotes of the cD galaxy. The background or sky value in each annulus was estimated using the distribution of pixel values (Fig. 1). The Gaussian peak in the histogram was identified with pixels near the sky value and the centroid and width of this peak were calculated in an interative fashion that excluded pixels falling further than 2σ from the centroid. This technique is very insensitive to the presence of bright stars or galaxies in the annulus. Fig. 2 shows the profile of surface brightness with semi-major axis. The photon noise limit is 30 magnitudes per square arc seconds, however the scatter in the profile suggests systematics that are several times larger. The profile clearly shows a continous fall in surface brightness to 28 mag./square arc-seconds at a distance of 600 h_{50}^{-1} kpc and then a slower roll-off or plateua extending to more than twice that distance. The extended halo may be an artifact produced by the scattered light from very bright stars and awaits confirmation. If the feature is real, its total luminosity is about $25L_*$. Further work will include corrections for scattered light and determining the elliptical bin parameters directly from the diffuse light rather than fixing them.

I thank David Buote, Claude Canizares, Chuck Steidel, and John Tonry for useful comments and advice, and the staff of MDM Observatory for their assistance.

References

Fabian, A.C., Nulsen, P.E.J., and Canizares, C.R., 1991, *ARAA 29*

Melnick, J., White, S.D.M., and Hoessel, J., 1977, *MNRAS* 180, 207-218

Melott, A.L., 1984, *Sov. Astron.*, 28, 478

Meritt, D., 1984, *ApJ* 276, 26

Miller, R.H., 1983, *ApJ* 268, 495

O'Connell, R.W., and McNamara, B.R., 1988, in *Cooling Flows in Clusters and Galaxies*, A.C. Fabian (ed.), Dordrecht: Kluwer Academic Publishers

Oemler, A., Jr., 1973, *ApJ* 180, 11-23

Partridge, R.B., 1990, in *The Galactic and Extragalactic Background Radiation*, S. Bowyer and C. Leinert (eds.), Netherlands : IAU

Sciama, D.W., 1982 *MNRAS*, 198, 1P

Thuan, T. X., and Kormendy, J., 1977, *PASP* 89, 466-473

Uson, J.M., Boughn, S.P., and Kuhn, J.R., 1991, *ApJ* 369, 46-53

Zwicky, F., 1933, *Helvetica phys. acta*, 6, 110

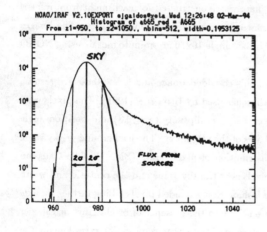

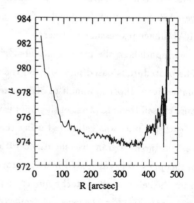

The Effect of the Cluster Environment on Galaxies

Bradley C. Whitmore
Space Telescope Science Institute
3700 San Martin Drive
Baltimore, MD 21218

ABSTRACT

Several galactic properties appear to be affected by the environment, especially the cluster environment. In this article we briefly review a wide variety of possible correlations, with a focus on the three *definite* effects, namely: 1) morphological fraction, 2) formation of cD galaxy, and 3) HI content. We then propose that these correlations can be explained by a unified picture of cluster evolution. In this simple model elliptical galaxies form first, and hence are largely unaffected by the collapse of the cluster core which occurs shortly thereafter. The collapse of the core results in the formation of the central cD galaxy by a giant merger event and results in a very small core radius for the cluster. The giant merger also results in the high specific frequency of globular clusters for the cD. The sharp, deep potential well of the cluster produces a strong tidal shear which destroys late forming disk and proto-disk galaxies. This results in the enhancement in the number of ellipticals, hence producing the morphology-clustercentric radius relation. The material from the shredded disk and proto-disk galaxies forms the ICM which then strips the gas from the spirals, hence producing the HI deficiencies.

1. INTRODUCTION

The topic of how the environment affects the structure and dynamics of galaxies is extremely broad and impossible to cover in a review of this length. In fact, the entire 27th Moriond meeting titled "Physics of Nearby Galaxies: Nature or Nurture" was devoted to this subject. Other recent reviews are White (1982, theoretical mechanisms), Dressler (1984, general review), Whitmore (1990, morphological fractions, size, internal kinematics), Kenney (1990, gas content), Oemler (1992, morphological fractions, colors, mechanisms), Whitmore (1992, group environment), and Balkowski (1992, observational evidence).

The first part of this review provides a cursory look at a wide range of observational parameters which may be affected by the cluster environment. A few key reference are included, but the reader is referred to various review articles for details, and for discussion of other aspects of the subject (*e.g.*, physical mechanisms, Butcher-Oemler effect, effect of the group environment). The second part of the review proposes a simple unified model which may explain several of the correlations.

2. PROPERTIES WHICH ARE DEFINITELY AFFECTED

2.1 Morphological Fractions
The fact that elliptical galaxies are more prevalent in clusters was already well established in the first half of this century (*e.g.*, Hubble and Humason 1931). This trend was quantified by Oemler (1974) and Melnick and Sargent (1977). The classic paper in this field is Dressler (1980) who classified over 6000 galaxies in 55 clusters. While Melnick and Sargent demonstrated the existence of population gradients as a function of clustercentric radius, Dressler argued that better correlations resulted when the local density was used.

However, Whitmore and Gilmore (1991) showed that Dressler's result was primarily caused by unequal binning, and Whitmore, Gilmore, and Jones (1993; hereafter WGJ) went on to show that the morphology-radius relation is the more fundamental correlation. Figure 1 shows the main result from WGJ. The elliptical fraction is nearly constant in the outer regions of the clusters, and then increases dramatically within 0.5 Mpc of the cluster center. The S0 fraction increases moderately as the center is approached, and then falls sharply within 0.2 Mpc of the center. The spiral fraction falls moderately as the clustercentric radius decreases, and then falls rapidly near the center. The spiral fraction is essentially zero at the cluster center, even though spirals dominate everywhere else in the universe.

These results led WGJ to conclude that some property of the cluster center is responsible for controlling the morphological fractions. They propose that the enhancement in the elliptical fraction near the cluster centers is due to the *destruction* of disk and proto-disk galaxies, rather than being due to some formation mechanism that favors ellipticals. In their model the material from the destroyed disks and proto-disks forms the intracluster medium (ICM), providing a link between the morphological fractions and the amount of x-ray gas in clusters. Figure 14 in WGJ shows that this idea works out quite well quantitatively, since the amount of x-ray gas in a cluster can be predicted by the strength of the elliptical enhancement. Although the exact physical mechanism for the destruction of disks and proto-disks is not defined by the model, WGJ suggest that a likely mechanism is the tidal shear produced by the mean gravitational field of the cluster, as proposed by Merritt (1984). Late-forming disk galaxies that are still in their protogalactic phase (*i.e.,* roughly 10 times larger; Fall and Efstathiou 1980) will be especially easy to destroy.

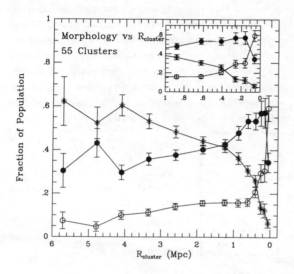

Figure 1: The morphology-clustercentric radius relation for the 55 clusters from the Dressler (1980) sample. Open circles are ellipticals; filled circles are S0's; and asterisks are spirals + irregular galaxies. Note the dramatic increase in the elliptical fraction within 0.5 Mpc of the cluster centers. (from WGJ)

2.1.1 Dwarf and Low Surface Brightness Galaxies

It is often assumed that dwarf galaxies should be particularly susceptible to environmental affects, because of their low binding energy. This is not the case, however, at least for nucleated dwarf ellipticals (dE's). A typical dE is about 5 times smaller and 100 times less massive (assuming dE's have 5 times the M/L of giant ellipticals) than a giant elliptical (Binggeli, Sandage, and Tarenghi 1984). Since the tidal influence scales as radius^3/mass, *already formed dwarf ellipticals with nuclei are as immune to tidal stripping as giant ellipticals.* This is consistent with the observational evidence which shows that nucleated dE's have the same spatial distribution as the E + S0 galaxies (Ferguson 1992). *Is this a coincidence, or does it indicate that the tidal shear is playing the main role in determining what types of galaxies can exist near the centers of clusters?*

The more extended dwarf irregulars (Im's) and nonnucleated dE's do avoid the centers of clusters, and have distributions similar to spiral + irregular galaxies. In the context of the WGJ model, this may simply indicate that the nucleated dE's formed earlier than the nonnucleated dE's and Im's which were still in their protogalaxy stage when the cluster collapsed, and were therefore destroyed by the strong tidal shear near the center of the cluster.

In a similar vein, Bothun *et al.,* (1993) find that low surface brightness galaxies are only found in very isolated environments and speculate that, "LSB disk galaxies have relatively long formation time scales and therefore must form in relative isolation".

2.2 cD Galaxies

cD galaxies are the largest, most massive galaxies in the universe. Their defining characteristic is an extended, low surface brightness envelope. They are nearly always found at the centers of rich clusters and have the same systemic velocity as the cluster (Quintana and Lawrie 1982, Oegerle 1994, Bird 1994). Although the specific physical mechanism responsible for their existence is still being debated, (*e.g.,* galactic cannibalism, accumulation of tidal debris from the cluster, preferred location without tidal shear) it is clear that they are only produced in rich clusters. Unlike normal ellipticals, their velocity dispersion profiles increase with radius (*e.g.,* Dressler 1979, see Figure 2 below), showing the presence of a deep potential well. cD galaxies also have the highest specific globular cluster frequency of any type of galaxy (Harris 1991).

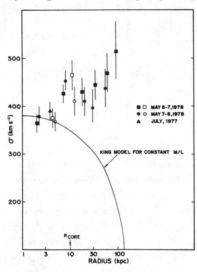

Figure 2: Velocity dispersion profile of the cD galaxy in Abell 2029. (from Dressler 1979)

2.3 HI Content

Early attempts to determine whether the neutral hydrogen content of cluster galaxies was affected by the environment were plagued by the difficulty of comparing similar samples of galaxies (*e.g.,* morphological types, luminosities, disk size). However, there is now good agreement that galaxies near the centers of cluster are deficient in their HI content (see reviews by Haynes 1990, Kenney 1990). Probably the most graphically convincing case is shown in Figure 3 (Cayatte *et al.* 1990), which shows how the HI disks have been truncated for the spirals near the center of the Virgo cluster. Again, it is uncertain what physical mechanism is responsible (*e.g.,* ram pressure sweeping, gas evaporation, tidal encounters).

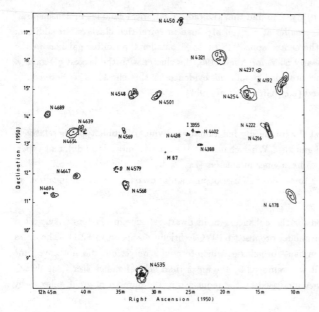

Figure 3: Neutral hydrogen map of the spirals near the center of the Virgo cluster. Each map has been magnified by a factor of five. Note the small sizes of the HI disks near M87, the center of the Virgo cluster. (from Cayatte *et al.* 1990)

3. PROPERTIES WHICH ARE POSSIBLY AFFECTED

3.1 Spiral Colors

Kennicutt (1983) reported that spirals in the Virgo cluster are about 0.1 mag redder than spirals in the field. Similarly, Oemler (1992) finds that cluster spirals are redder than their counterparts in the field, or in loose groups, by about 0.2 magnitudes in B-V. However, Gavazzi (1994) finds no difference in his sample, even though he uses the wider baseline provided by B-H colors.

3.2 Star Formation Rate

Kennicutt (1983) and Gavazzi (1992) have concluded, based on H_α and FIR observations, that cluster spirals have less star formation than field spirals. While this is true on the average, there appears to also be a small population of objects with abnormally large star formation rates, possible related to ram-pressure induced star formation (*e.g.,* Bothun and Dressler 1986, Gavazzi *et al.* 1992). van den Bergh (1976) finds that cluster spirals tend to be more "anemic", with smoother arms and less recent star formation. It is quite likely that several of these properties are related (*i.e.,* HI content, spiral color, star formation rate, anemic arms), and can all be explained by the removal of the gaseous reservoir.

3.3 Radius

Observational support for the existence of tidal stripping in clusters comes from the extensive study by Strom and Strom (1978), who find that the radii of elliptical galaxies in dense spiral-poor clusters are about 30 % smaller at a given M_V than in spiral-rich clusters. In addition, galaxies within 0.5 Mpc of the center appear to be 15 % smaller than outer galaxies in the same cluster. The effect is nearly 60 % for Abell 2199, the cluster with the largest cD galaxy. Although several studies have provided supporting evidence for this effect, (e.g., Peterson et al. 1979) others have disagreed (e.g., Girardi et al. 1991).

3.4 Luminosity Function

Bingelli et al. (1988) find that the luminosity function for individual Hubble types is relatively constant for cluster and field galaxies. What changes is the relative mix of the different types. The faint end slope appears to be steeper in clusters (i.e., $\propto L^{-1.0}$ in the field and $\propto L^{-1.25}$ in clusters), primarily due to the presence of a large population of dwarf ellipticals (Bingelli et al. 1988, Ferguson 1992).

One possible explanation for the enhancement of dwarf galaxies in clusters is suggested by the proto-disk destruction model proposed by WGJ (briefly discussed in §2.1). The extra dwarfs may simply be the remnants of galaxies which formed a bulge, but did not have time for the disk to settle before it was removed by the mean tidal field of the cluster. The dwarf-to-giant ratio would be further increased by the reduction in the number of giant galaxies by the same mechanism.

3.5 Far Infra-Red Emission

Thuan and Sauvage (1992) and Gavazzi (1992) show that the far infra-red emission comes from two components in spiral galaxies; star formation, and the general radiation field (i.e., the "cirrus"), with star formation being more dominant in late-type spirals. Hence it will be important to carefully match the mix of morphological fractions when comparing cluster and field galaxies. Careful studies of how the FIR is affected by the environment have only recently begun. Early indications show that the high FIR/optical galaxies may be missing in some clusters (Gavazzi 1992), as would be expected if star formation in clusters is reduced.

3.6 Rotation Curves

Several early studies (e.g., Chincarini and deSouza 1985, Guhathakurta et al. 1988) found no differences between the rotation curves of cluster and field galaxies. Whitmore, Forbes, and Rubin (1988) found an apparent correlation between the outer gradient of the rotation curve and the position in the cluster, with galaxies within 1 Mpc of the cluster center having falling rotation curves. Although Amram et al. (1993) argued that they did not see a similar effect, their Figure 2 actually shows a clear, though less steep correlation. However, Amram's latest work (1994) shows no correlation. Perhaps the main conclusion to draw is that even if a correlation exists, it is relatively weak. This might indicate that the already formed spirals in clusters are only weakly affected by the environment, or are so strongly affected that they are no longer identifiable as spiral galaxies.

3.7 Tully-Fisher Relation for Spirals

Aaronson *et al.* (1986) find no difference in the infrared Tully-Fisher relation for cluster and field galaxies. Rubin *et al.* (1988) find some evidence for spiral galaxies to have lower rotational velocity dispersions in clusters. This effect, if real, may be limited to galaxies near the centers of clusters (see §3.6), hence the overall affect on the Tully-Fisher relation is probably quite small.

3.8 Radio Continuum

Gavazzi (1992) finds an excess of high radio/optical galaxies in clusters. This is somewhat surprising since radio emission is generally found to correlate with the star formation rate. It is unclear how to interpret this result at present since other parameters are also involved, such as the strength of the magnetic field.

4. PROPERTIES WHICH APPEAR TO BE UNAFFECTED

4.1 CO Content

Kenney and Young (1988) find that the CO content of spiral galaxies is not affected by the cluster environment, unlike the HI content where a clear affect is seen. This is probably because the CO is located closer to the center of the galaxy, and is therefore less susceptible to effects such as tidal encounters and ram-pressure sweeping. See Kenney (1990) for a review.

5. A UNIFIED MODEL ?

A wide range of physical mechanisms have been proposed to explain the various environmental effects discussed in this article. However, is it possible that all of the major correlations can be explained by a single unified scheme ? Figure 4 shows a simple model which might account for the observations, at least in a qualitative sense. The model is an enhancement of the scheme proposed in WGJ (the reader is referred to §2.1 for a brief discussion, or to WGJ for more details). The new wrinkles are:

1. The collapse of the cluster core is the site of a gigantic merger event. Conditions are very favorable for merging since the cluster velocity dispersion is still relatively low (*i.e.*, the galaxies have fallen in from relatively short distances and hence have not attained large velocities). In addition, many of the galaxies are still gaseous protogalaxies, hence their cross-sections are very large. Recent studies, both observational (Holtzmann 1992, Whitmore *et al.* 1993) and theoretical (Kumai, Basu, and Fujimoto 1993), have suggested that globular clusters can be produced during gas-rich mergers. We might therefore expect a high efficiency of making globular clusters, as observed for cD galaxies.

2. The formation of the central cD galaxy, plus the accompanying dark matter, produces a very strongly peaked gravitational potential. This results in a strong tidal shear near the cluster center which can shred nearby protogalaxies, as well as already formed disk galaxies if they are very near the center. Recent gravitational lensing observations have shown that the core radii of many clusters are $\approx$ 50 kpc, much smaller than previously believed (*e.g.*, Soucail 1994, Kaiser 1994), hence the tidal shear is much stronger.

EFFECT OF THE CLUSTER ENVIRONMENT: A UNIFIED SCHEME ?

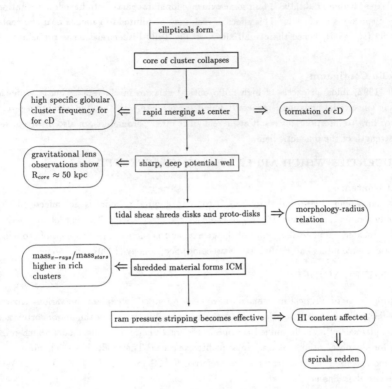

Figure 4: Proposed unified scheme of how galaxies may be affected by the cluster environment.

3. The material from shredded proto-disks forms the intra-cluster medium, which subsequently strips the neutral hydrogen from the spirals. This leads to the HI deficient galaxies, and eventually to redder spirals, lower star formation, and anemic spiral arms.

This simple model, while being primarily qualitative, does make a large number of testable predictions. For example, all of the following parameters should be correlated: morphological fraction, size/luminosity/mass of the cD galaxy, specific globular cluster frequency of the cD galaxy, R_{core} determined from gravitational lensing observations, $Mass_{x-ray}$, HI content of spirals, star formation rate and color of spirals, radii of inner galaxies. Only a few of these correlations have been looked at in detail. For example, WGJ (their Figure 14) show that the elliptical fraction can be used to predict $Mass_{x-ray}$. WGJ also showed that the tidal radii of both formed and unformed galaxies are consistent with this scheme, with already formed ellipticals relatively immune to tidal shear at all clustercentric radii while protogalaxies should be destroyed out to about 1 Mpc.

Other aspects of the model still need to be worked out. For example, what are the implications for the metalicity of the ICM? Are the time scales for the formation of different types of galaxies and the cluster collapse compatible with observations? Can the spatial distribution of the dwarf galaxies be explained by the model? One of the primary observational predictions is that gravitational lensing observations will find that clusters which have sharp, deep potential wells also have the greatest enhancement of elliptical galaxies. Perhaps the most exciting prospect is that HST observations may allow us to look back in time and actually see the collapse of the cluster core, the formation of the cD galaxy, and the destruction of disk and proto-disk galaxies.

REFERENCES

Aaronson, M., Bothun, G., Mould, J., Huchra, J., Schommer, R. A., Cornell, M. E. 1986,
 Ap. J., **302**, 536.

Amram, P., Sullivan, W. T. III, Balkowski, C., Marcelin, M. and Cayatte, V. 1993, *Ap. J.*,
 403, L59.

Amram, P. 1994, this conference.

Balkowski, C. 1992, *Physics of Nearby Galaxies: Nature or Nurture*, ed. T. T. Thuan,
 C. Balkowski, J. T. T. Van (Editions Frontieres, Gif-sur-Yvette Cedex).

Binggeli, B., Sandage, A., and Tammann, G. A. 1988, *Ann. Rev. Astron. Ap.*, **26**, 509.

Binggeli, B., Sandage, A., and Tarenghi, M. 1984, *Astron. J.*, **89**, 64.

Bird, C. M. 1994, *Astron. J.*, **107**, 1637.

Bothun, G. D. and Dressler, A. 1986, *Ap. J.*, **301**, 57.

Bothun, G. D., Schombert, J. M., Impey, C. D., Sprayberry, D., and McGaugh 1993, *Ap. J.*,
 106, 545.

Cayatte, V., van Gorkom, J. H., Balkowski, C., Kotanyi, C. 1990, *Astron. J.*, **100**, 604.

Chincarini, G. and de Souza, R. 1985, *Astron. Ap.*, **153**, 218.

Dressler, A. 1979, *Ap. J.*, **231**, 659.

Dressler, A. 1980, *Ap. J.*, **236**, 351.

Dressler, A. 1984, *Ann. Rev. Astron. Ap.*, **22**, 185.

Fall, S. M. and Efstathiou, G. 1980, *M.N.R.A.S.*, **186**, 133.

Ferguson, H. 1992, *Physics of Nearby Galaxies: Nature or Nurture*, ed. T. T. Thuan,
 C. Balkowski, J. T. T. Van (Editions Frontieres, Gif-sur-Yvette Cedex).

Gavazzi, G., 1992, *Physics of Nearby Galaxies: Nature or Nurture*, ed. T. T. Thuan,
 C. Balkowski, J. T. T. Van (Editions Frontieres, Gif-sur-Yvette Cedex).

Gavazzi, G. 1994, this conference.

Girardi, M., Biviano, A., Giuricin, G., Mardirossian, F., Mezzetti, M. 1991 *Ap. J.*, **366**, 393.

Guhathakurta, P., van Gorkom, J. H., Kotanyi, C. G., and Balkowski, C. 1988, *Astron. J.*, **96**,
 851.

Harris, 1991, *Ann. Rev. Astron. Ap.*, **29**, 543.

Haynes, M. 1990, *Clusters of Galaxies*, ed. W. Oegerle, L. Danly, M. Fitchett, (Cambridge University Press, Cambridge).

Holtzman, J. *et al.* (WFPC team) 1992, *Astron. J.*, **103**, 691.

Hubble, E. and Humason, M. L. 1931, *Ap. J.*, **74**, 43.

Kaiser, N. 1994, this conference.

Kenney 1990, *The Interstellar Medium in Galaxies*, ed. H. A. Thronson and J. M. Shull (Kluwer, Dordrecht), 151.

Kenney, J. D. and Young, J. S. 1988, *Ap. J. Suppl.*, **66**, 261.

Kennicutt, R. C. 1983, *Ap. J.*, **272**, 54.

Kumai, Y., Basu, B., and Fujimoto, M., 1993, *Ap. J.*, **404**, 144.

Melnick, J. and Sargent, W. L. W. 1977, *Ap. J.*, **215**, 401.

Merritt, D. 1984, *Ap. J.*, **276**, 26.

Oegerle, W. R. 1994, *Astron. J.*, **107**, 857.

Oemler, A. 1974, *Ap. J.*, **194**, 1.

Oemler, A. 1992, *Clusters and Superclusters of Galaxies*, ed. A. C. Fabian, (Kluwer Academic Publishers, London).

Peterson, B. M., Strom, S. E., and Strom, K. M. 1979, *Astron. J.*, **84**, 735.

Rubin, V. C., Whitmore, B. C. and Ford, W. K. 1988, *Ap. J*, **333**, 522.

Quintana, H. and Lawrie, D. G. 1982, *Astron. J.*, **87**, 1.

Soucail, G. 1994, this conference.

Strom, K. M. and Strom, S. E. 1978, *Astron. J.*, **83**, 73, 732 and 1293.

Thuan, T. X., and Sauvage, M. 1992, *Physics of Nearby Galaxies: Nature or Nurture*, ed. T. T. Thuan, C. Balkowski, J. T. T. Van (Editions Frontieres, Gif-sur-Yvette Cedex).

van den Bergh, S. 1976, *Ap. J.*, **206**, 883.

White, S. D. M. 1982, *Morphology and Dynamics of Galaxies*, ed. L. Martinet, M. Mayor, (Geneva: Geneva Obs.).

Whitmore, B. C. 1990, *Clusters of Galaxies*, ed. W. Oegerle, L. Danly, M. Fitchett, (Cambridge University Press, Cambridge).

Whitmore, B. C. 1992, *Physics of Nearby Galaxies: Nature or Nurture*, ed. T. T. Thuan, C. Balkowski, J. T. T. Van (Editions Frontieres, Gif-sur-Yvette Cedex).

Whitmore, B. C. and Gilmore, D. 1991, *Ap. J*, **367**, 64.

Whitmore, B. C., Gilmore, D., and Jones, C. 1993, *Ap. J*, **407**, 489. (WGJ)

Whitmore, B. C., Forbes, D. C., and Rubin, V. C. 1988, *Ap. J.*, **333**, 542.

Whitmore, B. C., Schweizer, F., Leitherer, C., Borne, K., and Robert, Carmelle, 1993, *Astron. J.*, **106**, 1354.

SPIRALS IN CLUSTERS DO NOT HAVE FALLING ROTATION CURVES

Amram P. (1), Balkowski C. (2), Marcelin M. (1), Boulesteix J. (1), Cayatte V. (2), Sullivan III W.T.(3)

(1) Observatoire de Marseille, France
(2) Observatoire de Paris-Meudon, France
(3) University of Washington, USA

Abstract.
Whitmore, Forbes and Rubin (1988) presented a good correlation between the slope of rotation curves and their location within a cluster, in the sense that inner galaxies tend to have falling rotation curves, while outer and field galaxies, tend to have flat or rising rotation curves. Amram et al (1993) did not confirm this correlation. Here we present a more complete sample including new Pérot-Fabry observations of galaxies very close to the centers of clusters. From these data, we definitively find that rotation curves of spiral galaxies do not decrease in the center of clusters.

1. Introduction

Many effects of the cluster environment on member galaxies have been established (see Whitmore's rewiev in these proceedings) but the effect on the dynamics is still controversial. Rubin, Whitmore and Ford (1988) and Whitmore, Forbes and Rubin (1988; hereafter collectively referred to as RWF), Distefano et al. (1990) and Amram et al.(1992, 1993, 1994) have observed optical rotation curves (RCs) of cluster galaxies. Their conclusions differ substantially. RWF presented evidence for a correlation in the sense that inner cluster spirals tended to have falling RCs, unlike those of outer cluster spirals or the great majority of field galaxies. This correlation suggested to RWF that inner cluster environment can strip away some fraction of the mass in the outer halo of a spiral galaxy or, alternatively, may not allow the halo to form. Distefano et al. (1990) pointed out that the case of Virgo cluster is quite ambiguous. Amram et al. (1993) found no significant evidence for anything more than a very small influence of the cluster environment. We reobserved all RWF's galaxies with a decreasing RC located in the inner part of a cluster because our sample could suffer from a lack of very central galaxies.

In Amram et al (1992), we have shown *(i)* that the very inclined and interacting spiral galaxy NGC 6045 has to be traited with great caution and anyway do not have a decreasing RC ; *(ii)* the galaxy UGC 4329 is 3 times less decreasing than claimed by RWF. In Amram et al. (1994), we have shown that the RC of the interacting galaxy NGC 6054 is no more decreasing. In this paper, we present new observations of galaxies very close to the center of the cluster DC 1842-62, already observed by RWF.

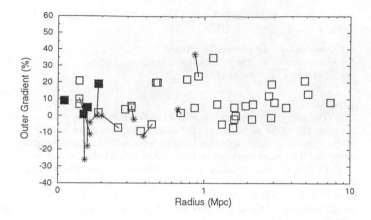

Figure 1. Outer gradient OG (see text for definition) for each galaxy versus its projected distance from the cluster center. Squares are for our data (filled square are for the galaxies of the cluster DC 1842-62 presented in this paper). Stars are for galaxies observed by RWF (a thin line links our data to RWF's ones for the same galaxy).

2. Observations and results

The already published observations have been obtained between November 1989 and April 1991 using the 3.6 m CFHT Telescope. The new observations presented here (table 1) have been made in May 1993 at the 3.6 m ESO Telescope in La Silla (Chili). The instrument CIGALE (CInématique des GALaxiEs) attached at the Cassegrain focus has been used. CIGALE is basically composed of a focal reducer (bringing the original f/8 focal ratio of the Cassegrain focus to f/2), a scanning Pérot-Fabry interferometer and an IPCS (2-D photon-counting system). The basic principles of this instrument are described in Amram et al. (1991).

The data reduction procedure have been extensively described elsewhere, but a major difference arises from using an IPCS (2-D photon-counting camera) instead of a CCD. Despite the fact that the quantum efficiency of the IPCS is 2 to 3 times lower than the one of a CCD, using an IPCS, one benefits of the multiplex advantages (fast scanning of the Pérot-Fabry). The spectral sampling of the data presented here is 16 $km.s^{-1}$ and the spatial sampling 0.91".

For a direct comparison with the results of RWF we used the same parameter OG (Outer Gradient) to define the slope of the RCs. OG is defined as the percentage of increase of the RC between $0.4R_{25}$ and $0.8R_{25}$, normalized to the maximum rotational velocity. OG is plotted versus the distance of each galaxy to the center of the different clusters in Mpc on figure 1. It is clear from this plot that RCs have roughly the same behaviour close to the center as in the outer parts of the clusters.

Table 1.   Parameters

(1)	(2)	(3)	(4)	(5)
Gal	$R_{Cluster}$	R_{25}	T	OG
DC 8	0.16	38.1	Sa	5
DC 10	0.11	23.2	Sc(pec)	9
DC 24	0.15	30.0	SBc	1
DC 39	0.19	40.2	SBc	19

(1) *All these galaxies belong to the Cluster DC*$1842 - 62$
(2) *Projected distance of each galaxy to its cluster center in Mpc*
    using $H_0 = 75 \ km.s^{-1}.Mpc^{-1}$
(3) *Corrected Radius in arcsec at the* 25 *mag.arcsec*$^{-2}$ *isophote in B* (*RC*3)
(4) *Morphological Hubble Type* (*RWF*)
(5) *Outer gradient of the rotation curve* (*see text*)

3.   The example of DC 24

The present subsection focuses on the kinematics of DC 24, the galaxy with the most decreasing RC, as an example. In fact, DC 24 is both the most decreasing RC (-26%) and the closest to the cluster center (0.15 Mpc, ($H_0 = 75$ $km.s^{-1}.Mpc^{-1}$)) in RWF's sample. So far, DC 24 is the ideal candidate to test in details the behaviour of the RC of galaxies in the very center of clusters.

The main results about this galaxy are summarized as follows: (i) both sides (receding and approaching) of the RC are in agreement and are **no decreasing**, permitting to derive the potential and the mass distribution of the galaxy; (ii) a position-velocity *(l-v)* diagram along the major axis is a good test to check the validity of the line-of-sight RC (*l* is the position along the major axis and *v* the radial velocity). When superimposing the projected RC onto the normalized *l-v* plot we obtain a very good agreement (see figure 2-left). (iii) the two-component mass model (using Carignan (1985)'s mass model) points out that the RC cannot decrease significantly before the end of the optical radius R_{25} even when the halo component is faint (see figure 2-right). This lead to the main conclusion : **the RC of DC 24 does not decrease within** R_{25}.

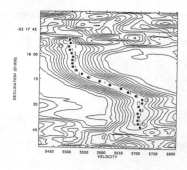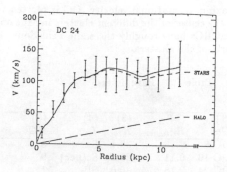

Figure 2.
(Left) : Rotation curve (RC) superimposed on a position-velocity map along the major axis of DC 24. Filled circles (•) represent the RC projected on the position-velocity map while open squares (□) represent the RC obtained within 5 degrees sector from both sides around the major axis PA. Isocontours are drawn from normalized individual profiles.

(Right) : Two-component (luminous and dark) mass model ("best-fitting" method). The search for the "best-fit" solution is made through an automatic procedure which consists in exploring a grid of values in the parameter 3-space and using the goodness-of-fit parameter χ^2 to orient the search (Carignan 1985).

4. Conclusion

Spiral galaxies located in the central part of clusters do not have decreasing RCs within the optical radius. Futhermore, the entire sample of galaxies do not present any correlation between the slope of the RCs (OG) and the radial location of the galaxy in the cluster. We are by now looking at the possible correlation between M/L of each galaxy with its distance to the cluster centers.

References

Amram, P., Boulesteix J., Georgelin Y.P., Georgelin Y.P., Laval, E., Le Coarer, E. and Marcelin, M., 1991, The Messenger 64, 44

Amram, P., Le Coarer, E., Marcelin, Balkowsky, C., Sullivan III, W.T. Cayatte, V., 1992, A&AS, 94, 175

Amram, P., Marcelin, M., Balkowski, C., Cayatte, V., Sullivan III, W.T. and Le Coarer, E., 1994, A&AS, 103, 5

Amram, P., Sullivan, WT., Balkowski, C., Marcelin, M., Cayatte, V., 1993, Ap. J.Let 403, L59

Carignan, C., 1985, Ap. J. 299, 59

Distefano, A., Rampazzo, R., Chincarini, G., de Souza, R., 1990, A&AS, 86, 7

Rubin, V.C., Whitmore, B.C. and Ford, W.K.,Jr 1988, Ap. J. 333, 522 (RWF)

Whitmore, B.C., Forbes, D.A. and Rubin, V.C. 1988, Ap. J. 333, 542 (RWF)

X-RAY EVOLUTION OF CLUSTERS OF GALAXIES

Alastair Edge

Institute of Astronomy, Madingley Road, Cambridge, CB3 0HA, U.K.

Abstract

Clusters of galaxies provide important clues to the nature and evolution of large scale structure in the Universe. X-ray observations of clusters have shown a dramatic decrease in the space density of the most X-ray luminous clusters with increasing redshift. In this talk I review these observations and compare them with those in the optical. I will attempt to review all the presently available and future ROSAT samples.

1 Introduction

Clusters of galaxies are ideal tracers of large scale structure as they can be identified with relative ease out to redshifts of 0.3 and beyond. Their average separation of 10–25 Mpc is a scale difficult to sample using galaxies (normal or exotic). Clusters also provide vital information about the evolution of the most massive systems and also the large scale structure. The fundamental restriction in determining changes in cluster mass is to find a faithful indicator of mass that can be measured with a precision of better than 10%. This restriction makes optical studies very difficult as the optical richness (the best optical estimate of mass) is sensitive to the background correction and the finite number of galaxies in the cluster and hence is never better than 20%.

Using X-ray measurements one would hope to use X-ray temperatures which should very closely match cluster masses. However, these were, until recently, rarely of measured to better than 10% accuracy and, even now, are available for a very restricted sample of clusters. On the other hand, the X-ray luminosity of a cluster is almost ideal for the task as it is highly non-linear with mass ($L_x \propto M^3$) and can be measured with reasonable accuracy. The non-linearity makes it much easier to measure changes in the mass of a cluster as a 20% increase in mass results in a 70% increase in X-ray luminosity. Therefore the best place to search for evolution in clusters of galaxies is an X-ray flux-limited sample.

2   Pre-ROSAT Samples

There have been two samples of clusters used to test for cluster evolution. The first is that of Edge et al. (1990). This sample was drawn from the All-Sky, scanning proportional counter surveys of UHURU, HEAO-1 and Ariel-V. From subsequent observations of these clusters with Einstein and EXOSAT, it was possible to identify sources that were confused with other X-ray sources or with other clusters, e.g. the Shapley concentration where 15% of the brightest clusters lie in 2% of the sky. The sample is essentially the brightest 50 clusters in ths sky and I shall refer to in the the rest of the text as B50.

From the B50 sample it was possible to detect a significant decrease in the number of high X-ray luminosity clusters at a redshift of greater than 0.1 (see Fig. 1). This represents a decrease in the space density of clusters of the order of five.

One great advantage of the B50 sample holds over other X-ray imaging samples is that it is a sample of luminosities *and* temperatures. Therefore is it possible to recalculate the X-ray luminosity function of the sample in any arbitrary passband. This is not possible for other samples such as the EMSS or ROSAT. It is important to make the comparison in the detection band used and not to make any temperature correction and conversion to 2–10 keV fluxes as information is lost in the process. To this end I present two new luminosity functions of the Edge et al. sample in the 0.1–2.4 keV and 0.3–3.5 keV bands correcting for galactic absorption and the contribution of any cooling flow (Edge, Stewart & Fabian 1992) in Figs 2 and 4. Taking the functions in the form of a Schecter function :

$$\frac{dN}{dL_x} = A \left(\frac{L_x}{10^{44}}\right)^{-\alpha} (10^{44}\,\mathrm{erg\,s^{-1}})^{-1}\mathrm{Mpc^{-3}}. \tag{1}$$

Then the coefficients are respectively $A = 10^{-6.41\pm0.14}$, $\alpha = -1.90 \pm 0.33$ and $L_0 = 4.8^{+\inf}_{-2.5} \times$

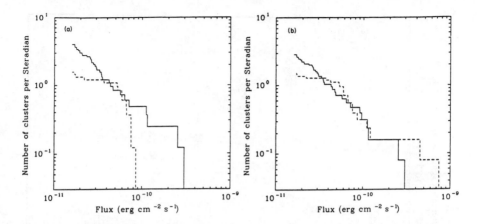

Figure 1: The source counts of the Edge *et al.* (1990) sample for a) high galactic latitude and b) all-sky samples. The counts are split on high ($L_x > 8 \times 10^{44}$ erg s^{-1}) plotted as dashed lines and low ($L_x < 8 \times 10^{44}$ erg s^{-1}) luminosity plotted as solid lines. Taken directly from Edge *et al.* (1990).

10^{44} erg s^{-1} for the ROSAT band (0.1–2.4 keV) and $A = 10^{-6.39 \pm 0.15}$, $\alpha = 1.86 \pm 0.33$ and $L_0 = 4.3^{+\inf}_{-2.1} \times 10^{44}$ erg s^{-1} for the EMSS band (0.3–3.5 keV). The compare to $A = 10^{-6.57 \pm 0.12}$, $\alpha = 1.65 \pm 0.26$ and $L_0 = 8.1^{+5.7}_{-2.3} \times 10^{44}$ erg s^{-1} for the 2–10 keV band of the original sample.

I encourage people to use these functions and not to either convert their data or convert older samples. Errors of factors of 2–3 can creep in if a crude luminosity-temperature conversion is used as the true scatter in the relation is not accounted for.

With the inclusion of temperatures in the sample allows the calculation of a temperature function (Edge etal 1990, Henry & Arnaud 1991) which provides one of our best limits in the mass function of clusters.

The other X-ray flux-limited sample is the Extended Medium Sensitivity Survey (EMSS) of Einstein. The results for clusters are presented in Gioia *et al.* (1990) and Henry *et al.* (1992). This sample also shows evidence for a decrease in the space density of high X-ray luminosity clusters but in this case out to redshifts of 0.3–0.6. The detection of evolution is made by the steepening of the luminosity function with redshift. However, there is an additional factor that must be included to interpret these results as the luminosity function itself is not a pure power law. This 'bent' power law results in samples of higher luminosity clusters (or in a flux-limited sample, higher redshift clusters) having *on average* steeper luminosity functions. Fig. 2 shows

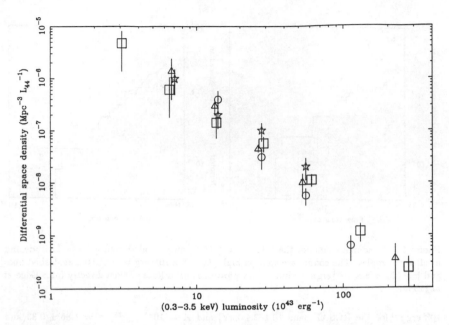

Figure 2: The luminosity function of the EMSS sample split into three redshift shells: 0.14–0.20 (stars), 0.2–0.3 (triangles), 0.3–0.6 (circles) plotted with the B50 luminosity function (squares) in the 0.3–3.5 keV band.

the EMSS results with the brightest 50 luminosity function. There is clearly a decrease in the space density of high luminosity clusters but it may not be as significant as 3σ as quoted by Gioia *et al.* and Henry *et al.*.

The evolution found in the B50 sample is most obvious in the source counts and not when plotted as a luminosity function directly. So as a test (and I stress this is not presented as a definitive comparison) I have examined the EMSS source counts. This is a very hazardous occupation as there are several very complex corrections made for sky coverage and for flux lost outside the detection cell. However, I am using the fluxes and sky coverage presented in Henry *et al.* (1992) which are used to determine the luminosity functions which are a similarly tricky transformation of the sample. Fig 3 shows the source counts of the EMSS and Brightest 50. The trend for the highest luminosity clusters ($L_x > 8 \times 10^{44}\,\mathrm{erg\,s^{-1}}$) to be a smaller fraction of a flux-limited sample as the flux-limit decreases is continued from the brightest 50 to the EMSS. Therefore I would argue that the EMSS and Brightest 50 are consistent with evolution although the absolute significance of the EMSS result *in isolation* is less than one would wish.

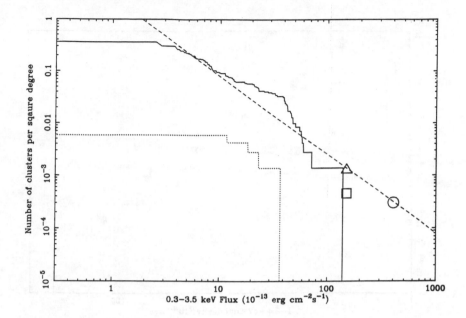

Figure 3: The source counts of the B50 sample high galactic latitude sample and the EMSS. The counts are split on high $(L_x > 8 \times 10^{44} \, \mathrm{erg\,s^{-1}})$ and low $(L_x < 8 \times 10^{44} \, \mathrm{erg\,s^{-1}})$ luminosity. The circle represents the B50 high and low luminosity at $5 \times 10^{-11} \, \mathrm{erg\,cm^{-2}\,s^{-1}}$ (2-10 keV) where the source counts are equal. The triangle marks the low luminosity and the square the high luminosity clusters in the B50 at the flux limit of the survey. The solid line is the low luminosity and the dotted line is the high luminsoity EMSS clusters. The dashed line is a Eucledian model for the low luminosity clusters alone.

3   Recent ROSAT results

Given the enormous amount of work required to complete an X-ray selected sample, it should not surprise the reader to discover that no complete RASS samples have been published. There are many in the latter stages, for instance, the SGP project (see Romer *et al.* 1994), the BCS (see Allen *et al.* 1992 and Crawford *et al.* 1994) and HYDRA (see Pierre *et al.* 1994).

The only published sample is the Brightest Abell Cluster Sample (BACS) of Ebeling (1993). This sample is a flux-limited sample of Abell clusters over the whole, high galactic latitude sky so is technically not a complete X-ray sample but at the flux-limit used $(6.1 \times 10^{-12} \, \mathrm{erg\,cm^{-2}\,s^{-1}})$ very few clusters this bright are not Abell clusters. This work is derived from the cross-correlation of the RASS catalogue with the Abell sample (Ebeling *et al.* 1993). The BACS contains 203 clusters within a redshift of 0.2. Ebeling (1993) demonstrates that the sample is

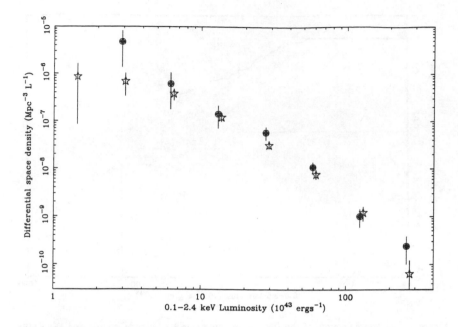

Figure 4: The BACS luminosity function from Ebeling (1993) plotted with the B50 luminosity function in the ROSAT band. The BACS points are plotted as stars and the B50 as solid circles. The BACS is plotted *without* the incompleteness correction added by Ebeling (1993) as the incompleteness is luminosity dependent.

consistent with the evolution of the X-ray luminosity function seen in the B50 and EMSS both in the luminosity function and in the source counts. Fig 4 shows the BACS luminosity function with the B50. There is a very clear agreement at luminosities above 4×10^{43} erg s^{-1} which is contrary to the original conclusion of Ebeling (1993) who used a simple band conversion to the B50 luminosity function which as shown above does not work reliably. The deficit in the BACS below 4×10^{43} erg s^{-1} results from the problems in detecting low luminosity sources and the higher proportion of non-Abell clusters at lower luminosities. The deficit also illustrates that despite the B50 being a 2-10 keV selected sample it still gives a 'fair' representation of the lowest luminosity and temperature clusters. The work on the BACS will soon be converted into a paper (Ebeling *et al.*, in preparation).

All other published ROSAT cluster samples (on cluster luminosity functions at least) are based on X-ray observations an optically selected sample.

Bower *et al.* (1994) have made PSPC pointed observations of 14 distant clusters ($0.2 < z < 0.55$) from the sample of Couch *et al.* (1991). Each cluster is richer, or as rich as, Abell Richness

Class 1. As the surveyed volume is known and all the clusters are observed, it is possible to calculate the X-ray luminosity function. They conclude that the normalisation of the X-ray luminosity function is significantly lower than nearby samples, especially at luminosities above $10^{44}\,\mathrm{erg\,s^{-1}}$. Again, Bower et $al.$ use an band-corrected luminosity function which has a slightly higher normalisation (20–40%) from the B50 function. While this does not significantly alter their conclusions, it lowers the apparent discrepancy. An additional point is that in the luminosity range $10^{43-44}\,\mathrm{erg\,s^{-1}}$, only half the B50 clusters are Richness Class 1 or above. Therefore the Bower et $al.$ sample should have half normalisation expected, again lowering the discrepancy.

An even more distant optical sample was studied by Castander et $al.$ (1994). They took 5 Gunn clusters $(0.7< z <0.95)$ of which 2 are clearly detected by the PSPC and another is a marginal detection. Following the same method as Bower et $al.$ (1994) they calculate a luminosity function that is significantly lower than that expected from lower redshift samples. However, in this sample the discrepancy is less severe than in the Bower et $al.$ sample and when allowance is made for the richness of the clusters it can be argued that the luminosity function at the $10^{43-44}\,\mathrm{erg\,s^{-1}}$ range is consistent with $z = 0$.

These two samples clearly indicate the importance of obtaining an X-ray selected sample of clusters to eliminate the uncertainties related to the original optical selection and richness. Optical samples are within a factor of two or three of the expected numbers so we can at least put an upper bound to the rate of evolution.

ROSAT pointed observations are important for establishing the presence of a cooling flow directly. As part of larger collection of ROSAT pointed observations as PI and from the public archives, I have gathered a sample of 22 clusters above a redshift of 0.15 of which 19 are cooling flows consistent with low redshift samples (Edge et $al.$ 1992). The fraction of cooling flows is plotted against redshift in Fig 5 and it is constant at all redshifts. This implies that there is no significant evolution in the fraction of clusters with cooling flows, although the sample cannot provide any information on whether the cooling flows themselves evolve, yet.

4 Future Prospects

There are a number of ROSAT samples from the Survey ($e.g.$ the ESO Key Project of Böhringer & Guzzo) which will provide an great deal of information about the luminosity function of clusters within 0.3. Deeper pointed observations will detect many more clusters with $z >0.3$ and constrain the luminosity function out to redshifts of as much as 1.

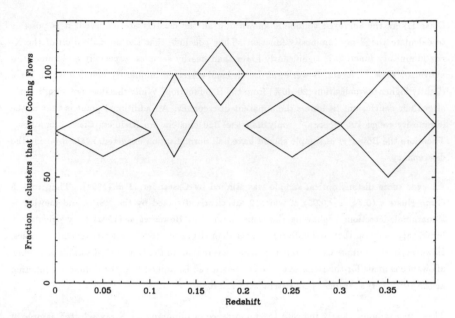

Figure 5: The percentage of cooling flows in clusters with X-ray images plotted against redshift. The lowest redshift point is from the Edge, Stewart & Fabian (1992) sample.

ROSAT pointed observations of clusters are providing an unprecedentedly clear picture of the presence of substructure in clusters (*e.g.* Briel *et al.* 1991). The relative frequency of X-ray substructure in clusters can give strong constraints on the rate of cluster evolution and cluster-cluster merger timescales. We await the results from complete samples of ROSAT images with great interest.

As was clear from the talks at this conference, ASCA is a great advance in the study of clusters. Unfortunately in the field of cluster evolution studies, ASCA will have a lesser impact. The work requires complete samples which will be difficult given the small number of clusters ASCA will observe even in a few years and the great competition for time. It may be possible to constrain the temperature function at higher redshifts with a well chosen sub-set of the EMSS sample (Henry, priv. comm.) but it will be difficult to compile the large samples required to constrain such a steep function well. It is only at the end of this decade with AXAF, XMM and ASTRO-E that large enough samples will be available to make significant improvements on ROSAT samples. It is to be hoped that we have learned enough about the X-ray properties of individual clusters from ASCA observations to make proper use of the results!

5 Conclusions

X-ray surveys of clusters of galaxies provide the clearest view of the evolution of the most massive objects in the gravitational hierarchy. These observations point to recent rapid merging of clusters. Both the overall statistics and observations of individual clusters indicate that cluster-cluster mergers are common. The implications of such rapid evolution range from the formation of central galaxies and cluster radio sources to the primordial power spectrum. Future observations will be fill in many of the finer details on individual objects but most of the future survey work has already been performed by ROSAT. The task now is to extract new samples quickly and uniformly.

Acknowledgments

I would like to thank the conference organizers for a very enjoyable meeting. I acknowledge the SERC for financial support. I thank Piers Millington-Wallace for the cartoon of 'Alice Dare, Pilot of the Future'.

References

Allen, S.W., Edge, A.C., Fabian, A.C., Böhringer, H., Crawford, C.S, Ebeling, H., Johnstone, R.M., Naylor, T. & Schwarz, R.A., 1992. MNRAS, 257, 67

Bower, R.G., Böhringer, H., Briel, U.G, Ellis, R.S., Castander, F.J. & Couch, W.J. 1994. MNRAS, 268, 345

Briel, U.G., Henry, J.P., Schwarz, R.A., Böhringer, H., Ebeling, H., Edge, A.C., Hartner, G.D., Schindler, S., Trümper, J. & Voges, W., 1991. A&A, 246, L10

Castander, F.J., Ellis, R.S., Frenk, C.S., Dressler, A. & Gunn, J.E. 1994 ApJ, 424, L79

Couch, W.J., Ellis, R.S., Malin, D.F. & MacLaren, I.1991, MNRAS, 249, 606

Crawford, C.S., Edge, A.C., Fabian, A.C., Allen, S.W., Böhringer, H., Ebeling, H., McMahon, R.G. & Voges, W. 1994, MNRAS, submitted

Ebeling, H., Böhringer, H., Voges, W.H. & Edge, A.C., 1993. A&A, 275, 360

Ebeling, H. 1993. PhD thesis, Universität München, MPE report 250.

Edge, A.C., Stewart, G.C., Fabian, A.C. & Arnuad, K.A. 1990. MNRAS, 245, 559

Edge, A.C., Stewart, G.C. & Fabian, A.C., 1992. MNRAS, 258, 177

Gioia, I.M., Henry, J.P., Maccacaro, T., Morris, S.L., Stocke, J.T., Wolter, A., 1990, ApJ, 356, L35

Henry, J.P. & Arnaud, K.A. 1991. ApJ, 372, 410

Henry, J.P., Gioia, I.M., Maccacaro, T., Morris, S.L. & Stocke, J.T. 1992, ApJ, 386, 408.

Pierre, M., Böhringer, H., Ebeling, H., Voges, W., Schuecker, P., Cruddace, R. & MacGillivray, H. 1994. A&A, in press

Romer, A.K., Collins, C.A., Böhringer, H., Ebeling, H., Voges, W., Cruddace, R.G. & MacGillivray, H.T. 1994. Nat, submitted

THE BUTCHER-OEMLER EFFECT IN RADIO SELECTED GROUPS OF GALAXIES

Esther L. Zirbel

Space Telescope Science Institute
3700 San Martin Drive, Baltimore, MD 21218

ABSTRACT

We re-state the result by AEZO [1] that the BO effect is observed in groups of galaxies that have at least 15 members (where $N_{0.5}^{-19}=15$ corresponds to 15 galaxies within 0.5 Mpc of the radio galaxy which are brighter than -19.0 V magnitude). We show the dependence of the fraction of blue galaxies as a function of group richness which agrees with Dressler's [2] morphology-density relationship, only at low redshifts (z~0.1). At high redshifts (z~0.4) rich groups ($N_{0.5}^{-19}>15$) have bluer colors. We thus infer that the color-density relationship is steepening with time.

We demonstrate that the blue galaxies in the high redshift rich groups (z~0.4, $15<N_{0.5}^{-19}<40$) can be divided into two classes: the bright blue galaxies ($M_V<-21.5$) that have disappeared today and the fainter blue galaxies whose evolution is more gradual. We suggest that the bright blue galaxies may be identified with the 'classical' BO galaxies, E+A galaxies, star bursting ellipticals or peculiar galaxies, while the fainter blue galaxies may be late type galaxies.

In addition, our data seems to indicate that the bright blue galaxies avoid the group centers. Moreover, the evolution of the blue fraction is independent of group-centric radius. However, these results need to be verified by a larger data set. If correct, the latter result would suggest that morphological segregation is dependent on global (not local) cluster properties.

Finally, we show that there are real differences between high redshift groups of the SAME group richness that are red (with $f_B<0.2$) and blue ($f_B>0.2$): (a) M* is brighter in red high redshift groups, (b) the red groups have no bright blue galaxies nor faint blue galaxies and (c) the blue groups have both, bright and faint blue galaxies. Since the existence of the bright blue and the faint blue galaxies seems to be coupled, we suggest that they may be genuine group members.

INTRODUCTION

Although the Butcher-Oemler effect [3] was regarded with a lot of skepticism 10 years ago, it is now well established that galaxies in high redshift (z~0.4) rich clusters show a population of galaxies that are significantly bluer than their lower redshift counterparts. However, the nature of these galaxies is still rather controversial. While spectroscopy [4] revealed that the blue galaxies are a combination of normal late type galaxies, type I Seyferts, starburst galaxies and post-starburst ellipticals with Balmer lines (named E+A galaxies), recent Hubble Space Telescope (HST) data showed that many of these "bluer" galaxies show a disturbed and peculiar morphology [5,6,7]. Moreover, explaining the cause of the BO effect and why this population of galaxies has disappeared today, still remains a major challenge. In fact, it is even uncertain if the blue galaxies are genuine cluster members [8] or if they are interlopers that are falling towards the cluster for the first time [9,10].

The aim of this paper is to analyze whether the BO effect is also observed in "poorer" environments and the general field. Since high redshift poor clusters (or loosely speaking "groups") are difficult to find, we decided to observe the fields surrounding powerful radio galaxies that are thought to inhabit density enhanced regions [11]. The suitability of radio-selected groups, the selection criteria, data reduction and conversion to rest frame colors and magnitudes is described in detail by AEZO [1]. Here, we shall first review one of the basic results from AZEO of how the fraction of blue galaxies, f_B, is affected by group richness, $N_{0.5}^{-19}$, and then proceed to three further questions: What are the magnitudes of the blue galaxies? What is f_B as a function of group-centric radius? How do high redshift groups that contain many blue galaxies differ from those high redshift groups that do not?

Quantitatively, we define f_B as the fraction of blue galaxies with colors that are -0.20 bluer than an early type galaxy of the same absolute magnitude, and $N_{0.5}^{-19}$ as the group richness which is the background subtracted number of galaxies surrounding the radio galaxy within a radius of 0.5 Mpc which are brighter than -19th rest frame V magnitude. 97% of our groups are Abell richness class 0. We use $H_0=50$ and $q_0=0.0$ throughout.

RESULTS

PART 1: The blue fraction as a function of group richness

In Figure 1a we see that the blue galaxy content of the low redshift (z~0.1) groups are a strongly decreasing function of their group richness. This is no surprise and reflects Dressler's [2] well-known morphology-density relationship (assuming a color-morphology relationship). However, at high redshifts (z~0.4) the color-density relationship is different (Figure 1b) from that at low redshifts: (a) the rich groups ($15<N_{0.5}^{-19}<40$) are on average bluer by $\Delta f_B=0.13\pm0.06$, (b) not all high redshift rich groups have a high blue fraction and (c) the poor high redshift groups ($N_{0.5}^{-19}<15$) have the same colors as the low redshift poor groups and as the field.

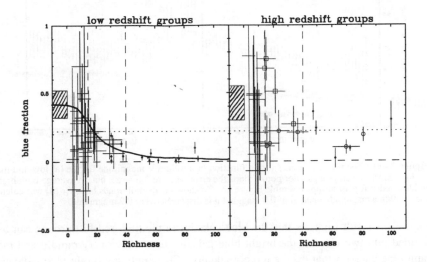

Figure 1a&b: The blue fraction, f_B, as a function of group richness, $N_{0.5}^{-19}$. The solid line in Figure 1a is an 'eyeball fit' to the data. At higher redshifts (Figure 1b) this eyeball fit appears flatter and may be shifted towards richer groups. The points with the horizontal and vertical error bars correspond to our radio groups and the filled circles correspond to the original BO clusters or CFA groups. The large circles represent red ($f_B<0.2$) groups, while the squares represent blue ($f_B>0.2$) groups. The hatched box shows f_B of the general field. The dashed lines distinguish between poor groups ($N_{0.5}^{-19}<15$), rich groups ($15<N_{0.5}^{-19}<40$) and clusters ($N_{0.5}^{-19}>40$). The dotted line separates blue and red groups. Notice that there are no blue rich groups at low redshifts.

As stated in AEZO, this result suggests that the evolution seen in rich clusters is not typical of that occurring in poor groups or the field. Evidently the evolution of galaxies is dependent on the group environment, and if the colors of galaxies at high redshifts are representative of their morphologies, one is forced to infer that the morphological segregation is of recent origin.

PART 2: The f_B as a function of absolute magnitude

In Figures 2a&b we display $f_B(M)$ for rich ($15<N_{0.5}^{-19}<40$) high and low redshift groups. The major difference between the high and the low redshift groups is the extra population of bright blue galaxies ($M_V<-21.5$) which is due to 13±3 bright blue galaxies in 8 high redshift groups. The fainter blue galaxies may also show a decrease in $f_B(M)$ with redshift, but this needs verification with a larger data set.

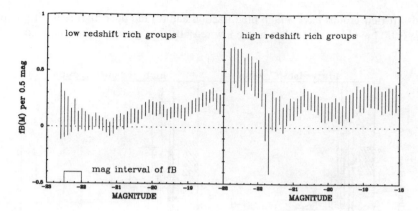

Figure 2a&b: The blue fraction, f_B, as a function of absolute V magnitude for the (a) low and the (b) high redshift rich groups. For poor groups the error bars are too large, but on average both high and low redshift poor groups resemble Figure 2b. To show the overall trends best, $f_B(M)$ was calculated within a magnitude interval of 0.5 mag, but it is displayed every 0.2 magnitude.

This result suggests that the blue galaxies in the high redshift groups can be divided into two classes: the bright blue galaxies that evolve very rapidly and the faint blue galaxies that evolve more gradually. Since only the bright blue galaxies have disappeared today, we speculate that these are the BO galaxies, while the fainter blue galaxies are probably late type galaxies.

PART 3: The f_B as a function of group-centric radius

We define $f_B(r)$ as the fraction of blue galaxies with absolute magnitudes ranging from -19 to -24 that are found within a ring of area $\Delta r^2 = (0.1\text{Mpc})^2$, centered on r, evaluated every 0.02Mpc.

In Figure 3a we display $f_B(r)$ for the high redshift bright blue galaxies (with $M_V < -21.5$) and we see that the bright blue galaxies seem to avoid the group centers. Interestingly, this behavior is consistent with that observed in the original BO clusters, where the BO galaxies avoid the cluster centers [8]).

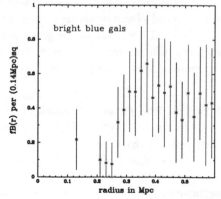

Figure 3a: $f_B(r)$ within a ring of area $\Delta r^2 = (0.14\text{Mpc})^2$ as a function of group-centric radius of bright galaxies ($M_V < -21.5$) only.

In Figure 3a&b we display $f_B(r)$ as a function of group-centric radius for all groups with $N_{0.5}^{-19}<40$. Comparing $f_B(r)$ of the low to the high redshift groups, we see that it is on average *higher* by $\Delta f_B(r)=0.13\pm0.10$ at high redshifts *regardless* of group-centric radius, *i.e.*, the overall shape of $f_B(r)$ remains constant with time.

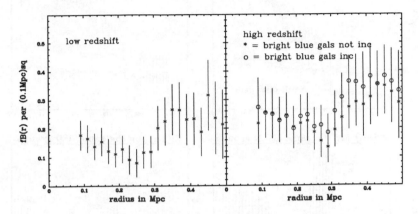

Figure 3b&c: We display $f_B(r)$ within a ring of area $\Delta r^2=(0.1Mpc)^2$ as a function of group-centric radius in intervals of $\Delta r=0.02Mpc$. We assume that the radio galaxy is in the center of the group, which needs to be tested separately. Note that the inclusion of the bright blue galaxies does not change the overal trend, mostly because the faint blue galaxies are more numerous.

Since the error bars are rather large this result needs to be verified with a larger data set. If we find that the blue fraction of the groups is indeed independent of group-centric radius it would imply that morphological segregation does not depend on the location of the galaxies within those groups, but rather on a more global property such as the overall cluster potential.

PART 4: Differences between high redshift blue and red groups

Comparing Figure 4a to 4b, we see that in the high redshift red groups (with $f_B<0.2$) the bright galaxies are on average brighter than the bright galaxies in the blue groups ($f_B\geq0.2$), i.e., red groups have a brighter M*. If we let the bright blue galaxies in the blue groups fade (since they have disappeared today) the difference in M* becomes even larger. In Figure 4d of the high redshift red groups, we see that almost all galaxies (22/24) that are brighter than -21.5 are also redder (with $\Delta(B-V)_0>-0.2$). Also, we see that red groups are not just deficient of bright blue galaxies, but they lack fainter blue galaxies, while the blue groups (Figure 4c) have a population of bright *and* faint blue galaxies. About half (13/25) of the bright galaxies (M<-21.5) in the blue groups are bluer than $\Delta(B-V)_0=-0.2$.

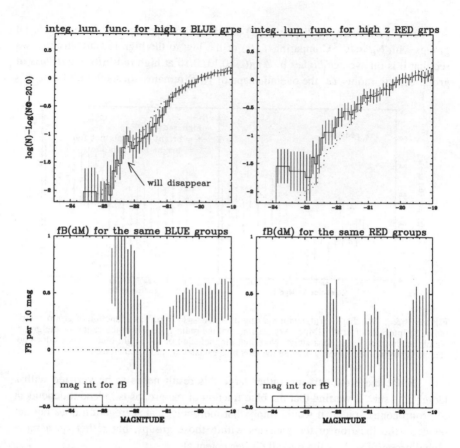

Figure 4: In Figures 4a&b we show the integrated luminosity functions for high redshift red (f_B<0.2) and blue (f_B>0.2) groups. The dotted line represents the shape of the overall luminosity function of all groups used in the analysis. Since its purpose is to illustrate the differences between the red and the blue groups more clearly, all luminosity functions are normalized such that log(N)=0.0 at -20th magnitude. Figure 4c&d show the corresponding blue fractions, f_B, as a function of magnitude. Note that f_B was calculated within a magnitude interval of 1.0 mag, but is displayed every 0.2 magnitude. Points with error bars larger than 1 magnitude are omitted.

We therefore claim that there are real differences between the groups that have the extra population of bright blue galaxies and those that do not. We suspect that the red and the blue groups are in different evolutionary states. Since the groups that have relatively more faint blue galaxies also have the extra population of bright blue galaxies, we suspect that these phenomena are coupled, and we suggest that the bright blue galaxies are genuine group members.

SUMMARY

We showed that the BO effect is observed at z~0.4 in clusters that have at least 15 members, but not in poorer environments. This suggests that morphological segregation happens only in rich environments and that it is of recent origin. It would be interesting to speculate what f_B as a function of richness looks like at higher redshifts. Do all the red rich clusters disappear $e.g.,$ 12), or does the eyeball fit in Figure 1 flatten and get shifted towards larger group richnesses?

Analyzing clusters of intermediate richness ($15<N_{0.5}^{-19}<40$), we showed that the blue galaxies in the high redshift groups can be divided into two classes: the bright blue galaxies that have disappeared today and the fainter blue galaxies whose evolution are more gradual. We speculate that the bright blue galaxies are starburst and post starburst galaxies and may correspond to the "classical BO" galaxies, while the fainter blue galaxies are mostly late type galaxies.

Finally, we show that there are real differences between high redshift groups of the SAME group richness that have the extra population of bright blue galaxies and those that do not: (a) M* is brighter in red high redshift groups, (b) red groups also have much less faint blue galaxies and (c) blue groups have both, bright and faint blue galaxies. Since the groups that have relatively more faint blue galaxies also have the extra population of bright blue galaxies, we speculate that these phenomena may be coupled, and we suggest that the bright blue galaxies may be genuine group members. Furthermore, we speculate that in contrast to the blue high redshift groups, the red high redshift rich groups may be DYNAMICALLY more evolved, and/or may have formed at earlier epochs, and/or may already have had a BO phase.

References

1) Allington-Smith J.R., Ellis R.S., Zirbel E.L. & Oemler A., 1993 (AEZO), Ap.J., **404**, 521
2) Dressler A., 1980, Ap.J., **236**, 251
3) Butcher H. & Oemler A., 1979, Ap.J., **226**, 559; 1984, Ap.J., **285**, 426
4) Dressler A. & Gunn J.E., 1983, Ap.J., **270**, 7
5) Ellis R.S., 1994, Space Telescope Science Institute Workshop on "*Quantifying Galaxy Morphology ar High Redshifts*"
6) Dressler A., 1994, Space Telescope Science Institute Workshop on "*Quantifying Galaxy Morphology ar High Redshifts*"
7) Dressler A., Oemler A., Gunn J. & Butcher H., 1994, Ap.J., in press
8) Oemler A. 1992, in "*Clusters and Superclusters*", ed. A.C. Fabian, (Dortrecht: Kluwer)
9) Dressler A. Gunn J.E. & Schneider D., 1985, Ap.J., **294**, 70
10) Evrard A., 1990, Ap.J., **363**,349; 1991, MNRAS, **248**, 8P
11) Pestage R.M. & Peacock J.A., 1988, MNRAS, **230**, 131; erratum 1989, MNRAS, **236**, 959
12) Ratos K.D. & Schombert J.M., 1994, preprint

RADIO PROPERTIES OF GALAXIES IN CLUSTERS

Giuseppe Gavazzi
Osservatorio Astronomico di Brera
via Brera, 28, Milano, Italy

Introduction.

The purpose of this talk is to discuss the subtle environmental differences found among the radio properties of radio galaxies, associated with E+S0 galaxies, and of spiral galaxies. The obvious issues that I will address are:

1) do cluster galaxies develop different radio morphologies than field galaxies?

2) is the frequency of occurrence as a function of radio luminosity of field galaxies different from that of galaxies in clusters?

1. *Radio Galaxies: Some Historical Background.*

Previous comprehensive reviews on this subject were given by Miley, 1975 and by Fanti, 1984.

Early interferometric studies of the Perseus and Coma clusters with the one-mile interferometer at Cambridge revealed the existence of asymmetric radio sources identified with bright Elliptical galaxies, which were named: "head-tail" radio galaxies (HT). Their brightness is peaked on the parent galaxy and gradually decreases along the tail, whose length may reach several hundred kpc. The spectral index increases as one moves along the tail. The polarization is as high as 60%, and the magnetic field is aligned with the tail. The prototypes of these sources are 3C83.1 (N1265) and IC310 in Perseus (Ryle & Windram, 1968), 5C4.81 in Coma (Willson, 1970).

Subsequent work at Westerbork in the early seventies led to better resolve these radio structures. The "head" was often resolved in two jets emerging from the galaxy nuclei, continuously bending in the direction of the "tail". It became apparent that the class of HT formed a continuum with that of classical double, Cygnus A-like radio sources, assuming that some external pressure was capable of bending the jets. A natural explanation was that the pressure was supplied by the galaxy motion itself (~ 1000 km/s), provided that the intergalactic space in clusters of galaxies contained a fair amount of gas, $\sim 10^{-3}$-10^{-4} atoms cm^{-3} and temperatures $\sim 10^8$ K (Jaffe & Perola, 1973). This was dramatically confirmed by early X-ray studies of clusters of galaxies which revealed the existence of large reservoirs of hot gas in the intergalactic space (Gursky et al., 1972).

Estimates of the external pressure (independent from X-ray measurements) were derived from observations of the low brightness regions of HT. They were generally found in static pressure equilibrium with the external medium (under the assumption of equipartition). Colla et al. (1975) confirmed an earlier result by Slingo (1974) that cluster radio galaxies contain a larger fraction of steep spectra sources than classical doubles. This was interpreted as an evidence for efficient confinement in clusters enabling us to see the aging of relativistic electrons due to synchrotron energy losses before the adiabatic losses would prevail (see also Feretti, Perola & Fanti, 1992).

Unlike narrow angle tails (NAT), sources with widely diverging tails (often called Wide Angle Tails or WAT) were found associated with the more dominant galaxies in clusters by Owen & Rudnick (1976). This is consistent with the drag model, since brighter galaxies are expected to have smaller velocities. In fact WAT have average velocities about 2 times smaller than NAT.

A radio continuum survey of a dozen of nearby, rich, northern clusters of galaxies was carried out in the seventies with the Westerbork telescope by C. Perola, W. Jaffe, E. Valentijn, G. Miley, R. Fanti, C. Lari and myself which proved that almost all clusters contained at least one HT. In total they represent about 30% of all radio galaxies found in clusters (Fanti, 1984).

Ekers et al., 1981 showed that sources with complex morphology (including HT) are predominantly found with intermediate-low radio luminosity (10^{23}-10^{24} W Hz^{-1} at 1.4 GHz), and that the departure from 180 deg of the angle of separation between the two extended components is larger and has a larger spread for galaxies in clusters than in the field.

Although the drag model gave a satisfactory explanation for the peculiar morphology radio galaxies in clusters, it was still unclear if HT formed a continuum with classical doubles as far as their frequency of occurrence: i.e. if the probability of developing radio sources with a given radio luminosity was enhanced or decreased in clusters galaxies, with respect to the field. A pioneer work by Auriemma et al. (1977) showed that the frequency of occurrence of radio sources, as a function of radio luminosity displays a break at P*. They claimed that the fraction of radio emitting galaxies increases with increasing optical luminosity, but P* remains constant. Fanti, 1984 found that the fraction of radio galaxies in clusters is consistent with that of field galaxies. In other words, the cluster environment which is capable of producing dramatic effects on the morphology of radio galaxies, has no measurable effect on the mechanism feeding the nuclear engine which provides the source for the relativistic material.

1.2 *The Vla Era.*

The advent of the VLA in the eighties gave a tremendous observational momentum to the study of radio galaxies in clusters and in groups, due to its superior sensitivity and resolution. Previously known HT were mapped with a resolution similar to optical and, thanks to the "self-calibration" technique, enough dynamic range was achieved to reveal thin bright jets feeding the low-brightness relaxed regions down the tail. Detailed studies of individual HT in the Coma cluster are for example in Dallacasa et al. (N4869); Venturi et al. (N4789, N4827). Recent deep surveys of individual nearby clusters complete to fractions of a mJy can be found for example in Kim et al., 1994a, 1994b, Kim 1994 for the Coma cluster; in Gavazzi & Contursi, 1994 for A1367. Thanks to the large sensitivity of the VLA at 327 MHz to large-scale emission, extended low-brightness radio sources on the scale of one Mpc were discovered at the SW periphery of the Coma cluster by Giovannini et al., 1991 Kim et al., 1989.

The work of Feretti & Giovannini, 1994 on a complete sample of 33 radio galaxies in clusters with linear size < 20 kpc, i.e. confined within the optical envelope of their parent galaxy gives another example of what the superior performance of the VLA made possible. They found 8 sources (24%) with bent (NAT, WAT) structure indicating that the effect of the pressure exerted by the intergalactic medium is influencing the interstellar gas within the galaxy.

The complete survey of 330 clusters carried on at 20 cm (Zhao, Burns, & Owen, 1989, Owen, White & Burns, 1992 and Owen, White & Ge, 1993) represents a major statistical improvement for the study of radio galaxies in clusters.

Based on these new observations, the Bivariate RLF of galaxies was re-determined (see de Ruiter, et al., 1990, Owen, 1993, Owen & Ledlow, 1994) confirming previous claims (Auriemma et al., 1977, Fanti, 1984) that cluster galaxies of a given optical luminosity develop radio sources with radio luminosity similar to "field" galaxies. Fig. 1 shows the frequency distribution of the quantity R/O=Radio/optical flux for a complete, optically selected (mp < 15.3) sample that I assembled for 158 nearly isolated E+S0 galaxies belonging to the bridge between Coma and A1367 compared with the one selected similarly, but containing 334 galaxies in the rich clusters: A262, Virgo, Coma, A1367, A2147, A2151, A2197, A2199. The two Radio/optical luminosity functions are in agreement over 4 decades of R/O.

A major contribution to the comprehension of the interaction between radio galaxies and their surrounding ambient was made possible by spatially resolved X-ray observations obtained with the Einstein and ROSAT observatories. Zhao, Burns & Owen, 1989 using a complete survey of

D < 3 Abell clusters discussed the lack of correlation between the radio and the X-ray luminosity.

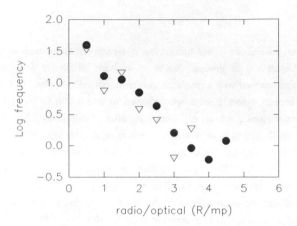

Fig.1: The frequency distribution of the radio/optical ratio of E + S0 galaxies in 8 clusters (filled circles) and of "field" galaxies in the bridge between Coma and A1367 (open triangles).

They showed that the internal pressure in cluster radio sources is correlated with the thermal pressure in the cooling flow, implying that cooling accretion confine the radio plasma. A complete radio/X-ray study at adequate resolution of cD galaxies with cooling flows is unfortunately not available (cf. Valentijn & Bijleveld, 1983). However some of these objects show bright compact radio sources which might be confined by the cooling flows (e.g. 3C338=N6166, Jaffe and Perola, 1974). A well studied example is Per-A (N1275) containing the bright radio source 3C84. Its radio jets bend where the thermal plasma is denser and find their way in correspondence with low X-ray surface brightness regions (Bohringer et al, 1993). Burns et al (1994a) compared the X-ray (Einstein) and radio (VLA) morphology of 41 rich clusters. They found evidence for a strong correlation between the positions of radio galaxies and clumps in the X-ray emission. The local environment seems more important in determining the radio properties of galaxies than the global cluster environment. Burns et al., 1987 did also a VLA survey of 139 poor groups. They found 9 HT radio galaxies, higher than expected from theoretical models. These observations led to predict the presence of a substantial intergalactic medium in these groups that should radiate significantly at soft X-ray energies. This proved to be actually true. Burns et al (1994b) used ROSAT X-ray data to show that around WAT in poor groups, such as those surrounding N4065 or N7503, there is substantial extended X-ray emission.

2. Radio Properties of Spiral Galaxies in Clusters

Spiral-Irregular galaxies in clusters are characterized by much lower luminosity than radio-galaxies ($P \sim 10^{20\text{-}22}$ WHz^{-1}). To compare the properties of this type of galaxies in clusters with normal "field" galaxies a well defined reference sample is needed. None of the radio luminosity functions available in the seventies (e.g. Cameron, 1971, Hummel, 1981) contained galaxies outside the local supercluster (therefore suffering from distance uncertainties due to the local peculiar velocity field). To overcome this difficulty Jaffe & Gavazzi, 1986, Jaffe, Gavazzi & Valentijn, 1986 undertook a survey of 400 spiral galaxies in the Coma Supercluster region. Gavazzi & Jaffe, 1986 determined the radio luminosity function of the spiral population in this survey and unexpectedly found that the probability of developing radio sources in the clusters A1367 and Coma was about 5 times higher than in the reference sample (later confirmed by Gavazzi & Contursi, 1994). In both cases they found a tight correlation between the radio luminosity and the B-V color of galaxies, indicating that blue galaxies have higher probability of becoming radio sources than red galaxies. This implies that the mechanism accelerating the cosmic ray electrons in galaxies is associated with the massive, rapidly evolving stellar population, therefore with type II supernovae events. Later studies confirmed this evidence using better indicators of high mass star formation rate, such as the equivalent width of the Hα+[NII] line (Gavazzi, Boselli & Kennicutt, 1991).

The question which remained to be explained was why cluster spiral galaxies, which appeared to be strongly hydrogen deficient (Giovanelli & Haynes, 1985), develop more luminous radio sources. Some galaxies at the NW periphery of A1367 were found with a radio morphology remarkably similar to that of HT radio galaxies suggesting an ongoing interaction with the intergalactic medium (Gavazzi & Jaffe, 1987). Meanwhile Gavazzi (1987, 1989) found evidence in these galaxies of abnormal HI content. The HI profiles of these galaxies were found with clear departures from the usual two-horned shape, suggesting asymmetries in the HI distribution, as if the gas content was removed on the up-stream side of the galaxy and was normal in the down-stream side. The CO distribution, however resulted symmetric, as expected in the ram pressure scenario, since the H2 gas usually resides deeper in the galaxy potential well, well shielded from the external pressure (Boselli et al, 1994).

High sensitivity/resolution VLA observations of these galaxies were recently obtained in B array. These are shown in Fig. 2 superposed to H band frames of the galaxies (showing the old stellar population in these objects) and to Hα frames (in which the young stellar population is enhanced).

97087, the edge-on Irregular, provides us with a good case for studying the correspondence between the radio emissivity and the young stellar population. Some of the resolved HII regions are clearly found associated with individual spots of enhanced radio emissivity.

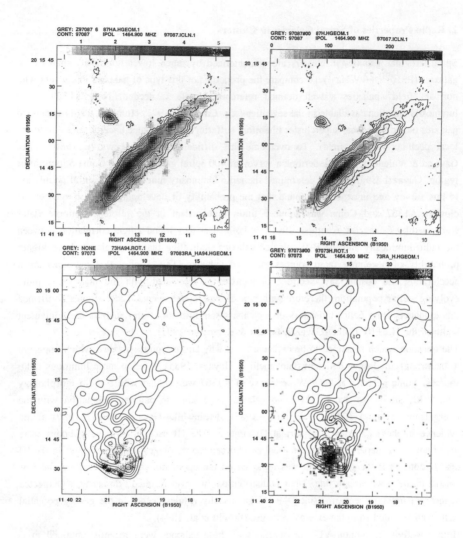

Fig.2: top: 1.4 GHz continuum map of 97087 (contour) superposed to a gray level representation of the Hα line map (left) and near IR 1.6 μ (right). Bottom: same for 97073.

97073 provides us with a spectacular example of a galaxy interacting with the cluster medium. The length of the radio trail exceeds by 3 times the optical extension of the galaxy.

The up-stream side of the galaxy is characterized by peripheral bright (10^{40} erg s^{-1}) HII regions which seem to have formed at the surface of a bow-shock. These data indicate that the high velocity motion of galaxies through the cluster gas might induce, along with radio morphology disturbances, conspicuous changes to the stellar evolution, by enhancing the star formation rate.

Stimulated by these paradigmatic examples, a search started for other cluster galaxies exhibiting similar properties, in order to establish if the drag model could give a sufficiently general explanation (Scodeggio & Gavazzi, 1993). The search would not be made possible if a systematic survey in the near Infrared H band was not undertaken. In the last five years we completed such a survey in the H and B bands for Coma, A1367 and for the "field" sample in the Coma supercluster bridge (Gavazzi, Randone & Branchini, 1994). There is a significant population of faint, blue systems which appears unique to the cluster environment (see Fig. 3). A remarkable property of these galaxies concerns their velocity relative to the cluster. Fig. 4 a and b show the B-H color and the Hα E.W. of galaxies in Coma+A1367 versus the modulus of their peculiar velocity. It is apparent that, while all red galaxies have small velocity dispersion (~300 km s^{-1}), the blue (high star formation rate) systems have a velocity dispersion twice as large (~600 km s^{-1}). This provides us with strong statistical evidence that the drag mechanism can alter the evolution of these spiral galaxies falling in the cluster environment for the first time.

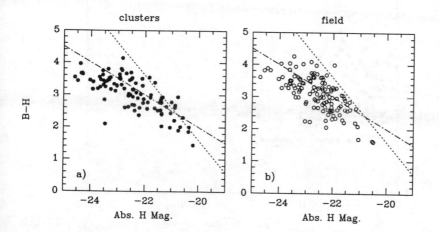

Fig.3: B-H color vs. H luminosity diagram of a complete ($m_p \leq 15.6$) sample of spiral galaxies in the Coma+A1367 clusters (left) and in the "field". Notice the relative overabundance of blue-faint systems in the two clusters.

108

Due to the tight correlation between the star formation properties and the radio emissivity in spiral galaxies, the radio luminosity (normalized to the near IR H luminosity) as a function of the peculiar velocity (Fig. 4c) shows a pattern similar to the one in Fig. 4a and b, confirming that the cluster environment can produce substantial perturbations to the evolution of spiral galaxies. This is important in order to better understand the evolution of galaxies in the local universe, and to establish the zero-point for the Butcher-Oemler effect.

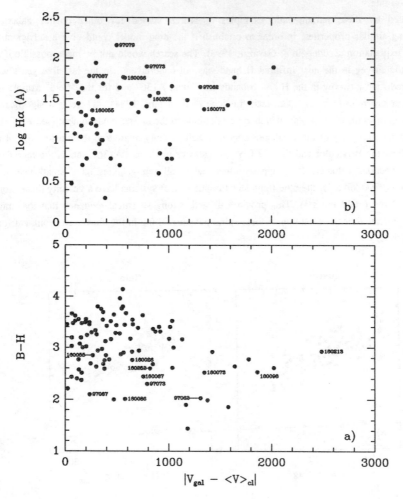

Fig. 4: Distributions of the star formation rate indexes B-H (a); Hα E.W. (b) vs. the deviation from the mean cluster recessional velocity $|V_{gal} - <V>_{cl}|$ (From Gavazzi, Randone & Branchini, 1994).

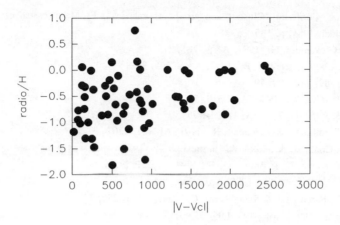

Fig. 4c: Distributions of the radio/H excess vs. the deviation from the mean cluster recessional velocity $|V_{gal} - <V>_{cl}|$.

ACKNOWLEDGMENTS. I wish to thank R. Fanti, F. Owen and J. Burns for providing me with unpublished material. I acknowledge partial financial support by EEC contract ERB-CHRX-CT92-0033.

REFERENCES

Auriemma, C., et al., 1977, A&A, 57, 41

Bohringer, H., et al., 1993, MNRAS, 264, L25

Boselli, A., Gavazzi, G., Combes, F., et al, 1994, A&A, 285, 69

Burns, J., et al., 1987, AJ., 94, 587

Burns, J., et al., 1994b. Proc. Conf. ROSAT science Symposium. ed. Schleger E. & Petre R., (in press).

Burns, J., et al., 1994a, ApJ (march 1, in press)

Cameron, M., 1971, MNRAS, 152, 403

Colla, G., et al., 1975, A&A, 38, 209

Dallacasa, D., Feretti, L., & Giovannini, G., 1989, A&A, 223, 379

de Ruiter, H., Parma, P., Fanti, C., & Fanti, R., 1990, A&A, 227, 351

Ekers, R., et al., 1981, A&A, 101, 194

Fanti, R., Proc. Conf. on "Clusters and groups of galaxies", F. Mardirossian et al. eds. Dordrecht: Reidel, 1984, p. 185

Feretti, L., & Giovannini, G., 1994, A&A, 281, 375

Feretti, L., Perola, C., & Fanti, R., 1992, A&A, 265, 9

Gavazzi, G., 1989, ApJ, 346,59

Gavazzi, G., & Jaffe, W., 1986, ApJ, 310, 53

Gavazzi, G., & Jaffe, 1987, A&A, 186, L1

Gavazzi, G., Boselli, A., & Kennicutt, R., 1991, AJ, 101, 1207

Gavazzi, G. & Contursi, A., 1994, AJ. in press.

Gavazzi, G., Randone, I., & Branchini, E., 1994, ApJ. in press

Giovanelli., R., & Haynes, M., 1985, ApJ., 292, 404

Giovannini, G., Feretti, L., & Stanghellini, C., 1991, A&A, 252, 528

Gursky, H., et al., 1972, ApJ., 173, L99

Hummel, E., 1981, A&A, 93, 93

Jaffe, W., & Gavazzi, G., 1986, AJ., 91,204

Jaffe, W., Gavazzi, G., & Valentijn, E. 1986, AJ., 91, 199

Jaffe, W., & Perola, C., 1973, A&A, 26, 423

Jaffe, W., & Perola, C., 1974, 31, 223

Kim, K., et al., 1989, Nat, 341, 720

Kim, K., et al. 1994a A&AS, in press

Kim, K., et al. 1994b A&A, in press

Miley, G., Proc. NATO School on Physics of nonthermal radio sources, 1975, ed. G. Setti

Miley, G., et al., 1975, A&A, 38, 38

Owen, F., & Rudnick, L., 1876, ApJ, 205, L1

Owen, F., Proc. Conf. "Jets in Extragalactic radio sources" eds. Roeser and Meisenheimer. Springer-Verlag, 1993

Owen, F., & Ledlow, M., 1994 (preprint)

Owen, F., White, R., & Burns, J., 1992, ApJS, 80, 501

Owen, F., White, R., & Ge, J., 1993, ApJS, 87, 135

Ryle, M., & Windram, M., 1968, MNRAS, 138, 1

Scodeggio, M., & Gavazzi, G., 1993, ApJ., 409, 110

Slingo, A., 1974, MNRAS, 168, 307

Valentijn, E., & Bijleveld, W., 1983, A&A, 125, 223

Venturi, T., Feretti, L., & Giovannini, G., 1989, A&A, 213, 49

Willson, M., 1970, MNRAS, 151, 1

Zhao J., Burns, J., & Owen, F., 1989, AJ, 98, 64

QUANTITATIVE RESULTS FROM WF/PC IMAGING
OF THE DISTANT, RICH CLUSTER 0016+16

Gregory D. Wirth
Board of Studies in Astronomy & Astrophysics
University of California, Santa Cruz
Santa Cruz, CA 95064 USA

ABSTRACT:

I present the first quantitative results on distant galaxy image structure as observed in the core of Cl0016+16 ($z = 0.55$), the most distant *bona fide* galaxy cluster targeted with the *Hubble Space Telescope's* WF/PC-1 camera. This cluster achieved initial notoriety in the early 1980's as the original "anti-Butcher-Oemler-effect" cluster: despite its high redshift, it contradicted Butcher & Oemler's observed trend toward higher-z clusters having more blue galaxies. Three hours of *HST I*-band observations contain data on 170 galaxies to $I = 24$ (corresponding to $M^* + 2$ for $h = 0.5$, $q_0 = 0.05$), providing our best pre-WFPC-2 information on the structural properties of $z = 0.5$ cluster galaxies. I compare the observed sizes and luminosities of ellipticals in Cl0016+16 with local counterparts to demonstrate the feasibility of testing cosmological models and luminosity evolution using WF/PC-1 images of distant clusters. By employing the image concentration index as a shape indicator, I show that the "E+A" population is consistent with an exponential disk model, and is morphologically distinct from the "k-type" population which is well represented by an $r^{1/4}$ model. Interest in Cl0016+16 will remain high due to its outstanding richness, high x-ray luminosity, and unusually large number of active "E+A" galaxies among its members.

Introduction

Improvements in our understanding of early-type galaxies over the last 15 years have led to the discovery of important correlations among the principal properties of cluster ellipticals. Among these "global scaling relations" are (1) the Faber-Jackson law, $L \propto \sigma^4$, [4] and (2) the "Fundamental Plane" relating radius r, surface brightness I, and velocity dispersion σ of cluster ellipticals. [7] Such correlations reveal what constrains galaxy formation, [5] and provide an important distance indicator for mapping large-scale flows. [10]

Given that global scaling relations in early-type galaxies are important, a key question is their universality; *i.e.*, do the same scaling relations hold in all environments and at all epochs? While one can investigate environmental effects by comparing cluster and field galaxies nearby, the age issue can only be addressed by studying galaxies at different evolutionary stages. Although recent evidence suggests that ellipticals differ in age, [6] no evidence yet shows that elliptical galaxies of the *same mass* have *different ages* at the current epoch. Thus, the best method at present for comparing galaxies of different ages is to study galaxies at different redshifts.

Cl0016+16: Ideal laboratory for studying evolution and cosmology

To compare distant and local E/S0's, we need a sizable, bright sample — just what a rich cluster provides. In fact, Cl0016+16 is arguably the best-suited of all distant clusters for studying evolution of elliptical galaxies, because it is:

★ Distant. At $z = 0.55$, we look back nearly halfway to the Big Bang when observing Cl0016+16, providing excellent leverage to measure evolutionary and cosmological effects.

★ Rich. The cluster contains over 200 galaxies to a magnitude of $M^* + 3$.

★ Massive. It ranks among the 3 most luminous x-ray clusters known. [8]

★ Well-studied. For 15 years it's been the target of numerous studies from the x-ray, optical, IR, and radio regimes (including new x-ray and radio maps presented at this conference).

★ Red. Cl0016+16 is the original "anti-Butcher-Oemler" cluster, having galaxies indistinguishable in rest-frame color from local E/S0's. [9]

The very red color of this cluster suggests that it may contain some of the oldest galaxies at the $z \approx 0.5$ epoch; thus, Cl0016+16 provides an opportunity to set *firm lower limits* on the amount of evolution occurring over the last half of the age of the universe, and simultaneously allows cosmological tests to be performed with the effects of evolution minimized.

HST WF/PC Observations

I've analyzed 3 h of WFC data taken in the core of Cl0016+16 using the $F785LP$ passband (rest-frame V). Deconvolution using 16 iterations of the Lucy-Hook algorithm improved the enclosed light within $0\rlap{.}''5$ from 37% to 85%. Over 170 galaxies are detected to a limit of $M^* + 1$. Of these, 24 are known cluster members, including 13 galaxies with "k-type" spectra typical of K giant stars, 8 having "a-type" (E+A) spectra featuring strong Balmer absorption, and 4 exhibiting "e-type" spectra with emission lines. [1]

Photometry of these objects proved challenging since their growth curves do not generally converge to an asymptotic "total magnitude," owing to the crowded field and low SNR. Galaxy radii were measured based on the $r(\eta)$ method, superior to other techniques in that it: (1) assumes no profile shape; (2) gives the same r, independent of brightness; (3) does not require knowledge of the total magnitude; and (4) is independent of redshift. [11]

Quantitative Results on Galaxy Morphology

Figures 1–2 summarize our quantitative results. Figure 1(a) shows how radius relates to luminosity for local ellipticals. The distribution has a distinctive "kink," enabling one to detect luminosity evolution or measure q_0. Can we measure the size and brightness of high-redshift galaxies well enough with HST to recover this information? Figure 1(b), showing red galaxies in Cl0016+16, suggests so: for these likely cluster E/S0's, we observe the same general trend in slope as for the Virgo galaxies in Fig. 1(a). Due to the short exposure time, our photometry is not deep enough to enable a detailed comparison with the local sample, but the potential of this approach is evident.

Figure 2 illustrates a second application for quantitative measures of galaxy structure: distinguishing disk and bulge-dominated galaxies using the concentration index $C \equiv 5\log(r_{80}/r_{20})$. Figure 2(a) shows where pure disk and pure $r^{1/4}$-law profiles lie in the concentration index vs. magnitude plane. We conclude that distinguishing between the galaxy types is feasible to $I \approx 22 \approx M^*$. Concentration indices for confirmed cluster members are shown in Figure 2(b). Galaxies with "k-type" spectra lie primarily in the region occupied by $r^{1/4}$ profiles in the simulations; thus, they are probably elliptical galaxies. The "a-type" galaxies are clearly less compact than the "k-type" population, and appear in the "disk" part of the diagram, while no conclusions can be drawn from the 2 "e-type" galaxies. Our finding that the "a-type" (E+A) galaxies form a class which is morphologically distinct from the "k-type" population is

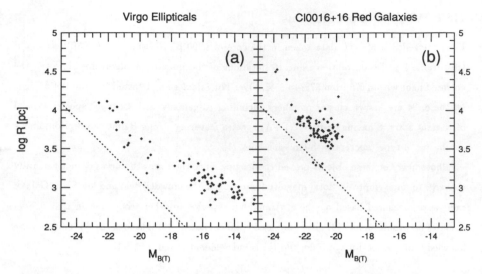

Figure 1: The radius-luminosity relation for Virgo and Cl0016+16. (a) Effective radius vs. total blue luminosity for Virgo ellipticals. [11] Note the "kink" in the distribution near $M^*_{B(T)} \approx -21$ where the slope changes from steep to shallow. The slanted line is a locus of constant surface brightness. (b) A similar diagram for red galaxies $(r - i) > 0.6$ in Cl0016+16, showing the half-light radius vs. total magnitude (within $r(\eta = 2.5 \text{ mag})$) measured from the *HST* data. The transformation assumes restframe $(B - V) = 1$, $q_0 = 0.5$, $h = 0.5$.

consistent with recent visual estimates from WFPC-2 images in Cl0939+47, [2] but differs from WF/PC-1 claims that "E+A" galaxies in AC114 and A370 resemble normal ellipticals. [3]

Conclusions

Obtaining meaningful quantitative information on distant galaxy morphology is possible using WF/PC-1 data, as demonstrated here by the discrimination of disk- and bulge-dominated galaxies, and by the general agreement of the local radius-luminosity distribution and that for E/S0 candidates in Cl0016+16. Other WF/PC-1 clusters at lower redshift can be expected to yield similar or better information. These quantitative results on distant cluster galaxy structure suggest that upcoming WFPC-2 imaging in Cl0016+16 and other clusters will provide a treasure trove of useful data on the shapes and sizes of high-redshift, early-type galaxies.

This study, a collaboration with David Koo and Richard Kron, was made possible by Ivan King, who provided the WF/PC-1 observations, and by Matthew Bershady, who wrote and supported the photometry routines and indulged me in many helpful discussions.

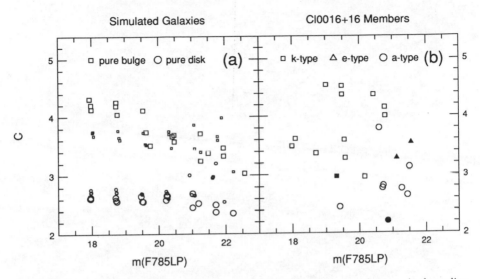

Figure 2: Concentration index $C \equiv 5\log(r_{80}/r_{20})$ vs. total magnitude, where r_N is the radius enclosing $N\%$ of the "total light," meaning light within $r(\eta = 2.5 \text{ mag})$. (a) Measurements for *simulated galaxies* using axisymmetric models of realistic size and brightness which are convolved with the deconvolved PSF, inserted into the Cl0016+16 image, and photometered with the program galaxies. Larger symbols denote longer scale length for model galaxy. Disk and $r^{1/4}$ models can be distinguished consistently for $m_{F785LP} \lesssim 21$, and statistically past 22. (b) Confirmed Cl0016+16 members, with different spectral types indicated. Galaxies with emission lines are shown as filled symbols. Scatter is higher than in the simulations due to greater size variation, non-axisymmetry, and deviation from perfect $r^{1/4}$ or disk profiles.

References

[1] Dressler, A., and Gunn, J. E. 1992, ApJS, 78, 1

[2] Dressler, A., Oemler, A., Butcher, H. R., & Gunn, J. E. 1994, ApJ, in press

[3] Couch, W. J., Ellis, R. S., Sharples, R. M., & Smail, I. 1994, ApJ, in press

[4] Faber, S. M., & Jackson, R. E. 1976, ApJ, 204, 668

[5] Faber, S. M., *et al.* 1987, in Nearly Normal Galaxies, ed. S. M. Faber (New York: Springer-Verlag), 175

[6] González, J. J. 1993, Ph.D. Thesis, University of California, Santa Cruz

[7] Guzman, R., Lucey, J. R., & Bower, R. G. 1993, MNRAS, 265, 731

[8] Henry, J. P., *et al.* 1992, ApJ, 386, 408

[9] Koo, D. C. 1981, ApJ, 251, L75

[10] Lynden-Bell, D., *et al.* 1988, ApJ, 326, 19

[11] Sandage, A., and Perelmuter, J. M. 1990, ApJ, 350, 481

INTERACTIONS AND THE BLUE GALAXIES IN DISTANT CLUSTERS

Russell J. Lavery
Department of Physics and Astronomy
Iowa State University
Ames, IA 50011
lavery@iastate.edu

ABSTRACT

High resolution images, obtained using the HRCam on the CFHT, of all the known star-forming galaxies in the two distant clusters Cl0016+1609 ($z = 0.54$) and Cl0303+1706 ($z = 0.41$) reveal a variety of morphological types. A number of the emission line galaxies in each cluster show evidence for having recently undergone a strong tidal encounter, yet none of these systems appear to be in the process of merging. These tidal encounters may have been responsible for inducing the enhanced star formation observed in these galaxies. The red Balmer absorption line population of Cl0016+1609, which is comprised by 7 of the 30 confirmed cluster members, are quite diverse in appearance, ranging from very compact systems interacting with fainter companions to disk-like galaxies with large bulges, possibly being S0 galaxies.

I. Introduction

Many rich, centrally concentrated, Come-like clusters of galaxies having redshifts greater than 0.2 have a significant (~20%) population of blue galaxies, i.e., the Butcher-Oemler effect.[1)2)] The spectroscopic observations of these distant clusters have revealed many of these blue galaxies to have undergone a period of intense star formation.[3)4)5)6)] There is now strong evidence, based on high resolution imaging of these galaxies from the ground and with HST, that the star formation in many of these blue galaxies has been induced by interactions and/or mergers with other galaxies.[7)8)9)10)11)12)] Here we present new high-resolution images of the spectroscopically confirmed star-forming galaxies in two additional distant clusters of galaxies, Cl0016+1609 and Cl0303+1706.

II. Observations

The high-resolution camera (HRCam)[13)] operates at the prime focus of the CFHT. It is a tip-tilt correction system that compensates for the first order image motion and routinely produces images with stellar FWHMs of 0.5 arcsec. The observations of Cl0016+1609 and Cl0303+1706 were made over two observing runs during the latter parts of 1992 and 1993. Two fields were observed in each cluster which included all the recent star-forming galaxies in these clusters. This observing program is in collaboration with M. Pierce (NOAO) and R. McClure (DAO).

III. Results

A) Cl0016+1609. While having a blue galaxy fraction of only ~2%, this cluster does have a number of blue galaxies with emission lines and/or Balmer absorption lines in their spectra. Cl0016+1609 also has a significant population of red galaxies with Balmer absorption lines,[14)] suggesting this cluster may have had a much large blue galaxy fraction than is presently observed. Of the five blue emission line galaxies, only one is a definite disk galaxy (also having a "companion" galaxy 2.2 arcsec away), with two others having a compact, but elongated appearance. The remaining two galaxies are also quite compact, though one of them, a galaxy with a very strong emission line spectrum, does show signs of having undergone an interaction with a smaller galaxy 2.3 arcsec away.

The Balmer absorption line systems of Cl0016+1609 consist of 3 blue and 7 red galaxies. Of the 3 blue galaxies, two are quite compact, revealing little detail. The third system, however, appears to be a very disturbed, though isolated, late-type disk system. Looking at the red galaxies, two are compact, isolated systems, two appear to be interacting with fainter companions, one may be interacting with the blue disk system discussed above, and two appear to be elongated galaxies with bright central regions. These later two could possibly be S0 galaxies.

At the present time, it is not known if these red galaxies are actually the later stage of the larger starbursts responsible for the blue galaxy populations in these distant clusters. It may be that at least some of these red galaxies with Balmer absorption lines have just accreted gas from a companion galaxy and have had a small amount for star formation, which produces the Balmer absorption lines.

B) Cl0303+1706. There are six known emission line galaxies in this cluster. Two of these show strong tidal tails, almost certainly due to a recent interaction, though their emission line strengths are relatively weak. Two additional galaxies are nearly edge-on late-type disk galaxies. One galaxy, which has a very strong emission line spectrum, is very compact and may be an AGN. The last emission line galaxy is elongated, but it is not possible to determine its morphology (elliptical or disk). This cluster does not have a population of red Balmer absorption line galaxies as exists in Cl0016+1609.

IV. Discussion

Overall, the morphological properties of the "active" galaxies, galaxies presently undergoing or having recently completed a period of enhanced star formation, span a broad range of galaxy types in these two clusters. But, in Cl0016+1609, 6 of these 15 active members (40%) appear to be interacting systems, which may have been responsible for inducing the star formation observed in these galaxies. In Cl0303+1706, while none of the galaxies are in obvious interacting systems, 2 of the 6 have strong tidal tails, likely produced by an interaction. For one of these galaxies, the tail points to a smaller galaxy 3 arcsec away. Surprisingly, none of the active galaxies, in either cluster, appear to merging systems consisting of roughly equal mass components, as seen in other clusters.[9)11)12)]

Previous HRCam observations of clusters at $z \sim 0.4$ have shown the importance of interactions and mergers in producing the blue galaxies in distant clusters.[9)] These new data provide additional support for the importance of galaxy-galaxy encounters. These interactions and mergers are sure to play a major role in determining the morphological mix of galaxies observed in centrally concentrated clusters of galaxies at low redshift.

V. What Is To Be Done?

With the high resolution imaging capabilities now available from the ground and with HST, spectroscopic observations of 100+ cluster members become a necessity. Such data will distinguish true cluster members from field galaxies and provide information on the present star formation rate in these cluster galaxies. Velocity information would also be useful for measuring relative velocities of the pairs and help determine whether the star-forming galaxies are recent arrivals into the cluster environment.

On the theoretical side, models for transforming Sc galaxies into earlier type galaxies are important. While merging galaxies are likely to produce a remnant similar to E galaxies, the transformation of Sc galaxies to earlier type disk galaxies, especially S0s, through the absorption of dwarf galaxies needs to be investigated. Such types of encounters, systems with relatively large mass ratios, are probably more likely than encounters of nearly equal mass systems. In nearby centrally concentrated clusters, small bulge late-type galaxies are very rare, yet such galaxies constitute a significant fraction of the blue galaxies in distant clusters.[10][11][12] Therefore, there must be some process capable of depleting the late-type galaxy populations in nearby rich relaxed clusters.

REFERENCES

[1] Butcher, H., & Oemler, A. Jr. 1978, ApJ, 219, 18

[2] Butcher, H., & Oemler, A. Jr. 1984, ApJ, 285, 426

[3] Dressler, A., & Gunn, J. E. 1983, ApJ, 270, 7

[4] Lavery, R. J., & Henry, J. P. 1986, ApJ, 304, L5

[5] Henry, J. P., & Lavery, R. J. 1987, ApJ, 323, 473

[6] Couch, W. J., & Sharples, R. M. 1987, MNRAS, 229, 423

[7] Lavery, R. J., & Henry, J. P. 1988, ApJ, 330, 596

[8] Lavery, R. J. 1990, in Dynamics and Interactions of Galaxies, ed. R. Wielen (Berlin: Springer), 30

[9] Lavery, R. J., Pierce, M. J., & McClure, R. D. 1992, AJ, 104, 2067

[10] Lavery, R. J., & Henry, J. P. 1994, ApJ, 426, 524

[11] Couch, W. J., Ellis, R. S., Sharples, R. M., & Smail, I. 1994, ApJ, in press

[12] Dressler, A., Oemler, A., Jr., Butcher, H. R. & Gunn J. E. 1994, ApJ, in press

[13] McClure, R. D., et al. 1989, PASP, 101, 1156

[14] Dressler, A., & Gunn, J. E. 1992, ApJS, 78, 1

THE DYNAMICAL STATE OF HIGH REDSHIFT CLUSTERS

Francisco Javier Castander, *Institute of Astronomy, Madingley Road, Cambridge CB3 0HA, UK*

Richard Bower, *Royal Observatory of Edinburgh, Blackford Hill, Edinburgh, UK*

Warrick Couch, *School of Physics, University of New South Wales, Kensington, NSW 2033, Australia*

Richard Ellis, *Institute of Astronomy, Madingley Road, Cambridge CB3 0HA, UK*

Hans Böhringer, *Max Planck Institut für extraterrestrische Physik, D-85740, Germany*

ABSTRACT

We present an ongoing study of a sample of galaxy clusters at a mean redshift $\bar{z}$=0.4. The sample was selected from high contrast prime focus 4-meter photographic plates. Subsequent images in X-rays with ROSAT revealed X-ray luminosities much lower than expected for local clusters of similar optical richness. Here we report further spectroscopic and photometric data for the sample. So far 3 clustres have been studied. One (the only one with no X-ray flux detected) appears to be a spurious effect caused by projection and the other two have velocity dispersions as expected from their richness according to local relationships. This suggests the low X-ray luminosities are not caused by their dynamical immaturity but by a lower gas density possibly caused by an epoch of gas reheating.

Subject Headings: cosmology: observations – galaxies: clustering – galaxies: evolution

1. INTRODUCTION

Clusters of galaxies are an invaluable tool in observational cosmology. As the largest gravitationally bound structures, they are good tracers of the large-scale structure of the universe and are also regions for efficient observations of galaxies in large numbers. As they can be detected over cosmological time scales, they are uniquely suited to evolutionary studies.

Although several catalogues of galaxy clusters have been compiled with different criteria, given the compromise of area covered and depth required, few have succeeded in providing a homogeneous sample of high redshift clusters for cosmological work. Such distant samples would provide a powerful test of hierarchical theories of structure formation that predict a rapid decline in the abundance of massive galaxy clusters with redshift.

A recent compilation of high redshift clusters with well-defined selection criteria was made by Couch, Ellis, Malin and MacLaren (CEMM)[1]. They searched deep, contrast-enhanced photographic plates taken at the AAT in two different bands (b_J and r_F) for significant surface density enhancements above the background fluctuations. They found a total of 112 cluster candidates. Spectroscopic follow up of the richest candidates demonstrated the reality of most of these clusters and the validity of the selection criteria. The number desities and redshift distributions obtained for the clusters selected in the red band, r_F, were consistent with no evolution. However, in the blue band, b_J, the number density was higher than expected and the redshift distribution was more extended than for the non-evolving case. In a detailed study, CEMM proposed that recent star formation within the distant cluster environments could explain these effects but they could not reject the possibility of contamination by spiral-rich foreground groups.

X-ray studies do not suffer from the above projection effects as the emission is proportional to the square of the density of the intracluster gas. Early X-ray studies found negative evolution in the X-ray luminosity function (XLF), i.e. fewer X-ray luminous clusters in the past[2,3,4], in apparent disagreement with conclusions derived from the CEMM sample. With the advent of ROSAT and its good imaging capabilities at low fluxes, it became possible to measure the X-ray luminosities of the CEMM sample and test the evolution of the XLF. Bower et al[5] imaged a complete subsample of the CEMM clusters in the redshift range $0.3<z<0.5$ and confirm that these clusters are less X-ray luminous that their nearby counterparts of similar optical richness. Their results are thus inconsistent with a non-evolving XLF.

We have now embarked in a spectroscopic and photometric follow up of these clusters to complement the somewhat contradictoty picture of low X-ray luminosities and high optical richness. We are obtaining velocity dispersions and photometric data to investigate the dynamical state and richness of the clusters more carefully.

In §2 we describe briefly the sample selection and the X-ray observations. In §3 we present our new observations and in §4 we discuss our results and summarise our main conclusions.

2. X-RAY OBSERVATIONS

From the CEMM spectroscopic sample we selected a subsample of 21 clusters with contrast* $\sigma_{cl}>4.0$ that have accurate positions and redshift spectra for more than one galaxy. (This contrast corresponds roughly to Abell richness class 1). This sample was selected to be imaged with the PSPC (position sensitive proportional counter) on board ROSAT. The 21 clusters span from 0.15 to 0.66 in redshift with a mean of $\bar{z}=0.42$, but the completeness drops off in the tails of their redshift distribution. We therefore chose a subset of 14 in the $0.3<z<0.5$

---

* see CEMM for definition of σ_{cl}

range that could be described by an approximately constant comoving number density. This subset covered an area of 27.8 deg^2 and was drawn from a volume of $2.1 \times 10^7 \ h_{50}^{-3}$ Mpc^3.

According to the present day XLF and the number density of the sample the luminosities expected for these clusters range between $\sim 5 \times 10^{43}$ and $\sim 5 \times 10^{44} \ h_{50}^{-2}$ erg·s^{-1} (q_o=0.5). However our X-ray measurements show that these clusters are underluminous by almost an order of magnitude[5].

For a more detailed analysis of the evolution of the X-ray luminosity function with this sample, Bower et al[5] developed a maximum likelihood method in which they took into account possible biases arising from the optical selection in the determination of the XLF evolution. Notwithstanding the uncertainty they found an amplitude of the XLF that is inconsistent with the present day normalisation at a 3σ level even if a factor of 3 scatter is allowed in the richness-luminosity relation.

3. OPTICAL OBSERVATIONS

To understand this apparent contradiction and hence the dynamical state of distant clusters we have embarked upon a new study. Spectroscopic and photometric data have been obtained for three clusters with the ESO 3.6m in La Silla, Chile. Each has been imaged in B and R to $B\sim 24.5$ and $R\sim 23.5$. Using multi-slit masks we have also secured spectra for 20-25 objects per cluster field. With typical exposures of ~ 6000s we have been able to determine redshifts for members down to $R\sim 21.0$.

Table 1 summarises the optical results together with the X-ray luminosities for these three clusters. Column 2 gives the redshifts, and column 3 the contrast values. In column 4 we show the number of objects in excess of the background counts in the magnitude range $R< m_3+2$ within a 0.5 h_{50}^{-1} Mpc projected radius from the cluster centre, $N_{0.5}$. Offset images were taken to determine the background counts. One dimensional rest-frame velocity dispersions are tabulated in column 5. These values are based on 9 and 12 members for J2175.23c and F1835.22c respectively. No value is given for F1835.2cl for which there are only 5 members. We believe that the number counts enhancement measured in this field, for which no X-ray emission is detected, is due to the superposition of three groups at 0.303, 0.377 and 0.442. The X-ray luminosities are shown in column 6.

Table 1: Summary of cluster parameters observed

Cluster	z	σ_{cl}	$N_{0.5}$	σ_o km·s^{-1}	L_x (0.4–2.5 keV) ($10^{44} h_{50}^{-2}$ergs^{-1})
J2175.23c	0.408	4.5	25±5	610±150	0.156
F1835.2cl	0.377	5.4	31±5	—	<0.141
F1835.22cr	0.473	4.9	25±5	620±130	0.228

4. DISCUSSION AND CONCLUSIONS

The availability of photometric, spectroscopic and X-ray data allows to check the reliability of the optical selection. The photometric data confirm that these regions of the sky are overabundant in objects compared to the background. Although one cluster out of three turned out to be a projection effect, F1835.2cl was the only cluster from which no x-ray flux was detected.

The richness estimates in the central parts of these clusters are the ones expected for Abell richness class 1 clusters. However, their X-ray luminosities are approximately one order of magnitude lower than clusters of similar richness and do not fall within the scatter of the L_x-$N_{0.5}$ relation. The one-dimensional velocity dispersions are somewhat lower and higher than expected from their richnesses and bolometric luminosities respectively but given the errors both values are within the scatter of the σ_o-$N_{0.5}$ and L_x-σ_o relations.

With few members it is difficult to assess the internal dynamical state of these clusters reliably, however the velocity dispersions together with the shape of the velocities distributions suggest that these clusters are in dynamical equilibrium and that they are not undergoing violent relaxion. We consider it implausible that their low X-ray luminosities are caused by a state of disequilibrium.

Given the range of parameters measured, these $\bar{z}$=0.4 clusters look in their optical properties as clusters at the present epoch. It seems therefore likely that their low X-ray luminosities are due to differences in the way the intracluster gas fills their potential wells. Their low X-ray emissivities arise from a lower density gas perhaps due to an epoch of gas reheating[6]. However further measurements are needed in other clusters to confirm and improve the statistical significance of these results.

Acknowledgements

We would like to ackowledge Alfonso Aragón-Salamanca for uselful discussions. FJC acknowledges the support of the Instituto Astrofísico de Canarias and Sidney Sussex College, Cambridge.

REFERENCES

1) Couch, W J, Ellis, R S, Malin, D F & MacLaren, I, 1991 *Mon. Not. R. astr. Soc.*, **249**, 606 (CEMM).
2) Edge, A C, Stewart, G C, Fabian, A C & Arnaud, K A, 1990 *Mon. Not. R. astr. Soc.*, **245**, 599.
3) Gioia, I M, Henry, J P, Maccacaro, T, Morris, S L, Stocke, J T & Wolter, A, 1990 *Astrophys. J.*, **356**, L35.
4) Henry, J P, Gioia, I M, Maccacaro, T, Morris, S L, Stocke, J T & Wolter, A, 1992 *Astrophys. J.*, **386**, 408.
5) Bower, R G, Böhringer, H, Briel, U G, Ellis, R S, Castander, F J & Couch, W J, 1994 *Mon. Not. R. astr. Soc.*, in press.
6) Kaiser, N, 1991 *Astrophys. J.*, **383**, 104.

FABRY-PEROT AND MULTI-FILTER OBSERVATIONS
OF DISTANT GALAXY CLUSTERS

Guido J. Thimm[1]
Max-Planck-Institut für Astronomie, Königstuhl 17
D-69117 Heidelberg, Germany

Abstract

We have applied a promising way of studying the galaxy population in distant clusters to Cl 1409+524 (3C 295) at $z=0.46$. A sequence of Fabry-Perot images (FWHM=1.0–1.3 nm) was used to search for redshifted [O II]λ372.7 nm- and [O III]λ500.7 nm line emission. We studied 144 galaxies with $m_{lim}(R)=22.5$ within 1 Mpc around the cluster center. Previously known emission-line galaxies in the cluster were confirmed and 17 new members with emission lines were found. Their star formation rate of 1–2 $M_\odot yr^{-1}$ is typical for normal spirals. We further observed this cluster with broad-band B, R and seven intermediate-band filters (FWHM=10.0–20.0 nm) in order to derive low-resolution spectral energy distributions of cluster galaxies. These were fitted by template spectra to estimate the principle Hubble class and redshifts. Based on this decomposition, we derived a percentage of emission-line galaxies of 40±11%. This method was extended to the high redshift clusters Cl 1602+4313 ($z=0.895$) and Cl 2155+0334 ($z=0.820$). In addition to standard galaxy spectra we fitted models for E+A-galaxies to the data. Cl 2155 turned out to be not a galaxy cluster but a random fluctuation of field galaxies. Deep Fabry Perot imaging with $f_{lim}=1.5\times10^{-17}$erg cm^{-2}s^{-1} also revealed only one flat spectrum emission-line galaxy about 1 Mpc off the assumed cluster center. The cluster characteristics of Cl 1602 were confirmed. No galaxies similar to an old elliptical were found in this cluster. Instead, there is strong evidence that several galaxies have recently ($\leq$2 Gyr) experienced an intense phase of star formation. Their spectral energy distributions are very well fitted with E+A-type spectra. This is the first possible detection of such post-starburst galaxies at $z>0.8$.

[1]present address: ESO, Karl-Schwarzschild-Str. 2, D-85748 Garching bei München, Germany

126

1. Introduction

There are many reasons why the study of clusters of galaxies far out in the universe is so exciting. For example, the origin of the fundamental morphology-density relationship [8] observed in our cosmic neighborhood, which is still not understood, seems to be hidden in the physical state and structure of high redshift galaxy clusters and their individual cluster members. The discovery of a blue wing in the color distribution of galaxies in distant clusters (the Butcher-Oemler effect [5]) provided first observational evidence for spectral evolution of the cluster population. It motivated further intense studies which have all shown that beyond $z=0.2$ all clusters seem to show this excess of blue galaxies. Some of the suspicious blue cluster members were subsequently studied via multi-object spectroscopy. These observations revealed that a blue wing in the color distribution is partly due to contamination by fore- or background galaxies which have not been taken into account due to imperfect statistics in the photometric field correction. In the case of the 3C 295-cluster (Cl 1409+524) at a redshift of $z=0.46$, only 40% of the blue objects turned out to be cluster members and the photometric blue galaxy fraction was thus reduced from 40% to 25%. In contrast, for Cl 0024+165 at $z=0.39$ the percentage of 25% was confirmed [9]. Although spectrosocopy is the chosen method for unveiling the galaxies' redshift and spectral peculiarities, its efficiency in identifying members of distant clusters is typically only 50%, a draw-back considering the typical three-nights typically allocation at 3m-class telescopes. Furthermore, at redshifts higher than about 0.4 late-type galaxies appear relatively brighter than ellipticals introducing a bias towards blue objects. Here, we present a more reliable and efficient method of deriving the fraction of emission-line (ELG) and quiescent galaxies in distant clusters up to redshifts of $z=0.9$. A tunable imaging Fabry-Perot interferometer (FPI) is used to observe an interval of about $\pm 5500\,\mathrm{km\,s^{-1}}$ around a strong, redshifted emission line. From these data, the specta of individual objects can be reconstructed and checked for the presence of emission lines. In order to estimate the redshift of quiescent objects, we used the 4000Å-break as a characteristic spectral feature [15].

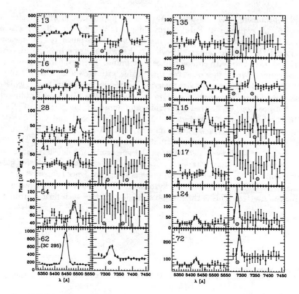

Figure 1. *Examples of Fabry-Perot spectra of objects with emission lines in the field of the 3C 295-cluster. Dotted circles in the [OII]-spectra mark the expected wavelength of the [OIII]λ495.9/500.7nm-doublet for the [OII]-emission taken as a reference redshift.*

It can be measured by placing a series of narrow-band filters around the mean position of the break. Together with additional broad band colors, these low resolution spectral energy distributions (SEDs) can be fitted by galaxy spectra to estimate Hubble class and redshift, a method pioneered by Couch et al. [7], Ellis et al. [14] and Loh & Spillar [13].

2. Fabry-Perot- and Filter-observations of the 3C 295-cluster ($\bar{z}$=0.46)

To find emission-line galaxies in the 3C 295-cluster we obtained a sequence of FP-images covering the redshifted [OII]λ372.7nm- and [OIII]λ500.7nm-emission at $-5500 - +5500\,\mathrm{km\,s^{-1}}$ and $-600 - +7600\,\mathrm{km\,s^{-1}}$ with a resolution of $550\,\mathrm{km\,s^{-1}}$ and $450\,\mathrm{km\,s^{-1}}$, respectively. The exposure time for each setting was 3000 s. These data were used to construct FP-spectra which were checked for the presence of emission lines. All galaxies with a limiting R-band magnitude of 22.5 within 1 Mpc around the center of the cluster were investigated. The 3σ flux limits are $5.6\times10^{-17}\mathrm{erg\,cm^{-2}s^{-1}}$ and $8.5\times10^{-17}\mathrm{erg\,cm^{-2}s^{-1}}$, respectively. All 6 previously known emission-line galaxies in the cluster [10] were confirmed and 17 new members with emission lines were found (Fig. 1). From the [OII]-flux we inferred a star-formation rate of $1-2\,\mathrm{M_\odot\,yr^{-1}}$ which is a value typical for normal spiral galaxies. The cluster was also observed with broad band B, R and seven narrow band filters (FWHM=10–20 nm) to derive low-resolution SEDs of cluster galaxies. Applying χ^2-method these low-resolution spectra were fitted by template spectra of types E/S0, Sbc, Scd and Irr [6] to estimate Hubble class and redshifts. A comparison of our redshifts with literature data [10] has shown that we achieved a mean accuracy of σ_z=0.009 for ellipticals and σ_z=0.07–0.10 for spirals and irregulars due to a less pronounced 4000Å-break. Based on this decomposition of the cluster population, we derived a percentage of ELGs of 40±11%.

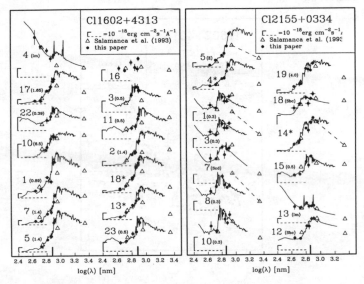

Figure 2. *Broad-band SEDs of objects in two distant clusters. Black dots show our photometry, open triangles indicate V, I and K-band data taken from SECC[1]. The best fitting SEDs are shown as full lines, zero-levels are indicated by dashed lines. The spectral type of time in 10^9 Gyr after the second starburst for E+A models is given in brackets behind each object number according to SECCs labeling. The location of the 4000Å-break at the redshift taken from Gunn, Hoessel & Oke[12] is shown as a bold tickmark at the bottom of both diagrams.*

3. High redshift clusters at $z \geq 0.8$

Fabry-Perot and filter-observations are an effective means of studying the galaxy population in distant clusters. We, therefore, started to apply this method to Cl 2155+0334 (z=0.820) and Cl 1602+4313 (z=0.895) using a new focal reducer/detector-setup at the Calar Alto 3.5 m telescope. While the FP-data for the latter cluster were not fully reduced at the time of writing of this paper, unprecedented deep FP-imaging covering ± 2500 km s^{-1} around redshifted [OII] is available for Cl 2155. The mean exposure time for each wavelength setting is 5600 s. In a field of 5'×5' all objects with a limiting R-band magnitude of 23.5 were checked for the presence of emission lines at a flux limit of 1.5×10^{-17}erg cm^{-2}s^{-1}. With reference to this limit we would have obtained the same results for the 3C 295-cluster described above if it had been at a redshift of 0.95. Despite this limit, we detected only one flat-spectrum ELG about 1 Mpc off the assumed cluster center. Therefore, the cluster members show very low or no signs of activity, or we do not see a cluster at the redshift measured by Gunn et al.[12] but merely an apparent clustering of projected field galaxies. We observed both clusters with broad-band B, R and four intermediate-band filters in order to derive low-resolution SEDs similar to our study of the 3C 295 field. In each case, two filters match the redshifted 4000Å-break. Photometric calibration was obtained via spectrophotometrically observed standard stars in both fields and independently checked by photometry of standard stars. Photometric errors are always less than 10%. In addition to standard galaxy spectra, models of E+A-galaxies provided by Bruzual[4] were fitted to the data. These peculiar E+A-galaxies which were discovered by Dressler & Gunn[9] show signs of a recent starburst reflected in strong Balmer absorption lines, indicative of a large population of A-stars. In the model, E+A-galaxies are assumed to be evolved ellipticals which experience a second burst of star-formation. The burst, which consumes 20% of the total mass of the galaxy, lasts 0.25 Gyr with subsequent passive evolution.

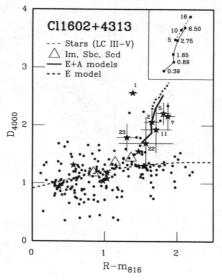

Figure 2. *4000Å-break versus (R-m$_{816}$) color index for all objects detected in the Cl 1602-subfield. The colors expected for various E+A-model galaxies redshifted to z=0.895 are indicated by a thick line. The timespan in units of 10^9 years after the second starburst is passively evolving elliptical at 5–16 Gyr after its birth are shown as a thick dashed line. Im-, Sbc- and Scd-galaxies have colors marked by triangles. The dashed thin line traces the position of galactic stars[13] in our filter system. Some galaxies of Fig. 2 are plotted with asterisks.*

We restricted our analysis to the central parts of the clusters which were also observed in V, I and K by Aragon-Salamanca et al.[1] (SECC). Figure 2 displays our spectral fits to all objects contained in the SECC sample. Indeed, most of the galaxies in the Cl 2155-field are not at a redshift of $z=0.82$. Their apparent 4000Å-break clearly differs from its expected position. This cluster is thus more a random fluctuation of field galaxies, rather than a distant cluster. In the case of Cl 1602, most of the objects appear to be at the redshift measured by Gunn, Hoessel & Oke[12]. The K-band flux measured by SECC matches very well the extrapolated infrared tail of the model spectra. Strong deviations appear only in the case of objects classified as stars by SECC (No. 4 and 14 for Cl 2155, No. 13 and 18 for Cl 1602). Hence, we assume that No. 5 in Cl 2155 and No. 17 in Cl 1602 are also galactic stars. Figure 3 shows the galaxies 4000Å-break as a function of $(R-m_{816})$-color for all objects in the total Cl 1602-field for which the neccessary data could be extracted. Several galaxies group around colors expected for E+A-galaxies seen at $z=0.89$ and appear significantly bluer than a passively evolving elliptical seen $5-10\times10^9$yr after its birth[3]. Although high signal/noise spectroscopy is required to reveal the nature of these objects, the quality of the spectral fits and the very well fitting K-band data lead us to the conclude that we are actually observing E+A-galaxies at redshifts $z>0.8$. Galaxies No. 1, 2, 7 and 5 are the best candidates for such objects in which a starburst occured about 2×10^9yr ago. Since E+As also exist in large numbers in medium redshift clusters at $z=0.4-0.5$ ($\approx20\%$ of the population[10,2]) we suggest that the triggering mechanism is linked not to cosmic time but to a local phenomenon. We probably witness the transformation of the galaxy population in the dense intracluster gas detected in this cluster.

4. Summary

We have applied a promising method of studying galaxy populations in distant clusters. Fabry-Perot imaging is used to detect members with emission lines, observations with intermediate band filters are used to estimate redshift and Hubble class of passive members. The 3C 295-cluster was observed to test our method. Within 1 Mpc around the cluster center, 144 objects with $m_{lim}(R)=22.5$ were checked for the presence of [OII]- and [OIII]-emission. 17 new ELGs were discovered. The flux radiated in the emission lines is typical for spirals with star-formation rates of a few solar massess per year. Using narrow-band filter observations, 52 ellipticals could be identified in this cluster. Based on this decomposition, we derived a fraction of ELGs of 40±11%. We extended our method to clusters at $z>0.8$. Cl 2155+0334 turned out to be not a cluster at $z=0.82$ but a random superposition of field galaxies. Cl 1602+4313 at $z=0.89$ was confirmed as a high redshift cluster. In its central region, several E+A-galaxies were identified. Considering that such post-starburst galaxies also a common occururence in medium redshift clusters, we suggest that the triggering mechanism responsible for the burst is a local phenomenon rather than one linked to cosmic time[16].

5. References

[1] Aragon-Salamanca A. et al., 1993, MNRAS 262, 764 (SECC)
[2] Belloni P. et al., 1994, this meeting
[3] Bruzual G., Charlot S., 1993, ApJ 405, 538
[4] Bruzual G., 1993, private communication
[5] Butcher H., Oemler A., 1978, ApJ 219, 18
[6] Coleman G.D. et al., 1980, ApJS 43, 393
[7] Couch W.J. et al., 1983, MNRAS 205, 1287
[8] Dressler A., 1980, ApJ 236,351
[9] Dressler A., Gunn F.E., 1982, ApJ 263, 533
[10] Dressler A., Gunn J.E., 1992, ApJS 78, 1
[11] Ellis R.S. et al., 1985, MNRAS 217, 239
[12] Gunn J.E. et al., 1986, ApJ 306, 30
[13] Gunn J.E., Stryker L.L, 1983, ApJS 52, 121
[14] Loh E.D., Spillar E.J., 986, ApJ 303, 154
[15] Thimm G.J. et al., 1994, A&A, in press
[16] Thimm G., 1994, A&A, submitted

COLOR EVOLUTION OF CLUSTER GALAXIES FROM z=0 to z=1

Karl D. Rakos
Inst. of Astronomy, University of Vienna

and

James M. Schombert
IPAC, J.P.L. Calif. Inst. of Technology

Abstract

Using the rest frame Stroemgren photometry of galaxies in rich clusters between z=0 and z=1, we have developed photometric signature for interacting starburst galaxies and AGN galaxies of IRAS-type. We believe that the majority of blue galaxies in clusters are triggered by interactions.

Introduction

We have published rest frame Stroemgren photometry (3500 A, 4100 A, 4750 A and 5500 A) for 509 galaxies in 17 rich clusters between z=0 and z=1 as a test of color evolution[1,2,3,4,5]. Our observations confirm a strong, rest frame, Butcher-Oemler effect where the fraction of blue galaxies increases from 20% at z=0.4 to 80% at z=0.9. This trend is much stronger than found by earlier studies and suggests that all cluster galaxies with disks (S0's and spirals) are involved in star formation 7 to 8 Gyr's ago.

We also find that a majority of these blue cluster galaxies is composed of E + A post-starburst systems based on color criteria. When comparing our colors to the morphological results from HST imaging we conclude that at least one part of the blue cluster galaxies is a population of late-type, LSB objects who fade and are then destroyed by the cluster tidal field. This proposed LSB population would also explain the high fraction of AGN activity in high redshift clusters[6]. In a study of nearby, giant LSB galaxies, Knezek and Schombert[7] found that 60% have low luminosity AGN activity. The weak emission is assumed to be due to the low surface density of gas in the cores of these systems, making a deficiency in fuel for the central engine. If the same event which triggers star formation in the blue

132

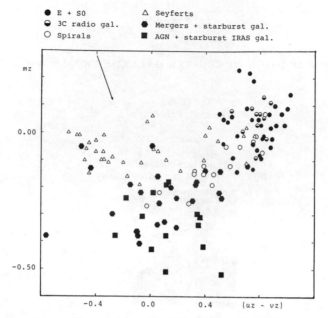

Figure 1: (uz–vz) for different types of galaxies.

cluster population also increases the core gas density the hidden AGN would increase in luminosity and the higher AGN fraction observed by Dressler and Gunn would be realised.

On the other hand our photometry is a powerful tool to recognize galaxies involved in a starburst by interaction and AGN galaxies of IRAS-type.

Photometric properties of active galaxies

The two color diagram (uz–vz) versus mz is very sensitive to different types of galaxies. We have calibrated this diagram using about 140 high resolution, high S/N ratio, spectra of galaxies available in the literature[8,9,10,11,12]. Synthetic colors uz, vz, bz and yz have been calculated using these spectra. Figure 1 shows the diagram. Starburst galaxies are well separated from ellipticals spirals and Seyfert galaxies. AGN, starburst galaxies and mergers have mz< −0.2 in almost each case. In general mz is influenced by reddening, metallicity and bimodal distribution of star colors in a galaxy. The metallicity of all plotted galaxies is not very different from the solar metalicity; the intrinsic reddening (arrow in Fig. 1) has the largest effect.

Our observations show, that for increasing numbers of blue galaxies also the number of galaxies with mz< −0.2 increases. For example, the HST results on CL0939.7+4317 at z=0.40[13] show that 34% are blue galaxies and 7% of observed galaxies are mergers. The same 7% galaxies have mz< −0.2, a photometric signature for mergers. One of our clusters CL317+1521, z=0.583 has 60% blue galaxies and also 42% have photometric signature for mergers. The morphological classification of such extreme

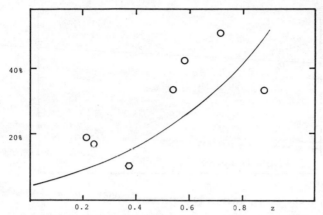

Figure 2: Fraction of galaxies with mz< −0.2 versus redshift.

clusters would be very valuable to solve the problem of blue galaxies in clusters. We intend to submit a proposal to HST for such observations. The fraction of blue galaxies is in the first aproximation a linear function of redshift:

$$f(B) = 1.2\,z - 0.28$$

The fraction of galaxies with mz< −0.2 follows rather a power law. On the other hand the rate of interactions increases as rapid as $(1+z)$ to the forth power[14]. The present day frequency of interactions is estimated by various authors to be around 4%. In the Figure 2 we have plotted the fraction of galaxies with mz< −0.2 in 6 observed clusters as a function of redshift, the solid line is the theoretical prediction from Carlberg[14]. We believe that the majority of blue galaxies is triggered by interactions. This view is also supported through the local distribution of blue galaxies within a cluster. We have drawn 3 circles around a cluster centre with radii of 0.5, 1.0 and 1.5 Mpc. The fraction of blue galaxies in cluster should be f(B), in the centre circle f(Bc), in the first ring f(B1), in the second ring f(B2) and outside the largest circle f(B3). To avoid statistics of small numbers we can apply this procedure only to three clusters:

cluster	z	f(B)	f(Bc)	f(B1)	f(B2)	f(B3)
CL0016+16	0.54	0.47	0.13	0.60	0.55	0.44
CL317+1521	0.58	0.60	0.57	0.74	0.63	0.48
CL0128+608	0.66	0.36	0.00	0.33	0.25	0.44

The maximum number of blue galaxies is placed in the distance between 1 and 0.5 Mpc from center. It would be very desirable to repeat the measurements with a larger number of galaxies.

Similar conclusion can be drawn from the behaviour of the 4000 A break. The amplitude of the break is simply related to the color index (uz−vz) by

$$2.5 \log D = 0.646\,(uz - vz) + 0.245, \; r = 91\%.$$

In the Figure 3 the amplitude of the break (measured in uz−vz) refers to a 1 Gyr burst model of a

134

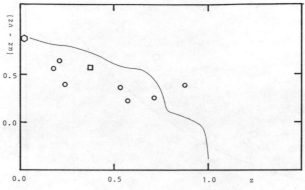

Figure 3: (uz–vz) versus redshift.

galaxy (continuous line) as a function of redshift for the redshift of galaxy formation at z=1.0 published by Bruzual and Charlot[15]. To the measurements by Kimble et al. for z=0[16] and Soucail et al. for z=0.37[17] we have added our measurements for 7 different clusters. In spite of a high change in the break we expect strong bursts induced by interactions between galaxies.

Acknowledgements

We wish to thank the generous support of KPNO and Lowell Obs. for collecting the high redshift data. Additional financial support from the Austrian Fonds zur Förderung der Wissenschaftlichen Forschung is gratefully acknowledged.

References

1. Fiala, N., Rakos, K. and Stockton, A. 1986 P.A.S.P. 98, 70.

2. Rakos, K., Fiala, N. and Schombert, J. 1988 Ap.J. 328, 463.

3. Rakos, K., Schombert, J.and Kreidl, T. 1991 Ap.J. 377, 382.

4. Schombert, J., Hanlan, P., Barsony, M. and Rakos, K. 1993 A.J. 106, 923.

5. Rakos, K. and Schombert, J. 1994 submitted for publication

6. Dressler, A. and Gunn, J 1983 Ap.J. 270, 7.

7. Knezek, P. and Schombert, J. 1994, in prep.

8. Gunn, J. and Oke, J. 1975 Ap.J. 195, 255.

9. Yee, H. and Oke, J. 1978 Ap.J. 226, 52.

10. Kennicutt, R. 1992 Ap.J. Suppl. 79, 255.

11. De Bruyn, A. and Sargent, W. 1978 A.J. 83, 1257.

12. Ashby, M., Houck, J. and Hacking, P. 1992 A.J. 104, 980.

13. Dressler, A., Butcher, H. and Gunn, J. 1994 Ap.J., in press.

14. Carlberg, R. 1992 Ap.J. 399, L31.

15. Bruzual, G. and Charlot, S. 1993 Ap.J. 405,538.

LARGE SCALE MORPHOLOGICAL SEGREGATION IN GALAXY CATALOGS

Rosa Domínguez-Tenreiro, Dpto. Física Teórica, C-XI, UAM, 28049 Madrid,Spain
Mª Ángeles Gómez-Flechoso, Dpto. Física Teórica, C-XI,UAM, 28049 Madrid, Spain
Ana Campos, Physics Department, Durham University, Durham DH1 3LE, England
Gustavo Yepes, Dpto. Física Teórica, C-XI, UAM, 28049 Madrid, Spain

Abstract

The morphological segregation of galaxies in the CfA1 and SSRS catalogs has been analyzed in detail through the scaling formalism. It has been positively detected at a statistical significative level, up to 15-20 h^{-1} Mpc in the CfA1 catalog and up to 20-30 h^{-1} Mpc in the SSRS catalog, with ellipticals and lenticulars more clustered than spirals. Moreover it is also present, at a statistical significative level, in areas of moderate density.

It is possible that two key questions to understanding the process of galaxy formation (of any type) are the following: why are there galaxies of different morphological types (MT)?, and how were the MT originated? The differences in the spatial distribution of galaxies of different MT (known as morphological segregation (MS)) could possibly provide us with very useful informations for this understanding.

Early studies on galaxy morphology have shown that galaxies of different MT do not share the same space distribution[1][2][3]. Later on, quantitative analyses demonstrated that there exist a correlation between the MT and the galaxy density[4]...[12] and that galaxies of different MT have different clustering properties (with ellipticals (E) more clustered than spirals (S) and lenticulars (SO) in an intermediate position)[13]...[21].

But MS is not well established at large scales (say $r > 10$ h^{-1} Mpc, see however[20][22]) and in regions of moderate or low density (see[14][20]). However, the existence or not of MS at scales larger than galaxy clusters and outside the densest areas of the galaxy distribution is an important question to understand the origin of MT, because a positive detection would suggest that the process of morphological differentiation is correlated with environmental effects in the field of primordial fluctuations, while its absence could indicate that the morphological differentiation is only caused by different evolutive processes undergone by structured galaxies in cluster cores and groups[23].

In this paper we present the results of an exhaustive analysis of MS in the CfA1[24] and SSRS[25] catalogs through the scaling formalism[26][27]. This formalism is particularly suited to our purposes because it allows for a separate description of regions of different density. Its formulation to describe small data sets can be found in [27][28]. Here we only recall some definitions. Let us consider a distribution of N points. We assign to each point i, a) a probability at radius r given by $p_i(r) = n_i(r)/N$, where $n_i(r)$ is the number of points in a ball centered at i and of radius r, and b) a scale $r_i(p)$ at probability p, such that the sphere of radius r_i centered at i contains $n_i = pN$ points. Then we form the sums

$$Z(q,r) = \frac{1}{N} \sum_{i=1}^{N} p_i(r)^{q-1} \tag{1}$$

$$W(\tau,p) = \frac{1}{N} \sum_{i=1}^{N} r_i(p)^{-\tau} \tag{2}$$

Eqs. (1) and (2) define the so-called correlation sum and n-nearest neighbor-distance algorithms, respectively. The moments $Z(q,r)$ describe preferentially regions of higher density as q increases (for example, for $q = 6$ the sum in (1) is dominated by the points in overdense regions, while for $q = 2$ it is dominated by points in areas of moderate density). The $W(\tau,p)$ sums describe preferentially areas of lower density as $|\tau|$ increases (for example, for $\tau = -1$ the relative weight of different density bins is maximum for regions of average density, while for $\tau = -5$ the major contribution comes from underdense areas).

We have calculated the $Z(q,r)$ and $W(\tau,p)$ moments for five parent samples extracted from each catalog. They are volume-limited complete samples and their redshifts are limited in the line-of-sight direction by distances 40 h^{-1} Mpc, 50 h^{-1} Mpc, 60 h^{-1} Mpc, 70 h^{-1} Mpc, and 80 h^{-1} Mpc. The galaxies in each parent sample have been placed in different morphological groups, according to their MT (see Table 1); two different classification schemes, 1 and 2, have been considered for spiral galaxies. The results of our calculations show that MS between E+S0 and S galaxies is present in overdense and moderate density areas (described by the $Z(q,r)$ moments) in any parent sample up to $r \simeq$ 15-20 h^{-1} Mpc for the CfA1 catalog and up to $r \simeq$ 20-30 h^{-1} Mpc in the SSRS catalog, with E+S0 more clustered than S galaxies. By contrast, no systematic differences have been detected between early- and late-type spirals. Concerning the $W(\tau,p)$ sums, the MS appears systematically between E+S0 and S galaxies in regions of moderate density, but it is not systematically present in underdense regions.

We have tested the null hypothesis $\mathcal{H}_0$ that any pair of morphological galaxy groups, A and B, have been drawn from the same underlying population, in order to quantify the statistical significance of the clustering differences we have found. To this end, for any pair A and B we have formed the sample $A \cup B$, and we have extracted from it M random subsamples with N_A objects and M random subsamples with N_B objects (N_A and N_B are the number of objects in samples A and B, respectively). We form the differences

$$\delta_{lk}(x) = S_l^A(x) - S_k^B(x) \tag{3}$$

$$\delta(x) = S^A(x) - S^B(x) \tag{4}$$

for any pair of random realizations of A and $B(l, k = 1, \ldots, M)$ and for the data, respectively. Here x is a particular value of r or p, and S are the $Z(q, r)$ or $W(\tau, p)$ statistics. We then define the critical statistics:

$$P_{ij} = \sum_{x\ bins} \log \frac{100}{M^2} \sum_{l,k=1}^{M} \theta \left(\frac{\delta_{lk}(x)}{\delta_{ij}(x)} - 1 \right) \tag{5}$$

and

$$P = \sum_{x\ bins} \log \frac{100}{M^2} \sum_{l,k=1}^{M} \theta \left(\frac{\delta_{lk}(x)}{\delta(x)} - 1 \right) \tag{6}$$

where θ is the Heaviside step function.

The confidence levels at which we can rule out the null hypothesis $\mathcal{H}_0$ for different pairs of morphological groups are given in Table 2. We have taken $M = 500$ realizations and $10\ h^{-1}$ Mpc $\leq r \leq 20\ h^{-1}$ Mpc and $0.025 \leq p \leq 0.3$. In the CfA1 catalog there exist many $T = 4$ spiral galaxies and the differences between spirals depend on the spiral classification scheme (1 or 2, see Table 1), so we show the results for the two classification schemes. In the SSRS catalog, the results are qualitatively stable against a change in the spiral classification, so that we only present the results for the classification scheme labeled as 2.

As can be seen in Table 2, the differences found between elliptical and spiral galaxies (of any type, or taken together) in the SSRS catalog for areas of high and moderate density, are statistically significant. In the underdense areas, the differences are neither systematic nor statistically significant. The same is true for the N40 and N50 volumes of the CfA1 catalog. This behaviour changes in the N60 and N70 volumes (only the differences between EL and ES2 are significative), presumably due to their lower density as compared with other volumes of this catalog when taken with the same absolute magnitude limit, and/or a possible misclassification of spirals for ellipticals in these volumes[22]. The differences between early- and late-type spirals are not statistically significant, except for areas of moderate and high density of the N50, N60 and N70 volumes, where late-type spirals are more clustered than early-type ones.

Table 1: Number of galaxies in the different morphological groups and volumes of the CfA1 and SSRS catalogs considered in this work.

Morphological group	T-type range	CfA1					SSRS				
		N40	N50	N60	N70	N80	S40	S50	S60	S70	S80
EL	$[-5, 0]$	102	87	71	67	75	40	57	70	58	40
ES1	$[1, 4]$	137	122	107	92	80	73	102	120	119	98
LS1	$[5, 7]$	74	57	39	30	20	81	92	102	83	71
ES2	$[1, 3]$	104	87	76	67	60	62	88	109	106	84
LS2	$[4, 6]$	103	84	68	54	40	89	104	113	96	85
St	$[1, 7]$	211	179	146	122	100	154	194	222	202	169

Table 2: Confidence levels at which the null hypothesis can be ruled out when the galaxy samples are described by the $Z(q, r)$ and $W(\tau, p)$ statistics.

Statistics	Morphological	CfA1					SSRS				
	Pair	N40	N50	N60	N70	N80	S40	S50	S60	S70	S80
$Z(2, r)$	ES2/EL	1.00	0.99	0.98	0.99	0.67	0.99	1.00	0.96	0.93	0.89
.	LS2/EL	1.00	0.49	0.58	0.29	0.63	0.99	0.99	0.94	0.97	0.94
.	St/EL	1.00	0.97	0.64	0.83	0.88					0.96
.	ES1/LS1	0.18	0.94	0.75	0.91	0.95					
.	ES2/LS2	0.77	0.95	0.98	0.99	0.50	0.11	0.63	0.04	0.47	0.47
$Z(6, r)$	ES2/EL	1.00	1.00	0.92	0.77	0.71	0.99	0.99	0.65	0.65	0.72
.	LS2/EL	0.99	0.65	0.81	0.90	0.76	0.95	0.99	0.72	0.79	0.78
.	St/EL	0.99	0.97	0.17	0.74	0.71					0.88
.	ES1/LS1	0.16	0.77	0.61	0.75	0.80					
.	ES2/LS2	0.92	0.95	0.96	0.96	0.92	0.40	0.65	0.04	0.72	0.54
$W(-1, p)$	ES2/EL	1.00	0.63	0.74	0.94	0.28	1.00	0.89	0.99	0.99	0.97
.	LS2/EL	1.00	0.50	0.16	0.14	0.92	1.00	0.88	0.96	0.97	0.96
.	St/EL	1.00	0.94	0.82	0.92	0.90					0.98
.	ES1/LS1	0.59	0.36	0.58	0.87	0.72					
.	ES2/LS2	0.18	0.76	0.59	0.88	0.59	0.68	0.63	0.36	0.32	0.04
$W(-5, p)$	ES2/EL	0.69	0.56	0.82	0.85	0.41	0.74	0.80	0.44	1.00	0.73
.	LS2/EL	0.60	0.63	0.80	0.89	0.89	0.47	0.76	0.31	0.53	0.53
.	St/EL	0.68	0.49	0.78	0.92	0.60					0.55
.	ES1/LS1	0.19	0.91	0.70	0.73	0.80					
.	ES2/LS2	0.42	0.81	0.36	0.22	0.36	0.78	0.32	0.04	0.94	0.33

REFERENCES

1. Hubble, E., & Humason, M.L., 1931. *Astrophys. J.* , **74**, 43.
2. Oemler, A., 1974. *Astrophys. J.* , **194**, 1.
3. Melnick, J., & Sargent, W.L., 1977. *Astrophys. J.* , **215**, 401.
4. Dressler, A., 1980. *Astrophys. J.* , **236**, 351.
5. Bhavsar, S.P., 1981. *Astrophys. J.* , **246**, L5.
6. de Souza, R.E., Capelato, H.V., Arakaki, L., & Logullo, C., 1982. *Astrophys. J.* , **263**, 557.
7. Postman, M., & Geller, M.J., 1984. *Astrophys. J.* , **281**, 95.
8. Einasto, M., & Einasto, J. , 1987. *Mon. Not. R. astr. Soc.* , **226**, 543.
9. Tully, R.B., 1988. *Astron. J.* , **96**, 73.
10. Maia, M.A.G., & da Costa, L.N., 1990. *Astrophys. J.* , **352**, 457.
11. Sanromà, M., & Salvador-Solé, E., 1990. *Astrophys. J.* , **360**, 16.
12. Whitmore, B.C., Gilmore, D.M., & Jones, C., 1993. *Astrophys. J.* , **407**, 489.
13. Davis, M., & Geller, M.J., 1976. *Astrophys. J.* , **208**, 13.
14. Giovanelli, R., Haynes, M.P., & Chincarini, G.L., 1986. *Astrophys. J.* , **300**, 77.
15. Domínguez-Tenreiro, R., & Martínez, V.J., 1989. *Astrophys. J.* , **339**, L9.
16. Santiago, B.X., & da Costa, N.L., 1990. *Astrophys. J.* , **362**, 386.
17. Börner, G., & Mo, H.J., 1990. *Astr. Astrophys.* , **227**, 324.
18. Mo, H.J., & Börner, G., 1990. *Astr. Astrophys.* , **238**, 3.
19. Maurogordato, S., & Lachièze-Rey, M., 1991. *Astrophys. J.* , **369**, 30.
20. Mo, H.J., Einasto, M., Xia, X.Y., & Deng, Z.G., 1992. *Mon. Not. R. astr. Soc.* , **255**, 382.
21. Iovino, A., Giovanelli, R., Haynes, M., Chincarini, G., & Guzzo, L., 1993. *Mon. Not. R. astr. Soc.* , **265**, 21.
22. Santiago, B.X. & Strauss, M.A., 1992. *Astrophys. J.* , **387**, 9.
23. Oemler, A. , 1992. in "Clusters & Superclusters of Galaxies", ed. A.C.Fabian (Kluwer), p. 29.
24. Huchra, J., Davis, M., Latham, D., & Tonry, J., 1983. *Astrophys. J. Suppl.* , **52**, 89.
25. da Costa, L.N., et al. , 1988. *Astrophys. J.* , **327**, 545.
26. Jones, B.J.T., Martínez, V.J. Saar, E., & Einasto, J., 1988. *Astrophys. J.* , **332**, L1.
27. Martínez, V.J., Jones, B.J.T., Domínguez-Tenreiro, R. & van der Weygaert, R., 1990. *Astrophys. J.* , **357**, 50.
28. Domínguez-Tenreiro, R., Gómez-Flechoso, M.A., & Martínez, V.J., 1994. *Astrophys. J.* , **424**, 42.

THE STRUCTURE OF CLUSTERS OF GALAXIES AS OBSERVED BY ROSAT

Hans Böhringer
Max-Planck-Institut für extraterrestrische Physik
85740 Garching, FRG

Abstract

The importance of clusters of galaxies in cosmological research is highlighted by two facts: clusters are dynamically young and still evolving and they are the largest clearly defined mass aggregates in the Universe. Therefore the study of their dynamical structure, their mass, and their composition is of prime importance. X-ray observations – in particular by means of the unique imaging capability of the ROSAT observatory – have enabled very detailed structural studies of galaxy clusters and have greatly advanced our understanding of their physics and their composition.

This paper illustrates the results of recent ROSAT studies of clusters and groups of galaxies for a few representative examples. Particular attention will be given to the nearest and very complex cluster in the constellation Virgo. Mass determination of clusters is discussed. And recent results of ROSAT observations of poor groups of galaxies are presented. These small groups seem to show the transition from X-ray properties of clusters to X-ray properties of single galaxies.

1. Introduction

Clusters of galaxies are not only the largest well defined mass aggregates that have clearly decoupled from the cosmological expansion and are now approaching their proper dynamical equilibrium state. They are also among those astronomical objects that show the most rapid evolution in the recent past, as is illustrated for example in the evolution of the X-ray luminosity function as shown by F. Canstander and discussed by A. Edge at this meeting. Thus they are not only individually dynamically young, but they are also as a population among the youngest astronomical objects. The later point is reflected by the fact that many clusters have not yet attained a dynamical equilibrium state. Clusters are most often found to be still evolving and growing by the accretion of surrounding material. Therefore the study of the dynamical structure of galaxy clusters and the determination of their mass are important current topics in cosmological research.

X-ray astronomy has provided us recently with a more detailed look at galaxy clusters than it was possible before at any other wavelength. In optical astronomy the structural studies of clusters are limited by the number of galaxies and measured galaxy redshifts that outline the cluster structure. The X-ray emission originates in a teneous hot intracluster gas that traces the mass distribution in the cluster and is therefore an ideal diagnostics of the cluster structure.

The intracluster gas has typical temperatures of 2 to 10 keV. The optically thin radiation that is emitted by the plamsa at this temperatures has its emission maximum in the soft X-ray region. It is also this wavelength region where current X-ray telescopes are operative. In particular the ROSAT observatory with its imaging X-ray telescope is currently providing very detailed observational data on galaxy clusters. Here some representative ROSAT studies will be discussed with particular attention to the Virgo cluster. The occurance of substructure and the mass determination of clusters is dicussed. ROSAT observations of two Hickson groups will illustrate how ROSAT studies have extended our knowledge about galaxy systems to the least massive units in the mass spectrum.

2. The ROSAT Observatory

The ROSAT observatory [1,2] which was launched in June 1990 carries on board an X-ray telescope which is an ideal instrument for the imaging of cluster of galaxies. It covers an energy range from about 0.1 to 2.4 keV. The two focal plane instruments, the PSPC (position sensitive proportional counter) and HRI (high resolution imager) reach an on axis resolution of about 20 arcsec and 5 arcsec in the otpical axis, respectively. The PSPC provides some energy resolution which amounts to about 40% at 1 keV [3].

The limited energy resolution of the PSPC instrument and the low upper end of the ROSAT window at 2.4 keV make temperature determinations from the X-ray spectra quite difficult for the temperature range of clusters. Thus reasonable results are only possible for very good photon statistics. On the other hand it is an advantage that the sensitivity of the PSPC instrument for the emission of hot gas with fixed emission measure is independent of the temperature in the range 2 to 10 keV. Thus the observed radiation is directly related to the emission measure.

3. X-ray Study of the Virgo Cluster

The most prominent cluster of galaxies in our immediate neighbourhood is the Virgo cluster, with a distance of about 20 Mpc. Its has been subject to many studies [4], and more than 400 cluster galaxy redshifts have been measured [5]. The cluster is an important milestone in establishing the cosmological distance ladder [6]. Thus an understanding of the morphology of this cluster and a mass determination are quite important. Unfortunately the Virgo cluster is a very complex, unrelaxed system and does not easily lend itself to modelling and to a virial mass estimate. Also the large field of view – the cluster extends over more than 10 degrees in the sky – makes a complete study difficult. Thus only selected fields were imaged with the EINSTEIN observatory [7], while scans with the non-imaging collimated detector on GINGA revealed extended emission on scales of serveral degrees [8].

The ROSAT All Sky Survey now provides for the first time an unlimited view at the sky with good imaging quality. Fig. 1 shows a contour plot of the X-ray surface brightness in the energy band from 0.4 to 2.4 keV. The image has been smoothed with a variable Gaussian filter featuring a large scale smoothing of up to 55 arcmin FWHM for the low surface brightness regions but causes little distortion to the point sources. The most prominent feature in the image of the Virgo cluster is the giant almost spherically symmetric X-ray halo around the bright elliptical galaxy M87. The X-ray halos around the ellipticals M86 and M49 are also clearly visible and M58 and M60 show up as X-ray sources. Faint non-symmetrical X-ray emission from the cluster extends over the whole region including both M87 and M49 with dimensions of more than 8 and 5 degrees in north-south and east-west direction, respectively. Fig. 1 also shows the density distribution of the galaxies in Virgo from the photometric survey of Binggli, Tammann, and Sandage [9]. The images are surprisingly similar which implies that the galaxy and gas distributions both follow the overall mass distribution in the cluster very well. In particular the asymmetric extension to the east and the sharp edge in the west are well visible in both contour maps. An even better correlation is obtained if one compares only the early type galaxies (ellipticals, dwarf ellipticals, and S0 galaxies) with the X-ray surface brightness distribtuion [10]. In the south-eastern corner of the Virgo image X-ray emission from the North Polar Spur (the rim of a Galactic superbubble) is also contributiong to the X-ray emission above the X-ray background. The contaminating emission is significantly softer and can therefore be distinguished from the cluster emission.

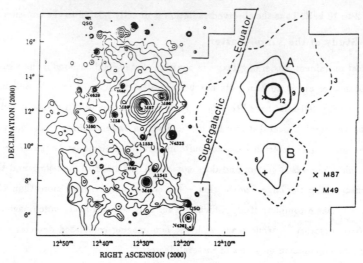

Figure 1: An X-ray image of the Virgo cluster of galaxies from the ROSAT All Sky Survey in the form of an intensity contour plot for the energy band 0.4 to 2.4 keV is shown on the left. On the right the density distribution of the galaxies from the photometric survey of Binggeli *et al.* [9] is shown for comparison.

In order to understand the structure of the Virgo cluster in more detail we have attempted to model the cluster by decomposing it into several components. We have assumed that a major part of the cluster consists of three roughly spherically symmetric X-ray halos around the galaxies M87, M86, and M49. Subtracting a model image from the observed surface brightness distribution in Virgo shows that about 80% of the emission can be accounted for by such a model [11]. Only the sharp cut-off at the western side of the cluster is not adequately modeled by a superposition of spherically symmetric halos. The residuals show faint, diffuse, irregular emission to the north of M87, to the west towards M60, between M87 and M49 and around M49 [11]. The X-ray halo of M87 is about one order of magnitude brighter than those of M49 and M86. In the halo of M87 the X-ray emission can be traced out to about 1.5 to 1.8 Mpc.

The halo of M87 is sufficiently bright in X-rays to allow a detailed spectroscopic analysis in concentric rings around M87 [11]. The resulting temperature profile shows a significant decrease of the temperature towards the centre inside a radius of $\sim$ 100 kpc consistent with predictions from earlier studies on the cooling flow structure in M87 [12]. In the region outside the cooling radius the combined data of GINGA and ROSAT are consistent with a uniform temperature between 2 and 2.4 keV.

With the given temperature and gas density distribution the integrated radial mass profile can be determined. For the core region of Virgo to a radius of 1.8 Mpc one finds a gravitational mass of $1.5 - 5.5 \cdot 10^{14}$ $M_\odot$. The large uncertainty of this value comes from the large errors in the measurement of the temperature profile. The gas density distribution can be determined with much higher precision - assuming again spherical symmetry of the cluster core - and one finds a gas mass of $4 - 5.5 \cdot 10^{13}$ $M_\odot$. Thus about 7 to 36% of the infered gravitational mass can be accounted for by the X-ray luminous gas.

The gravitational effect of the Virgo cluster is responsible for a peculiar acceleration of our galaxy and the local group. The " Virgo infall velocity" so produced is estimated to be about 250 km s^{-1} for which a Virgo mass of about 10^{15} $M_\odot$ is required [14]. The core region of Virgo as observed in X-rays accounts already for a major fraction of this infered mass.

4. Substructure in Clusters of Galaxies

The observational evidence and the implications of substruture in clusters of galaxies is discussed in several lectures and will therefore just be summarized here. Already in the first observations of clusters by ROSAT in the calibration and verification phase one of the nicest examples of a cluster with substructure – picturing a clusters that is just in the processes of the merging of two subcomponents – was found in Abell 2256 [15] (see also contribution by U.G. Briel). It was pointed out, among others, by Richstone et al.[16] that the frequency of subclustering, being a measure of the dynamical age of the cluster, can be used to constrain the possible value of the mean density of the Universe, Ω_0. Therefore tools are developped to quantify the significance of substructure in clusters.

An interesting method was recently presented by Mohr et al.[17], who analysed the change in the center, orientation and ellipticity of elliptical isophotes fitted to cluster images as a function of radius. To obtain a significance for the results the analysis has to be supplemented by Monte Carlo simulations. Mohr et al.[17] find that four out of five clusters analysed have significant substructure and are therefore dynamically young. In a more qualitative analysis Henry and Briel [18] find that four out of six of the brightest X-ray clusters have substructure. The results point towards a high value for Ω_0. The cosmological implications of these results are discussed in more detail in the contribution by A.E. Evrard.

5. The Mass of Galaxy Clusters

With the high sensitivity, the low internal background, and the possibility to discriminate against most of the very soft X-ray background in the 0.1 to 0.4 keV band, the ROSAT observatory provided an important advance in the study of cluster structure on large scales and in the determination of the masses for entire clusters. For the first time the X-ray emitting gas can be traced out to radii of about 3 Mpc in some nearby clusters. This corresponds to an "Abell radius" and is probably also very close to the edge of the virialized galaxy system.

The simultaneous knowledge of the gas density and temperature profile of a spherically symmetric cluster allows to determine the gravitational mass profile of the cluster on the assumption that the gas is in hydrostatic equilibrium. The technique of mass determination from X-ray data is discussed in other contributions and has been described in some detail [19] for the results summarized here.

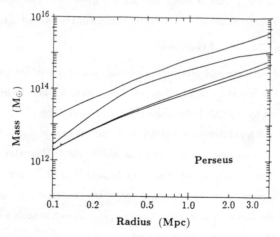

Figure 2: Integrated radial profiles for the gas and gravitational mass in the Perseus cluster of galaxies as determined from ROSAT X-ray data. The upper two curves indicate the constraint for the gravitational mass profile while the lower two curves bracket the gas mass profile.

Results for the gravitational and gas mass profiles for the example of the Perseus cluster

Table 1: Gas and Gravitational Masses of Galaxy Clusters

cluster	R_x (Mpc)	M_{grav} (10^{14}) $M_\odot$	M_{gas}/M_{grav}
Perseus	3.0	10 - 26	0.13-0.43
Coma	4.0	11 - 28	0.14-0.44
A2256	4.0	12 - 46	0.12-0.45
M 87	1.8	1.5-5.5	0.07-0.36
Centaurus	1.5	$\sim$ 1.9-3.8	0.13-0.37
AWM 7	1.6	2.4-4.6	0.17-0.32

are shown in Fig. 2. The gas mass is larger than the galaxy mass by more than a factor of 5 (assuming $M/L = 5M_\odot/L_\odot$ for the galaxies). The gas mass cannot account for the binding mass, however, and the major mass component has to be attributed to "dark matter". The gas density profile has a shallower form than the distribution of the galaxies. The uncertainties in the gravitational mass distribution are too large, however, to decide if the dark matter follows the distribution of the gas or that of the galaxies. Similar results for the gass mass and gravitational mass were derived from ROSAT data for some other nearby clusters. The results are summerized in Table 1 (see also [20,21]).

Two effects have been neglected in the above analysis. First the hydrostatic equation may have to be modified to account for pressure from turbulence, magnetic fields, and cosmic rays. Second if the gas is clumped on a scale smaller than the resolution of the telescope the gas mass is overestimated. We have estimated that both effects will probably lead to an overestimate of the gas to total mass ratio by no more than about 30% [19]. Taking these corrections into account one may conclude that the gas fraction in richer clusters is about 10 - 30%. The cosmological implications of these large gas mass fractions were discussed in detail in the contributions by S.D.M. White and C.S. Frenk.

6. The Structure of Compact Galaxy Groups

For poor groups of galaxies comprising only four or five group members a study of their structure, their dynamical state, and their mass is even more difficult if one has to rely on optical observations only. Before the launch of ROSAT very little was know about the X-ray emission of these smallest groups.

Recently Ebeling et al.[22] has conducted a search for X-ray emssion from Hickson's compact groups in the ROSAT All Sky Survey and found about 10% of these groups to be detected in the Survey above the detection limit (see also the contribution by T. Ponman). Two poor groups have been observed in early ROSAT pointed observations, one is Hickson's group HCG 62 [23] and a non-Hickson group around the galaxy NGC 2300 [24]. They both show extended X-ray emission of hot intragroup gas and the observations imply a large gravitational potential corresponding to masses of a few 10^{13} M$_\odot$. Here we will discuss some results of ROSAT pointed observations of two other Hickson groups, HCG 42 and HCG 97. Both also show extended X-ray emission from hot gas presumably bound in the gravitational potential well of the group.

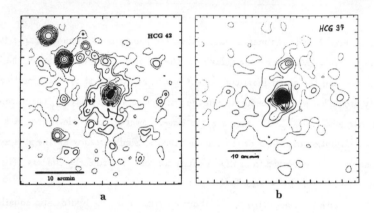

a   b

Figure 3: X-ray images of the two compact Hickson groups HCG 42 (a) and HCG 97 (b) in the form of contour plots. The images were constructed from the photons received in the 0.4 to 2.4 keV energy band. The galaxies are plotted symbolically on top of the X-ray contour plot.

The X-ray images of the two groups are shown in Fig. 3. Both groups are dominated by a giant elliptical galaxy that is located at the maximum of the X-ray emission. HCG 42 is more compact while HCG 97 shows a larger extend. Some diffuse X-ray emission can be traced in this group out to a radius of 0.6 Mpc. The ROSAT observations are deep enough for reliable temperature determinations. HCG 97 has a fairly uniform temperature around 1.05±0.1 keV. HCG 42 has a central temperature of about 0.8 keV whereas the temperature increases outside the central area (probably a cooling flow) to values of about 0.9 to 1 keV.

From these data mass estimates can be performed on the assumption of spherical symmetry which is not so nicely given for these groups as for the richer clusters discussed above. For

HCG 97 a total mass of $2 - 5 \cdot 10^{13}$ M$_\odot$ is obtained for an outer radius of 600 kpc and a mass of $1 - 2 \cdot 10^{13}$ M$_\odot$ for HCG 42 for an outer radius of 200 kpc.

The two objects show quite striking differences in their appearance. The smaller one of the two groups, HCG 42 with four galaxies at according redshifts, appears more compact in X-rays. The β-model fit yields a β-value of about 0.7. The X-ray emission is clearly concentrated on the giant elliptical galaxy which dominates the group. The X-ray halo around HCG 97 is more extended, with a value for the β-parameter of about 0.4. The dominant elliptical galaxy is also located in the center of the X-ray surface brightness distribution, but the emission is less peaked. Another interesting parameter to compare is the gas mass fraction for the two groups. For HCG 97 the gas mass to total mass ratio is 6 to 15% while a much smaller value of 0.5 to 2% is obtained for HCG 42.

These observational results lead us to the following conclusions. In going from rich clusters to smaller galaxy systems a flattening of the gas density profile seems to be observed (see also David et al.[25]) with typical values for the β parameter of 0.7 to 0.8 for very rich cluster as for example Coma and A2256 and values as small as 0.4 - 0.5 for poor clusters and groups as for example for the halo around M87. Also the gas mass fractions seem to decrease slightly from rich clusters to smaller systems. In this respect HCG 97 as a galaxy group fits nicely into these scheme of X-ray properties. HCG 42 on the contrary resembles in its properties very much to those of isolated elliptical galaxies which have more compact X-ray halos (larger β-parameters) and smaller gas mass fractions [26,27]. The X-ray properties noticed here for HCG 97 and HCG 42 are in fact similar to the X-ray halos around M86 and M49 in the Virgo cluster [11].

These conclusions are very interesting with respect to the question where the transition occurs between a collection of a small number of galaxies and a group with a very definite group character. The observations are indicating that Hickson groups as the smallest units in the cluster mass function may indeed sometimes fall into one and sometimes into the other category and that we are actually exploring here the transition region from individual galaxies to real galaxy groups.

Acknowledgements

I like to thanks my colleagues U.G. Briel, D. Neumann, H. Ebeling, G. Hartner, and W. Voges for the collaboration in the study of galaxy clusters with ROSAT. I especially also like to thank the ROSAT team for providing the ROSAT data and for the analysis software that makes the data analysis possible.

148

8. References

1 Trümper, J.: 1983, *Adv. Space Res.*, **2**, 142.
2 Trümper, J., 1992, *Q. J. R. astr. Soc.*, **33**, 165.
3 Briel, U.G., Pfeffermann, E., Hartner, G., and Hasinger, G., 1988, *Proc. SPIE*, **982**, 401.
4 Richter, O.-G. and Binggeli, B. (eds.), Workshop on *The Virgo Cluster of Galaxies*, 1985, ESO Conf. Proc. No. 20.
5 Binggeli, B., Popescu, C.C., and Tammann, G.A., 1993, *Astron. Astrophys. Suppl.*, **98**, 275.
6 Rowan-Robinson, M., 1991, in *Observational Tests of Cosmological Inflation*, T. Shanks *et al.*(eds.), Kluwer Publ., p 161.
7 Forman, W., Jones, C., and DeFaccio, M., 1985, ESO Workshop Proc. No. 20: *The Virgo Cluster*, O.-G.Richter, B. Binggeli (eds:), p. 323.
8 Takano, S., Awaki, H., Koyama, K., Kunieda, H., Tawara, Y., Yamauchi, S., Makishima, K., & Ohashi, T., 1989 *Nature*, **340**, 289.
9 Binggeli, B., Tammann, G.A., and Sandage, A., 1987, *Astron. J.*, **94**, 251.
10 Schindler, S.C. *et al.*, 1994, in preparation.
11 Böhringer, H., Briel, U.G., Schwarz, R.A., Voges, W., Hartner, G., and Trümper, J., 1994, *Nature*, **368**, 828.
12 Stewart, G.C., Canizares, C.R., Fabian, A.C., and Nulsen, P.E.J., 1984, *Astrophys. J.*, **278**, 536.
13 Koyama, K., Takano, S., and Tawara, Y., 1991, *Nature*, **350**, 135.
14 Davis, M., Tonry, J., Huchra, J.P., and Latham, D.W., 1980, *Astrophys. J.*, **238**, L113.
15 Briel, U.G., Henry, J.P., Schwarz, R.A., Böhringer, H., Ebeling, H., Edge, A.C., Hartner, G.D., Schindler, S.C., and Voges, W., 1991, *Astron. Astrophys.*, **246**, L10.
16 Richstone, D., Loeb, A., and Turner, E.L., 1992, *Astrophys. J.*, , **393**, 477.
17 Mohr, J.J., Fabricant, D.G. and Geller, M.J., 1993, *Astrophys. J.*, **419**, L9.
18 Henry, J.P. and Briel, U.G., 1993 *Adv. Space Res.*, **13**(12), 191.
19 Böhringer, H., 1994, in *Cosmological Aspects of X-ray Clusters of Galaxies*, W.C. Seitter (ed.), Kluwer Publ., in press.
20 Briel, U.G., Henry, J.P., & Böhringer, H., 1992, *Astron. Astrophys.*, **259**, L31.
21 Henry, J.P., Briel, U.G., and Nulsen, P.E.J., 1993, *Astron. Astrophys.*, **271**, 413.
22 Ebeling, H., Voges, W., and Böhringer, H., 1994, *Astrophys. J.*, (submitted).
23 Ponman, T.J. and Bertram, D. , 1993, *Nature*, **363**, 51.
24 Mulchaey, J.S., Davis, D.S., Mushotzky, R.F., and Burstein, D., 1993, *Astrophys. J.*, **404**, L9.
25 David, L.P., Forman, W., and Jones, C., 1990, *Astrophys. J.*, **359**, 29; **369**, 121.
26 Forman, W., Jones, C., and Tucker, W., 1985, *Astrophys. J.*, **293**, 102.
27 Nulsen, P.E.J., Stewart, G.C, and Fabian, A.C., 1984, *Mon. Not. R. astr. Soc.*, **208**, 185.

OBSERVATION OF THE X–RAY CLUSTER A2256 WITH ROSAT

Ulrich G. Briel

Max-Planck-Institut für extraterrestrische Physik

8574 Garching, FRG

Abstract

The *ROSAT* observatory with its high spatial resolution X–ray telescope in combination with the position sensitive proportional counter (PSPC) is an ideal instrument to study extended sources like X–ray clusters of galaxies.

One of the best studied nearby rich cluster is A2256, observed with the *ROSAT* PSPC altogether for 55ksec. The X–ray surface brightness distribution shows clear evidence for substructure in the center of A2256, interpreted as the result of an ongoing merger event of a subgroup with the main cluster. Integrating in azimuthal rings we detected X–ray emission out to a radius of 3 h_{100}^{-1} Mpc.

The observation was deep enough to obtain the first two-dimensional temperature distribution of a galaxy cluster. Compared with hydrodynamic simulations this 2D temperature map gives further stringent evidence of the ongoing merger.

1. Introduction

One of the best studied galaxy cluster in X–rays as well as in the optical is the Abell cluster A2256. Based on extensive studies with the *EINSTEIN* observatory [1,2] and on 115 measured galaxy redshifts [1,3], the cluster was considered to be a more distant version of the Coma cluster in terms of its properties and has well relaxed to a state of dynamical equilibrium, although it appeared to have a somewhat elliptical shape in X–rays. A2256 was one of the PCV targets of *ROSAT* . This observation led to the first unambiguous detection of a merger event of a galaxy group with the main galaxy cluster [4]. In addition, the exposure was sufficently deep to enable us to measure for the first time the radially integrated temperature profile of a rich cluster from which we could place stringent limits on the gravitating mass and its radial shape [5].

2. X–ray surface brightness distribution

Follow-up PSPC observations of A2256 led to a total integration time of 55ksec of the cluster and its surroundings which revealed a wealth of new X–ray sources in the close vicinity to the cluster. We have an ongoing optical observing program to identify those sources, of which a large fraction may be cluster members. In Figure 1 we show a contour plot of the X–ray surface brightness   distribution of the 55ksec observation after smoothing with an

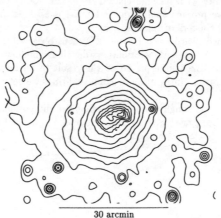

30 arcmin

Figure 1: Contour plot of the X–ray surface brightness distribution of A2256 after smoothing with an adaptive smoothing algorithm (see text for details).

adaptive smoothing algorithm (in which low surface brightness regions were smoothed using a 2D-Gaussian with large FWHM whereas high surface brightness regions were smoothed with small FWHM and intermediate regions correspondingly). The surface brightness is vignetting and exposure corrected. The contours are at the following flux levels in the energy band from 0.5 to 2.5 keV: 0.3, 0.6, 1.1, 1.8, 3.2, 4.8, 8.0, 12.8, 17.6, 22.4, 27, 32 10^{-3} PSPC-cts sec^{-1} arcmin^{-2}. This contour plot confirms our previous findings of the two maxima in the center of the cluster and reveals more details of the substructure. Even without further image reconstruction, it resembles very well the image obtained by the wavelet analysis of the A2256-PVC data [6].

In Figure 2 we show the azimuthally averaged surface brightness distribution in the 0.5 to 2.5 keV energy band from the region I (the region from PA 310° to 220°, excluding the X–ray emission from the infalling subgroup, as denoted by Briel et al., 1991[4]). We also have excluded obvious point sources and subtracted a background of 1.4 10^{-5} PSPC-cts sec^{-1} arcmin^{-2}. The solid line is the best fitting β model to the data. We found a core radius of 5.35 ± 0.07 arcmin and a β of 0.810 ± 0.007, both values in very good agreement with the previously determined parameters[4]. X–ray emission is detected out to a radius of 60 arcmin, corresponding to about 3 h_{100}^{-1} Mpc which is twice the Abell radius.

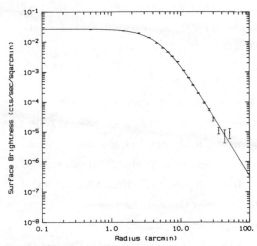

Figure 2: Azimuthally averaged surface brightness distribution of A2256 in the 0.5 to 2.5 keV energy band. The smooth curve is the best fitting β model (see text for details).

3. Spectral analysis

We have shown that is is possible to determine reliably X–ray temperatures of up to 8 keV with the *ROSAT* PSPC although its energy band is only from 0.1 to 2.5 kev (see Figure 3 and Table 1 of Henry, Briel & Nulsen [5]). What is needed is a high counting statistic to be able to see the temperature depended change of the shape of the continuum in the spectrum over the *ROSAT* energy band. With the new data we could determine the temperature in concentric rings out to one Abell radius [7].

In addition, this deep PSPC image enabled us to determine for the first time a two dimensional temperature map of the hot plasma of a rich galaxy cluster [7]. In this 2D temperature map one can clearly see the low temperature of the gas of the merging group, moving from the north-west towards the center of the cluster. North-east and south-west of the contact discontinuity are regions of statistically significant higher temperatures, indicating that the X-ray emitting plasma is not at all isothermal. Simulations of merger events using N-body and 3D hydrodynamic algorithms [8,9] can follow the evolution of a merger and reveal its signature in X-ray surface brightness distribution and projected plasma temperature [10]. The striking similarity between the measured 2D temperature map and the simulated maps is an other strong evidence of the ongoing merger of the subgroup with the main cluster.

4. References

1 Fabricant, D., Kent, S. & Kurtz, M. 1989, ApJ, 336, 77.

2 Fabricant, D., Beers, T.C., Geller, M.J., *et al.,* 1986, ApJ 308, 530.

3 Bothun G. & Schombert, R.E., 1990, ApJ, 360, 436.

4 Briel U.G., Henry J.P., Schwarz R.A., *et al.,* 1991, A&A, 246, L10.

5 Henry J.P., Briel U.G. & Nulsen P.J.E., 1993, A&A, 271, 413.

6 Slezak, E., 1994, *Clusters of Galaxies*, this Volume.

7 Briel, U.G. & Henry, J.P., in preparation.

8 Evrard G.: 1990, *Clusters of Galaxies*, Cambridge University Press, 287.

9 Schindler S., & Müller E., 1993, A&A, 272, 137.

10 Schindler S.: 1991, Ph.D. Thesis, LMU München.

ASCA DATA ON GALAXY CLUSTERS

Koujun Yamashita
Department of Physics, Nagoya University
Furo-cho, Chikusa-ku, Nagoya 464-01, Japan

ABSTRACT. X-ray astronomy satellite ASCA is suitable for imaging and spectroscopic observations of clusters of galaxies, having the angular resolution of 3 arcmin (HPD) and spectral resolution of 2-10% and covering the energy range of 0.5-10keV. Twenty five clusters were selected for PV phase observations, including 3 groups of galaxies, 3 poor clusters, 11 nearby rich clusters and 8 distsnt clusters. The Hubble constant was derived by using Sunyaev-Zeldovich effect clusters (CL0016+16 and A665). We report on the instrumentation and preliminary results of clusters of galaxies observed in PV phase.

1. Introduction

Spatially-resolved spectroscopic observations of clusters of galaxies is eagerly needed to investigate their structure, formation, evolution and the origin of intracluster gas[1]. Previous satellites, Einstein and ROSAT observed X-ray images below 4keV at maximum with good angular resolution, whereas spectral informations were poorly known due to the limited energy ranges and resolutions. The X-ray morphologies are divided into two categories, they are, centrally concentrated and spherically symmetric clusters with small core radii having cD galaxy at the center associated with cooling flows and largely extended clusters with large core radii and merging substructures. The morphological classifications of clusters observed by Einstein imaging were done by Jones and Forman[2], so called, single symmetric peak, offset center, elliptical, complex multiple structures, double, primary with small secondary and primarily galaxy emission. ROSAT All Sky

Survey detected thousands of clusters with the high angular resolution[3),4)]. These results are very useful and complimentary for ASCA observations.

David et al.[5)] compiled temperatures of 104 clusters ever observed. Ginga observations obtained temperatures and abundances of 45 clusters[6)]. The X-ray properties of clusters are represented by the morphological parameters of core radii and radial gradient of gas distribution, spectral parametes of temperature, abundance and luminosity, and the cosmological redshift. ASCA makes it possible to derive these parameters from the imaging and spectroscopic observations. It will promise the great advance of the understanding of clusters. Furthermore the stratific scheme of astronomical objects, such as galaxy, group of galaxies, poor cluster, rich cluster and large scale structure, hopefully gets in unified understandings related to the formation and evolution of clusters.

The Hubble constant will be derived by observing distant clusters which show Sunyaev-Zeldovich(hereafter S-Z) effect in microwave region. It has already reported that Hubble constant is less than 50 km/sec by combined analysis of X-ray data and S-Z effect. The gravitational lensing clusters are suited for investigating the dark matter relevant to the cosmological critical density.

Here we present the ASCA instrumentation, preliminary results of spectra and images of nearby and distant clusters, and the Hubble constant determination.

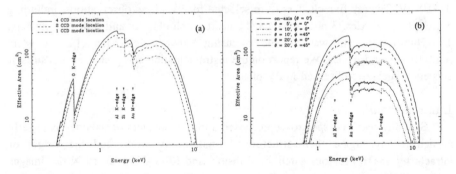

Fig.1 Effective area of one set of XRT+SIS(a) and XRT+GIS(b) within 12 mm diameter at focal plane. CCD modes correspond to the incident angle $\theta=0'$ for 4CCD, $\theta=5'$ for 2CCD and $\theta=7'$ for 1CCD.

2. Instrumentation

The fouth Japanese X-ray astronomy satellite ASCA was lauched on February 20, 1993 and put onboard four sets of multi-nested thin foil mirror X-ray telescope (XRT) incorporated with two X-ray CCDs(Solid state Imaging Spectrometer, SIS) and imaging gas scintillation proportional counters(Gas Imaging Spectrometer, GIS) for each two sets[7)]. XRT has the outer diameter of 35cm and focal length of 3.5m, which consists of 120 pieces of thin foil mirrors(0.15mm thickness) aligned at coaxial and confocal position by 1mm pitch in average[8]. The effective area of a telescope against X-ray energies are shown for XRT+SIS and XRT+GIS in Fig.1. SIS consists of four mosaic chips sensitive down to 0.5keV, having superior energy resolution (2% at 6keV)and small field of view(22x22 arcmin square)[9], whereas GIS is more sensitive up to 10keV with moderate energy resolution(8% at 6keV), covering wide field of view(50 arcmin in diameter)[10]. Both detectors are complimentarily functioned. The energy resolutions are shown in Fig.2. The angular resolution mostly depends on the point spread function of XRT with 30 acrsec(FWHM) and 3arcmin(HPD), as shown in Fig.3.

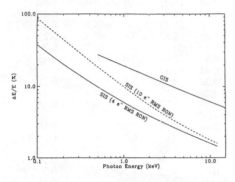

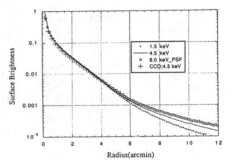

Fig.2 Energy resolution of SIS and GIS   Fig.3 Point spread function of XRT.

3. Observations

Twenty five clusters were selected for PV phase observations, which include group of galaxies, poor clusters, and nearby and distant rich clusters, referring to the observational results of Einstein, Ginga and ROSAT as listed in table 1. Eight distant clusters(z>0.1) include three S-Z effect clusters, A2218, A665 and Cl0016+16, and two gravitational lensing clusters, A370 and A963.

The standard observation time is 40ksec/target corresponding to one day observation. Multiple pointings were carried out for largely extended clusters to completely cover the whole cluster, such that 6 pointings for Coma and 5 pointings for Oph. Normally a target source on the focal plane is located at 5 arcmin away from the optical axis of a telescope to avoid the central dead area of SIS caused by gaps between chips and shadowing effect of supporting ribs of GIS window. Background data have been accumulated in blank sky for 300ksec, whereas the fluctuation of diffuse X-rays below 2keV should be taken into account .

PV phase observations were completed on October, 1993. After that 34 clusters were observed in AO1 and 37 clusters are scheduled in AO2 up to November, 1994.

Table 1 ASCA PV observations of clusters of galaxies

name	redshift	GINGA LAC (c/s)	kT (keV)	Ab	IPC (c/s)	GIS (c/s)	ASCA kT (keV)	Ab
			Group of Galaxies					
NGC1399(For)	0.00445	7.7	1.46	1.0	0.52	0.55	1.0	0.40
NGC2300	0.0076	-	-	-	r0.5	0.1	1.0	<0.2
WP23(NGC5044)	0.0087	7.4	1.07	-	1.24	0.43	0.96	0.26
			Poor Cluster					
AWM7	0.0179	44.4	3.8	0.47	3.88	-	4.0	0.5
MKW3s	0.0434	12.6	3.0	0.46	0.89	0.50	3.6	0.3
Hyd A	0.0522	15	3.85	0.41	1.17	0.89	3.7	0.4
			Nearby Rich Cluster(z<0.1)					
M87(Vir)	0.0038	173.7	2.34	0.44	14.3	5.2	2.8	0.41
Cen Cl	0.0107	65.5	3.54	0.54	9.33	3.0	3-4	1-0.2
A1060	0.0114	30.5	2.55	0.40	2.4	1.4	3.3	0.4
A426(Per)	0.0183	466.6	6.22	0.42	25.25	-	6.0	0.4
A1656(Coma)	0.0235	168.6	8.11	0.22	6.62	5.1	7.4	0.2
Oph Cl	0.028	292	9.1	0.29	r31	9.9	10.7	0.29
A2199	0.0305	40.6	4.22	0.41	2.67	2.0	4.1	0.45
A496	0.0316	33.1	3.91	0.42	2.11	-	-	-
A2319	0.0529	76.4	9.17	0.23	2.35	2.0	9.0	0.25
A2256	0.0601	35.2	7.51	0.28	1.37	1.4	6.4	0.24
A1795	0.0621	31.7	5.34	0.36	1.71	1.5	6.8	0.35
			Distant Cluster(z>0.1)					
A2218	0.1710	4.0	6.61	0.28	0.17	0.19	8.0	0.18
A1689	0.1747	9.0	7.16	0.34	0.6	0.5	8.7	0.28
A665	0.1816	7.5	9.53	0.44	0.29	0.19	9.0	0.33
A2163	0.201	12.6	12.9	0.33	0.49	0.39	11.8	0.30
A963	0.207	2.4	6.18	0.00	0.15	0.12	8.3	0.3
Zw3146	0.2906	-	-	-	r0.5	0.20	5.1	0.38
A370	0.373	-	-	-	0.05	0.06	8.8	0.5
Cl0016+16	0.545	<1	-	-	0.05	0.05	8.4	0.1

r: ROSAT PSPC(c/s), Ab: abundance relative to cosmic values

4. Spectral analysis

SIS has a capability to resolve emission lines of H-like and He-like ions of heavy elements. X-ray emissions from clusters are most likely originated from a thin hot plasma of intracluster medium in a collisional ionization equilibrium, so that the plasma temperature could be derived not only from a model fitting of whole spectra, but also from the intensity ratio of emission lines of different ionization stages of an element. Now the latter method becomes feasible by a spectroscopy with the SIS resolution. Intracluster medium consists of primordial gas and processed gas ejected from member galaxies. The abundance is different from cluster by cluster, depending on the temperature and total mass. The determination of an abundance of each element, especially O and Fe, gives a clue to know the origin of processed gas.

In Fig.4 there is shown an X-ray spectrum of M87 observed by one chip of SIS and fitted with a thermal bremsstrahlung of kT=1.9keV with an absorption of $N_H=9.8\times10^{20}cm^{-2}$ which exceeds the galactic column density in the direction of

M87. Residuals clearly show the existence of several emission lines, such as O, Si, S, Ar, Ca and Fe. If we introduce number of emission lines at expected energies of each element, we can get satisfactory fitting. The intensity ratio of H- and He-like emission lines of Si and S gives consistent temperature to that of the continuum. Strong enhancement around 1keV is due to Fe-L line complex mixed with Ne and Mg lines. Therefore Raymond-Smith model with a single temperature does not fit well to the data, so that we need at least two temperature components. Assuming an isothermality in the emitting region, emissivities of Fe-L lines could be checked by the spectral observations of an astrophysical plasma, especially Fe-L and Fe-K lines, which gives an impact to basic atomic processes.

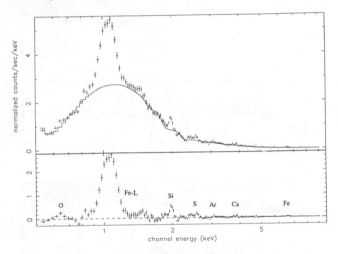

Fig.4 X-ray spectrum of M87 in Vir cluster observed by SIS

On the other hand GIS can more precisely determine temperatures higher than 6keV, since it has higher sensitivity in high energy region and most of atoms except for iron are fully ionized. In order to confirm the consistency of best fit parameters between SIS and GIS, the spectra of the central region of Coma cluster are shown in Fig.5, fitted with Raymond-Smith model. The best fit temperature and abundance are obtained to be 7.39(+0.76/-0.55)keV and 0.18(=0.09/-0.09) for SIS and 7.37(+0.26/-0.22)keV and 0.19(+0.04/-0.03) for GIS, respectively. Total counts are 17160 in 11x11 arcmin for SIS and 49518 in 30 arcmin diameter for GIS. When the temperature is higher than 4keV, only Fe-K lines contribute to the determination of abundance. The spectra of distant clusters, A665(z=0.1816) observed by SIS and CL0016+16(z=0.545) by GIS, are shown in Fig.6.The redshifted iron line is clearly recognized in A665 spectrum. The best fit temperatures of A665 and CL0016+16 were obtained to be 9.0(+/-1.0)keV and 8.4(+/-1.0)keV, respectively. Temperatures and abundances of 25 clusters observed in PV phase thus derived are listed in table 1 together with Ginga results. Some of clusters associated with cooling flow have radial distribution of temperatures and abundances(Ikebe and Mushotzky in this proceedings). These values are still preliminary at this moment. They would be changed by further analysis.

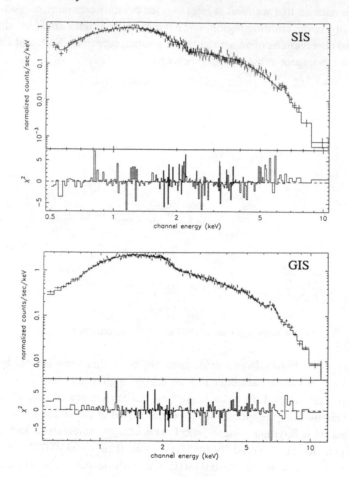

Fig.5 X-ray spectra of Coma observed by SIS and GIS

5. X-ray image

The denconvolution of X-ray image observed by ASCA is not so easy due to the complicated telescope imaging characteristics. Raw image of Coma cluster observed in 1-10keV by GIS is shown in Fig.7, which was constructed by adding together 6 pointing data. This is compared with ROSAT image[11],[12], which shows substructures over the whole cluster. Cross-shaped feature at the central region is caused by imaging properties of XRT. The subcluster obviously shows lower temperature compared to the central region. The spatially-resolved spectral analysis is now going on, results of which will be published elsewhere.

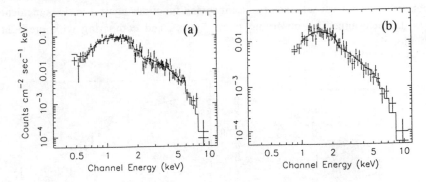

Fig.6 X-ray spectra of A665 observed by SIS(a) and Cl0016+16 by GIS(b)

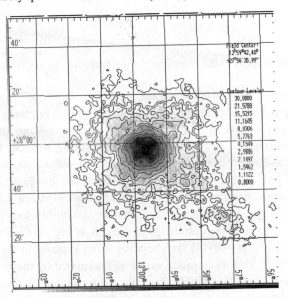

Fig.7 X-ray image of Coma(GIS)

The image of CL0016+16 observed in 0.5-10keV by one chip of SIS is made of 800 counts and shown in Fig.8. There exists an AGN in the north west direction 3 arcmin away from the cluster center, which was also observed by Einstein HRI[13]. This map just demonstrates ASCA imaging capability that such a distant cluster is identified as extended source with the ASCA angular resolution. Radial profile of surface brightness is shown in Fig.9, compared with the model calculations folded with ASCA response function. A solid curve is calculated with Einstein values, though fitting is not yet satisfactory. Point spread functions against various incident angles are determined by observing point sources and comparing with preflight calibration data.

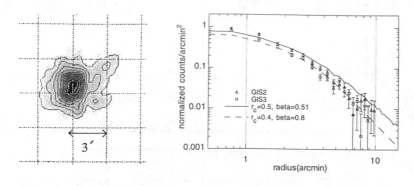

Fig.8 X-ray image of CL0016+16(SIS)   Fig.9 Radial profile of CL0016+16(SIS)

6. Determination of the Hubble constant

The determination of plasma temperatures and surface brightness profile of S-Z effect clusters is essential to derive the Hubble constant. Wang and Stocke have determined temperatures of 12 distant clusters by using Einstein IPC spectra[14]. Combining the S-Z effect in the microwave region[15], plasma temperature obtained by ASCA and the surface brightness profile observed by Einstein[13], we have derived the Hubble constant to be 41(+15/-12) km/s/Mpc for CL0016+16 and 47(+17/-17) km/s/Mpc for A665, which is consistent with previous result[16]. These values are plotted against the cosmological redshift in Fig.10. Optical observations give the value to be 83(+14/-14) km/s/Mpc by using galaxies in the distance up to Coma cluster[17],[18]. This discrepancy would be interpreted by means of introducing a peculiar motion of clusters which affects the decrement of the cosmic microwave background, although there is no observational evidence. Anyway X-ray observations and S-Z effect make it possible to derive the hubble constant in 20 times more distance scale Recently Jones et al.[19] have obtained an image of S-Z effect for several distant clusters by using the radio interferometer(Jones in this proceedings). Combining these results with ASCA observations, we have to confirm the determination method of the Hubble constant.

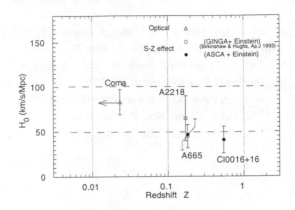

Fig.10 Hubble constant vs. redshift

7. Summary

ASCA is the most powerful instrument to investigate clusters of galaxies with wide energy coverage up to 10keV and superior energy resolution to distinguish emission lines of He-like and H-like ions, though the angular resolution is 3 arcmin(HPD). The calibration of instruments is going on for detailed imaging and spectral analysis. It is expected that further analysis reveals interesting problem concerning cooling flow and merging of clusters, cosmology and so on.

References

1) Mushotzky, R. 1992, NATO ASI Series vol.366 "Clusters and Superclusters of Galaxies", ed. A.C. Fabian, Kluwer, p.91.

2) Jones, C. and Forman, W., 1992, NATO ASI Series vol.366 "Clusters and Superclusters of Galaxies", ed. A.C. Fabian, Kluwer, p.49.

3) Boehringer, H., et al, 1992, NATO ASI Series vol.366 "Clusters and Superclusters of Galaxies", ed. A.C. Fabian, Kluwer, p.71.

4) Briel, U.G., and Henry, P.J., 1993, Astr. Astrophys., 278, 379.

5) David, L.P., Slyz, A., Jones, C., Forman, W., and Vrtilek, S.D., 1993, Astrophys. J., 412, 479.

6) Yamashita, K., 1992, Proc. Yamada Conference XXVIII "Frontiers of X-Ray Astronomy" eds. Y. Tanaka and K. Koyama, p.475.

7) Tanka, Y., et al., 1994, Publ. Astron. Soc. Japan, in press.

8) Serlemitsos, P.J., et al., 1994, Publ. Astron. Soc. Japan, submitted.

9) Ricker, G., et al.,1994 , in preparation.

10) Makishima, K. , et al., 1994, in preparation.

11) Briel, U.G., Henry, J.P. and H. Boehriger, 1992, Astr. Astrophys. 259, L31.

12) White, S.D.M., Briel, U.G., and Henry, J.P., 1993, Mon. Not. R. astr. Soc., 261, L8.

13) White, S.D.M., Silk, J., and Henry, J.P., 1981, Astrophys. J., 251, L65.

14) Wang, Q., and Stocke, J., 1993, Astrophys. J., 408, 71.

15) Birkinshaw, M., Gull, S.F., and Hardebeck, H., 1984, Nature, 365, 34.

16) Birkinshaw, M., Hughes, J.P., and Arnaud, K., 1991, Astrophys. J., 395, 466.

17) Jacoby, G.H. et al., 1992, Publ. Astron. Soc. Pacific, 104, 599.

18) van den Bergh, 1992, Publ. Astron. Soc. Pacific, 104, 861.

19) Jones, M., et al., 1993, Nature, 365, 320.

TEMPERATURE STRUCTURE AND HEAVY ELEMENT DISTRIBUTION IN THE X-RAY EMITTING ICM

Y. Ikebe, Y. Fukazawa, K. Makishima, T. Tamura, H. Ezawa
Depertment of Physics University of Tokyo, Bunkyo-ku, Tokyo 113, JAPAN

H. Honda, T. Murakami
Institute of Space and Astronautical Science, Sagamihara, Kanagawa 229, JAPAN

T. Ohashi
Department of Physics, Tokyo Metropolitan University, Hachioji, Tokyo, 192-03, JAPAN

R.F. Mushotzky
Laboratory for High Energy Astrophysics, NASA/GSFC, Greenbelt, MD 20771, USA

K. Yamashita
Department of Physics, Nagoya University, Chikusa-ku, Nakoya 464-01, JAPAN

and A.C. Fabian
Institute of Astronomy, University of Cambridge, Madingley Road, Cambridge, CB3 0HA, UK

Abstract

We report some first (preliminary) results on clusters of galaxies from observations with the **ASCA** satellite, Japan-US collaborating X-ray astronomical satellite launched on 1993 February 20.

1 Introduction

ASCA[15], which carries X-Ray Telescopes(XRT) and focal plane detectors GIS and SIS, enables spatially-resolved X-ray energy spectra to be obtained with good energy resolution. We can thus measure the temperature structure and the distribution of heavy elements in the ICM (intracluster medium) with a much improved accuracy than before.

The SIS sensor has a rectanguler FOV of 22 arcmin by 22 arcmin, while the GIS sensor has a round FOV of 52 arcmin diameter. Due to the decrease in the effective area of the XRT and the GIS performance towards the edge of FOV (for example, the gain dropping towards the outside), however, the practical area has roughly a 40 arcmin diameter. Thus we can observe up to 1Mpc from the center of the clusters which have redshift more than ~0.03 with just one pointing.

2 Centaurus cluster

The Centaurus (A3526) cluster of galaxies is an X-ray bright nearby cluster, at a distance of 64 Mpc (z=0.0107 and $H_0 = 50$ km s^{-1} Mpc^{-1}). The spectrum obtained with the HEAO-1 A-2 can be expressed with a two temperature model[10], at 2.3keV and 7-9keV. Ginga observations[17] gave a complex spectrum that is not well described by a single temperature model. Imaging observations from Einstein and ROSAT show the existence of cooling flow, with the cooling radius of 100 - 150 kpc and mass deposition rate of 20 - 90 $M_\odot$yr^{-1} [1),3),9)].

ASCA observation and results

X-ray emission from the Centaurus cluster covers the full field of view of the GIS. In the spectra obtained both by the SIS and the GIS, we can clearly see emission lines from highly ionized ions, including K-lines from O, Si, S, Ar, Ca and Fe, and Fe-L line complex. The data have been divided into several annular regions according to the angular distance R from the cluster center. Background was subtracted from pulse height spectrum in each region, using observations of blank sky (i.e. no bright sources), which contains both non-X-ray background and cosmic diffuse X-ray background.

Figure 1 summarizes the results from model fitting for the GIS pulse height spectrum from each annular region. The energy spectra of the regions beyond 8 arcmin radius can be well expressed with a single temperature thin thermal plasma emission model due to Raymond and Smith [12] (RS-model) with galactic absorption. We have fixed the abundance ratios between the elements to be at the solar ratios. The temperature is 3-4 keV and the heavy element abundance is 0.3-0.4 times solar. The energy spectra taken from the regions within 8 arcmin radius cannot be fitted with a single RS-model. We applied a two temperature RS-model for the inner-region spectra (the abundances of the two components are assumed to be the same), and obtained good chi-square values. Figure 1-c shows the fluxes of the hot component obtained from each spectrum and the relative amount of the emission measure of the cool compoment against that of the hot component.

Discussion

As we can see in Figure 1-a and 1-c, the cool component which has the temperature of 1 keV appears inside of 8' and the fraction of the emission measure of cool component increases towards the center. The standard inhomogeneous cooling flow model might be able to express the measured temperature structure. There might be cooled gas clumps distributing within the core which is filled with the hot gas having the temperature of ~4 keV.

As shown in Figure 1-b, the heavy element abundance profile shows a dramatic increase towards

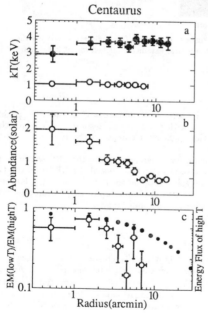
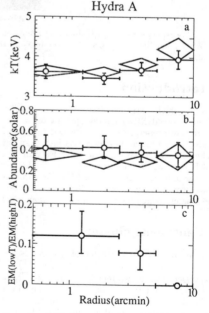

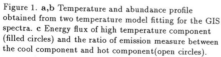

Figure 1. a,b Temperature and abundance profile obtained from two temperature model fitting for the GIS spectra. c Energy flux of high temperature component (filled circles) and the ratio of emission measure between the cool component and hot component(open circles).

Figure 2. a,b Temperature and abundance profile obtained from single RS-model fitting. Open circles show the GIS results and diamonds show the SIS results. c The ratio between the emission measure of cool component and that of hot component whose temperature is 4.0 keV.

the center. Since the overall abundance is predominantly determined by the iron K-line for which the cool component contribute little, the inferred abundance gradient cannot be an artifact caused by the two temperature structure. This central concentration of heavy elements is a new finding from ASCA, not predicted by the standard cooling flow model.

Further discussion is found in Fukazawa et.al.1994 [6].

3 Hydra A cluster

The Hydra A cluster(z=0.0522) is classified as a poor cluster, with a central radio source. Its X-ray luminosity measured with Einstein is 4.1×10^{44} ergs s^{-1} (0.5-4.5keV)[4] and Ginga gave the luminosity value of 4.8×10^{44} ergs s^{-1} [16] in the same energy band, which are the largest values among the poor clusters. The X-ray surface brightness profile obtained with the IPC on board the Einstein satellite has a large central concentration deviating from an isothermal β-model, which suggests the existence of cooling flow having one of the largest mass deposition rate at 600 ± 120 $M_{\odot}$yr^{-1} [4].

ASCA Observation and Results

We divided the data into 4 annular regions with different radii and obtained the background-subtructed energy spectra from each region. We performed model fitting for each spectrum. Each spectrum can be expressed by single RS-model with low energy absorption due to Galactic column density. The relative abundance ratios between each elements are fixed to the solar ratio. Figure 2-a,b shows the radial profile of the temperature and the heavy element abundance obtained from spectral fitting. There is some evidence of temperature gradient, with ths gas being cooler towards the center. The abundance distribution has no clear trend.

We also performed the spectral fitting for the spectrum taken from the region within 5.0 arcmin radius. Due to some problem with the responce matrices of the SIS, we only show here the results from the GIS. A single temperature RS-model with galactic absorption cannot explain the spectrum well. The best-fit χ^2 value is 107.3 for 43 degrees of freedom. Consequently we added another temperature to express the spectrum. This two temperature model gives an acceptable fit, $\chi^2 = 39.42$ for 41 degrees of freedom. The two temperatures obtained are $1.09^{+0.21}_{-0.13}$ keV and $4.25^{+0.52}_{-0.33}$ keV. The temperature measured with Ginga is $3.8^{+0.21}_{-0.18}$ keV[16] which is intermediate between the two temperature showm above. Although the individual spectra taken from the four regions do not require two temperatures, we applied a two temperature model to the spectra taken from the regions of $R=0-2.'5$ and $R=2.'5-5'$. By fixing the hotter temperature to 4.0keV(the same value as the temperature at $R=5'-10'$), we obtained the ratio of the emission measure between the cool component and the hot component (Figure 2-c).

We also used a varialble abundance RS-model, in which the abundances of each elements are free parameters. This gives a fair fit($\chi^2 = 24.41$, $\nu=37$), but abundances of Ne and Mg become extreamly high ($5.3^{+2.6}_{-1.8}$ and $2.0^{+1.8}_{-1.2}$ solar respectively). This means it is not realistic to consider the energy spectrum to be of single temperature.

Discussion

While the Einstein observation suggested the existence of cooling flow from the X-ray surface brightness profile, ASCA has finally distinguished the cool component with X-ray spectroscopy. The fact that the spectrum taken from the region within 5 arcmin is not explained with a single temperature but expressed well with two temperature model of 1.09keV and 4.25keV is direct evidence of existence of a cool component and shows that the ICM in the Hydra A cluster cannot be isothermal. The luminosity of cool component having the temperature of 1.09keV is 7.0×10^{43} ergs s^{-1} (0.5-4.5keV). This value is very close to 5.5×10^{43} ergs s^{-1} which is the luminosity of central excess emission above the isothermal β profile observed with Einstein IPC[4].

In contrast with the Centaurus cluster (Figure 1-b), the heavy element abundance does not have any clear trend (Figure 2-b). It may change at most by a factor of two from the outside to the center.

4   Short comments for some other clusters

Perseus cluster

The Perseus cluster is the brightest extragalactic X-ray source and has been observed in various X-ray astronomy missions. Recent remarkable advance shown by Rosat observation [13] is that the temperature gradient downword towards the center was clearly detected. Spacelab 2 mission[5],[11] and SPARTAN 1 mission [8] found a strong Fe abundance gradient, but BBXRT mission[2] did not confirm that.

The projected temperatures obtained from the ASCA observations within about 15′ from the cluster center is not constant, which change from ∼4keV to ∼8keV. The central region within ∼3′ radius is characterized by a significantly low temperature of ∼4keV. The iron abundances within 10′ from the center is almost constant which is 0.4 solar in average. Including the data points beyond 10′ from the center the iron abundances implys some scattering with the position and distributed from 0.3 to 0.6 (±0.2 as a typical 90% error) solar with no systematic concentration towards the cluster center. R.Mushotzky reported in this conference that the distribution of the equivalent width of Fe-K emission line is not uniform over a wide angular scale (K.Arnaud private communication).

A1060, AWM7, and MKW3s

A1060 is at distance of $z=0.0114$ and has the cD galaxy. The energy spectrum obtained with the HEAO A2 has two different temperature of 2.3 keV and 7-9keV[10]. The mass deposition rate has been estimated to be 6 $M_\odot yr^{-1}$ with the EXOSAT LE observation[14]. The ASCA observations do not detect significant temperature gradient nor abundance gradient, and the data are consistent with $kT \sim 3.2$ keV and abundance ~ 0.4 solar within 16′ from the center. In the ASCA spectrum, we did not find any additional component which has higher temperature. The hotter component indicated by the HEAO A2 observation may come from an contaminating source happened to be in the FOV of the HEAO A2 instrument.

AWM7($z=0.0179$) and MKW3s($z=0.0434$) are poor clusters having cD galaxies and probably suitable for investigation of the role of cDs in clusters. ASCA observation of AWM7 indicate that the central region within $\sim 2'$ radius has the temperature of 3.5keV and the iron abundance of 0.6-0.7 solar, while surrounding region has higher temperature of ∼4keV and lower iron abundaces of 0.4-0.5 solar. This concentration of metal is the third significant detection with ASCA after Centaurus and Virgo clusters.

MKW3s is 2.6 times more distant than AWM7, and the data do not show significant variation in the temperature or abundance. Measured temperature and abundance within 2′ are 3.6 ± 0.2 keV and 0.3 ± 0.1 solar and consistent to be constant within 10′ radius.

These features suggest that the key parameter for the metal concentration in clusters is not very simple. The 3 clusters where the concentration is observed all accomodate cD galaxies, but several other cD clusters show uniform abundance. Presence of a strong cooling flow may be related but the simple mass deposition rate is not simply correlating with the degree of metal concentration. Since the inhomogeneity in the abundance has important implication about the origin of hot intergalactic medium, we need to increase the number of ASCA sample of clusters.

References

[1] Allen,S.W and Fabian,A.C. 1994 MNRAS,in press
[2] Arnaud,K.A. etlal. 1991, FRONTIERS OF X-RAY ASTRONOMY, ed. Y.Tanaka and K.Koyama, p.481
[3] Canizares,C.R. et.al. 1987 in Cooling Flows in Clusters and Galaxies, ed. A.C. Fabian,p.63.
[4] David,L.P., Arnaud,K., Forman,W. and Jones,C. 1990 *Ap.J.* **356**,32.
[5] Eyles,C.J. et.al. 1991, *Ap.J.* **376**,23.
[6] Fukazawa,Y. et.al 1994, PASJ in press.
[7] Katilsky,T. et.al. 1985, *Ap.J.* **291**,621.
[8] Kowalsky,M.P. et.al. 1993, *Ap.J.* **412**,489.
[9] Matilsky,T., Jones,C. and Forman,W. 1985 *Ap.J.* **291**,621.
[10] Mitchell,R., Mushotzky, R.F. 1980 *Ap.J.* **236**,730.
[11] Ponman,T.J. et.al. 1990, Nature **347**,450.
[12] Raymond,J.C., and Smith,B.W. 1977 *Ap.L.Suppl* **35**,419.
[13] Schwarz,R.A. et.al. 1992, A&A, **256**, L11.
[14] Singh,K.P. et.al. *Ap.J.* **330**,620.
[15] Tanaka,Y. et.al., 1994 PASJ in press
[16] Tsuru,T. 1991 Doctral Thesis, University of Tokyo
[17] Yamanaka,M. 1994 Master thesis(in Japanese)

X-RAY SPECTRA OF CLUSTERS OF GALAXIES

Richard MUSHOTZKY
Laboratory for High Energy Astrophysics
Goddard Space Flight Center
Greenbelt MD USA 20771

ABSTRACT

We present ASCA spatially resolved spectra for several clusters. These data allow determination for the first time of the detailed mass profiles, abundance profiles and the ratio of elemental abundances. Preliminary analysis indicates that, with the exception of the cool central regions, these clusters are isothermal to within 15% out to ~ 1 Mpc. These data make possible model independent mass profiles out to ~ 1 Mpc for a reasonable number of clusters. It is also clear that while some low luminosity clusters show a clear Fe abundance gradient, many do not. In addition the best fit abundance ratios show overabundances, relative to Fe, of the α-burning products very similar to that seen in metal poor halo stars in our galaxy. This indicates that type II SN were the dominant contributors to the enrichment of the IGM. The ASCA spectra allow measurement of the redshifts of the clusters and show that the cluster gas and the optical galaxies lie at the same velocities. A temperature and abundance map of the Perseus cluster shows non-azimuthally symmetric effects which can complicate simple determinations of the mass profile.

1. Introduction

The x-ray emission from clusters of galaxies is due, primarily, to thermal bremsstrahlung from a hot, optically thin, gas enriched with heavy elements and contained in the cluster potential well (see Sarazin[1] for a comprehensive review). Spatially resolved x-ray spectroscopy, made possible for the first time for a large sample of objects by the ASCA satellite, gives directly the density law, $\rho(r)$, the temperature profile, $T(r)$, and the distribution and abundance of the heavy elements (O, Ne, Mg, Si, S, Ca, Ar, Fe). One must stress that the x-ray emission in the cluster is a dominant process. Most of the visible baryons[2,3] are in the hot gas with typical values inside 1-3 Mpc being $M_{gas}/M_{stars} \sim 2\text{-}10$ and $M_{gas}/M_{total} \sim 0.1\text{-}0.2$.

X-ray spectra of optically thin plasmas can be roughly divided into two regimes: $T < 2\times10^7$ degrees where line cooling dominates and $T > 2\times10^7$ where bremsstrahlung cooling dominates. Thus the emission from "low" kT plasmas is dominated by lines while hotter plasmas are dominated by the continuum. Because one expects variation in the temperature of the cluster IGM with position, the lines produced in the gas can have strongly variable equivalent widths. It is thus necessary to have both sufficient spectral resolution to measure the individual lines strengths and sufficient spatial resolution to isolate regions of different temperatures. ASCA is the first satellite to have these capabilities.

We shall only consider a subset of the topics for which spatially resolved x-ray spectroscopy is necessary. Topics include:

1) Determination of the Hubble constant by
   a) measuring the temperature profile of Sunyaev-Zeldovich clusters
   b) measuring the temperature profile of "arc" clusters
2) Measuring the dark matter distribution in clusters of galaxies
3) Determining the distribution and origin of the heavy elements in clusters of
   galaxies by
   a) determining the "O"/Fe ratio
   b) measuring the distribution of Fe
   c) measuring the variation of Fe with z and cluster type
4) The physics of cooling flows
   a) measure the temperature as a function of radius
   b) determine the cooling rate directly from the x-ray data
   c) measure the amount of cold matter formed by cooling flows
5) Measurement of the evolution of cluster properties (temperature, abundance, scale
   length etc.) with z to constrain theories of the origin and evolution of structure
6) Understanding the origin and nature of the IGM in poor clusters of galaxies

7) Constraining the nature of cluster mergers from measurements of the redshift of the gas compared to the galaxies and determination of non-radially symmetric structure in the temperature distribution

8) A search for concentrated mass profiles in the centers of clusters by examination of the temperature sensitive He to H-like Fe line ratios.

In this talk I will concentrate on items #2 and #3 and briefly mention #7 and #8. The other areas have been covered[4-10]. I would also like to stress that only a fraction of the ASCA PV data have been analyzed in detail and that the results presented here are a mere fraction of what will be available relatively shortly. Also while the ASCA calibration is not yet final I expect that the results presented here are relatively robust against the expected small changes.

2. General Cluster Properties

It has been shown in detail[11] that if the ICM is in hydrostatic equilibrium and the external pressure is negligible the total mass of the cluster can be expressed as

$$M(<r) = \frac{kT_g(r)}{Gmm_H}\left[\frac{d\log\rho}{d\log r} + \frac{d\log T}{d\log r}\right] \cdot r \tag{1}$$

where T(r) is the gas temperature and r the gas density. Small deviations from hydrostatic equilibrium might be expected in clusters due to mergers but detailed numerical simulations show that the effect on the cluster mass derived is not strong[12].

Thus one needs to determine the temperature and density at some fiducial radius and their distribution with radius. The determination of the mass using this method does not require assumptions about the form of the potential or a particular scale length and is numerically stable. Inspection of the Rosat data shows that the x-ray gas profile frequently extends to ~ 3 Mpc. This method can be used to determine the mass profile out to radii where the assumption of collisional equilibrium no longer applies. The ASCA GIS surface brightness parameters, fitted to the functional form

$$S(R) = S(0)\left[1 + \left(\frac{R}{a}\right)^2\right]^{-3\beta_{fit} + \frac{1}{2}} \tag{2}$$

(where a is a "core" radius) are in good agreement with those obtained by Einstein and Rosat data (Table 1). The GIS to Rosat ratio is temperature sensitive, due to the different responses of Rosat (E < 2 keV) and the ASCA GIS (Eavg >> 2 keV) indicating that the clusters are roughly isothermal inside the field of view of the GIS (~14', 1.2 Mpc at z ~ 0.05).

Table 1
Surface Brightness Parameters for ASCA Clusters

NAME	R(core)Mpc ASCA	R(core)Mpc Rosat/EO	b ASCA	b Rosat/EO
A 1795§	0.38(±0.02)	0.3±0.1**	0.81±0.01	0.72±0.07**
		0.44±0.02		0.80±0.02
WP 23	0.035±0.003	0.028±0.01*	0.54±0.03	0.54±0.02*
A 2256‡	0.48±0.063	0.45±0.02**	0.62±0.03	0.72±0.04**
		0.42±0.02***		0.75±0.03 ***
A 2199	0.197±0.006	0.14+/-0.02**	0.73±0.02	0.68±0.05**
A 2319†	~0.46	0.41±0.05**	~0.65	~0.65†
A 496§	0.183±0.008	0.133±0.011	0.60±0.03	0.57±0.023

§ A 496, A 1795 Rosat fit requires a central excess - without including this explicitly,
  structural parameters change - R(core) gets much smaller
† A 2319 - very large size, (R(core) ~ 5.5') makes ASCA estimates uncertain, also an
  apparent typographical error in the Jones & Forman[13] paper for the value of β
* Rosat value from David et al.[14]
** Einstein value from Jones & Forman[13]
*** Rosat value from Briel et al.[15]
‡ A 2256 does show a spatially dependent temperature [16]which may explain
  the different β value

The ASCA spectral resolution (Figure 1) also allows detailed measurement of
the redshift which is in good agreement with the optical data (Table 2). This indicates
that, at least for these systems, the galaxies are indeed moving about the center of mass
of the system and that recent mergers have not strongly effected the position of the
center of mass in velocity space.

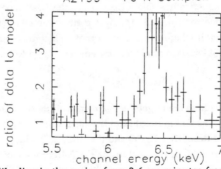

Figure 1. The Fe He-like line in the region from 3-6 arc minutes from the center of Abell 2199.
Notice that the energy of the Fe He-like line, whose rest energy is at 6.67 keV is at 6.45 keV
indicating a redshift of 0.03. The model used was a featureless bremsstrahlung.

Table 2
ASCA Redshifts for Selected Clusters

Cluster	z(optical)	z(ASCA)†	Velocity Difference km/sec (eV)	Maximum velocity offset (km/sec)
A 2199*	0.0305	0.0324(± 0.002)	570 (12.7)	1170
A 1795	0.063	0.0630(± 0.006)	0 (0)	1800
MKW3s	0.0450	0.052(± 0.003)	210 (47)	3390
A 496	0.0329	0.0326(± 0.0027)	90 (13)	720
A 426	0.0182	0.0190(± 0.0025)	240 (5.4)	1140

* cD galaxy at z = 0.03158, all others have cD galaxy within δz of cluster
† ASCA systematic error is δE ~ 15 eV, which corresponds to δz ~ 0.0022. Quoted errors are 90% confidence statistical errors only.

3. Mass Determination

Direct spectral fitting for several clusters (cf. Figure 2) shows that (with the exception of the central regions in some "cooling flow" clusters) the temperatures are isothermal to +/- 15% out to ~ 1 Mpc. Because most massive clusters are relatively hot (kT >> 2 keV) the derivation of temperature profiles from the Rosat data[17] has been relatively uncertain. However comparison (Figure 3) of the most precise Rosat temperature profile of a hot cluster (that of the 53 ksec observation of A 1795[18]) with 1/4 of the ASCA data (e.g. GIS 2 only) shows not only the small relative uncertainties of the ASCA data but relatively good agreement between Rosat and ASCA. For lower temperature clusters the Rosat data are quite good and very good agreement is found in the temperature profiles for WP 23. However, we find that the Rosat abundance estimates disagree with the ASCA values[14,19,20] and that use of χ^2+1 errors are not sufficient (Figure 4). At present, systematic calibration uncertainties do not allow determination of ASCA temperatures beyond radii of ~14'.

It is also noteworthy that the Ginga and ASCA temperatures are in very good agreement. The Ginga data average over a large beam while the ASCA data are derived only within a 14' radius indicating that the emission weighted temperature does not show a large gradient[21]. However ASCA observations of high z clusters[6] shows that at R > 1.5 Mpc there may be a significant temperature gradient for at least 2 clusters, as seen previously in the Exosat and Ginga data for Coma[22].

A systematic problem is that the temperatures for kT < 2 keV systems derived from the Mewe-Kaastra (MEKA) code differ from that of the Raymond-Smith (R-S) code. For example for WP 23 at 85 kpc the R-S code gives kT = 1.06±0.03 keV while the MEKA code gives 0.88±0.04. This is because each code treats the physics of the Fe L lines differently and in the χ^2 minimization most of the weight is assigned (in the ASCA fits) to the flux weighted centroid of the main Fe L lines which is a very strong function of temperature. The ASCA bandpass allows a fit at E >> 1 keV where the lines are much weaker and the physics is better, but the signal to noise is worse. For WP 23 a bremsstrahlung + lines gives kT ~ 1.030±0.15 keV in good agreement with the R-S plasma model.

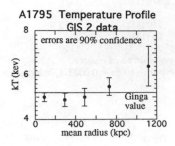 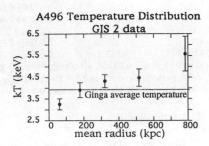

Figure 2. Temperature distribution for two clusters from GIS 2 data only . All errors are 90% confidence for one interesting parameter. The radius is in kpc with H_0 = 50 km/sec/Mpc.

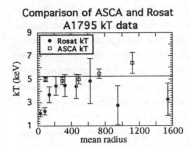 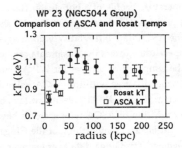

Figure 3. Comparison of the Rosat and ASCA spatially resolved temperatures for A 1795 and WP 23. For A 1795 the ASCA central point is the high temperature in a two component fit. The radius is in kpc with H_0 = 50 km/sec/Mpc. For A 1795 both the ASCA and Rosat errors are 90% confidence. For WP 23 the Rosat data[14] have been assigned 5% errors while the ASCA errors are 90% confidence.

The precise ASCA temperatures allow a direct measurement of the mass out to radii of ~1Mpc. If the gas is isothermal the mass can be approximated quite accurately at R >> a by

$$M(<r) \sim 10.8 \times 10^{14} \, (\beta_{fit}) T_{10keV} \, (R_{Mpc}) M_\odot \qquad (3)$$

while an estimate of the mass from optical velocity dispersions, assuming that the velocity dispersion is constant with radius, that mass follows light and that the galaxy

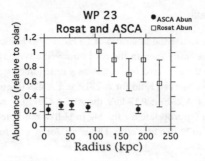

Figure 4. comparison of ASCA and Rosat abundance profiles for WP 23. Similar results are seen in other systems with kT ~ 1 keV such as NGC 4472. (ASCA errors are 90% while Rosat errors are χ^2+1[14].) The origin of this difference is unknown.

distribution is a King profile, is

$$M = 7.0 \times 10^{14} \sigma_{1000}^2 R_{Mpc} \, M_\odot \quad . \tag{4}$$

These values are not always in detailed agreement. However, for the data presented here the deviations are rather small (± ~ 30%) and consistent with the (rather small) uncertainties in the velocity dispersions and the mass model. For example for A 1795 with σ = 920(+73,-59) km/sec and T = 5.3+/-0.1 keV the estimators at 1 Mpc give masses of 5.9(+1.55,-1.14) x 10^14 M⊙ for the optical estimator and 4.6(+/-0.2) x 10^14 M⊙ for the x-ray estimator. For A 496 with σ = 714 km/sec, kT = 3.9+/-0.1 the x-ray and optical masses are 2.5 and 4.4 x 10^14 M⊙ while for A 2199 with σ = 794 and kT = 4.2+/-0.1 they are 3.3 and 3.6x 10^14 M⊙.

Thus for 2/3 of these systems the "x-ray mass" is ~ 30% less than the estimate from optical data. (The optical velocity dispersion are derived from the very precise recent determination by Oegerle & Hill[23]). Even with the new very precise data the well known "β problem" is still with us[24]. For A 1795, A 496 and A 2199, β_{spec} = 0.958, 0.78, 0.90 while β_{fit} = 0.81, 0.60, 0.73 respectively. The ASCA determination of the temperature distribution also lends weight to the large values of the mass in gas compared to the total mass found in many clusters[14]. If, as seems to be the case for several clusters, the temperature is decreasing beyond 1 Mpc the ratio of gas mass to total mass will rise beyond the isothermal limits.

Further analysis of the ASCA PV observations, using all four detectors and with final calibrations will be able to trace the temperature distribution out to R ~ 20' (2 Mpc at z = 0.06) and AO observations should be able to derive the mass profile out to the limits of the assumption of hydrostatic equilibrium.

4. He-like Fe K Line Ratio

We are also able to use the line ratio of Fe He-like to H-like lines to search for hot gas that may not be easily seen in the continuum fits. We have used the Mewe and Kaastra code to derive the expected line ratios as a function of temperature and have plotted this against the observed ratio for A 2319 and A 496 (Figure 5). While the Ginga average temperature for A 2319 is 9.17 keV the ASCA GIS fit temperature for the central 2' radius region (appropriate for the He to H-like ratio plot) is 10.66±1 keV, consistent with the He to H-like line ratio. However, for A 496 there appears to be a discrepancy

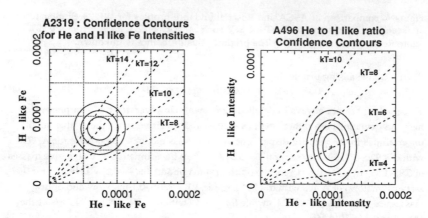

Figure 5. He-like and H-like Fe line fluxes for A2319 and A 496. Lines of constant temperature are indicated. The 3 outer contours correspond to 68, 90 and 99% confidence.

between the line ratios and the continuum temperature, with the line ratio indicating a higher temperature. This point is relevant to models of gravitational lenses[25,26] which show that if the measured ASCA central temperatures are correct and the observed x-ray surface brightness profiles are a measure of the shape of the potential, then there is a fundamental disagreement in the inferred potential from the x-ray and gravitational lens data. The "easiest" way out of the problem[6] is if there exists a deeper potential with much smaller scale length which is not well sampled by the low energy Rosat image and which has a relatively small amount of gas in it. In this case the temperature, as determined by the continuum form, would be lower than that shown by the He to H-like Fe line ratio because of the great sensitivity of this ratio to small amounts of high temperature gas. We anticipate that this method will be able to strongly constrain the high temperature range of the gas temperature distribution. Also cooling flow models predict that the gas should be multiphase[27] and thus there may exist a wide range of temperatures at a given radius.

5. Abundance distribution

There have been several recent papers on the distribution of Fe in the Perseus[28,29] and Virgo clusters[30]. Recently it has been shown that the Centaurus cluster shows a rather strong Fe abundance gradient within the central 100 kpc[31]. We have examined the possibility of an abundance gradient in A 496, A 1795 and A 2199 (see also Ohashi[8] for A 1060). For these 4 clusters there is no evidence of a gradient in Fe within the central 1 Mpc (Figures 4,6).

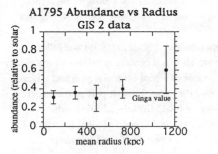
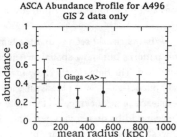

Figure 6. Abundance vs radius for A 1795 and A 496 derived from fits to GIS 2 data only. All errors are 90% confidence. The Ginga abundance values are from Yamashita[32]. When both Ginga and ASCA data exist, the abundance determinations are in very good agreement with each other when provision is made for the existence of spatial variation in the Fe abundance[31].

The discovery that at least some low luminosity clusters show an abundance gradient while such a gradient appears to be weak or absent in other clusters indicates that we are seeing a variety of phenomena. This property may be related to the "age" of these systems, the degree of merging or the relative effect of ram pressure striping versus initial winds in elliptical galaxies. If most of the material is injected over long periods of time (as might be expected in a ram pressure stripping hypothesis) then one expects a concentration of metals towards the center of the cluster[32]. On the other hand if the gas is ejected rather early in the cluster life or mergers cause the gas to become well mixed, then the central concentration should be small. The fact that we see both types of behavior indicates that we should be looking for other correlations: e.g. do clusters with strong central Fe concentrations have other properties that are strongly related? For example the Virgo and Centaurus clusters have a very high fraction of spiral galaxies and low central galaxy density (but so does A1060). However, based on optical data Virgo and Centaurus are *in the process* of merging (for Virgo we have the M 86 and M 49 concentrations of galaxies and for Cen the Cen I and II sub-clusters[34] while A 1060 could be a post-merger system. These data may suggest that clusters which have undergone strong mergers have had the gas "homogenized" while other, more isolated systems, which have not yet undergone a strong merger may show abundance gradients.

6. The Perseus Cluster (Abell 426)

The Perseus cluster is the brightest and one of the largest clusters and thus is an excellent candidate for detailed study by ASCA. With 3 ASCA GIS pointings[35] we have been able to derive temperatures and abundances in 4 x 4' bins in the central regions and 8 x 8' bins further out, covering a total solid angle of ~ 48 x 64' (Figures 7,8).

What is clearly seen is that the temperature and abundance do not follow simple patterns but show spatial structure which is not obviously related to the galaxy density field. The data clearly show the existence of a cool central region and a large "patch" of cool gas ~ 30' to the west. However the most unusual part of the structure is the existence of a "hot ridge" ~ 15' to the west of NGC 1275. In addition, while the equivalent widths do not vary not strongly across the full field of view (except to the southwest), the abundances vary by a factor of two because of the variance in the temperature.

7.6	7.7	10.6	13.6	11.4	6.6	4.6	2.7
8.1	6.8	6.3	8.6	9.9	9.2	7.5	4.7
7.6	6.5	(4.5)	6.6	8.3	9.4	5.8	4.7
7.5	8.5	6.9	8.6	8.7	9.7	5.5	5.0
X	6.7	8.3	12	8.4	6.7	4.8	2.3

48' (at left)

64 arc minutes

Figure 7. Temperature map of the central 48 x 64 arc minutes of the Perseus Cluster[35]. The circle marks the position of NGC 1275. Each box is 8 x 8' ; north is to the top and East to the left. The values are the temperatures in keV. The exact values are preliminary.

The physical origin of such a variation is unclear . There is no obvious x-ray or optical substructure[36] that is simply related to the temperature or abundance variations. Some of the simulations by[37] of a cluster merger show similar temperature variations if we assume that the merging component came from the east.

Clearly further work is necessary. The presence of large amplitude variations in the temperature in Perseus, the best observed cluster to date, may indicate that the simple azimuthally symmetric analysis done so far (sec 3,5) may have to be revisited.

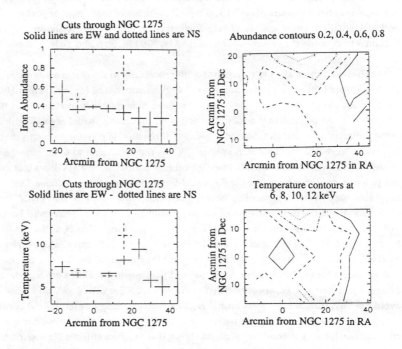

Figure 8. Temperature and abundance contours and slices of the Perseus cluster. Solid line is lowest contour and dashed, dashed-dotted and the dotted values are given in the figure. All values are preliminary.

7. Elemental Abundances

A. Data

The origin of the heavy elements in clusters is the subject of intensive investigation at the moment[38,39] and has fundamental implications for the history of star formation in galaxies, the epoch of cluster formation, the evolution of clusters and the rate of type I and type II supernovae. In brief, if most of the elements are formed early on, during the postulated initial burst of star formation in elliptical galaxies, one expects an abundance ratio most consistent with the type II supernova that would dominate the initial burst. Alternatively if much of the metals in the IGM are due to the continual process of stellar evolution and the removal of this gas from galaxies, one expects either a mixture of type I and type II abundances (e.g. solar) or perhaps a Fe enriched situation which would indicate dominance by type Is. ASCA allows us for the first time to examine the relative abundances of O, Ne, Mg, Si, S and Fe in a large sample of objects.

However, there are a few problems with proceeding to the direct analysis. First of all because of the strong dependence on EW with temperature for the He and H-like lines, which are the dominant lines, one must have rather small uncertainties in the temperature and be relatively certain that one is not including spatial regions with rather different temperatures. Secondly because of the atomic physics problems that have been "revealed" by the ASCA spectra[9,10] it is rather difficult to determine the Mg abundance because the He-like Mg lines are confused with the Fe XXIV lines that are not properly predicted by either the Raymond-Smith or Mewe-Kaastra codes. One must also "stay clear" of the cooling flow regions where the effects of the "extra" absorption make the determination of the oxygen abundances very uncertain. Finally one must pick clusters which are at the "correct" temperatures. That is, if the temperature is too low one is dominated by the Fe L lines which carry most of the cooling at $T < 2 \times 10^7$ degrees and if one is too hot the fraction of the O, Ne etc. ions that are in the He or H-like state is very low and the equivalent widths are too low to measure. In practice, then, we are limited to clusters with $2 < kT < 6$ keV and must avoid the high surface brightness central regions where cooling can (and does) occur.

With the ASCA PV sample we have attempted to derive abundances for 6 clusters (see Table 3). Preliminary analysis shows that for most clusters Ne ~ solar, Si ~ 1/2 solar and Fe is ~ 1/3 solar (using 4×10^{-5} for the Fe solar value rather than the 3.2×10^{-5} in use with Ginga/Heao-1 analysis). The WP 23 ratios and values are similar to those of some elliptical galaxies observed with ASCA[19]. WP 23 shows evidence of x-ray absorption out to radii of 120 kpc, similar to that seen in the Centaurus cluster[31].

For Type II supernova integrated over a "standard mass function" Thielemann et al.[40] "predict" that (normalized to solar values) O/Fe ~ 4.5, Ne/Fe ~ 5, Si/Fe ~ 2.5, S/Fe ~ 1-1.6. However these values[41] are somewhat sensitive to the exact nuclear physics used and the details of stellar evolution. These values are very close to the those seen in A 496, MKW3s and (perhaps) A 1795 and A 2199.

However Perseus clearly has a smaller Si/Fe ratio (due to enhanced Fe). Type II SN have a very different set of abundance ratios (O/Fe ~ 10^{-3}, Si/Fe ~ 0.3, S/Fe ~ 0.2) :

small admixtures of type I SN can increase the Fe abundance and lower the O, Si and S/Fe ratio. Stellar mass loss (e.g. red giant winds and planetary nebulae) can also

Table 3
Preliminary ASCA Abundances for Clusters†

Name	O	Ne	Si	S	Fe
MKW3s	1.27±0.45	1.13±0.3	0.45±.20		0.24±.06
A 496	0.52±0.2	1.33±0.20	0.49±0.16	0.22±0.13	0.32±0.02
A 1795	0.87±0.45	0.92±.045	0.93±0.35	<0.25	0.27±0.05
A 2199	0.66±0.50	1.04±0.4	0.77±0.2	~0.25	0.32±0.04
A 426	---	0.77±0.3	0.54±0.15	<0.3	0.37±0.03
WP 23*	---	---	0.16±0.06	0.18±0.11	0.26±0.03

notes:† All abundances are linear and relative to solar values. The 90% confidence errors are statistical only and have been symmetrized. Oxygen abundances for A 426 and WP 23 are not quoted due to the effects of x-ray absorption in these objects. Preliminary analysis of A 1060 shows similar patterns with Ne and Si having a larger abundance than Fe. *WP 23 has kT ~ 1 keV and so the result is sensitive to Fe L line.

change the abundance ratios away from "pure" type II abundances. While we are still not certain, we feel that type II supernova are probably responsible for most of the heavy element production in the IGM of clusters. However, given the uncertainties in the nuclear physics the good agreement may be fortuitous. A similar pattern of abundance ratios is seen in low metallicity halo stars[42]. At the same Fe/H abundance of 0.3 the observed ratio of O and a burning products to Fe is ~ 2.5:1, very similar to the average of (Ne+Si)/Fe ~ 2.7 seen in the cluster gas.

B. Theory

Recently a detailed summary of the theory of elemental abundances in clusters has been given by Arnaud[38]. "Type II" abundance ratios for some clusters are in "agreement" with theoretical calculations[39,43] of the origin of the metals from an early wind phase of ellipticals. We can summarize Arnaud's predictions as follows : If other sources of metals are important they can be due to :

1) ram pressure stripping - Metals would tend to be more centrally concentrated than the ASCA data show for rich clusters (see sec 5). However some nearby low luminosity clusters clearly show a gradient in the central 100 kpc.

2) winds from low mass galaxies enriched by type I SN - There would tend to be a higher Fe abundance and lower O, Si abundances than is observed in most systems. In addition the ASCA spectra of elliptical galaxies in Virgo[19] show a relatively low Fe abundance and solar abundance ratios. One also predicts[44] that low mass systems with flat density gradients due to injection of energy should be more metal rich.

A preliminary set of conclusions from the ASCA data analyzed so far is that
1) The lack of abundance gradients in massive clusters (at least in the central 1 Mpc)
   indicates that the gas is well mixed, thus stripping is relatively unimportant.
2) While the sample is not complete, consistency with type II abundances indicates
   continual enrichment effects are small.
In addition the ASCA results[7] show that the correlation seen in the Ginga data
between Fe and the x-ray luminosity, such that high Fe is associated with low L(x), may
have a strong contamination due to a Fe gradient in the center of some low L(x)
clusters. It is also clear that not all low luminosity nearby systems show an abundance
gradient (e.g. A 1060, Ikebe[7]). Thus the relationship between Fe abundance and other
cluster properties will have to be looked at more carefully. However it is clear that a
range of Fe abundance exists, as seen by Ginga,[45] with Perseus near the high end at ~
0.35 solar and A 2319 near the low end at 0.2 solar.

8. Conclusions

ASCA has fulfilled its promise of determining spatially resolved spectra of
clusters. Under the assumptions of spherical symmetry the abundance and
temperature profiles can be well determined. As with any successful experiment the
new ASCA data have resulted in a large number of new questions, such as, Why do
elliptical galaxies and WP 23 have much lower O and Ne abundances?, What is
different about the high Fe clusters (Perseus)?, Why are some clusters well mixed and
others not?, What is the variation in the abundance pattern and what is its cause?,
Given a wide (?) range of O, Si/Fe ratios why is the Fe abundance relatively constant
when theory indicates that the Fe abundance should be larger in low mass systems
which have a smaller ratio of gas to total mass?, How do the atomic physics
"problems" effect the actual abundances?, What is the cause of the non-azimuthal
temperatures variations in Perseus? - do these variations occur in other clusters
(preliminary analysis of the Rosat data for A 2256[16]) shows that it too has non-
azimuthal kT variations) and how do they effect the mass estimates derived under
symmetry assumptions? and What is the temperature profile at large radii? Many of
these questions can be answered with further analysis of the PV and AO ASCA data.

Acknowledgements: My thanks go to Prof. Tanaka and the entire ASCA PV team that
have made this research possible. In particular I would like to thank Dr. K. Arnaud for
communication of his results on the Perseus cluster and Drs. Yamashita, Fabian,
Makishima, and Bautz for collaborations on the ASCA analysis. I would also like to
thank Dr. M. Loewenstein for his useful comments and R. Gibbons for help with the
manuscript.

References:
1) Sarazin, C. L., 1986, Rev. Mod. Phys., 58, 1
2) Edge, A. C. & Stewart, G. C., 1991, MNRAS, 252, 428
3) Jones, C. & Forman, W., 1992, Clusters and Superclusters of Galaxies, p 49, ed. A. C. Fabian (Kluwer Academic Publishers)
4) Yamashita, K., 1994, Proceedings of the New Horizon of X-ray Astronomy Meeting, Tokyo Metropolitan University
5) Yamashita, K., 1994, these proceedings
6) Bautz, M., et al., 1994, P.A.S.J. in press
7) Ikebe, Y., 1994, these proceedings
8) Ohashi, T., 1994, Proceedings of the New Horizon of X-ray Astronomy Meeting, Tokyo Metropolitan University
9) Fabian, A. C., 1994, Proceedings of the New Horizon of X-ray Astronomy Meeting, Tokyo Metropolitan University
10) Fabian, A. C., 1994, these proceedings
11) Fabricant, D., Rybicki, G. B., & Gorenstein, P., 1984, ApJ, 286, 186
12) Evrard , A. E., 1994, these proceedings
13) Jones, C. & Forman, W., 1984, ApJ, 276, 38
14) David, L. P., Jones, C., Forman, W. & Daines, S., 1994 ApJ in press
15) Briel, U. G., Henry, J. P. & Böhringer, H., 1992, A&A, 259, L31
16) Briel, U. G., 1994, these proceedings
17) Henry, J. P., Briel, U. G. & Nulsen, P. E. J., 1993, A&A, 271, 413
18) Arnaud K., private communication
19) Awaki, H., et al., 1994, P.A.S.J., in press
20) Forman, W., Jones, C., David L., Franx, M., Makishima, K., & Ohashi, T., 1993, ApJ, 418, L55
21) Miyaji, T., et al., 1993, ApJ, 419, 66
22) Hughes, J. P., Butcher, J. A., Stewart, G. C. & Tanaka, Y., 1993, ApJ, 404, 611
23) Oegerle, W. R. & Hill, J. M., 1994, AJ, 107, 857
24) Gerbal, D., Durret, F. & Lachièze-Rey, M., 1994, A&A, in press
25) Loewenstein, M., 1994, ApJ, in press
26) Miralda-Escude, J., 1994, these proceedings
27) Allen, S. W., Fabian, A. C., Johnstone, R. M. & Nulsen, P. E. J., 1992, MNRAS, 254, 51
28) Ponman, T. J., & Bertram, D., 1993, Nature, 363, 51
29) Kowalski, M. P., Cruddace, R. G., Snyder, W. A., Fritz, G. G., Ulmer, M. P. & Fenimore, E. E., 1993, ApJ, 412, 489
30) Koyama, K., Takano, S. & Tawara, Y., 1991, Nature, 350, 35
31) Fukuzawa, Y., et al., 1994, P.A.S.J., in press
32) Yamashita, K., 1993, private communication
33) Metzler, C. A. & Evrard, A. E., 1994, University of Michigan preprint
34) Lucey, J., Dickens, R. J. & Dawe, J. A., 1980, Nature, 285, 303
35) Arnaud, K., et al., 1994, ApJ Lett, in prep
36) Bird, C. M., 1994, AJ, 107, 1637
37) Schindler, S. & Müller, E., 1993, A&A, 272, 137
38) Arnaud, M., 1994, these proceedings
39) Renzini, A., Ciotti, L., D'Ercole, A. & Pellegrini, S., 1993, ApJ, 419, 52
40) Thielemann, F.-K., Nomoto, K. & Hashimoto, M., 1993, in Les Houches, Session LIV, eds. S. Bludman, et al. (Elsevier Sci. Publ.)

182

41) Hashimoto, M., Nomoto, K. & Thielemann, F.-K., 1993, IAU Colloquium No. 145, Supernovae and Supernova Remnants, eds. R. McCray and Z. Wang (Cambridge University Press)

42) Wheeler, J. C., Sneden, C. & Truran, J. W., 1989, Ann. Rev. Astronomy & Astrophysics, p 279, eds. G. Burbidge, D. Layzer and J. G. Phillips (Annual Reviews Inc.)

43) David, L. P., Forman, W. & Jones, C., 1992, ApJ, 380, 39

44) White, R., 1991, ApJ, 367, 69

45) Stewart, G., 1992, Frontiers of X-ray Astronomy, p 447, eds. Y. Tanaka and K. Koyama (Universal Academy Press)

A SEARCH FOR SUBSTRUCTURES IN 11 ROSAT CLUSTERS

USING WAVELET TECHNIQUES

E. SLEZAK
Observatoire de la Côte d'Azur
BP 229 / F-06304 Nice cedex 4 / France

F. DURRET, D. GERBAL
Institut d'Astrophysique de Paris
98bis Bd Arago / F-75014 Paris / France

ABSTRACT :   We report on a search for subclustering in a small sample of X-ray clusters of galaxies observed by ROSAT. A multiscale analysis based on the wavelet transform allows us to observe very different morphologies in the X-ray maps, ranging from complex clusters (ABCG 401, ABCG 754, ABCG 2256) to regular ones (ABCG 478, ABCG 1413, ABCG 2029). The fact that morphological analyses of clusters depend on the resolution which is used is emphasized.

1. Introduction

As reviewed by M. West in this issue, subclustering in clusters of galaxies is of great importance since it is connected to the dynamics and evolution of clusters and gives constraints on the cosmological scenarios. But the extent of this subclustering has long been controversial due to the difficulty to assess its statistical significance from optical observations. Better information could be obtained from the X-ray emitting gas of the intra-cluster medium. Actually, strong evidences for subclustering have been found in X-ray maps[2,5,7], thereby emphasizing the dynamical young state of many clusters.

Recently new efforts have been done in order to quantify the amount of subclustering[3,4,8]. First applied to optical data, these methods are now used to analyze X-ray images[1,6,9,10,11]. We present here a search for substructures in a sample of 11 clusters observed by ROSAT using a wavelet-based method.

2. The Wavelet Analysis

The wavelet transform has been designed in order to localize the information provided by the Fourier transform without having a fixed resolution in the spatial and frequency domains. Owing to the properties of the so-called analyzing wavelet, the result of this transform can be viewed as a frequential examination of the signal around a set of locations and also as a spatial analysis for different scales. This peculiar space-scale analysis provides a scale-invariant description of the data the interpretation of which is quite easy : thinner and thinner details are displayed in the same way when smaller and smaller scales are investigated. The wavelet coefficients contain the information about all these details of different scales, so that adding them to the coarsest approximation of the signal is sufficient for recovering the initial data. From the image processing point of view, the result of the analysis looks like a set of unsharp maskings.

The wavelet transform can be used in order to achieve the detection of the whole range of structures which may exist in images, from large-scale patterns to small-scale features. It allows one indeed to assess a significance level to the detection of structures, to give their position in order to compare the result of the analysis with visual aspects in the image, and to introduce a scale notion in the detection. We made use of this unfolding of the data in the wavelet space in order to disentangle the various components which may be present in the X-ray images of clusters of galaxies and to design an algorithm for removing noise in the data while keeping all the details of the structures.

Assuming a Gaussian white noise, one can show that the knowledge of the noise-induced standard deviation on the coefficients of the first scale is enough to compute the influence of the noise at other scales. We have estimated it from the histogram of the wavelet coefficients of the first highest resolution scale since these coefficients describe mainly the small-scale noise features. The statistical significance of a coefficient is defined as the probability to get a higher value caused by a chance fluctuation of the underlying random process. Hence, the influence of the noise can be removed by selecting at each scale those coefficients for which this probability is lower than a given threshold. Even for the finest scale some coefficients will have large enough values to be kept and these small-scale details will be preserved. But now the mere addition of the thresholded wavelet coefficients is unadequate for recovering the data since ending up with an image which will give again the same wavelet coefficients is very unlikely. We have secured this relationship by minimizing at each scale the distance between the initial image and the processed one.

3. Results and Conclusions

Keeping in mind that our results are based on an image processing without any physics involved, very different morphologies in the X-ray maps are displayed by our multiscale close-up. For instance, a very complex hierarchical structure is detected for cluster ABCG 2256 (Figure 1, and also see Briel *et al.* 1991, and this conference). While it appears elliptical at

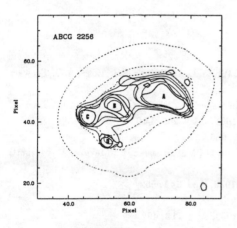

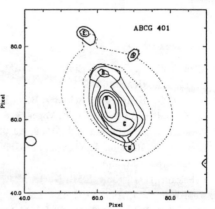

Figure 1.

Figure 2.

Image of ABCG 2256, with the following symbols : dashed line : 2σ, 3σ and 4σ contours of the reconstructed image; full thin line : 2σ, 3σ, 4σ and 6σ contours of the wavelet image at a 4 pixel scale; full thick line : 2σ and 4σ contours of the wavelet image at a 2 pixel scale.

Image of ABCG 401, with the following symbols : dashed line : 2σ and 4σ contours of the reconstructed image; full thin line : 2σ and 4σ contours of the wavelet image at a 4 pixel scale; full thick line : 2σ, 4σ, 10σ and 20σ contours of the wavelet image at a 2 pixel scale.

186

large scales, the close-up reveals first a bean-shaped central region where a large structure and a smaller one to the west are embedded, confirming the already described cooler substructure. Then, when looking at even smaller scales, it appears that this main component would not have a real existence since it breaks up into three smaller pieces. Complex structures are also exhibited for clusters ABCG 401 (Figure 2) and ABCG 754. ABCG 3558 is found to be bimodal while an offset centre is detected for clusters ABCG 426, ABCG 483, ABCG 2218 and ABCG 4059. Clusters ABCG 478, ABCG 1413 and ABCG 2029 appear regular for all the investigated scales.

We emphasize the fact that morphological analyses of clusters depend on the resolution which is used. While the coarse structure of most clusters is almost structureless, substructures can often be detected at smaller scales.

The existence of this small-scale clustering renders the determination of basic structural properties quite difficult and any confirmation of a merging hypothesis in the clusters which appear to have a complex structure would require further observations. We therefore plan to get a deeper insight into the dynamical state of these clusters by : i) deriving the physical properties of the X-ray gas taking into account the spatial structure displayed by our multiscale analysis, and ii) coupling this study with a dynamical analysis derived from optical data.

References :

1. Allen, S.W., Fabian, A.C., Johnstone, R.M., White, D.A., Daines, S.J., Edge, A.C., Stewart, G.C., 1993, MNRAS **262**, 901

2. Briel, U.G., Henry, J.P., Schwarz, R.A., Boehinger, H., Ebeling, H., Edge, A.C., Hartner, G.D., Schindler, S., Trümper, J., Voges, W., 1991, A&A 246, L10

3. Dressler, A., Schectman, S.A., 1988, AJ **95**, 985

4. Escalera, E., Biviano, A., Girardi, M., Giuricin, G., Mardirossian, F., Mazure, A., Mezzetti, M., 1994, ApJ **423**, 539

5. Fabricant, D.G., Kent, S.M., Kurtz, M.J., 1989, ApJ **241**, 552

6. Henriksen, M.J., 1993, ApJ **414**, L5

7. Mohr, J.J., Fabricant, D.G., Geller, M.J., 1993, ApJ **413**, 492

8. Salvador-Solé, E., Sanromá, M., González-Casado,G., 1993, ApJ **402**, 398

9. Schwarz, R.A., Edge, A.C., Voges, W., Böhringer, H., Ebeling, H., Briel, U.G., 1992, A&A **256**, L11

10. Ulmer, M.P., Wirth, G.D., Kowalski, M.P., 1992, ApJ **397**, 430

11. White, S.D.M., Briel, U.G., Henry, J.P., 1993, MNRAS **261**, L8

MODEL-FREE DERIVATION OF THE MASS DISTRIBUTION FROM X-RAY IMAGES OF CLUSTERS

Shigeru J. Miyoshi
Department of Physics, Faculty of Science, Kyoto Sangyo University
Kamigamo-Motoyama, Kita-ku, Kyoto 603, Japan

Abstract

We have established a method to derive from X-ray imaging data the model-free spatial distribution of binding mass of spherically symmetric cluster of galaxies as well as that of X-ray emitting hot gas. Subtracting the masses of hot gas and galaxies, we can get the model-free spatial distribution of intracluster dark matter. Since our method need not assume any functional form of mass distribution beforehand, the obtained dark matter distribution is free from the constraints or uncertainties concerned with model setting. Our method is applicable also to clusters having cooling flow. We tried to apply it to Abell 478 (having cooling flow) and Abell 2256 (having no cooling flow) observed with *ROSAT*. The results are also reported.

1. Introduction

It has been needed so far to set some assumptions or models for the functional form of gas or binding-mass distribution or of temperature distribution to obtain the dark matter distribution in clusters of galaxies from their X-ray imaging data. Because, the information on the temperature distribution of intracluster hot gas was incomplete. But, now it has become possible to obtain good temperature information from the *ASCA* satellite, and therefore the intracluster dark matter distribution is obtainable for spherically symmetric clusters of galaxies from X-ray imaging data only, in principle, without any model setting.

2. Mathematical treatment

The equation of motion for a steady-state cooling flow in a spherically symmetric cluster of galaxies and the equation of state for the cooling flow gas yield

$$M(r) = \frac{\dot{M}(r)^2}{(4\pi)^2 Gr^3\rho_g(r)^2}\left(2+\frac{d\log\rho_g(r)}{d\log r}-\frac{d\log\dot{M}(r)}{d\log r}\right)$$
$$-\frac{kT_g(r)r}{G\mu m_H}\left(\frac{d\log\rho_g(r)}{d\log r}+\frac{d\log T_g(r)}{d\log r}\right), \tag{1}$$

where r is the three-dimensional radial distance from the cluster center, $M(r)$ the binding mass within radius r, $\rho_g(r)$ the gas mass density at r, and $T_g(r)$ the gas temperature at r, k the Boltzmann constant, G the gravitational constant, μm_H the mean molecular weight (m_H is the atomic hydrogen mass), and $\dot{M}(r)$ is the mass inflow rate at radius r given by

$$\dot{M}(r) = -4\pi r^2\rho_g(r)\,u(r) \simeq \frac{2\mu m_H}{5kT_g(r)}L(r), \tag{2}$$

where $u(r)$ and $L(r)$ are the flow velocity and the X-ray luminosity at radius r, respectively. Scince the ratio of the first term to the second term of the right-hand side of equation (1) is of the order of the square of Mach number ($\ll 1$ in general), the following familiar formula is available even in the case where the cooling flow exists:

$$M(r) = -\frac{kT_g(r)r}{G\mu m_H}\left(\frac{d\log\rho_g(r)}{d\log r}+\frac{d\log T_g(r)}{d\log r}\right). \tag{3}$$

From the X-ray imaging data we get the X-ray surface brightness, $L_p(R)$, and the projected average gas temperature, $T_p(R)$, where R is the projected distance from the cluster center. Let $\varepsilon_\nu(r)$ be the volume emissivity of hot gas at frequency ν and radius r, and let z be the distance along the line of sight, i.e., $r=\sqrt{R^2+z^2}$. Then we have

$$L_p(R) = 2\int_0^\infty dz\int_{\nu_1}^{\nu_2}\varepsilon_\nu(r)d\nu = \int_{R^2}^\infty\int_{\nu_1}^{\nu_2}\frac{\varepsilon_\nu(r)d\nu dr^2}{\sqrt{r^2-R^2}}, \tag{4}$$

and

$$T_p(R) = \frac{1}{L_p(R)}\int_{R^2}^\infty\int_{\nu_1}^{\nu_2}\frac{\varepsilon_\nu(r)T_g(r)d\nu dr^2}{\sqrt{r^2-R^2}}, \tag{5}$$

where ν_1 and ν_2 are the observed lower- and upper-limit frequencies. These equations are of the form of Abel's equation, each of which is solved as

$$\varepsilon(r) \equiv \int_{\nu_1}^{\nu_2}\varepsilon_\nu(r)d\nu = -\frac{1}{2\pi r}\frac{d}{dr}\int_{r^2}^\infty\frac{L_p(R)dR^2}{\sqrt{R^2-r^2}}, \tag{6}$$

and

$$\varepsilon(r)T_g(r) = -\frac{1}{2\pi r}\frac{d}{dr}\int_{r^2}^\infty\frac{L_p(R)T_p(R)dR^2}{\sqrt{R^2-r^2}}. \tag{7}$$

The three-dimensional distribution of gas temperature is thus obtained as

$$T_{\rm g}(r) = \frac{d}{dr}\int_{r^2}^{\infty}\frac{L_{\rm p}(R)T_{\rm p}(R)dR^2}{\sqrt{R^2-r^2}} \Big/ \frac{d}{dt}\int_{r^2}^{\infty}\frac{L_{\rm p}(R)dR^2}{\sqrt{R^2-r^2}} . \tag{8}$$

The volume emissivity of thermal bremsstrahlung is well known:

$$\varepsilon(r) = \frac{32\pi}{3}\left(\frac{2\pi}{3}\right)^{1/2}\frac{e^6\overline{Z^2}n_e(r)n_i(r)}{m_ec^2}\left(\frac{m_ec^2}{kT_{\rm g}(r)}\right)^{1/2}\int_{\nu_1}^{\nu_2}\overline{g_{\rm ff}}(\nu,T_{\rm g}(r))\exp\left(-\frac{h\nu}{kT_{\rm g}(r)}\right)d\nu, \tag{9}$$

where $n_e(r)$ and $n_i(r)$ are the electron and ion number densities at r, respectively, e the electron charge, h the Planck constant, and $\overline{Z^2}$ is the averaged square of ion charge. Let Y be the helium abundance in weight of the intracluster gas, then we have

$$n_e(r) = \frac{2-Y}{2}\frac{\rho_{\rm g}(r)}{m_{\rm H}} , \quad n_i(r) = \frac{4-3Y}{4}\frac{\rho_{\rm g}(r)}{m_{\rm H}} , \quad \overline{Z^2} = \frac{4}{4-3Y} , \tag{10}$$

and this gives (by using $\eta \equiv h\nu/kT_{\rm g}(r)$)

$$\rho_{\rm g}(r) = m_{\rm H}\sqrt{\frac{3^{3/2}(m_ec^2)^{3/2}h\,\varepsilon(r)}{(2-Y)2^{9/2}\pi^{3/2}e^6(kT_{\rm g}(r))^{1/2}\int_{\eta_1}^{\eta_2}\overline{g_{\rm ff}}(\eta)\exp(-\eta)d\eta}} . \tag{11}$$

In most case $L_{\rm p}(R)$ and $T_{\rm p}(R)$ are obtained in the form of step function averaged over each annulus dividing the two-dimensional X-ray cluster image. In this case the integrals in equations (7) and (8) are analytically integrated to yield a simple sum of non-singular functions. By averaging these functions on each annulus we get the result of the integrals in the form of step function again, from which we can estimate $\varepsilon(r)$ and $\varepsilon(r)T_{\rm g}(r)$ using equations (6) and (7).

The observed errors could be reflected on the results by the method of assigning statistical errors to them by Monte Carlo regenerations of the original data[1]. Our method is applicable also to clusters of galaxies having intrinsic absorption, since the absorption-corrected surface brightness and temperature are obtained from the spectral analysis.

Finally it should be noted that in the estimate of the value of Hubble constant using Sunyaev-Zel'dovich effect the systematic error concerned with model setting will be highly reduced by using thus obtained $n_e(r)$ and $T_{\rm g}(r)$.

3. Application to Abell 478 and Abell 2256

In order to check the validity of our method, we tried to apply it to Abell 478 (having cooling flow) and Abell 2256 (having no cooling flow) observed with *ROSAT*. The data are from Allen et al.[2] for Abell 478 and from Henry et al.[3] for Abell 2256. The temperature data have been enhanced by using spline function so as to fit in our present analysis, and 10% errors are added to the enhanced temperature data of Abell 478 to test the Monte Carlo method. The details of the present analysis will be reported elsewhere[4]. The obtained radial distributions of electron number density and the integrated binding mass are shown in Figures 1 and 2,

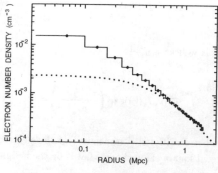

Fig.1. Radial distributions of electron number density for Abell 478 (solid line with dots) and Abell 2256 (dotted line).

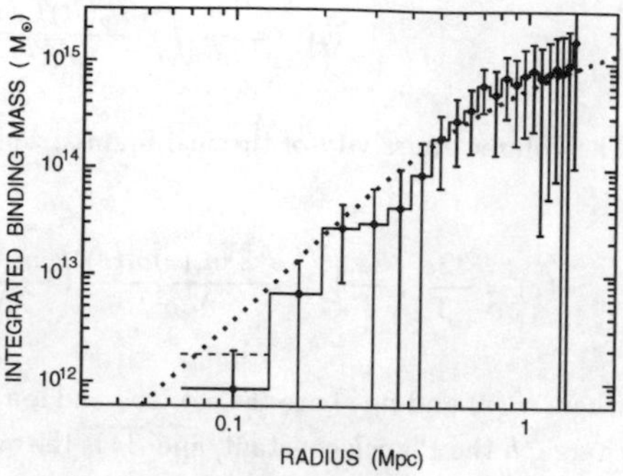

Fig.2. Integrated binding masses of Abell 478 (solid line with dots and error bars) and Abell 2256 (dotted line).

respectively. We can see that the radial binding-mass distributions of Abell 478 and Abell 2256 resemble each other in contrast with the significant difference in the distribution of electron number density. That is, the dark matter distribution in clusters of galaxies might be universal, whereas the distribution of intracluster gas is characterful, perhaps reflecting the diversity in the baryonic-matter environment.

4. Summary

1. We have established the method to obtain the model-free binding mass distribution in spherically symmetric clusters of galaxies from their X-ray images, which is applicable also to clusters having intrinsic absorption.

2. The radial distribution of binding mass obtained by our method for Abell 478 (having cooling flow) and Abell 2256 (having no cooling flow) resemble each other in contrast with the significant difference in the gas distribution. That is, the dark matter distribution in clusters of galaxies might be universal, whereas the distribution of intracluster gas is characterful.

3. X-ray imaging data obtained from *ASCA* will provide us more accurate information on the distribution of dark matter in clusters of galaxies.

References

1) Arnaud, K. A. 1988, in *Cooling Flows in Clusters and Galaxies*, ed. A. C. Fabian, Kluwer Academic Publishers, p. 31.
2) Allen, S. W., Fabian, A. C., Johnstone, R. M., White, D. A., Daines, S. J., Edge, A. C., & Stewart, G. C. 1993, *Mon. Not. R. Astron. Soc.*, **262**, 901.
3) Henry, J. P., Briel, U. G. & Nulsen. P. E. J. 1993, *Astron. Astrophys.*, **271**, 413.
4) Miyoshi, S. J. & Matsuura, M. 1994, in preparation.

GAS STRUCTURES IN THE CORES OF CLUSTERS

A.C. Fabian

Institute of Astronomy, Madingley Road, Cambridge CB3 0HA, UK

ABSTRACT

The intracluster gas in the cores of clusters of galaxies is mapped by its X-ray emission. The characteristic structure for such emission in most clusters is a steeply cusped peak about the central galaxy. Within that peak there may be smaller structures which are due to a central radio source. Also, the X-ray isophotes may wobble from side to side as the radius increases. These structures are reviewed and discussed in the context of cooling flows and the new spectra of clusters emerging from ROSAT and ASCA.

Global structures

The cores of most clusters are structured in both space and temperature. The commonest structure being the central cusp indicative of a cooling flow (Fig. 1) . The gas density, n, there rises inward as $n \propto r^{-1}$, where r is radius from the centre (usually the central cluster galaxy). The radiative cooling time of the gas $t_{cool} \propto T^{1/2}/n \propto rT^{1/2}$, where the gas temperature T is assumed to exceed 1 keV. Thus T_{cool} decreases inward unless $T \propto r^{-2}$ or steeper. X-ray spectra rule this out and instead show that $T \propto r$, approximately. Generally, $t_{.cool} \lesssim H_0^{-1}$ within the inner 100–200 kpc. This inner region is the cooling flow. It is common, occuring in at least 70 per cent of clusters (Edge et al 1992).

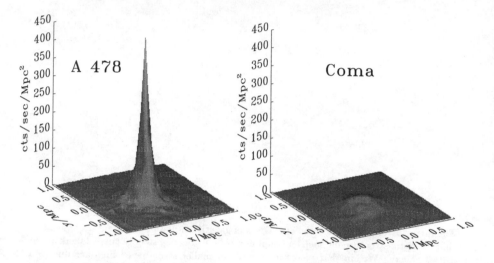

Fig. 1. Comparison of the X-ray surface brightness of A478, which has a strong cooling flow, with that of the Coma cluster, which does not. The surface brightness and radii have been adjusted to a common distance (that of the Coma cluster). Steve Allen and Harald Ebeling are thanked for kindly preparing this figure.

The properties of the cooling flow region in clusters are now being well studied spatially and spectrally with ROSAT and ASCA. Density and temperature profiles are obtained by, for example, the deprojection technique and the mass deposition rate, $\dot{M}$, from the luminosity profile (see e.g Allen et al 1993; White et al 1994; Fig 2).

$$\dot{M} \approx \frac{2}{5}\frac{Lm}{kT}.$$

Values of $\dot{M}$ range from 10 to $> 500\,M_\odot\,\mathrm{yr}^{-1}$. The presence of a cooling flow confounds measurement of an X-ray core radius to a cluster, especially from a soft X-ray image.

At larger radii and in many low-to-moderate luminosity clusters, substructure and large-scale assymetries are observed in the X-ray emission. Examples are the the infalling sub-clusters in A2256 (Briel et al 1991) and Coma (White et al 1993), the outer emission in the

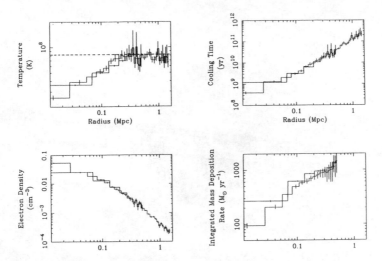

Fig. 2. Results obtained by deprojecting the X-ray images of A478 (White et al 1994).

Cygnus A cluster (Arnaud et al 1984) and the many examples shown in the work of Jones & Forman (1992). Here however we are concerned with the structures within the cores of clusters.

Local structures

Smaller scale structures are sometimes seen superimposed on the larger scale surface-brightness cusp. In the case of the massive flow in A478, no statistically significant structures are seen (White et al 1994). When structures are seen they are usually associated with the central radio source. Examples are;

- M87 (Böhringer et al in preparation). Here there are structures that follow the outer quasi-linear radio structures (see Schreier & Feigelson 1984 for Einstein Observatory images).
- NGC 1275 in the Perseus cluster (Fig. 3; Böhringer et al 1993) shows both holes and peaks of emission where the radio lobes have swept up the cooling gas.
- A0335+096 (Sarazin et al 1992) has structures that correlate with the radio emission.
- Cygnus A (Carilli et al 1994) has both peaks of emission at the edges of the radio lobes and holes in the inner parts.
- The NGC 5044 group (David et al 1994) has a wake following the central galaxy. This is not apparently related to any radio source.

    A major class of structure is that of 'wobbling isophotes'. Here the surface brightness isophotes are roughly centred on the central galaxy, but wobble from side to side as the radius increases. Good examples of this are seen in the Centaurus cluster (Fig. 4; Allen & Fabian 1994) and Shapley 8 (A3558; Jex et al, in preparation). Just what is happening here is not

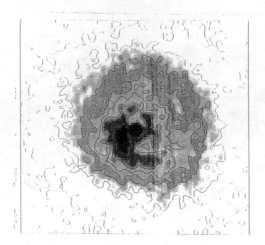

Fig. 3. The central 5 arcmin diameter region around the nucleus of NGC 1275 as imaged with the ROSAT HRI. The radio lobes sit in the 2 holes N and S of the nucleus. Note the large peak of X-ray emission to the SE of the nucleus.

certain, whether it is the gas slopping in the potential or the potential itself is oscillating. There is some similarity to the behaviour of shells around elliptical galaxies and a merger of the central galaxy (or the cluster core) with another massive galaxy (or cluster core) is a strong possibility. Perhaps the structures are caused by the masses oscillating to and fro or perhaps they orbit each other for a while. Since the mass density in an isothermal core varies as r^{-2} then the period of any orbit or oscillation should vary as r.

Even when the isophotes do not wobble, then the isophotes are often elliptical. They are usually aligned with the starlight of the central galaxy. This occurs even when the scales are quite different, being kpc for the starlight and tens to 100s kpc for the X-ray gas (see eg Allen et al 1994).

X-ray Spectra – Emission

Cool X-ray emitting components are commonly seen in cooling flow clusters. T decreases inward. The temperature inferred from deprojection in a cluster such as A478 agrees with the ROSAT-measured spectral temperature, indicating that the size of the dark matter core exceeds 150 kpc (Allen et al 1993). The small dark matter core radii required for the interpretation of some gravitational lensing observations are not seen in those nearer clusters which have been well studied in X-rays. Either the clusters are different or the geometry is not spherically symetric.

The distributed mass deposition inferred from cooling flows implies that the gas is inhomogeneous. The lack of observable features means that these inhomogeneities are very small ($\ll$ kpc).

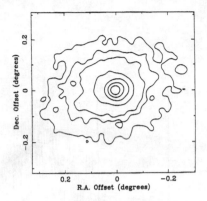

Fig. 4. X-ray isophotes of the central region of the Centaurus cluster (Allen & Fabian 1994).
Note how the contours shift to the W then to the E as the radius is increased.

The new data from ASCA confirms the presence of the cooler gas components expected
in a flow (Fukazawa et al 1994; Fabian et al 1994). This is shown in Fig. 5 where such spectral
components from 2 arcmin radius regions from the centre of the Centaurus and A1795 clusters
are shown. The raw spectra have been fitted above 2.5 keV with an isothermal gas and the
appropriate Galactic absorption and then extrapolated to lower energies. It is clear that there
is an excess of emission below 2 keV which requires gas at temperatures of about 1 keV.

Progress in studying the details of these spectra is currently stalled by the discovery
(using the Centaurus spectrum) that the current plasma models used to interpret them (Raymond & Smith 1977; Mewe & Gronenschild 1984) are inaccurate in predicting the important
iron L lines. The ratio of the 4–2 to 3–2 transitions is wrongly predicted and also the strength
of the lines below 0.8 keV (Liedahl et al 1994).

X-ray Spectra – Absorption

The presence of X-ray absorption in cooling flows was discovered by White et al (1991) using
the Einstein Observatory Solid State Spectrometer. It has since been confirmed with the
ROSAT PSPC (Allen et al 1993; 1994), BBXRT (Arnaud et al 1992; see also Mushotzky
1992) and now ASCA (Fukazawa et al 1994; Fabian et al 1994). The need for such absorption is illustrated in Fig. 5. Any emission spectrum which explained the positive spectral
residuals above 1 keV would also predict emission below 1 keV, where little positive emission
is observed. Absorption corrects this. Note that the ASCA spectra of a similar sized region
in the centre of the Coma cluster are consistent with the low Galactic column density in that
direction, demonstrating that the requirement for excess absorption is not an instrumental
effect.

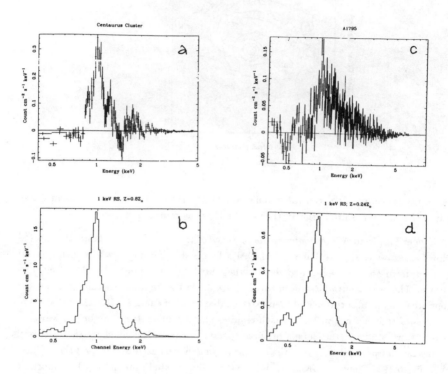

Fig. 5. a) Residuals from fitting the ASCA SIS spectrum above 2.5 keV from the central 2 arcmin radius of the Centaurus cluster with an isothermal Raymond-Smith (RS) model. The model has been extrapolated to lower energies and Galactic absorption included. The fitted abundance is $0.8\,Z_{\odot}$. Note the excess emission above 0.8 keV indicative of cooling gas and the lack of significant emission below that energy. Compare with b) which shows the spectrum of a 1 keV plasma folded through the response of the SIS (the absorption and abundance are the same as for a). Excess absorption is required to reduce the emission predicted from such gas below 0.8 keV. A similar comparison is shown in c) and d) for A1795, which has a lower abundance ($0.24\,Z_{\odot}$) and lower Galactic absorption.

Summary

The cusp-profile, high X-ray surface brightness of most cluster cores and the presence of cooler, and cold, spectral components both point to cooling flows (see Fabian 1994 for a recent review). Much of the cluster gas in the cores must be X-ray multiphase, with a spread of temperature of two or more. Within the inner 200 kpc or so the cooler phase cools out and a slow subsonic inflow, necessary to maintain pressure balance, occurs. Some of the cooled gas probably hangs around as small clouds absorbing the softer X-rays. The innermost 10 kpc may be dominated by cooled gas and pushed around by a central radio source, if present. This region is however less than one per cent of the volume of the whole flow.

Mergers with other clusters and subclusters will stir the gas from time to time and as the central galaxies merge they may orbit or oscillate through each other, giving rise to the wobbling isophotes seen in some clusters. The subclusters themselves often lead to observed clear X-ray structures at larger radii.

REFERENCES

Allen SW, Fabian AC. 1993. MNRAS in press

Allen SW, Fabian AC, Johnstone RM, White DA, Daines SJ, et al. 1993. MNRAS, 262, 901

Allen SW, Fabian AC, Böhringer H, Edge AC, White DA, 1994, MNRAS in press

Arnaud KA, Fabian AC, Eales SA, Jones C, Forman W. 1984. *Mon. Not. R. astr. Soc.*211:981

Arnaud KA, Serlemitsos PJ, Marshall FE, Petre R, Jahoda K, et al. 1992. In *Frontiers of X-ray Astronomy*, pp. 481, ed.s Tanaka Y, Koyama K. Tokyo: Universal Academy Press Inc.

Böhringer H, Voges W, Fabian AC, Edge AC, Neumann DM. 1993. MNRAS 264, L25

Briel UG, et al 1991, AaA, 246, L10

Carilli CL, Owen FN, Harris DL, 1994, AJ, 107, 480

David LP, Jones C, Forman W, Daines SJ, 1994, ApJ in press

Edge AC, Stewart GC, Fabian AC. 1992. MNRAS, 258, 177

Edge AC, Stewart GC, Fabian AC, Arnaud KA. 1990. MNRAS, 245, 559

Fabian AC, Arnaud KA, Bautz MW, Tawara Y, 1994, ApJ submitted

Fukazawa Y, et al 1994, PASJ in press

Jones C, Forman W. 1992. Clusters and Superclusters of Galaxies, ed A.C. Fabian, Kluwer

Liedahl D, Osterheld AL, Mewe R, Kaastra JS, 1994, Preprint

Mewe R, Gronenschild HBM, 1981, AaAS, 84, 511

Mushotzky RF. 1992. Clusters and Superclusters of Galaxies, ed A.C. Fabian, Kluwer, 91

Raymond JC, Smith BW, 1977, ApJS, 35, 419

Sarazin CL, O'Connell RW, McNamara BR. 1992b. ApJ 397, L31

White DA, Fabian AC, Johnstone RM, Mushotzky RF, Arnaud KA. 1991. MNRAS 252, 72

White SDM, Briel UG, Henry JP, 1994, MNRAS 261, L8

White DA et al. 1994. MNRAS in press

X-RAY, RADIO, AND OPTICAL STRUCTURES IN COOLING FLOW CLUSTERS

Craig L. Sarazin
Astronomy Department, University of Virginia
Box 3818, Charlottesville, VA 22903–0818 U.S.A.

ABSTRACT

New X-ray, radio, and optical observations of the central regions of the cD galaxy in the cooling flow cluster A2597 are discussed.

1. Introduction

The centers of rich clusters of galaxies are very dynamically active environments, which show evidence for interesting structures in the optical, radio, and X-ray spectral regions. Here, I discuss the central cD galaxy in the Abell richness class 0 cluster A2597 at a redshift of $z = 0.0852$. The central galaxy was found to have extensive optical and UV line emission filaments[1][2], suggesting that it is a cooling flow. Crawford et al. [3] analyzed the relatively short *Einstein* IPC observation of the cluster, and showed that it was indeed a cooling flow, with a total cooling rate of $\dot{M} = 370 \pm 95\,M_\odot$ yr^{-1} out to a radius of $r_c = 240 \pm 80$ kpc. (All distance-dependent values in this paper assume $H_o = 50$ km s^{-1} Mpc^{-1} and $q_o = 0.0$.) The cD galaxy in A2597 hosts the moderately luminous radio source PKS2322-122[4].

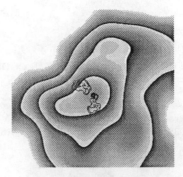

FIG. 1—Contours from the 3.5 cm VLA A array radio map are shown superimposed on the inner 24×24 arcsec of the ROSAT HRI X-ray image of A2597.

The colors of the central 15–20 kpc of the cD galaxy in A2597 are 0.7–1.0 magnitudes bluer in $(U - I)$ than a typical cD. The bluest regions lie in lobe-like structures which extend radially $\sim 5 - 7$ kpc on either side of the I-band nucleus, in a NE/SW orientation[5].

2. Observations

A2597 was observed in X-rays with the ROSAT HRI and PSPC[6][7]. These X-ray observations confirm that A2597 is a cooling flow. The PSPC spectra also directly show the decrease in the intracluster gas temperature with decreasing radius.

The central radio source PKS2322-122 in A2597 was observed with the VLA in A-array at a wavelength of 3.5 cm[7]. The spatial resolution of the observation is about 0.2 arcsec. The radio image shows emission from the nucleus, from a short jet to the SW, and from diffuse lobes to the NE and SW. There is a sharp bend ($\gtrsim 90°$) in the jet about 1 arcsec from the nucleus, and the jet is very bright there. The diffuse radio lobes have a very steep spectral index $\alpha \approx -1.5$. This suggests that the diffuse lobes are confined by the pressure of ambient gas, and have undergone significant synchrotron aging. The synchrotron lifetime of the lobes then implies that the age of the source is $t \gtrsim 5 \times 10^6$ yr. The pressure in the X-ray emitting gas at the smallest measured radii (3 arcsec) is $P_X \approx 5 \times 10^{-10}$ dynes cm^{-2}. The minimum pressures in the radio lobes are both $P_{radio} \approx 6 \times 10^{-10}$ dynes cm^{-2}. This confirms the idea that the lobes are confined by the ambient X-ray emitting gas.

Figure 1 show contours of the radio map superimposed on the central regions of the X-ray emission. The X-ray image shows an elongated structure of X-ray emission running roughly SE to NW. The radio jets appear to emerge perpendicular to this "bar" of X-ray emission.

FIG. 2—Contours from the 3.5 cm VLA A array radio map are shown superimposed on the inner 20×20 arcsec of the $(U - I)$ color map of the central cD in A2597.

The lobes of diffuse radio emission are both swept back in a southeast direction, parallel to the X-ray bar.

Figure 2 shows contours of the radio emission superimposed on an optical color map of the central cD galaxy in $(U - I)$. using data from McNamara & O'Connell[5]. This color map clearly shows the blue lobes discovered by McNamara & O'Connell. Figure 2 shows that the optical blue lobes are aligned parallel to the initial radio jet axis.

3. Discussion and Conclusions

The HRI X-ray image shows an elongation of the X-ray emission along a position angle of about 137°, perpendicular to the initial direction of the radio jets. Several other clusters with central radio sources and cooling flows show a similar effect[8][9][10][11]. One explanation of the X-ray elongation is that the X-ray emitting gas in the cluster has a small but non-zero amount of angular momentum. As the gas cools at the center of the cooling flows, the gas flatten into a disk. If the gas continues to cool and flow inward, it might eventually feed the central AGN. Radio jets might be expected to emerge perpendicular to the accretion disk.

The minimum pressures in the radio lobes are consistent with pressure confinement by the ambient, X-ray emitting gas. The plasma in the lobes would be much lighter than the ambient gas, and would rise buoyantly away from the center of the galaxy. However, the observed lobes both appear to have been deflected to the southeast, along the major axis of the cD galaxy. If the deflection of the lobes to the southeast is due to ram pressure from the motion of the ambient gas, the velocity of the ambient gas must be $\gtrsim 300$ km s^{-1}.

The blue optical lobes at the center of the cD in A2597 might be due to jet-induced star formation[5], or to scattered light from a beamed AGN at the center of the cD[12], or synchrotron radiation or inverse Compton radiation due to microwave background photons interacting with relativistic particles associated with the radio source. In the case of synchrotron or inverse Compton radiation, the blue lobes should be identical to the radio lobes in morphology. It is clear from Figure 2 that this is not the case.

In the jet-induced star formation model, the blue lobes are produced by young stars formed by the interaction between the radio emitting plasma and the ambient thermal gas. While the blue lobes and the radio lobes do have crudely similar spatial scales and orientations (Figure 2), the blue lobes extend considerably further out. Geometrically, the blue lobes are quite symmetric on either side of the nucleus, while the radio structure is very asymmetric. If the blue lobes were due to interactions with the radio jets, one might expect the SW lobe to be particularly bright because of the strongly disrupted jet in this direction.

Alternatively, the blue lobes could be scattered light from an anisotropically radiating, nonthermal active nucleus. The lobe structure would result from beamed radiation which is scattered into the line of sight by electrons in the X-ray emitting gas or by dust grains[12]. This model predicts that the blue lobes should align with the initial direction of the radio jets and be fairly symmetric, which is just the geometry observed in A2597. Moreover, Sarazin & Wise showed that the observed surface brightness of the blue lobes was consistent with that expected from electron scattering. If the lobes are due to electron scattering, the scattered light should be circumferentially polarized at roughly the 5% level.

This work was done in collaboration with Jack Burns, Kurt Roettinger, Brian McNamara, and Bob O'Connell. This work was supported by NASA Astrophysical Theory Program grant NAGW–2376 and NASA ROSAT grant NAG 5–1891.

4. References

[1] Hu, E. M. 1988, in Cooling Flow in Clusters and Galaxies, ed. A. C. Fabian, (Dordrecht: Reidel), 73
[2] Heckman, T. M., Baum, S. A., van Bruegel, W. J., & McCarthy, P. J. 1989, ApJ, 338, 48
[3] Crawford, C. S., Arnaud, K. A., Fabian, A. C., & Johnstone, R. M. 1989, MNRAS, 236, 277
[4] Ball, R., Burns, J. O., & Loken, C. 1993, AJ, 105, 53
[5] McNamara, B. R., & O'Connell, R. W. 1993, AJ, 105, 417
[6] Sarazin, C. L., O'Connell, R. W., & McNamara, B. R. 1994, preprint
[7] Sarazin, C. L., Burns, J. O., Roettinger, K., & McNamara, B. R. 1994, preprint
[8] Sarazin, C. L., O'Connell, R. W., & McNamara, B. R. 1992a, ApJ, 389, L59
[9] Sarazin, C. L., O'Connell, R. W., & McNamara, B. R. 1992b, ApJ, 397, L31
[10] Baum, S. A., O'Dea, C. P, & Sarazin, C. L. 1994, preprint
[11] Böhringer, H., Voges, W., Fabian, A. C., Edge, A. C., & Neumann, D. M. 1993, MNRAS, 264, L25
[12] Sarazin, C. L., & Wise, M. W. 1993, ApJ, 411, 55

OPTICAL SPECTROSCOPY OF THE ROSAT X-RAY BRIGHTEST CLUSTERS

C.S. Crawford

Institute of Astronomy, Cambridge University, UK

ABSTRACT

Results are reported from an optical follow-up study aimed at determining new redshifts for clusters of galaxies selected from the *ROSAT* All-Sky Survey. We have obtained spectra for the central galaxies of 71 'new' clusters out to a redshift of 0.3, and review here their optical properties. Thirty-four per cent of these galaxies exhibit optical spectral anomalies such as strong line emission and an excess UV/blue continuum, similar to those found in lower-redshift cooling flow clusters. We confirm a clear trend for the strongest line emitters to also have the bluest continua. Whilst the probability for such optical anomalies is increased for galaxies with associated radio sources, the strength of these features is not directly related to the power of the radio emission.

INTRODUCTION

The ROSAT All-sky survey (RASS) has detected several thousand clusters, from which we have selected a flux-limited sample of the $\sim$ 300 brightest X-ray cluster sources in the Northern Hemisphere. The flux limit of $f_X \geq 2 \times 10^{-12}\,\mathrm{erg\,cm^{-2}\,s^{-1}}$ corresponds to $L_X \sim 2 \times 10^{44}\,\mathrm{erg\,s^{-1}}$ at $z \sim 0.1$, or $L_X \sim 8 \times 10^{44}\,\mathrm{erg\,s^{-1}}$ at $z \sim 0.2$. The sample has been obtained by cross-correlating survey detections against both the Abell and Zwicky optical cluster catalogues, and also selecting extended RASS sources associated with an overdensity of galaxies on optical sky survey plates. The resulting ROSAT Brightest Cluster Sample (hereafter BCS) has an increased sample size and a lower flux limit compared to previous X-ray-selected flux-limited samples such as the 'brightest 50' (Edge et al.1992) and the EMSS (Stocke et al.1991). These two earlier samples both showed evidence for strong cluster evolution and for a high percentage of cooling flows. The larger volume of space sampled by the BCS will allow better constraints on the large-scale spatial distribution and evolution of clusters.

The first stage of compiling the new sample has been to obtain redshifts for those catalogued clusters where the distance is unknown, and for our newly-discovered X-ray-selected clusters. We have collected redshifts for the central dominant galaxies within 2 arcmin of the X-ray centroid for a total of 71 clusters (Allen et al.1992; Crawford et al.1994), and the redshift information for the BCS is now virtually complete. The majority of these 'new' clusters lie at redshifts 0.1-0.15, with the most distant at $z \sim 0.3$ – the apparent z cutoff does not reflect any real decrease in high-L_X clusters beyond $z \sim 0.3$, but rather the limitations of optical sky survey plates and the smaller X-ray extents in the RASS.

SPECTRAL ANOMALIES

The optical spectra of the central cluster galaxies in these 'new' clusters show some interesting anomalies. Some have strong ($L_{H\alpha} \sim 3 \times 10^{40} - 10^{43}\,\mathrm{erg\,s^{-1}}$) low-ionization emission lines ([OI], [OII], [OIII], Hα, [NII], [SII]) with velocity widths typically of a few hundred $\mathrm{km\,s^{-1}}$. The incidence of such line emission is $\sim 34\%$, and we find no evidence for redshift-evolution in the rate of occurrence of such systems, unlike as reported for the smaller-sized EMSS (Donahue et al.1992). The properties of this line emission (ie line luminosity, rate of occurrence, line intensity ratios) are very similar to those of low-z central galaxies in cluster cooling flows. In particular, they share the tendency for such properties to be related to the global *cluster* properties (Heckman et al.1989, Crawford & Fabian 1992, Allen et al.1992) – there is a general trend for the richer, higher-L_X clusters have both lower ionization spectra and higher $L_{H\alpha}$. There do not appear to be any differences in optical properties between the optically-selected and X-ray selected clusters. Mechanisms proposed for powering these luminous emission-line systems involve tapping the thermal energy of the hot gas entrained in mixing layers round cold clouds in the intracluster medium, as well as the kinetic energy released by deep molecular shocks driven through these clouds from either a contained radio source or recent subcluster merging activity due to the evolution of rich clusters of galaxies (Crawford & Fabian 1992).

The most luminous emission-line galaxies also have an excess (rest-frame) UV/blue continuum. Simple spectral synthesis suggests that the blue light is well fit by an extra component of massive stars (mainly B5 and around $10^6 - 10^8$ stars; Allen et al.1992; Crawford & Fabian 1993; Crawford et al.1994). The amount of excess blue light correlates well with $L_{H\alpha}$ (or L_X), suggesting that both the optical anomalies are due to the same process operating at the centre of richer clusters. If the blue light is due to massive stars, the universal nature of its spectrum is more consistent with a fading starburst than continuous star formation; in addition, the rate ($< 10\% \dot{M}_X$) and central location imply that it is not directly related any associated cooling flow. At low redshifts, blue-excess central galaxies are associated with powerful radio sources within cooling flows, sometimes displaying a bimodal structure that suggests the possibility of jet-induced star formation (McNamara & O'Connell 1993). However, the spectrum is also consistent with $F_\lambda \propto \lambda^{-1.5}, \lambda^{-2.5}$, so a contribution from a hidden nuclear continuum scattered into our line of sight by either dust or hot electrons cannot be ruled out (Wise & Sarazin 1992; Crawford & Fabian 1993).

OTHER WAVEBANDS

Follow-up ROSAT PSPC pointed observations of 8 of these emission-line clusters show that 7 are cooling flows, with $\dot{M} \sim 200 - 400 \, M_\odot \, yr^{-1}$ (Allen et al.1994), confirming the use of optical spectral signatures as good tracers of distant cooling flows. We have also correlated the 'new' clusters of the BCS against radio all-sky and Abell cluster surveys, and find a median detection of $\log(P_{1.4}) \sim 25 \text{WHz}^{-1}$ at a rate of 23%, consistent with lower-redshift samples (we plan follow-up VLA snapshots of the BCS to better quantify the radio properties).

There is a definite link between the radio and optical properties of the central cluster galaxies, in that the percentage of line-emitting systems with radio emission is higher than those without line emission. In low-z clusters, cooling flow nebulae are optically over-luminous for their radio power (Heckman et al.1989). Our sample shows that the presence of a central radio source increases the probability of the galaxy having line emission and excess blue light, but the strength of such features is not directly related to the radio power – indeed, there are specific exceptions in both the BCS and at lower redshifts (either line-luminous systems with no strong radio source, eg 0335+096, A1068, or vice-versa eg A2029). The emission-line systems from both the BCS and the EMSS span the full range of radio power (Crawford et al.1994). This lack of a detailed correlation poses a challenge to models of blue light generation that rely on a powerful radio source (jet-induced star formation, scattered nuclear emission). Our X-ray selection technique forms an interesting comparison to previous more radio-selected samples (Heckman et al.1989) which find an apparent correlation of $L_{H\alpha}$ with $P_{1.4}$ – radio-selection results in a bias to higher radio luminosity for the powerful line emitters. As the BCS clusters are selected to be X-ray-bright, it is possible instead that these are the most luminous due to evolution via subcluster mergers, and hence with the most recent input of energy.

WHERE NEXT?

So far, this analysis of the optical properties of the central cluster galaxies is only complete for the 'new' clusters in the BCS. We are now extending the analysis of the X-ray/optical/radio properties to the entire BCS, hoping to answer some of the questions raised by this preliminary study on a more statistical basis: Which of the optical and radio properties are dependent on L_X? Is the radio source necessary or available for all blue-excess galaxies? Is line emission an unambiguous indicator of a cooling flow? Why do some high-$\dot{M}$ flows not have optical anomalies (merger history, radio source...)? The entire BCS will enable us to sample a wide redshift range to test for any match between subcluster merging activity and the optical properties of the galaxy.

High resolution UV spectroscopy of the galaxies with HST will reveal definitive stellar signatures if the blue light is due to starbursts; alternatively, a detailed polarization spectrum of the blue continuum should also resolve whether hot electrons or dust are the possible scattering agent. The further members of the BCS are now at a similar distance to intermediate-z radio galaxies and quasars, known to lie in clusters of galaxies (Yee & Green 1984, 1987; Yates et al.1989; Hill & Lilly 1991). Such powerful radio galaxies also display similar luminous and extended low-ionization nebulae and an excess UV/blue continuum. Continuum imaging should reveal whether the blue BCS galaxies exhibit an alignment effect, and if so, whether they may be an important nearby lower-power analogue of the very distant 3CR systems.

REFERENCES

Allen, S.W. et al.1992, MNRAS, 259, 67

Allen, S.W. et al.1994, MNRAS, submitted

Crawford C.S., Fabian, A.C., 1992, MNRAS, 259, 265

Crawford C.S., Fabian, A.C., 1993, MNRAS, 265, 431

Crawford, C.S. et al.1994, MNRAS, in press

Donahue, M., Stocke, J.T., Gioia, I.M., 1992, ApJ, 385, 49

Edge A.C., Stewart, G.C., Fabian, A.C., 1992, MNRAS, 258, 177

Heckman, T.M., Baum, S.A., van Breugel, W.J.M., McCarthy, P., 1989, ApJ, 338, 48

Hill, G.J., Lilly, S.J., 1991, ApJ, 367, 1

McNamara, B.R., O'Connell, R.W., 1993, AJ, 105, 417

Stocke, J.T, et al.1991, ApJS, 76, 813

Wise, M & Sarazin C.L. 1992, ApJ, 395, 387

Yates, M.G., Miller, L. & Peacock, J.A., 1989, MNRAS, 240, 129

Yee, H.K.C. & Green, R.F., 1984, ApJ, 280, 79

Yee, H.K.C. & Green, R.F., 1987, ApJ, 319, 28

THE RELIABILITY OF X-RAY CONSTRAINTS OF INTRINSIC CLUSTER SHAPES

David A. Buote

Department of Physics and Center for Space Research 37-618A,
Massachusetts Institute of Technology, 77 Massachusetts Avenue,
Cambridge, MA 02139

John C. Tsai

NASA/Ames Research Center, Mail Stop 245-3, Moffett Field, CA 94035

Using the simulation of Katz & White[10] we have tested the viability of X-ray analysis for constraining the intrinsic shapes of clusters of galaxies considering the effects of both substructure and steep temperature gradients. We restrict our analysis to the aggregate shapes of clusters on scales of $r \sim 1-2$ Mpc in order to reduce our sensitivity to subclustering in the core. For low redshifts ($z < 0.25$) the X-ray method accurately measures the true ellipticity of the three-dimensional cluster dark matter provided the inclination of the cluster is known to within ~ 30 deg; assuming the gas is isothermal adds only small errors to the derived shapes. At higher redshifts the X-ray method yields unreliable results since the gas does not trace the cluster gravitational potential. We proffer some necessary conditions for the reliability of X-ray methods characterized by both the amount of substructure in the X-ray surface brightness images and the shapes of the isophotes. We conclude that measurements of the aggregate shapes of clusters on scales $r \sim 1-2$ Mpc are insensitive to core substructure representing scales of a few hundred kpc. Therefore our results suggest that the X-ray measurements of aggregate cluster shapes by Fabricant, Rybicki, & Gorenstein[7] and Buote & Canizares[4] are valid provided that they do not suffer from serious projection effects.

Introduction

We investigate the reliability of X-ray methods for determining the intrinsic shapes of galaxy clusters by analyzing the cluster simulation of Katz & White[10]; the effects of subclustering and temperature gradients on the shape determinations are examined. Katz & White (hereafter KW) modeled the formation and evolution of a Virgo-sized cluster ($M \sim 2 \times 10^{14} M_\odot$) in a standard flat, biased Cold Dark Matter universe ($\Omega = 1$, $H_0 = 50$ km s^{-1} Mpc^{-1}, b=2.6, $M_{DM}/M_{bary} = 10$). They modeled the dissipational gas component with smoothed particle hydrodynamics[9] allowing for cooling via radiative and compton processes; gravitational effects were modeled using the hierarchical tree method. Hence, KW constructed an X-ray cluster that formed and evolved in the context of large-scale structure and thus serves as a laboratory for testing X-ray methods for determining intrinsic cluster shapes. Using the KW cluster in its final time step Tsai, Katz, & Bertschinger[16] (hereafter TKB) tested the accuracy of spherically-symmetric X-ray analysis of the radial mass distribution. They concluded that the mass inferred from the X-rays matched the true mass of the simulation to within $\sim 25\%$ when the true temperature profile was used.

Do the peculiar features (i.e. biased CDM, no star formation) of the KW simulation preclude using it for studying real clusters? The primary virtue of the KW simulation is that it produces a "non-trivial" cluster: the KW cluster (1) is quite flattened having an ellipticity of about 0.55 within 1.5 Mpc, (2) has a steep temperature gradient that does not appear to be typical of real clusters (Mushotzky, these proceedings), and (3) has substructure at all redshifts. Surely if the KW simulation produced a round, isothermal, and smooth cluster the X-ray methods could not fail. Therefore, the KW cluster may not be a perfect representation of a real cluster but it provides a formidable test for the X-ray methods of shape determination.

We test the X-ray technique used by Buote & Canizares[4,3,5] (hereafter BC92), who built on the original study of Binney & Strimple[1,15], to constrain the shapes of the dark matter in five Abell clusters using *Einstein* images. The fundamental assumptions of this method are that the gas is a single-phase ideal gas in a state of quasi-hydrostatic equilibrium with the gravitational potential of the cluster. We solve the equation of hydrostatic equilibrium for the gas density and assume functional forms for the gas temperature and the gravitational potential; i.e. we use assume the gas is isothermal or use the true temperature profile from the KW simulation; for the potential we use spheroidal power-law models . From the gas density we construct the X-ray emissivity and then, by projection onto the sky, the X-ray surface brightness. Finally, we convolve the model surface brightness with the IPC PSF to compare to the "observed" images take from the KW simulation.

In order to reduce effects of small-scale substructure (few hundred kpc) we measure the aggregate shapes of clusters on scales of $1 - 2$ Mpc from the cluster center. We quantify shapes by computing the quadrupole moments (or equivalently the principal moments of inertia). We compute aggregate shapes of the X-ray images obtained from the KW simulation and compare to the X-ray models; we also compare azimuthally averaged radial profiles.

Results

For low redshifts ($0.13 \leq z \leq 0.25$) we find that the X-ray method accurately measures the true ellipticity of the cluster dark matter when the true inclination of the cluster is taken into account; in the figure we show the X-ray surface brightness for the KW cluster at $z = 0.13$. The X-ray models employing the true temperature profile deviate from the true cluster ellipticity ($\epsilon \sim 0.55$) by $\epsilon \sim 0.05$ while the isothermal models have slightly larger deviations $\epsilon \sim 0.10$; both of these deviations underestimate the true ellipticity but are less than the typical uncertainties obtained by BC92 for real clusters. When the inclination of the cluster is not taken into account we obtain results for the true temperature models in accordance with Binney & Strimple[1] and Fabricant et. al.[7]; of course, the effects of inclination on cluster shapes may be uncovered by analyzing a well-defined statistical sample of clusters[14] . Our results affirm the assertion that conclusions regarding the shape of the dark matter are not overly sensitive to the temperature gradient of the gas; i.e. the ellipticities of the true-temperature models differ from the isothermal models by less than the typical errors of BC92. We expect that the assumption is even more valid for real clusters since they likely do not have such a steep temperature gradient present in the simulation.

At higher redshifts ($0.38 < z < 0.83$) the X-ray method yields unreliable results. The gas at these early times does not trace the shape of the cluster gravitational potential as it must if it were in hydrostatic equilibrium. At $z \sim 0.83$ the gas traces the dark matter itself and for $z \sim 0.38 - 0.67$ it follows neither the dark matter nor the potential.

The X-ray images of the KW cluster exhibit general properties as a function of redshift that correlate with the reliability of the X-ray methods. The strong subclustering in the $z = 0.83, 0.67$ and $z = 0.38$ clusters and the distorted X-ray isophotes in the $z = 0.38$ cluster are not seen at the lower redshifts. Moreover, the isophotes of the lower redshift clusters ($z < 0.25$) are overall more regularly shaped and rounder than those at higher redshifts. If the gas was in

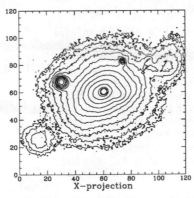

X−projection

Contour plot of the X-ray surface brightness of the KW cluster at $z = 0.13$ viewed nearly edge-on ($i = 80°$); the contours are separated by a factor of 2 in intensity and the coordinate axes are in arcminutes. The cluster is placed at a distance of 100 Mpc so that $1'$ represents 29.1 kpc.

hydrostatic equilibrium at the earlier times ($z > 0.38$) then the large ellipticities ($\epsilon_x > 0.4$) of their isophotes would imply dark matter ellipticities larger than 0.7 (cf. end of §5.1 of BC92); this is unphysical because dynamical considerations forbid such flat, non-rotating, ellipsoidal structures[11,12]. Thus a qualitative statement of necessary conditions for the reliability of the X-ray methods is that (1) there is no obvious subclustering on the same scale used to compute the aggregate shape and (2) the isophotes are regularly shaped and not too elongated ($\epsilon_x < 0.3$). Of course these conditions are not sufficient since they could both be the results of projection effects.

The clusters studied by BC92 satisfy these necessary conditions with the possible exception of Coma. Fitchett & Webster[8] have suggested that Coma is bimodal on scales of several hundred kpc, comparable to the scale used by BC92 to compute the aggregate shape. Davis & Mushotzky[6] have provided further evidence for such bimodality from analysis of *Einstein* X-ray data. For A2256, in contrast, the substructure appears to reside in the core on a scale of a few hundred kpc[2] which is substantially smaller than the aggregate scales (~ 1 Mpc) used by others[7,3] to measure the intrinsic dark matter shape. Moreover, the core substructure in A2256 appears to be very similar to that present in the $z = 0.13$ cluster of the KW simulation. *We thus conclude that core substructure representing scales of a few hundred kpc does not invalidate X-ray measurements of intrinsic aggregate (i.e. $r \sim 1 - 2$ Mpc) cluster shapes.*

We conclude that measurements of the aggregate shapes of clusters on scales of $1 - 2$ Mpc from the cluster center are practically unaffected by core substructure representing scales of a few hundred kpc. Therefore our results suggest that the X-ray studies of such aggregate shapes of clusters by Fabricant et. al.[7] and BC92 (Buote[3]) are valid provided that they do not suffer from serious projection effects.

We thank Neal Katz for allowing use of the KW simulation and Claude Canizares for useful discussions. A complete report of this work has been submitted to the Astrophysical Journal.

References

(1) Binney, J., & Strimple O. 1978, MNRAS, 187, 473
(2) Briel, U. G., et. al. 1991, A& A, 246, 10
(3) Buote, D. A. 1992, M.S. Thesis, Massachusetts Institute of Technology
(4) Buote, D. A., & Canizares, C. R. 1992, ApJ, 400, 385 (BC92)
(5) Buote, D. A., & Canizares, C. R. 1994, ApJ, in press
(6) Davis, D. S., & Mushotzky, R. F. 1993, AJ, 105, 409
(7) Fabricant, D., Rybicki, F., & Gorenstein, P. 1984, ApJ, 286, 186
(8) Fitchett, M. J., & Webster R. 1987, ApJ, 317, 653
(9) Hernquist, L., & Katz, H. 1989, ApJS, 70, 419
(10) Katz, N., & White, S. D. M. 1993, ApJ, 412, 455 (KW)
(11) Merritt, D., & Stiavelli, M. 1990, ApJ, 358, 399
(12) Merritt, D., & Hernquist, L. 1991, ApJ, 376, 439
(13) Mohr, J. J., Fabricant, D. G., & Geller, M. J. 1993, ApJ, 413, 492
(14) Plionis, M., Barrow, J. D., & Frenk, C. S. 1991, MNRAS, 249, 662
(15) Strimple, O., & Binney, J. 1978, MNRAS , 188, 883
(16) Tsai, J. C., Katz, N., & Bertschinger, E. 1994, ApJ, 423, 553 (TKB)

THE ENRICHMENT OF THE INTRA-CLUSTER MEDIUM

Monique ARNAUD

C.E.A., DSM, DAPNIA, Service d'Astrophysique, CE. Saclay, Orme des merisiers,
91191 Gif sur Yvette CEDEX, FRANCE

Abstract

The quantity of iron in clusters (both in the stars and in the Intracluster Medium) is an important clue for our understanding of formation and chemical/dynamical evolution of galaxies as well as the origin of the ICM. We discuss the problem of the ICM enrichment in view of recent theoretical and observational works, with particular emphasis on the global iron production and the relative role of SNI and SNII in the enrichment process. A major contribution from SNII is advocated. We show that bimodal star formation models, where high-mass stars are favored in violent star formation phases, can account for the observations on elliptical galaxies and on the ICM as well as on our Galaxy and starburst galaxies.

1. Introduction

The X-ray emitting hot intergalactic gas is the main visible component of clusters of galaxies: its mass is equal to 1-7 times the stellar mass present in the galaxies [1,2] and it can reach 30% of the total cluster mass - visible mass plus dark matter [3]. The detection of the iron K lines in the X-ray spectra has shown that the gas is enriched in metals and has been processed, at least in part, into the stellar content of the cluster galaxies. Typical abundances are about 0.35 solar [4,5] and decrease slightly with the ICM temperature [4,6,7,2]. A number of questions are prompted by these observations: what part of the ICM is primordial and what part has been ejected from the galaxies?, what type of galaxies enriched the ICM and how and when? To answer these questions a detailed modeling of the chemical evolution of galaxies and of the ejection process must be done, taking into account the constrains provided by observational data on both the ICM and the cluster galaxies. The difficulty but also the interest of the ICM enrichment problem come from the fact that it involves a large variety of important astrophysical issues, as emphasized and extensively discussed in the recent work of Renzini et al. [8]), and this at all astrophysical scales: star evolution and supernovae physics (the SN being the only iron producers), star formation, formation and chemical/dynamical evolution of galaxies and environmental effects, origin and heating of the ICM and cluster formation. If a general consensus has emerged that the ICM iron originated from elliptical galaxies and was ejected through SN driven wind/outflows, the relative role of type I and type II SNs is still a matter of controversy [8 -20]. In section 2 we review the relevant observational constraints, in section 3 we discuss the problem of the ICM enrichment in view of recent theoretical and observational works, with particular emphasis on the global iron production and the open issue of the relative role of SNI and SNII. In section 4 we briefly present a model [20], that we proposed recently, which is based on bimodal star formation.

2. The observational data

2.1. The key quantities

To understand the ICM enrichment process and the origin of the ICM it is essential to consider the relevant observational quantities [2,8]: the iron mass present in clusters (both in the ICM, M_{Fe}^{ICM} and in the stellar component of the galaxies, M_{Fe}^*), the stellar mass M^*(or luminosity, L_V) and the ICM gas mass, M_{Gas}^{ICM}. To provide a real constraint the cluster iron mass must indeed be compared (or normalized) to a global quantity, characteristics of the stellar component of the cluster, from which the iron is produced. We can consider the visible luminosity, a quantity which is directly observed but cannot directly constrain the chemical evolution model without a detailed follow-up of the luminosity evolution. Alternatively, the stellar mass is a direct parameter in any chemical evolution model but is not directly observed and requires a knowledge of the galaxy mass-to-light ratio, a quantity not precisely known.

Key informations are derived from:
- The M_{Fe}^{ICM} versus L_V relationship for each galaxy type. If a particular type of galaxy is playing a dominant role in this enrichment, this should be apparent in some specific correlation between the ICM iron mass and the cluster luminosity in that type.
- The M_{Fe}/L_V ratio or M_{Fe}/M^*. If a constant Initial Mass Function (IMF) is assumed, this ratio is directly linked to a fundamental quantity in chemical models, the iron mass that a given population of stars can produce, the so-called iron global yield, which depends only on the IMF. In any case it is a strong constraints on the proportion of iron producing stars in the IMF.
- The M_{Fe}^{ICM}/M_{Fe}^* ratio, i.e. the ratio of ejected iron over iron locked into stars. It sets a constraint on the iron production history and on the mass fraction lost by the galaxies.
- The M_{Gas}^{ICM}/L_V ratio. It only provides an upper limit to M_{Gas}^{Eject}/L_V, the ejected gas mass over luminosity ratio deduced from the enrichment model. In practice this limit is never reached and this constraint is used to deduce the proportion of primordial gas present in the ICM.
- Finally it must be recalled that the iron abundance by itself is not a meaningful constraint: it is a quantity that depends on the amount of primordial ICM gas, in which the iron mass ejected by the galaxies is diluted.

2.2 At Cluster scale

The new results from the X-ray satellite Ginga (see Figure 1) confirm that the iron mass measured in the ICM is correlated with the selected luminosity of E/SO galaxies, as was already shown in Arnaud et al [2]. No such correlation appeared for spirals. The best fit corresponds to a simple proportionality law with:

$$\frac{M_{Fe}^{ICM}}{L_V^{E/SO}} = 2 \ 10^{-2} \ \frac{M_\odot}{L_\odot} \qquad (1)$$

A value entirely consistent with the above value was found by Tsuru [7] who studied the typical ratio between the iron mass present in the ICM and the total stellar mass present in the galaxies irrespectively of their type (which allows him to consider a larger sample).

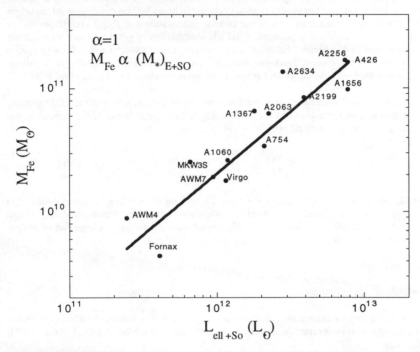

Figure 1: Correlations between iron mass and optical luminosities. The iron mass, the product of the iron abundance by the gas mass, has been computed using the very precise overall iron abundance determined by GINGA [4,6,7,21,this work] and the gas mass derived from EINSTEIN or ROSAT imagery data [2,6,25-28]. L_V, the visible luminosity, is obtained from the photometry of the galaxies, divided into E+SO and Sp [2,22-24]. This work is made in collaboration with researchers from Nagoya University, Kyoto University, Tokyo University and CfA.

There is some scatter in the correlation between the two quantities: M_{Fe}^{ICM} can vary by a factor of two for a given $L_V^{E/SO}$. This deviation from the best fit law does not present any obvious trend with cluster luminosity and could arise from the uncertainties on the iron mass determination. The first uncertainty comes from using global spectra and assuming an uniform iron abundance in the ICM. Were the iron distribution more peaked than the gas distribution we would overestimate the total iron mass. Spatially resolved spectroscopy is still scarce, but rapidly increasing with the new results from the ASCA satellite (see the contributions of K.Yamashita, Y. Ikebe and R. Mushotzky). The iron abundance seems fairly constant at large scale; however, in a few cases, an overabundance at the very center has been detected. The second source of uncertainty is on the gas mass determination, which depends on the assumed extent of the cluster atmosphere. In particular the gas mass over luminosity ratio increases with radius since the galaxy distribution is more peaked that the gas distribution.

The simple proportionality law between M_{Fe}^{ICM} and $L_V^{E/SO}$ naturally lead to the conclusion that the ICM iron originates in E/SO galaxies and that it is ejected through galactic winds. Other ejection processes, like ram pressure stripping, which depend on the environment, would imply a general variation of the iron mass over luminosity ratio with cluster richness [8]. This conclusion on the origin of the ICM iron is not surprising in view of our current understanding of ellipticals. Ellipticals are well known to contain an old stellar population and a low proportion of gas. These two observations are usually explained by considering that ellipticals have experienced a violent burst of star formation in the early stage of their evolution. The strong concentration of supernovae expected at the beginning of this evolution is likely to have driven an outflow, resulting in the metal enrichment of the ICM.

Finally the proportion of intergalactic gas relatively to the luminosity of the E/SO galaxies (or stellar mass content, for a given M/L ratio) increases with the richness of the cluster, in the following range, as shown by Arnaud et al. [2]:

$$20 \, \frac{M_\odot}{L_\odot} \leq \frac{M_{Gas}^{ICM}}{L_V^{E/SO}} \leq 50 \, \frac{M_\odot}{L_\odot} \qquad (2)$$

Similar results were obtained by David et al.[29] and Tsuru [7] on the whole galaxy population. The ICM is thus by far the major visible component in clusters and without any detailed modeling we can already tell that it is unlikely that it has been entirely ejected from the galaxies. A large part of this gas is primordial, at least in rich clusters.

2.3 At the galaxy scale

2.3.1 Metallicity of nearby ellipticals

The metallicity measurements in the gaseous and stellar components on elliptical galaxies are important constraints on their chemical evolution, in particular on the relative role of SNI and SNII (see section 3.2).

Data on stellar metallicity are derived indirectly from Mg (Mg_2 index) and Fe line strengths and some empirical or/and theoretical calibrations. The iron mass present in galaxies is therefore much more uncertain that the iron mass present in the ICM. Buzzoni et al. [30] derived a mean iron abundance in ellipticals of [Fe/H]= 0.15, corresponding to a Mg_2 index of 0.3, with a large spread of ± 0.5 among the galaxy population. [Fe/H] is the usual logarithmic abundance relative to the sun.

It is well established that the Mg_2 index is tightly correlated with the central velocity dispersion [31]. It indicates that more massive galaxies should have a higher metallicity. However the direct correlation between Mg_2 and luminosity shows a considerably larger scatter [32] and it is not really meaningful to derive a [Fe/H] versus L relationship from the Mg_2 versus L relationship and [Fe/H] - Mg_2 calibration. Let us just notice that the stellar metallicity can vary by about a factor of 2 either way around the mean value and that this mean value is roughly reached for a galaxy of $L_V = 3 \times 10^{10} \, L_\odot$, a luminosity close to the break luminosity in the Schechter luminosity distribution. This mean metallicity can be considered as typical for clusters in a first approximation, and one gets for the iron mass over luminosity ratio (for $M^*/L_V = 6$, see below):

$$\frac{M^*_{Fe}}{L_V} \approx 10^{-2} \frac{M_\odot}{L_\odot} \tag{3}$$

In conclusion the amount of iron in the stellar component and in the ICM of clusters are similar [2,8].

Further constraints on the variation of metallicity among galaxies are given by the recent data on Mg_2, Fe5270 and Fe5335 index[33], covering a Mg_2 index range of 0.2 - 0.35, i.e more than 2 orders of magnitude in luminosity. They seem to indicate that Magnesium is overabundant with respect to Iron in giant ellipticals (with again a large scatter): [Mg/Fe]= 0.2-0.3 and that it increases with galaxy luminosity or mass: the variation of [Fe/H] should be about half that of [Mg/H].

The measurements on the metallicity in the hot gaseous component of ellipticals, made in X-ray, are scarce. X-ray observations (Ginga, BBXRT, Rosat) of the hot corona of the bright elliptical galaxies NGC 4472, NGC 1399 and NGC 4636 indicate iron abundances less than twice solar, with best fit values around solar [6,7,34,35]. Recent ASCA data [36] seem to confirm this low metallicity with even smaller best fit values: 1/2 solar or below. However the studied sample is still small and only simple models for the galactic halos have been considered yet. We must note that, if such very low values are further confirmed, we shall be facing a serious problem: no chemical evolution model (with no inflow) can accommodate a metallicity in the ISM (below solar) lower than in the stellar component (above solar). For galaxies inside clusters, this discrepancy could be indicative of an important dilution effect by accretion from the ICM. There might also be a serious problem in the stellar metallicity determination.

2.3.2. Mass over luminosity ratio and gas content

The mass to light ratio (M/L) is an important constraint because it depends on the IMF. Enhanced formation of massive stars in more massive galaxies, leaving more remnants, have actually been invoked to explain the apparent increase of M/L with mass [37]. Typical values [38,20] are M/L_V of 6 ± 3 for a galaxy of $L_V= 3\ 10^{10}\ L_\odot$. The variation of M/L_V with luminosity is uncertain [38,39]. It seems to slightly increase with luminosity [32,38], $M/L_V \propto L_V^{0.2-0.3}$.

Finally most of the gas in elliptical galaxies is in the form of a hot halo, as revealed by X-ray measurements. The gas content is low [40], with typical gas over stellar mass ranging from 0.001 to 0.07. The presence and properties of this hot halo (density and temperature distribution) is an important constraint on the dynamical history of elliptical galaxies [13,15].

3. The problem of the heavy element enrichment in clusters

3.1 Modeling of the enrichment from the galaxies ; the iron yield

All the models proposed in the recent years [8-20] take into account the usual scenario for elliptical galaxies, i.e. a starburst phase soon in their evolution and ICM enrichment through SN driven outflow. The basic ingredients of such models are the star formation rate (SFR), the initial mass function (IMF), the stellar lifetimes and remnant masses, the heavy elements production versus stellar mass (yield), and the energetics of the gas (i.e., heating by SN, radiative cooling, gravitational potential) which rules the ejection process. The resulting iron and gas mass ejected by each galaxy depends on the galaxy mass and one must integrate the contribution from each galaxy over the galactic mass distribution inside a cluster. This distribution can be derived from the Schechter luminosity function of the cluster galaxies, if the M/L ratio is known.

We must first emphasise that the modeling of iron production is specially uncertain because fundamental information on the iron producers themselves, the SNe, are lacking. If we know with some confidence how much iron is produced by SNI, their rate in the past is uncertain due to the nature of their progenitor (WD in binary systems): it depends on the efficiency of formation for binary systems and on the distance of the two stars. Conversely the progenitors of SNII are known (stars more massive than 8 $M_\odot$) and the SNII rates is a direct consequence of the IMF and star formation rate assumed but the SNII Fe yield is uncertain.

The second difficulty stems from the intrinsic complexity of the problem. A realistic model for elliptical galaxies would require a full hydrodynamical treatment of the ISM, combined with a follow-up of the chemical and photometric evolution, on a multi-phase representation of the galaxy (including at least a hot phase and cold clouds where stars are formed). Not surprisingly the theoretical works, that we cannot review in details here, have concentrated on specific aspects: dynamical evolution of the ISM (and X-ray properties of the hot gaseous halo) or chemical evolution (modeling the ISM, stars and ICM metallicities). The first type of models [12-15] rely on detailed hydrodynamical simulations at the expense of a rather crude modeling of the chemical evolution. This is of course the opposite for the second ones [2,9-11,18-20]

Finally the potentially high number of parameters to be considered in the cluster enrichment problem must not hide the fact that there is actually one fundamental parameter [2]: the iron yield assumed, i.e the relative production of iron (or integrated SN rate) per stellar mass, directly constrained by the observed iron mass over stellar mass ratio. Let us first compare this ratio observed in our galaxy to that observed in clusters (from Eqs 1 and 2, and M/L =6 ratio for E/S0 galaxies):

$$\left[\frac{M_{Fe}}{M_*}\right]_{Galaxy} \approx 10^{-3} \text{ and } \left[\frac{M_{Fe}}{M_*}\right]_{Cluster} = \frac{M_{Fe}^{ICM}}{M_*} + \frac{M_{Fe}^*}{M_*} \approx 5.10^{-3} \qquad (3)$$

The iron mass over stellar mass ratio is thus about 5 times larger in clusters than in our Galaxy. Therefore one cannot account for the iron present in clusters by a "standard" iron yield, i.e. one adapted to our Galaxy [2]. This is a real challenge for any enrichment model. Considering directly the total iron mass to light ratio, Renzini et al.[8] (see also Ciotti et al.[15]) reached a similar conclusion: a high supernova activity in the past is required (i.e high iron global yield), either a much higher SNI past average rate as compared to the present value observed in ellipticals (at least a factor of 10) or a high SNII rate (due for instance to a very flat IMF). Thus the main issue is to understand the relative importance of SNI and SNII in the enrichment process (for both the gaseous and stellar components of clusters) and why their integrated rate has been so high.

3.2 SNI or SNII ?

A key observational quantity for this issue is the α elements to Fe ratio, relative to solar. Indeed α elements (O, Mg) are only produced by SNII while Fe can be produced by both SNI and SNII. Ratio above solar are typical of enrichment by SNII since SNIs play the major role for the iron enrichment in our Galaxy. The observation of α elements in the ICM is difficult: it requires a high sensitivity and good spectral resolution at low energy and generally spectro-imagery capability. Indeed these elements are completely ionised at typical ICM temperature (above 2 keV) and significant emission is only expected in cooling flows or possibly in poor clusters.

There are now more and more converging evidences that SNII play the major role both in the ICM enrichment and the establishment of the stellar metallicity observed in present day ellipticals:

1- The high (O/Fe) ratio observed in Virgo and Perseus [41] already pointed towards a metal enrichment mainly by SNII. This relative overabundance of Oxygen seems now confirmed by the last ASCA observations (see the communication of R.Mushotzky).

2- The same applies for stellar metallicities. A (Mg/Fe) ratio about twice solar is expected if SNII are a major contributor to the stellar metallicity, and again a high SNII rate seems to be required, at least to explain the observed iron overabundance in massive galaxies. If a normal IMF is assumed, detailed chemical evolution models predict stellar Fe abundances below solar [9] and flatter IMF (higher SNII rates) for more massive galaxies are in better agreement with the variation of the (Mg/Fe) ratio with galaxy mass [42].

3- If the low iron abundances in elliptical galaxies is confirmed models with high SNI rates in the past are rejected since they predict iron abundances much higher than solar [35]. Actually even assuming a constant SNI rate equal to its present value is hardly compatible with the observed stellar metallicity, while it falls short by an order of magnitude in explaining the ICM iron mass [7]

4- From a more theoretical point of view, enrichment models based on standard IMF and rapidly decreasing SNI rates are not fully satisfactory either. To account for the ICM Fe content, i.e. to insure both a correct global iron production and its further ejection, the models based on SNs require a rapidly decreasing SNI rate [15]: $s > 1.4$, when the SNI rates is empirically parametrized as $R_{SNI}(t) \propto t^{-s}$. Other models, directly based on a more specific modeling of SNI progenitors (C-deflagration in white dwarfs in binary systems), predict a much weaker time dependence of the SNI rate [9,12-14] and then a less efficient heating. Although they produce iron in enough quantity [10], David et al.[14] showed that a high SNII rate (flat IMF) in the past is further needed to explain the high Fe content of the ICM (the iron produced by SNI is not entirely ejected).

If SNII have indeed play the major role in the ICM enrichment, it would be interesting to understand why (rather than to simply assume an ad-hoc flat IMF). One major advantage of the standard picture, assumed by most authors till now (normal IMF and major contribution from SNI, as in our Galaxy) was its simplicity; moreover it left open the possibility of an Universal IMF, as emphasized by Renzini et al.[8]. Actually there are already indications both in our Galaxy and in starburst galaxies that the IMF may not be universal and in particular is linked to the Star Formation Rate (SFR) through the physical conditions in the star formation regions.

The observed characteristics of starburst galaxies seem to be fitted better by models where only high mass stars are produced with a lower cut-off for the IMF at m ~ 3 $M_\odot$ [43-45]. The existence of a truncated IMF in case of high SFR is further supported by some theoretical arguments [45-47]. Such a IMF could also apply at the beginning of the evolution of elliptical galaxies, supposed to have experienced an even more intense starburst phase at the scale of the whole galaxy [46]. This type of IMF at the early stage of the evolution, has also the advantage a priori that a very high SNII rate is obtained producing both iron and thermal energy very fast and thus inducing a SN-driven wind of enriched gas very soon, i.e. while the gas mass fraction is high and few of the iron is blocked into stars. We can thus expect to account for the ICM enrichment. However since we observe long living stars (m < 1 $M_\odot$) in present day ellipticals this first phase (high mass mode of star formation) must have been followed by a more quiescent phase, producing stars in the whole mass range (normal mode of star formation), requiring some gas to be still available after the wind phase. In a recent paper[20] we studied quantitatively such a bimodal model, which is briefly presented in the next section.

This type model can be also applied to our Galaxy. Larson [37] has proposed a bimodal star formation for our Galaxy, which combines linearly a high mass mode, which forms only high mass stars and which is preponderant at early times only and a normal mode which forms stars of all masses at a nearly constant rate. The underlying idea, supported by observational data in our Galaxy, was already that "the formation of massive stars are favored at times and in regions where the SFR is high". Furthermore François et al.[48] have shown that if the two modes appear sequentially (first the high mass mode) all the main observational constraints on our Galaxy are satisfied: the G-dwarf metallicity, the age-metallicity distribution and the abundances of Deuterium and other isotopes of single elements.

In conclusion bimodal models could be an alternative way to account for the observations on our Galaxy, starburst galaxies, elliptical galaxies as well as on the ICM.

4. Bimodal star formation model for ellipticals

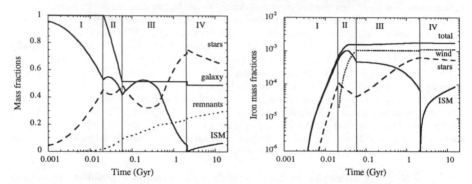

Figure 2: Variation with time of the mass fractions in the different components for a galaxy of initial mass $M_T = 3 \ 10^{11} \ M_O$ and $(v_1, v_2, \alpha) = (40, 18, 2) \ Gyr^{-1}$. Left Figure: Heavy full line: galaxy mass as compared to the initial mass, M_{Gal}/M_T. Full line, Dashed line, Dotted line: respectively gas mass, living stars mass and remnant mass fraction inside the galaxy: M_{Gas}/M_{Gal}, M_*/M_{Gal}, M_{rem}/M_{Gal}. Right Figure: Variation with time of the iron mass fractions. Heavy full line, Dotted line, Dashed line, Full line: respectively total iron mass fraction, iron mass fraction ejected outside the galaxy, iron mass fraction in the stellar component and in the ISM: M_{Fe}/M_T, M_{Fe}^{ej}/M_T, M_{Fe}^*/M_T, M_{Fe}^{ISM}/M_T. The thin vertical lines mark the different evolution phase: I = early burst phase; II = wind phase; III = quiescent star formation phase; IV = no star formation.

The galaxies are supposed to be formed from a "cloud" of gas with no pre-enrichment and the star formation is assumed to occur on a short time scale, following the standard picture of ellipticals. We assume that only high mass stars (Salpeter IMF truncated at 3 $M_\odot$) are formed during a first violent phase where the SFR is parametrised as $v_1 \exp(-t/\tau)$. Most of the heavy elements are produced, by SNII, during this phase (see Figure 2). This early phase ends with a strong galactic wind driven by SNII when the specific thermal energy exceeds the gravitational binding energy of the interstellar gas. Our model does not include a detailed hydrodynamical modeling of the wind and we introduce a simple parametrisation of the outflow: $dM_{Gal}(t)/dt = - \alpha M_{Gal}(t)$. During this wind phase we assume that star formation stops, due to a too hot environment. This phase typically last 0.04 Gyr, the lifetime of a 8 $M_\odot$ star: when the last SNII has exploded, the specific thermal energy decreases rapidly due to both cooling and mass input from longer living stars. A new star formation phase follows (phase III), where stars are formed from the pre-enriched gas left over during the wind phase and from the gas restored by the long living stars produced during the high mass mode. In this phase we assume a more quiescent star formation (SFR $\alpha v_1 \sigma$, where is the gas mass fraction), with a normal IMF (normal mode). The stars still alive today, which make the present measured stellar metallicity, are born during this very phase. The luminosity is followed throughout the evolution.

The evolution of the different components are illustrated on Figure 2, for a galaxy of initial mass $M_T = 3 \; 10^{11} \; M_\odot$ which ends with a luminosity of $3 \; 10^{10} \; L_\odot$. For $(\nu_1,\nu_2,\alpha)= (40,2,18) \; Gyr^{-1}$, we found a quite good agreement with observations: [Fe/H]= 0.16, [Mg/Fe]= 0.25, M_{lum}/L_v= 8.5 and a remaining gas mass fraction of about 6 %. The ISM metallicity is a little too high (twice solar). The galaxy has lost about half of its initial mass and the ejected iron mass over present luminosity ratio is $1.9 \; 10^{-2} \; M_\odot/L_\odot$.

The evolution depends on the galaxy mass due to the deeper gravitational potential for larger galaxies: the winds occurs later in more massive galaxies and star formation proceed further. As a consequence the final stellar metallicities increase with the galaxy mass: from 1.1 time solar to 1.6 time solar for Fe; from 1.9 time solar to 2.9 time solar for Mg. After integration over the cluster population (Schechter luminosity function) we also perfectly recover the ICM iron mass per unit luminosity of member galaxies: $2 \; 10^{-2} \; M_\odot/L_\odot$. However a possible weak point of the model is that [Mg/Fe] and [M/L] ratio vary only slightly with galaxy final luminosity.

We discuss the influence of the three main parameters in our model: astration rate in the burst phase (ν_1) and in the quiescent phase (ν_2), mass loss rate during the wind phase (α). We found that the global iron production is very robust with respect to the parameters: since most of the heavy element are produced during the high mass phase, it is ruled by the quantity of gas processed during that phase, which is regulated by the occurrence of the wind, multiplied by the global yield of the truncated IMF. This indicate that we have chosen a correct global iron yield and further support our choice of this type of IMF. On the other hand a key factor is the total mass lost during the wind. It must be 50 % in order to insure a correct share between present stars and the ICM as determined by the observed M_{Fe}^{ICM}/M_{Fe}^* ratio.

We computes the total contribution of the winds to the ICM and found $M_{Gas}^{Eject}/L_V=9.3$. It is concluded, as in previous works [10,14], that most of the cluster gas (50% for groups; 80 % for rich clusters) is of primordial origin. We also predict that the abundances of O and Si in the ICM, relative to Fe are higher than solar.

5. Conclusion

A large SN rate in the past is needed to explain the high iron mass present in the ICM. Available data seem now to favour SNII as the major contributors for the Iron production, at the expense of SNI. Whatever the model, the present ICM cannot be accounted for by the ejection from the galaxies: a large part of the ICM is of primordial origin (larger for richer clusters). Hence, the observed decrease of [Fe] with kT can be explained by a dilution effect.

In the future, it is essential to increase the number of clusters with measured luminosities (in each galaxy type), gas mass and iron mass and thus to perform Optical - X-ray (ROSAT, ASCA, XMM, AXAF) combined analysis. A better estimate of the ICM mass requires to observe far from the cluster center, while the Fe mass determination, which depends on the spatial variation of Fe, requires true spectro-imagery. Finally, in order to distinguish between SNI and SNII as a major source for the observed Fe, one must determine the relative abundances of O/Fe and Si/Fe in elliptical galaxies (halo) and clusters (cooling flows, groups), since only SNII produce O or Si. The results currently obtained by the ASCA satellite are of prime interest in that respect.

References

220

1   David, L, Arnaud, K., Forman, W., Jones,C., 1990, ApJ 356, 32
2   Arnaud, M., Rothenflug, R., Boulade, O., Vigroux, L., Vangioni-Flam, E., 1992, A&A, 254, 49.
3   Böhringer, H., 1994, in Cosmological Aspects of X-ray Clusters of Galaxies, W.C. Seitter (ed.), Kluwer Publ., in press
4   Hatsukade 1989, phD Thesis, ISAS RN 435
5   Edge, A., Stewart, G.,1991a, MNRAS, 252, 414
6   Ikebe, Y., Ohashi, T., Makishima, K., Tsuru, T., Fabbiano, G., Kim, D., Trinchieri, G., Hatsukade, I., Yamashita, K., Kondo, H., 1992, ApJ 384, L5
7   Tsuru, T., 1993, phD Thesis, ISAS RN 528
8   Renzini, A., Ciotti, L., D'Ercole, A., Pellegrini, S., 1993, ApJ, 419, 52
9   Matteucci, F., Tornambé, A., 1987, A&A 185, 51
10 Matteucci, F., Vettolani, G., 1988, A&A 202, 21
11 Matteucci, F., 1992, ApJ 397, 32
12 David, L., Forman, W., Jones, C., 1990, ApJ 359, 29
13 David, L., Forman, W., Jones, C., 1991, ApJ 369, 121
14 David, L., Forman, W., Jones, C., 1991, ApJ 380, 39
15 Ciotti, L., D'Ercole, A., Pellegrini, S., Renzini, A., 1991, ApJ 376, 380
16 White, R., 1991, ApJ 367, 69
17 Hattori, M., Terasawa, N., 1993, ApJ, 406, L55
18 Ferrini, F., Poggianti, B., 1993, ApJ 410, 44
19 Mihara, K., Takahara, F., 1994, preprint
20 Elbaz, D., Arnaud, M., Vangionni-Flam, E., 1994, A&A, submitted
21 Yamashita, K., 1991, 28th Yamada conference "Frontiers of X-ray Astronomy", p475
22 Fuchs, B., Materne, J., 1982, A&A, 113, 85
23 Wirth, 1983, ApJ, 274, 541
24 Richter , O.G., 1989, A&ASuppSeries, 77, 237
25 Böhringer, H., Schwarz, R., Briel, U., Voges, W., Ebeling, H., Hartner, G., Cruddace, R., 1992, in "Clusters and Superclusters of galaxies", A.C. Fabian ed., NATO ASI Series, vol 366, page.71
26 Schwarz, R., Edge, A., Voges, W., Böhringer, H., Ebeling, H., Briel, U.G, 1992, A&A 256, L11
27 Briel, U., Henry, J., Böhringer, H., 1992, A&A 259, L31
28 Henry, J., Briel, U., Nulsen, P., 1993, A&A 271, 413
            David, L, Arnaud, K., Forman, W., Jones,C., 1990a, ApJ 356, 32
30 Buzzoni, A., Gariboldi, G., Mantegazza, L.,1992, A&A 103, 1814
31 Bender R., Burstein, D., Faber, S.M., 1993, ApJ, 411, 153
32 Vader, J.P., 1986, ApJ 306, 390
33 Worthey, G., Faber, S.M., Gonzalez, J.J., 1992, ApJ 398, 69
34 Serlemitsos, P.J., Loewenstein, M., Mushotzky, R.F., Marshall, F.E., Petre, R., 1993, ApJ, 413, 518
35 Forman, W., Jones, C., David, L., Franx, M., Makishima, K., Ohashi, T., 1993, ApJ, 418, L55
36 Awaki, H., et al., 1994, PASJ, in press
37 Larson R., 1986, MNRAS, 218, 409
38 Bender R., Burstein, D., Faber, S.M., 1992, ApJ, 399, 462
39 Djorgovski, S., Davis, M., 1987, ApJ, 313, 59
40 Forman, W., Jones, C.,Tucker, W., 1985, 1 ApJ 293, 102
41 Canizares, C.R., Markert, T.H., Donahue, M.E., 1988, in Cooling Flows in Clusters and Galaxies, ed.2A.C. Fabian (Dordrecht:Kluwer), Page 63
42 Matteucci, F., 1994, A&A, in press
43 Wright, G.S., Joseph, R.D., Robertson, N.A., James, P.A., Meikle, W.P.S., 1988, MNRAS, 233, 1
44 Rieke, G.H., Loken, K., Rieke, M.J., Tamblyn, 1993, ApJ, 412, 99
45 Doane, J., Mathews, W.G., 1993, ApJ, 419, 573
46 Silk, ,J., 1993, in The Feedback of Chemical Evolution on the Stellar Content of Galaxies, ed.D.Alloin and G. Stasinska, page 299
47 Henriksen R.N., 1991, ApJ 377, 500
48 François P., Vangioni-Flam E., Audouze, J., 1990, ApJ, 361, 487

IRON AS A TRACER IN CLUSTERS OF GALAXIES

ALVIO RENZINI

Dipartimento di Astronomia, Università di Bologna, CP 596, I-40100 Bologna, Italy

Institute of Astronomy, University of Tokyo, Mitaka, Japan

ABSTRACT. Several astrophysical inferences are derived from the empirical *iron mass to light ratio* (IMLR) of the ICM and stellar components of clusters and groups of galaxies. The IMLR of the ICM appears to be independent of cluster richness, which indicates that no baryon degassing took place. A small group instead appears to have much smaller values of the IMLR, which argues for lesser groups having lost most of their original ICM, probably at early times. The total cluster IMLR is used to estimate the total kinetic energy injectd by supernovae, while the IMLR of the ICM allows a fairly precise estimate of the total energy input from galactic winds. It is found that $\sim 80 - 90\%$ of the SN energy is radiated away during galaxy formation, and the residual 10–20% is used to drive early galactic winds. This appears to be largely sufficient to have strongly affected the ICM evolution in groups and small clusters, while for large clusters the size of the effect is sensitive to the relative timing of galaxy and cluster formation. Finally, it is argued that existing data favor the notion of a systematic increase of the baryonic fraction of clusters with cluster mass, in apparent conflict with existing simulations for the structure and ICM evolution.

1. The Iron Mass to Light Ratio of the ICM and of Cluster Galaxies

The iron content of clusters of galaxies offers to us a powerful tool for the investigation of a number of interesting astrophysical issues, such as:

- The relative role of the various supernova types in manufacting all the iron that is observed.
- Iron as a tracer of baryon circulation on various scales.
- Iron as a record of the *integral* past SN heating, star light production, and galaxy winds.
- The iron to other elements ratios as indicators of the time scale of galaxy formation.

Most of these topics are extensively discussed by Renzini *et al.* (1993, hereafter RCDP). Here some of the main conclusions are reported, along with a few additional considerations. What follows is entirely based on data available before *ASCA*, and taking all published data (e.g., iron abundances) at face value. Newer data – some of which are being reported at this meeting – may affect some of the conclusions, but the inferences presented here are so simple and direct that the implications of new observations should become easily apparent.

The most effective way of quantifying the iron content of clusters is by their iron mass to light ratio (IMLR), i.e., by the ratio of the total mass of iron in a cluster over the total optical luminosity of the cluster galaxies. The IMLR can be defined separately for the ICM, for the galaxies themselves, as well as for the cluster as a whole.

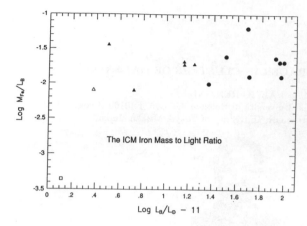

The ICM Iron Mass to Light Ratio

Fig. 1.- The iron mass to light ratio (IMLR) for the ICM of clusters and groups as a function of the total optical luminosity of the clusters. Data are taken as follows. Filled circles: Arnaud et al. (1992); filled triangles: Tsuru (1993); open triangle: David et al. (1994a); open square: Mulchaey et al. (1993), assuming $H_0 = 50$, i.e. $h = H_0/100 = 1/2$.

Fig. 1 shows the IMLR for the ICM of several clusters and groups. The IMLR is here given by the product of the central iron abundance as obtained from X-ray observations times the total mass of the ICM, i.e., chemical homogeneity is assumed. If gradients were present, then values in Fig. 1 may overestimate the actual IMLR. With one exception, the IMLR appears to be remarkably constant, irrespective of the cluster optical luminosity:

$$\left(\frac{M_{Fe}}{L_B}\right)^{ICM} \simeq 0.01 - 0.02 \qquad (M_\odot/L_\odot). \tag{1}$$

The exception is the small group NGC 2300 (Mulchaey et al. 1993), the faintest object in Fig. 1, that appears to have an IMLR some 50 times smaller than all other objects.

Two important implications follow from these data:

• No baryon degassing has taken place in (rich) clusters ($L_B \gtrsim$ few $10^{11} L_\odot$), as otherwise a trend of the IMLR with L_B would likely result. Accretion of primordial gas is instead allowed, as this would affect the ICM iron abundance, but not its IMLR.

• A major iron loss, and therefore baryon degassing along with it appears instead to have taken place in NGC 2300, probably at early times. Given its low iron abundance (~ 0.06 solar), most of the present intragroup medium would have been re-accreted at later times.

More and more accurate IMLR values are required to confirm these inferences, especially for small groups ($L_B \lesssim 10^{11} L_\odot$), so as to set a precise boundary between open groups (that have experienced baryonic degassing) and closed clusters.

The IMLR for the iron now locked into stars inside cluster galaxies is given by:

$$\frac{M_{Fe}^\star}{L_B} = <Z_{Fe}^\star> \frac{M_\star}{L_B} \simeq 0.01 - 0.02 \quad (M_\odot/L_\odot), \tag{2}$$

having adopted a solar abundance (~ 0.002) for the average iron abundance (by mass) in stars, and a value between 5 and 10 for the $M_\star/L_B$ ratio of the stellar component of galaxies. Thus, there appears to be a nearly equal amout of iron in the ICM as there is locked into stars. Note however that both IMLRs depend on the assumed value of the Hubble constant, and do so in different ways. If one assumes both IMLRs to be 0.015 for $H_0 = 50$ [thus with a total IMLR $\sim 0.03 (M_\odot/L_\odot)$], then the total IMLR becomes:

$$\left(\frac{M_{Fe}}{L_B}\right)^{TOT} \simeq 0.01 \, h^{-\frac{1}{2}} + 0.03 \, h \qquad (M_\odot/L_\odot), \tag{3}$$

where the first term on the r.h.s. refers to the ICM and the second to galaxies. Thus, for $H_0 = 100$ ($h = 1$) one would have a total IMLR $\sim 0.01 + 0.03 = 0.04$, and one concludes that the total IMLR is not very sensitive to the adopted value of the Hubble constant, but the relative share of iron between the two cluster components shows a significant dependence. The cluster iron share between the two components clearly sets a strong constraint on models of galaxy formation and evolution: nearly as much iron needs to be ejected from galaxies as must remain locked into stars.

3. Using Iron to Make Integrals

The total amount of iron in clusters represnts a record of the overall past supernova (SN) activity and past mass and energy ejected from cluster galaxies. These values of the IMLR are now used to set some constraint on these relevant cluster properties. Theoretical estimates of the overall SN and galactic wind activity in clusters are very model dependent. Here an *empirical* approach is presented. The total SN heating is given by the kinetic energy released by one SN ($\sim 10^{51}$ erg) times the number of SNs that have exploded. It is convenient to express this energy per unit present optical light L_B, i.e.:

$$\frac{E_{SN}}{L_B} = 10^{51} \frac{N_{SN}}{L_B} = 10^{51} \left(\frac{M_{Fe}}{L_B}\right)^{TOT} \frac{1}{<M_{Fe}>} \simeq 10^{50} \quad (\text{erg}/L_\odot), \tag{4}$$

where the total IMLR is taken to be 0.03 $M_\odot/L_\odot$ as derived above, and the average iron mass release per SN event is assumed to be 0.3 $M_\odot$. This is appropriate to the case where $\sim 3/4$ of all iron is made by Type Ia SNs, and $\sim 1/4$ by Type II and other SN types (see RCDP). Were all the iron made instead by SNIIs, the resulting SN energy would go up by perhaps a factor of 3 or 4, as the average SNII makes less iron than a typical SNIa. This estimate should therefore be accurate to within a factor of 2 or 3.

The presence of a large amount of iron in the ICM indicates that matter (and then energy) has been ejected from galaxies. Arguments are presented in RCDP supporting the notion that matter was ejected rather than swept by ram pressure stripping, as also indicated by the IMLR of the ICM being independent of cluster richness. The kinetic energy injected into the ICM by galactic winds, again per unit cluster light, is given by 1/2 the ejected mass times the typical wind velocity squared, i.e.:

$$\frac{E_w}{L_B} = \frac{1}{2} \left(\frac{M_{Fe}}{L_B}\right)^{ICM} \left\langle\frac{v_w^2}{Z_w^{Fe}}\right\rangle \simeq 1.5 \times 10^{49} \frac{1}{Z_w^{Fe}/Z_\odot^{Fe}} \cdot \left(\frac{v_w}{500\,\text{km s}^{-1}}\right)^2 \simeq 10^{49} \quad (\text{erg}/L_\odot), \tag{5}$$

where the empirical IMLR for the ICM has been used, the average metallicity of the winds Z_w^{Fe} is assumed to be twice solar, and the wind velocity v_w cannot be much different from the escape velocity from individual galaxies, as usual in the case of thermal winds. Again, this estimate may be regarded as accurate to within a factor of 2, or so.

A first inference from these estimates is that $\sim 5 - 10\%$ of the kinetic energy released by SNs must survive as kinetic energy of galactic winds, thus contributing to the heating of the ICM. A roughly similar amount should go into work to extract the gas from the potential well of individual galaxies, and the residual $\sim 80 - 90\%$ has to be radiated away.

One can further indulge in this kind of considerations by comparing the above energies to other relevant energies. The binding energy of the stellar (baryonic) component of elliptical galaxies (that dominate in rich clusters) is in the range $E_*^{BIN}/L_B \simeq 10^{49} - 10^{50}\,\text{erg}/L_\odot$, increasing within this range with galaxy luminosity. Thus $E_w \lesssim E_*^{BIN} \lesssim E_{SN}$ (see RCDP for a brief discussion on the implications for elliptical galaxy formation).

The energy input from galactic winds can also be compared to the present thermal energy of the ICM, that roughly increases with cluster luminosity as:

$$\frac{E_{ICM}^{TH}}{L_B} \simeq 2 \times 10^{51} \left(\frac{L_B}{10^{13}}\right) \quad (\text{erg}/L_\odot) \tag{6}$$

Thus, $E_{ICM}^{TH} \gg E_w$ in big clusters ($L_B \sim 10^{13} L_\odot$), and galactic wind heating may be irrelevant for the evolution of the ICM. On the contrary, $E_{ICM}^{TH} \simeq E_w$ in small groups ($L_B \simeq 10^{11} L_\odot$), and galactic winds may well have substantially degassed them at early times, which is indeed in qualitative agreement with the low IMLR observed in the NGC 2300 group.

224

Crucial for the evolution of the ICM is however the relative timing of galactic wind heating and cluster formation (Kaiser 1991; Cavaliere et al. 1993). Most of star formation in cluster elliptical galaxies – and therefore most SN activity and galactic winds – appears to be confined at very early times, i.e., at $z \gtrsim 2$ (Bower et al. 1992; Renzini & Ciotti 1993). Thus, if the heat given by Eq. (5) is released either too early or too late the predicted evolution of the ICM will be at variance with the constraints sets by the observed X-ray evolution of clusters as well as with the present state of the ICM.

The importance of heating of the ICM is perhaps most clearly shown by the radial trend of the baryon fraction (BF) within clusters. CDM models for the evolution of the ICM including baryon cooling, but not heating, predict a radially decreasing BF (Babul & Katz 1993), i.e., baryons become more centrally concentrated than the CDM. This is at variance with the observations, that show just the opposite trend, with baryons being more diffused than CDM (David et al. 1994b). Galactic wind heating may be responsible for this effect, though in big clusters a fine synchronization may be required between the epoch of galactic wind heating and cluster formation, the present thermal content of the ICM being ~ 200 times larger than the available heating. Alternatively, other heat sources may be at work (AGN jets? pre-heating of the baryons before being incorporated into clusters?). In any event, a scenario in which both galaxy formation and substantial clustering proceed at early times ($z \gtrsim 2$) appears to be favored over cosmological models in which structures grow slowly.

4. Does the Baryon Fraction in Clusters Increase with Cluster Luminosity?

A final question concerns the global value of the BF of clusters. White et al. (1993) have recently shown that under standard CDM assumptions clusters cannot accrete much baryons so as to significantly increase their BF above the cosmic value. If so, the BF should be nearly constant among clusters, since the constant IMLR indicates that no baryon degassing took place. There is however a hint that the BF may not be constant among clusters, and if so we would have the direct evidence that the BF can change with time. Indeed, in fairly big clusters most of the baryons are in the ICM, and the ICM mass to light ratio appears to increase with cluster luminosity: $(M_{ICM}/L_B) \sim L_B^{0.5}$, though with some uncertainty (Arnaud et al. 1992). Thus, BF$\sim M_{ICM}/M = (M_{ICM}/L_B) \cdot (L_B/M) \simeq L_B^{0.5}(L_B/M)$, and the run of the BF with cluster luminosity depends on the behavior of the cluster M/L_B ratio. From the apparent concentration of well studied clusters about a fundamental plane (Schaeffer et al. 1993), it appears that no significant trend of the cluster M/L_B ratio exists with cluster luminosity (Renzini & Ciotti 1993), as also indicated by X-ray observations (David et al. 1994b). Therefore, if really the baryon mass to light ratio scales as $\sim L_B^{0.5}$, and the cluster $M/L_B \sim$ const., then the BF would also scale with cluster richness as $\sim L_B^{0.5}$. If so, rich clusters of galaxies would have been more effective in absorbing baryons from the IGM than predicted by the models of White et al. (1993). It appears of crucial importance fot its far reaching implications to accurately establish the behavior of the ICM and total M/L ratios as a function of cluster luminosity.

I would like to express my deep gratitude to the *Japan Society for the Promotion of Science* for its kind hospitality, and to Dr.s Nobuo Arimoto and Masaru Hamabe for their invaluable assistence during my stage at the Institute of Astronomy of the University of Tokyo.

REFERENCES

Arnaud, M., et al. 1992, A&A, 254, 49
Babul, A., & Katz, N. 1993, ApJ, 406, L51
Bower, R.G., Lucey, J.R., & Ellis, R.S. 1992, MNRAS, 254, 613
Cavaliere, A., Colafrancesco, S., & Menci, N. 1993, ApJ, 415, 50
David, L.P., Jones, C., Forman, W., & Daines, S. 1994a, CfA Preprint No. 3780
David, L.P., Jones, C., & Forman, W. 1994b, CfA Preprint No. 3760
Kaiser, N. 1991, ApJ, 383, 104
Mulchaey, J.S., Davis, D.S., Mushotzky, R.F., & Burnstein, D. 1993, ApJ, 404, L9
Renzini, A., & Ciotti, L. 1993, ApJ, 416, L49
Renzini, A., Ciotti, L., D'Ercole, A., & Pellegrini, S. 1993, ApJ, 419, 52
Schaeffer, R., Maurogordato, S., Cappi, A., & Bernardeau, F. 1993, MNRAS, 263, L21
Tsuru, T. 1993, PhD Thesis, University of Tokyo, ISAS RN 528
White, S.D.M., Navarro, J.F., Evrard, A.E., & Frenk, C.S. 1993, Nature, 366, 429

ROSAT STUDIES OF COMPACT GALAXY GROUPS

Trevor Ponman
School of Physics & Space Research
University of Birmingham, Birmingham B15 2TT, UK

ABSTRACT

The ROSAT X-ray telescope has provided an improvement in sensitivity over previous X-ray imagers which makes the study of the hot gas in galaxy groups possible for the first time. We have established the basic properties of the X-ray emission from a sample of 17 Hickson compact galaxy groups, and compare these with the well-known correlations which are seen in cluster properties. The groups appear to be anomalous in two respects: small temperature range and low metallicity. Possible reasons for this are discussed briefly.

1. INTRODUCTION

In the local Universe, the majority of galaxies are found in dynamically bound groups[1]. An understanding of the group environment and its influence on galaxy evolution is therefore very important. Although the Einstein Observatory made a few preliminary studies of X-ray emission from galaxy groups, it is only with the increased sensitivity of ROSAT that it has become possible to study a reasonable sample of groups in any detail. X-ray emission arises both from individual galaxies, and from hot gas trapped in group potential wells.

A particularly interesting subclass is *compact galaxy groups*, in which the galaxies are separated in projection by only a few galactic radii, and implied galaxy densities are 10^3–10^6 Mpc^{-3}.

This high density reduces the problem of contamination by fore- and background galaxies, and compact groups have been intensively investigated at longer wavelengths over the past decade, since a useful systematic collection was compiled from study of optical plates by Hickson[2].

Here we concentrate on the diffuse X-ray emission from compact groups, which ranges in luminosity over more than two orders of magnitude. We have assembled a sample of 17 Hickson groups which have been detected in the X-ray by the ROSAT PSPC, and investigate the overall properties of this emission, comparing it with the analagous results for galaxy clusters.

2. CORRELATION OF PROPERTIES

The X-ray properties shown in the figures below derive, in four cases, from the short ROSAT survey exposures analysed by Ebeling *et al.*[3]. For the rest, longer pointed observations are available, and for seven of these, the statistics are sufficiently good that it has been possible to fit a hot plasma model[4] to the X-ray spectrum (fixing the column at the expected galactic value[5]) and derive a temperature and metallicity. X-ray luminosities are bolometric values derived from the fitted spectrum, or where this is not available, from a typical group spectrum with $T = 1\,\mathrm{keV}$ and metallicity $Z = 0.3$ solar. Emission from individual galaxies, which can be present at a level $\sim 10^{41}$ erg s^{-1}, has not been removed in all cases, and may significantly contaminate the flux in the case of three of the groups – however, this will not change the thrust of our results.

For comparison with the groups, we compiled the properties of a set of ten galaxy clusters, for which bolometric X-ray luminosities and velocity dispersions (with errors) are available from Edge & Stewart[6], and metallicities from Yamashita[7].

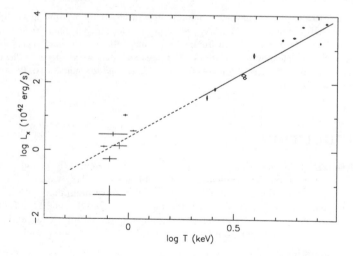

Fig.1: Relationship between X-ray temperature and (bolometric) X-ray luminosity for groups and clusters. In this and the following figures, clusters are represented by diamonds and groups by crosses, with sizes corresponding to 1σ errors. The solid line is the result of 2D regression over the cluster sample, and is extrapolated (dashed) for comparison with the groups.

$L_X : T$ **relation** – There is a tight correlation between X-ray luminosity and temperature for galaxy clusters. Fig.1 shows that the properties of groups fall fairly well on an extrapolation of the regression line ($L_X \propto T^{3.53}$) fitted through the clusters. However, it is worth noting that a selection effect is present, in that temperatures tend to be available only for the brighter groups, and the one really low luminosity group in the subsample (HCG90) falls well below the trend. In general there appears to be a very narrow spread in temperature within the groups, given the large range in luminosity.

$L_X : v$ **relation** – The looser relationship between luminosity and velocity dispersion in clusters reflects in part the difficulties of deriving reliable velocity dispersions. In the case of groups, a large error in v is inevitable, due to the small number of galaxies involved. We have adopted an error of 40%. On the other hand, the necessary information is available for the full sample of 17 groups. It appears from Fig.2 that the bulk of the groups fall off the cluster trend, having either lower v or higher L_X, though given the scatter, one would like larger samples to confirm the effect.

$T : v$ **relation** – The cluster data are reasonably well fitted by the $\beta = 1$ model (equal specific energy in gas and galaxies), which is shown dotted in Fig.3. However, it is clear that the group properties deviate strongly from this, in the sense that T varies very little for a considerable range in v. The low v groups are too hot.

$Z : T$ **relation** – Here the group results are particularly unexpected. A trend has been fairly clearly established from Ginga observations of clusters, whereby cooler clusters have higher metallicity. The galaxy groups, in contrast, seem to have remarkably *low* metallicities. It is

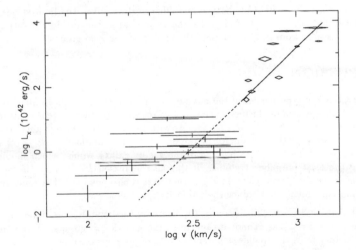

Fig.2: Relationship between galaxy velocity dispersion and X-ray luminosity for groups and clusters. The regression line is a fit to the cluster data.

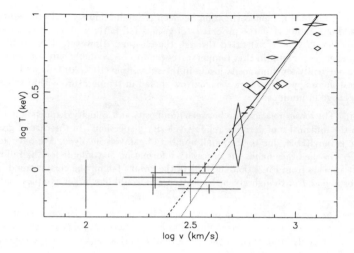

Fig.3: Relationship between galaxy velocity dispersion and X-ray temperature for groups and clusters. The solid regression line is a fit to the cluster data, extrapolated (dashed) to lower v, whilst the dotted line is the line along which the specific energy of gas and galaxies are equal.

wise to be cautious about ROSAT-derived metallicity values, given the limited spectral capability of the PSPC, and the possibility of temperature variations within the intragroup gas. However early results from ASCA[8] support the finding of low Z in groups.

3. DISCUSSION

In summary, the X-ray properties of the hot gas in compact groups seem to fit quite well onto the trends which are seen in clusters, except in two respects: (i) the gas temperature seems to have a lower bound at $\approx 0.8\,\text{keV}$, so that groups with low L_X and v have higher temperatures than expected, and (ii) the metallicity of the group gas is remarkably low ($Z \approx 0.2$). The first effect might result from extra heating of the gas by galaxy winds, which should be most apparent in the least luminous systems. If this also increased L_X it might account for the groups lying above the cluster trend in Fig.2, though it is also possible[9] that some groups have not yet virialised, which could reduce their velocity dispersion.

The second anomaly (low metallicity) might indicate that galaxy histories differ in groups and clusters, that metal-rich gas cannot escape from the galaxies in groups, or that much of it escapes altogether from the shallower potential wells of poor systems.

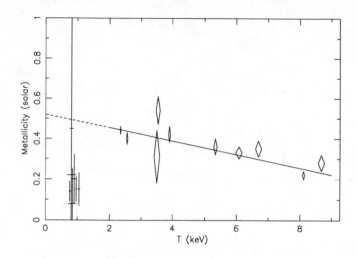

Fig.4: Relationship between gas temperature and metallicity for groups and clusters. The regression line is a fit to the cluster data.

REFERENCES

1. Tully R.B. *Astrophys. J.* **321**, 280 (1987).

2. Hickson P. *Astrophys. J.* **255**, 382 (1982).

3. Ebeling H., Voges W. & Böhringer H., submitted to *Astrophys. J.*(1994).

4. Raymond J.C. & Smith B.W. *Astrophys. J. Suppl.* **35**, 419 (1977).

5. Stark A.A. *et al. Astrophys. J. Suppl.* **79**, 77 (1992).

6. Edge A.C. & Stewart G.C. *Mon. Not. R. astr. Soc.* **252**, 428 (1991).

7. Yamashita K. in *Frontiers of X-ray Astronomy*, 475 (1992).

8. Mushotzky R.F., this meeting.

9. Mamon G.A. in *Gravitational Dynamics and the N-body Problem*, eds. Combes & Athanassoula (1994).

THE SUNYAEV–ZEL'DOVICH EFFECT IN CLUSTERS

Michael Jones

Mullard Radio Astronomy Observatory, Cavendish Laboratory, Madingley Road, Cambridge
CB3 0HE, UK

Abstract

The Sunyaev–Zel'dovich (S–Z) effect provides a way of measuring intrinsic properties of clusters of galaxies—their gas temperature and density, linear size and peculiar velocity—independently of the cluster redshift. However, the difficulty of observing the effect has until now limited the application of the S–Z effect to astrophysical problems. Recently, several groups using different observing methods (single-dish radiometry, single-dish bolometers and interferometry) have made detections with sufficient sensitivity, spatial resolution and frequency coverage to begin to exploit the potential of this technique.

Introduction

The Sunyaev–Zel'dovich (S–Z) effect[1,2] is the scattering of cosmic microwave background radiation (CMBR) photons off electrons in the gas that fills the gravitational potential well in clusters of galaxies. There are in fact two effects, a first-order effect due to the bulk velocity of the cluster with respect to the CMBR, and a second-order effect due to the thermal velocities of the electrons in the gas. Measuring these effects has considerable astrophysical benefits. The kinematic effect directly measures the cluster peculiar velocity. The thermal effect can be used, in conjunction with images and spectra of the X-ray emission from the same gas, to study cluster gas. Some clusters appear to have undergone recent mergers and are far from equilibrium; others seem to be dynamically relaxed. In the former, we can use S–Z measurements to help constrain the physical processes of the merger, with implications for the growth of large-scale structure in the universe. In the latter, where the gas may be characterized by only a few parameters, we can use the combination of S–Z data and X-rays to estimate the physical size of, and hence distance to, the cluster, thus yielding an estimate of the Hubble constant[3,4,5,6].

If the cluster has a peculiar velocity v_p along the observer's line of sight, the temperature of the CMBR spectrum is Doppler-shifted by an amount

$$(\Delta T)_{\text{kinematic}} = T_0 \frac{v_p}{c} \int n_e \sigma_T \, dl, \tag{1}$$

where n_e is the electron number density, T_0 is the temperature of the CMBR, σ_T is the Thomson cross-section and the integral is along the line of sight. In terms of Rayleigh-Jeans brightness temperature this is

$$(\Delta T_{\text{RJ}})_{\text{kinematic}} = T_0 \frac{v_p}{c} \int n_e \sigma_T \, dl \, \frac{x^2 e^x}{(e^x - 1)^2}, \tag{2}$$

or as an intensity

$$(\Delta I_\nu)_{\text{kinematic}} = \frac{k^3 T_0^3}{hc^2} \frac{v_p}{c} \int n_e \sigma_T \, dl \, \frac{x^4 e^x}{(e^x - 1)^2}, \tag{3}$$

where

$$x = \frac{h\nu}{kT_0}. \tag{4}$$

The thermal motion of the electrons also gives rise to a change in the spectrum which is second-order in the electron velocity, and does not preserve the black-body shape of the spectrum, with a brightness temperature change given by

$$(\Delta T_{\text{RJ}})_{\text{thermal}} = -2T_0 \int n_e \sigma_T dl \, \frac{kT_e}{m_e c^2} \frac{x^2 e^x}{(e^x - 1)^2} \left[x \coth\left(\frac{x}{2}\right) - 4 \right], \tag{5}$$

where T_e is the electron temperature. In terms of the intensity,

$$(\Delta I_\nu)_{\text{thermal}} = -2 \frac{k^3 T_0^3}{hc^2} \int n_e \sigma_T dl \, \frac{kT_e}{m_e c^2} \frac{x^4 e^x}{(e^x - 1)^2} \left[x \coth\left(\frac{x}{2}\right) - 4 \right]. \tag{6}$$

Thus the size of the thermal effect is proportional to the integral of $n_e T_e$, i.e. the electron pressure, along the line of sight.

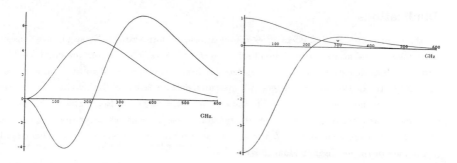

Figure 1: a) The frequency dependences of the thermal and kinematic S–Z effects, expressed as intensity. Note that the peak of the kinematic effect coincides with the null of the thermal effect. b) The frequency dependences of the thermal and kinematic effects expressed as brightness temperature.

The forms of the frequency dependances are shown in Figure 1. The maximum changes in *intensity* (Figure 1a) due to the thermal effect occur at 129 GHz (decrement) and 372 GHz (increment), with a null at 220 GHz. The kinematic effect, however, has a maximum at 220 GHz; these characteristic spectral signatures allow one to independently measure the two effects. Figure 1b shows the same frequency dependencies expressed as *brightness temperatures*: the thermal effect has a maximum decrement at low frequency, with a much smaller positive peak at 311 GHz.

What are the typical orders of magnitude of these effects? Substituting numbers into equations 2 and 5, we find

$$(\Delta T_{\text{RJ}})_{\text{kinematic}} \approx 0.1 \left(\frac{n_e}{5 \times 10^3 \, \text{m}^{-3}}\right) \left(\frac{l}{\text{Mpc}}\right) \left(\frac{v_p}{1000 \, \text{km s}^{-1}}\right) \, \text{mK} \tag{7}$$

$$(\Delta T_{\text{RJ}})_{\text{thermal}} \approx 1 \left(\frac{n_e}{5 \times 10^3 \, \text{m}^{-3}}\right) \left(\frac{l}{\text{Mpc}}\right) \left(\frac{T_e}{10 \, \text{keV}}\right) \, \text{mK} \tag{8}$$

in the low-frequency limit. So even for hot, dense cluster gas, the thermal effect is only a few parts in 10^4 of the CMBR, and for reasonable cluster velocities the kinematic effect is an order of magnitude smaller. Measuring such small temperature changes clearly presents a considerable challenge.

The magnitude of the S–Z effect depends only on the intrinsic properties of the cluster, n_e, T_e, l and v_p, not on the distance to the cluster. It is therefore possible in principle to observe clusters at very high redshifts. The angular size does change with distance, however, and this will affect the coupling to any particular telescope. However, angular size is a weak function of redshift for $z \gtrsim 0.5$ (assuming $\Omega_0 \simeq 1$). One could realistically have a telescope which could efficiently observe the S–Z effect in clusters at any redshift greater than, say, 0.2.

Implications

Cluster physics The S–Z effect gives complementary information to X-ray observations of the same gas, and is subject to different selection effects. X-ray observations are dominated by regions of high density (because X-ray surface brightness is proportional to n_e^2), and are most sensitive to the dense cores of clusters; S-Z measurements are sensitive to the outer, less dense, regions if they contribute significantly to the total pressure integral. Also, S–Z observations are not energy-band limited; one measures the integrated gas pressure whatever the temperature of the gas is. Complementary S–Z and X-ray observations will therefore help us understand the physics of the gas in individual clusters.

Hubble constant The S–Z effect can also be used to derive the Hubble constant. Consider the X-ray emission from a cube of gas of side l at a redshift z, with an electron number density n_e and temperature T_e. The observed X-ray surface brightness is

$$X_{SB} = \frac{K(T_e)ln_e^2}{(1+z)^4},\tag{9}$$

where $K(T_e)$ is an emissivity constant which includes the temperature and Gaunt factors together with the bandpass of the X-ray telescope, corrected for the redshift of the cluster. The S–Z decrement ΔT_{RJ} in the CMBR, is given by equation 5. Combining these, and using the angular-size–redshift relation for $q_0 = \frac{1}{2}$, we find

$$H_0 = \frac{8(T_0 k_B \sigma_T)^2}{m_e^2 c^3 K} \cdot \left(\frac{T_e}{\Delta T_{\mathrm{RJ}}}\right)^2 \theta X_{SB}\left((1+z)^3 - (1+z)^{3/2}\right),\tag{10}$$

giving H_0 in terms of the observables T_e, ΔT_{RJ}, the angular size θ, X_{SB} and z. This is a *physical* method which does not rely on local calibration of empirical relationships.

In practice, using this relationship presents many problems, not the least of which is measuring ΔT_{RJ}. One also needs an accurate gas temperature measurement (from X-ray spectroscopy), and a good model for the structure of the gas. If, for example, there were significant substructure in the gas below the resolution of the images, the X-ray emission would be enhanced relative to the S–Z decrement, leading to an overestimate of H_0. We have also assumed the same l for the transverse and line-of-sight sizes of the cluster, which is clearly not necessarily true. Reliable H_0 measurement by this method will only be possible using relaxed, near-spherically symmetric clusters. Although in principle it is possible to also measure q_0 using this method, the dependence on q_0 is weak for $z < 1$, and the X-ray measurements presently near-impossible for $z > 1$.

Cluster evolution Since ΔT is independent of z, it is possible to detect clusters via the S–Z effect back to their epoch of formation. Simulations of cluster evolution in different cosmological models, (e.g. Markevitch et al. (1991)[7]) give markedly different predictions for the population of S–Z "sources" in the sky. Detection of this "integrated S–Z effect" would strongly constrain theories of cluster evolution, and hence important cosmological parameters such as Ω_0 and the slope of the initial fluctuation power spectrum.

Table 1: S–Z detections by various groups, with approximate level of significance of detection.

	OVRO 40m	NRAO 140'	Ryle	OVRO 5.5 m	CSO/SUZIE
A2218	7σ		8σ		
A665	4σ	3σ	6σ		
0016+16	5σ	4σ	6σ		
A401		4σ			
A2163					5σ
Coma				6σ	
A773			5σ		
A1722			4σ		
A2142				5σ	
A2256				8σ	
A478				11σ	

Peculiar velocities The kinematic effect provides a direct measurement of cluster peculiar velocities. Simulations of cluster formation predict different mean peculiar velocities for different cosmological models; measurement of a sample of such velocities would provide additional constraints on the theories. If we were to measure a bulk flow in a large sample of clusters distributed around the sky, we could be forced to question our assumptions about the CMBR rest frame relative to the Hubble flow, or the assumption of homgeneity on large angular scales.

Observations

The history of observations of the S–Z effect is long and slightly disreputable. Many detections were claimed in the decade following Sunyaev and Zel'dovich's first paper, some of which were later retracted, but most of which have conveniently been forgotten, except by writers of review papers. The first detections which are widely accepted as being reliable were those of Birkinshaw, Gull & Hardebeck (1984)[8], in the three clusters Abell 2218, Abell 665 and 0016+16, and Uson (1987)[9] in A665, A401 and 0016+16. In the following decade Birkinshaw and his co-workers further refined their results, but no new detections were announced until 1992. In the past two years, however, there has been an explosion of results, due to years of careful work on new instruments by several groups, and the total number of clusters with detections (not all published yet) stands at eleven (see Table 1).

Most of the early work on the S–Z effect was done using radiometers mounted on large, single-dish telescopes. Since then results have also been obtained using bolometric receivers on single dishes, and using interferometry.

Radiometers

In principle measuring a temperature decrement of order 1 mK ought to be staightforward: a receiver system with a noise temperature of 50 K and a bandwidth of 100 MHz should achieve a 5-σ detection in only 10 minutes. In practice the atmosphere introduces fluctuating signals of order 1 K which mask the sky signal. Various switching schemes have been tried to reduce the atmospheric signal. Typically the telescope is fitted with two feeds, providing two beams on the sky separated by a few beamwidths, and the pointing of the telescope is switched so that one beam lies on the position just observed by the other. If the switching is in azimuth, to reduce the change in pick-up of ground radiation in the sidelobes, the reference beams either side of the central pointing will sweep out arcs as the parallactic angle changes. This *double differencing* scheme is efficient at removing the atmospheric signal, but also eliminates the DC term and the gradient of the sky signal; only the curvature of the sky signal is measured. The angular response of the system is limited: too small a cluster will only fill a small fraction of the beam and thus only contribute a small amount to the antenna temperature; too large a cluster and the reference arcs will lie inside the S–Z effect itself. Also, radio souces lying within the reference arcs will mimic the S–Z signal and must be corrected for, with separate higher-resolution observations.

Despite the problems of systematic effects from the atmosphere and ground-spill, this technique has had considerable success; as well as Birkinshaw's detections using the Owens Valley 40-m telescope at 20 GHz, Herbig et al. have detected the Coma cluster using a 5.5-m telescope at Owens Valley[10] and three more clusters (A478, A2256 and A2142) have also been detected using the same instrument (Readhead, private communication). The 5.5-m telescope operates at 30 GHz, with a 7-arcmin beam and 22-arcmin throw, using the double-differencing scheme described above. This beam throw is not sufficient to carry the reference arcs outside the cluster in the case of Coma; it is necessary to model the cluster gas in order to correct for this effect. In general, the derived central decrement for a cluster will always be model-dependent, since the observed quantity will be the convolution of the instrumental response with the actual structure of the S–Z effect.

Bolometers

To exploit the different frequency signatures of the kinematic and thermal S–Z effects, it is necessary to observe in the range 200–300 GHz. In this regime heterodyne techniques become extremely difficult and bolometers are the most efficient detectors. They have the advantages of very high bandwidth and sensitivity, and wide frequency coverage, but atmospheric effects remain a problem. Recently, the Berkeley group with their instrument SUZIE, mounted on the CalTech Submillimeter Observatory 10-m telescope on Mauna Kea[11] have detected the S–Z effect at 2.2 mm and 1.2 mm—the first observations of the thermal effect in increment. This instrument has two independent rows each of three detectors. Within a single row, the differential signal from each possible pairing of bolometers is measured by placing them in a Wheatstone bridge circuit in which the bias voltage is modulated, and the difference signal synchronously detected, equivalent to performing a square-wave chop on the sky. This, along with the mounting of the detectors on the same cold-plate in the cryostat, provides excellent immunity from instrumental offsets and drifts. Also, using three detectors means that both

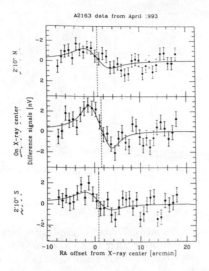

Figure 2: Three single-difference scans at different declinations through A2163 using SUZIE.

single- and double-difference signals are available without changing the pointing of the telescope, thus eliminating differential ground-spill; observations are made by parking the telescope and letting the cluster drift through the field. Figure 2 shows the results of three drift-scans through the cluster A2163, the hottest known cluster X-ray source[12], at different declinations. Clearly a set of such observations could provide a two-dimensional map of the S–Z effect.

Interferometry

This is a very different technique from the previous two. A single interferometer pair measures one Fourier component of the product of the sky brightness distribution and the primary beam of the antennas. From a number of pairs of different spacing and orientation the sky brightness can be reconstructed. Typically the Fourier plane is not fully sampled and no unique reconstruction is possible; techiques such as CLEAN and Maximum Entropy are used to effectively interpolate the unmeasured Fourier components. Interferometers have several significant advantages over single dishes for S–Z work[13]. They are not sensitive to total power and therefore not sensitive to fluctuations in atmospheric emission. Signals which do not have the rate of change of phase expected for the region of sky being studied are strongly attenuated, giving immunity from ground-spill. Also, an array including long and short baselines will simultaneously image the S–Z effect and any confusing radio sources.

However there also some problems. The sensitivity of an interferometer to an extended temperature feature like the S–Z effect is a very strong function of baseline. It is thus vital to use a telescope where the antennas can be packed as closely as possible. It also means that it is

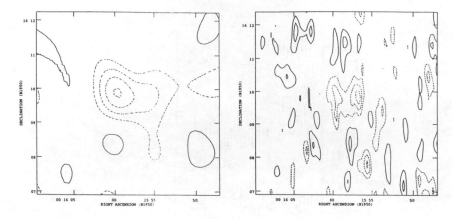

Figure 3: Ryle Telescope images at different resolutions of the cluster 0016+16. Both maps have had the point-spread function deconvolved using CLEAN. a) 100×60 arcsec resolution. Contour levels are $-560, -320, -280, -140, +140$ μJy beam^{-1}. b) 15×60 arcsec resolution. Contour levels $-150, -100, -50, +50, +100$ μJy beam^{-1}.

likely that a significant signal will only be detected on the one or two shortest baselines in a given array, and therefore there will be a problem reconstructing the image without additional information (for example, from an X-ray image).

The VLA has been used to search for the S–Z effect[14] but the baselines are too long (33-m minimum) to give good temperature sensitivity. The Australia Telescope has slightly shorter baselines (30 m in the most compact array) and sensitive recievers at 8 GHz; it has been used to search for the S–Z effect[15] but with limited success so far.

The Ryle Telescope (RT) in Cambridge has been developed as a specialised instrument for S–Z astronomy. It has eight 13-m antennas, five of which can be arranged into a compact, east–west array with spacings from 18 to 108 m. In this mode, at its operating frequency of 15.4 GHz, it is sensitive to angular scales of 30 arcsec–3 arcmin. We have so far mapped the S–Z effect in five clusters. Table 2 shows the maximum detected signal in Jy beam^{-1}, and the equivalent central temperature decrement under the stated assumptions about the structure of the cluster gas. The results from A2218 have been used to obtain a value of the Hubble constant[5] of 38^{+18}_{-16} km s^{-1} Mpc^{-1} (these errors include estimates of various systematic effects). A2218 appears to be nearly spherically symmetric and isothermal, making it a good candidate for estimating H_0.

The selection criteria for these clusters were high X-ray luminosity, $z > 0.15$, high X-ray temperature (if known), declination $> 15°$, and freedom from bright confusing radio sources, initially selected from the Green Bank 5 GHz survey, followed up by short RT observations. Integration times varied from 7×12 hours for A665 to 79×12 hours for A2218. The data

Table 2: Clusters observed with the Ryle Telescope. A665 and 0016+16 are significantly non-spherical; no model fit has been done for them yet. The model fits for the others assume spherical symmetry and an isothermal atmosphere with density given by $n_e = n_{e0} \left(1 + \theta^2/\theta_{cx}^2\right)^{-3\beta/2}$.

Cluster	Observed brightness (Jybeam^{-1})	Derived central temperature (μK)	Model
A2218	-500 ± 65	-900^{+60}_{-140}	$\beta = 0.65$, $\theta_{cx} = 60''$
A773	-590 ± 115	-790 to -990	$\beta = 0.65$, $\theta_{cx} = 25$ to $100''$
A1722	-520 ± 130	-700 to -870	$\beta = 0.65$, $\theta_{cx} = 25$ to $100''$
A665	-1080 ± 190		
0016+16	-620 ± 190		

reduction procedures have been described eleswhere[16,17,18]. As an example, Figure 3 shows two maps at different resolutions of 0016+16. There is clear evidence for a double structure to the core of the cluster; this structure only partially coincides, however, with the optical galaxy distribution and the mass map of Smail et al.[19] This cluster is clearly worthy of further study.

Conclusions

Sunyaev–Zel'dovich astronomy has arrived. We can obtain S–Z images with spatial resolution to determine structure, and spectral resolution to separate the kinematic and thermal effects. After two decades of largely inconclusive results, it is now possible to start solving real astrophysical problems.

Acknowledgements

The Ryle Telescope work was done in collaboration with Richard Saunders, Keith Grainge, Guy Pooley and Alastair Edge. I thank Andrew Lange, Sarah Church, Tony Readhead and Haida Liang for providing me with details of their work.

References

1) Sunyaev R.A. and Zel'dovich Ya. B., 1972, Comm. Astrophys. Sp. Phys., **4**, 173

2) Sunyaev R.A. and Zel'dovich Ya. B., 1980, Mon. Not. R. astr. Soc., **190**, 413

3) Birkinshaw M., Hughes J.P. and Arnaud K.A., 1991, Astrophys. J., **379**, 466

4) Birkinshaw M. and Hughes J.P., 1994, Astrophys. J., **420**, 33

5) Jones M., 1994, Astrophys. Lett. and Comm., in press

6) McHardy I., Stewart G., Edge A., Cooke B., Yamashita K. and Hatsukade I., 1990, Mon. Not. R. astr. Soc., 242, 215

7) Markevitch M. et al., 1991 Astrophys. J. **395**, 326

8) Birkinshaw M., Gull S.F. and Hardebeck H., 1984, Nat., **309**, 34

9) Uson J.M., 1987, in Radio Continuum Processes in Clusters of Galaxies, ed. Uson J.M. and

O'Dea, C P., NRAO, Greenbank, 255

10) Herbig T., Readhead A.C.S and Lawrence C.R., 1992, Bull. Amer astr. Soc., **24, 4**, 1263

11) Wilbanks T.M., Ade P.A.R, Fischer M.L., Holzapfel W.L. and Lange A.E., 1994, Astrophys. J., in press

12) Arnaud M. et al., 1992, Astrophys. J. **390**, 345

13) Saunders, R., 1986, in Highlights of Astronomy **7** ed. Swings, J-P., Reidel, Dordrecht, 325

14) Partridge R.B., Perley R.A., Mandolesi N. and Delpino F., 1987, Astrophys. J., **317**, 112

15) Liang H., this volume

16) Jones M. et al., 1993, Nat., **365**, 320

17) Grainge K., Jones M., Pooley G., Saunders R. and Edge A., 1993, Mon. Not. R. astr. Soc., **265**, L57

18) Saunders R., 1994, Astrophys. Lett. and Comm., in press

19) Smail I., Ellis R.S., Fitchett M.J. and Edge A.C., 1994, Mon. Not. R. astr. Soc., submitted

SIMULATIONS OF CLUSTERS OF GALAXIES

August E. Evrard

Department of Physics, University of Michigan, Ann Arbor, MI 48109-1120 USA

Abstract

The degree of complexity and, to a somewhat lesser degree, realism in simulations has advanced rapidly in the past few years. The simplest approach — modeling a cluster as collisionless dark matter and collisonal, non–radiative gas is now fairly well established. One of the most fruitful results of this approach is the *morphology–cosmology connection* for X–ray clusters. Simulations have provided the means to make concrete predictions for the X–ray morphologies of clusters in cosmologies with different Ω_o, with the result that low Ω_o cosmologies fair rather poorly when compared to observations. Another result concerns the accuracy of X–ray binding mass estimates. The standard, hydrostatic, isothermal model estimator is found to be accurate to typically better than 50% at radii where the density contrast is between 10^2 and 10^3.

More complicated approaches, which attempt to explicitly follow galaxy formation within the proto–cluster environment are slowly being realized. The key issue of *dynamical biasing* of the galaxy population within a cluster is being probed, but no conclusive understanding has been realized. The dynamics of multi–phase gas, including conversion of cold, dense gas into stars and the feedback therefrom, is the largest obstacle hindering progress. An example demonstrating the state–of–the–art in this area is presented.

1. Introduction

A typical rich cluster is a multi–component system containing many tens to hundreds of bright galaxies, a hot, metal–enriched intracluster medium (ICM) observed in X–rays, and dark matter whose presence has been inferred by application of the virial theorem for over 60 years [27]. The present relative distributions of these components reflect their full dynamical and thermal histories, which need not be the same. The role of simulations is to provide a tool to investigate the dynamical evolution of cluster components in a cosmological setting. A unique value of this tool is the ability to 'synthetically image' the results in a well–prescribed manner, providing direct, 'apples–to–apples' comparisons between theory and observation.

Nearly all viable large–scale structure models are 'bottom–up', in the sense that collapse of galactic–sized perturbations (= galaxy formation?) precedes the collapse of cluster–sized perturbations. In this way, aspects of cluster formation are intimately tied to galaxy formation which, of course, is linked to cooling and fragmentation of gas clouds and star formation [37]. Many unsettled issues regarding clusters (*e.g.*, the origin and distribution of metals in the ICM, whether or not galaxies fairly trace the cluster dark matter) persist because of the uncertainties in modeling, from both a physical and numerical perspective, galactic–scale star formation.

One can exploit the 'bottom–up' picture to simplify the problem considerably by assuming that the star formation within galaxies is largely finished before the collapse of the bulk of the cluster. One then thinks of the intracluster medium as the leftovers of galaxy formation which simply fall into and shock heat within the dominant, cluster potential well. This 'primordial infall' hypothesis, introduced by Gunn & Gott [15], has empirical reinforcement in the fact that the baryon content of the largest clusters is dominated by the intracluster gas rather than the galaxies [2]. Below, I present results using this approach applied to the problems of using the X–ray morphology of clusters to constrain the density parameter Ω_o (§3) and to the problem of the reliability of X–ray based binding mass estimates (§4).

Ideally, one would like to follow the formation of the galaxies directly within the proto–cluster environment. Physically, this requires adding, at a minimum, the dissipative mechanism of radiative cooling within the code. Physics associated with star formation can also be included, although with a large degree of parameterization uncertainty. Numerically, a wide dynamic range and enhanced spatial resolution are required since individual galaxies are factors $\gtrsim 10^3$ less massive than clusters and the optically bright regions of galaxies represent density enhancements a factor $\gtrsim 10^6$ over the cosmological background.

Some of the work presented in this article, in particular, the projects in §3 and §5, has been written up in another recent review [9]. There are recent developments in both projects which are included here. The work in §4 is new. Where needed, $h = 0.5$ is assumed throughout, with $h \equiv H_o/100$ km s^{-1} Mpc^{-1}.

2. Simulation Flavors

Simulations now come in a variety of flavors, as summarized in Fig. 1. Advances in the late 70's to mid 80's were made using N–body simulations which model the gravitationally dominant dark matter component. This approach is limited by its inability to follow directly observable components. One must make assumptions, such as galaxies fairly tracing the mass, in order to make contact with observations. The late 80's saw the advent of coupling gas dynamics with N–body codes, providing the capability to directly follow the baryonic component coupled to, but independent of, the dark matter. Multi–fluid approaches, incorporating several dynamically distinct components represent the current state–of–the–art.

In modeling the gas dynamics, one must choose whether to employ an Eulerian or Lagrangian approach. The simulations discussed in this article all use the Lagrangian method of smoothed particle hydrodynamics (SPH) [22, 16] coupled to the P3M N–body code[9]. Details of the P3MSPH can be found in ref [9]. Briefly, SPH is a Lagrangian scheme which uses a smoothing kernel $W(r, h)$ to determine characteristics of the fluid at a given point based on properties associated with the local particle distribution. For example, the density at the position of particle i is given by

$$\rho_i = \sum_j m_j W(r_{ij}, h_i) \tag{1}$$

where r_{ij} is the separation of the pair of particles i and j and h_i is the local smoothing scale. The kernel W has compact support on a scale of a few h; hence, h is a measure of the local resolution of the solution. Usually h is adaptively varied both spatially and temporally such that a constant number of neighbors in the range $\mathcal{O}(10^2)$ is involved in the above sum. This extends the dynamic range availbable in the experiment.

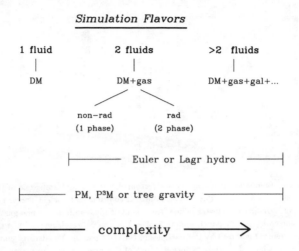

Figure 1. Schematic showing the variety of simulation approaches available for modeling structure formation.

The Lagrangian nature and wide dynamic range of SPH are well suited to the problem of large–scale structure formation. Schemes using Eulerian finite difference methods with fixed spatial resolution are limited in their ability to resolve objects of very high density contrast (such as galaxies) within a large–scale cosmological environment. Conversely, Lagrangian codes which employ particles of fixed mass have difficulty resolving low density regions where, by definition, there is not much mass.

Consider a region of space modeled by either N_{part} Lagrangian particles or N_{cell} Eulerian cells. Roughly speaking, the 'break–even' density contrast δ_{eq}, where Eulerian and Lagrangian approaches have comparable resolution, is that at which one particle in the Lagrangian calculation is contained in one cell of the Eulerian code. At densities above δ_{eq}, the Lagrangian method resolves one Eulerian cell with more than one particle (implying 'higher resolution') while for densities less than δ_{eq}, a single Lagrangian particle covers many Eulerian cells ('lower resolution'). It follows then that the 'break–even' density contrast is $\delta_{eq} = N_{cell}/N_{part}$.

In three dimensions, $\delta_{eq} = 256^3/64^3 = 64$ is a presently realistic value. A comparison of several cosmological gas dynamic schemes applied to structure formation in a cold dark matter universe supports this simple argument [18]. Examined at low spatial resolution, the codes produce very similar results for the thermal and spatial structure of the gas. When examined on smaller spatial scales, the Eulerian codes display superior resolution in low density contrast regions, whereas higher resolution is achieved by the SPH codes in high density contrast regions. An example of the latter is shown in Fig. 2. Since the mass within an Abell radius of rich clusters represents a significant ($\delta > 100$) local density enhancement, a Lagrangian approach is (arguably, of course) currently the most efficient and effective means to model them numerically. When estimating X–ray luminosities of clusters, resolution of high density regions is essential since the emission measure of bremsstrahlung scales as ρ^2.

3. A Morphology–Cosmology Connection

There are several ways clusters can be used as cosmological diagnostics (see West, White, Kaiser, Rhee and others in this proceedings). Their abundance as a function of, for example, velocity

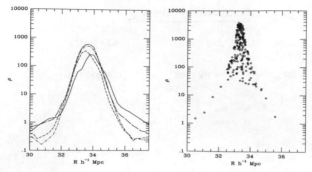

Figure 2. Density as a function of position along a rectangular region containing one of the larger clusters in the test simulation of Kang *et al.* (1994). The P3MSPH solution, in the right panel, under–resolves the low density 'wings' surrounding the cluster, where there is little mass and, hence, few particles. Conversely, the Eulerian code, shown in the left panel, under–resolves the central, condensed part of the cluster, where the bulk of the mass resides (as shown by the particles in the right panel). The density underestimate in the Eulerian code is due to a lack of spatial resolution; much of the cluster mass lies within one grid cell. The adaptive nature of the SPH smoothing kernel provides higher resolution in dense regions.

dispersion σ, is extremely sensitive to the normalization of the fluctuation spectrum (see den Hartog in this proceedings). The dependence of the shape of cluster density profiles to cosmology has also been recently re–examined [2] and is a potentially useful cosmological diagnostic.

A new approach to constraining Ω_o is based on the structure of the hot, intracluster gas. The motivating idea, pointed out by Richstone, Loeb & Turner [29], is that, because the linear growth of perturbations diminishes as Ω decreases, structure formation in a low Ω_o universe should occur earlier than if $\Omega = 1$. Their analysis based on a spherical model for cluster collapse yields an age difference between clusters in models with $\Omega_o = 0.2$ and $\Omega = 1$ of $\sim 0.3\ H_o^{-1} \sim 4 - 6$ billion years. The sound crossing time for 10 keV gas in the central 1 Mpc of a cluster is only 0.6 billion years, so this age difference corresponds to many sound crossing times within the region surveyed by X–ray imaging instruments. This leads to the expectation that clusters in low density models should have more relaxed X–ray isophotes than their critical counterparts.

This effect has now been verified and quantified with a set of 24 P3MSPH simulations [11]. Eight sets of initial conditions, two each in comoving periodic boxes of side 30, 40, 50 and 60 Mpc, were generated in a constrained manner [1] from an initial CDM fluctuation spectrum. Each initial density field was evolved in three different cosmological backgrounds: (i) an unbiased, open universe with $\Omega_o = 0.2$; (ii) an unbiased, vacuum energy dominated universe with $\Omega_o = 0.2$ and $\lambda_o = 0.8$ and (iii) a biased, critical density ($\Omega = 1$) universe with *rms* present, linear mass fluctuations in a sphere of $8\ h^{-1}$ Mpc equal to $\sigma_8 = 0.59$. A baryon content of $\Omega_b = 0.1$ was assumed for the models, with all the baryons in the form of gas. The rest of the mass was assumed to be collisionless dark matter.

Examples of present day X–ray images of the simulated clusters are shown in Fig. 3, along with corresponding *Einstein* IPC images of real Abell clusters. The simulated images show the IPC band–limited flux in a 68′ square field with an angular resolution of about 2′. The simulations were placed at the same redshift, scaled to have the same X–ray temperature and 'observed' for the same amount of time as the real clusters. Realistic detector noise was added. The low density models, shown in the last two rows, are much more centrally concentrated and display much less asymmetry than the critical universe clusters shown in the second row. These differences arise because the low Ω_o clusters suffer fewer merging events at late times, a result expected from a variety of analytic

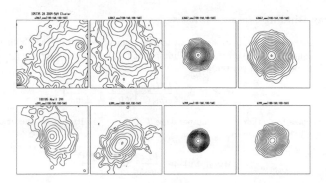

Figure 3. Examples of X–ray images for real and simulated clusters. The left column shows *Einstein* IPC archive images of Abell 3667 and 399 (upper and lower, respectively). The next three columns show randomly oriented views of randomly selected simulated clusters placed at the same redshift, scaled to the same X–ray temperature, and 'viewed' using the appropriate IPC instrument response for the same amount of time as the real clusters. Instrument noise (but no background sources) was introduced to the simulated images. Starting from the second to left, the columns are for the following models: $\Omega = 1$, $\Omega_o = 0.2$ with $\lambda = 0$ and $\Omega_o = 0.2$ with $\lambda = 0.8$. A CDM spectrum with $\Gamma = 0.5$ was used to generate the initial conditions.

arguments [29, 21, 19].

We have quantified the differences using statistics measuring the surface brightness fall-off (the familiar β_{fit} parameter), mean isophotal center shift [11, 25] and the mean eccentricity. The same measures have been made for both the simulated and observed clusters. Histograms of any of these show a distinct difference between the low and high density models, with the observations strongly favoring $\Omega = 1$ over either of the $\Omega_o = 0.2$ universes [24]. This result is supported by recent analysis of the abundance of rich clusters. In order to reproduce observations, an $\Omega_o = 0.2$ CDM dominated universe requires a very high fluctuation amplitude $\sigma_8 = 1.25 - 1.58$, which requires galaxies to be *less* clustered than the mass distribution [35].

Although there is more physics beyond this simple approach, it is difficult to finger a mechanism which would strongly distort in an *anisotropic fashion* the present cluster X–ray morphologies in the low Ω_o models. Feedback due to winds from early–type galaxies would have to occur very recently, and the winds would have to be coherently directed so as to distort the isophotes in a manner similar to that which occurs naturally by merging. Recent simulations incorporating winds in $\Omega = 1$ clusters show little effect on the overall morphology (Metzler in this proceedings). Adding radiative cooling would produce a large central cooling flow, but there is no reason to suspect this will strongly affect the morphology of the outer regions. Finally, unrealistically large tidal torques would be required to distort the structure of the X–ray gas in the inner ~ 1 Mpc region, where the bulk of the X–rays are observed.

It all boils down to this. Generating anisotropy in the gas distribution at late times requires a directed source of energy input with magnitude comparable to the binding energy of the cluster. The most natural source for such directed energy is the merging of two systems of roughly comparable mass. To save the low Ω_o models, one needs to come up with a mechanism(s) which replaces merging, but produces the same effects. It is not at all clear how to do this.

4. X–ray Binding Mass Estimates

We have used the above simulations to test the accuracy of estimating the binding mass of clusters using the assumptions of hydrostatic equilibrium and a 'beta–model' for the gas distribution [30]. The mass estimate can be written as

$$M(< r) = -\frac{kT(r)r}{\mu m_p G}\left[\frac{d \ln \rho}{d \ln r} + \frac{d \ln T}{d \ln r}\right]. \tag{2}$$

If the gas is close to isothermal at temperature T and the density follows the usual form of $\rho(r) = \rho_o(1 + (r/r_c)^2)^{-3\beta/2}$, this becomes

$$M_{bind}(< r) = \frac{kTr}{\mu m_p G} \; 3\beta \; \frac{(r/r_c)^2}{1 + (r/r_c)^2}. \tag{3}$$

ASCA observations reported at this meeting by Ikebe and Mushotzky indicate that the run of temperature with radius is close to isothermal. This need not imply exact isothermality throughout the cluster; only the azimuthal average need not vary strongly with radius. Briel showed data for A2256 from ROSAT which indicates a spatially varying temperature consistent with that expected from a recent merger. The simulated clusters generally show spatial variation, though the degree is dependent on the recent dynamical history (see Fig. 5 below). When radially averaged, the temparature profiles are usually weakly falling functions of radius out to the shock front separating the infall from hydrostatic regimes. Beyond this radius, which occurs at a density contrast $\mathcal{O}(10^2)$, the mean radial temperature drops rapidly.

To test the accuracy of the above estimators, the simulations used in the preceeding section were 'imaged' at $z = 0.04$ along each principal spatial axis with a 7200 sec exposure in the ROSAT passband. A Poisson photon noise field was added and then the mean value subtracted from the image. The radially averaged surface brightness maps were then fit to the standard form $\Sigma_x(\theta) = \Sigma_o(1 + (\theta/\theta_c)^2)^{-3\beta_{fit}+1/2}$. The central, emission weighted temperature T_e was similarly determined. The values of β_{fit}, r_c (from θ_c) and T_e were then used in equation (3) to estimate the binding mass as a function of radius. A total of 24 images for each cosmology were so generated.

We find that, at small radii where the density contrast is $\gtrsim 10^4$, the mass is typically underestimated, by factors up to 3. It is tempting to apply this result to the discrepancy raised by recent mass determinations from strong lensing (see Miralde-Escudé, Soucail and Babul in this proceedings). However, it is not clear whether this result is caused by physical or numerical effects, since it close to the resolution limit of these experiments. Also, the core of real clusters is a complicated place, with complex dynamics involving cooling flows which is not modeled in these experiments. It is, I believe, premature to claim that X–ray mass estimates are systematically low by large factors in the cores of rich clusters. It remains a real possiblity which should be pursued with future, high resolution simulations.

Farther out in the cluster, where the density contrast is between 10^3 and 10^2, the isothermal mass estimate is rather accurate. Fig. 4 shows histograms of the ratio of estimated to true mass measured at radii where the density contrast is 300. For all three cosmological models, the estimate is typically accurate to within 50% at this density contrast. Similar results are obtained for estimates at fixed metric radii of 1 Mpc in the $\Omega = 1$ models and 0.5 Mpc in the low density runs. (The low Ω_o clusters are more compact than their critical density counterparts.)

The upshot is that one should feel confident in trusting, at the 50% level, binding mass determinations based on the isothermal, hydrostatic model around radii of $0.5 - 1$ Mpc. Models incorporating ejection from early–type galaxies display similar behavior [23, 11]. As a consequence, the high baryon mass fraction in clusters [36] should not be construed as arising from a large factor underestimate in their binding masses.

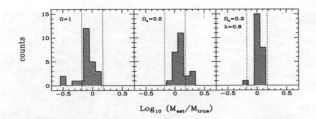

Figure 4. Histograms showing the decimal logarithm of the errors in isothermal binding mass estimates in a set of simulations. The estimates are at radii where the mean interior density contrast is 300, which is at a radius of of ~ 1 Mpc for rich clusters. The estimates are typically accurate to within 50% (dashed vertical lines).

5. Dynamical Biasing of Galaxies in Clusters

It is well known that dynamical mass estimates based on the virial theorem applied to cluster galaxy kinematics have yielded mass to light ratios around a factor 5 smaller than that required to reach closure density [14]. The two possible interpretations are: (i) the estimate is unbiased and $\Omega_o \sim 0.2$ or (ii) there is a systematic bias in the estimate which makes it consistent with $\Omega = 1$. One possibility for the latter is that the dark matter is very weakly clustered on comoving scales $\lesssim 10$ Mpc. Another is that the galaxies are condensed toward the cluster center, and that one is measuring only some inner fraction of the total cluster mass and missing an extended, outer dark envelope. The latter issue has been investigated numerous times with N–body experiments over the past decade. Unfortunately, the interpretation of these simulations is clouded by the rather naive way in which galaxies were represented within the cluster.

Ideally, one would like to form galaxies *in situ* and subsequently follow their hierarchically clustering to the scale of rich clusters. Since local gas temperatures and densities are known, radiative cooling rates can be calculated (with or without photoioniation heating). Gas which is sufficiently dense can cool rapidly, lose pressure support and sink toward the bottom of the local potential well. The standard lore is that copius star formation ensues once the baryons become self–gravitating, creating in the process some sort of galactic unit.

Uncertainty in calculating cooling rates arises from lack of resolution — the baryonic matter associated with a single particle or cell, which is typically $\gtrsim 10^8 M_\odot$, is assumed to be a single phase medium characterised by a single density and temperature. At very high redshifts, this may be a reasonable approximation. However, in strongly non–linear clustered regions, a complex multi–phase medium akin to our own interstellar medium will develop. If a typical galaxy is resolved by enough particles or cells, a crude multi–phase will develop, with cold, dense knots one associates with star forming regions surrounded by halos of hot, rarefied gas.

Simulations of this sort have been successful recently in producing clusters with anywhere from three [20] to several tens [12] of such 'galaxies' within them. An example is shown in Fig. 5. This cluster was modeled with P3MSPH using 2×64^3 particles to represent the dark matter and baryons. The simulation modeled a periodic cube 22.5 Mpc on a side in a standard cold, dark matter universe. The limiting spatial resolution was ~ 30 kpc and the mass per baryon particle was $3 \times 10^8 M_\odot$. An L_* galaxy would thus be modeled by about 300 particles.

The cluster shown in Fig. 5 forms from a merger at $z \sim 0.3$ (second row) involving roughly three major components. Prior to this, the dark matter and baryons trace each other well on scales resolved in the figure. During the merger, jets of hot gas can be seen squirting out in directions

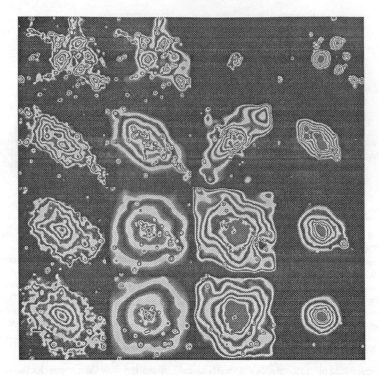

Figure 5. Formation of a cluster in a CDM universe (from Frenk, Evrard & White 1994). The columns show (left to right) projected dark matter density, projected gas density, emission weighted gas temperature and X–ray surface brightness in the ROSAT passband. The rows show the cluster at redshifts (top to bottom) $z = 0.7$, 0.3, 0.1 and 0. Each panel shows a physical 3 Mpc region. The X–ray images were made by fixing the observer—cluster distance to be equivalent to $z = 0.03$. The spacing between light or dark bands is approximately a factor of two except for the temperature maps where the spacing is $\sim 25\%$. See the text for further discussion.

perpendicular to the merger axis (compare the third with the first two columns of the second row). By $z = 0.1$, the hot gas has relaxed and is noticeably rounder than the dark matter distribution. A small group infalling from the lower right produces an X–ray emission feature and a fairly sharp temperature gradient in the cluster gas as the ram pressure of the infalling group compresses the gas intervening between it and the cluster core. The final X–ray structure of the cluster is quite regular, since no late mergers occur to stir up the gas. A mild, negative temperature gradient exists in the X–ray gas.

'Galaxies' are visible in the figure as small blips in the projected gas distribution. After the merger, the dark matter distribution has local density enhancements in the periphery of the cluster, but the central regions are relatively smooth. The central region in the baryons has much more structure due to the two–phase nature of the gas.

The galaxies represent a cooler and more concentrated population with respect to the dark matter. The ratio of velocity dispersions σ_{gal}/σ_{DM} (the 'velocity bias' parameter) is $\sim 75 - 85\%$. The ratio of the half–mass radii R_{gal}/R_{DM}, determined from the known 3D positions and using 1.6 Mpc as an outer radius, shows a much more pronounced bias. Application of the virial theorem to determine binding masses results in a large (factor $2-4$) underestimate of the total mass of the cluster.

What is worrisome about this treatment is that the galaxies are assumed to be purely gaseous throughout the evolution of the cluster. Their interactions with the surrounding medium and with each other during collisions entail viscous drag, which is unphysical for a galaxy comprised mainly of stars. Of particular concern is the fact that the largest galaxy in the center of the cluster ends up containing *more than half* of the total baryons in cluster galaxies. Although bright, central cD galaxies are not uncommon in rich clusters, it is not the norm for the central cD to be brighter than the sum of all the other galaxies in the cluster.

To test the effects of this purely collisional treatment on the galactic dynamics within the cluster, we performed another run in which the the SPH gas particles in galaxies at $z = 0.7$ were instantaneously turned into collisionless 'stars'. A collisionless, two–fluid run, using as initial conditions the dark matter particles and galaxies comprised of the star particles above, was then evolved from $z = 0.7$ to 0.

The galaxies in the collisionless treatment were generally more extended than their gas dynamic counterparts. Examination of galaxies' trajectories showed that the predominantly radial infalling orbits tended to take the galaxies very close to the cluster center on their first infall. In the gas dynamic case, the viscous gas interactions in the high density, central region braked the galaxies, effectively trapping them in the cluster core where they quickly merged with the central cD. In contrast, the galaxies comprised of collisionless stars flew through the center relatively undisturbed, as expected if the cluster velocity dispersion is larger than the internal velocities of the galaxies (which is the case here). No extremely large central galaxy formed. Instead, two galaxies of comparable mass separated by 0.5 Mpc were the most conspicuous objects in the cluster at $z = 0$. This situation is reminiscent in the Coma cluster.

There still remained some level of bias in the collisionless galaxies. A velocity bias of similar magnitude persisted, while the spatial distribution depended on the galaxy mass cutoff. The most massive galaxies were more concentrated than the dark matter while the set of all galaxies above a minimum 32 particle count ($10^{10}M_{\odot}$ in baryons) was spatially unbiased with respect to the dark matter. The different behavior of the two mass groups is not a transient result, since the same trend existed at earlier redshifts. It may be that the result is 'inherited' from the gas dynamic run via the initial conditions; the gravitational clustering being inefficient at erasing the memory of the initial bias. More details of these results are given elsewhere [9, xx].

To summarize, the issue of biases in the galaxy distribution within clusters remains uncertain. Observations of luminosity dependent clustering would be very helpful in constraining models.

6. Summary

Dynamical modeling of clusters of galaxies has improved significantly in the past few years, with the advent of simulation algorithms capable of handling the coupled evolution of multiple components representing dark matter, intracluster gas and galaxies. The new generation of experiments has opened up a new avenue for constraining Ω_o by using the X–ray morphology of rich clusters. They have also shed light on the accuracy of X–ray based binding mass estimates and the cluster baryon fraction inferred from them.

Issues which are more intimately linked to galaxy/star formation remain relatively poorly understood. Although definitive answers to the question of dynamical biases for galaxies in clusters remain elusive, results emerging from a variety of independent treatments suggest that galaxies should give a velocity dispersion estimate biased slightly (10−30%) low with respect to the dark matter. Optical mass estimates are likely to underestimate the total binding mass, but the magnitude of this effect is fairly uncertain. A firmer understanding of the star formation history of galaxies is required to significantly advance beyond our present position.

This work was supported by a NATO International Travel Grant, NASA Theory Grant NAGW-2367 and NSF via supercomputer resources.

References

[1] Bertschinger, E. 1987, ApJ, 323, L103.
[2] Crone, M.M., Evrard, A.E. & Richstone, D. 1994, ApJ, in press.
[3] David, L.P., Arnaud, K.A., Forman, W., & Jones, C. 1990, ApJ, 356, 32.
[4] Evrard, A.E. 1988, MNRAS, 235, 911.
[5] Evrard, A.E. 1994, in Numerical Simulations in Astrophysics, eds. J. Franco et al. , (Cambridge : Cambridge Univ. Press), in press.
[6] Efstathiou, G. & Eastwood, J.W. 1981, MNRAS, 194, 503.
[7] Evrard, A.E., Metler, C. & Navarro, J.F. 1994, in preparation.
[8] Evrard, A.E., Mohr, J.J., Fabricant, D.G. & Geller, M.J. 1993, ApJ, 419, L9.
[9] Evrard, A.E., Summers, F.J. & Davis, M. 1994, ApJ, 422, 11.
[10] Frenk, C.S., Evrard, A.E. & White, S.D.M. 1994, in preparation.
[11] Geller, M.J. 1984, Comments on Astr & Sp Sci, 2, 47.
[12] Gunn, J.E. & Gott, J.R. 1972, ApJ, 176, 1.
[13] Gingold, R.A. & Monaghan, J.J. 1977, MNRAS, 181, 375.
[14] Kang, H., Ostriker, J.P., Cen, R., Ryu, D., Hernquist, L., Evrard, A.E., Bryan, G. & Norman, M.L. 1994, ApJ, in press.
[15] Kauffmann, G. & White, S.D.M. 1993, MNRAS, 261, 921.
[16] Katz, N. & White, S.D.M. 1993, ApJ, 412, 455.
[17] Lacey, C. & Cole, S. 1993, MNRAS, 262, 627.
[18] Lucy, L.B. 1977, AJ, 82, 1013.
[19] Metzler, C.A. & Evrard, A.E. 1994, ApJ, submitted.
[20] Mohr, J.J., Evrard, A.E., Fabricant, D.G., & Geller, M.J. 1993, in preparation.
[21] Mohr, J.J., Fabricant, D.G., & Geller, M.J. 1993, ApJ, 413, 492.
[22] Richstone, D., Loeb, A., & Turner, E. L. 1992, ApJ, 393, 477.
[23] Sarazin, C.L. 1986, Rev Mod Phys, 58, 1.
[24] White, S.D.M., Efstathiou, G. & Frenk, C.S. 1993, MNRAS, 262, 1023.
[25] White, S.D.M., Navarro, J.N., Evrard, A.E. & Frenk, C.S. 1993, submitted to Nature.
[26] White, S.D.M. & Rees, M.J. 1978, MNRAS, 183, 341.
[27] Zwicky, F. 1933, Helv. Phys. Acta, 6, 110.

MODELS OF THE ICM WITH EJECTION FROM GALAXIES

Christopher A. Metzler & August E. Evrard

Department of Physics, University of Michigan, Ann Arbor, MI 48109-1120 USA

Abstract

We have conducted N–body + hydrodynamical simulations of rich clusters of galaxies, to examine the effects of supernova–driven galactic winds on cluster evolution. These simulations assumed an $\Omega = 1$ CDM cosmogony, and explicitly model gas, dark matter, and galaxies as separate fluids. The galaxies were placed at peaks in the initial overdensity field. During the simulations, galaxies acted as sources for energetic, iron–enriched gas. An extreme choice for the superwind energy budget was used, to emphasize the directions in which evolution is driven. We compared the results of these ejection models with similar runs, drawn from equivalent initial condtions but lacking galaxies or winds. We find that sufficiently strong winds drive cluster gas onto higher adiabats, resulting in decreased X–ray luminosity at higher redshift, and more rapid luminosity evolution to the present, than models without galactic feedback. Iron abundance gradients in the ICM are a universal feature of these ejection models; the gradients result from an existing gradient in the galaxy distribution compared to the primordial gas distribution, and thus may be sensitive to our technique for including galaxies. In many cases, the gradients are sufficiently shallow that multiple spectra from non–imaging X–ray telescopes with poor spatial resolution would be unable to detect them. Correlations of observables such as X–ray luminosity and temperature show both success and failure in reproducing results from real data.

1. Why Care About Winds?

To understand cluster gas, we must examine the effects of interactions with cluster galaxies. Galactic superwinds should deposit energy and mass into the ICM. It seems observationally established that superwinds can occur [2]; how important have they been in rich clusters?

There exists some evidence for energy input to the intracluster medium beyond that from infall. Of the 23 clusters in Edge & Stewart's [1] sample with observed X–ray temperatures and measured galaxy velocity dispersions, 15 seem to show more specific energy in gas than in cluster galaxies;

only 7 of these are 1σ consistent with equal energies. Meanwhile, of the 8 clusters evidencing a larger specific energy in galaxies, only one deviates from equality by greater than 1σ. Measuring the relative magnitude of specific energies by the β–parameter, $\beta = \frac{\sigma^2}{(kT/\mu m_p)}$, the data seem skewed towards $\beta < 1$. There are several possible interpretations of this result, but one is that velocity dispersions sample the depth of cluster potential wells, while cluster gas has received additional energy.

More suggestive of the importance of winds is the presence of heavy elements in the ICM. Iron abundances near solar are characteristic of cluster gas, and the recent detection of large abundances of neon, silicon, and magnesium in the ICM by the ASCA satellite [4] suggest enrichment is primarily by Type II supernovae. It seems likely that early, supernova–driven galactic superwinds have accounted for cluster metal enrichment; these winds should deposit energy into the ICM as well. How would this energy input affect the cluster gas? What sort of metal distribution should winds produce?

2.   Simulation Program

The initial conditions and simulation algorithm used are explained in Metzler & Evrard [3]. Eighteen runs were prepared, in boxes with comoving side lengths from 20 Mpc to 60 Mpc, allowing simulations of clusters of a range in richness. It was assumed: that the galaxies in our simulations all have a mass–to–light ratio of 8; that the galaxies eject half of their initial mass by the present, at a flat rate; and that the wind luminosity for an individual galaxy scales with the galaxy luminosity, and for a $10^{10} L_\odot$ galaxy was $L_{wind} = 4 \times 10^{42}$ erg s^{-1}. This results in an overall energy output that is likely an order of magnitude too high; but by such excess, we clearly show by comparison the differences between ejection models and those with no winds.

3.   Summary of Results

Figure 1 summarizes three of the results from our ensemble of runs. The upper left corner shows simulated ROSAT PSPC images of a cluster comparable in richness to A2142. The images are from two separate times in each simulation, corresponding to redshifts of 0.25 and 0.06; the cluster has been placed at the appropriate redshift for viewing. The contour levels are the same in each case. The two–fluid model is obviously more X–ray luminous. Galactic winds drive cluster gas onto higher adiabats, and the two–fluid runs thus achieve higher densities than their ejection model counterparts.

The upper right corner shows the evolution of the ROSAT band–limited X–ray luminosity within a projected 1 Mpc metric distance of the center of the cluster, for one member of the ensemble. The three curves represent three models: a two–fluid model (2F), where no galaxies were inserted and no winds occured; our standard ejection model (EJ), and a model with the same parameters as model EJ, but with ejection abruptly cut off after one–third the total time, about 3.5 Gyr (TR). The ejection runs display rapid luminosity evolution, with stronger winds resulting in stronger evolution. Energy input from winds primarily affects the central, low–adiabat gas, thus decreasing the emission from the cluster core. Gas which infalls later is less affected by ejection, so the low–redshift X–ray luminosities for the three models are closer than the high–redshift luminosities.

On the lower left are projected, emission–weighted iron abundance maps for a member of the ensemble, as it might be observed by the ROSAT PSPC and the EXOSAT ME. The EXOSAT ME was not an imaging detector; a spot on the map gives the value obtained from a pointing in that direction. Also shown are the effects of two scenarios for the mixing of ejected iron with the ICM: one in which the iron is well mixed, and one not. The abundance contours are normalized to the wind abundance. For the ROSAT PSPC, the contours shown are at 0.13, 0.27, 0.4, and 0.53; for the EXOSAT ME, the contours vary from 0.35 centrally to 0.3 in the no mixing case, and has a

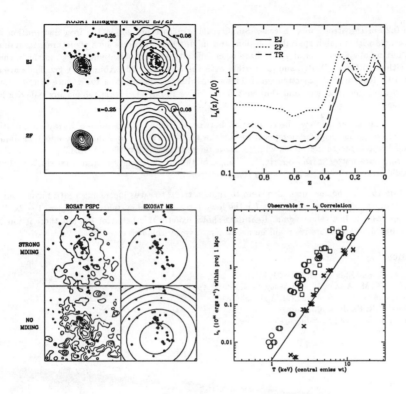

Figure 1. Four figures showing various results from the ensemble. The upper left corner shows simulated ROSAT PSPC images of the same cluster at redshifts of 0.25 and 0.6, for the run with galaxies and ejection, EJ, and the equivalent initial conditions with two fluids only (without galaxies or winds), 2F. The contours shown are 1, 2, 4, 8, 16, 32, 64, and 128σ. The dots indicate the projected locations of cluster galaxies. The upper right corner shows the redshift evolution of an ensemble member's X–ray luminosity, as a fraction of its final luminosity, for the EJ and 2F models, and for an additional model where only one–third as much energy and mass is ejected by galaxies, commencing at $z = 4$ and proceeding at the same rate, TR. The lower left corner is a map of the emission–weighted iron abundance distribution for an ensemble member, as it would be measured for the ROSAT PSPC and pointings of the EXOSAT ME detectors, and for two scenarios for mixing of the iron subsequent to ejection. The lower right corner shows the correlation between central, emission–weighted temperature and X–ray luminosity in the EXOSAT passband for the members of the ensemble as ejection (crosses) and two–fluid (circles) runs, as well as real data (squares). The solid line is a best–fit to the ejection runs, excluding the four lowest temperature systems from the fit as little of their X–ray emission falls within the EXOSAT passband.

value of 0.25 in the strong mixing case. Small scale structure present in the iron distribution is not detectable without high spatial resolution, and mixing tends to erase such structure. Assuming efficient mixing of ejected iron, it would have been difficult to detect the abundance gradient in this cluster with the ROSAT PSPC, and impossible with the EXOSAT ME. Abundance gradients are a characteristic feature of the ejection runs. This seems due to a gradient in the galaxy distribution relative to the primordial gas, and thus may be sensitive to our algorithm for placing galaxies in the volume.

The lower right corner displays the correlation between EXOSAT band–limited X–ray luminosity and central, emission–weighted temperature for the ejection runs, two–fluid runs, and real data. Excluding low temperature systems which have little emission within the EXOSAT passband, the ejection runs fare better in reproducing the slope of the $L_x - T$ relation from real clusters, but underpredicts the luminosities for a given temperature.

The ejection runs in the ensemble also seem to show a trend towards increasing central iron abundance as temperature decreases, except for the lowest temperature systems with $T_x = 1 - 2keV$, which drop down to low values again. Real data shows exactly this behavior [5], but there is much scatter in our data and more runs will be necessary to verify this agreement.

References

[1] Edge, A. C., and Stewart, G. C. 1991, MNRAS, **252**, 428.
[2] Heckman, T. M., Armus, L., and Miley, G. K. 1990, *Ap. J. Suppl.*, **74**, 833.
[3] Metzler, C.A. & Evrard, A.E. 1994, ApJ, submitted.
[4] Mushotzky, R. F., these proceedings.
[5] Ponman, T. J., these proceedings.

SIMULATIONS OF CLUSTERS USING HYDRA: ADAPTIVE PPPM+SPH

P. A. Thomas[1], F. R. Pearce[1] & H. M. P. Couchman[2]
[1] Astronomy Centre, University of Sussex, Brighton, BN1 9QH, UK.
[2] Dept. of Astronomy, University of Western Ontario, London, Ontario, N6A 3K7, Canada

We have used our new HYDRA code to study cluster formation. It is based on our earlier PPPM+SPH code but places sub-refinements in regions of high density so that the costly PP calculation can be replaced by additional PMs.

We first tested the self-similar hypothesis often invoked in hierarchical cosmologies by merging halos of collisionless particles at various speeds. The central density in te merger remnants is close to the maximum value allowed by phase-space constraints, indicating that there is no reason to expect a dark-matter core in clusters.

When gas is added to the merger simulations, it is found to behave in a qualitatively different fashion. The core gas shocks, irreversibly converting its kinetic energy into heat, then picks up more kinetic energy from the dark matter and shocks again. The gas is therefore 'heated' more than the dark matter and forms a resolved, constant-density core.

We have also performed a cluster collapse from more realistic initial conditions. The final density profile is more extended than that in the merger simulations, probably because of the continuous accretion of matter by 'secondary infall' at late times, but the core properties confirm our earlier results.

1. HYDRA: Adaptive PPPM+SPH

We have used our new HYDRA code to study cluster formation. It is based on our earlier PPPM+SPH code but places sub-refinements in regions of high density so that the costly PP calculation can be replaced by additional PMs[1]. This means that the code slows only by a factor of 2–3 when it bcomes heavily clustered, making it faster (or more accurate for a given speed) than TREE-based codes.

2. Merger simulations

We start with a variety of density profiles of the form $(r^2 + 2.5^2)^{-s/2}$ (solid lines in the above Figure) all of which tend towards a single homologue which in our case resembles a de Vaucouleurs' profile. In the final profiles, shown by the broken lines, the core radii have decreased relative to the half-mass radii and the central density is close to the maximum value allowed by phase-space constraints, indicating that there is no reason to expect a dark-matter core in clusters.[2]

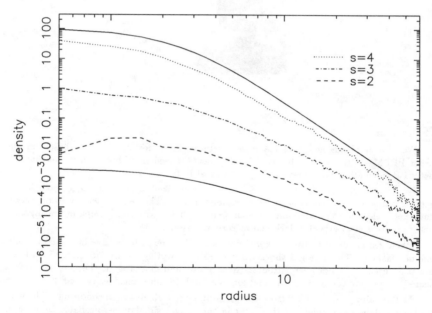

A mixture of gas and dark matter behaves differently.[3] The gas shocks converting its kinetic energy into heat, then picks up more kinetic energy from the dark matter and shocks again. It is 'heated' more than the dark matter and forms a resolved, constant-density core, as shown by the lower two panels of the Figures on the next page. We expect this to be a generic result, independent of the details of the merger process. The effect is not seen in a

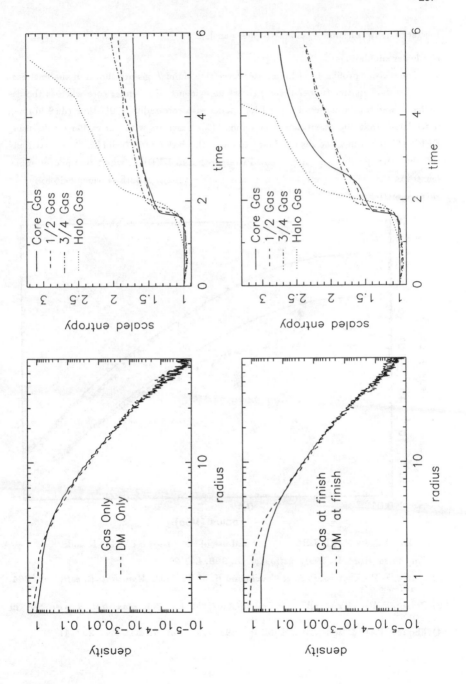

258

merger of halos containing gas only (upper panels).

3. Cluster simulations

The density profiles from the cluster formation simulations are shown in the final Figure. The dark matter (upper points) shows no evidence of an inner core whereas the gas profile (lower points) is well-fit by a King model with core radius $200h^{-1}$kpc (dashed line), much larger than the gravitational softening. This contrasts with our earlier results using PPPM+SPH in which the gas was found to follow the dark matter (solid lines). We attribute this difference partly to an improved SPH algorithm in HYDRA, which was poorly implemented in our earlier scheme, and partly to a smaller timestep, both of which help to reduce entropy-scatter.

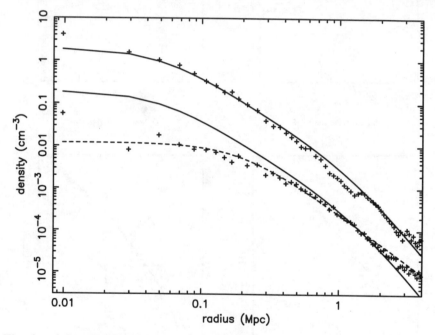

We acknowledge a NATO CRG 6920182 and use of the Sussex STARLINK node.

1) Couchman, H. M. P., 1991. *Astrophys. J.*, **368**, L23–26.

2) Pearce, F. R., Thomas, P. A. & Couchman, H. M. P., 1993. *Mon. Not. R. astr. Soc.*, **264**, 497–508.

3) Pearce, F. R., Thomas, P. A. & Couchman, H. M. P., 1994. *Mon. Not. R. astr. Soc.*, in press.

4) Thomas, P. A. & Couchman, H. M. P., 1992. *Mon. Not. R. astr. Soc.*, **257**, 11–31.

THE MASS FUNCTION IN THE ADHESION MODEL

B. DUBRULLE[1,2], U. FRISCH[3], A. NOULLEZ[3] and M. VERGASSOLA[3]

[1] *CNRS, UPR 182, SAP, L'Orme des Merisiers, 709, F-91191 Gif sur Yvette, France*
[2] *CNRS, URA 285, OMP, 14 av. E. Belin, F-31400 Toulouse, France*
[3] *CNRS, URA 1362, Observatoire de Nice, BP 229, F-06004 Nice Cedex 4, France*

Abstract

We present an analytical and numerical derivation of the mass function in the adhesion model. The scaling properties of the mass function at small masses are shown to be connected with the existence of a Devil's staircase in the Lagrangian map.

One important characteristic of large-scale structures in the Universe is the number density of masses, here referred to as the 'mass function'. Observations suggest that it follows a power law at small masses followed by a rapid cut-off at larger masses [1]. It is shown here that this property can be understood within a simplified model of the dynamics of the large scale structures, called the adhesion model. It is an extension of the so-called Zeldovich approximation. This approximation transforms the Jean-Vlasov-Poisson equations into a 'free-flight' problem (equivalent to a Burgers equation with no viscosity). Its main conditions of applicability are i) non-crossing of the particles orbits; ii) equivalence of the Vlasov-Poisson and the hydrodynamical Euler description; iii) Lagrangian invariance of the gravity; iv) proportionality of the initial velocity and gravitational acceleration (see [6]). Solutions of the Zeldovich approximation can be obtained by a simple mapping between initial (Lagrangian) position and present (Eulerian) position. However, after some time, this mapping develops singularities, corresponding to situations where particles, thrown with large initial velocities, catch up with slower particles and overtake them. This situation corresponds to the formation of a caustic in the density field.

This situation is not very realistic. In a true Universe with self-gravitating particles, caustic are avoided by the mutual interactions, which modify locally the gravitational acceleration and the velocity of the particles. To take into account this effect (and also to remove the singularity

260

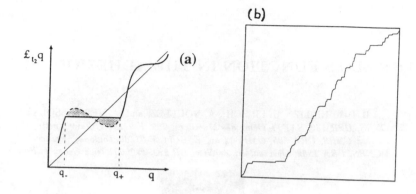

Figure 1: (a) Lagrangian map in the presence of a shock; (b) Lagrangian map for Brownian initial velocities ($h = 1/2$).

in the mapping), Gurbatov and Saichev [2] suggested to introduce an infinitely small viscosity, to mimick gravitational sticking. The caustics are then replaced by shocks, corresponding to formation of "clumps" in the density field (fig 1a), and the dynamics can then be described by a Burgers equation

$$\partial_t v + (v\nabla)v = \nu\nabla^2 v, \tag{1}$$

where $v(x, t)$ is the velocity field and ν is the velocity. In the limit $\nu \to 0$, the shape of the shocks is independent of the details of the dissipation mechanism, and exact solutions of the Burgers equation can be obtained via Legendre transforms (see [6]). This allows both analytical predictions on the behaviour of the solutions, via probabilistic tools developed by Sinai [5], and high resolution numerical solutions, thanks to an efficient Legendre transform algorithm developed by Noullez and Vergassola [7]. All the simulations presented here were performed on a Sun workstation, using the Fast Legendre Transform algorithm.

In the cosmological context, the initial density field is often taken as scale free, with a power law power spectrum of index n. This corresponds in the adhesion approximation to scaling initial velocities:

$$v_0(x + \lambda l) - v_0(x) = \lambda^h(v_0(x + l) - v_0(x)), \tag{2}$$

where h is the scaling exponent, so that, in a d-dimensional space, $n + d = 2(1 - h)$. With such scaling initial conditions, shocks occur everywhere, and the Lagrangian mapping initial $\to$ present position takes a very special shape, shown in Fig.1b. This shape is characterized by successive increasing 'plateaus' of different size (corresponding to the shocks), which are organized in a self-similar way: successive zooms inside the structure always lead to the same structure. This self-similarity is the signature of a fractal behaviour. The structure seen in Fig. 1b is called a Devil's staircase. This is a non-decreasing function which varies only over a fractal set of zero measure. The most famous Devil's staircase is obtained by computing the mass of a Cantor set as a function of the position. The corresponding shock structure in the

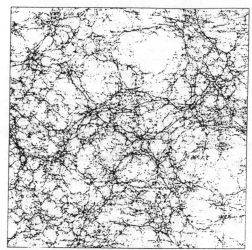

Figure 2: Mass density field in 2D for Brownian initial conditions ($h = 1/2$).

Eulerian space (at a given time), is depicted in Fig. 2, for a 2D simulation. A complex pattern of thin shock lines intersecting at nodes can be observed, reminiscent of what is observed in complete N-Body simulations.

Using these simulations, the mass function of the shocks $n(m)$ was computed for various initial conditions (various h) (see fig. 3 for the 1D case). It was found to obey a simple scaling behaviour, depending on the dimension d and of the scaling exponent of the initial velocity field, h:

- at small masses, $n(m)$ follows a power-law:

$$n(m) \sim m^{-h-1};\tag{3}$$

Note that the power-law is independent of the dimension. It might be due to the fact that the smallest masses belong to $d-1$ dimensional structures (nodes in 1D, shock lines or walls in 2D or 3D), so that the dynamics transverse to the shock is 1D in all cases. This is however a mere speculation.

- at large masses, $n(m)$ is a streched exponential:

$$\log(n(m)) \sim -m^{-2(1-h)/d}.\tag{4}$$

In that case, the result depends on the dimension. This is because strong shocks are made of nodes in any dimension, which correspond to d-dimensional polyhedra of mass m and length $L \sim m^{1/d}$ in the Lagrangian space.

The scaling properties of the mass function in the adhesion approximation, reminiscent of what is observed in the real Universe, is actually the signature of the Devil's staircase appearing in the Lagrangian map. The (analytical) proof of this result requires complex probability tools and can be found in [6]. A heuristic insight of the result can however be given, if one accepts that initial conditions with scaling exponent h give rise to a Devil's staircase of dimension h in the Lagrangian map. The underlying Cantor set, obtained by removing recursively smaller and smaller intervals, is then of dimension $d_F = h$. Since the Lagrangian map increases only

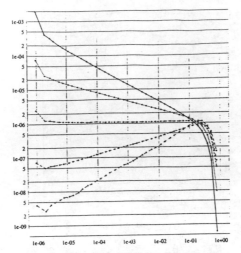

Figure 3: Cumulated mass function for 1D solutions of the adhesion models. The scaling exponent range from $h = 1/2$ to $h = -1/2$ from top to bottom, in steps of 0.25. Observe the wide range of scales, which has the exponent $-h$.

at regular points and remains constant at the location of shock points, the regular points correspond to the points in the Cantor set, while shocks correspond to the removed intervals. A well known result in fractal theory is that the distribution of the removed intervals (number of removed intervals of size l) follows a power-law $N(l) \sim l^{-d_F}$, where d_F is the dimension of the corresponding Cantor set. Since the mass was initially uniformly distributed over the space, the length of the removed interval (shock) is directly proportional to its mass. This means that the cumulated mass distribution obeys $N(m) \sim m^{-d_F}$, or, since $d_F = h$ and $n(m) = dN/dm$, $n(m) \sim m^{-h-1}$.

The present study provides a complete understanding of the mass function in the adhesion model. It is interesting to compare our results with the outcome of a heuristic theory of structure formation by Press and Schechter [4], which predicts a mass function:

$$n(m) \sim m^{-2+(1-h)/d} \exp\left(-\left(\frac{m}{m_*}\right)^{2(1-h)/d}\right). \tag{5}$$

We find therefore that the Press and Schechter and the adhesion model predictions agree in their functional form at large masses for any space dimension, but agree only in one dimension at small masses. The reasons for this agreement/discrepancy are not firmly established yet. We may note that Press and Schechter theory is based on isotropic collapse, which may be adequate to describe node (large mass) formation, but not structures with small masses, which are formed by a compression in one direction. Also, Press and Schechter theory is based on local collapse arguments, leading to the so-called "cloud in cloud problem": one cannot discriminate between real strutures, or structures which appear locally bounded but which actually belong to a larger structure. In the adhesion model, the theory is based on conditions of non-collapse of an extended halo, which avoids this problem.

It is yet not clear why Press and Schechter theory has been so succesfull in explaining mass functions derived from real N-Body experiments. Maybe the structure formation in N-Body simulations is more isotropic and more local than in the adhesion model, and so closer to the Press and Schechter assumptions. Maybe it is just an artefact of the N-Body mass function definition (based on friend of friend algorithm) which does not coincide with the adhesion definition, based on the Lagrangian map.

References

[1] Bahcall N and Cen R *Astrophys. J.* **407**, L49 (1993).

[2] Gurbatov S. and Saichev A. *Radiophys. Quant. Electr.* **27**, 456 (1984).

[3] Noullez A. and Vergassola M. *J. Sci. Comput.* in press (1994).

[4] Press W. and Schechter P. *Astrophys. J.* **187**, 425 (1974).

[5] Sinai Ya. *Commun. Math. Phys.* **148**, 601 (1992).

[6] Vergassola M., Dubrulle B., Frisch U. and Noullez A. *A&A* in press (1994).

THE FUNDAMENTAL PLANE OF GALAXY CLUSTERS

ALBERTO CAPPI

Osservatorio Astronomico di Bologna, via Zamboni 33, I-40126 Bologna, Italy

Abstract

In the three–dimensional space defined by the logarithms of central velocity dispersion σ, effective radius R_e and mean effective surface brightness I_e, elliptical galaxies are confined in a narrow plane (Dressler et al. 1987; Djorgovski & Davis 1987). I will discuss the observational evidence for the existence of a Faber–Jackson relation and, more generally, of a fundamental plane for galaxy clusters (Schaeffer et al., 1993). The existence and tilt of such a FP have interesting implications which will be briefly outlined.

1 Observational evidence for the fundamental plane of clusters

The relations between global observables in stellar systems are important both from a theoretical and a practical point of view. The Tully–Fisher relation for spirals and the Faber–Jackson relation for ellipticals involved two observables. In the case of ellipticals, the residual scatter has suggested the introduction of a third parameter, resulting in the definition of the so–called fundamental plane (Djorgovski & Davis 1987; Dressler et al. 1987; for a review, see Kormendy & Djorgovski 1989).

From the virial theorem we expect a relation involving the three observables R, L and σ, which can be expressed in the following way (see Djorgovski & Santiago 1993):

$$L \propto K R \sigma^2 \left(\frac{M}{L}\right)^{-1} \tag{1}$$

where K is a structural parameter. Notice that the existence of the FP for a given class of objects is *not* a trivial consequence of the virial theorem; it requires also that the class of objects under study has a similar dynamical structure and a tight mass to light ratio with a small dispersion.

The study of relations between global observables in galaxy clusters has been difficult until recently, because of the lack of data. In a previous work (Schaeffer et al. 1993) we could dispose of effective radii and total luminosities for a sample of 29 *regular* galaxy clusters, measured after an accurate and homogeneous reduction of high–quality photometric data by West et al. (1989). From these data, among other results, West et al. found a well–defined radius–luminosity relation, discussing also –and excluding– some possible selection effects. I point out that the redshifts of the clusters in their sample are well determined, and cluster peculiar velocities are not large enough to generate a spurious relation (this might happen because both R and L are estimated assuming a distance derived from the cluster redshift).

For 16 of these clusters we found reliable measures of velocity dispersion (Struble & Rood 1991). As a first step, we checked the existence of a relation between velocity dispersion and luminosity, and we found $L \propto \sigma^{1.9}$. Previous work had shown that velocity dispersion increased with richness (Danese et al. 1980; see also Girardi et al. 1993), and an indirect hint that such a relation exists is given by a "Malmquist bias" in a σ–z diagram for nearby galaxy clusters (Cappi et al. 1994). The relation L–σ for clusters, which is the equivalent of the Faber–Jackson law for ellipticals. is interesting, because the optical luminosity traces the stellar component, and in clusters the total mass is dominated by dark matter, while hot gas represents the major component of baryonic matter.

The above relations show anyway a quite large scatter. Is it due simply to observational errors, or does it depend on the effect of a third parameter? Indeed, we found that the second hypothesis is the right one: the above 16 clusters follow very tightly a FP (Schaeffer et al. 1993; see fig.1). We found $L \propto R^{0.89\pm0.15}\sigma^{1.28\pm0.10}$ or, defining a surface brightness $I_e = L/R_e^2$, $R_e \propto I_e^{-0.81}\sigma^{1.15}$, with the best fit parameters quite similar to the elliptical ones. Anyway the cluster FP cannot coincide with the elliptical one, because of the different M/L ratio. Notice that the qualitative analogy with ellipticals extends to all the two–parameter relations. For example, the relation σ–I_e is very poor, and this is true also for clusters. It seems that we have found a real property of regular galaxy clusters, and not a spurious one.

Analyzing their new sample of clusters, Zabludoff et al. (1993) notice that there is a big scatter in the relation between the velocity dispersion σ and N_{20} – a parameter they defined in such a way as to represent a sort of cluster "surface–brightness" –. Anyway, that result is not at variance with the existence of a cluster fundamental plane, for various plausible reasons: the N_{20}–σ relationship has only one independent parameter, like the L–σ or L–R relationships, and part of the dispersion can be ascribed to the lack of a second independent parameter (a relation of the type surface brightness–σ is equivalent to impose $L \propto R^2\sigma^\beta$, instead of the virial relation $L \propto R\sigma^2$ or the FP relation); moreover, while a valuable indicator, N_{20} is not so accurate as the results of true photometric analysis; finally, the new sample of Zabludoff et al. includes regular as well as irregular clusters, while the FP relation holds for more or less regular clusters.

2   Implications of the cluster fundamental plane

We conclude that regular clusters are confined in a FP comparable to that of elliptical galaxies, reflecting the virial theorem *but* giving also information about formation time dispersions, mass to light ratios (we found a very small trend of M/L with L, with $M/L \propto L^{0.3\pm0.1}$), or cluster peculiar velocities.

Another way to look at the data is using the coordinates defined by Bender et al. (1992) (see fig.2). These new coordinate system is not the FP, but represents a complementary and useful tool. This visualization gives directly $k_3 \propto \log(M/L)$ vs. $k_1 \propto \log(M)$. It is clear that M/L of these clusters has a small dispersion. Renzini & Ciotti (1993) argue from the approximate constancy of k_3 that richer clusters have collected more baryons per unit of dark matter mass, but have been less efficient to convert them in stars.

We can also have a rough estimate of the cluster peculiar velocity $V_p = V_{obs} - H_0 D$ (assuming that the deviation from the FP is entirely due to V_p, which is certainly not true). We find that a large dispersion in V_p is apparent in clusters beyond 0.05. This is not surprising: uncertainties on radius, luminosity and velocity dispersion increase with distance. The 10 clusters within $z = 0.05$ give reasonable results (Cappi et al. 1994). All of them have peculiar velocities (in absolute value, relative to the CMB) ≤ 1000 km/s. In fig.3 we show their peculiar velocities in the CMB frame as a function of the cosine angle between clusters and the GA direction (Faber & Burstein 1989). The behaviour of V_p is consistent with the recent results of Han (1992), Han & Mould (1992). We find also as an upper limit $\Delta H/H \leq 15\%$ for $z \leq 0.05$, consistently with Lauer & Postman (1992). Of course, these are only very rough results, which simply show the potentiality of the cluster FP as a distance indicator.

3 Conclusions

I have shown the observational evidence which suggests that regular clusters follow a fundamental plane analogous to the elliptical one. A critical point is the quality of the data, especially the photometry, to allow an accurate determination of the effective radius and the total luminosity. Therefore a large observational effort is needed to address some important issues. For example, available data do not tell us if M/L really changes with cluster mass or is constant. The exact location of the FP is needed, if we want to use it as a distance indicator. Moreover, the combination with X-ray data is essential to understand the role of the different matter components in galaxy clusters.

References

Bender R., Burstein D., Faber S.M., 1992, ApJ **399**, 462

Cappi A., Held E.V., Marano B., 1994, AA, submitted

Cappi A., Maurogordato S., Schaeffer R., Bernardeau F., 1994, in 9th IAP meeting on *Cosmic velocity fields*, F.Bouchet & M.Lachièze–Rey eds., in press

Danese L., De Zotti G., di Tullio G., 1980, AA **82**, 322

Djorgovski S., Davis M., 1987, ApJ **313**, 59

Djorgovski S., Santiago B.X., 1993, in ESO workshop on Structure, Dynamics and Chemical Evolution of Elliptical Galaxies, eds. I.J.Danziger, W.W.Zeilinger, K.Kjär, Garching, p.59

Dressler A. et al., 1987, ApJ **313**, L37

Faber S.M., Burstein D., 1989, in *Large–Scale Motions in the Universe*, ed. V.C.Rubin & G.Coyne, Princeton University Press, p.115

Girardi M., Biviano A., Giuricin G., Mardirossian F., Mezzetti M., 1993, ApJ **404**, 38

Han M., 1992, ApJ **395**, 75

Han M., Mould J.R., 1992, ApJ **396**, 453

Kormendy J., Djorgovski S., 1989, ARAA **27**, 235

Lauer T.R., Postman M., 1992, ApJ **400**, L47

Renzini A., Ciotti L., 1993, ApJ **416**, L49

Schaeffer R., Maurogordato S., Cappi A., Bernardeau F., 1993, MNRAS **261**, L21

Struble M.F., Rood H.J., 1991, ApJS **77**, 363

West M.J., Oemler A., Dekel A., 1989, ApJ **346**, 539

Zabludoff A.I., Geller M.J., Huchra J.P., Ramella M., 1993, AJ **106**, 1301

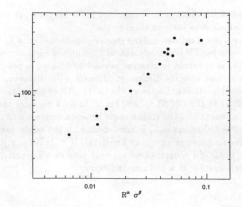

Figure 1: The fundamental plane of galaxy clusters: $\alpha = 0.89$, $\beta = 1.28$.

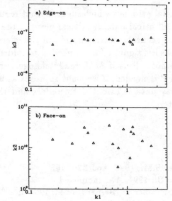

Figure 2: The same galaxy clusters in the coordinate system k_1, k_2, k_3.

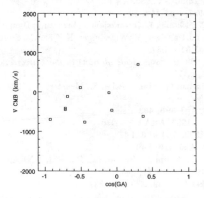

Figure 3: Peculiar velocities of galaxy clusters inferred from the FP.

MAPPING THE DARK MATTER IN CLUSTERS

Nick Kaiser[1,2], Gordon Squires[1]
Greg Fahlman[3] and David Woods[3]

[1] CITA, University of Toronto, Canada
[2] Canadian Institute for Advanced Research Cosmology Programme
[3] Astronomy and Geophysics, UBC, Vancouver, Canada

ABSTRACT

Massive clusters of galaxies gravitationally shear the images of faint background galaxies. At large impact parameters the shear is weak, but can still be measured, to a reasonable degree of significance, as a statistical anisotropy of the faint galaxy images. We describe techniques for measuring the shear and discuss the interpretation of the shear field. We have applied this analysis to ms1224+007. We find a clear detection of the shear, but, puzzlingly, we find a mass about three times that obtained by application of the virial theorem, and obtain a very large mass-to-light ratio. Similar results have been obtained by other groups, and we discuss their implications.

Giant arcs in clusters provide a very clean probe of the mass distribution in the central parts of clusters (see e.g. the reviews of Soucail and Miralda-Escude in these proceedings). The work we shall describe here follows the pioneering study of A1689 by Tyson, Valdes and Wenk (1990) where they measured for the first time the statistical anisotropy of the background galaxies at much larger radii.

MEASURING THE IMAGE SHEAR

From deep photometry of a field containing a massive cluster we first find the faint galaxies and measure their central second angular moments: $Q_{ij} = \int d^2\theta W(\theta)\theta_i\theta_j f(\vec{\theta})$, where f is the surface brightness, and form the "polarization"

$$e_\alpha = \left[\begin{array}{c} (Q_{11} - Q_{22})/(Q_{11} + Q_{22}) \\ 2Q_{12}/(Q_{11} + Q_{22}) \end{array} \right]$$

The window function $W(\theta)$ we use is a gaussian with scale length matched to that of the galaxy. In the absence of lensing the e_α values will scatter around a mean of zero on the e_1, e_2 plane, but a gravitational shear acting coherently over some angle will displace the distribution. Provided the shear is weak — and we will be measuring shears of typically 10% — the shift in the mean polarization is $\langle e_\alpha \rangle = P_{sh}s_\alpha$, where the shear $s_\alpha \equiv \{\phi_{,11} - \phi_{,22}, 2\phi_{,12}\}$ and the surface potential ϕ satisfies $\nabla^2\phi = 2\sigma$ with dimensionless surface density $\sigma = \Sigma_{phys}/\Sigma_{crit}$. The effective critical surface density is $\Sigma_{crit}^{-1} = 4\pi G a_l w_l \langle \max(0, 1 - w_l/w_g) \rangle$ with the average being taken over the distribution of comoving distances w_g to the faint galaxies. The proportionality constant P_{sh} — which we call the shear polarizability — depends on the details of the shapes of the galaxies, and can be estimated either for the population as a whole or, as we do, individually for each galaxy.

Each galaxy therefore provides an estimate of the shear along a particular line of sight, though a rather noisy one as there is a substantial scatter in the intrinsic polarizations. These can be averaged together to produce e.g. a smoothed shear map $s(\vec{\theta})$ with statistical uncertainty $\sim \sqrt{\langle s^2 \rangle_{intrinsic}/N}$ where N is the number of galaxies being averaged. An interesting feature of cluster studies is that the signal to noise varies rather slowly with radius; at large radii the signal becomes small, but the number of galaxies goes up and these cancel if the surface density varies as $\Sigma \propto 1/r$ for instance.

A minor complication is that distortion of the images can arise in the telescope and in the earth's atmosphere. Luckily there are sufficiently many foreground stars to provide a control sample with which to measure the point spread function quite precisely. One could imagine reconvolving the image with a psf designed to recircularise the stars and this would then null out the systematic error in the galaxies. In fact what we do is to calculate for each galaxy a 'smear polarizability' P_{sm} analogous to P_{sh} which tells us how the polarization shifts in response to smearing by an anisotropic psf (P_{sm} is essentially a measure of the inverse area of the galaxy), and use this to null out the systematic error. This approach is easier if, as in the data we describe later, the psf anisotropy varies across the chip. An ultimate limit on this technique — which one might eventually hope to apply to very large fields where it is vital to cancel even very tiny systematic effect — may possibly arise due to effects such as atmospheric dispersion and chromatic aberrations of the optics which cause the psf to depend on the spectrum of the objects, but with present data such effects are small compared to the statistical error.

INTERPRETATION OF THE SHEAR

Assuming we have a map of the shear $s(\vec{\theta})$ how do we infer from this the surface density σ? First, there is no local relation between the shear and σ. Physically, this reflects the fact that a constant density sheet lens does not produce shear. As one might expect, however, there is a local relation between the angular gradients of s and of σ:

$$\partial\sigma/\partial x = \tfrac{1}{2}\left[\partial s_1/\partial x + \partial s_2/\partial y\right]$$
$$\partial\sigma/\partial y = \tfrac{1}{2}\left[\partial s_2/\partial x - \partial s_1/\partial y\right]$$

This means that in principle one can construct any *differential* measurement of the surface density; for instance one can calculate the surface density difference between two points simply by integrating $\nabla\sigma$ along some line: $\delta\sigma_{12} = \sigma(\vec{\theta}_1) - \sigma(\vec{\theta}_2) = \int_{\theta_1}^{\theta_2} \vec{dl} \cdot \nabla\sigma$. The arbitrariness of the line chosen reflects the inherent non-uniqueness of any σ determination method. This arises essentially because one has two inputs s_1, s_2 from which we only want to recover the single scalar function σ. In the example here one could estimate $\delta\sigma_{12}$ by averaging over any combination of paths from θ_1 to θ_2 — and one would presumably try to find some optimum weighted combination of these — and one could also use loop integrals in some way to provide a check on the quality of the data, though how best to do this has yet to be worked out in any systematic way.

The ambiguity in the baseline surface density is something of a problem, particularly when the data coverage is limited. The ambiguity can be resolved to some extent by studying clusters with giant arcs, though this involves some uncertain interpolation of the surface density from the radii where the arcs lie out to the radii where the weak shear analysis can be safely applied. An alternative is to try and measure the perturbation of the background galaxy counts $n(m)$ (Broadhurst, Peacock and Taylor, 1994) to determine the surface density, though this is quite difficult, as we show below. We have developed a number of tests derived from the relation above between $\partial\sigma/\partial\theta_i$ and $\partial s_\alpha/\partial\theta_i$:

Mass Imaging

Kaiser and Squires (1992, hereafter KS93) provide an algorithm to reconstruct a smoothed 2-dimensional mass image. In the present context, this can be viewed as an average over all radial paths from infinity (or some large radius where the surface density and the shear can be assumed small) to the point in question. This becomes a two dimensional integral $\hat{\sigma} = \langle\int dl \cdot \nabla\sigma\rangle_{\text{radial paths}} \rightarrow \int d^2\theta\ldots$ which in turn can be replaced by a sum over the background galaxies (provided these are sufficiently dense on the sky).

An important practical limitation of this method comes from boundary terms introduced when the data are finite. Near the centre of the mass reconstruction this causes a constant negative shift which can be expressed in terms of the surface density and shear on the boundary (for a circular field the shift is the mean of σ plus half the mean tangential shear around the boundary). Further out nearer the edge of the field one finds a spurious negative trough;

the lack of observed shear beyond the field effectively introduces an integral constraint which forces the total mass in the lens to be zero. A nice feature of the method is that while the estimator is a convolution of the observed shears with an extended kernel, the noise has a white spectrum and, provided we average over a scale containing several galaxies, should be quite accurately gaussian. This makes assigning significance to features in the mass reconstructions fairly straightforward.

A weakness of the method is that it does not appear to make full use of the redundancy in the data described above. We have developed an alternative method which creates the most probable density field compatible with the data, under the prior assumption of gaussian noise with user specified colour and amplitude. This should incorporate the extra information. The results appear quite similar in *shape* to those obtained with the KS93 method, but there is a bias in amplitude in the reconstructed $\sigma(\vec{\theta})$ which is hard to calibrate.

Laplacian Map

An alternative is to construct a map of the laplacian of σ:

$$\nabla^2 \sigma = D_\alpha s_\alpha$$

where $D_\alpha \equiv \{\partial^2/\partial x^2 - \partial^2/\partial y^2, 2\partial^2/\partial x\partial y\}$. As we want a smoothed map of the laplacian we implement this as a filter in fourier space, the D_α operator becoming an algebraic function which multiplies the smoothing filter transfer function. This relation is local, so we don't need to worry about boundary terms. This method is probably going to be most useful for attempting to find clusters blindly in future large survey fields; a cluster will appear as a negative dip. A nice feature of this method is that one can also use the redundancy in the input data to calculate a map of $\nabla \times \nabla \sigma$ — which is simply obtained by applying the 'rotation' $s_1 \rightarrow s_2$, $s_2 \rightarrow -s_1$ to the data before applying the D_α operator — and which should of course be zero. This provides a useful check on the consistency of the data.

Aperture Massometry

It is possible to put a rigorous lower bound on the mass contained within a circular aperture. This method uses the mean tangential shear around a circular path of radius θ:

$$\langle s_T \rangle = \int \frac{d\phi}{2\pi} [s_1 \cos 2\phi + s_2 \sin 2\phi] = -\frac{d\bar{\sigma}}{d\ln\theta}$$

where $\bar{\sigma}$ is the mean surface density within the circle and the second equality (which is trivial for a circularly symmetric lens) follows in the general case from the 2-dimensional version of Gauss' law. It is then easy to show that the statistic

$$\zeta(\theta_1, \theta_2) \equiv (1 - \theta_1^2/\theta_2^2)^{-1} \int_{\theta_1}^{\theta_2} d\ln\theta \langle s_T \rangle = \bar{\sigma}(< \theta_1) - \bar{\sigma}(\theta_1 < \theta < \theta_2)$$

where the last symbol represents the mean surface density in the annulus $\theta_1 < \theta < \theta_2$. Since this is necessarily non-negative ζ provides a lower bound on $\bar{\sigma}(< \theta_1)$. The $\int d\ln\theta \langle s_T \rangle$ can again be replaced by an area integral and thereby by a discrete sum over galaxies and, as with the massmap determination, the error analysis is straightforward.

An interesting feature of this analysis is that it uses only data which lie in the control annulus, so provided a sufficiently large field, this can be placed outside of most of the cluster light, greatly simplifying the problem of distinguishing background galaxies from cluster members.

Unless the ratio of inner and outer radii θ_2/θ_1 is made very large, in which case we will only be able to estimate $\bar{\sigma}$ in a very small region, the systematic underestimation of $\bar{\sigma}$ can be quite substantial. For a power law surface density profile $\sigma \propto \theta^{-\gamma}$ and with $\theta_2 = a\theta_1$, $\zeta/\bar{\sigma} = (a^2 - a^{2-\gamma})/(a^2 - 1)$, so for $\gamma = 1$, ζ underestimates the true $\bar{\sigma}$ by 33% and 25% for $a = 2, 3$ respectively.

As with the laplacian map, it is possible to obtain a check on the consistency of the data by 'rotating' the inputs, $s_1 \to s_2$, $s_2 \to -s_1$ which should result in $\zeta = 0$ within the statistical error.

The ζ statistic is really a special case of the KS93 method for a particular choice of smoothing kernel; in this case a 'compensated top-hat'. In fact, from $d\bar{\sigma}/d\ln r = -\langle s_T \rangle$ one can show that an estimator for the surface density smoothed with an arbitrary circular window function with zero total weight: $\int d^2 r W(r) = 0$ is

$$\int d^2 r W(r)\sigma(\vec{r}) = 2\pi \int dr \langle s_T \rangle W'(r)$$

where

$$W'(r) = \frac{1}{r} \int_0^r dr' r' W(r') - \frac{rW(r)}{2}$$

which provides a simple way to construct the window function W' for e.g. any mexican hat type $W(r)$. Note that if W vanishes beyond some radius then so does W', which again is nice if one is dealing with finite data.

Dilution of the Counts

The ambiguity in the baseline surface density is a nuisance. This can be resolved in principle by measuring the dilution of the background counts $\delta n(m)$ caused by the amplification (BPT). Under the weak lens assumption, the perturbation to the counts is just proportional to the surface density, though with a rather small constant of proportionality since the amplification bias for faint galaxies is rather small. There are clearly some technical difficulties in applying this method; here one must look for a perturbation under the lens, so to speak, rather than around it as in the shear measurement, so one must be careful to correct for the faint cluster galaxy counts. This can be aided by using colour information, but getting accurate colours is expensive. One would also have to correct for masking of background galaxies by the high surface brightness parts of foreground galaxies, and perhaps subtle effects in the image detection and photometry where the extended diffuse light around the cluster galaxies overlays the background.

With effort these problems can perhaps be overcome, but the following example suggests that the method will still suffer from rather low signal to noise: If we use the ζ statistic to estimate $\overline{\sigma}$, the statistical uncertainty is $\langle \hat{\overline{\sigma}} \rangle^{1/2} = (1 - 1/a^2)^{-1} \sqrt{\langle s_1^2 \rangle / (4\pi \overline{n} r_1^2)}$ where $r_2 = ar_1$, $\overline{n}$ is the surface number density of galaxies, and the rms shear noise (with both instrumental and intrinsic contributions) is $\langle s_1^2 \rangle^{1/2} \simeq 0.43$ for the data described below. From the observed faint galaxy counts, the amplification bias appears to be quite small; $\simeq -0.25$. The amplification is $2\overline{\sigma}$, so the corresponding estimator is $\hat{\overline{\sigma}} \simeq -2\delta n(m)/n(m)$ (BPT describe alternatives such as looking for a change in the slope of the counts, but the simple example here illustrates the basic idea and it is hard to imagine that the noise in any other estimator is likely to be significantly different). Assuming a poisson distribution for the background galaxies, the noise in this estimator is then $\langle \hat{\overline{\sigma}}^2 \rangle^{1/2} = 2/\sqrt{\pi \overline{n} r_1^2}$. Clustering of the background galaxies will inflate this by an uncertain but probably appreciable factor, but the minimal poisson error is already about a factor 8 larger than that for the ζ statistic, so for the ms1224 data described below, for example, the expected S/N is below unity.

MS1224

This cluster was chosen for its high X-ray luminosity, its high redshift ($z = 0.33$) making it possible to survey a $\sim 2h^{-1}$Mpc square field in a reasonable time, and because it was also a target of the CNOC cluster project. The optical spectroscopy studies (Carlberg, Yee and Ellingson, 1994, hereafter CYE) gave a modest velocity dispersion of $\simeq 750$km/s, and apparently consistent with this, a low richness, though as we shall see, the mass found from the lensing appears to be much greater.

As described in Fahlman et al., 1994 (hereafter FKSW), we took 1 hr total I-band integrations on each of four fields surrounding the cluster centre under excellent seeing conditions. Our software found ~ 5000 objects over an area (after allowing for masked regions around bright foreground stars) of about 120 square arcmin, from which we extracted a 'faint-extended' subsample of about 2000 galaxies covering a range of about 3 magnitudes to I=23.4. As a test, these data were artificially stretched, rebinned onto a 2× coarser pixel grid and then degraded to simulate the effects of seeing. These synthetic data were then analysed in the same way as the real data. This verified that the analysis software was indeed able to detect the artificial shear, and also allowed us to estimate a small, but critical 'signal loss factor' due to seeing and other biases in the analysis. The anisotropy of the psf was measured and the correction applied as described above.

In the real data a clear shear signal was seen: the mass-map has a peak which coincides quite well with the bulk of the smoothed cluster light measured by CYE, and the tangential shear was also clearly seen (as a significance level of about 5-sigma). The ζ-statistic gave $\overline{\sigma}(< 2.7') \geq 0.06 \pm 0.012$. The signal was also seen repeatedly in independent magnitude sub-samples. A mysterious dark peak also appears repeatedly in the mass-map. This is not seen in the cluster light, but as it is only a $\simeq 3$-sigma detection it should not be taken too seriously.

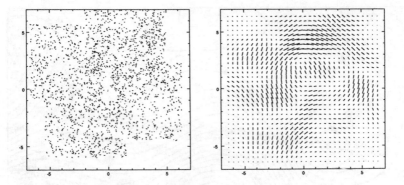

Fig. 1.—Spatial distribution and polarization (or ellipticity) parameters for the ms1224 faint galaxy subsample. The left panel shows the individual galaxies to be fairly uniformly distributed on the sky, though with some holes around bright foreground stars and galaxies. No particularly strong coherent distortion is apparent to the eye. However, in the panel on the right we have smoothed the polarizations to make a map of the shear, and the characteristic shear pattern is now clearly seen.

While the *location* of the main mass peak is in nice accord with the optical measurement, the *amplitude* is not. The mass scale calibration depends on the effective inverse critical surface density which in turn depends on the redshift distribution of the background galaxies. For our brighter galaxies we can measure $\Sigma_{\rm crit}^{-1}$ directly using the data of Lilly, 93 and Tresse *et al.*, 1993; the much larger CFRS redshift survey has recently been completed, increasing the sample size by an order of magnitude, and seems to reinforce the results obtained from the smaller published samples. For the fainter galaxies we need to extrapolate. Extrapolating the trend at brighter magnitudes suggest a very slow increase in $\Sigma_{\rm crit}$ of about 30% per magnitude. A similar or even more modest increase is indicated by the slow variation of shear with magnitude limit seen in our studies of ms1224 and now of several other similar clusters.

The upshot of all of this is a lower bound (aside from statistical error, of course) on the mass within a radius of 2.76' (or roughly $0.5h^{-1}$Mpc in physical radius) of $M_{\rm lens} \geq 3.5 \times 10^{14} M_\odot/h$. This can be compared with the virial mass in the same aperture — obtained by taking the total virial mass estimate and multiplying by the fraction of the total cluster light lying within the aperture — of $M_{\rm virial} = 1.15 \times 10^{14} M_\odot/h$; a factor 3 smaller than $M_{\rm lens}$. We can also use our photometry (or that of CYE) to obtain a mass to light ratio $(M/L)_V \simeq 800h$, much larger than the values typically obtained for nearby optically selected clusters.

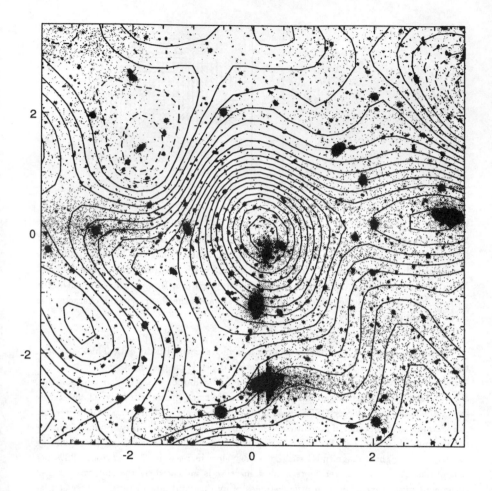

Fig. 2.—Contour plot of the projected mass reconstruction superposed on the summed I-band image of the central 7' square region of ms1224.

We have thought long and hard about possible errors or biases in our analysis which might have corrupted our mass estimates. Here is a non-exhaustive list of factors we have considered, though most of these can be safely discounted: *i) Biases:* There are a number of biases: $\zeta < \overline{\sigma}$; the optical light estimate includes projected material in the centre beam, but does not cover the entire control aperture, and no attempt has been made to remove the cluster galaxies, which will tend to dilute the shear signal. Allowing for these biases would only exacerbate the discrepancy. *ii) Statistical Uncertainty:* The statistical uncertainty in $\overline{\sigma}$ is about 20%. At the time we submitted FKSW there was a larger statistical uncertainty arising from the rather small size of the redshift surveys, but the larger CFRS survey seems to give similar results. The redshift surveys are, of course, not 100% complete and the missing 10% or so of the galaxies are most probably at higher redshift. However, even if we put these at redshift 2 say, the effect on our mass estimate is small. We found that in order to reconcile the mass estimates would require a median galaxy redshift ~ 4, which is clearly unreasonable. There is some variation in the redshift distribution from field to field in the z-surveys, and while the fluctuations expected for the larger field here are smaller, there is a remote possibility that we hit an extreme statistical fluctuation in $n(z)$ due to large-scale structure. However, it is relevant to note that the *counts* of galaxies we find agree well with those of e.g. Lilly, Cowie and Gardner (1991). *iii) Contamination:* Our method measures the total projected mass (excess) within our aperture. It is possible (though extremely improbable) that there is another high mass object within the aperture. However, if this lies at a redshift > 0.33 then the projected mass-to-light ratio for the combined system only increases, and if it lies at lower redshift it is hard to see why it was not detected. If we had no knowledge at all of the lens redshift, the lowest mass to light ratio is obtained by placing the lens at a somewhat lower redshift, and is only marginally less than our quoted value. We consider the effect of adding mass around the cluster itself below. *iv) Inhomogeneous Sampling:* Our massmap algorithm assumes uniformly sampled data, whereas in fact there are some masked holes which can result in a bias in the shape of real observed signal (though they do not create a bias in the sense of causing spurious detections where there is no real signal). Could this have created the dark-blob? We have explored this with simulations obtained by using the real galaxy positions but by shuffling the shear estimates and adding a known lensing signal, and we find any such bias to be very small. *v) Weak Shear Assumption:* If the shear becomes strong then the assumed linear response of the population mean polarisation will fail. In particular one might worry that gravitational amplification might have increased the mean redshift of the background galaxies behind the cluster. However, the measured shear in ms1224 is in fact very weak: $s \sim 10\%$ or so after correction for seeing; the light in the cluster is compact (more than half the light lies within our central aperture) so if mass traces light at least, the amplification for the galaxies we actually use is very small and in any case all indications are that the median redshift increases very weakly with increasing magnitude. One might worry that even though the mean surface density is low, the dark matter has clumpy substructure giving localised regions of non-linearity which somehow bias the mean shear estimation. This possibility probably deserves detailed study, but one argument against this is that one often sees very long smooth arcs, suggesting the dark matter in clusters is actually smoothly distributed, and, as emphasised by Tyson (1990), if one makes the dark mass too clumpy this produces a large number of conspicuous arcs which are not seen. *vi) Cosmological Model:* Our calculation of Σ_{crit} assumes a flat, zero cosmological constant model. Changing these assumptions makes only a very slight change to our results. *vii) Correlated intrinsic ellipticities:* Our error analysis assumes that the intrinsic ellipticities are uncorrelated. Flin (1993a,b) finds a tendency for galaxies in physical pairs and triplets to be aligned, but this is a weak statistical effect seen at the $\simeq$ 2-sigma level in a sample of $\sim 10^3$ galaxies, and would negligibly effect the noise level in our mass-maps. We are currently analysing some blank fields where we can check for spurious detections. None have been found as yet. *viii) Signal loss factor:* Our simulations, which show that due to seeing etc. we recover only about 70% of the input shear, assume that the faint galaxies are simply scaled down replicas of their brighter cousins. This may be false, but the sizes of the synthetic and real galaxies at least are quite similar. A better way to establish this calibration factor would be stretch and then degrade deep images from HST, which will shortly become possible. We are confident however, that seeing does not *increase* the shear.

None of these loopholes appear very promising and it is therefore hard to escape the conclusion that, in this cluster at least, the mass and the mass-to-light ratio are indeed very large. We have subsequently obtained similarly extensive data on A2218, and smaller fields on A2163 and A2390. These clusters all have arcs with measured redshifts, and while our analysis is still ongoing, we see no indication that the weak shear analysis overestimates the mass as compared with the arcs.

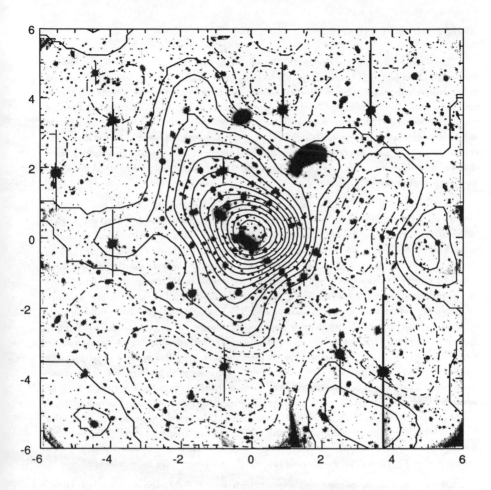

Fig. 2.—Contour plot of the projected mass reconstruction superposed on the photometry in A2218.

WHAT DOES IT MEAN?

There are really two puzzles here: Why is $M_{\text{lens}} \gg M_{\text{virial}}$ and why is the lensing derived M/L so large. It is quite possible to imagine that the observed velocity dispersion underestimates the mass: after all, the well documented 'beta-discrepancy' problem seems to indicate a sizeable scatter in σ_v^2/T_X and we might just be seeing a low-beta cluster. Perhaps the cluster consists of two clumps merging along a direction perpendicular to the line of sight and that is why we see a low σ_v. It is interesting that the conspicuous giant elliptical in the cluster does not lie near the centre of the main cluster concentration, reinforcing the suspicion that we are not dealing with a well relaxed system. This might explain a low virial mass, but would not reduce the M/L.

Another possibility is that the galaxies are relaxed, but that they suffer from velocity bias because their scale length is shorter than that of the mass. The key question is what is the mass profile derived from the shear? Unfortunately this is rather difficult to answer as with the current data we only have a 5-sigma detection, so there is considerable noise as well as bias in the mass profile. In addition, one should be wary of dilution of the shear signal by cluster galaxies which will further bias the profile in the centre. Our lower bound on the projected aperture mass applies if the projected mass vanishes in the control annulus: i.e. implicitly assuming a very *steep* mass profile. The lensing data themselves would be quite compatible with a more extended mass distribution. Under the empty annulus assumption the shear should fall off within the annulus as $s \propto 1/r^2$ whereas in fact it appears to be remarkably flat with radius, suggesting, at face value, a very flat surface density profile indeed. However, we must emphasise that invoking an extended mass profile will *increase* the mass to light ratio if one self-consistently corrects for the bias in the ζ statistic. With an isothermal sphere type mass profile, for example, $\overline{\sigma}$, and therefore M/L *within our aperture* would increase by about 30%, and the M/L within $1h^{-1}$Mpc would increase even more. Nor is it clear that this type of solution can really explain the low observed velocity dispersion; in the isothermal sphere example, the 1-D velocity dispersion for any population of finite radial extent is $\sigma_v^2 = V_{\text{rot}}^2/3 = \theta\overline{\sigma}(< \theta)/(6\pi) = (940\text{km/s})^2$, still larger than that observed.

Even our minimal mass gives a surprisingly high mass-to-light ratio (or essentially equivalent, but easier to measure, a very high mass per galaxy). However, the value is not at all out of line with other studies using the same technique: Bonnet *et al.*, 1993 claim the large scale shear around cl0024 requires a mass roughly 3-times larger than the virial mass, and Smail *et al.*, 1994 quote M/L of $\simeq 550h$, from their studies of cl1455, cl0016, quite comparable to the value here. What makes these high M/L ratios more surprising is when we allow for the considerable *increase* in the comoving number density of $\sim L_*$ galaxies inferred from the faint galaxy redshift surveys. We can clearly measure the excess cluster counts N_c in our central aperture over about a two magnitude range below L_*, and thereby obtain $(M/N)_{\text{cluster}}$. Similarly, we can readily estimate the comoving number density of field galaxies over the same magnitude range at this redshift and thereby obtain a estimate of (M/N) for a closed universe. An estimate of Ω then follows if one assumes that the mass-per-galaxy in the cluster is representative of the universe as a whole:

$$\Omega = \frac{(M/N)_{\text{cluster}}}{(M/N)_{\text{universe}}} = \frac{\overline{\sigma} d\Omega \sqrt{1 + z_c}(dn/dz)_{z_c}}{3N_c w_l \langle \max(0, 1 - w_l/w_g) \rangle} \simeq 1.8$$

This is very large compared to the typical values found applying the same kind of analysis to low redshift, optically selected clusters. The difference stems roughly equally from the high cluster M/L and from the evolution of the field galaxy population. There is of course considerable uncertainty in this estimate due to the uncertain $n(z)$ for the background galaxies, and, as with any Ω estimate of this kind, one is really under no obligation to believe that the mass-per-galaxy of this particular cluster, or indeed of clusters in general, is representative.

How do we understand the high M/L's if they are indeed real? Does the mass-to-light ratio of a cluster decrease with time; implying either that galaxy rich matter falls in later or that somehow galaxy formation is stimulated within the cluster? Or perhaps is the explanation simply that there is really a wide variation in M/L's for clusters; the well studied optically selected clusters at low redshift preferentially seeing the low M/L cases and the arcs selected clusters naturally sampling the higher end. This is attractive, but it is not easy to see why ms1224 should have been biased in this way; the highly speculative possibility that ms1224 got into the EMSS sample by macro-lensing a background AGN will shortly be testable with ROSAT and ASCA spectra.

How could a strong variation in M/L on cluster scales arise? Could it be that in an early stage of explosive galaxy formation the bulk of the gas was disturbed in the manner envisaged by Ostriker and Cowie (1981), resulting in a highly inhomogeneous gas entropy and density distribution? The evolution of the dark-matter clustering would proceed essentially undisturbed, but there will be DM concentrations which happen to lie in regions of high entropy gas where galaxy formation might plausibly have been impeded. An appeal of this idea is that this might also help explain the 'baryon catastrophe' problem (White, et al., 1993). The dark-clumps seen in some of the mass reconstructions are certainly of interest in this regard, but the significance of the dark feature in the ms1224 map at least is only marginal.

The results described here and those of Tyson's group, the Toulouse group and the Durham/Caltech group clearly show that these observations are a practical way to directly map the dark matter in clusters. The high mass-to-light ratios obtained are admittedly somewhat puzzling. The calibration of this method, on which these results rest, is not perfect, but we have argued that it is very hard to make the discrepancy with the virial mass in ms1224 go away and indeed, at face value, the lensing data are quite compatible with an even larger mass. The great strength of this method is that it makes no assumptions regarding the shape, dynamical stability or state of relaxation of the cluster. There are still uncertainties in e.g the redshift distribution of the faint galaxies, which affects the calibration, but these are small and of an 'engineering' nature and should be solvable with a combination of HST imaging, ground-based spectroscopy to fainter limits and a much larger sample of weak-shear cluster studies.

These observations are currently limited by detector technology. It would be of great value to obtain data out to large radii. CFHT has a corrected field $\sim 50'$ across, yet we currently use only use a $7'$ square 2048^2 chip. The 4096^2 MOCAM array will speed observations by a factor 4. With a thinned mosaic of this size on a 10m telescope the ms1224 study could be made in about 4-minutes, so it would be quite practical to go much fainter, increasing the number of background galaxies substantially, and thereby boosting the precision of the measurement. A further boost in signal to noise can be obtained by studying clusters at somewhat lower redshift, though to explore the same physical radius becomes more expensive and one also becomes more sensitive to how well correlated psf variations and other systematic effects can be corrected for. With these developments it should be quite feasible to obtain detailed individual mass profiles and shapes for the most massive clusters and also, with large random field surveys, to obtain a mass-selected sample of clusters. Galaxies, groups and poor clusters will be hard to detect individually, but by stacking results it should be possible to determine e.g. the galaxy-mass cross-correlation function directly. Another window of opportunity is to study coherent shear on the scale of superclusters; current observations being right at the level of precision where we expect to see a signal appearing. This will potentially provide a direct measure of the mass power spectrum $P_\rho(k)$, giving a strong test of cosmogonical theories and, combining with COBE type measurements on a similar scale, giving us a handle on the relative contribution of tensor and scalar modes and/or the ionisation history. Finally, a further spin-off from these studies will be quite accurate measurement of the mean relative geometrical distances to faint galaxies as a function of their size and magnitude. Combining these with directly measured redshifts should allow a fundamental test of the cosmological world model.

REFERENCES

Tyson, J., Valdes, F., and Wenk, R., 1990. ApJ, 349, L19

Broadhurst, T., Peacock, J., and Taylor. 1994, preprint

Kaiser, N., and Squires, G., 1993. ApJ, 404, 441 (KS93)

Fahlman, G., Kaiser, N., Squires, G., and Woods, D., 1994. to appear in ApJ. Available by anonymous ftp from ftp.cita.utoronto.ca in /cita/nick/ms1224/ms1224.ps

Carlberg, R., Yee, H. and Ellingson, E., 1994. To appear in ApJ

Lilly, S., Cowie, L, and Gardner. 1991. ApJ, 369, 79

Flin, P., 1993a. AJ, 105, 473

Flin, P., 1993b, ApJ, 406, 395

Ostriker, J. and Cowie, L., 1981. ApJ Lett, 285, L127

Bonnet, H., Fort, B., Kneib, J-P., Mellier, Y., and Soucail, G., 1993. A&A, 280, L7

Smail, I., Ellis, R., Fitchett, M. & Edge, A., 1994. Preprint

Tyson, J., 1990. In proceedings of AIP meeting "After the First Three Minutes", eds Holt, Bennet and Trimble

Tresse, L., Hammer, F., le Fevre, O., and Proust, D., 1993 A&A, 277, 53

Lilly, S.J., 1993. ApJ, 411, 501

White, S., Navarro, J., Evrard, G., and Frenk, C., 1993. Nature, 366, 429

X-RAY EMISSION AND S-Z EFFECT FROM CLUSTERS OF GALAXIES: IMPLICATIONS FOR COSMOLOGY

SERGIO COLAFRANCESCO

Osservatorio Astronomico di Roma
Via dell'Osservatorio, I-00040 Monteporzio, Italy

Abstract

We discuss the cosmological impact of clusters of galaxies as X-ray sources that also contribute to the CMB anisotropies on subdegree angular scales through the Sunyaev-Zeldovich (S-Z) effect.

1 Cosmological Relevance of Clusters of Galaxies

Clusters of Galaxies are good laboratories for cosmological studies. In fact, they can probe different aspects of the gravitational instability scenario: the shape and amplitude of the initial perturbation spectrum, the scenario of structure formation and also the role of non-linear mechanisms leading to the matter segregation in bound, collapsed structures.

Studies of the evolution of galaxy clusters are nonetheless complicated by several aspects: *i)* these structures are the largest bound aggregate of material in the universe and show evidences of both the linear phase of clustering in their outer regions where the halo collapse times are $\gtrsim H_o^{-1}$ and non-linear phenomena occurring predominantly in their central regions; *ii)* clusters contain large quantities of diffuse baryons in the form of hot ($T \sim 10^7 \div 10^8$ K), dense ($n_e \sim 10^{-3}$ cm^{-3}) and optically thin intra cluster medium (ICM). This shines in the X-rays with specific power $\epsilon \propto n_e^2 T^{1/2}$ and contributes to the CMB anisotropy through a microwave dip $\Delta \equiv \Delta T/T = -2(k\sigma_T/m_e c^2) \int dl n_e T$ (in the RJ region) generated by S-Z effect (Sunyaev & Zeldovich 1972). Moreover, the baryon fraction $f_g \equiv M_{gas}/M_{tot}$ of these structures is expected to evolve with epoch and/or with the mass scale (see CCM and CV for a discussion); *iii)* the observed distributions of X-ray clusters contain informations on the intrinsic evolution of the cluster population, and specifically on the evolution of their mass distribution (MD) and of their X-ray luminosity. In the following, we will use the ICM properties (X-ray emissivity and S-Z effect) to test some aspects of gravitational instability theories and of galaxy formation scenarios.

2 From Theory to Observations

We assume here a hierarchical scenario in which cosmic protostructures on the scale R form preferentially around the high peaks of the initial density field. Following the results of the simple model for the collapse of a uniform, self-gravitating sphere, we can select those fluctuations that will eventually collapse, requiring that their linear density contrast is $\delta \geq \delta_c \approx 1.7$.

The mass distribution $N(M,t)$ of the collapsed clumps can be derived from the kinetic equation

$$\frac{\partial N}{\partial t} = \frac{N}{\tau_+} - \frac{N}{\tau_-} + F \tag{1}$$

where τ_+, and τ_- are the statistical timescales for the *source* (formation) and *sink* (destruction) term, respectively. For the simple hierarchical merging scenario these time scales are specified by: $\tau_+ = 2t_* m^{-\Theta}/\delta_c^2 b^2 \Theta$, $\tau_- = 2t_*/\Theta(1 + dlnG/dln\nu_c)$, where $m \equiv (M/M_*)$, $\Theta = (n+3)/3$ and $M_*(z)$ is the characteristic mass going non-linear at redshift z. Here n is the index of the power law spectrum $P(k) = Ak^n$. The function G takes into account the details of the peak probability distribution (see AC). The characteristic time scale for clustering is $t_* \equiv M_*/\dot{M}_*$. The balance between the rates N/τ_+ and N/τ_- in eq.(1) is determined by the *flux* term $F = -\partial \left(\dot{M} N \right)/\partial M$

which describes the inertial shift of that part of the MD in which mass accretion by the original halos occur. Observations and numerical simulations (see White, these Proceedings) indicate that the cluster MD is well fitted by the Press & Schechter (1974, hereafter PS) result. In the present formalism, this can be recovered when dynamical phenomena occurring on time scales $\lesssim H^{-1}$ have rates that balance out as to give: $-N/\tau_- + F \approx -N\Theta/2t_*$. In fact, the PS result is the solution of the simple equation: $\partial N/\partial t = N/\tau_+ - N\Theta/2t_*$ and reads:

$$N(M,z) = N_o \frac{\mathcal{I}}{\sqrt{2\pi}} \frac{(n+3)}{6} \left(\frac{M}{M_*}\right)^{a-2} \frac{\delta_c b}{D(z)} \exp\left[-\frac{\delta_c^2 b^2}{2D(z)^2}\left(\frac{M}{M_*}\right)^{2a}\right] \quad (2)$$

for a power-law spectra $P(k) = Ak^n$, where $a = (n+3)/6$, $N_o = \rho_b/M_* \approx 1.8 \cdot 10^{-4} h^2 Mpc^{-3}/(10^{15} M_\odot)$, and $M_* \approx 10^{15} \Omega_o (R_*/8h^{-1} \text{ Mpc})^3 M_\odot/h$. Normalizing the density fluctuation spectrum by requiring $\sigma_\rho = b^{-1}$, the MD depends upon the combination $\delta_c b$ and $\mathcal{I}$.

Going from theoretical quantities like mass M - or filtering scale R - to observables requires to assume a self-similar density profile $\rho(r) = \rho_o[1+(r/r_o)^2]^{-3\beta/2}$ (with observed values $\beta \sim 0.6 \div 0.8$, see Jones & Forman 1991) during clusters evolution. This is synchronized to cosmology assuming $\rho \propto \rho_b(z)$ and normalizing the core radius $r_o = 0.15 M_{15}^{1/3}(1+z)^{-1} h^{-1}$ Mpc to a fiducial rich cluster with mass $M = M_{15} 10^{15} h^{-1} M_\odot$ at the present epoch. Then one obtains the total mass of the clump, the central electronic density $n_e(0) = f_g \rho_o(1+X)/2m_p$ and the virial temperature $T = -\mu m_p U/3kM$ inside the cluster potential well (see CMRV for details).

From these quantities it is easy to derive the predicted X-ray luminosity:

$$L \propto n_e^2 R^3 T^{1/2} \propto f_g^2 M_{15}^c \rho^d \quad (3)$$

with $c = 4/3$ and $d = 7/6$, and the microwave distorsion at frequency $x = h\nu/kT_r$:

$$\Delta_o \propto n_e RTg(x) \propto f_g M_{15} \cdot g(x) \quad (4)$$

with $g(x) = s(x)x^4 e^x/(e^x-1)^2$ and $s(x) = [x\coth(x/2) - 4]$. The baryon fraction f_g is considered to evolve as $f_g \propto M^\eta t^\xi$ following the predictions of biased scenarios (see CCM and CV for a discussion). The value $\eta \sim 0.15$ is consistent with the decrease of M/M_{lum} with the mass scale as derived by David et al. (1994) and the epoch dependence $\xi \sim 1.2$ is motivated by compression and heating of infalling baryons into the cluster potential wells (see CCM).

3   X-ray vs S-Z

The cluster X-Ray luminosity function (XRLF) can be derived in hierarchical scenarios as:

$$N(L,z) \equiv N(M,z)\frac{dM}{dL} \propto \frac{1}{M_* L_*}\ell^{-\gamma} \exp\left(-\frac{\delta_c^2 b^2 \ell^\theta}{2}\right) \quad (5)$$

and we compare it with the more extended, local database (Kowalski et al. 1984). Here $\ell \propto L/L_*(z)$ where $L_*(z) = L_o D(z)^{c/a}(1+z)^{3d-s}$ is the luminosity of clusters of mass M_*. Moreover, $\gamma = 1 + (3-n)/6c$ and $\theta = (n+3)/3c$. We also test our predictions against another set of observables, the X-ray cluster counts (XRC) as derived by the EMSS (Gioia et al. 1990). These are obtained as a convolution of the distant XRLFs with the cosmological volume element using the flux-luminosity relationship $L = 4\pi F D_L^2$, where D_L is the luminosity distance (see CV).

We are then left with two sets of observables and only two free parameters, $\mathcal{I}$ and the product $\delta_c b$, that we determine through a Chi-squared analysis. These two data set can be considered independent as the clusters used for studying the local XRLF have not been used in the EMSS. In Fig.1 we plot in the $\delta_c b - \mathcal{I}$ plane the best-fit values (full circles) for the local XRLF. We also plot a χ^2-isocontour (continuous line) at the 97.5% c.l. The full squares represent the best fit values to the XRC and the dotted line the relative χ^2-isocontour at the 97.5% c.l. To take into account the quality of the fits we add to the best-fit points labels indicating the corresponding values of χ_{min}^2. The standard flat CDM model ($\Omega_o = 1$, $h = 0.5$, $n = 1$) and a "tilted" CDM model ($\Omega_o = 1$, $h = 0.5$) with $n = 0.8$ can be rejected as there is not a region of the $\delta_c b - \mathcal{I}$ plane where both the local XRLF and the XRC data can be accounted for. For the low-density CDM model there is a narrow region of the $\delta_c b - \mathcal{I}$ plane where it is possible to fit at once the local XRLF and the XRC. BDM models are clearly rejected as they provide the worst scenario for fitting the XRLF and the XRC in the region of the parameter space we work with. Hybrid models present a narrow

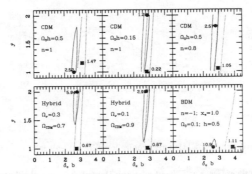

Figure 1: The combined fit to the XRLF and to the XRC

overlapping region, but the fit to the local XRLF is very poor, so poor that the case $\Omega_\nu = 0.3$ is rejected. The situation improves slightly if $\Omega_\nu = 0.1$.

Using the previous normalizations we derive predictions for the CMB temperatute anisotropies for the closed models we consider, on scales from a few arcmin to a few degree:

$$\bar{\Delta} \equiv \langle (\frac{\Delta T}{T})^2 \rangle^{1/2} = \int \frac{dV}{dz} dz \int dM \, N(M, z) \Delta_o(M, z) \bar{\zeta}(M, z) \tag{6}$$

where $\bar{\zeta}$ is the sky averaged cluster profile and dV/dz is the cosmological volume element. In Fig.2 we plot the predictions for $\bar{\Delta}$ for different beamsize experiments. We found that the secondary anisotropies due to S-Z effect from galaxy clusters contribute at most $\lesssim 30\%$ of the total anisotropy level (see CMRV for a more extended discussion).

4 Discussion: ... beyond the spherical model.

The previous results indicate that X-ray data require $\delta_c b \sim 3$ for the successful models. A value of b can be obtained only by assuming a specific value for δ_c. In the spherical collapse model $\delta_c = 1.7$: the corresponding values of the biasing factor, b_{Xray}, are given in Table 1. In the same Table we also give the values of the biasing factor, b_{COBE}, obtained by normalizing the amplitude of density fluctuations of the LSS models to the rms fluctuation value of $30\mu K$ of the COBE/DMR maps. Note that the values of the biasing factor derived from the XRLF and from COBE are quite consistent only for the hybrid models with $\Omega_\nu = 0.3$ (CV estimate that the errors in the deriving $\delta_c b$ is at most 5% at the 1 sigma level). However, these conclusions are based upon the spherical collapse model, which may be quite unrealistic. So let us impose $b_{Xray} = b_{COBE}$ and recover δ_c from the XRLF. The values derived in this way, δ_c^{COBE} say, are also given in Table 1. Having $\delta_c^{COBE} > 1.7$, as for the standard CDM or the hybrid $\Omega_\nu = 0.1$ models, implies that the collapse and virialization of groups and clusters occur on time scales longer than those predicted by the spherical model. On the contrary, having $\delta_c^{COBE} < 1.7$ implies that the collapse occur on time scales smaller than that of a spherical model. This is expected for a non spherical collapse (Bertschinger & Jain, 1993; Matarrese, Pantano & Saez, 1993).

Table 1

Model	$b\delta_c$	b_{Xray}	b_{COBE}	δ_c^{COBE}
CDM ($n = 1$)	2.6	1.53	0.95	2.74
CDM ($n = 0.8$)	2.8	1.65	2.22	1.26
MDM ($\Omega_\nu = 0.1$)	2.8	1.65	1.18	2.37
MDM ($\Omega_\nu = 0.3$)	2.8	1.65	1.60	1.75

There are good reasons to expect delays in cluster collapse times. For instance in the hierarchical clustering scenario, clusters form by merging of subunits, and these may survive inside the cluster

286

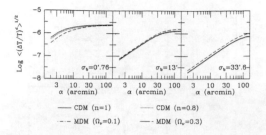

Figure 2: The cluster induced CMB anisotropies for different values of the antenna beam σ_b

for several crossing times (see, e.g., CV and references therein). To follow the cluster dynamics CA considered the evolution of a gravitating collisionless medium of size R, in which substructure is identified with the peaks of the density field smoothed on scales $\ll R$. In this case dynamical friction (d.f.) arises as a consequence of the "discrete" nature of the phase space structure. The collapse of a spherical shell of initial radius r_i is described by the equation: $d^2a/dt^2 = -4\pi G\bar{\rho}_i/3a^2 - \eta da/dt$ where η is the d.f. coefficient and $a(r_i, t) = r(r_i, t)/r_i$ is the expansion factor (see AC). The presence of a drag force determines an *increase* in the shell collapse time scale that, for $\bar{\delta} \ll 1$, reads: $T_c \approx T_{c0} \left\{ 1 + \lambda_o \frac{\sqrt{2\pi}}{3c} \bar{\delta}^{-3/2} \right\}$ where $\lambda_o \propto \eta T_{c0}$ and c is a constant depending on the average overdensity $\bar{\delta}$. From an asymptotic development of the solution of the eq. of motion in terms of the (usually small) coefficient η, the critical overdensity $\alpha = (a_f/a_i)\delta_c$ at the time of collapse, reads

$$\alpha = \frac{3}{5} \left[\frac{\omega\,(T, \bar{\delta})\,3\pi}{2} \right]^{2/3} = 1.69\omega^{3/2} \tag{7}$$

where $\omega\,(T) = \left[1 - \frac{6}{\pi}c \left(\frac{|1-\beta|}{\beta} \right)^{3/2} T \right]^{-1} \geq 1$ (see CA for details). So, the effect of d.f – and hence of substructure, in principle – is to increase the critical overdensity for collapse with respect to the case of a uniform sphere for which $\omega = 1$.

The main conclusions of this paper can be summarized as follows: *i)* Cluster abundance and evolution out to intermediate redshifts $z \lesssim 0.7$ are best fitted by a low density universe $\Omega_o h \sim 0.2$. *ii)* High values of the threshold for collapse $\delta_c > 1.69$ are inferred by X-ray data and imply delayed collapses. This result is also confirmed by N-body experiments and is expected considering non-linear effects of substructure in the theoretical description of the cluster collapse. *iii)* Higher threshold for collapse and the finding $b\delta_c \sim 3$ on cluster scales, tend to indicate low biasing factor $b \gtrsim 1$ that are more consistent with the LSS observations.

References

Antonuccio-Delogu, V. & Colafrancesco, S. 1994, ApJ, in press (AC)
Bertschinger, E. & Jain, R. 1993, preprint
Cavaliere, A., Colafrancesco, S., & Menci, N. 1993, ApJ, 415, 50 (CCM)
Colafrancesco, S. & Antonuccio-Delogu, V. 1994, preprint (CA)
Colafrancesco, S. & Vittorio, N. 1994, ApJ, 422,443 (CV)
Colafrancesco, S., Mazzotta, P, Rephaeli, Y & Vittorio, N. 1994, ApJ, in press (CMRV)
David, L.P. et al. 1994, preprint
Gioia, I.M. et al. 1990, ApJS, 72, 567: EMSS
Jones, C. & Forman, W. 1991, in *Clusters and Superclusters of Galaxies*, A.C. Fabian *et al.* eds., (Cambridge: Cambridge University Press), p. 49
Kowalski, M.P., Ulmer, M.P., Cruddace, R.G., & Wood, K.S. 1984, ApJS, 56, 403
Matarrese, S., Pantano, O., & Saez, D. 1993, preprint
Press, W.H., & Schechter, P. 1974, ApJ, 187, 425 (PS)
Sunyaev, R.A. & Zeldovich, Y.B., 1972, Comm. Astrophys. Sp. Phys., 4, 173

DOMINANT GALAXIES IN BIMODAL CLUSTERS

F. W. Baier, University of Potsdam, Germany

ABSTRACT. The existence of central dominant galaxies in clusters is well known. The investigation of the evolution of cD clusters and the formation of their dominant galaxies may provide a key for the understanding of the evolution of galaxy clusters overall. The most promising scenario for the formation of central dominant galaxies in clusters is not the growth by cooling flows but cannibalism of surrounding galaxies.

1. COOLING FLOWS AND FORMATION OF cD GALAXIES

Many clusters of galaxies are strong X-ray sources. Spectral investigations of the intracluster gas show that this emission originates as thermal bremsstrahlung from a diffuse intracluster gas with densities of $10^{-4} - 10^{-2} cm^{-3}$ and temperatures of $10^7 - 10^8 K$. There is observational evidence for cool gas in the cores of a certain number of galaxy clusters and a central excess X-ray emission above the hydrostatic–isothermal model. It is assumed that the radiative energy loss due to the X-ray emission in cluster cores often may be sufficient to cool the gas and to initiate a slow subsonic inward "cooling flow". If a central dominant galaxy moves slowly relative to the centre of gravity of the cluster, the cooling intracluster gas may be accreted by the central galaxy. Accretion rates of roughly hundred solar masses per year or more are inferred from X-ray measurements for some clusters. Taking into account a constant mass flow rate during the life of a cluster, some authors assume that all of the mass of central dominant galaxies may be due to such cooling flows (Fabian et al. 1984; O'Connel and McNamara 1989). In order to check this assumption we have to consider not only the greatest accretion rates observed in some clusters but the distribution of observed accretion rates. Mushotzky (1993) concluded from the investigation of 51 clusters that most of the accretion rates of the cooling flows are between 5 and 200 solar masses per year, with a substantial fraction up to 500 solar masses per year. Similar arguments are given by other authors, too. But we have to accept that the data tell their own tale. From the distribution of Mushotzky, it is evident that a fraction of 25 %

of clusters are without any cooling flow, 50 % of clusters exhibit mass flow rates lower than 50 solar masses per year, and only 15 % show mass flow rates larger than 250 solar masses per year. Arnaud (1988) presented the distribution of accretion rates among a sample of 43 cooling flows. She found that most cooling flows have an accretion rate less than 100 $M_\odot/yr$.

From the work of Mushotzky (1993), Arnaud (1988), and Edge (1991a,b;1992) it is evident that the distribution of accretion rates is based on relatively small samples (51, 43, and 55 clusters, respectively). In order to check the results we have attempted to enlarge the sample by investigating a homogeneous sample of 160 clusters of galaxies with known central dominant galaxies from the northern Abell catalogue with $z < 0.1$. Assuming an upper envelope of the X-ray luminosity–mass flow rate–plot, mean values for the mass flow rate for additional 82 cD clusters in the same redshift interval have been estimated from the X-ray luminosities determined from Einstein observations (Kowalski et al. 1984). From a sample of 160 clusters we determined a fraction of nearly 18 % without any cooling flow, 50 % of our sample possess mass flow rates lower than 50 solar masses per year, and only 10 % show mass flow rates larger than 100 solar masses per year. Our discussion is based on conservative estimates of accretion rates for cooling flows. But with the results of Braine and Dupraz (1994) from CO observations of dominant cluster galaxies the values of accretion rates proposed by the "standard model" of cooling flows should be reduced by a factor 5 on average. Assuming the mass of a cD galaxy to be greater than 10^{12} solar masses the formation of the observed large number of dominant galaxies in clusters by cooling flows can be explained only if we assume a substantially larger accretion rate in the past for z larger than 0.1.

2. EVOLUTION OF COOLING FLOWS

There are hints for a secular evolution of cooling flows: Donahue et al. (1992) observed extended $H\alpha$ emission in 14 distant clusters of galaxies between z=0.07 and z=0.37 and found that the fraction of X-ray clusters with a massive cooling flow has decreased by a factor of two since z=0.3. Furthermore, Luppino and Gioia (1994) found 21 X-ray clusters with $z > 0.2$ and $4*10^{44} erg/sec < L_x(0.3 - 3.5keV) < 20*10^{44}\ erg/sec$ in a sample of 41 X-ray selected clusters. Other examples of high X-ray luminous clusters with $L_x(0.3 - 3.5keV) > 2*10^{44}$ erg/sec and $z > 0.15$ are given by Henry et al. (1992). Obviously there is a high probability for such luminous clusters to lodge strong cooling flows.

However, there are also opposite arguments. Nesci and Altamore (1990) searched for cooling flows in 20 southern X-ray clusters at $z \sim 0.15$ and found no strong cooling flows in these clusters. Lastly there are many reports concerning a significant deficit in high luminous X-ray clusters in the redshift range $z \sim 0.1 - 0.2$ compared with nearby clusters (Gioia et al. 1990a,b; Edge et al. 1990; Edge and Stewart 1991a,b; Pierre 1991; Cavaliere et al. 1991; Henry et al. 1992 and others). Therefore, we should expect lower values of the mass flow rate in many clusters in the past because of the relation between X-ray luminosity and mass flow rate.

From this we may accept that cooling flows are short–lived phenomena on a cosmic time scale. These results are in contrast to the arguments from the high percentages of cooling flows in nearby clusters. Obviously the situation on this problem is controversial. We suggest, therefore, that the properties of a cooling flow may rather be determined by the dynamical evolutionary stage of a cluster.

3. CANNIBALISM AND FORMATION OF cD GALAXIES

A deficiency of bright galaxies in the central regions of many cD clusters is observed (Lugger 1984a,b; 1989; Baier and Schmidt 1992; Baier and MacGillivray 1993). Such results favour the idea that at least many cD galaxies formed in poor and low–dispersion subclusters which later merged to form rich clusters (Merritt 1984a,b; 1985). Moreover we have found different degrees of radial luminosity segregation in cD–clusters and clear correlations between the degree of radial mass segregation in clusters and some properties of their dominant galaxies as velocity offset, colour gradients, and envelope luminosity. This result confirms the assumption that there are different kinds of dominant galaxies in clusters according to their evolutionary stage by galactic cannibalism.

4. DOMINANT GALAXIES IN BIMODAL CLUSTERS

Considering the 160 northern Abell clusters with central dominant galaxies in the redshift range $0 < z < 0.1$ at least 50 % of them are bimodal clusters or show strong deviations from symmetry appearence. Very often the dominant galaxy is placed in only one subcluster. Sometimes even the other subcluster without a dominant galaxy contains a cooling flow (as in Abell 754). It is assumed that both these subclusters can merge as in the case of Abell 2256. Such a merging of clusters was discussed by Ulmer (1992) et al. and others. We have evidence for large numbers of cases of asymmetries in the galaxy distribution in cD-clusters. Moreover there are offsets between the position of the dominant galaxy and the maximum of the galaxy distribution as well as the X-ray distribution in a large number of clusters.

Therefore, we assume that such offsets are indicators for cluster merging. The dominant galaxy could be formed in a poor subcluster and the gravitational potential of this poor cluster was not strong enough to bind a large amount of gas. The merging process with a rich cluster – which often may contain a cooling flow – should be accompanied by a merging of the gaseous components with following increased X – ray emission and stronger cooling flow. During this process velocity offsets and positional offsets between the dominant galaxy and the X-ray center are quite normal.

5. CONCLUSION

From our discussion it follows that a large percentage of bimodal clusters contain cD galaxies. Furthermore it is known from previous investigation that a high fraction of galaxy clusters – even of cD clusters – shows substructure. This result favours the scenario proposed by Merritt (1984a,b) that dominant galaxies evolved in low dispersion components of binary clusters which later merged to rich clusters. In such a scenario we may explain some well–known observations:

The cD galaxy must not be at rest at the centre of the merged cluster for a certain time interval although it was at the kinematical centre of the premerger subcluster. In this way the observed velocity offset in many cases may be understood. There may be a displacement between the cD and the "center" of the merged cluster – especially between the cD and the center of a prior existing cooling flow which can be formed irrespective of the presence or absence of a central dominant galaxy in a deep cluster potential (Friaca 1993), for instance A 754, A 2256. Cluster elongation observed in many clusters can be explained, too.

After the cluster merging, the same focussing potential that had given rise to the cooling flow might attract the massive galaxy to the cluster centre. In such a way the cD moves eventually towards the kinematical centre of the merged cluster. At this central position within the cooling flow – which formed previously and indepedently of the entered dominant galaxy – mass accretion from the cooling flow may influence its final evolution. Such a final evolution by accretion should mainly feed the envelope of this galaxy. It would evolve in direction towards a "real" cD galaxy.

References

Arnaud, K. A.: 1988, in : Cooling Flows in Galaxies and Clusters, p. 31, ed. Fabian, A. C., Kluwer Academic Publishers, Dordrecht

Baier, F.W., and Schmidt, K.-H.: 1992, Astron. Nachr. **313**, 275

Baier, F.W., and MacGillivray, H.T.: 1993, International Scientific Meeting of the NATO Advanced Study Institute, Velen, in Press

Braine, J., and Dupraz, C.: 1994, Astron. Astrophys. **283**, 407

Cavaliere, A., Burg, R., and Giacconi, R.: 1991, Astrophys. J. Lett. **366**, L61

Cavaliere, A., Colafrancesco, S., and Menci, N.: 1991, Astrophys. J. Lett. **376**, L37

Donahue, M., Stocke, J. T., and Gioia, I. M.: 1992, Astrophys. J. **385**, 49

Edge, A. C., Stewart, G. C., Fabian, A. C., and Arnaud, K. A.: 1990, Mon. Not. R. Astron. Soc. **245**, 559

Edge, A. C., and Stewart, G. C.: 1991a, Mon. Not. R. Astron. Soc. **252**, 414

Edge, A. C., and Stewart, G. C.: 1991b, Mon. Not. R. Astron. Soc. **252**, 428

Edge, A. C., Stewart, G. C., and Fabian, A. C.: 1992, Mon. Not. R. Astron. Soc. **258**, 177

Fabian, A.C., Nulson, P.E., and Canizares, C.R.: 1984, Nature **310**, 733

Friaça, A.C.S.: 1993, Astron. Astrophys. **269**, 145

Gioia, I. M., Henry, J. P., Maccacaro, I., Morris, S. L., Stocke, J. T., and Wolter, A.: 1990a, Astrophys. J. Lett. **356**, L 35

Gioia, I. M., Maccacaro, T., Schild, R. E., Wolter, A., Stocke, J. T., Morris, S. L., and Henry, J. P.: 1990b, Astrophys. J. Suppl. **72**, 567

Henry, J. P., Gioia, I. M., Maccacaro, T., Morris, S. L., Stocke, J. T., and Wolter, A.: 1992, Astrophys. J. **386**, 408

Kowalski, M. P., Ulmer, M. P., Cruddace, R. G., Wood, K. S.: 1984, Astrophys. J. Suppl. Ser. **56**, 403

Lugger, P.M.: 1984a, Astrophys. J. **278**, 51

Lugger, P. M.: 1984b, Astrophys. J. **286**, 106

Lugger, P.M.: 1989, Astrophys. J. **343**, 572

Luppino, G. A., Gioia, I. M.: 1994, University of Hawaii, Institute of Astronomy, Preprint IfA-94/6

Merritt, D.: 1984a, Astrophys. J. **276**, 26

Merritt, D.: 1984b, Astrphys. J. Lett. **280**, L5

Merritt, D.: 1985, Astrophys. J. **289**, 18

Mushotzky, R.F.: 1993, in The Environment and Evolution of Galaxies, KLUWER ACADEMIC PUBLISHERS, Dordrecht, 1993, Proceedings of the THIRD TETON SUMMER SCHOOL HELD IN GRAND TETON NATIONAL PARK, WYOMING, U.S.A., July 1992, p. 383

Nesci, R., and Altamore, A.: 1990, Astron. Astrophys. **234**, 60

O'Connel, R.W., and McNamara, B.R.: 1989, Astron. J. **98**, 180

Pierre, M.: 1991, Astron. Astrophys. **252**, L23

Ulmer, M.P., Wirth, G.D., and Kowalski, M.P.: 1992, Astrophys. J. **397**, 430

THE GALAXY GROUP/COSMOLOGY CONNECTIONS

Gary A. Mamon, *IAP, Paris, & DAEC, Obs. de Paris, Meudon, FRANCE*

Abstract

Groups of galaxies are highly linked to cosmology: 1) groups are tidally destroyed by the tidal field of the cluster they fall into; 2) spherical infall leads to the young cosmo-dynamical state of loose groups, a fundamental surface for groups, $\Omega_0 \simeq 0.3$, and the mixed nature of compact groups (virialized groups, groups at full collapse, and chance alignments within collapsing loose groups, for decreasing compact group velocity dispersion) ; 3) X-ray analyses lead to $\Omega_0 \lesssim 0.5$.

1. Introduction

Whereas clusters of galaxies have often been used to provide cosmological constraints on the Universe, such as the density parameter, Ω_0, and the primordial density fluctuation spectrum, little similar effort has been applied to small groups of say 4 to 30 galaxies, as these suffer from small number statistics in a severe way: their properties (membership, virial M/L, dynamical state) are function of the algorithm used to define the groups, and vary tremendously from group to group.

Roughly half of all galaxies lie in groups that are probably bound (*e.g.,* ref. 1]), in contrast with the $\simeq 5\%$ that lie within rich clusters. Much interest has been provoked by the observation of groups that appear very compact in projection on the sky. A well-defined sample of 100 *compact groups* has been generated[2] from visual inspection of POSS plates. These groups appear denser than the cores of rich clusters, and seem now to be the best observed sample of galaxy systems.

Relative to field galaxies, the galaxies in compact groups show a higher level of dynamical interactions[3],[4], ongoing merging[5], and star formation[6]. Also, the morphologies of compact group galaxies are more correlated with group velocity dispersion than with any other group parameter[7],[8],[9],[10], which cannot be explained in simple models where galaxy merging generates elliptical morphologies[11].

Groups are subject to numerous myths, listed below, as should become clear to the reader by the end of this contribution.

Myth 1: Groups are virialized.

Myth 2: Group dynamics imply $\Omega_0 < 0.1$.

Myth 3: X-rays in groups imply $\Omega_0 \simeq 1$.

Myth 4: Groups are the preferential site for galaxy evolution.

Myth 5: Compact groups are nearly all as dense in 3D as they appear in projection.

2. Groups within clusters

The high level of small-scale substructure observed in clusters[12] is usually thought to be caused by groups falling into clusters. The frequency of substructure in clusters is a test on Ω_0[13],[14],[15], since in a low density universe, structure should freeze out early, and then reach internal equilibrium and become smooth, but one needs to know the dynamical survival time of the substructure, which can be destroyed by the tidal field of the cluster, or merge into other ones. This has been analyzed for X-ray isophotes using dynamical simulations with gas[16]. Simple calculations[17] show that the cluster tidal field is strong enough to destroy infalling groups (except for groups as dense as compact groups appear to be), as is confirmed by more detailed dynamical simulations (Capelato & Mazure 1994 in these proceedings).

The statistics of the primordial density field tell us that small dense systems (high peaks) will form preferentially near large dense ones[18]. Therefore, one expects dense groups to form near rich clusters. Dynamical friction will force these groups to fall to the center of the cluster. The galaxies in the group will merge into ellipticals, either before dynamical friction is completed or afterwards. Such dense groups may thus be the progenitors of a substantial fraction of the elliptical galaxies lying in the cores of clusters[19].

3. Spherical infall applied to groups

Groups, as everything else, partake initially in the general Hubble expansion. Because they are selected to be overdense objects, they go through a range of *cosmo-dynamical states*, reaching a maximum expansion (*turnaround*), then collapsing, and finally possibly virializing and/or coalescing into a single galaxy.

3.1 How small and how hot must a virialized system be?

From spherical infall, the mean density of a system at turnaround must be[20] $\bar{\rho}_{\rm ta} = (9\pi^2/16)/(6\pi Gt_0^2)$, and that of a system that has virialized must be $\bar{\rho}_{\rm vir} \geq 8\rho_{\rm ta}(t_0/\eta) = \Delta_{\rm vir}/(6\pi Gt_0^2)$, where for $\eta = 3$, $\Delta_{\rm vir} = 81\pi^2/2 \simeq 400$ ($\forall\Omega_0$). Combining this result with the virial theorem, $\sigma_v^2 = \gamma GM/R$, yields a system size $R \leq \sigma_v t_0/(\pi\eta\gamma^{1/2}) = 100\,(\sigma_v/100\,{\rm km\,s^{-1}})h^{-1}\,{\rm kpc}$, for $\eta = 3$, a singular isothermal ($\gamma = 1/2$) and $\Omega_0 = 1$ ($H_0 t_0 = 2/3$). So loose groups (which have $R \geq 1\,h^{-1}\,{\rm Mpc}$) are not virialized. Similarly, one obtains $\sigma_v \geq \gamma^{1/2}(\pi\eta GM/t_0)^{1/3} = 278\,(h\,M_{13})^{1/3}\,{\rm km\,s^{-1}}$ with the same parameters as above. For the typical compact group, $M = 3.8\,h^{-1}10^{12}M_\odot^{[21]}$, yielding $\sigma_v \geq 201\,{\rm km\,s^{-1}}$, which happens to be the median compact group velocity dispersion[21], and over twice the median loose group velocity dispersion[1],[22].

3.2 The fundamental surface

If a group has not yet virialized, one will incorrectly estimate its mass and crossing time. In spherical infall cosmology (and in other cosmologies too) the *biases* in these estimates are well-defined functions of the cosmo-dynamical state. Figure 1a shows *fundamental tracks* for the mass bias versus the crossing time (see ref. [23] for more details on the fundamental surface).

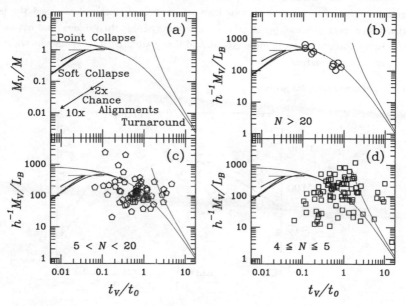

Figure 1. The fundamental surface for loose groups, where t_V and M_V are the measured crossing time and virial mass, while M is the true mass.

To compare with observed groups[22], the true M/L of groups is assumed to be a universal constant, hence M_{vir}/L is proportional to the mass bias. Using the observed high multiplicity groups to scale the y-axis, one obtains (Fig. 1b) $M/L = 440\,h$, which extrapolated to large scales would yield $\Omega_0 = 0.3$. Figures 1c and 1d show the groups of lower multiplicity, for which the statistical noise on the mass and crossing time estimators becomes increasingly important. The tracks in Figures 1b,c,d are cuts through a non-planar *fundamental surface*, where the third dimension is the scale of the system (*e.g.*, luminosity).

For low N, there is an excess of groups below the fundamental track, which is interpreted as favorable projections of elongated prolate groups. Alternatively, this can be caused by enhanced star formation in very small groups (*i.e.*, $M/L \sim N^\alpha$, $\alpha \approx 1/2$, but then many low N groups would still be expanding [upper right track]), or else the spherical infall scenario is far off. Note that only a minority of groups are off below the fundamental track (a negligible number are off above the track, and those are probably unbound groups). And one expects that favorable projections of elongated groups will be more frequent at low multiplicity.

In the standard picture, the low median M_{vir}/L ($100\,h$) is caused by a combination of *near-turnaround bias* and favorable projections. The collapse time of each group can be determined, and from their distribution, one can infer Ω_0 and the primordial density fluctuation spectrum. No loose groups have yet completed their collapse, and the large majority have negligible interpenetration of their galaxy halos. Hence, one does not expect strong environmental effects in loose groups, and if any are present, they may be tracers of effects at galaxy formation.

3.3 The nature of compact groups

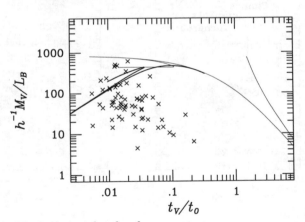

Figure 2. The fundamental surface for compact groups

Figure 2 shows that compact groups[21] occupy the lower left part of the fundamental track diagram, because they are selected to be compact, hence small. With this selection criterion, the high velocity dispersion compact groups (upper left) are the ones that are virialized and/or coalescing (see §3.1), next are the groups that are near full collapse, and the low velocity dispersion compact groups (lower right) are caused by chance alignments within *collapsing* loose groups. Alternatively, the low velocity dispersion compact groups could be caused by favorable projections lowering the line-of-sight velocity dispersion, *i.e.,* decreasing $\beta_{\rm spec} = \mu m_p \sigma_v^2/(kT)$, well below the typical values of 0.4. However, first indications[24] yield only few groups with very low $\beta_{\rm spec}$, despite the fact that the *ROSAT* data may select against the very cool groups. Moreover, there is little intergalactic hot gas in low σ_v compact groups, but this may simply be an extension of a general $L_X^{\rm IGM}$ vs. σ_v relation seen for groups and clusters (Ponman, in these proceedings).

The dynamically cold compact groups account for roughly half of the sample, consistent with the idea that compact groups are mainly caused by chance alignments within larger loose groups[8],[25], in which the high expected frequency of binaries[26] can explain the high level of interactions and star formation (§1). The morphology-velocity dispersion relation in compact groups (§1) merely reflects the fact that the high velocity dispersion compact groups are the only groups that have had enough *time* to reach virialization and see their galaxies merge within them into ellipticals.

4. The baryonic fraction in groups of galaxies

The relatively high baryonic fraction (25–30%) in clusters has been used as an argument for a low Ω_0[27]. Similarly, the first observation of intergalactic hot gas in a group (NGC 2300) led to a very low baryonic fraction (4%)[28], consistent with $\Omega_0 = 1$, if extrapolated to large scales. Subsequent studies[29],[30] have yielded baryonic fractions of 10–15% in groups. A reanalysis of the NGC 2300 group[31] points to baryonic fractions of 20 to 30% using the same X-ray surface brightness profile (the discrepancy is caused by the too large background used by the first study), implying $\Omega_0 \lesssim 0.3\, h_{50}^{-0.92}$ if extrapolated to large scales. Moreover, it has been pointed out[31] that the baryonic fraction increases with radius in the best fitting models, so that deeper X-ray observations may yield even larger numbers. However, the group has been reobserved more deeply, and the baryonic fraction turns out to be of order $\simeq 12\%$ (Mushotzky, private communication), and the discrepancy with the second study would be caused by imperfect galaxy subtraction in the first study! At face value, this last baryonic fraction would extrapolate to $\Omega_0 \simeq 0.5\, h_{50}^{-0.9}$ on large scales.

Acknowledgements: I am indebted to Trevor Ponman for useful discussions, and providing me with a look at his and Harald Ebeling's data, in advance of publication.

296

References

1] Tully, R.B., 1987, *ApJ*, **321**, 280.

2] Hickson, P., 1982, *ApJ*, **255**, 382.

3] Rubin, V.C., Hunter, D. & Ford, W.K. Jr., 1991, *ApJS*, **76**, 153.

4] Mendes de Oliveira, C. & Hickson, P., 1994, *ApJ*, in press.

5] Zepf, S.E., 1993, *ApJ*, **407**, 448.

6] Moles, M., del Olmo, A., Perea, J., Masegosa, J., Márquez, I. & Costa, V., 1994, *A&A*, in press.

7] Hickson, P., Kindl, E. & Huchra, J.P., 1988, *ApJ*, **331**, 64.

8] Mamon, G.A.., 1990, *in IAU Coll. 124, "Paired and Interacting Galaxies"*, ed. J.W. Sulentic, W.C. Keel & C.M. Telesco (Washington: NASA), p. 619.

9] Whitmore, B.C., 1992, *in XIIth Moriond Astrophys. Mtg. "Physics of Nearby Galaxies: Nature or Nurture?"*, ed. T.X. Thuan, C. Balkowski & J. Tran Thanh Van (Gif-sur-Yvette: Eds. Frontières), p. 351.

10] Mendes de Oliveira, C., 1992, Ph.D. thesis, Univ. of British Columbia.

11] Mamon, G.A., 1992, *ApJL*, **401**, L3.

12] Salvador-Solé, E., Sanromà, M. & González-Casado, G., 1993, *ApJ*, **402**, 398.

13] Richstone, D.O., Loeb, A. & Turner, E.L., 1992, *ApJ*, **393**, 477.

14] Lacey, C. & Cole, S., 1993, *MNRAS*, **262**, 627.

15] Kauffmann, G. & White, S.D.M., 1993, *MNRAS*, **261**, 921.

16] Evrard, A.E., Mohr, J., Fabricant, D. & Geller, M.J., 1994, *ApJL*, in press.

17] González-Casado, G., Mamon, G.A. & Salvador-Solé, E., 1994, *ApJL*, in press.

18] Evrard, A.E., Silk, J. & Szalay, A.S., 1990, *ApJ*, **365**, 13.

19] Mamon, G.A., 1994, *in Groups of Galaxies*, ed. K. Borne & O. Richter (San Francisco: A.S.P.), in press.

20] Gunn, J.E. & Gott, J.R., 1972, *ApJ*, **176**, 1.

21] Hickson, P., Mendes de Oliveira, C., Huchra, J.P. & Palumbo, G.G.C., 1992, *ApJ*, **399**, 353.

22] Gourgoulhon, E., Chamaraux, P. & Fouqué, P., 1992, *A&A*, **255**, 69.

23] Mamon, G.A., 1994, *in "N-Body problems and Gravitational Dynamics"*, ed. F. Combes & E. Athanassoula (Meudon: Obs. de Paris), p. 188.

24] Ebeling, H., Voges, W. & Böhringer, H., 1994, *ApJ*, in press.

25] Mamon, G.A., 1986, *ApJ*, **307**, 426.

26] Mamon, G.A., 1992, *in 2nd DAEC Mtg. "Distribution of Matter in the Universe"*, ed. G.A. Mamon & D. Gerbal (Meudon: Obs. de Paris), p. 51.

27] White, S.D.M., 1992, *in "Clusters and Superclusters of Galaxies"*, ed. A.C. Fabian (Dordrecht: Kluwer), p. 17.

28] Mulchaey, J.S., Davis, D.S., Mushotzky, R.F. & Burstein D., 1993, *ApJL*, **404**, L9.

29] Ponman, T. & Bertram, D., 1993, *Nature*, **363**, 51.

30] David, L.P., Forman, W. & Jones, C., 1994, *ApJ*, in press.

31] Henriksen, M.J. & Mamon, G.A., 1994, *ApJL*, **421**, L63.

THE FILTERING EVOLUTION OF PEAKS

Eduard Salvador-Solé and Alberto Manrique
Departament d'Astronomia i Meteorologia, Universitat de Barcelona,
Laboratori d'Astrofísica, Societat Catalana de Física,
Institut d'Estudis Catalans.
Avda. Diagonal 647, E-08028 Barcelona, Spain.

Abstract

The evolution of peaks in a random Gaussian field of density fluctuations through spatial filtering with varying smoothing scale is followed by studying the trajectories they trace in the density contrast vs scale diagram. This allows us to prove in a very simple manner that a necessary condition for such a filtering process to correctly reproduce the subsequent gravitational clustering process is the use of a Gaussian window. We also show that the usual mass functions (MF) for bound objects based on Press & Schechter's (PS) prescription extended to peaks are manifestly wrong for they do not account for the effects of mergers. The correct strategy for obtaining the correct mass function of bound objects within the peak model framework is outlined.

1. Introduction

An important goal in cosmology is to obtain the MF of bound objects in the hierarchical gravitational clustering scenario. The classical approach is based on the spherical collapse model[1] according to which the collapse time of a shell of radius R in a monotonous decreasing spherically symmetric density fluctuation endowed with Hubble expansion only depends on the mean density contrast $\delta \equiv (\rho - \bar{\rho})/\bar{\rho}$ interior to the shell. Now, given a random density field, the previous simple model suggests that points with density contrast above some threshold δ_t when the field is smoothed with a top-hat filter of scale R will tend to accrete matter so to reach, at a time determined by that threshold, a mass which, for density fluctuations in the linear regime, is equal to or larger than essentially the mean density of the universe times the volume associate to the top-hat filter. By differentiating over R the volume ocupied by these points one is led to the well-known PS's[2] expression for the MF of bound objects.

But the real density field is far from purely decreasing and spherically symmetric. Therefore, the previous can just be considered as an heuristic MF. It is not clear, for example, why all points above the threshold in the smoothed density field should tend to form bound objects rather than only peaks (density maxima). Moreover, the use of a top-hat filter may then not be the best suited for filtering of the initial density field to correctly reproduce the subsequent clustering process. Yet, PS's MF agrees with N-body simulations. For this reason much effort has been done trying to justify it. This has been achieved by means of the "excursion set" formalism[3]. However, this formalism is not valid for peaks, the most natural seeds of bound objects.

So far there is no satisfactory proposal for the MF of bound objects within the peak model framework. The most severe well-known drawback with PS's prescription extended to peaks is that it cannot properly account for the cloud-in-cloud problem. But another as much important problem is that it completely ignores the effects of mergers. Indeed, PS's MF states that the change in mass from R to $R + dR$ associated to peaks with density contrast above δ_t is equal to that associated to peaks upcrossing the threshold δ_t in that range of scales. It is therefore presumed: 1) that the density contrast of peaks decreases with increasing scale (in agreement with the peak model ansatz that peaks trace bound objects at any time), and 2) the mass associated to peaks of whatever density contrast is conserved with varying scale. Actually, as shown below, the former assumption depends crucially on the form of the window used, while the second simply does not hold owing to mergers.

2. The Evolution of Peaks in Filtering Accretion and Merger Processes

A point which is a peak on scale R may keep on being so on scale $R + dR$, but, in general, it is not. Some neighboring point becomes the new peak, or there is simply no peak in the neighborhood. We are interested in finding those peaks on scale $R + dR$ which can be regarded as the result of the evolution, by *continuous accretion*, of peaks on scale R, and be identified to them so that the series of points they trace in the δ vs R diagram be regarded as the "trajectories of evolving peaks".

According to the peak model, in diminishing the value of δ, peaks should rearrange as the corresponding bound objects do in time. So the identification of peaks on different scales can be naturally done by following the evolution of the bound objects they are supposed to trace. As they accrete matter, the latter move in space in a continuous manner. Thus, a necessary condition for a peak on scale $R + \Delta R$ to be identified with one on scale R is to be located within a separation of the order of ΔR from it. As can readily be seen by taking the Taylor series expansion of the first order derivative of the density field smoothed at scale $R + \Delta R$ at any point around the position $\mathbf{r}_p$ of a peak, there can be no more than one peak in the neighborhood of any given point (there can obviously be none). Therefore, the previous *necessary condition* provides an *unambiguous* criterium for the identification of peaks on different scales. Of course, for this criterium to be consistent the peak on scale $R + \Delta R$ should have slightly lesser density contrast than on scale R (it traces the same bound object at a later epoch), which is still to be checked. Now, the density contrast of an evolving peak on scale $R + \Delta R$ is given by $\delta + (\partial \delta / \partial R) \Delta R$ in terms of the random variables on scale R. This is readily seen by taking its Taylor series expansion around the previous position and scale, and neglecting second order terms in ΔR $(O(|\Delta \mathbf{r}|^2) = O(\Delta R^2))$. Therefore, the total derivative $d\delta/dR$ of a peak trajectory at a point (R, δ) coincides with the partial derivative $\partial \delta / \partial R$ of the peak represented by that point. This allows us to check the consistency of the *natural* identification criterium above.

Taking the derivative on R of the Fourier transform of $\delta(\mathbf{r}, R)$ we obtain

$$\frac{\partial \delta(\mathbf{r}, R)}{\partial R} = -\frac{R}{(2\pi)^3} \int_{-\infty}^{\infty} d^3 k \, k^2 \, \delta(\mathbf{k}) \, J(k^2 R^2) \exp(-i\mathbf{kr}), \tag{1}$$

with $J(k^2 R^2) \equiv -2 [\partial W(k^2 R^2)/\partial(k^2 R^2)]$, and $\delta(\mathbf{k})$ and $W(k^2 R^2)$ the Fourier transforms of the unfiltered field $\delta(\mathbf{r}, 0)$ and of the smoothing window $W(r^2/R^2)$, respectively. So we have

$$\frac{\partial \delta(\mathbf{r}, R)}{\partial R} = R \nabla^2 [\delta(\mathbf{r}, 0) * J(r^2/R^2)], \tag{2}$$

with $J(r^2/R^2)$ the inverse Fourier transform of $J(k^2 R^2)$. So, for a Gaussian window $(W(k^2 R^2) \equiv \exp(-k^2 R^2/2))$ one has $\partial \delta(\mathbf{r}, R)/\partial R = R \nabla^2 \delta(\mathbf{r}, R)$, and since $\nabla^2 \delta$ is negative for peaks, we are then led to the fact that $\partial \delta(\mathbf{r}, R)/\partial R$ is also negative. So also is $d\delta/dR$ of peak trajectories as needed. However, for any other window $\delta(\mathbf{r}, 0) * J$ is different from $\delta(\mathbf{r}, R)$, and since peaks may not be peaks when smoothing with any other more or less peaked function, (a peak only remains a peak disregarding the smoothing function used provided exact spherical symmetry and a monotonous decreasing density profile) $\nabla^2[\delta(\mathbf{r}, 0) * J]$ may then easily be null or positive. So. only the Gaussian window recovers such a fundamental property of dynamical clustering as "the growth by accretion of objects in time". (When dealing with points as in the excursion set formalism there is no such necessary condition to be satisfied.) In consequence, *for the peak model to work one must use a Gaussian window* and, then, the consistency of natural identification criterium above of peaks on different scales is automatically guaranteed. This also proves that one fundamental assumption for PS's prescription to be extensible to peaks (point 1 above) does not work in general.

Let us focus now on mergers. Like in real gravitational clustering in filtering mergers of similarly massive peaks the scale of the emerging peak experiences *an appreciable increment*, with the window associated to the new emerging peak typically encompassing those of their respective progenitors, while the density contrast of both the merging and emerging peaks remain similar. Indeed, when regions with similar average density associated to nearby peaks on different scales get in touch (sufficiently overlap) a further small increase in their respective scales makes them to disappear (in the sense above), while a new peak will appear with the scale of the window encompassing the whole merging region with similar average density, with the resulting finite skip in scale R unabling any identification between merging and emerging peaks. Therefore, merging peak trajectories disappear, and emerging peak trajectories appear in mergers. Merger events therefore yield appreciable *discontinuities* essentially along the direction of the R axis in peak trajectories in the δ vs R diagram making the total mass associated to peaks not to be conserved in varying the scale. This therefore completely invalidates PS's prescription extended to peaks (point 2 above). Note that, like in real dynamical clustering, filtering accretion can be regarded as a concatenate series of infinitesimal filtering mergers in which all but one of the merging peaks have inifitesimal scale.

As a consequence of the above properties characterizing the filtering evolution (with a Gaussian window) of peaks, the δ vs R diagram for evolving peaks differs from the excursion set one dealing with points in three main aspects: 1) all peak trajectories have the same monotonous trend of decreasing density contrast with increasing scale (their slope is never null nor minus infinity), 2) peak trajectories have finite extent owing to mergers, and 3) the number of peak trajectories decreases with increasing mass scale. In the limit of vanishing scale the number of trajectories diverges (for a divergent rms density fluctuation), while for R tending to infinity there is just one trajectory reaching $\delta = 0$.

3. The Correct Strategy to Derive the Analytical MF of Bound Objects

But peaks along the δ_t line on scales between R and $R + dR$ are those contributing to the MF referring to the time associated to δ_t with masses ranging from M to $M + dM$. Therefore, to derive the MF one must simply count, as already pointed out by Bond[4], the density of such peaks. The previous formalism allows us to properly do it. We must count the density of peak trajectories upcrossing the δ_t line in each range of scales, or equivalently, as attempted by Apple & Jones[5], the density of peaks on scale R with density contrast larger than δ_t evolving into peaks on scale $R + \Delta R$, for ΔR arbitrarily small, with density contrast equal to or lower than δ_t (see details in Manrique & Salvador-Solé[6]).

Strictly, one must still correct the resulting expression from two effects owing to the fact that the density contrast of merging and emerging peaks in a merger, though similar, are strictly not identical. Indeed, a slight decrease in the density contrast of the emerging peak relative to those of the merging ones is forseeable, since the region subtended by the former necessarily includes matter located in small underdense (since compared to peaks) interstices between the latter regions. The fact that the scale of the emerging peak encompasses local underdense regions, populated by peaks with the same density contrast as the merging ones but more sparsely distributed, correctly reproduces a frequent event in real gravitational clustering: the capture by collapsing regions of material which has not yet collapsed by its own right. However, there are two aspects in such "non-conservative" filtering mergers (in the sense of strictly not preserving the density contrast) making them to differ from real dynamical mergers. First, the appreciable finite decrement in the final density contrast yields a gap in density contrasts where *the mass of the merging peaks is in no peak*. Second, peaks located in such low density regions keep on evolving in the δ vs R diagram without being aware of their "capture" until the density contrast of the emerging peak becomes small enough for them to formally merge. This is the well-known cloud-in-cloud problem. Thanks to the formalism presented here both effects can in principle be corrected, and a fully justified MF for bound objects within the peak model framework obtained.

References

[5] Appel, L., & Jones, B.J.T. 1990, MNRAS, 245, 522 (AJ)
[4] Bond, J.R. 1989, Large Scale Motions in the Universe, eds. V.C. Rubin & G.V. Coyne (Princeton: Princeton Series), p. 419.
[3] Bond, J.R., Cole, S., Efstathiou, G., Kaiser, N. 1991, ApJ, 379, 440
[1] Gunn, J.E., & Gott, J.R. 1972, ApJ, 176, 1
[6] Manrique, A., & Salvador-Solé, E. 1994, in preparation
[2] Press, W.H., & Schechter, P. 1974, ApJ, 187, 425

MASS DISTRIBUTIONS IN LUMINOUS X-RAY CLUSTERS

Ian Smail
California Institute of Technology, Pasadena, US

Richard S. Ellis & Alastair C. Edge
Institute of Astronomy, Cambridge, UK

We construct a photometric catalogue of very faint galaxies (I<25.5) using ultra-deep CCD images taken with the 4.2m William Herschel telescope of fields centred on two distant X-ray luminous clusters: 1455+22 (z=0.26) and 0016+16 (z=0.55). Using a non-parametric procedure developed by Kaiser & Squires (1993), we analyse the statistical image distortions in our samples to derive two dimensional projected mass distributions for the clusters. The mass maps of 1455+22 and 0016+16 are presented at effective resolutions of 135 kpc and 200 kpc respectively with a mean signal to noise per resolution element of 17 and 14. Although the absolute normalisation of these mass maps depends on the assumed redshift distribution of the I<25.5 field galaxies used as probes, the maps should be reliable on a relative scale and will trace the cluster mass regardless of whether it is baryonic or non-baryonic. We compare our 2-D mass distributions on scales up to ~1 Mpc with those defined by the spatial distribution of colour-selected cluster members and from deep high resolution X-ray images of the hot intracluster gas. Despite the different cluster morphologies, one being cD-dominated and the other not, in both cases the form of the mass distribution derived from the lensing signal is strikingly similar to that traced by both the cluster galaxies and the hot X-ray gas. We find some evidence for a greater central concentration of dark matter with respect to the galaxies. The overall similarity between the distribution of total mass and that defined by the baryonic components presents a significant new observational constraint on the nature of dark matter and the evolutionary history of rich clusters.

1. INTRODUCTION

The nature of the dark matter in clusters of galaxies has been a central theme in cosmological research since its existence was inferred over sixty years ago[1]. However, until recently most of the interest has focussed on determining the amount of dark matter rather than its distribution. In fact, careful studies of selected nearby clusters have revealed a much higher baryonic fraction than expected in the inflationary $\Omega_{tot}=1$ Universe whose baryonic component is constrained by primordial nucleosynthesis arguments[2]. This dilemma might be resolved if it could be demonstrated that the dark matter in clusters was less concentrated than the baryonic component. Such arguments indicate that the observations constraining the relative distribution of dark matter are as important as those which estimate its total amount. Both the classical spectroscopic and X-ray techniques are ill-suited to tackling this problem in the important outlying regions of clusters. However, the analysis of the gravitational lensing signals, derived from the distortion of background galaxies viewed through clusters, offers an independent probe of the mass distribution in clusters on the relevant scales. We have undertaken a joint X-ray and lensing study of two distant X-ray luminous clusters to test the viability of this technique[3].

2. DATASET

The two clusters chosen are two of the most luminous X-ray clusters in the EMSS[4]. They are 1455+22 (z=0.26) $L_X = 1.6 \ 10^{45}$ ergs sec^{-1} and 0016+16 (z=0.55) $L_X = 1.4 \ 10^{45}$ ergs sec^{-1}. The optical observations were taken in sub-arcsecond seeing using the 4.2m WHT. The final on-source integrations for each cluster are roughly 12ksec in V and 20-25ksec in I. These exposures are sufficiently deep to obtain reliable image shapes and colours to at least I~25.5. The high source densities available (~60 arcmin^{-2} at I=25.5) enables us to resolve mass structures on scales comparable to those available from our X-ray images.

3. ANALYSIS & RESULTS

Various statistical tools have recently been developed to analyse the weak lensing of faint galaxies by rich clusters. The non-parametric lensing statistic developed by Kaiser & Squires[5] (see also Kaiser's contribution to this meeting) is ideally suited to investigate the relative distribution of mass in the lensing cluster.

1455+22 Optically 1455+22 is a poor cluster dominated by a cD. The derived mass map for 1455+22 is illustrated in Figure 1 along with the three baryonic tracers available. The morphological similarities between the distributions of cluster members, X-ray gas and lensing mass are striking. By fitting elliptical contours to the various distributions we can quantify this comparison (Table 1). Whilst there is obviously excellent agreement between the projected morphologies of the three distributions, in terms of shapes and orientations, it is critical to know whether the lensing matter has the same characteristic scale length as that of the baryonic components. To quantify this we fit a modified Hubble profile to the projected distributions (Table 1). Due to the large errors the scale lengths of the distributions are formally indistinguishable. A more informative approach is to take the 2-D maps and calculate the effective mass to galaxy surface density ratio as a function of position. This confirms that the mass distribution is more centrally concentrated than the galaxies at the 3.3σ level.

Returning to Figure 1 we note a significant secondary maximum (containing roughly 10% of the cluster core mass) in the mass map ~500 kpc due east of the cluster centre. Interestingly this peak does not coincide with any strong feature in either the distributions of X-ray emission, cluster members or field galaxies. The absence of such dynamically important structures in the baryonic maps indicates the possible danger of relying solely on indirect tracers of the cluster mass when studying the evolution of rich clusters.

0016+16 This cluster is morphologically quite different to 1455+22 having no central cD and a considerably higher optical richness, although with a similar X-ray luminosity. Nevertheless, most of the conclusions derived for 1455+22 apply equally well to 0016+16. We show the three baryonic tracers and the mass map in Figure 2. The most striking feature common to both baryonic maps and the mass distribution is an elliptical peak with bimodal substructure straddling the optically-defined centre. The mass map indicates the two clumps have a projected separation of 600 kpc with the more concentrated sub-clump in the southwest. The galaxy distribution reveals at least 3 sub-clumps orientated similarly to the mass distribution. A fourth sub-clump to the south-east is not detected in the mass map. The orientations of the mass, X-ray gas and galaxy distribution agree well (Table 2).

4. CONCLUSIONS

• Firstly, in each cluster we have four independent estimates of the orientation of the major axis of the cluster projected upon the plane of the sky (Tables 1 & 2). These four estimates span a range in scales between the central galaxies (~ 20kpc) out to ~0.5 Mpc. In both clusters all four estimates are in good agreement. This implies that at least to first order the systems are relaxed in their central regions. This is the first time that such a comparison has been made and it is encouraging to find such good agreement.

• Secondly, we find from the lensing analysis that both clusters have moderately elliptical $\epsilon \sim 0.5$–0.6 mass distributions close to the average ellipticity predicted for clusters from the effects of tidal distortion on proto-clusters.

• Finally, from a direct comparison of ratio of mass to galaxy surface density distributions in 1455+22 we detect a factor of 3 drop within r<500 kpc implying that the mass is more concentrated than the galaxies.

ACKNOWLEDGEMENTS

This work was partially supported by SERC. IRS acknowledges a NATO Advanced Research Fellowship.

REFERENCES

1) Zwicky, F. 1933, Helv. Phys. Acta. **6**, 489.

2) White, S.D.M., Navarro, J.F., Evrard, A.E. & Frenk, C.S. 1993, Nature, **366**, 429.

3) Smail, I., Ellis, R.S., Fitchett, M.J. & Edge, A.C. 1994, MNRAS, submitted.

4) Henry, J.P., Gioia, I.M., Maccacaro, T., Morris, S.L., Stocke, J.T. & Wolter, A. 1992, ApJ, **386**, 408.

5) Kaiser, N. & Squires, G. 1993, ApJ, **404**, 441.

Table 1

1455+22	Mass	Galaxies	Gas	Central Galaxy
ϵ	0.47±0.03	0.52±0.03	0.46±0.18	—
θ (deg.)	146±2	145±2	136±8	148±2
r_c (kpc)	100^{+80}_{-50}	180^{+70}_{-50}	150^{+100}_{-50}	—

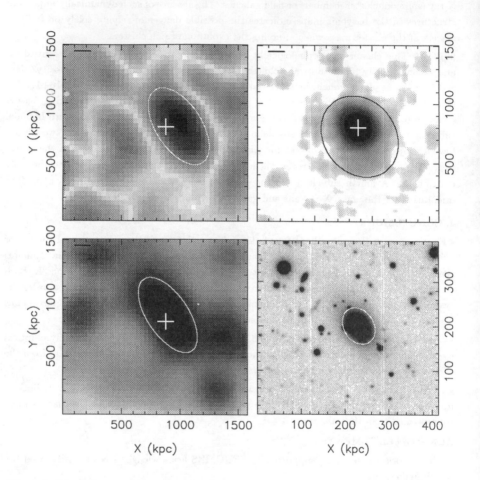

Figure 1: The four separate tracers available in 1455+22 to map the mass distribution. Over-layed on these are the best-fit ellipses to high-light the strong similarities between the ori-entations of the distributions over a range of scales. The ellipse shown for the X-ray surface brightness map has not been converted into the value for the mass (c.f. Table 1). Upper-left panel, the lensing derived mass map. Upper-right panel, the X-ray surface brightness distribution from our deep ROSAT HRI exposure. Lower-left, the number density of the red colour-selected cluster members. The panel at lower-right shows the central galaxy. The smoothing scale (135 kpc) used to construct both distributions is marked and the position of the cluster cD is indicated (+).

Table 2

0016+16	Mass	Galaxies	Gas	Central Galaxies
ϵ	0.59±0.01	0.21±0.02	0.61±0.06	—
θ (deg.)	131±6	124±8	127±4	125±10
r_c (kpc)	~210	~330	400^{+200}_{-150}	—

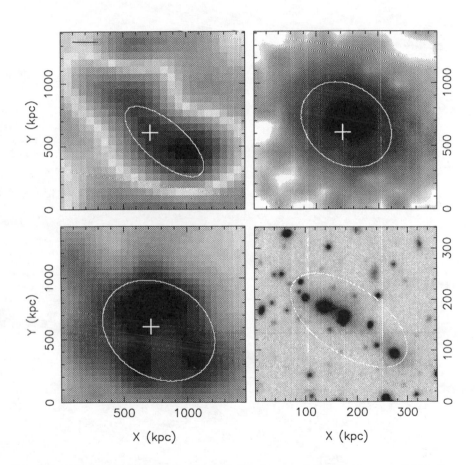

Figure 2: Maps for 0016+16 of the four possible tracers of the cluster mass distribution. Contoured over these are the best-fit ellipses showing the strong similarities between their orientations on scales from 200 kpc to 1.5 Mpc. The ellipse shown for the X-ray surface brightness map has not been converted into the value for the underlying mass. The lensing derived cluster mass distribution is shown in the upper-left panel. The upper-right panel is the X-ray surface brightness map from an archival ROSAT PSPC exposure. Lower-left, the distribution of colour-selected red cluster members. The central galaxy distribution is the lower-right panel. The smoothing scale (200 kpc) used to construct both distributions is marked and the position of the optical cluster centre is indicated (+).

THE ZERO-POINT OF THE CLUSTER CLUSTER CORRELATION FUNCTION

George Rhee[1] and Anatoly Klypin[2]
1. Department of Physics
University of Nevada, Las Vegas
Las Vegas NV 89154-4002
2. Department of Astronomy
New Mexico State University
Las Cruces NM 88005-8001

ABSTRACT

We propose the zero-point of the cluster-cluster correlation function r_0 as a sensitive test for the shape of the power spectrum of initial fluctuations. It is now possible to go beyond the power law description to measure the point at which the correlation function becomes zero. A number of measurements indicate that the zero point lies in the range $(40\text{-}60)h^{-1}$Mpc. The large value of r_0 at which the zero-point occurs rules out conventional CDM models independently of the assumed amplitude. The most severe constraints are imposed on the CDM models with the cosmological constant. Models with $\Omega < 0.25$ should be rejected because they predict too large r_0. If the age of the Universe is assumed to be larger than 15 Gyr, models with either $\Omega < 0.5$ or $h > 0.55$ are rejected. We present the results of numerical simulations of clusters in the mixed model (Cold-plus-Hot-Dark-Matter or CHDM). The correlation function of clusters in the model has a zero-point, $r_0 = 55h^{-1}$Mpc that matches the zero-point of the observed function and is very close to the zero-point predicted by the linear theory. The shape of the function on all available scales (up to $100h^{-1}$Mpc) is reproduced for both the Abell and the APM clusters.

INTRODUCTION

The clustering properties of rich clusters of galaxies can provide a powerful constraint for theories of galaxy formation. In particular the cluster spatial two-point correlation function provides a useful quantitative measure of clustering for comparison with theories. Now that cluster catalogs containing redshifts for several hundred clusters have become available it is possible to determine the scale at which the cluster correlation function has a value of zero (we refer to this as the ξ_{cc} zero-point). We argue in this paper that this is a key observation for comparison with models. We conclude from the published data that there is good evidence that the correlation function goes to zero at $r \sim 50h^{-1}$Mpc.

MODELS AND N-BODY SIMULATIONS

We study the CHDM model, which assumes that the Universe has the critical density and the Hubble parameter is H= 50 km s^{-1} Mpc^{-1}, and the cosmological constant is zero. The CHDM model has the following parameters. The mass density of the Universe in the form of neutrinos is $\Omega_\nu = 0.30$, the density of baryons is $\Omega_b = 0.1$. The amplitude of fluctuations is normalized so that our realization is drawn from an ensemble producing the quadrupole in the angular fluctuations of the cosmic microwave background at the $17\mu K$ level measured by COBE. Numerical simulations are done using a standard Particle-Mesh (PM) code (Hockney & Eastwood 1981, Kates, Kotok, & Klypin 1991). We use a 256^3 mesh for the gravitational force resolution, 128^3 "cold" particles and two additional sets of 128^3 particles to represent "hot" neutrinos. The particles have different relative masses: each "cold" particle has relative mass 0.7 and each "hot" particle has relative mass 0.15.

The size of the computational box for the simulations is 400Mpc ($h = 0.5$). The simulations were started at redshift $z = 7$ and were run to redshift zero with a constant step $\Delta a = 0.01$ in the expansion parameter a. The smallest resolved comoving scale in these simulations is $0.78h^{-1}$Mpc and the mass of a "cold" particle was $7.33 \times 10^{11}h^{-1}M_\odot$.

CORRELATION FUNCTIONS

In a number of recent papers it has been found that the cluster correlation function becomes negative on large scales (Peacock and West 1992, Dalton et al. 1992, Cappi & Maurogordato 1992, Postman et al. 1992 and Postman 1993, Scaramella et al. 1993). The zero point we infer from these studies is $r_0 = (50\pm10)h^{-1}$Mpc. This seems to be a robust result as the correlation functions have been computed using different samples and different methods. The correlation function of Abell clusters of richness $\mathcal{R} \geq 0$ is shown in figure 1. We show the data of Postman et al. (1992) scaled to $\Omega = 1$ with the addition of more accurate redshifts (Postman, 1993) and a more accurate estimator for the correlation function: (DD-2DR+RR)/RR (Landy & Szalay 1993). For the mass limit of CHDM clusters we chose $M > 2.5 \times 10^{14} h^{-1} M_\odot$. This is a compromise between the number density of the Abell clusters and mass of the clusters estimated by Bahcall & Cen. The power law $\xi_{cc}(r) = (r/20h^{-1}\text{Mpc})^{-1.8}$, at scales less than $(20 - 30)h^{-1}\text{Mpc}$ gives a reasonably good fit for both the observational points and theoretical predictions. At larger radii the correlation function falls below the power law and becomes negative at $r > 50h^{-1}\text{Mpc}$.

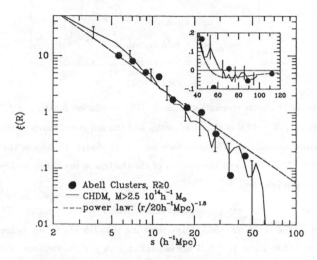

Fig 1. The Abell cluster correlation function. The correlation function of Abell clusters of richness $R \geq 0$ is shown as big circles (Postman et al. 1992, Postman 1993). The full curve shows predictions of the CHDM model. The dashed line in the plot shows the standard power law correlation function with a correlation length of $20h^{-1}\text{Mpc}$. The dashed line on the linear part of the plot presents the correlation function of the dark matter predicted by the linear theory.

Figure 2 shows the correlation function of APM clusters The mass limit for these clusters in the model was $M > 1.05 \times 10^{14} h^{-1} M_\odot$. It is clear from previous studies that the CDM model cannot reproduce the cluster-cluster correlation function (Bahcall and Cen, 1992, Olivier et al. 1993) because it has a zero point of $r_0 = 33h^{-1}\text{Mpc}$. For the CDM model with a cosmological constant (Kofman et al. 1993) the zero point occurs at $r_{0,CDM+\Lambda} = 16.5(\Omega h^2)^{-1}\text{Mpc}$.

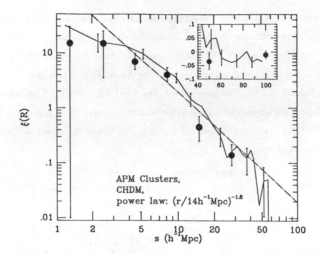

Fig 2. The APM cluster correlation function. The correlation function of APM clusters (Dalton et al. , $N = 190$) is shown as circles and the full curve shows predictions from the numerical simulations. The mass limit for the APM-style clusters in the model was $M > 1.05 \times 10^{14} h^{-1} M_{\odot}$ and the number of the clusters in the simulation box was 203 and 206 for the two runs.

The observed limits on the zero point put severe constraints on this model. The observed zero point lies in the range $40 - 60 h^{-1} Mpc$ implying that Ωh lies in the range 0.27–0.41. Thus models with $h < 1$ and $\Omega < 0.25$ are in conflict with the observations. Assuming the age of the universe to be larger than 15 Gyr rejects all models with $\Omega < 0.5$ or $h > 0.55$. For the tilted CDM model the constraint on the zero point implies that the large scale slope of the power spectrum should be in the range $h = 0.6 - 0.8$. The CDM $+ \lambda$ model and low Ω models claimed by Bahcall and Cen (1992) to fit the data at $r < 25 h^{-1} Mpc$ do not account for the key observation of the cluster zero point (their model correlation functions go negative only beyond $r = 100 h^{-1} Mpc$ in conflict with the observations). We conclude that the CHDM model provides an excellent fit to the APM and Abell cluster correlation functions over the range $5 < r < 100 h^{-1} Mpc$ for which the function has been determined.

REFERENCES

Bahcall, N.A., and Cen, R., 1993, ApJL, 398, L81

Cappi, A., & Maurogordato, S., A&A 259,423, 1992

Dalton, G.B., Efstathiou, G., Maddox, S.J., & Sutherland, W., 1992, ApJ, 390, L1

Hockney, R.W., & Eastwood, J.W., 1981, *Numerical simulations using particles (New York: McGraw-Hill)*

Kates, R.E., Kotok, E.V., & Klypin, A.A., 1991, A&A, 243, 295

Landy, S.D., Szalay, A.S., 1993, ApJ, 412, 64

Olivier, S.S., Primack, J.R., Blumenthal, G.R., & Dekel, A., 1993, ApJ, 408, 17

Peacock, J.A., & West, M.J., 1992, MNRAS, 259, 494

Postman, M., Huchra, J.P. & Geller, M.J., 1992, ApJ, 384, 404

Postman, M., 1993, private communication

Scaramella, R., Zamorani, G. and Vettolani, G., 1993, preprint

RICH CLUSTERS OF GALAXIES AND
THE ORIGIN OF STRUCTURE IN THE UNIVERSE

G. Efstathiou

Department of Physics, University of Oxford, England.

ABSTRACT

Rich clusters of galaxies provide powerful constraints on theories for the origin of large-scale structure in the Universe. The abundance of rich clusters of galaxies can fix the amplitude of the mass fluctuation spectrum, and its shape can be well constrained from the two-point correlation function of rich clusters of galaxies. Our results provide strong evidence for more large-scale power in the universe than expected in the standard cold dark matter (CDM) model. The peculiar velocities of rich clusters of galaxies can differentiate between variants of the CDM model. The observations conflict with low-density ($\Omega \sim 0.2$) scale-invariant CDM models by a wide margin, but are consistent with $\Omega = 1$ models if we ignore a small number of clusters with estimated peculiar velocities $\geq 1000 \mathrm{kms}^{-1}$.

1. Introduction

To model the formation of structure in the Universe we need to know the amplitude and shape of the mass fluctuation spectrum, and the background cosmology. Clusters of galaxies can provide important information on these parameters that is easier to interpret, and less model dependent, than analogous studies of galaxy surveys. In this article, I describe how clusters of galaxies can be used to answer three topical problems in cosmology:

The amplitude of the mass fluctuations: Conventionally, the amplitude of the mass fluctuations is specified by the *rms* mass fluctuation, σ_8, in a sphere of radius $8h^{-1}$Mpc. From surveys of the distribution of galaxies, we know that the *rms* fluctuation in the galaxy distribution in excess of Poisson noise is about unity on a scale of $8h^{-1}$Mpc[1]. However, since galaxies may be distributed differently to the mass, the value of σ_8 could differ substantially from unity, *i.e.* galaxies could be biased or antibiased with respect to the mass distribution. The abundance of clusters of galaxies as a function of mass provides an almost model free method of fixing σ_8. The argument is presented in more detail in Section 2, but can be summarized as follows. The average mass contained within a sphere of radius $8h^{-1}$Mpc is $5.9 \times 10^{14}\Omega h^{-1}M_\odot$ which is close to the mass contained within $1h^{-1}$Mpc of the centre of a rich cluster of galaxies. Since these masses are so similar, it follows that rich clusters of galaxies would be abundant in the Universe if σ_8 were as large as unity, independent of the shape of the fluctuation spectrum.

The shape of the mass fluctuation spectrum: The two-point correlation function of galaxies, or equivalently the power-spectrum, has been determined from angular catalogues[2−4] and from galaxy redshift surveys[5−8]. However, we need to know how the galaxy distribution is related to fluctuations in the mass if we are to test theoretical models of structure formation. Some authors have argued that the galaxy formation process might lead to non-linear biasing, so complicating the comparison between theory and observation[9−11]. In Section 3 I argue that the two-point correlation function of rich clusters in CDM-like models is insensitive to the amplitude of the mass fluctuations and to the cluster richness and so can provide a nearly parameter free measure of the shape of the mass fluctuation spectrum. Furthermore, if rich clusters of galaxies form at concentrations in the mass distribution, as seems reasonable, we can use dissipationless N-body simulations to model the spatial distribution of clusters

Large-scale peculiar velocity fields: Peculiar velocities on large-scales are dependent on the shape and amplitude of the mass fluctuation spectrum and on the growth rate of linear density fluctuations which is fixed by the background cosmology. If we know the shape and amplitude of the fluctuation spectrum, say from the methods described in the previous two paragraphs, we can use measurements of the peculiar velocity field to estimate the value of the cosmological density parameter Ω. We can therfore differentiate between models of structure formation such as an $\Omega = 1$ mixed dark matter model[12] and a low density CDM model[13] which have very similar power-spectra on large scales but predict different peculiar velocity fields. In Section 4 we argue that the peculiar velocities of rich clusters of galaxies are particularly useful for this type of comparison.

2. The Amplitude of the Mass Fluctuations

The abundance of rich clusters of galaxies as a function of mass or X-ray temperature has been used by a number of authors to estimate properties of the mass fluctuation spectrum [14-17]. Here I summarize the arguments presented in ref [18].

Figure 1 shows the abundance of rich clusters as a function of mass measured from two sets of cosmological N-body simulations. The initial mass fluctuation spectra in these simulations are from the family

$$P(k) = \frac{Bk}{(1 + [ak + (bk)^{3/2} + (ck)^2]^\nu)^{2/\nu}},\tag{1}$$

where $a = (6.4/\Gamma)h^{-1}$Mpc, $b = (3.0/\Gamma)h^{-1}$Mpc, $c = (1.7/\Gamma)h^{-1}$Mpc and $\nu = 1.13$. Equation (1) is motivated by the scale-invariant CDM model in which $\Gamma = \Omega_0 h$ if the baryon density can be neglected[19]. The panel to the left in Figure 1 shows results for an $\Omega = 1$ model with $\Gamma = 0.5$, as appropriate for the standard CDM model[20]. The panel to the right shows results for a spatially flat low density CDM universe with $\Gamma = 0.2$; in these models (hereafter refered to as LCDM) $\Omega_0 = 0.2$ at the final output time and the cosmological constant has the value $\Lambda_0 = 3H_0^2(1 - \Omega_0)$). The clusters in the simulations were found by locating high density regions with a percolation alogorithm [18] and counting the number of particles within a sphere of radius r_c. We then repeated the cluster finding by counting particles within r_c of the centre of mass of each cluster, recomputing the centre of mass and deleting overlapping clusters. This step was repeated twice to determine the final list of clusters. For the results presented here we have chosen $r_c = 0.5h^{-1}$Mpc. The simulations follow the evolution of 1 million particles in a cubical computational box $300h^{-1}$Mpc on a side. The force resolution of the models is $0.08h^{-1}$Mpc and so they have adequate resolution and particles to resolve the formation of clusters of galaxies.

The cluster abundances derived from the simulations are shown by the filled circles in Figure 1 for several values of σ_8. The solid lines in Figure 1 show analytic results[18] derived from a simple application of the Press-Schechter[21] model of structure formation which gives for the number density of clusters with masses greater than M (where the mass is measured within a sphere of radius $0.5h^{-1}$Mpc)

$$N(> M) = \frac{3}{2\pi^{3/2}r_8^3}\left(\frac{\delta_c}{\sqrt{2}\sigma_8}\right)^{3/\gamma}\int_{y_{min}(M)}^\infty y^{-3/\gamma}\exp(-y^2)\,dy,\tag{2}$$

$$y_{min}(M) = \delta_c\sqrt{2}\sigma_8\left[0.95(M/2\times10^{14}M_\odot)\Omega_0^{-0.8}\right]^{\gamma/2},$$

where $r_8 = 8h^{-1}$Mpc, γ measures the local slope of the fluctuation spectrum on scales near r_8 and is given by $\gamma = 0.68 + 0.4\Gamma$ for the family of spectra of equation (1); δ_c is a critical density contrast indicative of the formation of virialized structures and is set to 1.68 irrespective of the value of Ω_0. Equation (2) is in excellent agreement with the N-body results.

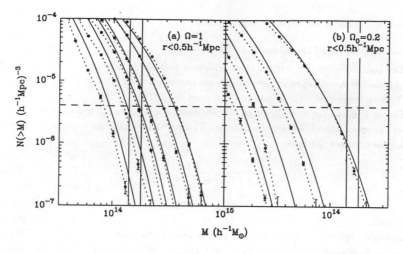

Figure 1: Abundances of rich clusters for various amplitudes of the mass fluctuations as a function of cluster mass. The mass is measured within a radius of $0.5h^{-1}$Mpc. The filled symbols in the Figure show the results of three simulations of an $\Omega = 1$ CDM model with $\Gamma = 0.5$ (Figure 1a) and for a spatially flat low density CDM model with $\Gamma = 0.2$ (Figure 1b). The solid lines show the predictions of the Press-Schechter model (equation 2). The curves plotted are for linear amplitudes (from left to right) $\sigma_8 = 0.4$, 0.5, 0.59, 0.67, 0.83 and 1.0 in Figure 1(a) and $\sigma_8 = 0.4$, 0.5, 0.67 and 1.0 in Figure 1(b). The horizontal dashed lines show an abundance of $4 \times 10^{-6}h^3$ Mpc^{-3}, which is about half the mean space density of Abell $R \geq 1$ Abell clusters. The vertical lines show the cluster masses inferred from X-ray temperatures and velocity dispersions.

From catalogues of velocity dispersions[22−23] and X-ray temperatures of Abell clusters[15,24], the median velocity dispersion of $R \geq 1$ clusters is estimated to be between 810 and 850 kms^{-1} and the median X-ray temperature to be between $kT = 3.5$ and 3.7 keV. From these numbers we infer masses within $0.5h^{-1}$Mpc of

$$M = 1.8 \times 10^{14}h^{-1}M_\odot, \quad (\sigma = 850 \text{ kms}^{-1}), \tag{3a}$$

$$M = 1.4 \times 10^{14}h^{-1}M_\odot, \quad (kT = 3.6 \text{ keV}), \tag{3b}$$

where we have assumed that the velocity dispersions of rich clusters of galaxies are isotropic and independent of radius and that the intracluster gas is isothermal. Figure 1 and equation (2) show that the abundance of rich clusters at these masses is equal to half the observed abundance of Abell $R \geq 1$ clusters, $n \approx 4 \times 10^{-6}h^3$Mpc^{-3} (see ref [25]) if the amplitude of the mass fluctuations is equal to

$$\sigma_8 = (0.57 \pm 0.05)\Omega_0^{-0.56}, \quad \Omega_0 \leq 1. \tag{4}$$

This constraint is almost independent of the primordial spectral index. This arises because a sphere of radius equal to the normalization scale of $8h^{-1}$Mpc encloses a mass comparable to the mass of a rich cluster of galaxies and so y_{min} in equation (2) is insensitive to the value of γ.

Equation (4) is consistent with previous work[14-17]. The main uncertainty in this estimate of σ_8 comes from the mass estimates of Abell clusters, but it seems unlikely that the estimated masses within $0.5h^{-1}$Mpc could be very much in error. Two interesting consequences of equation (4) are worth pointing out: (i) if $\Omega_0 = 1$, equation (4) implies that galaxies are biased tracers of the mass distribution on scales of a few Mpc; (ii) if the COBE observations of temperature anisotropies[26] arise from scalar perturbations, we require $\sigma_8 = 1.1 \pm 0.2$ according to the standard CDM model, which is about twice the value required by equation (4). Thus either the standard CDM model is incorrect or the COBE fluctuations are caused largely by tensor perturbations.

3. The Shape of the Mass Fluctuation Spectrum

There is a large amount of evidence that galaxies are more strongly clustered than expected in the standard CDM model[2-8]. In fact, the power-spectrum of the galaxy distribution can be well approximated on scales $\gtrsim 10h^{-1}$Mpc, by equation (1) with $\Gamma \approx 0.2$, rather than the value $\Gamma \approx 0.5$ expected according to the standard CDM model. This is illustrated in Figure 2 which shows the angular correlation function measured from the APM galaxy survey[2] compared to the angular correlation functions computed from the power-spectrum of equation (1) for values of Γ in the range 0.1-0.5. There are at least three possible interpretations of this result:

[i] The APM correlations are affected by systematic or sampling errors and are artificially high. This seems unlikely because: (a) independent checks of the APM survey suggest that the systematic errors in $w(\theta)$ are $\lesssim 2 \times 10^{-3}$ and so are small; (b) the clustering measured in redshift surveys of IRAS[5,8] and optical[6,7] galaxies suggest a power-spectrum with $\Gamma \approx 0.2$. There is consistency between the results from different samples of galaxies and between two- and three-dimensional surveys.

[ii] Galaxies are clustered in a different way to the mass distribution, so although $\Gamma = 0.2$ provides a good fit to the galaxy distribution, the mass distribution might be better fitted by a different value of Γ. This requires 'non-linear' biasing, i.e. biasing that is a function of scale. Such biasing might conceivably arise if the efficiency of galaxy formation is modulated by physical processes correlated on large scales. However, the modulations required are large ($\sim 30\%$ in $\delta\rho/\rho$ on scales of $\sim 10h^{-1}$Mpc) and the physics of such effects is extremely uncertain. (There is no consensus on even the sign of any modulation, let alone on the magnitude and coherence scale).

[iii] The power-spectrum of the mass distribution is best fitted by equation (1) with $\Gamma \approx 0.2$ on large-scales. The standard CDM model is therefore a poor match to the real universe and a different theory is required, perhaps a low-density spatially flat CDM universe, or a combination of hot and cold dark matter (hereafter MDM).

Of these possibilities, (iii) seems the most plausible and has been the one most widely discussed in the literature. However, (ii) deserves to be taken seriously and can be checked by using other methods to estimate the power-spectrum of the mass distribution, for example, via measurements of peculiar velocities, or the clustering properties of other tracers such as radio galaxies, quasars or rich clusters of galaxies.

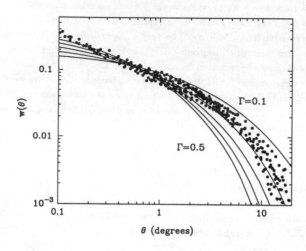

Figure 2. The angular correlation function $w(\theta)$ of APM galaxies measured in six magnitude slices in the magnitude range 17 to 20.5 scaled to a common depth at which an angle of 1° corresponds to a physical length scale of about $5h^{-1}\text{Mpc}$. The solid lines show angular correlation functions computed from the power-spectrum of equation (1) for $\Gamma = 0.5$ to $\Gamma = 0.1$ in steps of 0.1. The power-spectra were normalized to have $\sigma_8 = 1$.

Rich clusters of galaxies are especially interesting tracers of large-scale structure for several reasons. Firstly, clusters of galaxies in CDM-like models should be much more strongly clustered than the dark matter and so their clustering properties should be sensitive to the shape but not the normalization of the mass fluctuation spectrum. Secondly, it seems reasonable to identify rich clusters of galaxies with concentrations in the dark matter distribution, *i.e.* we should be able to model the formation of rich clusters of galaxies with a dissipationless N-body code. Theoretical predictions of the clustering of rich clusters should therefore be less sensitive to uncertainties associated with the physics of galaxy formation than predictions of the spatial distribution of galaxies. Thirdly, N-body simulations[27] show that the amplitude of the rich cluster correlation function is relatively insensitive to cluster richness and to the way in which clusters are identified from the mass distribution. It is therefore possible to make reliable predictions for the rich cluster correlation functions without having to model the exact criteria used to define clusters.

The main difficulty in using rich clusters to measure large-scale clusters lies in defining homogeneous samples from catalogues of galaxies. There has been much debate about the uniformity of the Abell cluster catalogue[28], which was compiled by visual inspection of uncalibrated photographic plates, and how strongly inhomogeneities affect the correlation function of Abell clusters[25,29−30]. Some of these problems are discussed by Sutherland in these proceedings. Rather than using the Abell catalogue, several groups have attempted to produce more uniform samples by applying computer algorithms to select rich clusters on calibrated photographic plates[31−32], or by constructing X-ray flux limited samples[33−34]. The largest of these samples has been compiled from the APM galaxy survey[31,35].

Figure 3 shows the two-point correlation function ξ_{cc} of a new redshift survey of 364 APM clusters. The new sample is an extension of an earlier survey to more distant clusters[35]. The mean space density of these clusters is $3.4 \times 10^{-5} h^3 \mathrm{Mpc}^{-3}$. The three panels in Figure 3 show the data points plotted together with predictions of the standard CDM model (Figure 3a), the LCDM model with $\Gamma = 0.2$ (Figure 3b) and the MDM model in which CDM contributes $\Omega_{CDM} = 0.6$, massive neutrinos contribute $\Omega_\nu = 0.3$, and baryons contribute $\Omega_B = 0.1$. The theoretical curves were made by identifying rich clusters of galaxies in the N-body models as described in the previous section and computing their masses within $r_c = 0.5 h^{-1} \mathrm{Mpc}$. The clusters were ordered in decreasing mass and a lower mass limit was applied to produce a sample of clusters with a mean space density equal to that of the observed sample. The theoretical predictions for ξ_{cc} depend sensitively on the shape of the fluctuation spectrum but are almost independent of the amplitude of the mass fluctuations (Figure 3).

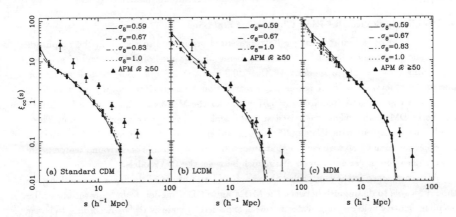

Figure 3. The triangles in each of the panels show the two-point spatial correlation function for a sample of 364 APM clusters of galaxies plotted as a function of redshift space separation s. The error bars on the points show one standard deviation. The data points are compared with the rich cluster correlation function determined from N-body simulations of three CDM models: (a) the standard CDM model; (b) a spatially flat low density CDM model with $\Gamma = 0.2$; (c) an MDM model (see text). The theoretical predictions are plotted for various values of the amplitude of the mass fluctuations σ_8, as indicated in the panels.

From the comparison shown in Figure 3, we conclude that the standard CDM model predicts a significantly lower amplitude than observed *over the entire range of scales plotted in the figure*. In contrast, the LCDM and MDM models plotted in Figures 3(b) and 3(c) provide acceptable fits to the observations. This is encouraging because the linear theory power-spectra of the LCDM and MDM models provide a good match to the galaxy two point correlation function (Figure 2). Figure 3 provides a powerful argument against the idea that the discrepancies between the standard CDM model and observations of galaxy clustering are caused by non-linear biasing. If that were the case, non-linear biasing must modulate the spatial distribution of rich clusters of galaxies in just such a way as to match the $\Gamma = 0.2$ power-spectrum that fits the galaxy distribution. Furthermore, the discrepancy between the standard CDM model shown in Figure 3(a) would require a large modulation on scales $\lesssim 10h^{-1}$Mpc where the cluster correlation function exceeds unity and a much smaller modulation on larger scales so as to produce a multiplicative change in the amplitude of ξ_{cc}; this seems highly contrived. It seems much more economical to suppose that the formation of galaxies and rich clusters of galaxies is dependent only on local properties of the mass density field and so the galaxy-galaxy correlation function and the cluster-cluster correlation function are multiples of the mass autocorrelation function. This hypothesis accounts naturally for the observations shown in Figures 2 and 3 and also for the amplitude and shape of the galaxy-cluster cross correlation function measured from the APM survey, which is approximately the geometric mean of the galaxy and cluster two-point correlation functions[36].

4. Peculiar Velocities of Rich Clusters of Galaxies

In the previous two sections we have presented arguments to constrain the amplitude and shape of the mass fluctuation spectrum using observations of rich clusters of galaxies, concluding that the MDM model with $\Omega_\nu \approx 0.3$ and the LCDM model with $\Gamma \approx 0.2$ can match the observations. If we ignore any contribution from gravitational waves, the COBE temperature anisotropies require $\sigma_8 = 0.67 \pm 0.11$ for the MDM model, and $\sigma_8 = 1.05 \pm 0.18$ for the LCDM model, where we have assumed a scale-invariant fluctuation spectrum. These results are consistent with the amplitudes inferred from the abundances of rich clusters of galaxies (equation 4), so we conclude that observations of the cosmic background temperature anisotropies do not yet allow us to distinguish between the two models.

However, since we have specified the shape and amplitude of the mass fluctuations, we should be able to distinguish between the MDM and LCDM models from observations of the peculiar velocity field on large scales as this is expected to scale as $\Omega^{0.6}\sigma_8$ according to linear perturbation theory. An example is given in Figure 4(a) from reference [37], which shows the distribution of three dimensional cluster peculiar velocities computed from MDM and LCDM simulations normalized to match the COBE temperature anisotropies ($\sigma_8 = 0.67$ for MDM and $\sigma_8 = 1.0$ for LCDM). The histograms are shown for two cluster samples of different richnesses, one with a mean intercluster separation $d_c = 30h^{-1}$Mpc, which is approximately the intercluster separation of the APM sample discussed in the previous section, and the other with $d_c = 55h^{-1}$Mpc, which is approximately the intercluster separation of Abell $R \geq 1$ clusters. The peculiar velocity distributions are almost independent cluster richness but strongly dependent on the model of structure formation. The *rms* of the MDM histogram is 751 ± 12 kms^{-1} and for the LCDM histogram it is 415 ± 5 kms^{-1}.

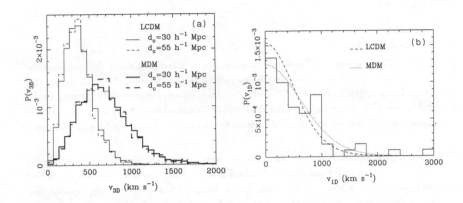

Figure 4: (a) Histograms of the distribution of three dimensional cluster peculiar velocities in the MDM and LCDM models for two cluster richnesses. (b) The histogram shows the distribution of one dimensional peculiar velocities estimated for 60 clusters of galaxies. The lines show the one dimensional velocity distributions in the MDM and LCDM model broadened by the observational errors.

Figure 4b compares the distribution of one dimensional cluster peculiar velocities expected in the MDM and LCDM models compared to the distribution of peculiar velocities with respect to the microwave background reference frame measured by various authors for 60 clusters of galaxies (see ref [37] for further details on the observational sample and on the statistical tests summarized below). The theoretical predictions have been convolved with the observational errors. The LCDM prediction is clearly a poor match to the observations. The MDM model provides a better match but fails to predict the observed number of clusters with peculiar velocities $\gtrsim 1000$ kms^{-1}. If we ignore correlations between the peculiar velocities, we find that the MDM model has a probability of 0.024% of matching the observations while the LCDM model has a negligible probability ($\ll 10^{-5}$). If we remove two clusters from the sample with peculiar velocities $|v_{CMB}| \geq 2000$ kms^{-1} (these are A2199 and A2197) the probability of the MDM model matching the data rises to 0.54% while the probability of LCDM model matching the data remains negligible.

Evidently, neither model seems capable of accounting for the data if we accept the observations at face value. However, we should be skeptical about the clusters with very high peculiar velocities. For example, new observations of A2199 by Lucey *et. al.*[38] give a peculiar velocity of -600 ± 600kms^{-1} compared to the value of -2919 ± 723kms^{-1} measured by Faber *et al.*[39] (and used in the histogram plotted in Figure 4b). The statistics are sensitive to the small number of clusters with high peculiar velocities and to the accuracy of the measurement errors.

The MDM model may be acceptable if some of the high peculiar velocities are caused by systematic errors, or the observational errors have been severely underestimated. Correlations between the peculiar velocities would further enhance the probability of the MDM model matching the data.

5. Conclusions

We have shown the following:

[1] The abundance of clusters of galaxies as a function of mass provides a constraint on the amplitude of the mass fluctuations that is insensitive to the shape of the mass fluctuation spectrum. The amplitudes derived in this way (equation 4) are consistent with the amplitudes required by the COBE anisotropies for MDM and LCDM models, but not standard CDM, if we assume a scale-invariant spectrum and ignore temperature anisotropies from gravitational waves.

[2] N-body simulations show that the two-point correlation function of rich clusters of galaxies should be insensitive to the amplitude of the mass fluctuation spectrum, weakly dependent on cluster richness, but strongly dependent on the shape of the spectrum. The spatial two-correlation function of a new redshift survey of 364 APM cluster of galaxies is well matched by either the MDM or the LCDM models, but not by the standard CDM model. The shape of the mass fluctuation spectrum that best fits the rich cluster correlations also provides a good match to the galaxy two-point correlation function on scales $\gtrsim 10h^{-1}$Mpc.

[3] Cluster peculiar velocities are observed to be higher than expected in the LCDM model. The observations are probably compatible with the MDM model if we ignore a small number of clusters with high peculiar velocities ($|v_{CMB}| \geq 1000$kms^{-1}), which might conceivably be overestimates caused by systematic errors in the data.

These results are consistent with the simplest versions of the inflationary model, which predict that the primordial fluctuations are nearly scale-invariant and that the universe is spatially flat with $\Omega = 1$. The excess large-scale power observed in the galaxy and cluster distributions is most plausibly explained by excess power in the mass fluctuation spectrum. The origin of the excess power is still very uncertain, it may be caused by a mix of dark matter as in the MDM model, but there are other possibilities[40-42]. It is also worth commenting that the above arguments provide nearly model independent contraints that point strongly to an $\Omega = 1$ universe; however, this conclusion conflicts with value $\Omega \approx 0.3$ inferred from the baryonic mass fraction of rich clusters of galaxies and the standard model of primordial nuceosynthesis[43]. It is not inconceivable that this discrepancy might also be related to the nature of the dark matter[44].

Acknowledgements I thank my collaborators, especially Rupert Croft, Gavin Dalton and Will Sutherland for their contributions to the projects described in this review. This work has been supported by the UK Science and Engineering Research Council.

325

REFERENCES

[1] Davis, M. & Peebles, P.J.E., 1983, Ap.J., **267**, 465.

[2] Maddox, S.J., Efstathiou, G., Sutherland, W.J. & Loveday, J., 1990, MNRAS, **242**, 43p.

[3] Collins, C.A., Nichol, R.C., Lumsden, S.L., 1992, MNRAS, **234**, 245.

[4] Baugh, C.M. & Efstathiou, G., 1993, MNRAS, **265**, 145.

[5] Efstathiou, G., Kaiser, N., Saunders, W., Lawrence, A., Rowan-Robinson, M, Ellis, R.S. & Frenk, C.S., 1990, MNRAS, **247**, 10p.

[6] Vogeley, M.,S., Park., C., Geller, M.J. & Huchra, J.P., 1992, Ap.J., L5.

[7] Loveday, J., Efstathiou, G., Peterson, B.A. & Maddox, S.J., 1992, Ap.J., **400**, L43.

[8] Feldman, H, Kaiser, N. & Peacock, J.A., 1994, Ap.J., in press.

[9] Rees, M.J., 1986, MNRAS, **218**, 25p.

[10] Babul, A. & White, S.D.M., 1991, MNRAS, **253**, 31p.

[11] Bower, R.G., Coles, P., Frenk, C.S. & White, S.D.M., 1993, Ap.J., **405**, 403.

[12] Klypin, A., Holtzmann, J., Primack, J. & Regos, E., 1993, Ap.J., **416**, 1.

[13] Efstathiou, G., Sutherland, W.J. & Maddox, S.J., 1990, Nature, **348**, 705.

[14] Evrard, A.E., 1989, Ap.J., **341**, L71

[15] Henry, J.P. & Arnaud, K.A., 1991, *Ap. J.*, **372**, 410.

[16] Lilje, P.B., 1992, *Ap. J.*, **386**, L33.

[17] Bond, J.R. & Myers, S. 1994, Ap.J., in press.

[18] White, S.D.M., Efstathiou, G. & Frenk, C.S., 1993, MNRAS, **262**, 1023.

[19] Bond, J.R. & Efstathiou, G., 1984, Ap.J., **285**, L45.

[20] Davis, M, Efstathiou, G., Frenk, C.S. & White, S.D.M., 1985, Ap.J., **292**, 371.

[21] Press, W.H. & Schechter, P.L, 1974, Ap.J., **187**, 425.

[22] Frenk, C.S., White, S.D.M., Davis, M., & Efstathiou, G., 1988, Ap.J., **327**, 507.

[23] Zabludoff, A.I., Huchra, J.P. & Geller, M.J., 1990, Ap.J.Supp., **74**, 1.

[24] Edge, A.C., Stewart, G.C., Fabian, A.C., & Arnaud, K.A., 1990, MNRAS, **245**, 559.

[25] Efstathiou, G., Dalton, G.B., Sutherland, W.J. & Maddox, S.J., 1992, MNRAS, **257**, 125.

[26] Smoot, G.F., Bennett, C.L., Kogut, A., Wright, E.L., Aymon, J., Boggess, N.W., Cheng, E.S., De Amici, G., Gulkis, S., Hauser, M.G., Hinshaw, G., Lineweaver, C., Loewenstein, K., Jackson, P.D., Jansen, M., Kaita, E., Kelsall, T., Keegstra, P., Lubin, P., Mather, J., Meyer, S.S., Moseley, S.H., Murdock, T., Tokke, L., Silverberg, R.F., Tenorio, L., Weiss, R., Wilkinson, D.T.,1992, Ap.J., **396**, L1.

[27] Croft, R.A.C. & Efstathiou, G., 1994, MNRAS, **267**, 390.

[28] Abell, G.O., 1958, Ap.J. Suppl., **3**, 211.

[29] Sutherland, W.J., 1988, MNRAS, **234**, 159.

[30] Bahcall, N.A. & West, M., 1992, Ap.J., **392**, 419.

[31] Dalton, G.B., Efstathiou, G., Maddox, S.J. & Sutherland, W.J., Ap.J., **390**, L1.

[32] Nichol, R.C., Collins, C.A., Guzzo. L. & Lumsden, S.L., 1992, MNRAS, **255** 21p.

[33] Romer, A.K., Collins, C.A., Bohringer, H., Ebelius, H., Voges, W., Cruddace, R.G. & MacGillivray, H.T., 1993, preprint.

[34] Nichol, R.C., Briel, U.G. & Henry, J.P., 1994, MNRAS, in press.

[35] Dalton, G.B, Croft, R.A.C., Efstathiou, G., Sutherland, W.J., Maddox, S.J. & Davis, M., 1994, MNRAS, submitted.

[36] Efstathiou, G, 1993, Proc. Nat. Acad. Sci. USA, 90, 4859.

[37] Croft, R.A.C. & Efstathiou, G., 1994, MNRAS, 268, L23.

[38] Lucey, J.R., Guzman, R., Steel, J. & Carter, D., 1994, in *Cosmic Velocity Fields*, eds. F. Bouchet and M. Lachieze-Rey, Editiones Frontiers, p43.

[39] Faber. S., Wegner, G., Burstein D., Davies. R.L., Dressler, A., Lynden-Bell, D. & Terlevich, R., 1989, Ap.J. Supp., 69, 763.

[40] Hill, C. & Ross, G., 1988, Nucl. Phys. B, 311, 253.

[41] Bond, J.R. & Efstathiou, G., 1991, Phys. Lett. B, 265, 245.

[42] Kaiser, N., Malaney, R. & Starkman, G., 1993, preprint.

[43] White, S.D.M., Navarro, J.F., Evrard, A.E. & Frenk, C.S., 1993, Nature, 366, 429.

[44] Kaiser, N., 1994, in *Cosmic Velocity Fields*, eds. F. Bouchet and M. Lachieze-Rey, Editiones Frontiers, p411.

SUPERCLUSTERS ON THE SKY

Roberto Scaramella
Osservatorio Astronomico di Roma, 00040 Monteporzio Catone (Roma), Italy

Abstract

The possible presence of hot, not very dense gas outside clusters of galaxies might be revealed by estimating and studying the diffuse X–ray emission or the Sunyaev–Zel'dovich effect from nearby superclusters of galaxies. In turn, these informations can yield useful data or constraints on the cosmic abundance of baryons, on the thermal history of the IGM and on the efficiency of galaxy and cluster formation. Besides general considerations and estimates based on statistical assumptions, it is then important to have a picture based on the *locally observed* distribution of superclusters.

We present here some preliminary results, that is examples of all-sky maps of supercluster. These are derived as projections along the line of sight of the overdensity field of clusters of galaxies limited to a depth of $300\,h^{-1}\,\mathrm{Mpc}$. We also show the angular autocorrelation functions of these maps, which in some cases show coherence over a wide range of scales.

Today one finds superclusters at the top of the clustering hierarchy of astronomical objects. However, a major problem is given by *how superclusters are operationally defined*, since there is some latitude among the possible choices and definitions. In turn, this reflects into different methods and compilations appeared in the literature over the years, starting with the first 3D catalog of Bahcall and Soneira (1984). Since, there has been a number of papers presenting supercluster catalogs, with increasing cluster redshift information. These papers basically used a percolation mechanism to define the superclusters. Even though the systematic effects due to intrinsic biases in the starting catalogs (i.e. the mostly used so far Abell catalog) can be taken into account by appropriate weighting the percolation radius (Zucca *et al.* 1993), this method yields a bitwise answer (yes/no) on possible memberships as a function of the linking parameter. Accordingly, also results on volumes, shapes and richness of superclusters vary discontinuously.

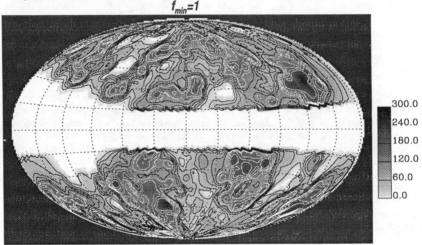

Figure 1.   *Map with* $w(\mathbf{x}) = 1$ *in galactic coordinates* (l^{II} *increasing to the right). Units:* h^{-1} Mpc.

This problem of identification is likely to reflect into the parameters derived from studies which try to constrain the possible presence of a hot, tenuous intra–supercluster plasma (eg Fabian & Barcons, 1991). Constraints on the possible abundance of ionized gas and its temperature come from early studies on the X-ray emissivity from candidate superclusters (Persic *et al.* 1988, 1990), as well as the "Great Attractor" direction (Jahoda & Mushotsky 1989). Even more promising is the cross–correlation of X-ray and microwave temperature fluctuation maps (Boughn & Jahoda 1993), since hot gas, if present, can yield Cosmic Microwave Background [CMB] anisotropies through the Sunyaev–Zel'dovich effect. Indeed it was argued by Hogan (1992) that the entire CMB anisotropy signal observed by the COBE

DMR experiment (Smoot *et al.* 1992) could be due to hot gas present in superclusters.

Infact, the CMB anisotropy studies are likely to be the most sensitive way of probing the presence of this gas, since the SZ effect is proportional to the first power of the electron density ($y \propto n_e T_e$), while the X-ray emissivity, being due to Brehmsstrahlung, is proportional to the square of the density ($\epsilon \propto n_e^2 T_e^{1/2}$). So, if one were to have an homogeneous intrasupercluster medium with, say, density $\times 10^{-2}$, temperature $\times 10^{-1}$ and linear dimensions $\times 10^1$ with respect to those of a rich cluster, then the X-ray surface brightness would be lower by a factor of $10^{-3.5}$, while the Compton parameter would decrease only by a factor 10^{-2}, and probably still be in the range detectable by sensitive CMB anisotropy experiments. Therefore it is of interest to produce actual maps on the sky of possible anisotropies due to nerby superclusters, trying different weights and then to cross-correlate them with present X and CMB data, and to indicate preferred areas on the sky as targets for future experiments.

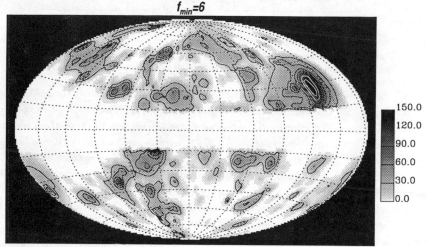

Figure 2. *Map with $w(\mathbf{x}) = 1$ in galactic coordinates.*

As initial step, we produced an all–sky overdensity field of clusters of galaxies limited to a depth of $300\,h^{-1}$ Mpc through the use of the Abell and ACO catalogs of clusters of galaxies, taking properly into account different biases present into the original catalogs. The field is obtained by Gaussianly smoothing clusters placed on a 128^3 grid of pixel spacing $p = 5\,h^{-1}$ Mpc and then dividing by the average field analogously derived from 100 pseudorandom catalogs which have the same biases as the original catalogs (Scaramella *et al.* 1990). It must be noticed that the form and the coherence length of the smoothing chosen here are likely to influence the final results, and other profiles for the clusters at large distances, like isothermal profiles or those given by the cluster–galaxy cross–correlation, will be examined in future work.

330

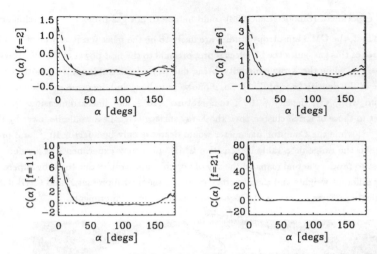

Figure 3. *Solid lines:* $w(\mathbf{x}) = 1$; *dashed lines:* $w(\mathbf{x}) = f(\mathbf{x})$. *At high f_{min} the lack of correlation at large angles reflects the fact that only few blobs are present on the sky.*

We then obtained all-sky maps with latitude $|b| \geq 15°$ of integrals along the line of sight by considering only those 3D regions which have values $> f_{min}$ times their *local* expected average. The grater the value for the threshold f, the smaller and the rarer these regions are. So we produce maps given by $\mathcal{I}(\hat{\theta}) = \int_{f(r\hat{\theta}) > f_{min}} w(r\hat{\theta})\, dr$, where $w(\mathbf{x})$ is a dimensionless weight function. Since $f(\mathbf{x})$ denotes the ratio $n_c(\mathbf{x}) / \langle n_c(\mathbf{x}) \rangle$, this translates in values of $(f - 1)$ for overdensities. Then, to values of $\mathcal{I}$ can correspond values of comptonization paramenter y, when a constant value of temperature and an electron density is assumed for the above–threshold regions, yielding values such as $y(\hat{\theta}) \sim 5 \cdot 10^{-9} h\, \mathcal{I}(\hat{\theta})(T_e/keV)(\Omega_B/0.1)$.

In Figure 1 and in Figure 2 we present maps for values $f_{min} = 1, 6$, and in Figure 3 results for the angular autocorrelation function of some maps for different values of f_{min} and different weighting on the integral along the line of sight.

Acknowledgments This work acknowledges partial financial support from the EC HCM programme (contract # EC ERBCHRX CT92 0033)

References

Bahcall, N.A., and Soneira, R., 1983, ApJ 270, 20

Fabian, A.C., & Barcons, X., 1991, Rep. Prog. Phys 54 1069

Boughn, S.P., and Jahoda, K., 1993, ApJ 412, L1

Hogan, C, 1992, ApJ 398, L77

Jahoda, K., & Mushotsky, R.F., 1989, ApJ 346, 638

Persic, M., *et al.*, 1988, ApJ 327, L1

Persic, M., *et al.*, 1990, ApJ 364, 1

Scaramella, R., *et al.*, 1990, AJ 101, 342

Smoot, G., *et al.*, 1992, ApJ 396, L1

Zucca, E., *et al.*, 1993, ApJ 407, 470

OBSERVATIONS OF CLUSTER CORRELATIONS

WILL SUTHERLAND and GAVIN DALTON

Department of Physics, University of Oxford,
1 Keble Road, Oxford OX1 3RH, U.K.
Draft: 27 May 94

ABSTRACT

We provide an overview of recent observational measurements of the spatial correlation function of rich clusters, from a variety of samples selected using both optical and X-ray criteria. Although some uncertainty remains concerning the correlations for the richest clusters, there is good agreement between several samples of clusters of intermediate richness. This provides strong evidence that the correlation function has a larger amplitude on scales $\sim 10 - 40\,h^{-1}$Mpc than in the standard CDM model. This is consistent with the excess power seen in a number of recent galaxy surveys, and provides significant evidence in favour of structure formation via gravitational instability with Gaussian initial conditions.

1. Introduction

As well as the wide range of cosmological information derived from the composition, dynamics and properties of individual clusters, the space distribution of galaxy clusters provides a very interesting probe of large-scale structure in the Universe. Although their space density is low, $\sim 10^{-5}\, h^3 \mathrm{Mpc}^{-3}$, they represent rare peaks in the density field and hence cluster surveys can provide a useful complement to galaxy surveys for measurements of structure on large scales $\gtrsim 10\, h^{-1} \mathrm{Mpc}$. In this article we will concentrate only on the spatial correlation function of clusters $\xi_{cc}(r)$, which provides the simplest description of superclustering, since existing samples are mostly too small for more refined analysis.

Until recently, most measurements of cluster correlations have been based on the Abell catalogue[1] , and its Southern hemisphere extension[2]. Abell noted that the distribution of clusters on the sky was non-random, one of the earliest indications for the presence of superclustering, and this was later supported by the power-spectrum analysis of Hauser & Peebles[3] .

Using a redshift survey of 104 Abell clusters, Bahcall and Soneira[4] (hereafter BS) estimated the correlation function ξ_{cc} for clusters of Abell richness class $R \geq 1$ to be $\xi_{cc}(r) \approx (r/r_0)^{-1.8}$, with a 'correlation length' $r_0 \approx 25\, h^{-1} \mathrm{Mpc}$, and found evidence that ξ_{cc} remained positive to $r \gtrsim 100\, h^{-1} \mathrm{Mpc}$. This correlation function is much larger than that for individual galaxies, and although Kaiser[5] showed that the clustering of high peaks in a Gaussian field is enhanced over the underlying mass clustering, it became clear that the measured ξ_{cc} was substantially larger than predicted by the standard CDM model[6] , motivating both alternative theoretical models and tests of the robustness of these results.

2. Results from the Abell / ACO Catalogues.

The selection of clusters from two-dimensional sky survey photographs is not a straightforward procedure. At a meeting such as this, many spectacular optical and X-ray images of rich clusters are shown, which may lead to the impression that these systems are very easy to locate. However, it should be borne in mind that the canonical Coma cluster is over twice as rich and $\sim 1/5$ as distant as the typical cluster samples at $z \sim 0.1$ used in most determinations of cluster correlations; so the surface density enhancement of galaxies is far less dramatic for most systems (e.g. Figure 1), and the contrast to the eye is further diluted by the foreground stars.

At this point, it is worth recalling the selection criteria of the Abell catalogue; for each cluster, Abell defined a characteristic magnitude m_{10} to be the magnitude of the 10th brightest galaxy within an angular radius corresponding to $r_A = 1.5\,h^{-1}$Mpc at the estimated distance of the cluster, and a richness N to be the number of galaxies in this radius above estimated background, in a magnitude slice $[m_3, m_3 + 2]$. This procedure is intended to provide a distance-independent sample; unfortunately it is difficult to independently replicate the catalogue, since

a) The magnitude estimates are visual, hence subjective.

b) The cluster definition is recursive, in the sense that the m_{10} depends on the adopted radius and vice versa, and

c) The richness is not strictly defined since the 'background' count for each plate was taken from "a region free of clusters" which is unspecified.

Despite these difficulties, it is known that most Abell clusters do correspond to physically bound systems[7]; however, the level of homogeneity required for large-scale structure measurements is much more stringent than for the study of individual clusters, and it is unclear whether the catalogue meets these demands.

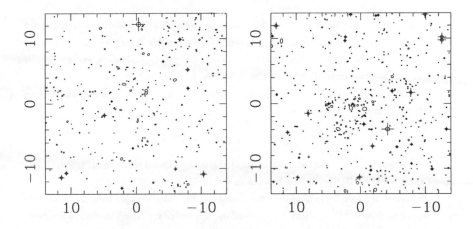

Figure 1: Finding charts of two typical clusters from the APM cluster redshift survey, also in the ACO catalogue. Axes show offsets in arcminutes. Bright stars are marked by crossed symbols, while other objects are galaxies (faint stars are omitted for clarity). The left panel shows A3095 (ACO richness $N = 49$, APM richness $\mathcal{R} = 30$); the right panel shows S112, from the ACO supplementary list, $N = 16$, APM richness $\mathcal{R} = 54$).

A reanalysis of the Abell data[8] (hereafter S88) cast some doubt on the reliability of the BS result[4]. This analysis investigated ξ_{cc} as a function of both projected and line-of-sight separations, and found that it was significantly elongated in the line-of-sight direction. This effect had been noted by BS but attributed to large cluster peculiar velocities $\sim 2000\,\mathrm{km/s}$. However, S88 found that the elongation extended to very large line-of-sight separations $\gtrsim 100\,h^{-1}\mathrm{Mpc}$, too large to be explained by peculiar velocities. This suggests that spurious clustering on the plane of the sky is more likely to be the cause; such an effect will give rise to excess pairs of clusters at small angular separations which are at widely different redshifts, i.e. an apparent 'projection effect'.

A possible cause of such effects was suggested to arise from the fact that clusters are not isolated systems but are merely the most prominent peaks in overdense superclusters. As a result, when two clusters at distinct redshifts appear close on the sky, the additional galaxies around one cluster will lead to an apparent enhancement in the richness of the other cluster. Since cluster catalogues must be selected above a richness threshold, this may 'promote' some poor clusters into the catalogue if they happen to lie behind an unrelated supercluster, i.e. a 'projection effect'; since the cluster number-richness relation is rather steep, a small systematic richness error can translate into a substantial error in the observed number of clusters. Such an effect will also enhance the number of neighbouring cluster pairs, hence biasing the correlation function upwards.

We note that there are other plausible causes of spurious 2-D clustering which are not 'projection effects' in a strict definition but will cause a similar elongation in the clustering pattern; these include sensitivity variations between sky survey plates[9], and subjective variations in the observer's efficiency during the visual scanning of the plates.

An empirical correction for these projection effects was applied by S88, and the derived correlation function was reduced to

$$\xi_{cc}(r) \approx \left(\frac{r}{r_0}\right)^{-1.8}, \qquad r_0 = 14^{+4}_{-3}\,h^{-1}\mathrm{Mpc},$$

with no clear evidence for positive correlations at $r \gtrsim 40\,h^{-1}\mathrm{Mpc}$. This estimate is marginally above the standard CDM prediction but not in severe disagreement.

This result led to a lively debate in the literature; the suggested projection effects were modelled analytically[10,11] by using estimates of the cluster-galaxy cross correlation function, with results in approximate agreement with S88. Some other authors concluded that such effects were negligible; e.g. Postman et al. [12] used a larger survey of Abell clusters to derive $r_0 \approx 20 \pm 4\,h^{-1}\mathrm{Mpc}^*$ and used a test based on the distribution of angles of cluster pairs

---

* Hereafter we shall concentrate on r_0 rather than the full $\xi_{cc}(r)$; since most estimates find a power-law slope consistent with -1.8, over the range $5 \leq r \leq 50\,h^{-1}\mathrm{Mpc}$, this is a convenient parametrisation which does not introduce much uncertainty.

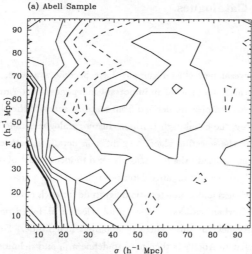

Figure 2:   A contour plot of ξ_{cc} as a function of projected separation σ and line-of-sight separation π, for a sample of Abell clusters, taken from ref. [13]. Contour levels are -0.4, -0.2 (dashed), 0, 0.2, 0.4, 0.6, 0.8, 1 (bold), 2, 3, 4.

relative to the line-of-sight to conclude that projection effects were almost absent. However, this test is not very sensitive and it was found by[13] that this sample did in fact show evidence for excess line-of-sight clustering, and a corrected correlation length of $14\,h^{-1}$Mpc was estimated. A small subsample of the BS clusters containing cD galaxies was analysed by West & van den Bergh[14] to derive $r_0 \approx 22 \pm 7\,h^{-1}$Mpc; but while this test does ensure that the sample consists of real 3-D clusters and not chance alignments, it has no sensitivity to systematic richness errors as proposed by S88, and the statistical uncertainty is large. Further tests claiming no contamination in the Abell samples have appeared[15,16], but these are also negative in the sense of failing to prove that the biases exist, rather than clearly proving that biases are absent, an important distinction. The elongation seen in Figure 2 is hard to explain by any other mechanism than projection effects, and has now been seen in several samples[8,13,17,18], so it appears that alternative cluster samples with more rigorous selection criteria are highly desirable to provide an independent measurement of the large-scale cluster distribution.

3. New Cluster Catalogues.

3.1 OPTICAL SAMPLES

In recent years, several new cluster samples have become available, based on objective selection criteria, which can provide an important independent determination of cluster correlations. Two of these samples are derived from machine scans of the UK Schmidt Telescope southern sky survey; the Edinburgh-Durham cluster catalogue[19] and the APM cluster catalogue[20] . Although the selection algorithms differ in detail, in both cases a two-stage cluster selection algorithm is used ; the first stage is used to locate a set of overdense regions in the 2-D galaxy distribution as candidate cluster centres, and then a more refined procedure is used to estimate a richness and characteristic magnitude for each cluster.

In the Edinburgh-Durham catalogue, the initial selection is based on selecting peaks in the smoothed density field in three slices of apparent magnitude. For each peak, an iterative procedure similar to Abell's is then used to define m_{10} and richness. Internal errors are estimated from clusters detected in more than one magnitude slice, and duplicates are removed to produce a catalogue of ~ 700 clusters over 2000 sq.deg. A redshift survey of a subsample of 89 clusters has been completed by Guzzo et al. [21], and this sample shows a correlation length of $16 \pm 4\,h^{-1}$Mpc[22].

In the APM cluster catalogue[20], initial cluster centres are defined by a percolation algorithm, and the iterative cluster definition differs somewhat from Abell's; a smaller counting radius of $0.75\,h^{-1}$Mpc is used to improve contrast above background, and m_{10} is replaced by 'm_X' where X is a function of the richness, to avoid a correlation between m_{10} and richness. A redshift survey of these clusters has been carried out by Dalton et al. [23]. The survey mostly uses a long-slit technique, where typically 2 or 3 galaxy redshifts are measured per cluster; the likelihood function for the cluster redshift based on the full distribution of apparent magnitudes is used to reject redshifts arising from foreground galaxies, and additional galaxies are observed in ambiguous cases. The method has been tested using a subsample of clusters with > 10 galaxy redshifts obtained from multi-fibre spectroscopy; it gives a substantial saving of telescope time since it avoids both the fibre losses and the need to observe fainter galaxies to use many fibres. The initial sample of 226 clusters has been analysed by Dalton et al. [23], and has recently been extended to a somewhat greater depth giving a sample of 364 clusters; the correlation function from this extended sample is shown in Figure 3, along with theoretical predictions[24] for standard CDM, mixed dark matter and low-density CDM models. Although the correlation length for the extended sample is significantly lower

$(r_0 = 14.5 \pm 1.75\,h^{-1}\mathrm{Mpc})$ than for the Abell cluster samples, it is consistent with the "corrected" Abell values and with our earlier results. However, the reduced error bars from the enlarged sample now give rise to a strong discrepancy with the standard CDM prediction, though the measurements are consistent with the mixed DM or low-density CDM models, which have been found to give a good match to large-scale clustering of galaxies[25,26].

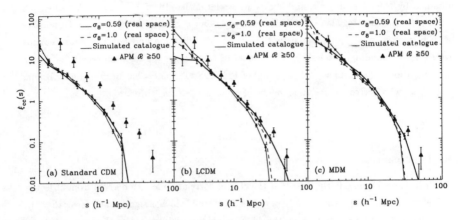

Figure 3:   The cluster correlation function from the extended APM sample of 364 clusters. Observed data points are the same in each panel, compared with simulated results for (a) Standard CDM, (b) Low-density CDM, and (c) Mixed DM.

In addition, to investigate the dependence of clustering strength with the richness cutoff of the cluster samples, we have carried out a deeper survey of 164 of the richest APM clusters, to a mean redshift of $z \approx 0.15$. This sample has a space density similar to Abell $R \geq 1$ clusters, and shows a correlation length of $r_0 \approx 17.5 \pm 4\,h^{-1}\mathrm{Mpc}$. A sub-sample with space density comparable to Abell $R \geq 2$ clusters gives $r_0 \approx 19 \pm 6\,h^{-1}\mathrm{Mpc}$, so there is little evidence for a strong dependence of the correlation length on cluster richness.

3.2 X-Ray Selected Samples

The selection of clusters in X-rays is probably the cleanest method for defining uniform samples for measurement of large-scale structure. The X-ray emission from clusters is very centrally concentrated, and is much stronger than that from field galaxies, hence it is straightforward to define a flux-limited sample of clusters without problems due to background subtraction or overlap of clusters seen in projection. A sample of 53 clusters detected by EXOSAT was studied by Lahav *et al.* [27] , who found a correlation length of $r_0 \approx 21\,h^{-1}$Mpc; however the number of clusters is very small, and their result drops to $17\,h^{-1}$Mpc if the galactic plane is masked; hence this sample is insufficient to resolve the uncertainties discussed in § 2.

The ROSAT all-sky survey is much more sensitive than any earlier wide-angle X-ray survey, and clearly provides an ideal database for cluster surveys, since it is expected to detect ~ 3000 clusters. A subsample of distant Abell clusters detected by ROSAT has been obtained by Nichol *et al.* [28], and shows a correlation length of $r_0 \approx 16 \pm 4\,h^{-1}$Mpc. Of course, the ideal strategy is to select clusters purely on the basis of X-ray data, and a number of such surveys are in progress; since the optical identification and redshift measurements are rather demanding in telescope time, most of these have yet to produce results, but a determination of ξ_{cc} from a redshift survey of 128 ROSAT clusters has been made by Romer *et al.* [29] , who derive a correlation length of $r_0 = 13.7 \pm 2.3\,h^{-1}$Mpc.

4. Discussion

It has now become fairly clear that the cluster correlation length derived from objective optical and X-ray samples is typically $r_0 \approx 15 \pm 3\,h^{-1}$Mpc, which is significantly lower than the BS value $\sim 25\,h^{-1}$Mpc derived from the Abell catalogue. However, even the lower estimates of ξ_{cc} remain significantly higher than the predictions of the standard CDM model, and all samples find that ξ_{cc} remains positive to a scale at least $r \gtrsim 40\,h^{-1}$Mpc.

The reason for the difference between Abell and other samples remains in dispute. Some authors[13,17] maintain that systematic inhomogeneities in the Abell catalogue cause the derived ξ_{cc} to be biased upwards, as discussed in § 2, while Bahcall & West[30] propose that the difference arises from the different richness of the cluster samples, combined with a strong trend in clustering strength with cluster richness, and hence with cluster abundance. Bahcall & West suggest that the data can be well fitted by a relation $r_0 = 0.4\,\bar{d}$, where $\bar{d} = \bar{n}^{-1/3}$ is the mean separation of the cluster sample for a given richness threshold.

Some trend in ξ_{cc} with cluster richness is expected theoretically; Bahcall & Cen[31] have claimed that the relation $r_0 = 0.4\bar{d}$ is reproduced in N-body simulations, but they use a model with $\Omega_0 h = 0.1$ which is disfavoured by COBE and galaxy clustering measurements[32]; also, their estimate for the richest clusters is uncertain due to the size of the simulation volume. In most models this dependence should be slower than a linear relation, as shown from analytic calculations by Mann *et al.* [33], and investigated by large N-body simulations by Croft & Efstathiou[24] and Efstathiou (this volume). The N-body and analytic results agree that the that the $r_0/\bar{d}$ relation flattens considerably below a linear relation at large $\bar{d}$, though the

N-body results predict slightly lower values of r_0. It is found that ξ_{cc} from simulations is reasonably insensitive to details of the cluster identification procedure.

In Figure 4 we show the observed values of r_0 for various cluster samples discussed previously, compared with the N-body results[24]. The observational evidence for $r_0 \sim 0.4\overline{d}$ is rather weak, resting mainly on the point for the $R \geq 2$ Abell clusters[18]. The rich APM clusters show a more modest increase in r_0, and are consistent with the N-body predictions.

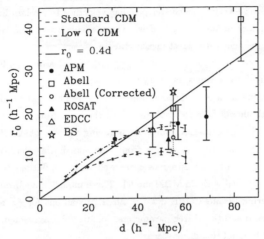

Figure 4:   The cluster correlation length r_0 as a function of the mean separation $\overline{d}$. Data points show observations from various samples as indicated, with Abell results from refs.[12,18]. The thick line shows the relation $r_0 = 0.4\overline{d}$, and thin lines show estimates from N-body simulations[24] for standard CDM (lower) and low-density CDM (upper).

We can briefly summarise our conclusions as follows:

i) There is clear evidence for systematic bias in the correlation function of the Abell catalogue, which is most clear-cut in the $R \geq 0$ samples, but is also apparent in the smaller $R \geq 1$ samples.

ii) After correction for these effects there is good agreement between results from Abell clusters and several independent samples. The correlation function for moderate richness clusters, with $\overline{n} \sim 2 \times 10^{-5}\, h^3 \mathrm{Mpc}^{-3}$ or Abell richness class $R \geq 0$ is well approximated by

$$\xi_{cc}^{R\geq 0} \approx \left(\frac{r}{r_0}\right)^{-1.8}, \qquad r_0 \approx 14.5 \pm 1.75\, h^{-1}\mathrm{Mpc}.$$

This result is seriously discrepant with the standard $\Omega h = 0.5$ CDM model for any value of b.

iii) For richer clusters the situation is less precise, but the richer APM clusters indicate a modest rise in clustering amplitude, with $r_0 \approx 17.5 \pm 4 \, h^{-1}$Mpc for these systems. At least some of the discrepancy with the "standard" value of $r_0 \approx 25 \, h^{-1}$Mpc may be attributed to small number statistics, since recent samples of Abell clusters have generally found values $\approx 21 \, h^{-1}$Mpc prior to correcting for projection biases. A moderate degree of bias in the Abell $R \geq 1$ clusters can easily account for the remaining difference.

iv) There is no need to invoke very large cluster peculiar velocities to explain line-of-sight anisotropy in ξ_{cc}. The lack of anisotropy in newer samples constrains such velocities to be $\lesssim 1000$ km/s, in agreement with direct measurements.

v) There is rather good evidence that ξ_{cc} remains positive to scales of $r > 40 \, h^{-1}$Mpc, beyond which scale the data becomes too noisy to be clear.

In the next few years, much larger samples should become available, particularly of X-ray selected clusters, which should help to resolve some of the remaining uncertainties for the richest systems. Overall, these results appear encouraging for the general framework of structure formation via gravitational clustering from Gaussian initial conditions. The observed ξ_{cc} for moderate richness clusters agrees quite well with simulations from a low-density CDM model and very well with an MDM model. These models have been proposed earlier to fit galaxy clustering[25] and COBE data[32]; their predictions for ξ_{cc} are almost independent of b and have no additional free parameters, so this good agreement is a non-trivial success for the gravitational clustering scenario.

ACKNOWLEDGEMENTS:

We thank our collaborators, Rupert Croft, Marc Davis, George Efstathiou and Steve Maddox for allowing us to quote results from the extended APM cluster survey in advance of publication. We are grateful to the AAT and CTIO for allocations of observing time.

References

1   Abell, G.O., 1958. *ApJS*, 3, 211.

2   Abell, G.O., Corwin, H.C., Olowin, R.P., 1989. *ApJS*, 70, 1.

3   Hauser, M.G., Peebles, P.J.E., 1973. *ApJ*, 185, 757.

4   Bahcall, N.A., Soneira, R.M., 1983. *ApJ*, 270, 20.

5   Kaiser, N., 1984. *ApJ*, 284, L9.

6   White, S.D.M., Frenk, C.S., Davis, M., Efstathiou, G., 1987. *ApJ*, 313, 505.

7   Struble, M.F., Rood, H.J., 1991. *ApJ*, 374, 395.

8   Sutherland, W., 1988. *MNRAS*, 234, 159.

9   Dalton, G.B., *D.Phil. Thesis*, Oxford University.

10   Dekel, A., Blumenthal, G.R., Primack, J.R., Olivier, S., 1989. *ApJ*, 338, L5.

11   Olivier, S., Primack, J.R., Blumenthal, G., Dekel, A., Stanhill, D., 1990. *ApJ*, 356, 10.

12   Postman, M., Huchra, J., Geller, M.J., 1992. *ApJ*, 384, 404.

13   Efstathiou, G., Dalton, G.B., Sutherland, W., Maddox, S., 1992. *MNRAS*, 257, 125.

14   West, M.J., van den Bergh, S., 1991. *ApJ*, 373, 1.

15   Jing, Y., Plionis, M., Valdarnini, R., 1992. *ApJ*, 389, 499.

16   Batuski, D., Bahcall, N.A., Olowin, R., Burns, J.O., 1989. *ApJ*, 389, 499.

17   Sutherland, W., Efstathiou, G., 1991. *MNRAS*, 248, 159.

18   Peacock, J.A., West, M.J., 1992. *MNRAS*, 259, 494.

19   Lumsden, S.L., Nichol, R.C., Collins, C.A., Guzzo, L., 1992. *MNRAS*, 258, 1.

20   Dalton, G.B., Efstathiou, G., Maddox, S.J., Sutherland, W., 1994. *MNRAS*, 269, 151.

21   Guzzo, L., Collins, C.A., Nichol, R.C., Lumsden, S.L., 1992. *ApJ*, 393, L5.

22   Nichol, R.C., Collins, C.A., Guzzo, L., Lumsden, S.L., 1992. *MNRAS*, 255, 21P.

23   Dalton, G.B., Efstathiou, G., Maddox, S.J., Sutherland, W., 1992. *ApJ*, 390, L1.

24   Croft, R.A.C., Efstathiou, G., 1994. *MNRAS*, 267, 390.

25   Efstathiou, G., Sutherland, W., Maddox, S.J., 1990. *Nature*, 348, 705.

26   Davis, M., Summers, F.J., Schlegel, D., 1992. *Nature*, 359, 393.

27   Lahav, O., Fabian, A., Edge, A.C., Putney, A., 1989. *MNRAS*, 238, 881.

28   Nichol, R.C., Briel, U., Henry, J.P., 1994. *MNRAS*, 267, 771.

29   Romer, A., Collins, C., Bohringer, H., Ebeling, H., Voges, W., Cruddace, R., MacGillivray, H., 1994. *Nature*, submitted.

30   Bahcall, N.A., West, M.J., 1992. *ApJ*, 392, 419.

31   Bahcall, N.A., Cen, R., 1992. *ApJ*, 398, L81.

32   Efstathiou, G., Bond, J.R., White, S.D.M., 1992. *MNRAS*, 258, 1P.

33   Mann, R., Heavens, A., Peacock, J.A., 1993. *MNRAS*, 263, 798.

ARCS AND ARCLETS IN CLUSTERS OF GALAXIES

G. SOUCAIL[1],
H. BONNET[1], B. FORT[1,2], J.P. KNEIB [1,3], J.F. LEBORGNE[1],
G. MATHEZ[1], Y. MELLIER[1], R. PELLO[1], J.P. PICAT[1]

[1] *Observatoire Midi-Pyrénées, URA 285, 14 Avenue E. Belin, F-31400 Toulouse, France*
[2] *DEMIRM, Observatoire de Paris, 61 Avenue de l'Observatoire, F-75014 Paris, France*
[3] *European Southern Observatory, La Silla, Chile*

Abstract

Gravitational lensing in clusters of galaxies is a recent topic which brought a large number of original results in the understanding of clusters of galaxies, as well as of distant galaxies. Cluster dark matter distribution are explored with the help of lens modeling, and faint field galaxies are observed with gravitational telescopes. In this paper we sumarize some of the most exciting results and discuss their implications in the context of observational cosmology.

1 Gravitational lensing in clusters of galaxies

1.1 Scientific interests of arcs and arclets

Detected for the first time less than 10 years ago [1, 2] the giant arcs in clusters of galaxies were first considered as rather exotic phenomena, demonstrating that rich clusters may act as strong lensing agent on distant background galaxies. But it became rapidly clear that cluster-lensing is a common effect as soon as one considers not only the high amplification events but also the weak shear of extended sources. This directly results from the existence of a large population of very faint and blue galaxies [3] spread all over the sky, which are potential sources for any lens because of their high number density. One of the major advantage of cluster lensing is the angular scales of the phenomenon, much are larger than those fixed by an individual galaxy lens. As an example, with a typical cluster core mass of $10^{14} M_\odot$ at $z_L = 0.3$, the Einstein radius (which fixes the angular scales of the lens) is $R_E \sim 30''$ to $1'$ for a source at $z_S \simeq 1$. This is much larger than the spatial resolution usually obtained on ground-based optical telescope ($\lesssim 1''$). Consequently the distribution of light along the arcs can lead to some spatial informations in the deflector, up to mass scales of individual galaxies.

The main output of the study of giant arcs and arclets concerns the mass distribution in cluster of galaxies. The rather crude estimation of the central mass inside the Einstein radius is robust, even if it does not give indications on its distribution. All cases of giant arcs presently analysed show evidence for a large amount of dark matter in the center of the clusters, with a mass-to-light ratio ranging from 50 to 300 in solar units. More refined models are useful to determine the core radius and the mass profile of the dark matter, which can be compared to other mass distribution estimates: mass traced by the luminous galaxies or X-ray gas distribution. In fact, since gravitational lensing acts on all scales, we should be able to probe a wide range of masses: the main lensing agent is a rich cluster with typical mass of $10^{14} M_\odot$ and core radius of $r_c \sim 100$ kpc, but some local deformations observed in giant arcs can be interpreted in terms of "mini-lensing" by masses ranging from 10^6 to $10^{11} M_\odot$ and scales of about 10 kpc. Moreover, as the sources are extended objects, the shear is directly measurable (contrary to lensing on ponctual sources such as quasars) giving access to mass gradients at large distance from the center. The weak shear effects are sensitive up to a level of a few percent of magnification and can trace masses of $10^{15} M_\odot$ in the outer parts of clusters (see part 2.3.). It is hoped that in a near future, the weak shear effect of the very large scale structures will even be detectable with the new generation of large array detectors [4, 5, 6].

Concerning the background sources, the use of clusters of galaxies as giant gravitational telescopes is a powerful tool to look at some very distant galaxies which are typical field galaxies. The spectroscopy of giant arcs, although a difficult task, is the best confirmation of the lensing origin of the observed structures. It also fixes the angular scales of the lensing configuration, useful for any modeling. However a few arclet candidates were later identified with blue cluster galaxies probably seen edge-on! After a few years of spectroscopic survey of giant arcs, we have been able to obtain a sample of distant field galaxies with a measured redshift and some information on their spectral content (see part 3.1.). For the faintest arclets, spectroscopy is out of reach of present-day telescopes and instrumentation but when possible multi-color photometry is an efficient way to study the high redshift field galaxies, their number counts and their photometric evolution.

In order to understand in more detail the formation of images through a gravitational lens, we remind shortly the different configurations which can be expected. An extensive study of the image formation by gravitational lenses can be found in Schneider, Ehler and Falco [7], especially in the case of the most simple potential distributions, such as the pseudo-isothermal elliptical potential with finite core radius. This distribution can create a large fraction of the possible image configurations, although more complex lenses or bimodal potentials have their own caracteristic images. Figure 1 summarizes these image configurations, which can easily be recognised in subarcsecond seeing images of giant arcs [9]. The terminology comes from the theory of catastrophes and was introduced initially by Blandford and Narayan [8].

1.2   Observations of gravitational lensing in clusters of galaxies

It is out of the scope of the paper to extensively review all the cases of gravitational lensing in clusters of galaxies presently identified, and we may refer to the review by Fort and Mellier [10] for a complete list. Anyway, we can remind here some key points concerning the observing conditions required and the criteria of selection presently used to optimise the rate of detection of giant arcs. In optical imaging, it is necessary to observe in high resolution mode with sub-arcsecond seeing conditions: the detailed morphology of giant arcs and the detection of possible intensity breaks is fundamental to recognize the image configuration and to try to reconstruct the brightness distribution of the source. The detection of some *multiple images* in a given lens is the best way to constrain any lens model (see below the case of MS2137–23). Most of the background sources are very faint objects, so the detection and photometry of as many arclets as possible require ultra-deep imaging and photometry in good seeing conditions, to increase the statistics of the distorted objects. Some specific observing modes and data reduction procedures have been developped in order to reach detection levels as low

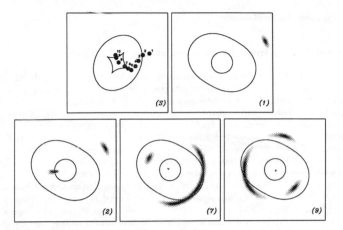

Figure 1: Some typical image configurations in the case of a non-singular elliptical potential. As the source moves in the source plane with respect to the caustics, the image deformation can take the different configurations: a "radial arc" in case (2), with a counter-image on the opposite side of the potential; a "cusp arc" in case (7), corresponding to the merging of 3 images, with two counter-images; the "fold arc" in case (9) corresponding to 2 merging images with 3 counter-images, although some of them can be too deamplified to be detectable. Case (1) corresponds to an arclet, when the source is rather far from the caustics and the deformation is small.

as a few 10^{-3} of the sky brightness with typical exposure times of 4 hours on a 4-m telescope.

The selection criteria for the detection of giant arcs or arclets are not well defined, and except for the EMSS survey [11, 12], there is no well defined samples of observed clusters. The strategy used by most of the "arcs hunters" is to select very rich clusters, most generally with a strong X-ray emission (this is the case for about 70 % of the known cluster lenses) and in the redshift range 0.15 to 0.5 or 0.6. Indeed, if most of the background sources are assumed to be at a redshift of 0.7 to 1.2 (see Table 1 below), this is the optimal redshift range for the lens. Moreover, the background sources are uniformily distributed so the expected number of arclets can be set proportional to the square of the Einstein radius (corresponding to the surface where the amplification is maximal). The Einstein radius beeing proportional to the square of the velocity dispersion for an isothermal sphere, the number of arclets is related to the 4th power of the velocity dispersion. The richness of the cluster is consequently a strong argument in favour of the existence of arcs and arclets.

We mention here the survey followed by the "Hawaian team" (Gioia, Luppino, Le Fèvre, Hammer) an a selected sample of 41 clusters from the EMSS survey, with a lower flux limit of $2\,10^{44}$ erg/s and a lower redshift range of 0.15. Their high rate of detection of extended arcs in their CCD images confirms the fact that X-ray luminosity is probably the best criterium for arc selection. Some results on the arcs statistics and their implications on the clusters mass distribution are coming, although still preliminary. We can also mention some new cases of arcs and arclets, now coming from the ROSAT X-ray clusters: the giant arc in S295 found in the course of an ESO Key-Programme of optical identification of ROSAT sources [13] is a typical case of 3 merging images which certainly include the local distorsion by the nearby galaxy. Abell 2104, also selected from the ROSAT All-Sky survey shows a bright and long arc centered on the central cD and rather close to it [14]. Finally, one should mention the recent detection by Bonnet et al. [15] of a weak shear pattern in the field of the double quasar Q2345+007, known for many years as the "dark lens" as no deflector was clearly identified. The weak shear pattern detected from the statistical weak distorsion of the background sources is compatible with the existence of a strong amount of matter, probably in the form of a very distant and massive cluster of galaxies.

2 Mass distribution from the modeling of arcs and arclets

Some examples of models for the matter distribution in clusters of galaxies are described below, but we can first remind briefly the main ingredients which are to be put in a model. Three families of parameters can be analysed: those corresponding to the lens, or the gravitational potential, those which characterize the source and its shape parameters, and finally the cosmology: the ratio D_{LS}/D_{OS} between the angular diameter distance Lens-Source and Observer-Source depends explicitly although weakly on the cosmological parameters q_0, Λ and Ω. The important parameters which characterize the potential distribution are its center, ellipticity and orientation, the total mass (or equivalently the velocity dispersion of the cluster) and the core radius. The pseudo-isothermal elliptical potential is most often used because it has a simple analytical value and its derivative are easy to compute in the lens equation. But in case of large ellipticity, the surface mass distribution derived from this potential through the 2D Poisson equation gives negative values in some regions, which are of course unphysical. Kassiola and Kovner [16] have demonstrated that there exists some slightly more complex elliptical distributions with core radius which can avoid the difficulties related to the mass distribution. But their results are recent and have not been fully tested yet for lens modeling.

2.1 MS2137–23: an optimal case for lens modeling

The arc systems in this cluster were initially detected by Fort et al. [17]. The first radial arc candidate was identified, about 5" from the center of the central galaxy, with very blue colors compared to the envelope of the galaxy, as well as a long tangential arc, 15" from the center, and several arclets located around the central giant galaxy. The model of this complex arc system (at least two independent systems, one corresponding to each large arc) was proposed by Mellier, Fort and Kneib [18]. They used a standard pseudo-isothermal elliptical potential (PIEP) with a finite core radius for the main deflector, as required by the existence of a radial arc. The other underlying hypothesis of this model is that *the light of the cD extended envelope traces the total mass* (including the dark matter). The other parameters of the lens were then fixed by the position and the elongation of the multiple images of the large arc as well as those of the radial arc. The results of the best modeling show that the core radius in this cluster must be very small ($r_c \simeq 40$ *kpc*) and the velocity dispersion of the order of 1000 km/s, depending mainly on the unknown redshift of the source. One of the main success of this procedure was its predictive power, in the sense that the 2 counter-images of the tangential arc and that of the radial arc were predicted, then found in the CCD images, and used to carefully adjust the lens parameters in a second iteration. The major astrophysical consequence is the peaked dark matter distribution, with a core radius significantly smaller than the one typically found from the X-ray analysis of the hot gas distribution in clusters. But more complicated matter distribution may occur in more complex clusters, such as A370, described below.

2.2 Abell 370: a new model from high resolution images

Many attempts to model the giant arc in A370 have been proposed by different groups since its first observations in 1986 (see [10] for a complete review of the models in this cluster). In this paper, we shall insist on the last one developped by Kneib et al. [19] as it gives some quantitative results on the potential and dark matter distributions. The model was derived from ultra-deep CCD images of the cluster obtained at CFHT in exceptional seeing conditions (0.5"). The structures observed within the giant arc reveal two significant breaks which favors the idea of a typical "cusp arc" with the merging of 3 components. Moreover the detection and the identification of a pair of faint objects with triangular shape in between the two dominant giant elliptical galaxies was considered as an evidence for a double potential cluster and used to probe the critical line in the central region of the cluster. Again the

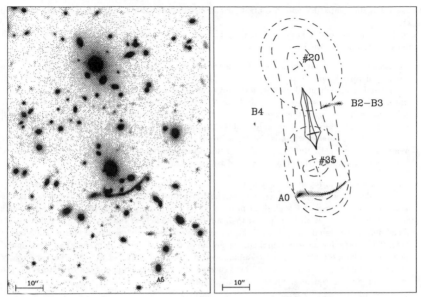

Figure 2: *(left)* : Deep CCD image of A370 in the I band, from CFHT, showing the full frame where arcs and arclets were detected and used for the modeling. *(right)* : Image reconstruction of the giant arc A0 and the B2-B3 pair with the predicted counter image B4.

assumption that the dark matter follows the light distribution of the extended envelopes of the two dominating galaxies of the cluster was introduced in order to reduce the number of free parameters of the lens. This assumption was justified a-posteriori by a convincing image reconstruction of the giant arc, the redshift prediction of the merging pair at $z = 0.865 \pm 0.01$, and maximum mass limits on the galaxies located near the giant arc (Figure 2). Moreover, Abell 370 is a double cluster, with two sub-components centered on the two main galaxies, each having a small core radius of the order of 100 kpc. This last property was also confirmed recently by the ROSAT HRI map of the cluster, which displays two peaks located exactly on the two giant galaxies (Böhringer et al., in preparation) !

2.3 Conclusions: dark matter and cluster-lenses

Up to now, there are only a few cluster-lenses for which a detailed model of a giant arc have been proposed, and all are cD and rich clusters dominated by one or two giant galaxies: in addition to the two previous cases, there are some preliminary results from the modeling on the clusters Cl2236–04 [20] and A2218 (in preparation). It seems that in all cases, the core radius of the dark matter distribution is quite small (30 to 100 kpc) and that the ellipticity and the orientation of the potential follows that of the dominant galaxy. The main problem in the interpretation of this result is that the determination of the potential concerns only the very central part of the cluster. It is presently difficult to separate the effects of the large scale mass distribution of the cluster from the influence of the central galaxy. Even if the dark matter associated with the central cD can be supposed baryonic and peaked, it is more speculative in the case of the cluster dark matter itself. The problem of the dark matter distribution is more complex in the case of rich clusters for which there is a high central concentration of galaxies, without the formation of a dominant one. In particular, in the clusters Cl2244–02 and Cl0024+17, a reanalysis of the lens configuration is expected with high resolution images. Preliminary results in the last case are again compatible with a central peaked distribution with a core radius smaller than 100 kpc [21].

The determination of the large scale mass profile in clusters will come from the analysis of both the intermediate and the weak distorsion regime:

- the arclet regime is intermediate between the arc and weak distorsion regimes. Objects are slightly distorted, with axis ratio ranging typically form 2 to 5. Even with ultra-deep images, their number in individual clusters does not exceed a few tens, and statistical analysis is quite uncertain. Anyway, some clusters such as A1689 and Cl1409 [22] have been investigated by different authors. Again they support the idea of peaked distributions of matter. Hammer [23] pointed out that the statistical analysis of the thinness of the arcs could give a similar conclusion. The velocity dispersion which is the other important parameter of a lens was also explored by Wu and Hammer [24]. But Wu [25] showed that the measurement of a velocity dispersion profile would not disentangle the different mass distributions used in lens modeling.

- the weak distorsion regime: although theoretically investigated since two to three years [5, 26], its first observational detection is quite recent ([27], Kaiser, this conference). It consists in the statistical detection of the weak shear pattern, at level of a few percents, for the faintest objects in the field. Bonnet et al. [27] applied their method in the field of the rich cluster Cl0024+1654. They detected a signal up to 1.5 h_{100}^{-1} Mpc from the center, implying a total cluster mass larger than $2 \ 10^{15} \ M_\odot$ for an isothermal sphere profile, a value 3 times larger than the virial mass! Similar results were also found by Falhman et al. [28] and Smail et al. [29], but at slightly smaller distance. A similar study is now expected at a distance large enough to distinguish the effects due to different mass profiles ($> 3h_{100}^{-1}$ Mpc).

It has been demonstrated now that gravitational lensing in clusters of galaxies is an efficient tool to probe the different mass scales. The central mass-to-light ratio in clusters determined this way is quite similar to the value found with the other standard methods: virial mass, X-ray mass ... but gravitational lensing offers more information concerning the mass distribution and in particular the estimation of the core radius. Moreover, the fine analysis of the morphology of giant arcs and their spatial structures are interpreted in terms of "mini-lenses" and local lensing effects, with masses ranging from 10^6 to $10^{11} \ M_\odot$ and typical size of 10 kpc. The importance of high quality data has been stressed, in particular the high resolution imaging and the deep photometry. In that sense, more constraints are strongly expected from HST images !

In conclusion, the future improvements of the modeling procedures and the mass distribution determination in clusters will come from the addition of optical data from the HST (identification of multiple images, distorted arclets, etc ...), with ROSAT X-ray images (constraints on the shape of the potential or the mass distribution in the clusters), and from wide field imaging in excellent seeing conditions (detection of the weak shear effect at a level where it will be possible to distinguish between the mass profiles at large distance).

3   Redshift survey of arcs and arclets

Two complementary approaches of the properties of the sources of the arcs are considered in this section. The first one corresponds to the redshift survey of the brightest and largest arcs, the second is a photometric survey and a statistical analysis of the arclets. Both surveys must be compared to other ones followed in different conditions: blank field redshift surveys or deep number counts in selected areas. The main output will concern galaxy evolution (in number density or in luminosity) and the age of galaxy formation.

3.1 Spectroscopic survey of giant arcs

The redshift determination of arcs and arclets has always been considered as a difficult observational task, mainly because of the low surface brightness of such objects. But it is of first importance for many reasons. It is obviously the best confirmation of the gravitational lens effect for a given structure which could be mistaken with some blue disk galaxy belonging to the cluster and seen edge-on! Moreover, arcs redshifts are necessary to infer the total mass of the lens because it fixes the geometrical scales of the lens and the global scaling factor; finally, as there is now an increasing number of spectra available for these arcs, they form a sample of very distant galaxies ($z > 0.7$) with some specific selection biases, useful for their cosmological implications. The use of the gravitational magnification (from 3 to 20 ...) is very efficient to observe distant galaxies, and clusters of galaxies are now extensively used as "gravitational telescopes". The main questions adressed by the study of distant galaxies are related to their redshift distribution, and their spectrophotometric history (galaxy formation and history of star formation). Indeed, since the discovery of the numerous faint and blue population of galaxies, the discussions about the redshift distribution of these objects have been quite extensive (see [31] for a review): does it correspond to a population of intrinsically faint and nearby galaxies for which the local counterparts still have to be searched, or is it a population of more distant objects? In that case, what is the history able to produce such an excess number in the faint end of the magnitude distribution (number density evolution with an increase of the merging rate with redshift, or luminosity evolution with a higher rate of star formation in the past). The recent redshift surveys of field galaxies [30, 31, 32, 33, 34, 35], seem to exclude the hypothesis of a nearby population of dwarf galaxies, as well as the idea that only luminosity evolution occured in the past: up to $B \sim 24.5$ or $I \sim 22.5$ there is no excess of galaxies at low redshift, neither a large number of high redshift galaxies. On the contrary, most of the data are consistent with the fact that the number density of galaxies decreased significantly between $z = 0.5$ and now. The redshift-magnitude relation (Hubble diagramme) predicted by different cosmological models of galaxy evolution shows that the behaviour is different enough to rule out some of them [31], at magnitudes fainter than $B = 25$.

In this context we can consider the sources of the giant luminous arcs as an interesting sample of distant field galaxies for which a spectrophotometric analysis is available. But we know *a priori* that the sample is limited in surface brightness ($\mu_B < 24.5$ to 25 mag $arcsec^{-2}$) and intrinsically biased towards galaxies at large redshift because they are lensed by clusters at intermediate redshift. Moreover, there exists an intrinsic difficulty to measure a redshift between $1 < z < 2.2$, because in "normal" (non-active) galaxies, there is no strong spectral feature expected in the UV rest-frame, which appears in the optical band for such redshifts. Fortunately, it has been possible to obtain a redshift measurement in some cases, and the results are summarised in Table 1. This is a compilation of existing results, and only a few of them are still unpublished. A more detailed analysis of the spectrophotometric properties of the galaxies will be published elsewhere (Soucail and Pelló, in preparation).

A short analysis of the sample shows that most of the source galaxies are not in a violent stage of their evolution, such as a burst of star formation. The equivalent widths of the [OII]λ 3727 emission line are typical of nearby spiral galaxies and in most cases there is no sign of nuclear activity. To confirm this result, we hope to derive more detailed morphological informations (HII regions, luminosity profiles, rotation curves ...) from several techniques: either with high resolution images of arcs (HST) and image reconstruction [36], or high resolution spectroscopy of arcs with emission lines, in order to study the spatial variations of the lines, both in position and intensity [37, 38]. In addition to optical observations, Smail et al. [39] began a near IR K-band survey of this sample and detected 7 of these arcs. The optical-to-infrared colors are compatible with the color distributions found in deep field surveys, and there is some evidence for an enhanced star formation in these sources. The authors seem to favour a continuous star formation scenario, with a peak at a redshift of about 1, instead of a single burst.

Table 1: Summary of the results from the spectroscopic redshift survey of giant arcs. In addition to the redshift of the arcs and their corresponding lens, global photometric properties are given, as well as an estimate of the magnification factor γ, and the intrinsic magnitudes of the sources corrected from it. Note also that the R magnitudes given with a * are Gunn-r magnitudes.

Cluster	z_{cl}	z_S	B	R	B–R	μ_B	γ	B_{int}	R_{int}
A370 (A0)	0.374	0.725	21.1	19.4	1.7	24.6	12	23.8	22.1
A370 (A5)	0.374	1.305 ?	22.7	22.3	0.4	25.4	6	24.7	24.2
Cl2244–02	0.336	2.237	21.2	20.4	0.8	25.3	20	24.5	23.7
A2390	0.231	0.913	21.9	20.0	1.9	25.3	12	24.6	22.7
A2218 (# 359)	0.176	0.702	24.3	21.4*	2.9	25.0	4	25.8	22.9
A2218 (# 289)	0.176	1.034	22.5	21.7*	0.8	24.2	5	24.2	23.4
A963 N	0.206	0.771	23.6	23.1	0.5	25.5	4	25.1	24.6
Cl0024+1654	0.391	—	23.0	22.3	0.7	25	4	24.5	23.8
S506 (Cl0500-24)	0.321	—	21.0	19.8	1.2	—	8	23.2	22.0
A2163 (A1)	0.203	0.742	24.2	21.8	2.4	—	3	25.4	23.0
A2163 (A2)	0.203	0.728	23.1	21.2	1.9	—	3	24.3	22.4
S295	0.303	0.931	22.4	21.5	1.0	—			
MS2137–23 (Tangential arc)	0.315	—	22.0	21.5	—	—			
MS2137–23 (Radial arc)	0.315	—	23.3	—	—	—			

3.2 Photometric survey up to $B_J = 27$ in Abell 370

In the case of arclets, which are generally too faint to be observed spectroscopically, we can look at their morphological and photometric properties to probe faint objects redshift distribution. This can be applied only in some well selected clusters in which their number is large enough for statistics. Such an analysis has been recently proposed by Kneib et al. [40] from their study of ultra-deep B, R and I images of Abell 370 and of a reference blank field. With a photometric sample complete up to $B = 26.5$ and some well defined selection criteria, they obtained a sample of 34 arclet candidates for which two estimates of the redshift were proposed. The first one is a rather classic one derived by comparing the observed colors with those predicted by spectrophotometric evolution models. The second one is called a "lensing redshift": it is valid only for clusters in which an accurate model of the matter distribution is previously obtained from the analysis of large arcs and multiple images. In that case, the "lensing" or "ellipticity redshift" of a given arclet corresponds roughly to the source redshift for which the intrinsic ellipticity is the most probable. From a detailed discussion of the error sources and a comparison between the two redshift estimates, a sample of 19 arclets or image pairs was extracted. After correction for the magnification factor, the magnitude of the sources lie in the range $25 < B < 27$ and they correspond to the deepest sample of field galaxies for which a tentative redshift was obtained.

The preliminary results of this analysis show that the redshift distribution of the faint galaxies is still centered at $z < 1$ for $25 < B < 27$, and that less than 40 % are at larger distance. Moreover as shown of Figure 3, there is no sign of "discontinuity" between the "true" redshift distribution at $B < 25$, measured spectroscopically, and this one. This is in contradiction with some suggestions that there could appear a change in the population of galaxies at faint magnitudes, due to a numerous population of very distant objects. On the contrary, the diagramme is compatible with "passive evolution" of the galaxies $z \simeq 1$. In that case, the decrease of the number density of galaxies at low redshift could be due to some processes. Deep HST images of blank fields would confirm this hypothesis, as up to now only marginal signs of interaction have been observed [33]. This discussion is still preliminary, and the sample used in Kneib et al. [40] is far from complete, the detection and

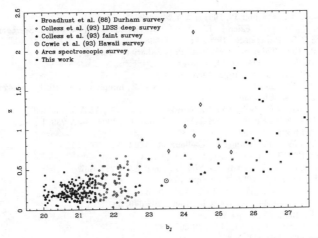

Figure 3: Redshift versus b_J magnitude for different samples of faint objects. Except this work on the arclets, all the data come from spectroscopic surveys.

identification of arclets in crowded fields beeing a difficult task. It is also strongly dependent on the image seeing, in particular when determining the shape parameters of the arclets. Moreover, the "lensing redshift" depends on the model of the potential, and its extension rather far from the center. In the case of Abell 370, we presently know, from the X-ray map analysis, that there are several subclumps in the cluster, which could distort the arclet distribution! Last but not least, the arclet sample is by definition limited to galaxies at $z \geq 0.5$ and cannot be compared directly to number counts of redshift distributions in deep fields, integrated all along the line-of-sight. Note that other approaches on the estimate of the mean redshift of arclets were developed from the analysis of the weak shear [41, 27], and also lead to the conclusion that the mean redshift can be hardly larger than 1 for sources as faint as $B \sim 27$. Anyway the method presented in Kneib et al. [40] will have to be applied on several other cases of well studied cluster-lenses to reinforce the statistics of the arclet sample and to average the individual effects of the clusters. The extension towards the near IR of the photometric analysis will constrain more securely the photometric redshifts, the study of the spectral content of the source galaxies, their age and their star formation history (Pelló et al. in preparation).

4 Conclusion

In conclusion, we are convinced and hope to have convinced the reader that gravitational optics is a fantastic tool for cosmologists!

References

[1] Soucail G., Fort B., Mellier Y., Picat J.P., 1987, A&A 172, L14

[2] Lynds R., Petrosian V., 1986, BAAS 18, 1014

[3] Tyson J.A., 1988, AJ 96, 1

[4] Blandford R.D., Saust A.B., Brainerd T.G., Villumsen J.V., 1991, MNRAS 251, 600

[5] Miralda-Escudé J., 1991, ApJ 370, 1

352

[6] Bartelmann M., Schneider P., 1991, A&A 248, 349
[7] Schneider P., Ehlers J., Falco E. E., 1992, in Gravitational Lenses. Berlin. Springer Verlag
[8] Blandford R.D., Narayan R., 1986, ApJ 310, 568
[9] Kneib J.P., 1993, Thèse de l'Université Paul Sabatier, Toulouse, France
[10] Fort B., Mellier Y., 1994, A&AR in press
[11] Luppino G.A., Gioia I.M., 1992, A&A 265, L9
[12] Le Fèvre O., Hammer F., Angonin M.C., Gioia I.M., Luppino G.A., 1994, ApJ 422, L5
[13] Edge et al., 1994, A&A submitted
[14] Pierre M., Soucail G., Böhringer H., Sauvageot J.L., 1994, A&A submitted
[15] Bonnet H., Fort B., Kneib J.P., Mellier Y., Soucail G., 1994, A&A 280, L5
[16] Kassiola A., Kovner I., 1993, ApJ 417, 450
[17] Fort B., Le Fèvre O., Hammer F., Cailloux M., 1992, ApJ 399, L125
[18] Mellier Y., Fort B., Kneib J.P., 1993, ApJ 407, 33
[19] Kneib J.P., Mellier Y., Fort B., Mathez G., 1993, A&A 273, 367
[20] Kneib J.P.,Melnick J., 1994, A&A submitted
[21] Kassiola A., Kovner I., Fort B., 1992, ApJ 400, 41
[22] Tyson J. A., Valdes F., and Wenk R., 1990, ApJ 349, 381
[23] Hammer F., 1991, A&A ApJ 383, 66
[24] Wu X.-P., Hammer F., 1993, MNRAS 262, 187
[25] Wu X.-P., 1993, ApJ 411, 513
[26] Kaiser N., Squires G., 1993, ApJ 404, 441
[27] Bonnet H., Mellier Y., Fort B., 1994, ApJ 427, L83
[28] Fahlmann G.G., Kaiser N., Squires G., Woods, D., 1994, preprint
[29] Smail I., Ellis R.,Fitchett M., Edge A.C., 1994b, in press
[30] Colless M.M., Ellis R.S., Taylor K., Hook R.N., 1990, MNRAS 244, 408
[31] Colless M.M., Ellis R.S., Broadhurst T.J., Taylor K., Peterson B.A., 1993, MNRAS 261, 19
[32] Cowie L.L., Songaila A., Hu E.M., 1991, Nature 354, 460
[33] Lilly S.J., Cowie L.L., Gardner J.P., 1991, ApJ 369, 79
[34] Lilly S.J., 1993, ApJ, 411, 501
[35] Tresse L., Hammer F., Le Fèvre O., Proust D., 1993, A&A, 277, 53
[36] Wallington S., Narayan R., Kochanek C.S., 1994, ApJ 426, 60
[37] Pello R., Le Borgne J.F., Soucail G., Mellier Y., Sanahuja B., 1991, ApJ 366, 405
[38] Soucail G., Fort B., 1991, A&A 243, 23
[39] Smail I., Ellis R., Aragón-Salamanca A., Soucail G., Mellier Y., Giraud E., 1993, MNRAS, 263, 628
[40] Kneib J.P., Mathez G., Fort B., Mellier Y., Soucail G., Longaretti P.Y., 1994, A&A in press
[41] Smail I., Ellis R.,Fitchett M., 1994a, in press

APPLICATIONS OF GRAVITATIONALLY LENSED LONG ARCS
IN CLUSTERS OF GALAXIES

Jordi Miralda-Escudé

Institute for Advanced Study, Olden Lane, Princeton NJ 08540

email: jordi@guinness.ias.edu

ABSTRACT

A brief summary of the theory of gravitational lensing needed to analyze the observations in clusters of galaxies is given. We outline some of the main results from present observations of gravitational lensing on the structure of clusters of galaxies, concerning the total mass, mass profiles, substructure, and cD galaxies.

Subject headings: gravitational lenses - galaxies: clustering - X-rays

1. INTRODUCTION

Astronomers are interested in learning about several components that are present in a galaxy cluster, such as the galaxies, the hot gas, and the dark matter. The galaxies and the hot gas can be studied from their optical and X-ray emission. However, in order to achieve a full understanding of their dynamical state, it is also necessary to know about the distribution of the total mass, which determines the gravitational potential.

Up to now, galaxy clusters have been studied by attempting to infer the mass distribution from observations of the galaxies and the hot gas alone. This has generally been based on several assumptions and simplifications: requiring the cluster to be in a stationary equilibrium state, absence of substructure, spherical symmetry, models for the mass radial profile, homogeneity of the hot gas, absence of any motions or pressure on the gas other than thermal, and maxwellian equilibrium.

Gravitational lensing in clusters of galaxies allows us to observe the mass distribution directly for the first time. Most of this mass is dark matter, and therefore it is not observed by other means. Consequently, it should now be of interest to combine any constraints obtained from gravitational lensing on the mass distribution, with the observations of galaxies and the intracluster medium, and see what we can learn on their physical and dynamical state. At the same time, the determination of cluster mass profiles will provide a test for cosmological theories of cluster formation.

2. BASIC THEORY OF GRAVITATIONAL LENSING

Gravitational lensing can be described as a mapping of the surface brightness of any source of radiation from the source plane to the image plane (see Schneider, Ehlers, & Falco 1992 for a detailed description). The source plane, with angular coordinates $\vec{\theta}_s$, contains the source as would be observed in the absence of lensing. The image plane, with angular coordinates $\vec{\theta}_i$, contains the lensed images that are observed. The lens equation gives this mapping:

$$\vec{\theta}_i = \vec{\theta}_s + \vec{\alpha}(\vec{\theta}_i) \ . \tag{1}$$

In the case of the single screen approximation (where it is assumed that most of the lensing mass is at the same distance from the observer, D_l), the angle $\vec{\alpha}$ is equal to the physcial deflection angle of the light rays as they pass by the lens, times the ratio D_{ls}/D_s, of the distance from the lens to the source and the distance from the observer to the source. It is given by:

$$\vec{\alpha} = \nabla\phi \ ; \qquad \nabla^2\phi = 2\frac{\Sigma(\vec{\theta}_i)}{\Sigma_{crit}} \equiv 2\kappa \ ; \qquad \Sigma_{crit} = \frac{c^2}{4\pi G}\frac{D_s}{D_l D_{ls}} \ . \tag{2}$$

Here, ϕ is the two-dimensional gravitational potential, and Σ is the surface density. As seen from these equations, the action of gravitational lensing depends only on the projected surface density Σ, but not on the distribution of matter along the line-of-sight.

The amplification matrix gives the transformation from the source plane to the image plane of a small element of area: $A^{-1} = (\partial\vec{\theta}_s/\partial\vec{\theta}_i) = 1 - (\partial\vec{\alpha}/\partial\vec{\theta}_i)$. Since $\vec{\alpha} = \nabla\phi$, the matrix A is symmetric and can be diagonalized. From equation (2), the average of the two eigenvalues of A^{-1} is $1 - \kappa \equiv 1 - \Sigma/\Sigma_{crit}$. Thus, the two eigenvalues can be written as $1-\kappa-\gamma$, and $1-\kappa+\gamma$, where γ is called the shear. The magnification in the area (and flux) of a source is $|A| = (1-\kappa-\gamma)^{-1}(1-\kappa+\gamma)^{-1}$, and the axis ratio of the image of a circular source is $q = (1-\kappa-\gamma)(1-\kappa+\gamma)^{-1}$.

When the surface densities are small, so that $\kappa \ll 1$, $\gamma \ll 1$, then we are in the regime of "weak lensing". Each source produces only one image, which experiences only a small distortion of its shape. In this limit, the amplification is $A = 1 + 2\kappa$, while the ellipticity given to a source is 2γ. Weak lensing has been detected in clusters of galaxies, using optical galaxies as sources (Tyson, Valdes & Wenk 1990; see also the contributions by Kaiser, Smail and Soucail in these proceedings). Since the original shape of the background galaxies is unknown, one can only measure the average shear over a certain area by averaging the ellipticities of several galaxies, and assuming that the orientations of the major axes of the sources are random and uncorrelated. Once the shear is obtained at several points, the surface density of the cluster can be recovered with an accuracy and resolution that is ultimately limited by the number of background sources and their intrinsic ellipticities (Tyson et al. 1990; Kochanek 1990; Miralda 1991; Kaiser & Squires 1993).

When one of the two eigenvalues of the matrix A^{-1} is equal to zero (i.e., $\kappa + \gamma = 1$ or $\kappa - \gamma = 1$), two new images appear around a "critical line". Since the magnification is very large along the principal axis of the vanishing eigenvalue, the images appear very elongated. Such strongly distorted images were discovered by Soucail et al. (1987, 1988) and Lynds & Petrosian (1989), and by now they have been seen in ~ 30 clusters (Fort 1992). They were originally called "arcs" because they are often curved, owing to the change of the orientation of the principal axis of the shear along the image (it has later been shown, however, that this curvature can be very small in many cases). When κ, $\gamma \sim 1$, "arclets" are generally produced (Fort et al. 1988).

3. WHAT HAVE WE LEARNED

FROM GRAVITATIONAL LENSING IN CLUSTERS?

3.1 Dark matter and core radii

First of all, gravitational lensing has given us the best evidence we have for the presence of dark matter. The first observations of the long arcs showed that the mass within $\sim 100h^{-1}$ kpc is indeed much larger than what can be accounted for from visible stars and gas, by a factor of about 10. In a spherical cluster, the condition $\kappa + \gamma = 1$ to form a long arc is equivalent to $\bar{\Sigma} = \Sigma_{crit}$, where $\bar{\Sigma}$ is the average surface density within the radius of the arc. This condition remains approximately correct for more complicated potentials.

This large amount of dark matter in the center implies that any flat core of the mass distribution should be smaller than the radius of the observed arcs (see Grossman & Narayan 1988). The basic reasons are that, if the surface density varied only slowly with radius near the arcs, then a very small decrease of the critical surface density (corresponding to a small increase in the redshift of the source) would allow for arcs to appear at much larger radii; moreover, the large masses that would be implied at large radius would be inconsistent with other dynamical measurements. At the same time, a lens with a very shallow profile would tend to produce arcs with very low curvature (Miralda 1993).

The narrow widths of the arcs have also been used as an argument against large cores; in particular, Hammer (1991) has claimed that the observed widths also imply a very steep profile. Here, we notice that such conclusions are very sensitive to the assumed properties of the background galaxies being lensed, and the way that the arc widths are measured. For example, a barred spiral galaxy will typically produce very thin arcs, because the arc width will be determined mostly by the minor axis of the source. The sources will typically be clumpy (they probably are star-forming galaxies and are seen in their rest-frame ultraviolet); if only the bright, small clumps are observed, this will also cause the arcs to appear thinner.

Elliptical galaxies with bright cusps in the center may also produce apparently thin arcs if their outer envelopes are below the limiting observable surface brightness.

3.2 Do all the clusters have similarly concentrated mass profiles?

A question which has proved particularly hard to answer is the following: do all clusters of galaxies have similar density profiles, and is the small core radius of the lensing clusters a general feature, or are the lensing clusters only a special class, having a much more centrally concentrated mass than the majority of clusters? This can be addressed by analyzing the frequency of highly distorted arcs in well-defined samples of clusters. Two such samples have been published so far, an optically selected one by Smail et al. (1991), and an X-ray selected one by Le Fèvre et al. (1994), and they seem to indicate that the fraction of clusters which are able to lens with large critical radii, typical of the observed arcs, is not very small. There are, however, several difficulties of interpretation: the probability that a cluster with a fixed mass distribution will lens a background source and produce an observable arc is rather uncertain, because it depends on the number counts of faint galaxies, their angular sizes, and their redshift distribution. Thus, if long arcs are not observed in some massive clusters, this may only be due to the absence of any background source sufficiently close to the caustics of the cluster and sufficiently extended to produce a long arc.

From a theoretical point of view, if clusters were formed via hierarchical gravitational collapse, and baryon dissipation has not increased the mass significantly within the radius of the observed arcs, one would expect that all relaxed clusters should have similar density profiles (Efstathiou et al. 1988; Navarro, Frenk & White 1994). However, there should be different degrees of relaxation, so that relaxed clusters may have most of their mass concentrated in one central clump, and would therefore be better able to lens, while clusters with several merging units will have several massive clumps, each one of them having a smaller critical radius, and a lower probability of producing long arcs. Occasionally, however, various clumps may appear superposed in projection, and this should enhance the lensing effects.

In fact, substructure on small scales is indicated by the morphology of the arcs in several clusters (e.g., Pelló et al. 1991, 1992; Kassiola, Kovner, & Blandford 1992; Miralda 1993).

3.3 Correlation of the Mass and Light Distribution

Gravitational lensing also allows us to test the correlation between mass and light substructure. One would generally expect that any merging clump of mass in a cluster would be associated with either a large elliptical at the center of the clump, or a group of galaxies which had collapsed before merging into the cluster. This suggests a general approach to be taken in modeling arcs lensed by clusters of galaxies: to assume that the cluster is made of mass clumps associated with the brightest cluster galaxies. Moreover, such galaxies are often cD galaxies, with stellar envelopes extending to radii similar to the observed arcs, and in these cases the ellipticity of the stellar envelope gives us the ellipticity of the gravitational potential. This method was suggested by Mellier et al. (1993) and Kneib et al. (1993), and applied to the cases of A370 and MS2137 very successfully. There may be, however, some exceptions: the arcs in A2390 require the presence of two mass clumps, but only one of them can be associated with a bright cluster galaxy, while there is no obvious concentration of galaxies that could be identified with the second clump (Pelló et al. 1991). Clearly, the long arcs, as well as weak lensing (see Soucail, these proceedings) can be a good tool to find out if there are any dark clumps of mass in clusters of galaxies.

3.4 cD Galaxies

Since the long arcs are often seen embedded in the stellar halos of cD galaxies at the center of the lensing potentials, this implies that the velocity dispersion of the stellar halos must rise to a high value consistent with the observed splitting angles. The velocity dispersions required are typically $\sim 1000\,\mathrm{km\,s^{-1}}$, much higher than the observed dispersions in the center of cD galaxies. Therefore, one can predict that velocity dispersions of cD galaxies (at least in the lensing clusters) will be observed to rise very fast at radii of $\sim 50h^{-1}\,kpc$, contrary to what is observed in other galaxies, where velocity curves are generally flat. This also implies that the inner profiles of clusters *must* be flatter than isothermal, otherwise even the central velocity dispersions of cD galaxies would need to be similar to that of the whole cluster. This flattening of the density profile towards the center has been confirmed from the observation of a "radial arc" in MS2137 (Fort et al. 1992; Mellier et al. 1993), which is a gravitationally lensed image very close to the center of the potential, and radially elongated. The position of this radial arc gives a powerful constraint on the form of the density profile in the inner $50h^{-1}$ kpc (Miralda 1994). This allows one to predict the velocity dispersion profile of the cD galaxy, and is consistent with a velocity dispersion in the range $300 - 400\,\mathrm{km\,s^{-1}}$ at the center, but which should rise to $700\,\mathrm{km\,s^{-1}}$ at a radius of only $30h^{-1}$ kpc (Fig. 9 in Miralda 1994).

This fast rise of the velocity dispersion of a cD galaxy may lead to a problem for their formation through mergers: how is it possible to maintain a population of cold stars within such a small region of the cluster center? Simulations of the formation of cD galaxies are usually done assuming that galaxies merge by dynamical friction within a cluster profile with a large core (e.g., Richstone 1990). New N-body simulations are needed to see if a cold cD galaxy can be formed within a small cluster core, or if one would always produce cluster stellar halos with much lower surface brightness and much higher central velocity dispersions.

3.5 Lensing masses and X-ray masses

Gravitational lensing measurements of the masses of clusters of galaxies can be compared with the values obtained from other methods. The long arcs give us the projected mass within the radius where the arcs are observed, usually $\sim 50h^{-1}$ kpc. Miralda & Babul (1994a,b) have compared these masses with the ones obtained from X-ray observations, assuming the gas is in hydrostatic equilibrium at the observed X-ray temperature, in the clusters A2218, A1689 and A2163. The mass obtained from lensing is at least a factor of ~ 2 larger than that obtained from the X-ray analysis in A2218 and A1689, while in A2163 the lensing mass is the same as the maximum mass consistent with the X-ray analysis (there is some uncertainty in the comparison since the detailed mass profile is not known). The disagreement arises from the fact that the gas distribution has a core radius of $\sim 100h^{-1}$ kpc, while the mass is more concentrated. This could be understood if the gas was hotter than the dark matter in the center, but the observed X-ray temperatures suggest it is not. There are two classes of explanations for this difference: the first is to assume that the lensing clusters are all highly elongated along the line of sight, either due to a prolate shape of the central clump or to the superposition of several clumps. In this case, the masses derived from X-ray observations could be basically correct, and most X-ray selected clusters should not show this difference, since only a small fraction of clusters can be pointing towards us. One should notice, however, that strong lensing will always be seen more easily in clusters where the surface density is enhanced by projection.

The second class of explanations is to say that the masses from the X-ray analysis are underestimated. This could be due to several things, all of which invalidate the assumption of hydrostatic equilibrium at the observed X-ray temperature: hydrodynamic motions of the gas (with the corresponding substructure in the gas distribution), a multiphase medium with an effective temperature higher than the observed one in the X-ray spectrum (a hot phase, with lower density, would emit less X-rays than cooler phases), rotation of the gas, magnetic pressure,... At some level, both types of effects must be present. The question is, which one is more important? In retrospect, it should not be too surprising that the lensing and X-ray masses are different by a factor of 2. In fact, it is reassuring that all the effects one can think of tend to make the lensing mass larger than the X-ray mass.

Many of the reasons why the X-ray masses could be underestimated might be even more important at large radius. If that was true, it would have profound implications for cosmology: clusters would be more massive than what we thought, and the ratio of gas mass to total mass in clusters could come to much better agreement with nucleosynthesis and a dark matter density corresponding to a flat universe (see White et al. 1993). Observations of weak lensing in X-ray selected samples of clusters are needed to measure lensing masses at large radius. The very preliminary present detections of weak lensing (see Kaiser, Smail, Soucail, these proceedings) seem to be reminiscent of the conclusions from the discovery of the long arcs: masses are large.

REFERENCES

Efstathiou, G. P., Frenk, C. S., White, S. D. M., & Davis, M. 1988, MNRAS, 235, 715

Fort, B. 1992, in *Gravitational Lenses*, ed. R. Kayser, T. Schramm & L. Nieser (Springer-Verlag), p. 267

Fort, B., Le Fèvre, O., Hammer, F. & Cailloux, M. 1992, ApJ, 399, L125

Fort, B., Prieur, J. L., Mathez, G., Mellier, Y., & Soucail, G. 1988, A&A, 200, L17

Grossman, S. A. & Narayan, R. 1988, ApJ, 324, L37

Hammer, F. 1991, ApJ, 383, 66

Kaiser, N. & Squires, G. 1993, ApJ, 404, 441

Kassiola, A., Kovner, I., & Blandford, R. D. 1992, ApJ, 396, 10

Kneib, J. P., Mellier, Y., Fort, B. & Mathez, G. 1993, A&A, 273, 367

Kochanek, C. S. 1990, MNRAS, 247, 135

Le Fèvre, O., Hammer, F., Angonin, M. C., Gioia, I. M., & Luppino, G. A. 1994, to be published in ApJLet

Lynds, R., & Petrosian, V. 1989, ApJ, 336, 1

Mellier, Y., Fort, B. & Kneib, J. P. 1993, ApJ, 407, 33

Miralda-E., J. 1991, ApJ, 370, 1

Miralda-E., J. 1993, ApJ, 403, 497

Miralda-E., J. 1994, to be published in ApJ

Miralda-E., J., & Babul, A. 1994a, in *Cosmological Aspects of Clusters of Galaxies*, ed. W. Seitter (Kluwer), in press

Miralda-E., J., & Babul, A. 1994b, submitted to ApJ

Navarro, J. N., Frenk, C. S., & White, S. D. M. 1994, submitted to MNRAS

Pelló, R., Le Borgne, J. F., Sanahuja, B., Mathez, G. & Fort, B. 1992, A&A, 266, 6

Pelló, R., Le Borgne, J. F., Soucail, G., Mellier, Y., & Sanahuja, B. 1991, ApJ, 366, 405

Richstone. D. 1990, in *Clusters of Galaxies*, ed. W. R. Oegerle, M. J. Fitchett, & L. Danly, Cambrigde: Cambridge Univ. Press, p. 231

Schneider, P., Ehlers, J. & Falco, E. E. 1992, *Gravitational Lenses* (Berlin: Springer-Verlag)

Smail, I., Ellis, R. S., Fitchett, M. J., Norgaard-Nielsen, H. U., Hansen, L., & Jorgensen, H. E. 1991, MNRAS, 252, 19

Soucail, G., Fort, B., Mellier, Y., & Picat, J. P. 1987, A&A, 172, L14

Soucail, G., Mellier, Y., Fort, B., Mathez, G., & Cailloux, M. 1988, A&A, 191, L19

Tyson, J. A., Valdes, F., & Wenk, R. 1990, ApJ, 349, L1

White, S. D. M., Navarro, J., Evrard, A. & Frenk, C. S. 1993, Nature, 366, 429

SIMULATIONS OF GRAVITATIONAL LENSING
BY CLUSTERS OF GALAXIES

Joachim Wambsganss[1,2], Renyue Cen[2] & Jeremiah P. Ostriker[2]

[1]Max-Planck-Institut für Astrophysik [2]Princeton University Observatory

Abstract

We present simulations of lensing by clusters of galaxies. We fill the universe densely with realistic matter distributions from large scale structure simulations. We follow a bundle of light rays with an opening angle of roughly 6 arcmin from the observer through a large number of lens planes, determining the deflection angles of the light rays in each plane due to the matter in this plane. A strongly overdense clump of matter at a redshift of $z_L = 0.72$ is by far the most important lensing structure along the light path of the realization presented here. We interpret this as a cluster of galaxies and study its lensing properties: magnification distribution, weak lensing, strong lensing (giant arcs), shear distribution. We show how high redshift galaxies would be mapped by this matter distribution.

I. Introduction

Recent observations of the effects of strong and weak lensing around rich clusters of galaxies (Tyson *et al.* 1990, Fahlmann *et al.* 1994, Smail *et al.* 1994a,b; Bonnet et al. 1994; Fort & Mellier 1994, Soucail, this volume) show the importance of gravitational lensing by clusters of galaxies. Lensing provides direct information about the total mass in the cluster and about its clumpiness at the same time, and it helps to study the population of background galaxies. Since mass determinations by lensing are sensitive only to the total mass distribution (cf. Miralda-Escude, this volume), not distinguishing the nature of the matter (baryonic or non-baryonic), it is an important means for supplementing the mass determinations of clusters via temperature of the X-ray gas in the cluster and via measuring the velocity dispersion of the galaxies. With very deep exposures by the refurbished HST or the Keck-Telescope, it is now possible to determine the fraction of lensed arcs in the sky. This may give us an idea of the number density of clusters at moderate redshifts, which in turn will put strong constraints on the cosmological models.

Simulations of lensing by clusters is usually done in two ways. One can try to model a certain observed cluster with a detailed lens model and to understand the exact observed lensing configuration. This approach can yield predictions of positions of arcs and arclets and is quite powerful in constraining the mass distributions, though it is not easy to show the uniqueness of a model. Here we attempt a second way: we use a realistic mass distribution of a cluster and its surroundings, follow the light rays as deflected by the cluster as well as by foreground and background matter, and determine the lensing properties of this mass distribution. Then we apply techniques similar to what observers do in order to get mass estimates and compare with the input mass distribution. In the linear regime different authors have studied the effects of weak lensing, e.g. Miralda-Escudé (1991) or Bartelmann & Schneider (1991). With the method outlined below we can treat weak and strong lensing at the same time, we are only limited by the dynamical range of current large scale structure simulations.

II. Method

We follow light rays in a cone of fixed angular size (about 6 arcmin) through realistic matter distributions in many lens planes, determine their deflection angles in each plane and collect them at source planes of different redshifts. We follow the light rays according to the multi-plane lens equation as described in Schneider, Ehlers & Falco (1992). The deflection angles are calculated for 500^2 rays in each plane, according to all the matter inside this plane. Subsequently we study the lensing properties of the matter in these lens planes.

The lens planes are obtained by "filling the universe densely" with matter cubes of comoving side length of $5h^{-1}$Mpc, obtained for a standard CDM, $\Omega = 1$ model with COBE normalization ($\sigma_8 = 1$). The underlying large scale structure simulations (cf. Cen *et al.* 1994) use 250^3 particles, the nominal resolution is $10h^{-1}$kpc, the real resolution is about $25h^{-1}$kpc. For lensing purposes, the matter inside each cube is projected on a two-dimensional screen. The rays are followed then through many screens, corresponding to different lens redshifts. The power from scales larger than $5h^{-1}$Mpc is folded in by a method similar to the one described in Cen *et al.* (1994): the density distribution of $(5h^{-1}\mathrm{Mpc})^3$ cubes inside a $(400h^{-1}\mathrm{Mpc})^3$ cube is used and convolved with the density distribution of the $(5h^{-1}\mathrm{Mpc})^3$ cubes.

It turns out that for most realizations the lensing pattern is dominated by one highly overdense cube or plane; usually the matter is concentrated in single or double-peaked structures, with masses of a few times 10^{13} M$_\odot$ or more, which we interpret as central region of a (rich) cluster of galaxies. A more detailed description of the method can be found in Wambsganss (1994).

III. Results

We show here results for one particular realization of the method described above, which is dominated by a single dense mass concentration. In Figure 1 contours of the surface mass density are shown for the integrated matter along the line of sight. The sidelength of the field is 343 arcsec (the scale is in 500 pixels of size 0.686"). The thick contour line marks the "average" surface mass density for a CDM, $\Omega = 1$ model, the level of the second thin line is the critical surface mass density for lensing, i.e. matter inside the second contour line is able to produce multiple images of background sources. The strongest mass concentration is clearly the dense clump in the middle of the top part. It turns out that it is a massive cluster at a redshift of $z_L = 0.72$.

The "shear field" is overlayed as short straight lines in a regular grid. The shear field is obtained from measuring the ellipticities of the images of circular background galaxies in squares of $(20 \text{ arcsec})^2$ and subsequent averaging. The relative lengths of the shear-lines reflect the relative strength of the shear at these locations, the direction of the line shows the direction of the local shear (i.e. a circular source would be deformed into an ellipse with major axis parallel to the line). We chose a source redshift of $z_S = 3$ for this figure, because the effect is most striking. It is obvious that the shear distribution is closely following the mass distribution. Note that there are regions of coherent shear as large as a few arcmin. The rms-value of the shear for the whole field is 9.7% (for $z_S = 1$ it is about 3.5%).

In Figure 2 one sees the magnification distribution for the matter field displayed in Figure 1. It is easy to see that the high magnification regions (white) correlate very well with the high density regions. That indicates that most of the lensing action is due to "convergence", rather than due to external shear. The magnification is higher than one magnitude at the positions close to the cluster. The black color in the inner part of the cluster (and few other locations) indicates that here the magnification is formally negative, i.e. that this is a region of multiple images.

In Figure 3 one sees the positions and shapes of high redshift galaxies as seen through this matter field. The galaxy density corresponds to 100,000 per square degree.

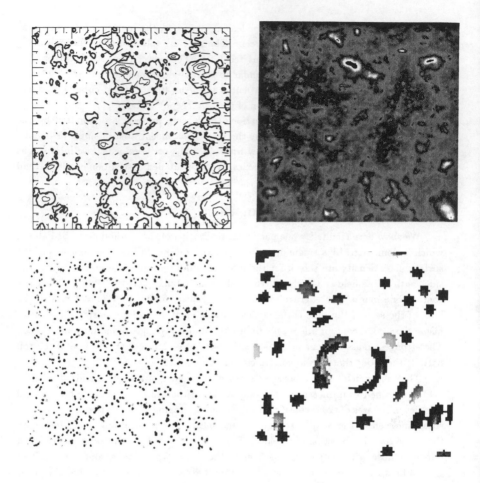

Figure 1 (top left): Contour map of the surface mass density integrated through all lens planes. The thick line indicates average density. The second thin line represents roughly the critical density for lensing. Superimposed is the shear distribution produced by the matter, i.e. the net ellipticity induced on high redshift galaxies. The length and direction of the lines show the direction and strength of the shear. The field is 343 arcsec at a side.

Figure 2 (top right): Lens-induced magnification map for the same matter distribution. Black indicates formally negative magnification, i.e. regions with multiple images.

Figure 3 (bottom left): Map of (intrinsically circular) distorted galaxies. The relative sizes indicate the relative magnifications. Note the two giant arcs in the middle of the top part, produced by the cluster seen in Figure 1.

Figure 4 (bottom right): Region around the giant arcs in Figure 3, zoomed by a factor 5. All the ellipticies are lens-induced.

Each deviation of an image from sphericity is due to lensing, for this idealized source population. The relative magnification of images is given by their relative area. Most striking in this map of distorted background galaxies are the two arcs, seen close to the location of the cluster in Figure 1 or the high magnification in Fig.2. The image region around these arcs is magnified by a factor of five and reproduced in Figure 4. From the two different gray scales it can be seen that the arc at the left actually consists of two galaxies that happen to be projected on top of each other. This would naturally produce color changes along the arc. Notice also the change in width of the right arc, although the source is circular (better: has a pixel representation of being spherical).

Assuming the two arcs form part of an "Einstein ring", we can determine the mass necessary to produce such an Einstein ring. With the lens and source redshifts of $z_L = 0.72$ and $z_S = 3$ and an opening angle of $\theta_0 \approx 10$", one obtains a mass of 5.3×10^{13} $M_\odot$. The actual mass inside the beam turns out to be 3.2×10^{13} $M_\odot$, if one determines it from the input mass distribution. Although the two numbers are quite close, they are not in perfect agreement. However, what we see is not a real Einstein ring, but it consists of two arcs originating from two different sources. A real Einstein ring would be formed by a source position in between the two, and therefore have slightly smaller radius, which would make the agreement between calculated and input mass even better.

One of the natural future application of the results obtained here is the mass reconstruction as proposed by Kaiser & Squires (1993). We can, e.g., study the quality of the reconstruction of the cluster mass distribution as a function of foreground and background matter, seeing, galaxy density or galaxy distribution. A statistical analysis of weak and strong lensing by groups and clusters of galaxies for a large number of different matter realizations can be found in Wambsganss, Cen & Ostriker (1994).

References

Bartelmann, M. & Schneider, P. 1991 *Astron. Ap.* **248**, 349.

Bernstein, G.M., Tyson, J.A., Kochanek, C.S. 1993 *A. J.* **105**, 816.

Bonnet, H., Mellier & Y. Fort, B. 1994 preprint

Cen, R., Gott III, J.R., Ostriker, J.P., & Turner, E.L. 1994 *Ap. J.* **423**, 1.

Fahlmann, G.G., Kaiser, N., Squires, G., & Woods, D. 1994, preprint

Fort, B. & Mellier, Y. 1994 preprint

Kaiser, N. & Squires, G. 1993, *Ap. J.* **404**, 441.

Miralda-Escudé, J. 1991 *Ap. J.* **380**, 1.

Schneider, P., Ehlers,J. & Falco, E.E. "Gravitational Lenses" (Springer, 1992)

Smail, I., Ellis, R.S., Fitchett, M.J. 1994 preprint

Smail, I., Ellis, R.S., Fitchett, M.J. & Edge, A.C. 1994 preprint

Tyson, J.A., Valdes, F., & Wenk, R. 1990, *Ap. J.(Letters)* **349**, L1.

Wambsganss, J. 1994 (in preparation)

Wambsganss, J., Cen, R. & Ostriker, J.P. 1994 (in preparation)

Poster papers

DETECTABILITY AND INCIDENCE OF E+A GALAXIES IN THE DISTANT CLUSTER Cl0939+47

Paola Belloni

Max-Planck-Institut für Astronomie, Königstuhl 17, D-69117 Heidelberg, Germany

Abstract

We present results of a study of E+A galaxies in the cluster Cl0939+47 (z=0.41). With a series of narrow-band (FWHM$\simeq$ 90–200 Å) and broad band (B-R-I) filters we have constructed low resolution spectra for all galaxies brigther than R=22.5 mag in a 5′ x 5′ field centered in this cluster. In particular, two of the narrow-band filters have been chosen to measure the 4000 Å break index. This index is a powerful tool for distinguishing a normal passively evolving elliptical from one with a recent episode of star formation. Three filters were centered on the H_β,H_γ and H_δ lines whose absorption features also indicates recent star formation. Template spectra were fitted to the low-resolution spectral energy distributions (SED) thus derived to determine the galaxies' Hubble class and redshift. We have computed models for the spectral evolution of an early-type galaxy that experiences a burst of star formation 1–2 Gyr before its observational epoch (post-starburst models). They provided us with E+A templates necessary to systematically identify this cluster population. By means of them, we detected *35 E+A galaxies in this cluster, 21±7%* of the total number of galaxies investigated. Their projected radial distribution shows that they are less concentrated than ellipticals, suggesting that *environmental effects may be a trigger mechanism for the starburst episode.* Moreover, we identified 14 of them on high resolution HST images [6]. Their morphology indicates that this kind of activity is associated with disk-like systems or mergers. Two cluster members, an unusually blue elliptical galaxy and a merger, evidence an earlier phase of the post-starburst temporal sequence, when the second burst is still ongoing.

E+A galaxies are characterized by a typical elliptical spectrum but unusually strong Balmer absorption lines, due to a large population of A-stars. These galaxies, rare in nearby clusters, represent another kind of activity in high redshift galaxy clusters as important as that manifested by emission lines for the *Butcher-Oemler effect* [4]. Our goal is to systematically identify E+A galaxies by means of multifilter photometry, using theoretical models and indices sensitive to recent star formation.

Models of E+A galaxies

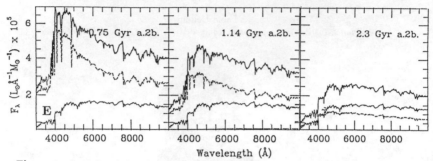

Figure 1. *Spectral evolution of an E+A SED (upper line). The contribution of the underlying elliptical galaxy (E) and the burst component (dashed line) to the E+A spectrum is shown. Note how the burst component dominates continuum and features in the resulting spectrum.*

In modelling E+A galaxies we made a basic assumption, i.e. that they are the result of a strong star formation episode occuring in an early-type galaxy (post-starburst picture). In building up a post-starburst galaxy we used the isochrone population synthesis models in [3]. We assumed that an elliptical formed the bulk of its stars in the first Gyr with a Salpeter IMF. At the age of 9.5 Gyr (corresponding to a passively evolved galaxy at the cluster redshift), it experiences a second burst of star formation. It lasts 0.25 Gyr and involves 20% of the initial galaxy's mass. The choice of the free parameters in the models was driven by their ability to reproduce the UV continuum (our bluest filter samples a central rest frame wavelength of 2500 Å) and the Balmer absorption line strengths of the few known post starburst galaxies. The grid of post-starburst SED's we used as templates covers a range in age spanning 0.5 to 2.5 Gyr after the second burst. Indeed, no signatures of the burst phase can be detect in galaxies with burst more than 3 Gyr old.

Figure 2. *The projected radial distribution of elliptical and E+A members. The zero value of the coordinates marks the cluster center. A King profile, characterized by a core radius $r_c = 50$ " and a central density $\sigma_o = 29$, can be fitted to the elliptical galaxies counts [2]. Instead, for the E+A no central concentration is evident. If any, an overdensity is visible in the outermost regions.*

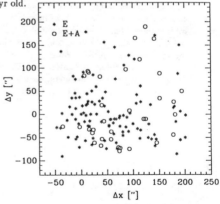

Table 1: Galaxy population in Cl0939+47

Spectral type	DG	This work	B-R	B-I	D_{4000}
Elliptical	22	110	2.40±0.17	3.55±0.26	2.21±0.35
E+A	6	31	2.03±0.17	3.01±0.32	1.81±0.23
Spiral & Im	2	24	1.37±0.34	2.11±0.34	1.30±0.22

Results & Discussion

In order to select a statistically complete sample, a very deep R-band frame of the Cl0939+47 (z=0.41) has been processed with INVENTORY, an automatic searching algorithm. All the objects with $m_R \leq 23.5$ in a $5' \times 5'$ field (2.2×2.2 Mpc; $H_0 = 50$ km s^{-1} Mpc^{-1}, $q_o = 0$) have been extracted and analyzed. Some of the filters have been chosen to reproduce the 4000 Å break index (D_{4000}) and to center the H_β, H_γ, and H_δ Balmer lines. The D_{4000} amplitude is an indicator of *variations* in the stellar content of normal ellipticals; the contribution of the light coming from hotter A- and F-stars increases the UV flux and then lower this index. For details on the photometric analysis see [7],[2]. Out of 323 objects, 275 (85%) could be classified with redshift and morphological type. By means of E+A templates, we have systematically identified E+A galaxies members. We correctly classified the six E+A already known [5] and found 29 new ones. Our results confirm, with a large statistical improvement and a systematic approach the incidence of the E+A galaxies in Cl0939+47. **21±7% of all member galaxies are E+A galaxies.** Tab.1 shows the B-R, B-I and D_{4000} mean values for all galaxies classified as members. The improvement achieved in the statistics in comparison with the most complete study to date for Cl0939+47 [5] is evident.The galaxy populations are characterized by values significantly different of these indices. Compared with the ellipticals, E+A galaxies have bluer colors and lower D_{4000}. They separate themselves from the spiral population too, having redder colors and higher D_{4000}. Ellipticals and E+A galaxies have also different spatial distributions (Fig.2).

HST images [6] provided the Hubble type for 14 of our 35 classified E+A members. The six E+A galaxies known from [5] are mergers or irregular galaxies and the newly found E+A turned out to be disk-systems, spiral or irregular types. This morphology correlates fairly well with the E+A age sequence after the second burst (mergers and irregular galaxies appear to be the youngest post-starburst galaxies). We suggest that we are observing the E+A phenomenon in its different phases. Moreover, the SED of a very blue elliptical galaxy and a merger that we confirmed as cluster members, could be successfully fitted by E+A models that reproduce earlier phases of the second burst, when it is still ongoing [2]. Therefore, the activity in the cluster indicated by the E+As takes place in both the active and fading phases. This suggests that the trigger mechanism responsible for the E+A phenomenon is not linked to a particular cosmic time, but instead dependent on cluster properties such as density and environment. This work was made in collaboration with G.Bruzual for the theoretical aspects, and H.-J.Röser and G.Thimm who provided the software used for the photometric analysis.

References

[1] Belloni P. et al., 1994, Mem.S.A.It. in press

[2] Belloni P.,G.Bruzual,H.-J. Röeser, 1994, A&A, submitted

[3] Bruzual G., Charlot S., 1993, ApJ 405, 538

[4] Butcher H., Oemler A., 1978, ApJ 219, 18

[5] Dressler A., Gunn J.E., 1992, ApJS 78, 1

[6] Dressler A.,1992,*STSI Newsletter* 9,2

[7] Thimm G. et al., 1994, this meeting

Comparing the Ambient Sunyaev-Zeldovich Effect from Clusters with Primary CMB Anisotropies

J.R. Bond[1], S.T. Myers[2]

[1] CITA, University of Toronto, Toronto ONT M5S 1A1, Canada

[2] Department of Astronomy, Caltech, Pasadena CA 91125, USA

ABSTRACT We use large-angle very deep peak-patch catalogues to make simulated skies, for a CDM model normalized in amplitude to match the cluster X-ray distribution and 4 Einstein-deSitter models normalized to match the COBE anisotropy data. These illustrate the promise of CBI-style degree field interferometry with few arcminute resolution and SAMBA-style large field low resolution ($\sim 10'$) mapping both for cleaning the CMB maps of the SZ and moving cluster effect to reveal the more fundamental primary CMB sky and for learning about evolution of the cluster system.

The Peak-Patch Picture is the natural generalization of the Press-Schechter approach to include the non-local coherence of collapsed structures and also of the BBKS single-filter peaks theory to allow a mass spectrum and solve the cloud-in-cloud problem. Both statistical and dynamical clustering of the peaks are included. Peak-patch catalogues accord well with N-body cluster and group catalogues, both statistically and spatially. For a detailed exposition see Bond and Myers (1993), *The Hierarchical Peak-Patch Picture of Cosmic Catalogues I: Algorithms; II: Validation and Application to Clusters*, Ap. J., in press.

Sample Catalogues: To construct the group and cluster catalogue for the maps of Fig. 1, a region extending to $z = 1.5$ covering $16° \times 16°$ was simulated, using 62 boxes, each of comoving volume $(200 \, h^{-1} Mpc)^3$ and 128^3 resolution, rather more than is feasible with current N-body or hydro codes. A standard CDM model with $\Omega = 1, h = 0.5$ and an initially scale invariant (Zeldovich) spectrum (index $n_s = 1$) was normalized to $\sigma_8 = 0.7$ — so that the X-ray temperature distribution of clusters comes out approximately correctly. The final catalogue had 52525 clusters and groups. Fig. 2 used similar catalogues for 4 inflation-inspired Gaussian structure formation theories with a critical density in clustering matter and whose σ_8 was chosen to fit the COBE anisotropy within about 1 sigma: (A) standard CDM with $n_s = 1$ as above, but now with $\sigma_8 = 1$ (COBE gives $\sigma_8 \approx 1.13 Q_{rms,PS}/(17.6\mu K)$ for $\Omega_B = 0.05$ and the large scale bulk flow normalization also gives $\sigma_8 \approx 1$); (B) $\sigma_8 = 0.71$ standard CDM, but with a tilt, $n_s = 0.8$; (C) $\sigma_8 = 0.71$ hot-cold hybrid ($\Omega_\nu = 0.3$, hence $m_\nu = 7$ ev and $\Omega_{cdm} = 0.65$, $\Omega_B = 0.05$); (D) $\sigma_8 = 0.45$ CDM, but with a flattened shape, parameterized by $\Gamma = 0.2$ rather than the $\Gamma = 0.5$ of the standard CDM spectrum. The models (C)–(D) reproduce the large scale galaxy clustering data with linear biasing (which the standard CDM model does not do, and the tilted model (B) also does not quite do). Model (D) is an example of a class of models with extra large-scale power, where the power on large scales ($300 \, h^{-1} Mpc$) relative to that on galaxy-clustering scales ($8 \, h^{-1} Mpc$) is parameterized by the shape factor Γ, which should be in the range 0.15–0.3 to explain large scale clustering; a preferred recent value is 0.25. An example is a model with a decaying neutrino of mass m_ν and lifetime τ_d, which has $\Gamma = 1.08\Omega h (1 + 0.96(m_\nu \tau_d/\text{kev yr})^{2/3})^{-1/2}$.

Internal Peak-patch Physics and the X-ray Test: The peak-patch catalogues can give only gross characterizations of the cluster properties, such as virialized mass, internal energy, baryon number, and (linear) bulk-flow velocities. Until hydro/N-body simulations tell us how these quantities are distributed within a large statistical sample of clusters, we use observed internal distributions, but scaled with the measured peak-patch parameters. For the figures we assume the gas profiles in the clusters are spherical, with density $\propto (1 + (r/r_{core})^2)^{-1}$ (a $\beta = 2/3$ profile), with the core radius a fixed fraction of the cluster radius (0.1) up to a maximum allowed value of 300 kpc. The temperature distribution is assumed to be isothermal, taken to be proportional to the internal energy of the clusters (an outcome of the peak-patch method), with a constant $C_T \approx 1 - 1.2$ translating between the two. SZ anisotropies are proportional to the line-of-sight pressure integral, hence will be uncertain to an order-unity correction factor $C_{SZ} = (\Omega_{Beff}/(2\Omega_B))C_T$, which depends as well upon an effective baryon abundance Ω_{Beff} which takes into account separation of gas from the dark matter and so may be higher than the primordial Ω_B (thus the factor of 2 enhancement factor was adopted).

For X-ray emission, another order-unity correction factor enters, $C_X = (\Omega_{Beff}/(2\Omega_B))^2 C_T^{1/2}$ (for bremsstrahlung emission). For nonlinear Thomson scattering from the moving cluster, the correction factor is $C_V \propto (\Omega_{Beff}/(2\Omega_B))$. There is also an error on the peculiar velocities of the clusters because of nonlinear effects which is typically 20%.

We have shown that the current X-ray temperature data for the Edge *et al.* (1990) cluster sample, the Henry and Arnaud (1991) distribution, and the constraint arising from having at least one cluster with 13.6 keV within $z = 0.2$ supports σ_8 in the range $\sim 0.6 - 0.8$, and that models with more large scale power (and hence flatter fluctuation spectra in the cluster regime) fit the X-ray

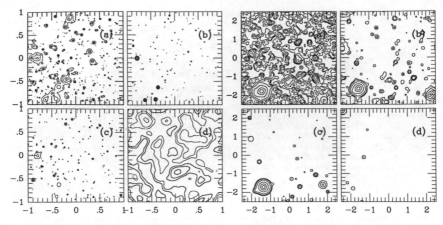

Fig. 1: $2° \times 2°$ maps for the $\sigma_8 = 0.7$ CDM model.   **Fig. 2:** $5° \times 5°$ SZ maps for models (A)-(D).

bright end better — in basic agreement with what many other authors have also found using the Press-Schechter formula. Thus (B) and (C) fit *much* better than (A) and (D). The luminosity and flux distributions also support a flatter spectrum and are compatible with σ_8 in this range, but there is a large uncertainty because the relative abundance of baryons in gaseous form compared with dark matter seems to be higher than primordial nucleosynthesis predicts. The flattening can be characterized by the effective index $n_{\rho,eff}(4\,h^{-1}\text{Mpc})$, which needs to be ~ -2 to (naively) match dn/dL_X, but could be a little steeper ($\lesssim -1.6$) to match dn/dT_X. Galaxy clustering data requires ≈ -1.6, derived assuming $\Gamma \approx 0.25$. By contrast,(A) gives -1.2, (B) gives -1.4, (C) gives -2.2 (with a 3 ev rather a 7 ev neutrino this rises to -1.6), and (D) gives -1.7.

Maps: Fig. 1 consists of 4 square-degree simulated fields that could be probed by the Cosmic Background Imager (CBI) being proposed by Caltech: an 8 small-dish interferometer to map scales from $\sim 2' - 20'$, with optimal sensitivity $\gtrsim 5'$, using HEMTs to cover frequencies $30 - 40$ GHz, with a 15 GHz channel to help to remove contamination. 1(a) shows the SZ effect for 30 GHz, with contours $-5 \times 10^{-6} C_{SZ} \times 2^{n-1}$; 1(b) the associated ROSAT map $(0.1 - 2.4$ keV$)$, with contours $10^{-14} C_X \times 2^{n-1}$ erg cm^{-2} s^{-1}, so the minimum contour level is similar to the ROSAT 5σ sensitivity for long exposure pointed observations; 1(c) the Thomson scattering anisotropy induced by the bulk motion of the clusters, with contours now $\pm 1.25 \times 10^{-6} C_V \times 2^{n-1}$; 1(d) primary anisotropies, with contour levels at $\pm 10^{-5} \times 2^{n-1}$. Negative contours are dotted. The hills and valleys shown are natural (not beam-smoothed): mapping them will give a direct probe of the physics of how the photon decoupling region at redshift ~ 1000 damped the primary signal. The maps of Fig. 1 have the following minima, maxima, mean offsets, and *rms*, in units of 10^{-6}: (a) $(-47, 0, -2.0, 3.0)C_{SZ}$; (b) $(0, 12, 0, -0.05, 0.23) \times 10^{-14} C_X$; (c) $(-7.57, 6.03, -0.04, 0.36)C_V$; (d) $(-53, 48, -0.06, 18)$. Thus the SZ effect is competitive with the much larger primary anisotropies expected in this model only in the cores of clusters; and the moving-cluster anisotropies are disappointingly small, even when nonlinear corrections are included. Using the information in a deep field cluster catalogue such as 1(b) will clearly be invaluable for separating SZ from primary. Even so, since the true sky will be the sum of 1(a,c,d) – plus Galactic and extragalactic synchrotron and bremsstrahlung sources for CBI, and plus dust for SAMBA, some possibly cold — separation will not be easy especially without many widely-spaced frequency bands.

SAMBA is a satellite experiment proposed by Puget *et al.* to map the entire sky using bolometers, with angular sensitivity to modes in the range from $\sim 10' - 20'$ to $\sim 1.5°$. With bolometers, one can straddle the frequency where the SZ effect changes sign, providing a valuable discriminator of SZ from primary $\Delta T/T$. In Fig. 2, we used a $7'$ beam, a little better than the resolution SAMBA is likely to achieve, on 25 square-degree simulated fields to show how different the SZ sky looks in the COBE-normalized models. The Compton y-parameter contours shown are $1.25 \times 10^{-6} C_{SZ} \times 2^{n-1}$, not unreasonable for SAMBA ($\Delta T/T = -1.5y$ at 3 mm and $1.3y$ at 1 mm).

DYNAMICAL EVOLUTION OF INFALLING GROUPS
ON CLUSTERS OF GALAXIES

Hugo V. Capelato[1] & Alain Mazure[2]

1.Divisão de Astrofísica – INPE/MCT
Caixa Postal 515 – 12201-970 — São José dos Campos,SP, Brasil.
2. Laboratoire d'Astronomie -USTL - CNRS
34095 Montpellier Cedex

1. Introduction

It is now commonly accepted that the subclustering found in a number of clusters of galaxies is a real phenomenon and not due to mere projection effects or even the only statistical fluctuations of the general density field of the cluster[9]. The origin of these clumps of galaxies may be two fold:

1. Clumps are young structures living within a recently formed and as yet not virialized cluster of galaxies, as suggested by early numerical simulations[3,10]. If this is the case, the cluster when seen in detail appears rather as a cluster of clumps of galaxies, as exemplified by the Hydra and the Cancer cluster of galaxies[2,5], and also maybe by the Shapley-8 (A3558) cluster[4]. It has also been suggested[13] that at last some of these clumps, before merging among themselves, may have enough time to suffer some internal dynamical evolution leading to the formation of bright galaxies which may be the seed of cD galaxies observed in rich clusters of galaxies. The double structure of the central region of the Coma cluster[6,11], that of A3558, or the two evolved clumps of galaxies, both centered on cD galaxies, of A3667[12], may be the prototypes of this evolutionary stage of

The figure displays the evolution of the bound mass of the group (normalised to its initial mass), as a function of the time. As it can be seen the most dramatic changes occur for groups in radial orbits (RW1 and RW5), by the time they attain their periastron ($\simeq$ 2Gyr). This is due to the tidal shock produced by the rapid passage of the group through the cluster core. The more compact group ($W_o = 1$) naturally resists better to this tidal shock than the more extended one. However, because of its compactness and also because it stays more massive for a longer time, it suffers a greater deceleration during its passage by the cluster core which causes the more rapid dissolution of this group after periastron. Groups in non-radial orbits (CW1 and CW5), display a much less dramatic behaviour, with a more or less constant rate of mass-loss which is clearly high for the less compact group. We find that except for the case of most compact group in radial orbit discussed above, groups may survive (at least with half of its initial mass) up to the time of its apostron but are completely disrupted just after.

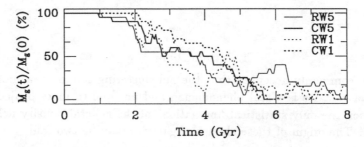

Fitchett[7] has qualitatively discussed the results of similar numerical experiments. His initial group is about 2.5 more massive than ours and he starts the experiments with the group at rest relative to the cluster center. In spite of these small differences, his basic conclusions seem to be consistent with our results. However, in variance to Fitchett's conclusions, we do not favour a more rapid destruction of non-radial infalls (C) as compared to the radial infalls cases (R). We also find that more compact configurations in radial orbits may be more rapidly disrupted because of an enhanced dynamical friction produced by the cluster galaxies.

clusters of galaxies.

2. Clumps are groups of galaxies which still survive after the secondary infall towards the already relaxed cluster. For instance it is argued[9] that at least part of the substructures found in the periphery of rich clusters may be identified to such groups. The clump of galaxies around N4839 in the Coma cluster may well be a prototype of this case.

Here we place ourselves in this last hypothesis and discuss the fate of such infalling groups. In order to do this we start running a series of numerical simulations of the dynamical evolution of an initialy bound group of a few galaxies which infalls toward the cluster centre under a variety of initial conditions. In this poster we report the results of the first 4 run's already completed.

2. Simulations setup

We modelled the background cluster as a 1024-particles random realization of a King sphere with central potential $W_o = 7.5$, total mass $3 \times 10^{15} M_\odot$ and core radius of 0.4Mpc. These values are nearly those found by Kent & Gunn[6] for the Coma cluster.The two initial groups were constructed as random realizations of King spheres of 20 particles with a fixed half-mass radius of 0.2Mpc and central potentials $W_o = 1$ and $W_o = 5$ and. This allows producing group models with two degrees of compactness (the greater the central potential a less compact group is obtained). The particles masses were set the same as that for the cluster particles, $m_* = 3 \times 10^{12} M_\odot$.

The groups were always released from a radial distance of 3.50Mpc from the cluster center with radial velocity of 500km/s. These values roughly match those for N4839 group at the Coma cluster. Non-radial infalling orbits were obtained by setting an initial tangential velocity to the groups of also 500km/s

The simulations were made using a C translation of the Barnes and Hut TREECODE[1]. The softening parameter were set at 13kpc a value which is about the half-mass radius of giant galaxies. Total energy and angular momentum were conserved to better then 0.5%.

3. Results and Discussion

4. References

1. Barnes, J. , Hut, P., 1986, Nature,**324** , 446

2. Bothun, G.D., Geller ,M.J, Beers, T.C., Huchra, J.P., 1983, ApJ.,**283**, 33

3. Cavaliere, A., Santangelo, P., Tarquini, G., Vittorio, N., 1986, ApJ., **305**, 651

4. Dantas, C.C., de Carvalho, R.R., Capelato, H.V., 1994, poster presented at this meeting

5. Fitchett, M.J., Merrit, D., 1988, ApJ., **335**, 18

6. Fitchett, M.J., Webster, R., 1987, ApJ.,**317**, 653

7. Fitchett, M.J. 1990, in *Clusters of Galaxies*, STScI Symposium, eds. Oergerle, W.R.,*et al.*; Cambridge Univ. Press, p. 111

8. Kent, S.M., Gunn, J.E., 1982, AJ.,**87**, 945

9. West, M.J., Bothun, G.D., 1990, ApJ.,**350**,36

10. Lima Neto, G.C.B., 1989, MSc Thesis, University of Sao Paulo

11. Mellier, Y., Mathez, G., Mazure, A., Chauvineau, B., Proust, D., 1988, A&A, **199**, 67

12. Sodre, L., Capelato, H.V., Steiner, J.E., Proust, D., Mazure, A., 1992, MNRAS,**259**, 233

13. Tremaine, S., 1990, in *Dynamics of the Interactions of Galaxies*, ed. R. Wielen; Springer-Verlag, p. 394

HIGH–ORDER CORRELATIONS OF RICH GALAXY CLUSTERS

ALBERTO CAPPI[1] & SOPHIE MAUROGORDATO[2]

[1] *Osservatorio Astronomico di Bologna, via Zamboni 33, I-40126 Bologna, Italy*
[2] *CNRS; Observatoire de Paris-Meudon, LAM, 5 Place J.Janssen, F-92195 Meudon, France*

Abstract

We have analysed the two and three–dimensional all–sky distributions of rich Abell and ACO galaxy clusters by using counts in cells. We have measured the volume–averaged angular and spatial correlation functions. Confirming previous results, we find a well defined hierarchical relation between the two and three–point correlation functions, remarkably constant with scale. We find that the hierarchical relation is followed up to the sixth order at angular scales between $\sim 2^o$ and $\sim 4^o$. Anyway, northern and southern subsamples give different results. The inferred values of S_J, where $S_J = \bar{\xi}_J/\bar{\xi}_2^{J-1}$, are comparable to those measured for the galaxy distribution. These results are confirmed to the 4th order by our analysis of a complete 3D sample of Abell and ACO clusters; they indicate that the statistical properties of the cluster distribution originate from the underlying galaxy distribution, and that the biasing between clusters and galaxies is non–linear.

In scale–invariant models (hereafter SIMs; see Balian & Schaeffer 1989), the void probability function (VPF) normalized to the Poissonian expectation, $\log(P_0)/nV$, rescales with $N_c = nV\bar{\xi}$. This property of the VPF is verified for galaxies, and also for galaxy clusters (Jing 1990; Cappi, Maurogordato, Lachièze-Rey 1991). In SIMs, one expects also a hierarchy of the volume–averaged correlation functions (corresponding to the reduced moments):

$$\bar{\xi}_J = S_J\bar{\xi}_2^{J-1} \tag{1}$$

It is therefore natural to extend the statistical analysis and measure the higher–order moments.

We have calculated the moments of the cluster distribution from counts in cells (see Bouchet, Davis & Strauss 1992, Gaztañaga 1992, and Bouchet et al. 1993). From the $P(N)$ we can estimate the reduced moments of order J.

3–D samples are yet quite small, and it is difficult to go beyond order 4, while 2–D samples are larger and can give more significant results. We selected all clusters with richness $R \geq 1$ and distance class $D = 5 - 6$, at galactic latitude $\mid b_{II} \mid \geq 45^o$. This sample includes $N = 1569$ Abell & ACO clusters (717 in the north and 852 in the south). From the analysis of this sample we find (Cappi & Maurogordato 1994) that the rich cluster distribution is consistent with the correlation hierarchy up to $J = 6$ at scales between 2° and 4° degrees, corresponding approximately to the range $20 - 40 \ h^{-1}$ Mpc, where we find $s_3 \sim 2.9$ and $s_4 \sim 14$ (see fig.1). The analysis of a smaller 3–D sample of nearby clusters (281 clusters, $R \geq 0$, $\mid b_{II} \mid \geq 40^o$, $z \leq 0.08$) gives $S_3 \sim 2.5$ between 22 and 38 h^{-1} Mpc, and $S_4 \sim 12$ between 30 and 35 h^{-1} Mpc. However, there is a discrepancy between southern and northern,

382

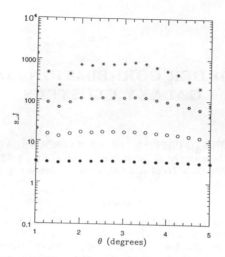

Figure·1: s_J, J=3,...6, for the 1569 Abell+ACO clusters with richness $R \geq 1$, distance class $D = 5 - 6$, and $\mid b_{II} \mid \geq 45^o$

which deviate from the hierarchical behaviour. Gaztañaga (1994) estimated S_J –up to the 9th order– from the galaxy angular distribution in the APM Survey. At scales between 7 and 30 h^{-1} Mpc, he finds $S_3 = 3.1 \pm 0.14$, $S_4 = 22.0 \pm 2.5$. While uncertainties (depending also on the deprojection factors) do not allow a detailed comparison, these results suggest that the APM Galaxy Survey and rich clusters are sampling the same underlying large–scale distribution. The absence of any strong effect on the values of S_3, which are remarkably similar for clusters and optical galaxies, equal within ~ 10 %, rules out a linear biasing –where $S_3 \propto 1/b$–. The fact that the values of Q_J are around unity for both galaxies and clusters is consistent with models where a natural bias comes out from gravitational interaction of the matter field (see Bernardeau & Schaeffer 1992).

References

Balian R., Schaeffer R., 1989, AA **220**, 1

Bernardeau F., Schaeffer R., 1992, AA **255**, 1

Bouchet F., Davis M., Strauss M., 1992, in *The Distribution of Matter in the Universe*, IInd DAEC meeting, Mamon G.A. and Gerbal D. eds., Observatoire de Paris–Meudon, p.287

Bouchet F., Strauss M.A., Davis M., Fisher K.B., Yahil A., Huchra J.P., 1993, ApJ **417**, 36

Cappi A., Maurogordato S., 1992, AA **259**, 423

Cappi A., Maurogordato S., 1994a, in 9th IAP meeting on *Cosmic velocity Fields*, eds. F.Bouchet and M.Lachièze–Rey, in press

Cappi A., Maurogordato S., 1994b, ApJ, submitted

Cappi A., Maurogordato S., Lachièze–Rey M., 1991, AA **243**, 28

Gaztañaga E., 1992, ApJ **398**, L17

Gaztañaga E., 1994, MNRAS, in press

Jing Y.P., 1990, AA **233**, 309

Tóth G., Hollósi J., Szalay A.S., 1989, ApJ **344**, 75

NO ARC IN THE DOUBLE QUASAR?

H. Dahle[1], S.J. Maddox[2] and Per B. Lilje[1]

[1]Institute of Theoretical Astrophysics, University of Oslo,
P.O. Box 1029, Blindern, N-0315 Oslo, Norway

[2]Royal Greenwich Observatory, Madingley Road,
Cambridge CB3 0EZ, UK

Abstract

A gravitational arc system near the double QSO 0957+561 has recently been reported by Bernstein et al. (1993). If real, it is probably caused by a massive z=0.5 group of galaxies near the line-of-sight in addition to the cluster of which the lensing galaxy is a member. This sets strong constraints on determinations of the Hubble constant from the time delay in the double quasar. Here we present new results from extremely deep, high-resolution images of these arc candidates.

Both the morphology and the colours show that these objects are probably only chance alignments of three and two different objects, and not gravitationally lensed arcs. Hence, the z=0.5 group is most likely insignificant, and the constraints of Bernstein et al. on H_0-determinations are not valid.

Introduction. The "double QSO" 0957+561, discovered by Walsh et al. (1979), remains the best studied example of a gravitational lens system. As shown by Borgeest & Refsdal (1984), a value for the Hubble constant which does not rely on the steps of the local distance ladder may be determined from systems like these. This will require a reliable value for the time delay between the two quasar images as well as a well-constrained model for the lensing mass distribution. The main problem is the complicated mass distribution of this lens, due to the fact that the lensing galaxy is immersed in a galaxy cluster at z=0.36 which gives a significant contribution to the total lensing potential. There is also another galaxy group at z=0.5 present in the field, centered on a galaxy 1.5' from the lens center.

Bernstein et al. (1993) have recently reported a pair of elongated objects ~ 20" from the lens center, interpreted as strongly lensed background galaxies. This interpretation relied solely on morphological evidence. The existence of these arcs reduced the allowed classes of models to only two:

1. Single-screen models with very small lensing galaxy masses (giving unreasonably low values for H_0), or
2. Two-screen models which need to include a large mass ($\sim 10^{14} M_\odot$) in the z=0.5 group.

If (2) is correct, we would be forced to accept that a rather unassuming group of 4-5 galaxies has a total mass which rivals that of a well-sized cluster with ~ 100 galaxies.

Observations and results. The field around QSO 0957+561 was observed in January 1994 with the 2.56 meter Nordic Optical Telescope (NOT). We employed the 1024x1024 IAC CCD with an image scale of 0.14" pixel^{-1}. Using the shift-and-stare technique, we added a large number of frames (each of typically 1200 s) to get a combined 24,600 s V-image and a 27,000 s I-image. The combined I frame has a seeing of 0.76"(FWHM), and the combined V frame has a seeing of 0.81".

We find that the morphology of the arc candidates of Bernstein et al. (1993), called A1 and A2, suggests that they are not strongly gravitationally lensed, stretched-out images of background galaxies.

384

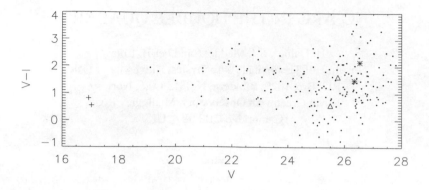

Figure 1: Colour-magnitude diagram for objects in the field of QSO 0957+561. The two quasar images are marked with crosses, the two brightest components in A1 are marked as asterisks and the two components in A2 are marked as triangles.

Rather, they seem to be a triplet (A1) and a pair (A2) of separate objects which may be interacting galaxies or chance alignments of galaxies at different redshifts.

We can not completely rule out these objects as arcs based on morphology only: A gravitational arc may be quite clumpy, depending on the structure of the lensing potential. The colours of the various substructures must, however, be the same if the lensing hypothesis is correct, that is, if all the light in the arcs originate from the same galaxy.

The photometry (see figure 1) shows a considerable difference in colour ($\Delta(V - I) > 1.0$) between the components in A2. The photometry also gives different colours for the two brightest components in A1, but the differences are not as dramatic as for the components in A2. If A1 and A2 are stretched-out images of single galaxies, one would certainly not expect to see large colour differences between the various parts of the arcs.

Conclusions. Based on photometric as well as morphological evidence, we can exclude A1 and A2 as gravitational arcs. This means that the z=0.5 group probably has a rather insignificant mass and that the constraints imposed on determinations of H_0 by Bernstein et al. (1993) (model 1 and 2 above) are not valid.

Further analysis of weak lensing of faint background galaxies in the field to constrain the lens model is in progress. Tentative results support the conclusion that the lensing contribution from the z=0.5 group is negligible and indicate that the peak in the field mass distribution is situated within 20" from the lensing galaxy.

References

Bernstein, G. M., Tyson, J. A., Kochanek, C. S. 1993, AJ, 105, 816
Borgeest, U., Refsdal, S. 1984, A&A, 141, 318
Walsh, D., Carswell, R. F., Weymann, R. J. 1979, Nat, 279, 381

DYNAMICAL AND STRUCTURAL PROPERTIES OF A3558

Christine C. Dantas[1], Reinaldo R. de Carvalho[2,3] & Hugo V. Capelato[1]

1.Divisão de Astrofísica - INPE/MCT
Caixa Postal 515 - 12201-970 — São José dos Campos, SP, Brasil.
2. California Institute of Technology
Astron. Dept. 105 24, Pasadena CA 91125, USA
3. On Leave of absence from Observatório Nacional/CNPq

Abstract

We study the fundamental physical properties of the cluster of galaxies A3558 (Shapley 8). We obtained a statistically complete catalogue for 255 galaxies (B_{lim} = 18.75). The radial velocity data already published in the literature have been added to our catalogue. This match provided a radial velocity catalogue containing 141 galaxies. From the analysis of this catalogue we report the existence of significant subclustering in A3558. The presence of two main central concentrations not identified previously is established and confirmed by the wavelet analysis of ROSAT X-ray maps [7]. The cD galaxy is at rest in one of these condensations.

The photometric catalogue was obtained from a 2048 × 2048 pixels (1.67 " per pixel) scan of a ESO/SRC IIIa-J plate, available at STScI, centered on the dominant cD galaxy. Magnitudes were measured with FOCAS. The radial velocities catalogue was obtained matching the photometric catalogue to the radial velocity catalogues determined by [1], [2] and [3], and then applying the iterative procedure described in [4] . The 129 galaxies with velocities in the interval 11700 and 17100 $km\ s^{-1}$ are probably cluster members. We find $\langle V \rangle$ = 14389 ± 83 $km\ s^{-1}$, z = 0.048, and $\sigma_{corr} = 899^{+\ 62}_{-\ 51}\ km\ s^{-1}$.

The isodensity contour map of A3558 (cf. figure) shows that the cluster is broken in several smaller concentrations. Most of these features also appear to be kinematically distinct. The statistical significance of the southeastern subclustering has been previously confirmed applying the Lee statistics[5].

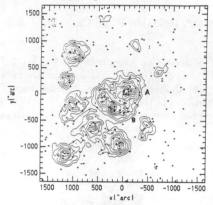

We find that the 2 central concentrations (A and B) have mean velocities which are different by a factor 3 of their combined variances. The wavelet analysis of the ROSAT HRI X-ray map by Slezak[7] shows the existence of 2 central pics of emission at positions that coincide with the condensations A and B . The mean velocity of condensation B differs by less than 20 $km\ s^{-1}$ from that of the cD galaxy, suggesting that the cD is dynamically bound to this condensation rather than to the A one. This explains the apparent discrepancy between the mean velocity of the cluster and the velocity of the dominant galaxy[6], and is in agreement with the hypothesis that the giant central galaxies are probably formed in their host substruture. No luminosity segregation was found in these substructures.

References

[1] Bardelli S., et al., 1993, MNRAS, in press.

[2] Teague P. F., Carter D., Gray P. M., 1990, ApJS, 72, 715.

[3] Metcalfe N., Godwin J. G. & Spenser S. D. 1987, MNRAS, 225, 581.

[4] Yahil A., Vidal N. V., 1977, ApJ, 214, 347.

[5] Dantas C. C., de Carvalho, R. R. & Capelato H. V., 1994, in preparation.

[6] Gebhardt K., & Beers T. C., 1991, ApJ, 383, 72.

[7] Slezak E., 1994, this Conference.

THE INADMISSIBILITY OF
RADIAL NUMBER DENSITY PROFILES
OF
GALAXY CLUSTERS

F.W. Baier[1], H.T. MacGillivray[2], P. Flin[3], J. Krywult[3]

[1] University of Potsdam, Potsdam, Germany
[2] Royal Observatory, Edinburgh, Scotland
[3] Cracow Pedagocical University, Cracow, Poland

The study of density profiles of galaxy clusters has a long history. The main interest in density profiles is connected with the asssumption that such investigations may contribute to the knowledge of origin and dynamics of galaxy clusters (Bahcall 1977, Sarazin 1988). But the parameters used for describing clusters strongly depend on many conditions, e. g. the assumed cluster center or the limiting magnitude of counts. Usually, after constructing the number density profile a fit is made using the isothermal, Hubble or King formulae. Presently, due to the large number of data arriving from automatic scans it is possible to study galaxy distributions in clusters in greater detail.

We used data from automatic scans of Schmidt plates made in the Royal Observatory, Edinburgh, and from the work of Hickson (1977) for an investigation of 13 clusters. The cluster centres were determined using a maximum likelihood method (Sarazin 1980), assuming the brightest cluster member in the centre as a first approximation. Later on, the counts of galaxies were obtained in circular rings which radii increase with the step $0.1 * n$ Mpc ($H_o = 55 kms^{-1} Mpc^{-1}, q_o = 0.5$). Three independent counts were performed, accepting n=1, 2, and 3. Each number density plot has been fitted by a King function, minimizing χ^2 function similar to the approach used by Semeniuk (1982). Such a procedure gives the new cluster centre together with structural parameters, i.e. central cluster density, core radius and background density.

From this investigation it follows that the structural parameter "core radius" may depend on the size of the circular rings. There are some clusters with an extremely small influence of the ring width on the structural parameters, e.g. A 754 or A 1139. On the other hand there are clusters with a greater influence, e.g. A 151. Such a dependence may reflect the existence of substructure. But the agreement among values of the core radii determined by counts with different ring widths does not indicate the lack of some more detailed subclustering. This becomes very clear in the case of A 754. In Figure 1 we present a contour plot for the galaxy distribution in this cluster. The extremely complicated structure of this cluster shows the questionableness of structure parameters deduced from counts of galaxies in circular rings for this case. The same is right in other cases. Moreover it is known from independent investigations (Baier et al. 1978 - 1983, Geller and Beers 1982, Baier and MacGillivray 1994) that most galaxy clusters – even cD clusters – display substructure. The present analysis confirms the former results and shows that structural parameters are very sensitive to several factors – especially to substructure. Therefore, we think that before applying full analysis of radial projected cluster density distributions to the growing number of data, it will be necessary to check the influence of these factors to the result.

388

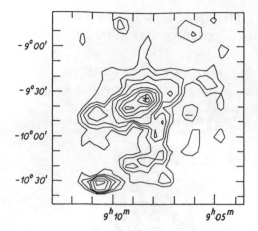

Figure 1. Number density distribution for the cluster Abell 754 down to $m_j = 20.0$. The isolines correspond to 0.80, 0.70, 0.60, 0.50, 0.40, 0.30, 0.25, 0.20, and 0.15 galaxies per $arcmin^2$. Coordinates are for the epoch 2000.0. The position of the cD galaxy is marked by a cross.

References

Bahcall, N. A., 1977, Ann. Rev. Astron. Astrophys. **15**, 505
Baier, F.W., and Mai, W.: 1978, Astron. Nachr. **299**, 69
Baier, F.W., and Mai, W.: 1978, Astron. Nachr. **299**, 197
Baier, F.W.: 1979, Astron. Nachr. **300**, 85
Baier, F.W.: 1979, Astron. Nachr. **300**, 133
Baier, F.W.: 1979, Astron. Nachr. **300**, 243
Baier, F.W., and Ziener, R.: 1977, Astron. Nachr. **298**, 87
Baier, F.W.: 1980, Astron. Nachr. **301**, 17
Baier, F.W.: 1980, Astron. Nachr. **301**, 165
Baier, F.W.: 1983, Astron. Nachr. **304**, 211
Baier, F.W., and MacGillivray, H.T.: 1994, in progress
Geller, M.J., and Beers, T.C.: 1982, Publ. Astron. Soc. Pacific **94**, 421
Hickson, P.: 1977, Astrophys. J. **217**, 16
Sarazin, C.L.: 1980, Astrophys. J. **236**, 75
Sarazin, C.L.: 1988, X-ray Emission from Clusters of Galaxies, Cambridge University Press
Semeniuk, I.: 1982, Acta Astron. **32**, 357

Addresses of the authors:

F.W. Baier, WIP–Working Group "Galaxy Clusters", University Potsdam,
c/o Astrophysikalisches Institut Potsdam
An der Sternwarte 16
D–14482 Potsdam, Germany

H. T. MacGillivray, Royal Observatory, Blackford Hill, Edinburgh EH9 3HJ Scottland, UK

P. Flin, J. Krywult, Cracow Pedagogical University, ul. Podchorazych 2, 30–084, Cracow, Poland

NON-POLYTROPIC MODEL WITH GALACTIC WINDS
FOR CLUSTERS OF GALAXIES

R. Fusco-Femiano

Istituto di Astrofisica Spaziale,CNR, Via E.Fermi 21-C.P.67,I-00044 Frascati RM,Italy

Abstract

The intracluster gas of clusters of galaxies shows a metal enrichement with nearly solar abundances of metals. Two possible mechanisms are indicated for the injection of material by member galaxies: ram pressure stripping and protogalactic winds. In this article it is proposed a new static model that with respect to the non-polytropic model formulated by Cavaliere & Fusco-Femiano[1] (hereafter CFF), utilized to jointly fit all the available X-ray and optical imaging and spectroscopic data of the Coma cluster[2];hereafterFFH, includes also the contribution of supernovae-driven protogalactic winds to the heating and mass of the intracluster medium. The use of this model for the analysis of spatially resolved X-ray spectra should allow to discriminate between the wind and ram-pressure stripping scenario, regarding the injected energy and the metal enrichment of the intracluster gas. A complete treatment can be found in Fusco-Femiano[5].

The model

The CFF non-polytropic model assumes that the intracluster medium is composite of primordial gas that is compressed and heated by gravity during the cluster collapse and by gas stripped from galaxies by the ambient medium. Most of the ICM must be primordial since the gas mass is much greater than the observed stellar mass of the cluster galaxies[3,4]. In this model the relation

$$kT(R) = \mu m_H \sigma^2(R)/\beta \qquad (1)$$

holds everywhere throughout the cluster. Two objections at this relation are that the heating of the primordial gas is a very complex issue (the processes that heat this gas would be probably different from those which would have heated the galaxies) and that simulations of cluster formation indicate that the galaxy velocity anisotropy should vary with radius. However, FFH have demonstrated, for the first time, how a physically- motivated static model in which the heating is controlled by local conditions, can jointly fit all the actual X-ray and optical data on the Coma cluster. With respect to the CFF non-polytropic model, we introduce in this model the possibility that a contribution to the heating of the ICM may derive from the ejection of material via galactic winds. The relation (1) is modified including this effect

$$kT(R) = \mu m_H (\sigma^2(R) + \epsilon_{wind})/\beta$$

where ϵ_{wind} take into account of the heating by galactic winds.

The distributions for the gas density and temperature are:

$$n/n_o = (\rho_G/\rho_{Go})^\beta [(\sigma^2/\sigma_o^2 + q)/(1+q)]^{\beta-1} e^{-f_{wind}}$$

$$T/T_o = (\sigma^2/\sigma_o^2 + q)/(1+q)$$

where $(W(R) = G \int_R^{R_t} M(r) r^{-2} \sigma^{-2} dr$ is the normalized gravitational potential and R_t the cluster radius)

$$q = \epsilon_{wind}/\sigma_o^2$$

$$\rho_G/\rho_{Go} = e^{W-W_o} I_{3/2}(W)/I_{3/2}(W_o)$$

$$\sigma^2/\sigma_o^2 = I_{5/2}(W)/I_{5/2}(W_o) * I_{3/2}(W_o)/I_{3/2}(W)$$

$$I_q(W) = \int_0^W e^{-\eta} \eta^q d\eta$$

$$f_{wind} = q\beta \int_{W_o}^W \frac{(1 + e^{-x} x^{3/2}/I_{3/2}(x)) dx}{(\sigma^2/\sigma_o^2) + q}$$

References

[3] Blumenthal,G.R.,Faber,S.M.,Primack,J.R.,&Ress,M.J.1984,Nature,311,517

[4] David,L.P.,Arnaud,K.A.,Forman,W.,&Jones,C. 1990,ApJ,356,32

[1] Cavaliere, A., & Fusco-Femiano, R. 1981, A&A, 100, 194 (CFF)

[2] Fusco-Femiano, R., & Hughes, J. P. 1994, ApJ, *in press* (FFH)

[5] Fusco-Femiano, R. 1994, A&A, *in press*

ARCS IN X-RAY SELECTED CLUSTERS

I. Gioia[1,2], G. Luppino[1], J. Annis[3], O. Le Fèvre[4], and F. Hammer[4]
[1] Institute for Astronomy, Honolulu, HI USA 96822
[2] Istituto di Radioastronomia del *CNR*, 40129, Bologna, ITALY
[3] Fermilab Astrophysics Center, Batavia, IL USA 80510
[4] *D.A.E.C.*, Observatoire de Paris, Meudon, FRANCE

Abstract

We present results from an imaging survey carried out at the University of Hawaii to search for gravitational lenses in X-ray selected clusters of galaxies. We have imaged 41 clusters extracted from the *EMSS* in two colors, and we have found 8 giant arcs and a similar number of mini-arcs and/or candidates. Spectroscopy is needed to confirm the gravitational lensing hypothesis.

1. Introduction

Deep imaging with *CCD*'s has revealed that clusters act as gravitational lenses producing distorted and magnified images of background galaxies. Arc redshifts are systematically measured to be greater than the cluster redshifts[1,2] and very similar to those of galaxies found in deep redshift surveys. This fact, combined with the symmetry and locations of the arcs, confirm the gravitational lensing idea. As the physics of the lensing is understood, we may use the properties of the arcs to probe the mass distribution in rich clusters. Another promising field of investigation is the study of the properties of very distant normal galaxies which are the "source" of the lensing. The determination of their redshifts would be otherwise impossible with present day technology. A large number of clusters needs to be observed to derive global properties of either the lens or the sources and large amounts of telescope time need to be allocated for both imaging and spectroscopy. A high efficiency procedure to search for arcs is then required.

2. The Hawaii Arc Survey results

We have been involved in an observational program to image in B and R a sample of 41 of the highest X-ray luminosity $EMSS^{2,3}$ clusters ($L_x > 2 \times 10^{44}$ ergs/s) with redshifts $z > 0.15$ in order to search for gravitational lensing. We assume that the hot, X-ray emitting gas is a tracer of the total gravitational potential of the cluster, both visible and dark matter. High X-ray luminosity is therefore a sign of a deep potential well and thus is an indicator of a true massive cluster, likely to exhibit the lensing phenomenon.

Of the 41 clusters in our sample, 8 contain spectacular "giant arcs" ($l > 10$") and 9 more contain arclets or arc candidates. The high incidence of lensing obtained (at least 29%) is a better success rate than achieved with surveys of optical selected clusters[5,6]. The lensing frequency and the thinness of the arcs, are strong evidence for compact mass density profiles for the lensing clusters. We have completed the imaging part of the survey and are concentrating now on obtaining spectra of the newly discovered arcs with the *CFH* and the Keck telescopes. We present here the results of the imaging survey which was carried out in excellent seeing conditions, using the University of Hawaii 2.2m telescope equipped with a Tektronix 2048 × 2048 *CCD*. Figure 1 shows a mosaic for the 7 of the 8 giant arcs. The top right *CCD* image is a 2-hour long exposure of the cluster MS0451.6−0305 which, at a redshift of $z = 0.55$, is the most X-ray luminous cluster source known ($L_x(0.3 - 3.5) = 2.0 \times 10^{45}$ ergs/s [$H_0 = 50$; $q_0 = 0.5$]. This value is 1.4 times the X-ray luminosity of CL0016+16, the archetypical high redshift X-ray cluster. In our recent 2.2m run we discovered a giant arc in the core[7]. Also worth mentioning is the cluster MS0302.7+1658 (top left). The "straight" arc in this *EMSS* cluster at $z = 0.424$ was discussed in Mathez et al. 1992 [8]. In our deep images taken on the *UH* 2.2m telescope, the straight arc is seen as the brighter, eastern extension of a long structure visible between the two bright galaxies. Another arc is seen to the south of the brightest galaxy. Spectroscopic determination of the redshifts of the brightest arcs is the next step in this study. *HST* and *ROSAT* data of the lensed clusters will also be obtained.

3. References

1) Soucail, G., Mellier, Y., Fort, B., Mathez, G. and Cailloux, M. 1988, A&A, 191, L19.
2) Pello, R., Le Borgne, J.F., Sanahuja, B., Mathez, G. and Fort, B. 1992, A&A, 266, 6.
3) Gioia, I.M. et al., 1990, ApJS, 72, 567.
4) Stocke, J.T. et al., 1991, ApJS, 76, 813.
5) Lynds, R. and Petrosian, V. 1989, ApJ, 336, 1.
6) Smail, I. et al., 1991, MNRAS, 252, 19.
7) Luppino, G.A. et al. 1994, in preparation.
8) Mathez, G., Fort, B., Mellier, Y., Picat, J.-P., Soucail, G. 1992, A&A, 256, 343

This work has received partial financial support from *NASA* grants NAG5-1752, NAG5-1880 and from *NSF* grant AST91-19216. The *CCD* development at *IfA* has been supported by *NSF* grant AST 90-20680.

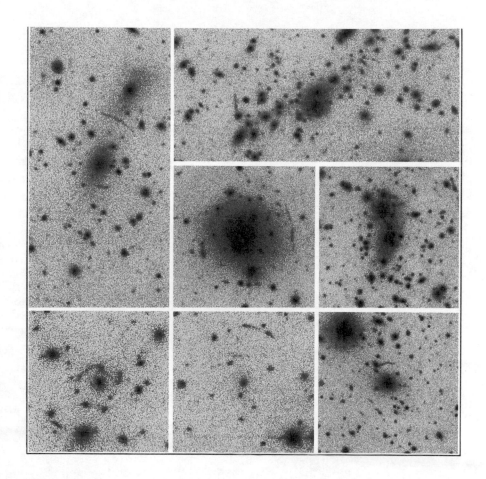

Figure 1 - CCD mosaic of seven EMSS clusters with gravitationally lensed arcs.

DYNAMICS OF SUBSTRUCTURES IMMERSED IN GALAXY CLUSTERS

Guillermo González-Casado,[1] Gary A. Mamon,[2,3] and Eduard Salvador-Solé[4]

[1]Dep. Matemàtica Aplicada II, Univ. Politècnica de Catalunya,

Pau Gargallo 5, 08028 Barcelona, Spain

[2]DAEC, Observatoire de Paris-Meudon, 92195 Meudon, France

[3]Institut d'Astrophysique, 98 bis Blvd Arago, 75014 Paris, France

[4]Dep. Astronomia i Meteorologia, Univ. de Barcelona,

Avda Diagonal 647, 08028 Barcelona, Spain

ABSTRACT

We present the results of a study of the dynamical survival of small-scale substructure immersed in relaxed galaxy clusters.

1. INTRODUCTION

Small-scale substructure in the central regions of apparently relaxed clusters seems to be quite common. The observed frequency of small-scale substructure may be used as a constraint to cosmological models provided that we know the time that such substructures survive immersed in a relaxed cluster. To derive this time we consider the dynamical evolution of small-scale substructure in clusters within two extreme alternate scenarios for its possible origin: 1) the accretion of a group (or small cluster) on a quasi-radial orbit, and 2) the merger of two clusters of similar masses, followed by the decoupling of their dense cores.

2. DYNAMICS

In the accretion scenario it is assumed that a group or small cluster of galaxies is accreted by the cluster from its turnaround radius in an elongated orbit. In the merging scenario it is assumed that two clusters of similar mass have merged together, and in this process their central cores have detached from their main body. If the initial clusters have cuspy cores, these are indeed likely to survive the tidal processes during the violent relaxation phase. After violent relaxation the detached cores are left off-center with a random angular momentum.

Accreted groups and detached cores following elongated orbits will both suffer a tidal shock when passing near the cluster center. Computing the effects of the tidal shock by means of an impulsive approximation, it can be demonstrated that the relative internal energy gain after a pericenter passage scales as the ratio of the mean density of the cluster within the pericenter to the mean density of the group or detached core: $|\Delta U/U| \propto \bar{\rho}_{cl}(R_p)/\bar{\rho}_{sub}$. Since the mean density of a cluster core is much higher than the mean density of a whole group, the latter systems are more prone to tides. However, the orbits of clumps surviving to cluster tides (as well as those of very massive clumps) will decay towards the cluster center by dynamical friction. In these cases, one can define the survival time of the clump as the time taken by its orbit to settle within the cluster core radius.

3. RESULTS

Infalling groups and small clusters are tidally disrupted at first passage through the core of a rich cluster, regardless of their initial orbital parameters, since their internal energy gain is more than one order of magnitude larger than their binding energy. The time spent by groups within the cluster, before they reach the pericenter and are disrupted by the cluster tidal field, never exceeds one cluster crossing time.

Since detached cores of clusters are much denser than groups, they are considerably more robust to tides. Detached cores with more than 5% of the total cluster mass always survive to tides. They are not disrupted by impulsive tides when passing near the cluster center in an elongated orbit. Neither they are severely limited by tides when following nearly circular orbits. Detached cores can spend more time in the central regions of relaxed clusters than accreted groups, although dynamical friction causes the more massive detached cores of merged clusters to fall directly into the cluster center. Anyway, if the mass of detached cores is in the range of 5% to 20% of the total cluster mass, they may have a survival time longer than one cluster crossing time provided that their initial orbits are not too elongated.

ON THE DARK MATTER DISTRIBUTION AROUND A CLUSTER OF GALAXIES IN THE COSMIC STRING SCHEME

Tetsuya HARA[1], Masakazu MATSUURA[1], Hideki YAMAMOTO[1],
Petri MÄHÖNEN[2] and Shigeru J. MIYOSHI[1]

[1] Department of Physics, Kyoto Sangyo University, Kyoto 603, Japan
[2] Department of Astrophysics, University of Oxford, Oxford, UK

1. INTRODUCTION

The cosmic string model seems to have developed to be one of the viable models for the cosmogony and here we investigate the distribution of cold dark matter (CDM) around a cluster of galaxies in this scheme. A cluster of galaxies is considered to be formed at the crossing site of three wakes of infinitely long cosmic strings. The simulated line-of-sight velocity dispersion and projected surface number density of galaxies are compared with the observations in a simplified case. Some features seem to be in good agreement with the observation, although the detail structures require a more refined investigation. A characteristic pattern of density inhomogenities is expected to exist within a cluster, which might be related to the substructures observed in many clusters of galaxies. The brightest cluster member such as gE, D or cD galaxy is naturally expected to reside at the cluster center in this scheme.

2. ASSUMPTIONS AND EQUATION OF MOTION OF DARK MATTER

We calculate the motion of CDM in the configuration that three cosmic strings passed through and triggered the formation of three orthogonally crossing wakes at $1+z=10^4$. The equation of motion of CDM particle in the flat Friedmann universe is given in Hara et al. (1993). The numerical calculations are made with the PM method with CIC mass assignment scheme, using 64^3 particles and cells. We treat the dark matter only.

We investigated the case that three wakes intersected orthogonally like the x-y, y-z, and x-z planes in the Cartesian coordinates. To compare the results of simulation with the observations of Coma cluster, we adopted the value $G\mu\beta\gamma=5\times10^{-6}$ and the box length 48Mpc in the following analysis.

3. THE VELOCITY AND DENSITY DISTRIBUTIONS

The simulated present-day distribution of dark matter around and within a cluster is displayed in Fig. 1, where the local to background density ratio ρ/ρ_b is used to discriminate the iso-density contours. The iso-density contours of $\rho/\rho_b=4$, 64, 512 and 1536 are displayed in Figures 1a-d. The central region is magnified by four times in Fig. 1c-d, that is, the box size is 12Mpc in them.

As expected, dark matter has accumulated to the three wakes as seen in Fig. 1a. The density is higher in each bar-like intersected region of two wakes as seen in Fig. 1b. It can be understood that dark matter falls into each wake and at the same time accumulates toward the bar-like intersected region. A considerable part of CDM particles in the bar-like part contract towards the center and to form a cluster there.

It must be noted that there are considerable density inhomogenities around and within a cluster of galaxies. Each of Figures 1a, 1b and 1c show in total 6 horns or lumps, reflecting the structure of the three crossing bars. The motion of dark matter is determined by the initial condition and the relatively dense bar-like part of dark matter falls into the center. Dark matter passes through the center and returns. Such features are also derived in the case that three wakes intersected with crossing angle $\sim 75°$ and the case that each wake was triggered at different epoch as $1+z=3\times10^4$, 10^4 and 3×10^3.

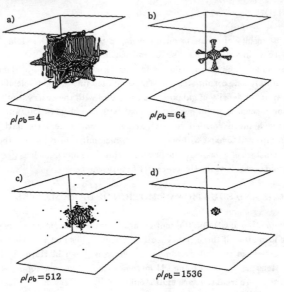

a) $\rho/\rho_b=4$

b) $\rho/\rho_b=64$

c) $\rho/\rho_b=512$

d) $\rho/\rho_b=1536$

4. CONCLUSION

Although the adopted model is rather simple, we believe that some characteristic features of clusters of galaxies are derived (see Hara et al. 1994) in the long cosmic string scheme such as
1) the surface number density of galaxies around a cluster of galaxies,
2) the velocity dispersion and number density of galaxies in a cluster of galaxies,
3) the existence of a giant galaxy such as cD galaxy in the cluster center, having a similar shape with the cluster itself.

Moreover our simulation shows that there is a characteristic length for cluster of galaxies and that clusters of galaxies are accumulating dark matter even now.

References
Hara, T., Mähönen, P., & Miyoshi, S., 1993, ApJ, 412, 22
Hara, T., Matsuura, M., Yamamoto, H., Mähönen, P., & Miyoshi, S., 1994, ApJ in press

MEDIUM REDSHIFT CLUSTERS OF GALAXIES:
M/L in CL0017-20 and CL0500-24

L. Infante, P.Fouque, G. Hertling, M. Way, H. Quintana
P. Universidad Católica de Chile, Casilla 104, Santiago 22, Chile
Edmond Giraud, European Southern Observatory

Abstract

The photometric and kinematic properties of two clusters of galaxies, namely CL0017-20 and CL0500-24, are presented. These two clusters seem alike in terms of dynamical properties, richness, compactness, luminosity function and both present arc-like structures.

1 Introduction

Clusters of galaxies are the largest collapsed mass aggregates known in the Universe. They provide both a direct estimate of the amplitude of the spectrum of fluctuations in the Universe and an estimate of Ω. Although current estimates of the mass-to-light ratios in clusters is $\sim$ 200-400 $M_\odot/L_\odot$ in medium z clusters it ranges from 90 to 200 $M_\odot/L_\odot$[1,2,3] These values are well below what is required to close the Universe. Several independent methods to determine the mass distribution in clusters have been tested, each resulting in somewhat different answers; velocities provide virial masses, photometry provides luminous mass, X-ray luminosities explore the distribution of gas in the cluster potential, lensing probes directly this potential and more recently the application of the S-Z effect have provided temperature maps[4,5,6,7,8]. Velocities only measure the mass within the orbits. Although cluster virial masses imply low values of Ω (0.1-0.2)[9] there is independent evidence for $\Omega \sim 1$[10,7] An open question is whether the dark matter is concentrated more in the outer haloes of the clusters than in the core. A rise of a factor of about 8 in the M/L is necessary to reach $\Omega \approx 1$. Infante[2] discuss the difficulties in estimating M/L in medium z clusters, in particular the estimates of the virial radius which differ by factors of 2 to 3 depending on the background, external radius used to estimate the virial radius, etc.

The existing data is insufficient for a reliable estimate of M/L in medium z clusters (0.18 < z < 0.5). According to our information, based on a bibliographic search, there are 253 clusters with measured redshifts larger than 0.18. Among them, only 14 clusters have more than 13 measured velocities.

The results in this paper are part of an ongoing program aimed at the study medium redshift clusters in the southern hemisphere. Here we present a summary of the results obtained in two clusters, CL0017-20 and CL0500-24.

2 Results

Observations were carried out with the LCO 40" and ESO 3.6m telescopes in Chile.

Magnitudes and colours were obtained for 213 galaxies in CL0017-20 and 759 galaxies in CL0500-24. Care was taken to correctly remove the background galaxies. Galaxy number counts in the surrounding field of CL0500-24 are consistent with results in other studies. The colour-magnitude diagram of CL0500-24, when contrasted with the colour-magnitude diagram of the field, shows that most of blue objects in the central area are probably field galaxies and not B-O objects. Further spectroscopy is required for the blue objects in the central region.

The luminosity functions of the two clusters have been fitted by a Schechter function. The Schechter parameters n^* and M^* (74, -20.99 in g for CL0017-20 and 52, -21.71 in V for CL0500-24) are consistent with those obtained in other studies.

Velocities were obtained for 26 galaxies in CL0017-20 and 4 in CL0500-24. Moreover, we have used 24 extra velocities from Giraud[11]. The distribution of velocities in both clusters are very close to Gaussian, in particular if CL0500-24 is split into two subconcentrations. Observed mean redshifts are $< z >_{CL0017-20} = 0.272$ and $< z >_{CL0500-24} = 0.322$, and observed line-of-sight velocity dispersions are $\sigma_{CL0017-20} = 1510$ km s^{-1} and $\sigma_{CL0500-24} = 1911$ km s^{-1}, or $\sigma_{CL0500-24C} = 917$ km s^{-1} and $\sigma_{CL0500-24N} = 1152$ km s^{-1}, when CL0500-24 is split into its subconcentrations.

A group finding algorithm was applied to the data in both clusters. No subconcentration is found in CL0017-20. However, our algorithm clearly detects two subconcentrations in CL0500-24.

Evolutionary and K – corrections were applied to the luminosities of both clusters. After correcting all quantities for relativistic effects, we obtain $(M/L)_{CL0017-20} = 127$ M$_\odot$/L$_\odot$ and $(M/L)_{CL0500-24} = 157$ M$_\odot$/L$_\odot$. Although both clusters show conspicuous arc-like structures centered on the cluster, they have low mass-to-light ratios.

A determination of Abell richness class has been done. CL0017-20 appears to be class 2 (88 galaxies in one Abell radius) and CL0500-24 class 1 (65 galaxies).

This work was supported in part by FONDECYT grant #1930570.

References

[1] Mellier, Y., Soucail, G., Fort, B., & Mathez, G., 1988, A&A, 199 , 13. [2] Infante, L., Fouque, P., Hertling, G., Way, M., Giraud, E. & Quintana, H., 1994, A&A, in press. [3] Sharples, R.M., Ellis, R.S., Couch, W.J., & Gray, P.M., 1985, MNRAS 212 , 687. [4] Wu and Hammer, 1993, MNRAS 262 , 187 [5] Smail et al. 1994, this conference. [6] Jones, 1994, this conference. [7] Kaiser, 1994, this conference. [8] Tyson 1992, Physics Today Vol 45, N° 6, 24. [9] Kent and Gunn 1982, AJ 87 , 945. [10] Bertschinger et al 1990, ApJ 364 , 370 [11] Giraud, E. 1990, A&AS 83 , 1

A MULTI-WAVELENGTH MASS ESTIMATE OF A z=0.31 CLUSTER

HAIDA LIANG
Mount Stromlo and Siding Spring Observatories, The Australian National University, Private Bag, Weston Creek Post Office, ACT 2611, Australia

RONALD D EKERS
Australia Telescope National Facility, P.O. Box 76, Epping 2112, Australia

The Cluster MS2137-23

MS2137-23 was first discovered in the Einstein Extended Medium Sensitivity Survey (EMSS).[2)3)7)] It is a strong X-ray source with a luminosity $L_X \sim 10^{45}$ ergs s^{-1} and has a redshift of $z = 0.31$. A giant gravitational 'arc' ($15.5''$ from its centre), a radial arc ($5''$ from its centre) and a number of smaller 'arclets' have been found by Fort *et al.* (1992). Mellier *et al.* (1993) modelled the cluster potential using both these arcs and successfully predicted the positions of the arclets. The cluster velocity dispersion and core radius deduced from the model were $800 < \sigma_{los} < 1100$ km/s (for 'arc' redshift of 0.5 to 3) and $6'' < r_c < 8.5''$, respectively.

An attempt to detect the Sunyaev-Zel'dovich effect [8)] in the direction of this cluster has been made using the Australia Telescope (AT) because of the cluster's high X-ray luminosity and the presence of the giant arc. We obtained an effective integration time of 40 hrs at 8.7GHz in the ultra-compact configuration of the AT (maximum baseline of 122m). There were 7 discrete radio sources in the field with the strongest having a flux of 0.8 mJy at 8.7 GHz. After the subtraction of the radio sources, we obtained a flux decrement of -0.132 ± 0.039 mJy at the cluster centre.

Modelling

The cluster gravitational potential and thus the total mass is well constrained by the lensing 'arcs' as modelled by Mellier *et al.* within the radius of the giant tangential arc (85 kpc). The only X-ray information published is the luminosity. In the X-ray image the cluster fell close to the edge of the Einstein IPC detector where the resolution is low. Analysis of the data showed that the cluster is unresolved which places an upper limit of 0.1 Mpc on the X-ray core radius [5] which is consistent with the core radius deduced from lensing. Since there is no X-ray temperature information available, we can not constrain the total mass or gas mass using this X-ray data alone. However, we can construct a self-consistent model of the gas properties from the X-ray luminosity, results of the SZ effect and the potential deduced from lensing data [5].

We will assume here that the gas is isothermal, spherically symmetric and in hydrostatic equilibrium. From the equation of hydrostatic equilibrium, the gas density profile is given by

$$\rho_{gas}(r)/\rho_o = \exp[\frac{\mu m_p}{kT_{gas}}(\phi(r) - \phi_o)] \tag{1}$$

where $\phi(r)$ is the cluster potential which is given by the lensing models.[6] Since the ellipticity of the deduced 2-D cluster potential is small, we will approximate it by a circular potential and de-project it to a spherically symmetric 3-D potential. The X-ray luminosity is given by $L_x \propto \rho_{gas}^2 \Lambda(T_{gas})$ and the SZ decrement $\Delta T \propto \rho_{gas} T_{gas}$, thus given L_x, ΔT and $\phi(r)$, we can determine the gas temperature T_{gas} and central electron density for the gas. Analysis show that $T_{gas} < 1.2 \times 10^8$K for the range of r_c and σ_{los} given by Mellier *et al.*. The best fit model gives $T_{gas} = 9 \times 10^7$K and $n_{e,0} = 0.68$ cm^{-3}. Thus the mass of various components within 85 kpc are $M_{tot} \sim 4.1 \times 10^{13} M_\odot$, $M_{gas} \sim 1.9 \times 10^{12} M_\odot$ and $M_{gal} \sim 6.5 \times 10^{12} M_\odot$. The $M_{tot}/L_B \sim 100 M_\odot/L_\odot$ and $(M_{gas} + M_{gal})/M_{tot} \sim 0.18$ which are similar to nearby clusters. Within the central 85 kpc this cluster has similar mass as Coma[4] even though it is poorer than Coma. The optical number counts from I band AAT CCD images show that the cluster is very diffuse with an Abell richness class of 1.

Conclusions

1. We have been able to construct a self-consistent model for the cluster gas properties using the available data from X-ray, SZ effect and the gravitational potential deduced from lensing effects.
2. The gas temperature is $< 1.2 \times 10^8$K and the best fit temperature is 9×10^7 K assuming that the gas is not clumpy.
3. The hot gas is $> 5\%$ of the cluster total mass and the baryonic fraction in the central 85 kpc is > 0.15.
4. The cluster MS2137-23 has a relatively small X-ray core radius (< 0.1Mpc) consistent with the lensing deduced core radius.

References

1. Fort B. *et al.*, 1992, *Ap. J.*, **399**, L125.
2. Gioia I. M. *et al.*, 1990 *Ap. J.*, **356**, L35.
3. Henry J. P. and Arnaud, K. A.,1991, *Ap. J.*,**372**, 410.
4. Hughes J. P., 1989, *Ap. J.*, **337**, 21.
5. Liang H. & Ekers R., 1994, to be submitted to ApJ.
6. Mellier Y., Fort B. & Kneib J., 1993, *Ap. J.*,**407**, 33.
7. Stocke J., Morris S., Gioia I., Maccacaro T., Schild R., Wolter A., Fleming T. and Henry J., 1991, *Ap. J. Suppl.*, **76**,813.
8. Sunyaev, R. A. and Zel'dovich, Ya. B., 1972, *Comments Astrophys. Space Phys.*, **4**, 173.

ESO KEY-PROJECT "CLUSTERS OF GALAXIES"

A.Mazure, E.Escalera (Montpellier University, France)
P.Katgert, R.Den Hartog, (Leiden Observatory, Netherlands)
P.Dubath (ESO, Munich, Germany)
D.Gerbal , A.Biviano (IAP, France)
P.Focardi (Bologna University, Italy)
G.Giuricin (SISSA, Italy)
B.Jones (Niels Bohr Institute, Denmark)
O. Lefevre (Meudon Observatory, France)
M.Moles, J.Perea (Institute of Astrophysics,Grenade, Espagne)
G.Rhee (University of Nevada,Las Vegas, USA).

Abstract

More than 5000 radial velocities among 106 rich ACO clusters have been obtained in the frame of an ESO Key Project. Results are presented concerning kinematics of galaxies within clusters as well as on Large Scale Structures.

I. PROPERTIES OF EMISSION LINE GALAXIES IN CLUSTERS

A well known morphology segregation is present in clusters of galaxies: Spirals are found preferentially in low dense regions, while Ellipticals and Lenticulars are in denser ones (Dressler 1980). Is it possible to detect also differences between these two classes when considering kinematics? This problem has been already addressed within the last decade on limited samples (Moss & Dickens 1977 Sodré et al 1989 Tully & Shaya 1984...) and updated with recent redshift surveys: Zabludoff et al (1993).

The possible scenario for the two populations is the following:

E and S0 are lying inside the virialized core , Sp and Irr are falling on the potential well (secondary infall) either in outer layers (symmetric infall) or in groups (asymmetric infall) and then could appear in sub-clumps.

Then , differences for the 2 classes could appear when looking at:

-Velocity dispersions which could be different since Sp and Irr have V-infall.

- Mean velocities which could be different in the case of asymmetric infall (Zabludoff et al 1993, Van Harlem 1993), and not different in the case of symmetric infall.

- Spatial distribution since Sp are expected to be on the outskirts of the cluster.

More than 5000 reliable velocities in direction of 106 ACO clusters have been obtained in the frame of the ESO K-Project on clusters of galaxies. No morphological types are so far available for our sample but 2 populations could be defined:

-Emission line galaxies (ELG)

and

- Non Emission Line Galaxies (NELG).

The mean fraction of ELG is around 10 to 15 % (with large variations from cluster to cluster) in agreement with the mean spiral population found in clusters. From our sample, it appears that both velocity dispersions and spatial distribution (harmonic mean radius) differ significantly in a statistical way . The velocity dispersion for ELG is found greater than that of NELG (about 14%) and their harmonic mean radius also (20%) in agreement with Sodré et al results. We found no statistical differences between $< V_{ELG} >$ and $< V_{NELG} >$ although in some clusters large differences appear. Moreover, a first analysis shows no obvious correlation of ELG with subclustering. As a consequence, NELG appear as " well virialized " , and ELG not virialized in the same potential well.

Although no systematic difference appears between mean velocities, it is still difficult to conclude concerning a-/symmetric infall. However the fact that the harmonic mean radius of ELG is found greater than that of NELG is rather inconsistent with ELG concentrated in sub-groups.

Finally, looking at luminosity functions for ELG/NELG shows that they are significantly different with less bright galaxies for ELG.

II.PROBING LARGE SCALE STRUCTURES

II.a. New superstructures.

About 9 hours in alpha and 60 degrees in delta have been covered up to a redshift z=0.1. Using the KPGM and litterature data a uniform sampling in volume and Abell richness is obtained up to z=0.08. Examination of the distribution of the systems observed leads to the detection of cluster concentrations including the Shapley concentration and others (Grus-Indus, Horologium-Reticulum...) with new redshifts of clusters added. As far as we know, we identify a new concentration at z = 0.08-0.09. This superstructure could include about 10 (rich) clusters, of which 7 have measured redshifts from the KPGM within a region of 20x20x20 Mpc^3. This system is located at 270 Mpc (H_0 =100) and would correspond to an overdensity of 10 to 20. Another concentration is also found at z=0.1. Only one redshift is measured but the other redshifts estimated using m_{10} are in agreement with the distance.

Such concentrations seem comparable to the Great Attractor region where 5 clusters are found within 25 Mpc. The concerned clusters here are the following: A3671, A3677, A3681, A3682, A3690, A3691, A3693, A3694, A3705, A3706, A3734, A3752, A3764, A3778, A3795, A3813, A3814.

II.b. Distribution of Large Scale Structures

Analysing redshifts obtained along 106 lines of sight in direction of ACO clusters we detect many systems detected along each line of sight. We then calculate inter-galaxy distances along each one and put all together. Several (broad) peaks appear more or less regular with some inter distances avoided.

Separations in z about 0.013 (40 Mpc, H_0 = 100) appear the most probable with may be some harmonics between 0.03-0.04 and 0.04-0.05. No significative peak appears around 128 Mpc. Work is in progress to

406

compare with more or less organized models (Poisson, hierarchical clusters, Voronoi foam).

REFERENCES

Capelato et al, AA, 117, 17, 1983
Dressler, ApJ Supp, 236, 351, 1980
Moss & Dickens, MNRAS, 178,701, 1977
Sodré et al, AJ, 97, 1279, 1989
Tully & Shaya, AJ, 281, 31
Van Harlem, PhD Thesis, Leiden, 1992
Vettolani et al, Preprint, 1993
Zabludoff et al, AJ, 106, 1314, 1993

NON-SPHERICAL COLLAPSE AND THE MASS FUNCTION

P. Monaco

SISSA, via Beirut 4, 34013 - Trieste, Italy
Dipartimento di Astronomia, Università degli Studi di Trieste, Trieste, Italy

Abstract

A first attempt to obtain an expression for the mass distribution of collapsed clumps was made by Press & Schechter[3] (hereafter PS), who assumed that any overdensity, taken from a smoothed Gaussian density field, follows the spherical collapse model. The PS mass function has generally been found to fit reasonably the results of N-body simulations. More recently, Jain & Bertschinger[1] have claimed that the PS mass function significantly underestimates the number of high-redshift high-mass objects. This can be explained[2] by using non-spherical models for the collapse of generical perturbations.

The relevant quantity for the construction of a mass function is the instant of collapse of a given mass element, i.e. when the Lagrangian density diverges, so that the mass function can be regarded as an intrinsically Lagrangian quantity. For a cold irrotational fluid element, a general non-spherical perturbation is characterized by a non-vanishing shear, whose evolution equation is non-local. In this brief report we describe how to find reasonable approximations for the collapse time from local initial conditions, and the consequences on the mass function.

408

In the framework of Zel'dovich[4] approximation (ZEL), the evolution of a perturbation is local. However, ZEL predicts a spherical perturbation to collapse slower than the exact spherical solution. To overcome this problem, I propose[2] to take as the collapse time the minimum between the spherical and ZEL predictions (ZEL *ansatz*). Moreover, I have used the homogeneous ellipsoid model (HEM) to describe the collapse of a perturbation from local initial conditions.

It is possible to express the mass function as the product of the PS one times a correction factor $\mathcal{I}(\sigma)$, which is a function of the mass variance σ. It turns out that non-spherical perturbations reach high densities faster than spherical ones. As a consequence, more high-mass objects are predicted to form. In Fig. 1 the $\mathcal{I}(\sigma)$ curves are showed for the ZEL *ansatz* (dashed curve) and HEM (continuous curve). Both models predict a bump to appear in the mass function around M^*, while HEM predicts also a shift of M^* toward large masses (see Fig. 2).

In conclusion, while the PS mass function remains a good first approximation, our prediction of an enhancement of high-mass objects is consistent with Jain & Bertschinger's findings[1], but only at high redshifts. At later times, highly non-linear events, such as dynamical friction or previrialization, can effectively slow down the collapse rate, especially for non-spherical collapse, so as to erase the excess of high-mass objects.

References

1) Jain, B., & Bertschinger, E. 1993, preprint IAS-AST-93/70
2) Monaco, P., in preparation
3) Press, W.H., & Schechter, P. 1974, ApJ 187, 425
4) Zel'dovich, Ya.B. 1970, Astrofizika 6, 319 (trad.: 1973, Astrophysics 6, 164)

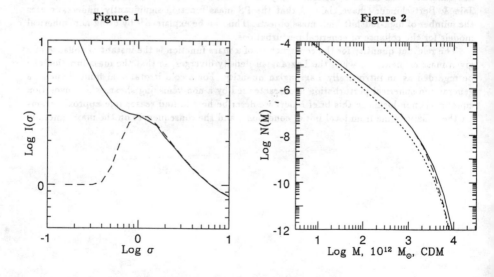

Figure 1   Figure 2

OBSERVATIONAL SUPPORT FOR THE GURZADYAN-KOCHARYAN RELATION IN CLUSTERS OF GALAXIES

P. Monaco

SISSA, via Beirut 4, 34013 - Trieste, Italy
Dipartimento di Astronomia, Università degli Studi di Trieste, Trieste, Italy

Abstract

It is well known that the Hausdorff (fractal) dimension d_H of a system, such as a cluster of galaxies, is related to the slope γ of the two-point correlation function by the relation

$$d_H = 3 - \gamma \simeq 1.2. \tag{1}$$

Gurzadyan & Kocharyan[3], by means of the theory of dynamical systems, have succeeded in deriving the following formula for an autogravitating system of galaxies:

$$d_H \simeq 3(1 - 2/3 \ \exp(-T/\tau_{GS})), \tag{2}$$

where T is the Hubble time and τ_{GS} is the Gurzadyan-Savvidy[4] relaxation time:

$$\tau_{GS} = \left(\frac{15}{4}\right)^{2/3} \frac{1}{2\pi\sqrt{2}} \frac{v}{Gmn^{2/3}}. \tag{3}$$

Here v is the velocity dispersion, m the mean mass of the objects and n the number density (related to some well-defined size of the system). Eq. 2 gives us a very general dynamical explanation of the Hausdorff dimension of a galaxy system, and, furthermore, it connects the geometric observable d_H to the dynamical properties of the system itself. In this brief report we check observationally the validity of Gurzadyan-Kocharyan relation for certain well-studied rich clusters of galaxies[5].

It has been shown[2] that the observable velocity dispersion of bright galaxies is a meaningful estimate of the true velocity dispersion v. As an estimate of the cluster density, the Bahcall's[1] counts of core galaxies, $N_{0.5}^c$, are taken: we assume $n = \alpha N_{0.5}^c$. Moreover, it is assumed that all the mass of the Universe is in collapsed clumps, with masses ranging from about $10^6 M_\odot$ to about $10^{13} M_\odot$ according to some mass function which is universal.

We can sum up all our ignorance in the determination of the quantity τ_{GS}/T in the following way:

$$\tau_{GS}/T = 1.46\, v\, (N_{0.5}^c)^{-2/3}\, p, \tag{4}$$

(v in km/s), where p is an "uncertainty" parameter whose value is $p = 1/(mh\alpha^{2/3})$ (m in units of $10^{10} M_\odot$). The stability of p for different clusters of the same richness class is the only assumption we need. Moreover, an order-of-magnitude estimate of p gives[5] a value of $10^{-2\pm1}$.

Samples of cluster galaxies with known redshifts have been taken for four Richness 2 Abell clusters, namely Abell 401, Abell 426 (Perseus), Abell 1656 (Coma) and Abell 1795. For every cluster the galaxy angular correlation function $w(\theta)$ has been estimated. At small angular scales, up to some tenths of degree, the correlation function can be fitted by a power law, $w(\theta) \propto \theta^{-\beta}$. Limber equation gives $\beta = \gamma - 1$. At larger scales the correlation function steepens and then becomes negative, just because of the geometry of the cluster profile.

Table 1 lists the obtained small-scale slopes β and Hausdorff dimensions d_H (Eq. 1) for the four clusters: in all cases the Hausdorff dimension is marginally or significantly greater than 1.2, which is consistent with Eq. 2. To verify whether Eqs. 2 and 3 give a consistent dynamical picture, estimates of the uncertainty parameter p have been obtained by comparing the estimates of the relaxation time τ_{GS} given by Eq. 2 and Eq. 4. Table 1 shows that these estimates p_{est} are consistent among themselves and are of the order of magnitude predicted.

It is concluded[5] that the Gurzadyan-Kocharyan relation gives a dynamical description of the space distribution of cluster galaxies which is consistent with our data. The study of large samples of galaxies in clusters and in other systems will be able to give more precise answers.

Table 1: Results

	$N_{0.5}^c$ (1)	v (km/s) (2)	$(\tau_{GS}/T)_{Eq.4}$ (3)	d_H (4)	$(\tau_{GS}/T)_{Eq.2}$ (5)	$p_{est} \times 10^2$ (6)
A 401	34	1254	$174 \times p$	1.43 ± 0.10	$4.13^{+1.42}_{-0.88}$	$2.4^{+1.6}_{-0.8}$
A 426	32	1253	$181 \times p$	1.57 ± 0.09	$2.98^{+0.66}_{-0.48}$	$1.6^{+0.9}_{-0.4}$
A 1656	28	1049	$166 \times p$	1.71 ± 0.13	$2.28^{+0.64}_{-0.44}$	$1.4^{+0.8}_{-0.5}$
A 1795	27	899	$146 \times p$	1.73 ± 0.20	$2.20^{+1.14}_{-0.60}$	$1.5^{+1.3}_{-0.6}$

References

1) Bahcall N.A., 1981, ApJ 247, 787
2) Girardi M., Biviano A., Giuricin G., Mardirossian F., Mezzetti M., 1993, ApJ 404, 38
3) Gurzadyan V.G., Kocharyan A.A., 1991, Europh. Lett. 15, 801
4) Gurzadyan V.G., Savvidy G.K., 1986, A&A 160, 203
5) Monaco, P., 1994, A&AL, accepted

Mass Determination of Clusters of Galaxies with ROSAT/PSPC Data

Doris M. Neumann
Max-Planck-Institut für extraterrestrische Physik
85740 Garching, FRG

Abstract

The determination of the total mass of clusters of galaxies is an important goal in modern astronomy. The X–ray ROSAT/PSPC data provide sufficient spatial and energy resolution to estimate not only the total mass of galaxy clusters but also the distribution of the total mass. Therefore new methods of mass determination are necessary, which make no a priori assumptions on the cluster's gravitational potential. We developed such a method using a Monte–Carlo–Simulation.

Mass Analysis of Two Galaxy Clusters

The mass determination is based on the assumptions of hydrostatic equilibrium of the ICM and approximate spherical symmetry of the cluster. In a first step the gas density distribution is determined by fitting a β-model[1] to the surface brightness profile of the cluster. The temperature distribution is obtained spectroscopically in concentric rings around the centre

412

of symmetry. Due to the large uncertainties in the temperature, a direct solution of the hydrostatic equation is impracticable. In using a Monte–Carlo–Simulation we are able to take into account all possible shapes of the temperature profile within the given error bars and the requirement of increasing total mass with radius. The combination of all solutions provides the uncertainties of the mass profile[2].

For the application of this method we used AWM7, a poor cluster with 33 galaxies[3]. and the Perseus cluster of galaxies (about 187 galaxies[4]) as first candidates. Figure 1 shows the results for AWM7. For the Perseus cluster we determine a total mass of 4–8 $\cdot 10^{14} M_\odot$ at a radius of 1200 kpc. The total amount of gas is approximately $6 \cdot 10^{13} M_\odot$.

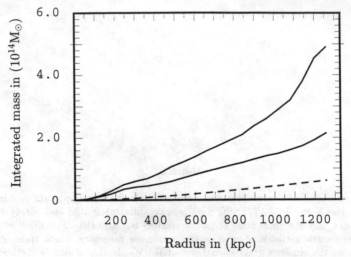

Figure 1: Total mass profile of AWM7 (solid lines: upper and lower limit). The dashed line indicates the mass of the ICM

References

1 Gorenstein P. D., Fabricant D., Topka K. *et al.*, 1978 Ap. J., 224, 718.

2 Neumann D. M., *Cosmological Aspects of X-ray Clusters of Galaxies*, Kluwer, in preparation.

3 Malumuth E. M., 1992, Ap. J., 386, 420.

4 Kent S. M., Sargent W. L. W., 1983, A. J., 88, 697.

THE DETECTION OF EXTENDED HI ABSORPTION IN ABELL 2597

C. O'Dea[1], S. Baum[1], & J. Gallimore[1,2]

[1] Space Telescope Science Institute, 3700 San Martin Dr., Baltimore, MD 21218
[2] University of Maryland, Astronomy Program, College Park, MD 20742

ABSTRACT

We have detected HI in absorption towards the bright radio source PKS 2322-123 associated with the central cD galaxy in the rich cluster A2597.

We detect a 'narrow' velocity width component with FWHM $\sim$ 220 km s^{-1} (towards the nucleus only) which is spatially unresolved and redshifted by $\sim 200 - 300$ km s^{-1} from the systemic velocity. We suggest that this component may be associated with ongoing cannibalism in the cD galaxy.

We detect a 'broad' velocity width component with FWHM $\sim$ 410 km s^{-1} which is spatially extended over the $\sim 3''$ extent of the radio source and which is at the systemic velocity of the optical emission lines. We suggest that this component is associated with the bright Hα nebula (Crawford & Fabian 1992; Heckman et al. 1989). Our derived parameters suggest that there is much more mass in the HI than in the Hα implying that the nebula is photon bounded.

The basic observational parameters of the broad component, (e.g, systemic velocity, low optical depth, broad line width) are very similar to the absorption found in NGC1275 (3C84) in the Perseus cluster.

OBSERVATIONS AND RESULTS

The VLA results are summarized in Tables 1 and 2. For details, see O'Dea, Baum, & Gallimore (1994).

Table 1. Results

Broad Component	
Peak	3.0 ± 0.3 mJy
FWHM	412 ± 40 km s^{-1}
Center velocity (heliocentric)	24604 ± 17 km s^{-1}
$\Delta S/S$	0.0056
Narrow Component	
Peak	7.7 ± 0.3 mJy
FWHM	221 ± 10 km s^{-1}
Center velocity (heliocentric)	24886 ± 5 km s^{-1}
$\Delta S/S$	0.0187

Table 2. Derived Parameters of the HI

Parameter	Broad Component	Narrow Component
Optical Depth τ	0.006	0.019
Covering factor	$0.006 < c_f < 1$	$0.019 < c_f < 1$
Column Density N_H/T_s cm^{-2} K^{-1}	4.5×10^{18}	8.2×10^{18}
Mass M/T_s M$_\odot$ K^{-1}	7×10^5	3.5×10^5
Cloud radius pc	$2.6 \times 10^{-2} < r_{cl} < 4.4$	
Number of clouds	$4 \times 10^3 < N_{cl} < 2 \times 10^{10}$	

ACKNOWLEDGEMENTS

JG was partially supported by the STScI DDRF. The VLA is operated by NRAO which is operated by AUI under cooperative agreement with NSF.

REFERENCES

Crawford, C. S. & Fabian, A. C. 1992, MNRAS, 259, 265

Heckman, T., Baum, S., van Breugel, W., & McCarthy, P. 1989, ApJ., 338, 48

O'Dea, C. P., Baum, S. A., & Gallimore, J. 1994, ApJ, in press

A ROSAT SEARCH FOR CLUSTERS
AROUND POWERFUL RADIO GALAXIES

C.P. O'Dea[1], D.M. Worrall[2], D. Gilmore[1], S.A. Baum[1], E. Zirbel[1], C. Stanghellini[3]

[1] Space Telescope Science Institute, 3700 San Martin Dr., Baltimore, MD 21218, USA
[2] Harvard-Smithsonian Center for Astrophysics, 60 Garden St., Cambridge, MA 02138, USA
[3] Istituto di Radioastronomia del CNR, Stazione di Noto C.P. 169, I-96017 Noto (SR), ITALY

ABSTRACT

We have obtained ROSAT PSPC observations of three powerful radio galaxies in order to search for extended x-ray emission from a surrounding cluster of galaxies.

We detect extended emission (a β model fit gives FWHM $\simeq$ 165 kpc for $\beta = 2/3$ and $H_o = 75$ km s^{-1}Mpc^{-1}) from the classical double radio galaxy 2053–201 ($z = 0.156$) with a luminosity of $L_x \sim 3 \times 10^{43}$ ergs s^{-1}. This is in agreement with the expected emission from an Abell cluster (e.g., Henry et al. 1982) and also with previous detections of closer 3CR FRII radio galaxies (Fabbiano et al. 1984; Feigelson & Berg 1983).

We also observed two GHz Peaked Spectrum Radio Galaxies (O'Dea, Baum, & Stanghellini 1991) 1345+125 ($z = 0.122$) and 2352+495 ($z = 0.237$). The 3σ upper limits to the x-ray luminosity are on the order of $L_x < 3 \times 10^{42}$ ergs s^{-1} and are about an order of magnitude below the detection of 2053–201. These observations support the hypothesis that GPS radio galaxies and their environments are not strong x-ray emitters. The upper limits are too low to be consistent with emission from a typical Abell cluster, but are consistent with the x-ray luminosity of poor clusters with central dominant galaxies (Kriss et al. 1983) or from groups of galaxies (Dell'Antonio et al. 1994).

The limits on x-ray luminosity are near the low end of the distribution for FRII radio galaxies, but are in agreement with the lower x-ray luminosity FRI radio galaxies (Fabbiano et al. 1984). This is puzzling since the high radio power and host galaxy properties are in general similar to those of FRII rather than FRI radio galaxies (e.g., Stanghellini et al. 1993; O'Dea, in preparation). Thus, the active nuclei are either intrinsically weak in the soft x-rays (compared to typical FRII radio galaxies) or are heavily obscured.

OBSERVATIONS AND RESULTS

The results are summarized in Table 1 for the case of a Raymond-Smith (RS) model for the x-ray emission and will be discussed elsewhere in more detail (O'Dea *et al.* in preparation). Upper limits are 3σ and are given for two apertures corresponding to (1) a point source and (2) a 200 kpc radius extended source.

Table 1. Results

Source	model	aperture radius (arcsec)	PSPC counts	flux 0.2 - 2 keV 10^{-13} ergs/cm^2/s	luminosity 0.2 - 2 keV 10^{42} ergs/s
(1)	(2)	(3)	(4)	(5)	(6)
2053–201	RS	120	492.3 ± 28.3	6.61	32.2
1345+125	RS	35	< 25.7	< 0.58	< 1.7
1345+125	RS	100	< 35.9	< 0.98	< 2.9
2352+495	RS	35	< 16.9	< 0.12	< 1.4
2352+495	RS	61	< 19.8	< 0.15	< 1.7

ACKNOWLEDGEMENTS

This research was partially supported by NASA grant NAG5-2158. We are grateful to Bob Mutel for his enthusiasm and encouragement.

REFERENCES

Dell'Antonio, I. P., Geller, M. J., & Fabricant, D. G., 1994, AJ, 107, 427

Fabbiano, G., Miller, L., Trinchieri, G., Longain, M., & Elvis, M., 1984, ApJ, 277, 115

Feigelson, E. D. & Berg, C. J., 1983, ApJ, 269, 400

Henry, J. P., Soltan, A., Briel, U., & Gunn, J. E., 1982, ApJ, 262, 1

Kriss, G. A., Cioffi, D. F., & Canizares, C. R., 1983, ApJ, 272, 439

O'Dea, C. P., Baum, S. A., & Stanghellini, C. 1991, ApJ, 380, 66

Stanghellini, C., O'Dea, C. P., Baum, S. A., & Laurikainen, E., 1993, ApJS, 88, 1

ROSAT HRI OBSERVATION OF THE GRAVITATIONAL LENS CLUSTER A2390

M. Pierre   (CE Saclay, SAp, F-91191 Gif sur Yvette)

J.-F. Leborgne, G. Soucail   (Obs. Midi-Pyrenées, F-31400 Toulouse)

Abstract

We present a preliminary analysis of a 30 ksec ROSAT HRI image of A2390 which is a remarkable gravitational lens. The X-ray data confirm the presence of a strong cooling flow and indicate that the underlying gravitational potential is very elongated, as suggested by the galaxy distribution.

Introduction

The rich cluster of galaxies Abell 2390 is a well known gavitational lens, exhibiting a giant arc and numerous arclets. The giant arc has the remarkable property of having a straight shape; it is made of three clumps, covers at total size of 15"x1.3" and has a redshift of 0.913 (Pelló et al 1991).

The cluster has a mean redshift of 0.231 and a velocity dispersion of 2122 km/s (Le Borgne et al 1991). It is dominated by a large cD in its center and a central radio source was detected by Owen et al (1982). Optical spectroscopy of the central galaxy (Le Borgne et al 1991) revealed an extended region with emission lines caracteristic of a cooling flow.

The distribution of the cluster galaxies is clumpy and strongly elongated in the SE-NW direction which coincides with the cD's main axis. A velocity gradient is also observed along this direction which may explain the large velocity dispersion; however, the velocity histogramme does not allow to assign peculiar velocities to the substructures observed in the galaxy distribution.

It is possible to model the underlying gravitational potential by fitting the straight arc, either with a bimodal potential (Pelló et al 1991) or a very ellongated potential (Kassiola et al 1992). This cluster is a strong X-ray emitter (McMilian et al 1989 and references therein) but the Einstein image did not allow to constrain further the potential shape. This has motivated a 30 ksec ROSAT HRI pointing. With a spatial resolution of 5" it will be possible to map in detail the gas distribution and constrain the gravitational potential responsible for the observed features. Values of 50 $km/sec/Mpc$ and 0.5 were assumed for H_o and q_o respectively.

X-ray analysis

The X-ray image of Abel 2390 is shown on Fig. 1. The X-ray centroid coincides with the cD position and the ellipticity of the contours follows closely that of the galaxy. A bump about 45" in the North-West is associated to a galaxy density enhancement were the gravitational arc is located. On a larger scale, the direction of the galaxy's main axis seems also to be favored by the overall galaxy distribution: 4 clumps of galaxies are conspicuous at 2.3' to the South-East and 1.8' to the North-West (two on each side). They are likely to be associated to the X-ray clumps observed at the periphery (the significance of these X-ray clumps is from 3 to 5 σ above local background). All of this seems to suggest that the cluster is not in a relaxed state, but is undergoing some merging events with a preferential direction strongly characterized, which could be related to structures on much larger scales. This could be investigated in a more detailed analysis of the galaxy velocities. Moreover, the detailed contour plot shows clearly a high, almost circular, peak at the very cluster center, confirming the presence of a cooling flow. The total cluster luminosity is $\sim 2 \; 10^{45}$ erg/sec in the ROSAT band (assuming a mean temperature of 5 keV).

The radial surface brightness distribution (assuming in first approximation spherical symetry) was fitted by means of two King profiles, in order to disentangle the cooling flow contribution from that of the cluster and to further derive the potential. This gives core radii of 112 kpc and 335 kpc and β of 0.83 and 0.60 for the cooling flow and the proper cluster diffuse contribution respectively. Corresponding gas density distribution were derived and, assuming a cluster age of 10^{10} years we calculated the maximum radius up to which cooling is efficient ($t_{cool} = 7\ 10^{10}T^{1/2}\rho^{-1}$ $years$, where T is in units of $10^8 K$ and ρ of $10^{-3}cm^3$). For a mean temperature of 5 keV, this yields 186 kpc and corresponds exactly to the point where the cooling flow's contribution becomes negligible. The fraction of the total luminosity enclosed within this radius is $\sim 20\%$. Corresponding mass flow rate is 300 Mo or 754 Mo for a cooling flow temperature of 5 or 2 keV respectively.

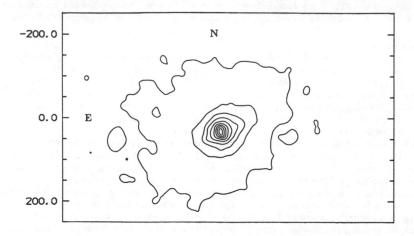

Figure: ROSAT HRI image of A2390. It revealed an overall elongated morphology as well as a highly peaked central emission indicating the presence of a strong cooling flow. First contour and contour increment are 0.08 and 0.15 $counts/arcsec^2$ respectively. Y-axis is in units of 0.5".

Conclusions

The cluster A2390 shows numerous remarkable properties, making presently an unified view of the cluster premature. Two main aspects can be stressed:

-1- There are X-ray evidences for a strong cooling flow which is certainly related to filaments detected in optical. This makes the study of the inner cluster potential even more delicate.

-2- The mass distribution (optical, X-ray) is very elongated along the cD main axis direction. In the assumption where the overall dark matter distribution follows that of the gas, the hypothesis of a bimodal potential is therefore excluded. The elliptical potential proposed by Kassiola et al (1992) seems presently the only viable solution. However, the model parameters need to be carefully determined using both optical and X-ray data; special care is to be given to the amount, compactness and ellipticity of the dark matter with respect to that of the gas.

References

Kassiola A., Kovner I., Blandford R.D., 1992 ApJ 396, 10

Le Borgne J.F., Mathez G., Mellier Y., Pelló R., Sanahuja B., Soucail G., 1991 A& AS 88, 133

McMilian S.L.W., Kowalski M.P., Ulmer M.P., 1989 ApJS 70, 723

Owen F.N., White R.A., Hilldrup K.C., Hanisen, 1982 AJ 87, 1083

Pelló R., Le Borgne J.F., Soucail G., Mellier Y., Sanahuja B., 1991 ApJ 366, 405.

BUTCHER – OEMLER EFFECT:
BURSTS OR TRUNCATED STAR FORMATION?

B.M. Poggianti and G. Barbaro
Dipartimento di Astronomia, vicolo dell'Osservatorio 5, 35122 Padova, Italy

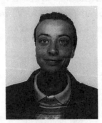

THE BUTCHER – OEMLER EFFECT

Butcher and Oemler (1978, 1984) found in several distant rich galaxy clusters a much larger fraction of blue galaxies than in similar nearby clusters. Their chief conclusion has been made stronger by further investigations, but a more complex behaviour concerning galaxies in distant clusters has emerged, revealing that a larger number of them have or have had recently a relevant activity of star formation. Hereafter we will restrict our discussion to galaxies lacking present activity, but with an anomalous recent star formation witnessed by either strong Balmer absorption lines ("E+A") or by an UV excess (Euvx). In both cases the continuum spectrum longward λ=3000 Å can be fitted with an elliptical.

A detailed analysis is needed in order to clarify whether bursts in ellipticals or truncated star formation in spirals (or both) are responsible for these observed anomalous galaxies and to suggest discriminating future observations. An evolutionary synthesis model, based on the code of Barbaro and Olivi (1989), is employed: each burst model represents an elliptical galaxy with exponential SF rate with time scale of 1 Gyr to which a second episode of SF is added (for a classification of the bursts see PB (1994)). Spirals models with and without burst prior to the interruption of the SF are also considered. The well studied cluster A370 at z=0.37 is taken as an example.

It will be interesting to compare models predictions with the direct morphological HST classification that are becoming available for some clusters (Couch et al.,1994, Dressler et al., 1994, Wirth, 1994). Preliminary results of this work suggest that starbursts are effective in both ellipticals and spirals: a detailed theoretical analysis is then even more valuable.

COLOURS

An elliptical with burst cannot be distinguished from a spiral with truncated star formation (with or without a burst) in any colour with effective wavelenght $\lambda > 2500$ Å. This is valid also for the Euvx galaxies in A370, that are equally well fitted by the two kinds of models. However there is a range of wavelenght where the two spectra differ significantly. This is illustrated in Fig.1, which shows the spectra of the models of a normal Sc (solid line), an elliptical with burst (long dashed line) and an Sc where the star formation ended 1

Gyr ago (short dashed line) in the rest frame at z=0.38. The truncated spiral is *redder* for $\lambda < 2500$ (rest frame) than the elliptical with burst but they have the same observed (U-685) and (418-685) colours of an Euvx in Abell 370. The spiral is missing the significant presence of metal – rich P-AGB stars that in ellipticals belong to the populations of the old bulk of star formation and are the main contributors to the UV flux.

Therefore a *far UV – visible colour* (like (1550-V) in A370) *would allow to discriminate if an observed object with UV excess originates from an elliptical or from a spiral-like galaxy.*

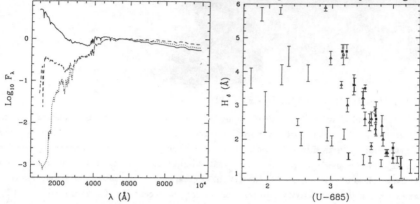

Figure 1. Models spectra.   Figure 2. H_δ vs. (U-685).

H_δ EQUIVALENT WIDTH

Fig.2 shows the relation between the $EW(H_\delta)$ and the colour (U-685) for a set of models at z=0.38: truncated spirals(triangles), ellipticals with a burst ended at least 0.5 Gyr ago (squares) and with a more recent burst (R). A burst added to a spiral before the truncation has the effect to mimic a later morphological type. There is a correlation between H_δ and (U-685), although a quite large spread is found in the case of recent bursts: the EW is affected mainly by type A dwarf stars and therefore is sensitive to star formation 1-2 Gyrs old. On the contrary, the U band reveals in particular more recent bursts; this explains why such a spread is not found in the case of old bursts. The knowledge of the H_δ of the Euvx's in A370 could distinguish between burst ellipticals and truncated spirals only in the case R. *In a more general way, a blue colour and H_δ alone are not discriminating between the two possibilities unless the burst is recent (<< 0.5 Gyr). Viceversa, if the morphology (HST) is known, H_δ gives indications on the detailed characteristics of the burst.*

REFERENCES

Barbaro, G., Olivi, F.M.: 1989, ApJ 337, 125
Butcher, H., Oemler, A.Jr.: 1978, ApJ 219, 18
Butcher, H., Oemler, A.Jr.: 1984, ApJ 285, 426
Couch, W.J., Ellis, R.S., Sharples, R.M., Smail, I.: 1994 preprint
Dressler, A., Oemler, A., Butcher, H.R., Gunn, J.E.: 1994 ApJ in press
Poggianti, B.M., Barbaro, G.: 1994, Mem. SAIt n.66 (PB)
Wirth, G.D.: 1994, this volume

DYNAMICAL PARAMETERS IN TWO cD RICH CLUSTERS

H. Quintana, L. Infante and M. Way

Grupo de Astrofísica, P. Universidad Católica de Chile

Casilla 104, Santiago 22, Chile.

Abstract

We report observations of $\sim$150 velocities in each of the clusters A119 and A133, obtained with a multiobject fiber spectrograph. The cluster A133 shows a complex velocity structure. We derive values for the velocity dispersions and dynamical masses of both clusters. From a preliminary analysis of the velocity fields we note the presence of substructures.

1 Introduction

New facilities to obtain large numbers of radial velocities of galaxies in clusters have brought hopes for an increased understanding of the dynamics of rich clusters of galaxies. From suitable velocity data it is possible to derive dynamical parameters and analyze the velocity fields to evaluate the degree of relaxation, merging, infall and evolutionary process. A limited number of clusters in the literature reach over 100 measured members, while just a handfull have over 200 velocities. It is an urgent matter to raise the number of cluster with such data.

Most evolved clusters seem to be of type cD, where the X-ray image usually shows a peaked symmetric structure. They are also X-ray luminous permitting a study of the gas structures to fairly large distances, providing good tools to study evolution. Clusters at all distances need to be observed for evolutionary studies. However, to compare clusters at different epochs we first need to attain good knowledge of nearby clusters.

Among several clusters under study (i.e. A3266, A3391/95, A3558) here we present a progress report of data obtained on A119 and A133. Velocities in A119 were published by Melnick and Quintana[1] and by Fabricant et al[2], who also analyze X-ray data. Little information is known for A133. X-ray images of this cluster are presented by Harris et al[3].

2 Results

Observational data include the following.

- Positions measured with ESO's Optronics with 0.3 arcsec internal accuracy, of ~400 galaxy in each cluster, covering areas of $\sim 1.7° \times 1.7°$ centered on the cD's and down to $\sim 17^m$.

- Spectroscopy. A total of ~ 150 spectra were obtained for each cluster at Las Campanas Observatory 100" telescope. We used S. Shectman's fiber spectrograph and 2D-Frutti detector on October 1990. The configuration with 64 fibers was used ($\sim$50-54 objects and 8 fibers for sky). Spectra resolution: 5 Å over $\lambda\lambda$ 3800-6800 Å. Three exposures of 80-120 min. were taken of partly overlapping $1.5° \times 1.5°$ fields in each cluster.

Reductions were performed with IRAF, using RV and RVSAO cross-correlation packages. Line identification and gaussian fitting by eye was also done, to corroborate cross-correlations results for spectra with low Tonry and Davis (1979) R parameter: $R < 4$.

Combining data from the literature (for A119), we obtained:
- 170 velocities in the A119 region, over a 1.5° x 1.5° area.
- 147 velocities in the region of A133, over a 1.8° x 1.3° area.

Many foreground and background galaxies are detected. Applying a naive 3 σ clipping algorithm, we obtain for the likely members:
- A119 : 150 members, which gives $\bar{v} = 13318$ kms^{-1} and a dispersion $\sigma_v = 823$ kms^{-1}.
- A133 : 117 members, if the velocity center is set disregarding a secondary peak at 17400 - 17600 kms^{-1}. From this we derive $\bar{v} = 16670$ kms^{-1}, and a dispersion $\sigma_v = 760$ kms^{-1}.

Both clusters histograms look fairly gaussian with some perturbations:
- A119 is very flat topped.
- A133 has strong secondary spike at 17400 kms^{-1}, indicative of substructures.

Applying the virial mass and other mass estimators from Heisler et al[4], values are obtained as follows:

Preliminary Mass Estimators

	Autogravitating System				cD as Mass Center	
	M_{virial}	$M_{projected}$	M_{aver}	M_{median}	M_{virial}	$M_{projected}$
			$10^{14} M_\odot$			
A119	24.8	29.1	30.1	19.9	5.9	14.5
A133	21.2	27.6	22.4	19.6	5.6	13.7

Further details and results of the analysis can be found in Quintana et al[5].

This work was supported in part by FONDECYT grant #1930572.

References

[1] Melnick and Quintana 1981 AJ 86, 1567. [2] Fabricant, Kurtz, Geller and Zabludoff 1993 AJ 105, 788. [3] Harris et al 1990, The Einstein Observatory Catalog of IPC X-ray sources, Vol. 2, Smithsonian Astrophysical Observatory, Cambridge. [4] Heisler, Tremaine and Bahcall 1985 ApJ 298, 8. [5] Quintana, Way and Infante, 1994, in preparation.

VELOCITIES IN THE SHAPLEY SUPERCLUSTER

H. Quintana, A. Ramírez

P. Universidad Católica de Chile, Casilla 104, Santiago 22, Chile

J. Melnick, European Southern Observatory, La Silla, Chile

S. Raychaudhury, Center for Astrophysics, Cambridge, USA.

and E. Slezak, Observatoire de la Cote d'Azur, France.

Abstract

New 367 velocities were obtained and, together with literature values, used for a preliminary analysis of the dynamics of several supercluster members and for an evaluation of the supercluster shape and mass. Further and future observations are briefly described.

1 Introduction

The Shapley supercluster (SC) is the densest region in the Universe within $z \leq 0.1$. Its distance allows a detailed study of galaxies in this region, important as a testbed for cosmological conditions and for studies of galaxy evolution in dense systems. The main, long term objectives of this work are to map the SC extention and isolation, disentangle the supercluster structure, evaluate the SC mass and its influence on the local global motion, to study member clusters evolution and to set constraints for cosmological models. Immediate objectives are to enlarge the velocity sample, to obtain cluster redshifts and dispersions, and to get preliminary estimates of the SC mass.

2 Results

We summarize these first observations and results, more fully reported by Quintana et al[1]. The observations and velocity data comes from different sources: 367 new velocities in SC central area were obtained at Las Campanas (LCO), La Silla (ESO) and Cerro Tololo Observatories (CTIO) (mainly ESO 1.5m and LCO 2.5m telescopes). Positions and photographic photometry come from APM scans of J SRC Survey plates, complemented by MAMA machine scans of ESO R Survey copies, plus CTIO 4m prime focus plates (for some clusters). Including published velocities, we extend the sample to 1087 velocities over the area Dec = -26° to -36°, RA = 12^h:30 - 14^h:00. The sample with measured velocities is non-homogeneous, in space and in magnitude and is mostly concentrated in clusters. The present data show interesting features, but is inapropriate for a complete statistical analysis.

A simple analysis of these data shows some interesting results, such as follows:
- The SC apparently extends in velocity from $\approx$ 10000 kms^{-1} to 19000 kms^{-1}, with a complex structure. There is a rather sharp cut-off at 20000 kms^{-1}. There is a superposition of a foreground wall type structure, centered in velocity at $\sim$ 5.000 kms^{-1}.
- We derive velocity parameters for 15 SC likely cluster members, having 10 or more velocities. New dispersions for A3528, A3532, A3556 are derived from $\sim$30-40 velocities. A new A3558 dispersion is based on 145 velocities.
- Standard mass estimators can be calculated, using new velocities and positional information for all cluster galaxies (to estimate the gravitational radius). For the complex we deduce a lower limit of $10^{16} M_\odot$ (for H$_o$=50 kms^{-1} Mpc^{-1}), with a direct, sum-over clusters, best estimate of $2 \times 10^{16} M_\odot$.
- From an analysis of cluster separations in dec, ra and cz, we deduce that the SC is likely flattened in dec, but of similar extention in ra and in the radial direction. We also show that Abell distance class is a poor distance indicator in the area, result expected due to the richness and complexity of the region.
- If Ω_0 is small ($\sim$0.1) and H$_0$=100 kms^{-1} Mpc^{-1}, the SC could explain up to 50% of the CMWB dipole. However, for $\Omega_0 = 1$ and H$_0 \sim$ 50kms^{-1} Mpc^{-1}, of order 8.8 $\times 10^{17} M_\odot$ for SC are needed to account for the 606 kms^{-1} dipole motion, implying lots of intra SC dark matter. This is very unlikely if Hudson [2] results concerning the contribution of galaxies within 8000 kms^{-1} are confirmed.

3   Ongoing and future work

Fiber velocity observations using the DuPont 100" telescope over a $5° \times 5°$ region have recently been obtained for galaxies down to R $\simeq$ 16.5 magnitude. The ESO 3.6m telescope is also being used to secure redshifts for all possible cluster members in a $15° \times 15°$ area. CCD fields are being observed with several telescopes to accurately calibrate the APM and MAMA scans of J and R SRC/ESO survey plates of the area. The immediate aim is to increase the number of velocities to several thousands, covering homogeneously the cluster and intercluster region, to carry out a more detailed dynamical analysis.

This work was supported in part by FONDECYT grant #1930572.

References

[1] Quintana, Ramírez, Melnick, Raychaudhury and Slezak, 1994, A.J., submitted. [2] Hudson, 1993, MNRAS 265, 72.

GRAVITATIONAL LENSING BY THE RICH CLUSTER AC114

Ian Smail
California Institute of Technology, Pasadena, US

Warrick J. Couch
School of Physics, University of New South Wales, Sydney, Australia

Richard S. Ellis
Institute of Astronomy, Cambridge, UK

David Hogg
California Institute of Technology, Pasadena, US

Deep Hubble Space Telescope images of superlative resolution obtained for the distant rich cluster AC114 (z=0.31) reveal a variety of gravitational lensing phenomena for which ground-based spectroscopy is available. Of greatest interest is a remarkably symmetrical pair of compact blue images separated by 10 arcsec and lying close to the cluster cD. We propose that these images arise from a single very faint background source gravitationally lensed by the cluster core. Deep ground-based spectroscopy confirms the lensing hypothesis and suggests the source is a z=1.86 compact star-forming system. Taking advantage of the resolved structure around each image and their very blue colours, we have identified a candidate third image at a separation of 49 arcsec. This separation is nearly an order of magnitude larger than the previous widest separation multiply-imaged system and reflects the massive nature of the lensing cluster. The location, parity and properties of each image promises to strongly constrain the mass concentration in the inner regions of the cluster.

1. INTRODUCTION

We have started a deep imaging programme with HST designed to reveal the morphological nature of star-forming galaxies in distant clusters[1]. The first target of this programme was the cluster AC114 (z=0.31) the data for which reveals the remarkable potential of HST for providing new results on a variety of gravitational lensing phenomena seen in rich intermediate redshift clusters[2]. The cluster was observed with the HST's WFC-I in a series of exposures totalling 6 hours in each of F555W (V) and F814W (I). These images are complemented by a series of deep ground-based multi-colour (UBVRIK) frames.

2. A RESOLVED WIDE SEPARATION MULTIPLY-IMAGED PAIR

The most interesting candidate lensed system in AC114 is a pair of symmetrical compact images, S1 and S2, about 12 arcsec north of the central cD (Figure 1(a)). Both images have similar blue colours, a bright compact source and an L-shaped extension (D1/D2). Although separated by 10.0±0.2 arcsec, the images are highly symmetrical. The two faint objects in between (E1/E2) are much redder, with colours similar to those of cluster members. We suggest that S1+D1/S2+D2 represent two images of a single compact background source, possibly a star forming galaxy with a companion.

The relative parity displayed by S1+D1 and S2+D2 indicate that the lensing mass is not located between them. The proximity of the system to the cluster core and cD, coupled with its extreme separation, indicates that the cluster potential is likely to be playing a central role in creating this system. Moreover, in any viable model it is likely that there are more than two observable images, with the remaining fainter images on the other side of the cD. The blue colours and distinctive morphologies of S1+D1/S2+D2 should enable us to easily locate any other suitably-magnified images.

Within a radius of 1 arcmin from the cD there are only 4 suitable candidates images satisfy our joint colour/morphology criteria. The most promising of these is C3 (Figure 1(b)). The angular separation of C3 from the mid-point of S1/S2 is 48.7 arcsec.

Unlike C3, S1 and S2 are just within reach of faint object spectrographs on 4-m class telescopes, We have attempted to measure a redshift for the source and confirm the lensing hypothesis. A 34 ksec exposure using EMMI on the 3.5m NTT shows a number of weak absorption features which occur in the spectra of both S1 and S2, confirming that they arise from the same source. These features identify the source redshift as z=1.86.

3. DISCUSSION AND CONCLUSIONS

Multiply-imaged sources with spatially extended features provide extremely strong constraints on the shape and depth of the lensing potential. The constraints are so strong that our current modelling of this system with simple multi-component mass distributions has yet to determine a viable solution. Nevertheless, even without such sophisticated models it is possible to derive some interesting results about the the source and lensing cluster from our observations. To begin with, from the lensing configuration and lack of other bright images it is likely that the magnifications of the observed images is high, requiring the source to have a very faint intrinsic apparent magnitude ($B \geq 27$). Moreover, given that we have a pair of images rather than an arc, that the source must be extremely compact, this contrasts with the the bulk of the faint field population which have scale sizes of ~0.5 arcsec. Both these facts point towards the possible existance of a new population of ultra-compact high redshift galaxies[3]. Finally, if we accept C3 as the third image we obtain an estimate of the cluster velocity dispersion of $\sigma \sim 1600$ kms/sec, remarkably close to the spectroscopic value[4], $\sigma = 1650\pm220$ kms/sec. Such a massive cluster at this redshift is uncomfortably large for standard CDM.

ACKNOWLEDGEMENTS

This work was partially supported by SERC. IRS gratefully acknowledges a NATO Advanced Research Fellowship. WJC acknowledges financial support from the Austrailian Research Council.

REFERENCES

1) Couch, W.J., Ellis, R.S., Sharples, R.M. & Smail, I. 1994, ApJ, in press.
2) Smail, I., Couch, W.J. & Ellis, R.S. 1994, MNRAS, in prep.
3) Fort, B. & Miralda-Escudé, J. 1993, Ap.J., **417**, L5.
4) Couch, W.J. & Sharples, R.M. 1987, MNRAS, **229**, 423-455.

Figure 1: Major tick marks are 1 arcsec. (a) Lucy-Richardson deconvolution of the HST F555W image of the candidate multiply-imaged source close to the cD of AC114, with structures marked. (b) A comparison of the candidate third image (C3) found on the basis of colours and morphology compared to a suitably demagnified copy of S1.

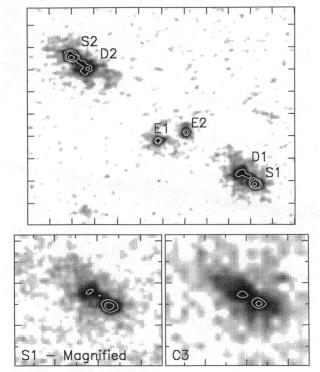

Detection of diffuse hot ionized gas in groups with central early type galaxies

I. Thiering[1], M. Dahlem[2], S. Döbereiner[3]

[1] Landessternwarte, Königstuhl 12, 69117 Heidelberg, Germany
[2] Johns Hopkins University, Homewood Campus, Baltimore, MD 21218, U.S.A.
[3] MPI für Extraterrestrische Physik, Giessenbachstr., 85740 Garching, Germany

We report on the detection of hot ionized gas in three groups or poor clusters of galaxies at distances above 100 Mpc (recession velocities above 8000 km s^{-1}). In all three cases the emission is centered on the dominant member of the group (NGC 4104, NGC 6269, NGC 6329). In each case, the spectrum can be represented by a thermal Raymond-Smith spectrum with kT $\simeq$ 1.1 to 1.5 keV. This suggests that none of them hosts an AGN that contributes significantly to their emission in the ROSAT band (0.1 to 2.4 keV). The soft X-ray luminosities are on the order of 1.6×10^{42} (NGC 6329), 2.2×10^{42} (NGC 4104), and 4.7×10^{42} erg s^{-1} (NGC 6269). This scatter in L$_x$ for gas at almost equal temperatures indicates that the three groups have different total gas masses. The soft X-ray luminosities and the temperatures of the gas are typical of single E/S0 galaxies or small groups, while for clusters L$_x$ $\sim 10^{44...45}$ erg s^{-1} and kT of a few keV would be expected. We find some evidence for an ultrasoft thermal component near 0.3 keV.

In Fig. 1 we show as an example the ROSAT PSPC image of NGC 4104 (contours), superimposed onto a digitized POSS (blue-) plate. The contours represent the 7, 10, 14, 20, 28, 40, 56,8 0, 113, and 160 σ levels.

One can clearly see diffuse emission in addition to the central peak. The diffuse X-ray emission and the optical image of NGC 4104 are elongated along the same direction. At the distances of the group which is about 110 Mpc[1], the diameter of its hot gaseous halo corresponds to >350 kpc, i.e. 4 times its Holmberg diameter, D$_{25}$. Since a more detailed analysis (in combination with data of more galaxies) is still underway (Thiering et al. 1994, in prep.), which – after subtraction of the pointsources and further smoothing – will lead to a higher sensitivity for extended emission, these values are lower limits.

Fig. 2 shows the spectrum of NGC 4104 and a fitted Raymond-Smith model. For the column density of neutral hydrogen N$_H$ the Galactic value in direction of NGC 4104 is used, from the Dwingeloo survey (Hartmann & Burton 1995). Above 0.3 keV, all spectra can be well-fitted with single-component Raymond - Smith (1977) models, which suggests that there is practically no other emitting mechanism contributing in the 0.3 to 2.4 keV range than diffuse hot gas with a temperature of about 1.5×10^7 K. For lower energies some exess emission is visible. Higher N$_H$ values would only increase the discrepancy, and so this speaks for the presence of an ultrasoft emission component as recently suggested by Pellegrini & Fabbiano (1994). For the three galaxies the reduced χ^2-values for the residuals of a best fit to a power-law energy distribution are two to four times as high than those of their Raymond-Smith model fits. The most important results of the spectral fits are presented in Table 1.

We thank Dap Hartmann for providing us with Galactic HI column densities prior to publication. MD is supported by NASA grant no. G002-72900.

References:
Hartmann D. & Burton W.B. 1995, "The Leiden-Dwingeloo Atlas of Galactic Neutral Hydrogen", Cambridge University Press (in prep.)
Pellegrini S. & Fabbiano G. 1994, ApJ (in press)
Raymond J. C., Smith B. H. 1977, ApJ Suppl. 35 419
Thiering I., Dahlem M., and Döbereiner S. 1994, ApJ (in prep.)
Tully R. B. 1988, Nearby Galaxies Catalog (Cambridge: Cambridge University Press)

---

[1] Based on H$_o$ = 75 km s^{-1} Mpc^{-1} and on recession velocities corrected for the Virgocentric flow, as described by Tully (1988)

Table 1: Results of Raymond-Smith fits to the observed spectra

Galaxy	type	M_B^i [mag]	kT [keV]	ΔkT [keV]	EM 4π d^{-2} [10^{-18} cm^5]	ΔEM 4π d^{-2} [10^{-18}cm^5]	χ^2/ν	Gal. NH# [10^{20} cm^{-2}]
NGC 4104	S0	-22.78	1.36	0.10	5.44	0.59	1.56	1.81
NGC 6269	E	-22.80	1.36	0.07	3.66	0.53	1.09	5.32
NGC 6329	E	-21.63	1.16	0.04	3.08	0.27	1.27	1.24

values from Hartmann & Burton (1995; in prep.)

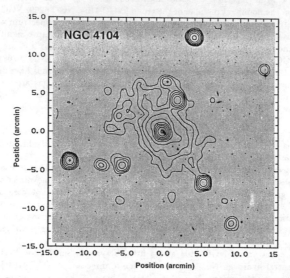

Figure 1: Contour map of the ROSAT PSPC image of NGC 4104. The angular resolution is about 40". The contours represent the 7, 10, 14, 20, 28, 40, 56, 80, 113, and 160 σ levels. standard deviation of the single pixel variation, above the mean. The field of view is: 29'×29'.

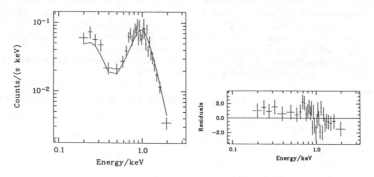

Figure 2: **Left** panel: Observed ROSAT spectrum and best-fitting single-component Raymond-Smith model of NGC 4104. We use the Galactic neutral hydrogen value from Hartmann & Burton (1995). **Right** panel: residuals of the spectral fit.

THE POPULATION OF GALAXIES IN THE DISTANT CLUSTER Cl 1613+310

R. Vílchez-Gómez[1], R. Pelló[2] and B. Sanahuja[1]

[1]Departament d'Astronomia i Meteorologia, Av. Diagonal 647, E-08028 Barcelona, Spain

[2]Observatoire Midi-Pyrénées, 14 av. Édouard Belin, F-31400 Toulouse, France

Abstract: We study the photometric properties and galaxy content of the distant cluster Cl 1613+310 (z = 0.415). It is a very rich and concentrated cluster which shows a strong evidence for segregation in luminosity and color. We use the photometric information to classify galaxies in spectro-morphological types. This analysis leads to the conclusion that this cluster contains a high fraction of S/Im star-forming galaxies. The results are discussed in terms of evolution of galaxy populations.

1. INTRODUCTION

The photometric study of rich clusters of galaxies at high redshift is one of the most important tools to understand the evolution of galaxies in dense environments. The discovery of the "Butcher–Oemler effect" has been understood as an evidence of a strong, recent evolution of galaxies in clusters (Butcher & Oemler 1984, hereafter BO). The interpretation of the blue galaxy excess is a difficult challenge because the galaxy content varies from cluster to cluster. As suggested by Dressler at al. (1985), the difference can arise from several reasons: different initial conditions, a difference on the time scales for cluster formation, and/or environmental influences. The presence of luminosity and color segregation in nearby clusters (Capelato et al. 1980) as well as in high redshift clusters (Mellier et al. 1988) is often interpreted in terms of dynamical friction and sweeping. Nevertheless, it is not still clear in what extent these properties are innate or the result of later evolutionary processes. It is evident that more information is needed and that it is essential to enlarge the sample of well known high redshift clusters. This is the aim of this paper.

In the present paper we concentrate on the photometric results obtained for the rich distant cluster Cl 1613+310 (z = 0.415; Sandage et al. 1976), which is known to exhibit X-ray and radio emission (Henry et al. 1982 and Jaffe 1982, respectively). The existence of a diffuse stellar component in the center of this cluster has been reported by Vílchez–Gómez et al. (1994). All along this paper, we assume $H_0 = 50$ km s^{-1} Mpc^{-1} and $q_0 = 0.1$ in a standard Friedmann cosmology.

2. OBSERVATIONAL PROCEDURE AND DATA ANALYSIS

The photometric observations reported here were carried out in two different runs (in May 1987 and July 1988) at the F/3.4 prime focus of the 3.5 m telescope of the C.A.H.A (Calar Alto, Almería, Spain). The detector used was an RCA CCD, with an equivalent field of 4.4×2.8 and a pixel size of 0.506. All the details concerning these observations can be found in Pelló & Vílchez–Gómez (1994), hereafter referred as Paper I. The filters used were Johnson B and Thuan–Gunn g and r (Thuan & Gunn 1976).

To evaluate the degree of central concentration of the clusters, the concentration index (C), R_{30} and N_{30} are used, as defined by BO. We also use the average central galaxy density, $N_{0.5}$, given by Bahcall (1981). The projected densities of this cluster (number of galaxies per surface unit or surface brightness) have been fitted by an analitic King law using a Gauss–Newton χ^2 minimization algorithm. Only galaxies brighter than the completeness limit in magnitude were considered in these calculations. The center of the cluster is defined by the optical barycenter of the whole central group of galaxies.

In order to investigate the existence of subclustering and, eventually, the presence of segregations in luminosity and color, we have performed an angular-separation test following the method proposed by Capelato et al. (1980). The set of objects used in these calculations is defined by the completeness limit of the sample in magnitude. The size of the bins in magnitude or color has been imposed to contain the same number of galaxies in each bin. After correction for contamination by means of the comparison field, we have fitted a Schechter luminosity function (Schechter 1976) to the distribution of galaxies in B, using the χ^2 minimization algorithm. Besides, we calculate the distribution of galaxies in morphological types through the distribution in colors and we determine the importance of the fraction of blue objects, according to the definition given by BO. Using the Bruzual's code for the spectro-photometric evolution of galaxies, we have obtained the SED corresponding to 6 spectro-morphological types: E/S0, Sa, Sbc, Scd, Im and a single starburst.

3. THE 2D DISTRIBUTION OF GALAXIES

As it is shown by Vílchez–Gómez et al. (1994), the shape of Cl 1613+310 is basically circular. Then, we can safely assume circular symmetry along the subsequent calculations. We have calculated the cluster profile. The cutoff radius is taken as the distance where the projected density coincides with the density in the comparison field. The radius obtained with this definition is $101''$ (0.718 h^{-1} Mpc). Assuming that galaxies are ellipticals, a magnitude of completeness $r = 24$ (see Paper I) is equivalent to $M_V = -17.0$, taking into account the distance modulus and the K correction. With this limit in magnitude, the concentration parameter is $C = 0.372$, with $R_{30} = 40''$ (284 h^{-1} kpc) and $N_{30} = 37$. The central galaxy density, $N_{0.5}$, is 24 and the estimated velocity dispersion is about 1200 km s^{-1}. All these results confirm that we are dealing with a rich and compact cluster. The fit of the cluster profile gives a radius smaller than those found for other rich clusters, with similar redshifts, such as A 370 (Mellier et al. 1988).

We have found, using the λ_1 method (Capelato et al. 1980), that the luminosity and color segregations in this cluster are important. The general result is that the brightest and reddest objects are more concentrated: their length scales are always smaller than those of the faint and blue objects. In addition, it is possible to show that these red and luminous galaxies preferentially lie in the central part of the cluster.

4. THE POPULATION OF GALAXIES

We have calculated the luminosity function in B with a mean K-correction for all the galaxies which corresponds to an E/S0 type. The result of the Schechter luminosity function fit is: $n^* = 41\pm19$, $\alpha = -0.79\pm0.64$ and $M^* = -20.77\pm0.78$. These values are compatible, within the errors, with those derived by Colles (1989), using also a χ^2 method, for a sample of rich and nearest clusters.

The distribution of galaxies in colors clearly shows a double peak in g – r. This configuration divides the sample of galaxies into blue ($0.0 \lesssim$ g – r $\lesssim 1.0$) and red ($1.0 \lesssim$ g – r $\lesssim 2.0$) populations. The confusion between the two peaks in B – g is more important and the separation into populations is less evident. The red sequence for the color–magnitude distribution of E/S0 galaxies is less important than expected. An important blue population appears in these diagrams, as a first evidence in favor of an important fraction of star–forming galaxies.

We calculate the fraction of blue galaxies, (f_B), according to the definition given by BO. After the correction for the color-magnitude effect and the statistical correction for contamination due to blue objects (using the comparison field), we obtain a blue fraction $f_B = 0.21\pm0.03$. This value is compatible with the f_B–z relation obtained by BO for a rich cluster at $z = 0.415$ (Fig. 3 of BO).

We determine the excess of galaxies in the cluster per bin in the color-color plane with respect to the comparison field. When we consider the complete sample of galaxies, we find that 40% of them are E/S0 galaxies, about 17% are S/Im galaxies and 43% are bluer than the predicted values for the Im type. These "blue" galaxies correspond to objects bluer than g – r = 0.4 and B – g = 0.1. The importance of this population of blue galaxies in the color-color diagram increases with the magnitude. When we consider the population within the completeness limit in magnitude ($r = 24$), 55% of galaxies are E/S0, 24% are S/Im "normal" star-forming galaxies and 22% are bluer than the Im type. The fraction of E/S0 galaxies increases to 77% when the sample reduces to objects brighter than $r = 22$. In this case, we have 20% of normal S/Im galaxies and less than 3% of extremely blue objects.

References

Bahcall N.A., 1981, ApJ 247, 787
Butcher H., Oemler A., 1984, ApJ 285, 426
Capelato H.V., Gerbal D., Mathez G., Mazure A., Salvador–Solé E., Sol H., 1980, ApJ 241, 521
Colles M., 1989, MNRAS 237, 799
Dressler, A., Gunn J.E., Schneider D.P., 1985, ApJ 294, 70
Henry J.P., Soltan A., Briel U., Gunn J.E., 1982, ApJ 262, 1
Jaffe W., 1982, ApJ 262, 15
Mellier Y., Soucail G., Fort B., Mathez G., 1988, A&A 199, 13
Pelló R., Vílchez–Gómez R., 1994, A&AS, in preparation (Paper I)
Sandage A., Kristian J., Westphal J.A., 1976, ApJ 205, 688
Schechter P., 1976, ApJ 203, 297
Thuan T.X., Gunn J.E., 1976, PASP 88, 543
Vílchez–Gómez R., Pelló R., Sanahuja B., 1994, A&A 283, 37

XIVth RENCONTRES DE MORIOND ASTROPHYSIQUE
CLUSTERS OF GALAXIES
List of participants

Dr. Nabila Aghanim
Institut d'Astrophysique Spatiale
Université Paris XI Bat. 121
F - 91405 Orsay Cedex
France
E-mail : aghanim@iaslab.ias.fr

Dr. Philippe Amram
Observatoire de Marseille
2, Place Le Verrier
F - 13248 Marseille Cedex 4
France
E-mail : amram@obmara.cnrs-mrs.fr

Dr. Monique Arnaud
CEA/DAPNIA/SAp
C E - Saclay L'Orme des Merisiers 709
F - 91191 Gif-sur-Yvette Cedex
France
E-mail : arnaud@sapvxg.saclay.cea.fr

Dr. Frank W. Baier
University of Potsdam WIP-Group"Galaxy Clusters"
An der Sternwarte 16
D - 14482 Potsdam
Germany
E-mail : fbaier@aip.de

Dr. Matthias Bartelmann
MPI für Astrophysik
Postfach 1523
D - 85740 Garching
Germany
E-mail : msb@mpa-garching.mpg.de

Dr. Paola Belloni
MPI für Astronomie
Koenigstuhl 17
D - 69117 Heidelberg
Germany
E-mail : belloni@mpia-hd.mpg.de

Dr. Andrea Biviano
Institut d'Astrophysique
98bis, Boulevard Arago
F - 75014 Paris
France
E-mail : biviano@iap.fr

Dr. Hans Böhringer
MPI für Extraterrestriche Physik
Giessenbachstrasse
D - 85748 Garching
Germany
E-mail : hxb@mpe.mpe-garching.mpg.de

Dr. Dick Bond
C I T A - University of Toronto
McLennan Labs
ON M5S 1A7 Toronto
Canada
E-mail : bond@cita.utoronto.ca

Dr. François R Bouchet
Institut d'Astrophysique
98bis, Boulevard Arago
F - 75014 Paris
France
E-mail : bouchet@iap.fr

Dr. Ulrich Briel
MPI für Extraterrestriche Physik
Giessenbachstrasse
D - 85740 Garching
Germany
E-mail : ugb@mpe.mpe-garching.mpg.de

Dr. David Buote
M I T
Center for Space Research Rm 37-618a
MA 02139 Cambridge
U.S.A
E-mail : dbuote@space.mit.edu

Dr. Hugo Capelato
Inst. Nac. Pesq. Espaciais
Divisao de Astrofisica C.P. 515
12201-970 S. José dos Campos
Brazil
E-mail : hugo@das.inpe.br

Dr. Alberto Cappi
Osservatorio Astronomico di Bologna
Via Zamboni , 33
I - 40126 Bologna
Italy
E-mail : cappi@alma02.bo.astro.it

Dr. Francisco Javier Castander
Institute of Astronomy
Madingley Road
CB3 0HA Cambridge
U.K
E-mail : fjc@mail.ast.cam.ac.uk

Dr. Rosa Dominguez-Tenreiro
Dpto. Fisica Teorica - CXI
Univ. Autonoma Madrid Cantoblanco
E - 28049 Madrid
Spain
E-mail : rosado@emduam11

Dr. Sergio Colafrancesco
Osservatorio Astronomico di Roma
Via dell' osservatorio, 5
I - 00040 Monteporzio
Italy
E-mail : cola@astrmp.astro.it

Dr. R. Hank Donnelly
Wellesley College
Dept. of Astronomy/Whitin Observatory
MA 0281 Wellesley
U.S.A
E-mail : donnelly@annie.wellesley.edu

Dr. Françoise Combes
Observatoire de Paris - D E M I R M
61, Avenue de l'Observatoire
F - 75014 Paris
France
E-mail : bottaro@mesioa.obspm.fr

Dr. Bérengère Dubrulle
CEA/DAPNIA/SAp
C E - Saclay L'Orme des Merisiers 709
F - 91191 Gif-sur-Yvette
France
E-mail : dubrulle@obs-mip.fr

Dr. Carolin Crawford
Institute of Astronomy
Madingley Road
CB3 0HA Cambridge
U.K
E-mail : csc@mail.ast.cam.ac.uk

Dr. Florence Durret
Institut d'Astrophysique
98bis, Boulevard Arago
F - 75014 Paris
France
E-mail : durret@iap.fr

Dr. Hakon Dahle
Institute Theoretical Astrophysics
University of Oslo BOX 1029 Blindern
N - 0315 Oslo
Norway
E-mail : hdahle@astro.uio.no

Dr. Alastair Edge
Institute of Astronomy
Madingley Road
CB3 0HA Cambridge
U.K
E-mail : ace@mail.ast.cam.ac.uk

Dr. Antonella de Luca
Institut d'Astrophysique Spatiale
Université Paris XI Bat. 121
F - 91405 Orsay Cedex
France
E-mail : deluca@iaslab.ias.fr

Dr. George Efstathiou
University of Oxford
Keble Road
OX1 3RH Oxford
U.K
E-mail : gpe@astro.ox.ac.uk

Dr. Roland den Hartog
Sterrewacht Leiden
Niels Bohrweg 2 P. O. Box 9513
NL - 2300 RA Leiden
The Netherlands
E-mail : hartog@rulhl1.LeidenUniv.nl

Dr. August Evrard
2071 Randall Laboratory
Physics Department
MI 48109-1120 Ann Arbor
U.S.A
E-mail : evrard@pablo.physics.lsa.umich.edu

Dr. Andrew Fabian
Institute of Astronomy
Madingley Road
CB3 0HA Cambridge
U.K
E-mail : acf@mail.ast.cam.ac.uk

Dr. Piotr Flin
Krakow Pedagogical University
Institute of Physics ul. Podchorazych 2
PI - 30-084 Krakow
Poland
E-mail : sfflin@cyf-kr.edu.pl

Dr. Carlos Frenk
University of Durham
Physics Department
DH1 3LE Durham
U.K
E-mail : c.s.frenk@durham.ac.uk

Dr. Roberto Fusco-Femiano
Istituto di Astrofisica Spaziale
C.P 67
I - 00044 Frascati
Italy
E-mail : saxias::sci

Dr. Eric Gaidos
M I T
Center for Space Research Rm 37-616B
MA 02139 Cambridge
U.S.A
E-mail : ejgaidos@space.mit.edu

Dr. Giuseppe Gavazzi
Osservatorlo di Brera
Via Brera, 28
I - 20121 Milano
Italy
E-mail : gavazzi@bach.mi.astro.it

Dr. Isabella Gioia
Institute for Astronomy
2680 Woodlawn Drive
HI 96822 Honolulu
U.S.A
E-mail : gioia@galileo.ifa.hawaii.edu

Dr. Giuliano Giuricin
SISSA
Via Beirut 2
I - 34013 Trieste
Italy
E-mail : 38028::giuricin

Dr. Guillermo Gonzalez-Casado
Universidad Politecnica de Catalunya
Dept. Matematica Aplicada II Pau Gargallo, 5
E - 08028 Barcelona
Spain
E-mail : ggonzalez@ma2.upc.es

Dr. Vahe G. Gurzadyan
Yerevan Physics Institute
Department of Theoretical Physics
375036 Yerevan
Armenia
E-mail : 40174::gurzadyan

Dr. Ariane Hemming
University of Sydney
Physics Building A 28
NSW 2006 Sydney
Australia
E-mail : alh@physics.su.oz.au

Dr. Yasushi Ikebe
University of Tokyo - Cosmic X-ray Laboratory
7-3-1Hongo,Bunkyo-ku
113 Tokyo
Japan
E-mail : ikebe@miranda.phys.s.u-tokyo.ac.jp

Dr. Leopoldo Infante
Universidad Catolica de Chile
Facultad de Fisica Casilla 104
22 Santiago
Chile
E-mail : linfante@astro.puc.cl

Dr. Michael Jones
M R A O - Cavendish Laboratory
Madingley Road
CB3 0HE Cambridge
U.K
E-mail : mike@mrao.cam.ac.uk

Dr. Martine Joubert
Laboratoire d'Astronomie Spatiale
B.P. 8
F - 13376 Marseille Cedex 12
France
E-mail : joubert@astrsp-mrs.fr

Dr. Nick Kaiser
C I T A - University of Toronto
60, St George Street
M5S 1A7 Toronto
Canada
E-mail : kaiser@cita.utoronto.ca

Dr. Russell Lavery
Iowa State University
Dept. of Physics and Astronomy
IA 50010 Ames
U.S.A
E-mail : lavery@iastate.edu

Dr. Haida Liang
Australian National University
Institute Advanced Studies Private Bag
ACT 2611 Weston Creek P.O
Australia
E-mail : hliang@atnf.csiro.au

Dr. Vladimir Lukash
Astro Space Centre
Profsoyuznaya 84/32
117810 Moscow
Russia
E-mail : vlukash@esoc1.bitnet

Dr. Rainer Madejsky
Institut d'Astrophysique
98bis, Boulevard Arago
F - 75014 Paris
France
E-mail : madejsky@iap.fr

Dr. Gary Mamon
Institut d'Astrophysique
98bis, Boulevard Arago
F - 75014 Paris
France
E-mail : gam@iap.fr

Dr. Alain Mazure
Université Montpellier II - G R A A L
C.P 072
F - 34097 Montpellier Cedex
France
E-mail : 18068::mazure

Dr. Jorge Melnick
E S O
Casilla 19001
19 Santiago
Chile
E-mail : jmelnick@eso.org

Dr. Nicola Menci
Osservatorio Astronomico di Roma
Via dell' Osservatorio
I - 00040 Monteporzio
Italy
E-mail : 28903::menci

Dr. David Merritt
Rutgers University
Dept. Physics & Astronomy
NJ 08855 Piscataway
U.S.A
E-mail : merritt@physics.rutgers.edu

Dr. Christopher Metzler
University of Michigan - Department of Physics
500 E. University
MI 48109-1120 Ann Arbor
U.S.A
E-mail : metzler@pablo.physics.lsa.umich.edu

Dr. Felix Mirabel
CEA/DAPNIA/SAp
C E - Saclay L'Orme des Merisiers 709
F - 91191 Gif-sur-Yvette Cedex
France
E-mail : mirabel@sapvxg.saclay.cea.fr

Dr. Jordi Miralda-Escude
Institute Advanced Study
Princeton
NJ 08540 Princeton
U.S.A
E-mail : jordi@guinness.ias.edu

Dr. Shigeru Miyoshi
Kyoto Sangyo University - Department of Physics
Kamigamo-Motoyama, Kita-ku
603 Kyoto
Japan
E-mail :

Dr. Pierluigi Monaco
SISSA
Via Beirut 4
I - 34013 Trieste
Italy
E-mail : monaco@tsmi19.sissa.it

Dr. Richard Mushotzky
NASA - GSFC - Code 666
Lab. High Energy Astrophysics
MA 20771 Greenbelt
U.S.A
E-mail : mushotzky@lheavx.gsfc.nasa.gov

Dr. Julio Navarro
University of Durham
Department of Physics
DH1 3LE Durham
U.K
E-mail : j.f.navarro@durham.ac.uk

Dr. Doris Neumann
MPI für Extraterrestriche Physik
Giessenbachstasse 1
D - 85740 Garching
Germany
E-mail : don@rosat.mpe-garching.mpg.de

Dr. Chris O'Dea
STScI
3700 San Martin Drive
MD 21218 Baltimore
U.S.A
E-mail : odea@stsci.edu

Dr. Daniel Pfenniger
Geneva Observatory
University of Geneva
CH - 1290 Sauverny
Switzerland
E-mail : pfennige@scsun.unige.ch

Dr. Marguerite Pierre
CEA/DAPNIA/SAp
C E - Saclay L'Orme des Merisiers 709
F - 91191 Gif-sur-Yvette Cedex
France
E-mail : pierre@sapvxg.saclay.cea.fr

Dr. Bianca Maria Poggianti
Dipartimento di Astronomia
Vicolo dell' Osservatorio, 5
I - 35122 Padova
Italy
E-mail : poggianti@astrpd.astro.it

Dr. Trevor Ponman
University of Birmingham
Sch. Physics & Space Research Edgbaston
BI5 2TT Birmingham
U.K
E-mail : tjp@uk.ac.bham.sr.star

Dr. Karl D. Rakos
Institut für Astronomie
Tuerkenschanzstrasse 17
A - 1180 Wien
Austria
E-mail : rakosch@astro.ast.uniwie.ac.at

Dr. Alvio Renzini
Dipartimento di Astronomia
C.P 596
I - 40100 Bologna
Italy
E-mail : alvio@alma02.cineca.it

Dr. George Rhee
Univ. Nevada Las Vegas - Department of Physics
4505 S. Maryland Parkway
NV 89154 Las Vegas
U.S.A
E-mail : grhee@nevada.edu

Dr. Rachida Sadat
Observatoire d'Alger
C R A A G B.P 63
Bouzareah
Algeria
E-mail :

Dr. Eduard Salvador-Solé
Facultad de Física - Dpt. Astronomia Meteorologia
Av. Diagonal 647
E - 08028 Barcelona
Spain
E-mail : eduard@faess0.ub.es

Dr. Craig L. Sarazin
University of Virginia - Department of Astronomy
P.O. Box 3818
VA 22903-0818 Charlottesville
U.S.A
E-mail : cls71@coma.astro.virginia.edu

Dr. Roberto Scaramella
Osservatorio Astronomico di Roma
Monteporzio Catone
I - 00040 Monteporzio
Italy
E-mail : kosmobob@astrmp.astro.it

Dr. Eric Slezak
Observatoire de la Côte d'Azur
B.P. 229
F - 06304 Nice Cedex 4
France
E-mail : slezak@obs-nice.fr

Dr. Ian Smail
CALTECH
Rm 105-24
CA 91125 Pasadena
U.S.A
E-mail : irs@astro.caltech.edu

Dr. Geneviève Soucail
Observatoire Midi-Pyrénées
14, Rue Edouard Belin
F - 31400 Toulouse
France
E-mail : soucail@obs-mip.fr

Dr. William J. Sutherland
University of Oxford
Keble Road
OX1 3RH Oxford
U.K
E-mail : rlesis::oxvad::wjs

Dr. Roberto Terlevich
RGO
Madingley Road
CB3 0EZ Cambridge
U.K
E-mail : rjt@mail.ast.cam.ac.uk

Dr. Inge Thiering
Landessternwarte
Koenigstuhl 12
D - 69117 Heidelberg
Germany
E-mail : inge@topaz.mpia-hd.mpg.de

Dr. Guido J. Thimm
MPI für Astronomie
Koenigstuhl 17
D - 69117 Heidelberg
Germany
E-mail : thimm@dhdmpi50.bitnet

Dr. Peter Thomas
University of Sussex
Astronomy Centre, MAPS Falmer
BN1 9QH Brighton
U.K
E-mail : p.a.thomas@sussex.ac.uk

Dr. Dario Trevese
Univ. Roma "La Sapienza" - Istituto Astronomico
Via G. M. Lancisi, 29
I - 00161 Roma
Italy
E-mail : trevese@astrom.astro.it

Dr. John C. Tsai
N A S A - Ames Research Center
Mail Stop 245-3
CA 94035-1000 Moffet Field
U.S.A
E-mail : jcht@cloud9.arc.nasa.gov

Dr. Brent Tully
University of Hawaii - Institue of Astronomy
2680 Woodlawn Drive
HI 96822 Honolulu
U.S.A
E-mail : tully@ifa.hawaii.edu

Dr. Michiel van Haarlem
University of Durham - Physics Department
South Road
DH1 3LE Durham
U.K
E-mail : m.p.van-haarlem@durham.ac.uk

Dr. Koujun Yamashita
Nagoya University - Department of Physics
Furo-cho, Chikusa-ku
464 - 01 Nagoya
Japan
E-mail : a41271a@nucc.cc.nagoya-u.ac.jp

Dr. Rosendo Vílchez-Gómez
Univ. de Barcelona Fac. de Física
Dpt. Astronomia Meteorologia Av. Diagonal 647
E - 08028 Barcelona
Spain
E-mail : rosendo@fabsp1.ub.es

Dr. Esther Zirbel
STScI
3700 San Martin Drive
MD 21218 Baltimore
U.S.A
E-mail : zirbel@stsci.edu

Dr. Joachim Wambsganss
MPI für Astrophysik
Karl-Schwarzschildstrasse 1
D - 85740 Garching
Germany
E-mail : joachim@cvxastro.mpa-garching.mpg.de

Dr. Michael West
Sterrewacht Leiden
P. O. Box 9513
NL - 2300 RA Leiden
The Netherlands
E-mail : west@strw.strw.leidenuniv.nl

Dr. Simon White
Institute of Astronomy
Madingley Road
CB3 0HA Cambridge
U.K
E-mail : swhite@mail.ast.cam.ac.uk

Dr. Brad Whitmore
STScI
3700 San Martin Drive
MD 21218 Baltimore
U.S.A
E-mail : whitmore@stsci.edu

Dr. Gregory Wirth
University of California - Lick Observatory
1156 High Street
CA 95064 Santa Cruz
U.S.A
E-mail : wirth@lick.ucsc.edu